Politics and Government in the Middle East and North Africa

POLITICS AND GOVERNMENT

IN THE

MIDDLE EAST

AND

NORTH AFRICA

*Tareq Y. Ismael and
Jacqueline S. Ismael*

Foreword by Timothy Niblock

with contributions from
Kamel S. Abu Jaber
R. Hrair Dekmejian
Nassif Hitti
Bahgat Korany
Ann Mosely Lesch
Cyrus Amir Morki
Richard H. Pfaff
Walter Weiker
Manfred W. Wenner
Marvin Zonis

Florida International University Press / Miami

Printed in the U.S.A. on acid-free paper ⊗

Library of Congress Cataloging in Publication Data

Politics and government in the Middle East and North
    Africa / by Tareq Y. Ismael and Jacqueline S. Ismael with
    contributions from Kamel Abu-Jaber . . . [et al].
        p.   cm.
    Includes index.
    ISBN 0–8130–1043–8. — ISBN 0–8130–1062–4 (pbk.)
    1. Middle East—Politics and government—1979– 2. Africa,
North—Politics and government. I. Ismael, Tareq Y.
II. Ismael, Jacqueline S.
DS63.1.C644 1991
320.956—dc20   90–47983
                    CIP

The Florida International University Press is a member of University Presses of Florida, the scholarly publishing agency of
the State University System of Florida. Books are selected for
publication by faculty editorial committees at each of Florida's
nine public universities: Florida A & M University (Tallahas-
see), Florida Atlantic University (Boca Raton), Florida International University (Miami), Florida State University (Talla-
hassee), University of Central Florida (Orlando), University
of Florida (Gainesville), University of North Florida (Jackson-
ville), University of South Florida (Tampa), and University of
West Florida (Pensacola).

Orders for books published by all member presses should be
addressed to University Presses of Florida, 15 Northwest 15th
Street, Gainesville, Florida 32611.

To the people of Iraq and Kuwait,
both victims of the same tyranny
of dictatorship and militarism

Contents

Foreword: The Gulf Crisis (1990–1991) and the Comprehension of Middle Eastern Politics

Tim Niblock

As this book goes to press, the Middle East is witnessing events of crucial importance. These events seem destined to engender fundamental changes in the societies, polities, and economies of the region. However the crisis that has been set in train by Iraq's invasion of Kuwait ends, the challenge posed to the sociopolitical framework of regional states will be profound and sustained. The relationship between regional states and outside powers will be reshaped and refashioned. The Middle East will not be the same again.

Momentous events are, of course, not new to the area. The history of the Middle East during this century, indeed, seems to consist of a series of such events, each of which has transformed the pattern of regional politics. Each has unleashed new social and political forces, drawn new borders, and brought new regimes to power. World War I created the framework of states that currently holds sway in the eastern Mediterranean, the Arabian peninsula, and the Fertile Crescent. World War II weakened the grip of the colonial powers, giving new opportunities for national liberation. The Palestine war of 1948–49 and the Suez war of 1956 created and strengthened the Israeli state but also gave rise to a stronger and more militant strain of Arab nationalism. The Algerian war of independence (1954–62) both incorporated and reinforced this strain of nationalism. The 1967 Arab-Israeli war weakened many of the established regimes in the Arab world, facilitating the rise of new political movements (initially predominantly leftist, subsequently predominantly Islamist). The 1973 war and the associated rises in oil prices changed the balance of power and influence in the region. The regimes, and the regional and international standing, of the oil-producing countries of the Gulf (Saudi Arabia's, in particular) were strengthened. The Iranian revolution of 1978–79, establishing an Islamist regime in Iran, gave new vitality and confidence to Islamic political movements throughout the Middle East.

To compare the Gulf crisis of 1990–91 with these earlier events may seem premature—especially as, at the time of writing, no major military conflict has occurred. Yet the dimensions of the crisis, whether or not accompanied by war, ensure that its significance will be of a similar order. The issue, and the measures taken to resolve it, touch directly on the interests and concerns of all the peoples of the area: their security, livelihood, identity, political rights, and physical environment. Many of the region's most critical problems, long submerged but always exerting a malignant influence on developments, have been placed in the spotlight. New political movements, institutional structures, and balances of regional power will emerge in response to a deeper popular consciousness of these problems.

The publication of this book, then, comes at an apposite time. As the politics of the region begin to change under the impact of the Gulf crisis, it becomes more important than ever to understand the dynamics that have shaped the region, the forces that have kept governments in power, and the character of the institutions through which power is exercised. The information and analysis presented here, set within a comparative framework, make clear the particularities of every country while showing also the broader regional trends.

Crises tend to give prominence to a region's most critical problems and dilemmas. Academic analysis should perform a similar role. It is to the credit of this book, therefore, that the analysis presented illustrates, reflects, and documents problems that the

Gulf crisis also lays bare. Four such problems, revealed by both the crisis and the analysis, are worthy of particular attention. The first is that the system of states that World War I bequeathed to the eastern Arab world has an inherent instability. The reason is simple: the states have the same attributes of sovereignty, independence, and self-determination enjoyed by states anywhere, yet their interests, objectives, and identities are intertwined and overlapping. The policies that any one of these states pursues impinge crucially on the interests of its neighbors and depend for their success on how these states respond or react. Labor supply and demand, communications routes, strategic needs and requirements, water supply, communal and regional identities, the Palestine issue, the optimum means of exploiting resources, etc., constitute the fields of necessary interaction. For as long as the states concerned fail to establish an effective regional framework which can ensure that these shared interests become fields of cooperation and coordination, rather than grounds for conflict, the relations between them will be subject to sudden crises.

The Iraq-Kuwait issue abounds in shared interests—most crucially with regard to Iraq's access to the Gulf. It is, however, not only the shared interests between Iraq and Kuwait that have fed into the crisis. The intensity of the conflict that has been unleashed and the fervent maneuvering of every state in the region stem from the whole web of shared and overlapping interests. The critical attitude of the government of Yemen toward non-Arab military involvement in the issue, for example, has interacted with the dynamics of Yemeni unification and with long-standing Yemen-Saudi border differences to cause a sharp deterioration in Yemeni-Saudi relations.

It has often been assumed that, with the passage of time, the states of the eastern Arab world will become more separate, self-sufficient, and discrete. The truth is quite the opposite. As their economies develop, and as their populations become more politically and socially aware, their interests become more tightly interlocked. On all of the shared interests mentioned above, one state's policies impinge ever more closely on the security and well-being of others. The dangers of conflict, where incompatible policies are being pursued, steadily increase. While consciousness of the need for a regional framework may increase in the light of the Gulf crisis, the bitterness of the antagonisms engendered will make the approach to a cooperative and coordinative framework difficult.

A second problem is that of establishing political structures in which the freely articulated opinions, demands, and objectives of the populations form the foundation on which political action is built—in short, the problem of democracy. The Gulf crisis gives prominence to this issue in two respects: first, by raising doubts among liberal democrats over the appropriateness of acting to secure the survival of autocratic monarchies; second, by reinforcing a perception that dictatorship can encourage expansionist (and perhaps megalomaniac) ambitions in political leaders, pushing them toward aggressive foreign adventures which liberal democratic institutions would inhibit.

The chapters of this book show that the dilemma over democracy in Middle Eastern countries, as in underdeveloped countries generally, is not easy. Whereas developed countries have proved capable of combining political pluralism with strong and effective government, few underdeveloped countries have been able to do so. The dilemma does not rest on a dichotomy between the moral high ground of democracy and the practical effectiveness of dictatorship. Strong governments in the Middle East, providing no room for popular involvement in decision-making, have often proved ineffective in the long term: the policies pursued, not shaped by local needs and demands, can be unrealistic and inappropriate. On the other hand, liberal political institutions and free expression may, in a society marked by extreme inequality, simply provide the channel through which the rich and powerful maintain their position.

The negative effects of the absence of democracy in much of the Middle East is clearly apparent today—whether in the monarchies of the Gulf (where organized political activity is absent), the single party or military-backed regimes (where political activity is restricted to the one track), or in Palestine (where Israel has claimed rights over the territory of the occupied West Bank and Gaza while denying the population political representation). Authoritarianism has had a deadening effect on political spontaneity, individual creativity, and cultural vitality. It has enabled elites to further their own interests with no risk of exposure or criticism. Popular needs have been discounted in favor of objectives that satisfy the interests and self-image of ruling elites.

A third problem is the Palestine issue. Even while international opinion has been focused on the Gulf, the conflict over Palestine has shown its ability to mold the framework within which regional politics develop. The supportive following that Saddam Hussain has attracted in some sectors of Arab opinion, for example, can be understood only in the light of the resentment and frustration engendered by the Palestine issue. Israel's refusal to accommodate the demand for Palestinian Arab statehood, and the reluctance of the Western powers to insist on Israel's compliance with United Nations resolutions, has created the basis for Saddam Hussain— prepared to threaten Israel and to disregard the blandishments of Western powers—to garner some popular support. In some corners of popular consciousness, hopes rise that Saddam's strong leadership may, directly or indirectly, yield benefits for the Palestinian cause. Less combative approaches, it is contended, have failed: the PLO's recognition of Israel's existence, and its renunciation of terrorism, have not drawn the United States into an effective mediatory role; and the sacrifices of Palestinians during the Intifadah have not diminished the Israeli government's resistance to Palestinian Arab statehood. However forlorn and misplaced the hopes, they nonetheless exert an influence on popular opinion.

Western military support for the defense of Saudi Arabia and for the restoration of Kuwait's sovereignty may be conceived in terms of upholding a principle of international law, yet the policy's success will be crucially affected by regional views on the propriety of Western policy in the wider area. The scope within which Western policy can proceed, and within which governments allied to the Western powers can operate, is limited and constrained by this factor. A feature of Middle Eastern politics that is made apparent in some of the chapters of this book is exposed: even where the Palestine issue does not actually cause Middle Eastern conflicts, it nonetheless imposes itself on a conflict's dynamics, shaping the options which regional and external powers can adopt. The importance of solving the problem of Palestinian Arab dispossession gains renewed emphasis.

A fourth problem is the unequal distribution of wealth within and between the states of the Middle East and the social and inter-state tensions to which it gives rise. The Gulf crisis has focused attention on the extent and value of the resources that the city-state of Kuwait owned, the uses to which the wealth was put, the con-trast between Kuwait's wealth and the poverty of some Arab peo-ples, and the unequal benefit that different categories of Kuwait's population (national and nonnational) drew from the state's re-sources. Yet the fundamental issues raised do not relate only to Kuwait and the Gulf states; they are not the responsibility of any one state or political system. They are issues with regional dimen-sions, needing treatment within a regional framework.

The hope must be that, with attention now drawn to the region's underlying problems, the gradual resolution of these prob-lems may ensue, creating a more stable region and one that caters more effectively to the needs of its peoples. The information and analysis found in this book provide the basis on which a thorough reconsideration of the region's prospects can be undertaken.

Exeter, December 1990

Preface

Slaves to foreigners they are,
but lions on the people of their kin.

Ma'ruf al-Rusafi (Iraqi poet, 1875–1945)

On January 17, 1991, war erupted in the Gulf, sanctioned by UN resolutions and initiated by the United States and its allies in Operation Desert Shield with a blitzkreig air assault on Iraq. In the first three days of Operation Desert Storm (the American code name for the offensive), over 7,000 sorties were flown against Iraq. Initial expectations of scenario like the Six-Day War of 1967 gave way to more cautious projections by the end of the first week as Iraq's military capabilities proved more resilient than anticipated. Then, the air bombardment of Iraq intensified to an average of a raid a minute. When hostilities stopped after 43 days, about 110,000 sorties had been flown, dropping between 110 and 120 million pounds of bombs on Iraq and Kuwait. Military experts observed that the United States dropped more bombs and missiles on more targets in Iraq than at any time in history. With Iraq's economic, transportation, communications, utilities, water, and sewage infrastructures demolished, military entrenchments in and around Kuwait became primary targets of the air offensive in preparation for a ground offensive to drive Iraqi occupation forces from Kuwait.

While a ceasefire is being negotiated as this book goes to press, the political fallout from the war is already taking form. At the popular level, the war has inflamed Arab opinion against the United States. There is widespread conviction throughout the Arab world (indeed, throughout the Muslim world) that the assault on Iraq is aimed at its destruction, not at the liberation of Kuwait, and is in fact part of a broader American strategy to establish military hegemony over the region. Mass demonstrations in the Maghreb, Jordan, Sudan, and Yemen protesting the relentless air bombardment of Iraq's cities and towns reflect the strong reaction among the majority of Arab people to the air bombardment of Iraq.

At the political level, Arab states are polarized into those who actively support the war, and those who don't. For the most part, the two sides correlate with the polarization of wealth in the Arab world. The rich oil-producing states of the Gulf are active supporters of, and indeed are financially underwriting, the American military operation in the Gulf, estimated to cost $56 billion in the first three months alone. Saudi Arabia pledged $13.5 billion dollars to the United States, the Kuwaiti emir a like amount. The poor states, on the other hand, are generally opposed (some actively, others only passively). Syria, Egypt, and Morocco are the only non-oil producing Arab states actively supporting the military operation, but each faces growing popular opposition to the war generally, and their participation particularly, on their home fronts. On February 2, 1991, for example, the king of Morocco expressly forbade protests of Morocco's participation in Operation Desert Storm. The next day, between 300,000 and half a million protesters defied his injunction and took to the streets of Rabat in the largest mass demonstration the country had ever experienced.

Other regional actors—Turkey, Iran, Israel—have struggled with popular political and strategic currents that threaten to draw them into the conflict. Turkey, a member of NATO closely allied with the United States, resisted American pressures to take a more active role in Operation Desert Shield (the defensive stage of the operation) but inevitably became more enmeshed. Large Turkish troop concentrations along the Iraq-Turkish border were reported to be solely defensive, but they effectively prevented the deployment of several divisions of Iraqi troops to the main theater. On January 17 (with the initiation of Operation Desert Storm), American B-52 bombers began using Incirlik, Turkey's NATO air base, for bombing missions against Iraq, in effect formalizing Turkish participation in the operation.

Iran adopted an official policy of neutrality but, in reaction to the ferocity and scope of the air bombardment of Iraq, warned that it would not tolerate the territorial dismantling of the country. It also gave notice that Iran would enter the war in defense of

Iraq if Israel entered the conflict. In the meantime, Iran initiated an intense diplomatic drive to find a formula for peace within the framework of UN Resolution 660.

Israel resisted Iraq's efforts to draw it into the war. Iraq fired 35 SCUD missiles armed with conventional warheads at Israel in the first five weeks of the war. Posing no serious military threat to Israel, the missile attacks in fact proved counterproductive to Iraq's strategy: Israel's agreement to forestall retaliation evoked substantial sympathy and support internationally and resulted in the deflection of concern over the plight of 1.6 million Palestinians in the occupied territories suffering from Israel's imposition of a relentless curfew on them from the onset of the war. While Palestinians celebrated their bravado, the missile attacks in fact weakened the international momentum building to force Israel to accept an international conference to address the Palestinian problem.

Internationally, the twenty-eight-nation alliance participating in Operation Desert Storm held together in spite of serious strains. The threat of Israeli retaliation to the SCUD missile attacks posed the first serious challenge. While all of the Arab states in the alliance agreed that an Israeli retaliation would not affect their participation, in fact it was feared that this would cause such a backlash in the Arab world that the stability of these governments would be seriously compromised.

The ferocity of the bombardment of Iraq proved the most serious strain on the multinational alliance. Participants feared that it was exceeding the mandate of the UN resolution legitimating the use of force to expel Iraq from Kuwait. As popular opposition to the massive scale of the military intervention into the Middle East and the bombardment of Iraq spread through the Arab, Islamic, and Third worlds, the pace of diplomatic activity intensified. First France, then Iran, and finally the USSR launched diplomatic initiatives to find a peace formula within the framework of Resolution 660 and avert a ground war.

However, diplomatic initiatives proved unsuccessful, and on February 23 the United States and its allies in Operation Desert Storm launched a massive ground offensive against Iraqi forces in Kuwait. On February 26, in the face of imminent military defeat,

Saddam Hussain announced the withdrawal of Iraqi forces from Kuwait in compliance with Resolution 660. George Bush refused to call a ceasefire, and allied military units moved into Iraq in pursuit of an Iraqi military surrender. On February 27 Kuwait was formally liberated from Iraqi occupation when Kuwaiti contingents of the multinational force entered Kuwait City and hoisted the Kuwaiti flag.

The scope of Iraq's military defeat opens serious questions about the fate of Iraq. Will Saddam Hussein's regime survive? If not, what will replace it, or will Iraq be dismembered? Furthermore, while it is clear that the United States and its allies won the war, it is not clear who will win the peace. As Timothy Niblock points out in the foreword, the nation-state system in the Middle East is fragile, and the Gulf conflict brought a number of inherent tensions in it to the fore. While it is still too early to assess the impact of the Gulf war on politics and government in the Middle East and North Africa, Oliver Wendell Holmes's dictum "What is past is prologue" highlights the utility of the pedagogical approach adopted in this volume: that the patterns of politics over time are more important in understanding Middle East politics at any given point in time than vice versa. Political events in the Middle East in themselves generally appear irrational, illogical, or chimerical; and indeed, journalistic approaches to the region tend to emphasize these appearances. But events examined from the perspective of patterns over time are perceived in terms of their underlying dynamics rather than their sensational characteristics.

Thus, the perspective adopted here takes the approach that the Middle East today is related to the Middle East yesterday, or yesteryear, or yesterera for that matter, by patterns through time, or changes in patterns over time, not by events in time. Singular events or chains of events, in other words, are significant as markers of patterns, or changes in patterns, rather than because of their intrinsic characteristics, no matter how interesting these may be.

The organization of this volume reflects the effort to set events in the context of patterns of continuity and change. Part I introduces the dynamics of history, Islamic culture, and nationalism that have been dominant forces in shaping the patterns of Middle East politics in the twentieth century. The remaining five parts organize the fifteen case studies by geographic subregions. Each case study attempts to elucidate the patterns of political continuity and change that have evolved in the state over the post–World War II era. Current events are thus placed in the perspective of patterns of continuity and change within the state in particular, and within the region in general.

The case study approach used in this volume brings together some of the leading scholars on the region's politics. This reduces any tendency to trade off depth for breadth, a common problem in an area like the Middle East where specialized knowledge of so many cases really requires a team approach. The case studies build on the foundation presented in Part I. The volume as a whole is an attempt to make it possible for students of Middle East politics to grasp better the events in the region as they unfold by understanding the patterns of continuity and change that have evolved. Care has been taken to examine each state as fully as possible within the unavoidable limitations of space, the only limitation imposed on contributors.

Since this is an introductory text and a general body of knowledge of the subject is well established, the principle of parsimony dictated that a list of bibliographic references was sufficient to serve the reference function. Thus, unless the topic is controversial, or the information is contentious from the author's perspective, or there is a direct quote, footnotes have been eliminated and bibliographic references have been provided at the end of each chapter.

By the same principle, computerized library search techniques render the provision of extensive bibliographies anachronistic and redundant. In the firm pedagogical belief that students should be encouraged to develop the necessary library skills for research, bibliographic references have been limited to those necessary but not sufficient to supplement the text.

There are many systems of transliteration of names from Middle Eastern languages, and no particular standards prevail. Transliteration used in this book followed popular usage in the media rather than a formal system. This was to simplify recognition of names and places.

1

Introduction

Tareq Ismael and Jacqueline Ismael

The Middle East, located roughly between southwestern Asia and the eastern Mediterranean, does not constitute a distinct geographic region. Although it is chiefly distinguished from Europe by religion, from the Far East by culture, and from central Asia by geography and is generally considered to center in the Fertile Crescent, its periphery is not clearly demarcated. For this reason the term *Middle East*, along with the term *Near East*, has never applied to a specific region or group of countries. Its meaning has been determined by political rather than geographic factors and therefore has changed in correspondence to the growth of Western interest and involvement in the area. The very term *Middle East* is not a product of the region but a Western creation.

Near East is an antiquated concept, originating around the fifteenth century with the early European explorations to find new routes to the East. The lands farthest from Europe were called the Far East; the Near East was the term used to designate the lands ruled by the Ottoman Empire after 1453. Moreover, European archaeologists use the term Near East to distinguish the ancient civilizations of Mesopotamia, Egypt, and Persia from those of the Far Eastern civilizations of China and Japan. Clearly, both terms are European in origin and have little meaning at all from an Asian or African geographic point of view.

The term *Middle East* came into popular usage during World War II with the establishment of the British Middle East Command and the Allied Middle East Supply Center. Both served the North African and Asian countries west of India. Since then, the appellation has become increasingly popular while that of Near East has become somewhat obsolete. Thus, the terms are sometimes used interchangeably, or the Near East may refer only to the Balkans or to the Balkans and Egypt plus those lands near to and east of the Mediterranean, including southwestern Asia. Similarly, the Middle East has been variously defined: the broadest view considers it to be the area from Morocco on the Atlantic coast to Pakistan in Asia and from Turkey to Sudan; the narrowest definition concedes only the Arab countries on the eastern Mediterranean, plus Turkey, Israel, and Iran.

The problems caused by such a confusion of nomenclature become apparent when one examines the U.S. government's use of the terms *Near East* and *Middle East*. For example, Secretary of State John Foster Dulles, in his statements on the Eisenhower Doctrine to House and Senate committees in 1957, defined the Middle East as the area extending from Libya in the west to Pakistan in the east, from Turkey in the north to the Arabian peninsula in the south, and including Ethiopia and Sudan. He also indicated that the terms *Middle East* and *Near East* are interchangeable. A year later, on August 13, 1958, President Dwight Eisenhower, in his address to the emergency special session of the United Nations General Assembly dealing with the Lebanese and Jordanian crises, used the term *Near East* but did not mention the Middle East. The State Department, in answering reporters' queries, indicated that the terms are reciprocal but that they included only the countries of Egypt, Syria, Israel, Jordan, Lebanon, Iraq, Saudi Arabia, Yemen, the Gulf Emirates of Abu Dhabi, Dubai, Sharjah, Ras al-Khaymah, Umm al-Qaiwain, Ajman, and Fujairah, Bahrain, Oman, and Kuwait. Thus, the secretary of state and the State Department each defined the Middle East quite differently, and in 1959 a geographer in the State Department concluded that the Middle East could not be defined.[1] Great Britain, which has had a long history of involvement in the area, has also had difficulty with these amorphous terms, and in 1947 its government commented, "Where precision would be required we should not use these terms."[2]

Because of the confusion about the proper use of the term *Middle East*, the first task is to specify clearly the area in question. The view most commonly held in the literature, and the one adhered to in this book, is that the Middle East is that area centered on the Fertile Crescent (including the states of Iraq, Syria, Lebanon, Israel, Jordan), the northern belt (Turkey and Iran), the Nile Valley (Egypt and Sudan), the Arabian Peninsula (Saudi Arabia, Yemen, and the Gulf states), and North Africa (Libya and the states of the Maghrib). This division, like any other, is rather arbitrary, but it takes into account the major characteristics shared by the included states.

The Importance of the Middle East in World Affairs

The historic role of the Middle East in world affairs is derived from its location as the cultural and economic intermediary between Europe, Asia, and Africa. Far Eastern commodities such as silk, sugar, spices, paper, gunpowder, and the compass were introduced to Europe through the Middle East. The Middle East preserved, expanded, and passed on to the West the philosophic and scientific ideas of the Greeks and Hindus; and it was there that the three great monotheistic faiths, Judaism, Christianity, and Islam, were born. The area has been contended by every conqueror moving from one to another of its three neighboring continents and has been successively incorporated into the Persian, Greek, Roman, Arab, Mongol, Tartar, and Turkish empires. It has been the key to the Orient, the bridge connecting Africa, Asia, and Europe, and a chief trade center for millennia.

The importance of the position of the Middle East as a corridor of East-West communication, somewhat diminished by the fifteenth-century discovery of a sea route to India, has been revived in modern times by the Suez Canal and the advent of air travel. Today, the area is a center of air and sea traffic. The value of its waterways—the Turkish Straits, the Suez Canal, the Red Sea, the Bab-al-Mandeb, the Straits of Hormuz, and the Gulf—for communication, travel, and trade is illustrated by the difficulties to outside powers caused by the 1956 and 1967–75 blockages of the Suez Canal and the "tanker war" in the Gulf in the late 1980s. Today, ships from most major international shipping lines plough the vital waterways of the Middle East. A major portion of the world's oil, Europe's in particular, moves through Middle Eastern waterways, especially the Gulf.

Air routes across the Middle East are as vital to communications and trade today as its age-old caravan routes were earlier. All of the region's major international airports—Amman, Baghdad, Beirut, Cairo, Dhahran, Istanbul, Jiddah, Tehran, and Tel Aviv—serve almost every international airline. Moreover, domestic flights have contributed to a significant growth in air traffic in the region. Thus, both air and sea traffic together have conferred a special cultural, political, and economic importance to the Middle East vis-à-vis the rest of the world.

Oil production in the Middle East overshadows any other global concerns. For the industrialized nations in general, Western Europe and Japan in particular, the uninterrupted supply of energy is a major concern. The oil cartel and the rise of the Organization of Petroleum Exporting Countries (OPEC) and the aftermath of the 1973 Arab-Israeli war created a profoundly new and heightened interest in the region. Because Middle Eastern oil is the key to the economy of Western Europe and a basic global resource, its continued availability is of vital economic and strategic importance. According to the distinguished scholar John S. Badeau, "The first and foremost [interest of America] is that the Middle East, or any vital part of it, shall not be occupied or controlled by a foreign power hostile to the United States and the free world. Such a power could either deny oil and passage to the West, or use access to them as diplomatic blackmail to force changes in Western policy"[3] (fig. 1.1).

The accumulation of petrodollars engendered lucrative economic opportunities, especially for the advanced industrialized nations. Consequently the expansion of trade and commerce gained considerable importance for countries desiring to expand their market in the region. The concentration of large oil reserves in the region and the question of energy security imposed vital political and strategic importance on the Middle East vis-à-vis the world powers— the United States and the Soviet Union. In fact, during World

Fig. i.i. *OPEC (13 members)*[a] *and OAPEC (11 members)*[b]

OPEC

Algeria	Libya
Ecuador	Nigeria
Gabon	Qatar
Indonesia	Saudi Arabia
Iran	United Arab Emirates
Iraq	Venezuela
Kuwait	

OAPEC

Algeria	Qatar
Bahrain	Saudi Arabia
Egypt[c]	Syria
Iraq	Tunisia
Kuwait	United Arab Emirates
Libya	

Note: Out of the 13 OPEC members, seven are from OAPEC and, with the exception of Algeria and Libya, five are from the Middle East as defined in this text. Besides, a total of six Middle East states comprise OPEC membership. This emphasizes the influence of the Middle East on OPEC separate from OAPEC.
a. Organization of Petroleum Exporting Countries.
b. Organization of Arab Petroleum Exporting Countries.
c. Egypt's membership was suspended from April 17, 1979.

War II, both Germany and the Allies were already attempting to secure Middle East oil for themselves while denying it to the enemy. The end of the war brought a compromise arrangement for sharing Middle East oil. Given that the Soviet Union continues to be a net exporter of oil, it probably does not view oil as its major priority in the region. More recent illustrations of the geostrategic importance of the Middle East to the world powers were the buildup of the U.S. military presence in the Gulf during the late stages of the Iran-Iraq war and the massive buildup precipitated by Iraq's invasion of Kuwait on 2 August 1990.

In addition to the question of energy security, the Middle East is important to world affairs for other reasons. (1) States in the Middle East form an important part of the Third World. The Mid-

Fig. 1.2. *The League of Arab States (21 members)*

Algeria	Lebanon	Saudi Arabia
Bahrain	Libya	Somalia
Djibouti	Mauritania	Sudan
Egypt	Morocco	Syria
Iraq	Oman	Tunisia
Jordan	Palestine	United Arab Emirates
Kuwait	Qatar	Republic of Yemen

dle East countries closely align themselves with the Non-Aligned Movement, or NAM. The NAM bloc is significant in both political and economic terms. (2) The Arab countries of the Middle East and North Africa (as delineated here) constitute 85 percent of the members of the League of Arab States (fig. 1.2). The league functions in the collective interests of the Arab world. In this context it has particular political and economic implications for the foreign policy deliberations of other countries with regard to the Arab world. (3) Within the Arab world, a number of political, economic, and strategic groupings were formed in the 1980s: the Gulf Cooperation Council (GCC), formed in 1981, included Bahrain, Kuwait, Oman, Qatar, Saudi Arabia, and the United Arab Emirates; the Arab Cooperative Council, formed in 1989, included Egypt, Jordan, Iraq, and Northern Yemen; the Arab Maghrib Union, formed in 1989, includes Tunisia, Algeria, Libya, Morocco, and Mauritania. (4) Of further concern to international relations is the Islamic Conference Organization (ICO). All of the countries of the Middle East, except, of course, Israel, make up more than a third of the membership of the ICO. Moreover, Arab states constitute more than half its membership (fig. 1.3). (5) The Middle East is the religious center of Islam. Mecca is the land of the holiest shrine of Islam, the Ka'abah, and millions of pilgrims visit it annually. Medina is revered as the second holiest place of Islam because it is the place of the Prophet's Mosque and was the seat of government for the first Islamic government. Jerusalem is considered the third holiest place of Islam. It contains the Mosque of Umar, the second Khalifah, and the Dome of the Rock. Other religions also have roots in the Middle East. Jerusalem is a sacred place for

Fig. 1.3. *Islamic Conference Organization (45 members)*

Afghanistan[a]	Indonesia	Pakistan
Algeria	Iran	Palestine Liberation
Bahrain	Iraq	Organization
Bangladesh	Jordan	Qatar
Benin	Kuwait	Saudi Arabia
Brunei	Lebanon	Senegal
Burkina Fasso	Libya	Sierra Leone
Cameroon	Malaysia	Somalia
Chad	Maldives	Sudan
The Comoros	Mali	Syria
Djibouti	Mauritania	Tunisia
Egypt[a]	Morocco	Turkey
Gabon	Niger	Uganda
Gambia	Nigeria	United Arab Emirates
Guinea	Oman	Republic of Yemen
Guinea-Bissau		

Note: Observer status has been granted to the "Turkish Federated State of Cyprus" (which declared independence as the "Turkish Republic of Northern Cyprus" in November 1983). a. Egypt's membership was suspended in May 1979 and restored in March 1984. Afghanistan's membership was suspended in January 1980.

Jews. Christendom also stakes a claim on Jerusalem; it is the city where Christ died and was resurrected and has remained a city of religious importance for Christians. (6) The importance of the Middle East in world relations is reflected in the Arab-Israeli conflict. Since the proclamation of the State of Israel in Palestine, the region has experienced four major wars. This conflict has caused very serious concern for the world community, igniting fears of an escalation of the conflict, a superpower confrontation, and the use of nuclear weapons.

Physical Geography

The Middle East is an area of contrasting geographical features that range from swampy regions, where coal beds are formed, to steep cliffs and jagged peaks. Most of Arabia is a slanted coastal block that climbs gradually from sea level in the northeast to 12,000 feet in the southwest until it reaches Yemen, where a sharp drop occurs and the land rushes down into the troughs and rifts that constitute the Red Sea and the Gulf of Aden. The southern plateaus, other than the break at Yemen, continue into North Africa without much change or disturbance in the landscape, creating a region of seemingly endless, relatively flat, sand-covered surfaces. Central Turkey and central Iran are also elevated plateaus that sometimes reach a height of 8,000 feet. But it is the various systems of rugged mountains with their formidable peaks, deep valleys, and sheer drops to narrow coastal lowlands that vividly command the Middle Eastern scene. The Caucasus Mountains, which divide the Black and Caspian seas, tower to 19,000 feet; the Zagros Mountains, a wide system of ranges, thrust to the southeast across the face of Iran; and in Turkey the Toros Daglari (the Taurus Mountains) overshadow the Anatolian Plateau, and the Elburz range commands the southern shores of the Caspian coast.

Two other important physical features of the Middle East are its rivers and waterways, which have played eventful political, economic, and social roles in their respective regions. The Nile River is made up of several streams that flow from central Africa and Ethiopia and merge to amble over a relatively flat territory in the Sudan and to roar through a cataract zone north of Khartoum. Then, below Aswan and during the rest of its journey through Egypt, the river follows a long, fertile valley until it reaches Cairo, where it separates into two branches and enters the Delta. The Nile follows a seasonal variation in the volume of water it transports. Every summer the river rises, and during the month of August it reaches a high point that is some 18 feet above the annual low in April and May. In the process it deposits over 100 million tons of silt, a sedimentary material rich in minerals and other substances vital to plant life.

The Tigris-Euphrates is the other important river system in the Middle East. These two rivers begin in the mountains of eastern Turkey and grow as they wind through tortuous channels, until they reach the plains of Syria and Iraq. Thousands of years ago rich sediment carried by the Tigris and Euphrates created, between Baghdad and what is now the present shoreline of the Gulf, a broad, fertile valley out of the basin that once held waters of the Gulf. Today, the rivers join approximately 230 miles south of Baghdad to form the Shatt-al-Arab, which flows 70 miles farther to the Gulf.

The waterway from the Black Sea to the Aegean, which separates Europe from Asia and is commonly referred to as the Straits, has been significant in human affairs throughout history. At the southwestern outlet of the Black Sea lies the Bosphorus, which extends for 16 miles between Asiatic and European Turkey. The Bosphorus is a deep channel ideally suited for the docking and unloading of heavily laden, deep-draft vessels. On the shores of the inlet where the Bosphorus enters the Sea of Marmara stands Istanbul, one of the legendary cities of the Middle East. Istanbul, known variously throughout history as Byzantium and Constantinople, has been an important city in the history of civilization.

The Sea of Marmara, which is 60 miles wide, marks the second stage of the passage to the Mediterranean from the Black Sea and extends for some 125 miles to the southwest, where it joins the Dardanelles, an ancient strait that accounts for the final 25 miles to the Aegean. The Dardanelles is two and a half to four and a half miles wide and is referred to in Greek mythology as the Hellespont, the sea where Helle fell from the ram with the golden fleece and drowned.

Climate

There has been little documentation of climatic change during the last 5,000 years in the Middle East. Generally speaking, the Middle East experiences a Mediterranean climate. Winter precipitation, caused by the westward flow of maritime air, is the rule along the coasts of the Black, Caspian, and Mediterranean seas, and many areas experience as much as 30 inches yearly. In the summer this flow of air is largely inhibited by the appearance of higher pressures in the western Mediterranean, and sunny days with blue skies prevail. The territories that receive the most rain during the winter months are those whose coastlines face west and are backed by rapidly rising highlands, like those found in Lebanon, Israel, and western Asia Minor. Where these geographic features are missing, rainfall in any season lessens and it is always scarce in the interior. Egypt, the Maghrib, and the plateaus of Arabia, Iran, and Turkey have vast expanses of desert. In addition, the rains in these areas are not only seasonal but extremely erratic. Damascus has an annual rainfall of about ten inches, but it has received as much as four inches in one morning. In the mountains of eastern Turkey and Iran greater precipitation occurs, but winter is still by far the wettest season, with additional months of snow contributing significantly to the yearly average. There are two climatic exceptions to the rhythm of moist winters followed by summer droughts: the monsoon region of southern and southwestern Arabia, which acquires most of its precipitation during the months of July, August, and September, and the Black Sea coast of Turkey, which receives rain throughout the year.

The temperatures of the various regions depend greatly on altitude and latitude. In the mountainous areas of Arabia, winters can be quite harsh and cold. This can also be said of Asia Minor and a major portion of Iran because of their vulnerability to the cold air pockets formed over the Eurasian land mass. To the south, however, the seas exert a tempering influence. During the daylight hours of summer, temperatures often exceed 100° F in Egypt, Arabia, Iran, and the interior of Turkey, but nights are generally cool everywhere except in some lower valleys and along the coasts of the Gulf, the Red Sea, and the Mediterranean, where the humidity is extremely high.

Ethnic Geography

Just as there is little accord among scholars as to the exact boundaries of the Middle East, there is also little agreement among anthropologists concerning the definition of the term *race*. Most modern writers feel that if true biological divisions ever did exist among humans, they were obscured and diffused long before the advent of recorded history as early humans wandered extensively over the broad reaches of their natural environment and intermixed freely with the peoples of other regions. Since the intermingling of races is especially characteristic of the Middle East, any attempt to group these peoples racially would be virtually impossible. They will, therefore, be grouped according to the languages they speak and the religions they practice, and even these overlap.

There are three major distinct linguistic/cultural groups in the region—Arab, Turkish, and Persian—and a number of smaller groups—Kurdish, Berber, and Assyrian. Arabs constitute the single largest majority, numbering about 200 million, or two-thirds of the region's population.   Turkish inhabitants make up the second largest group. The population of Turkey is estimated at more than 51 million. Persians rank as the third largest group, numbering over 47 million. Their modern national identity is Iranian.

In order to understand the political dynamics of the Middle East, it is as essential to discern the distinctions between groups as it is necessary to recognize the similarities among them. For instance, Arabs may be Christian, Jewish, Muslim, or some other faith; generally what determines ethnic identification is language. On the other hand, what determines religious identification is declaration of belief. Muslims may or may not be Arabs; and so too Christians, Jews (or any of the other religions extant in the Middle East). Thus, Kurds are Muslims but not Arabs; Christians may or may not be Arabs or Kurds; and so on.

Religion

Religion has played an important role in the affairs of the Middle East for centuries and has provided not only a basis for national and cultural unity but also a source of diversity. Islam, Judaism, and Christianity—which originated in the Middle East—are the dominant religions, and a significant number of adherents to these faiths are more likely to identify with their religion than with their political state. Both Christianity and Islam are universal religions, embracing followers from all ethnic groups. Only Judaism is an exclusivist religion, limiting membership on the basis of ascriptive criteria.

With more than 200 million Muslims in the Middle East, Islam is, at least numerically, the most influential religion. Early in its history, Islam was divided into two major sects, the Shi'a and the Sunni. The Shi'a sect, found predominantly in Iraq and Iran, is divided into a number of subsects, among them Imami, Isma'ili, and Zaydi. In addition, there are a number of Islamic heterodox and offshoot sects, which include Druze, Yazidi, Ibahdi (modern Kharijite), Alawi (Nusayri), Ali-Ilahi or Ahl al-Haqq, and Bahai. With the overthrow of the Pahlavi dynasty in Tehran in 1979, Shi'ism has risen to political prominence.[4] The Khomeini administration dismantled the last remnants of what was perceived as a repressive, Western-styled monarchy. In its place, Iran was transformed into an Islamic republic according to the Shi'ite school of thought (see chapter 6). It is the Sunni sect of Islam, however, that predominates. This sect represents 90 percent of all Muslims and is the principal faith of Egypt, Syria, Jordan, the Arabian peninsula, and Turkey. The Sunni branch of Islam is divided into four "schools of law": the Hanifite, the Malikite, the Shafite, and the Hanbalite. Each has its distinct interpretation of scripture and tradition, but there is agreement on the fundamentals.

Members of the Coptic church in Egypt and the Greek Orthodox church in Syria and Lebanon constitute the largest Christian organizations found in the Middle East. In addition, there are small groups of Armenian and Syrian Orthodox and Nestorians scattered throughout the area. Originally, the Coptic church evolved in Alexandria, the Greek Orthodox in Constantinople, and the Syrian or Jacobite in Antioch. The Roman Catholic church, currently represented in the Middle East by various uniate churches, such as the Greek Catholic, Coptic Catholic, and Syrian Catholic, first arose in Rome.

The Jewish faith is the third most significant religion in the Middle East and, aside from traces of the lost Samaritan and Daraite sects, generally follows the traditional canons set forth by a native orthodox Rabbinate Judaism. The principal canonical scripture is the Torah. Although there is disagreement over the precise number of divisions in Judaism, it can be broadly divided into two major sects: Orthodox and Reform. Jewish communities can be found in most Middle Eastern states, but since 1948 the largest concentrations have, of course, been found in Israel. The creation of Israel in 1948 may be viewed as a product of the politicization of Judaism in the form of a national movement. See chapter 4 for an examination of this and chapters 11 and 12 for its political ramifications.

Economic Geography

Agriculture

Harsh climatic conditions have long been a source of concern to agricultural specialists in the Middle East. Farming has been generally restricted to those regions that lie outside the vast stretches of desert and steppe, and thus it has been confined to relatively small areas. Probably only 7 to 10 percent of the total area is suitable for cultivation. However, this estimate is changing with the introduction of advanced farming technology.

The seasonal concentration of rainfall seriously limits the amount of ground that can be used productively. Except in the mountains, most precipitation occurs during only one or two months; the rest of the year remains virtually arid. Moreover, except for the Euphrates, Tigris, Nile, and Karun rivers, Middle Eastern rivers are small, and the lakes have a high saline content. Therefore, in many areas dry farming is necessary, and a system of two or three years' rotation of the land is often unavoidable. Another difficulty is that in territories like Iraq the rivers flood every spring when additional water is least needed.

Agriculture was carried on in a primitive fashion until modern systems of irrigation, flood control, and farming were developed to offset the long summer droughts and the unequal distribution of water. At present, chemical fertilizers and scientific methods of grazing and harvesting are being rapidly introduced. Although many farmers still use handmade, manual tools to cultivate the soil, land redistribution in Iran, Syria, and Egypt was accompanied by the introduction of modern farming techniques. Following the oil boom of the 1970s, the agricultural sectors have rapidly expanded, and considerable industrialization is under way.

Farming is largely for local consumption except for the raising of cotton, which was Egypt's chief export. Now cotton is superseded by oil. Also, a fourth of Israel's agricultural produce is exported. Though the region boasts an extensive grain belt, it was still unable to produce the amount of food required to sustain its population. However, this trend is rapidly changing. For instance, Saudi Arabia is now a net exporter of wheat. Generally, Turkey, Iraq, and Syria harvest a surplus of wheat and even manage to export some barley and rice. However, Iran, Israel, and Egypt must import grain.

The principal plants that have been developed from the flora native to the area—besides wheat and barley—are broad beans, rye, leeks, onions, lentils, grapes, figs, garlic, apricots, peaches, apples, plums, pears, pomegranates, melons, dates, olives, walnuts, and almonds. Wheat and barley are by far the most important grains cultivated in the Middle East and are largely produced in the north, where climatic conditions are favorable to their growth. Barley is favored in Iraq, Iran, and Syria because of its greater resistance to insects and environmental extremes. Rye is a crop that does well in the foothills and the colder regions of Iran and Turkey. As one moves south toward southern Arabia, corn and drought-resistant cereals, such as millets and sorghums, become the principal plants grown. In those areas of the desert where water is available and in other regions where irrigation is possible, such as in Lower Egypt, Iran, and southern Iraq, rice (which requires a great deal of heat and moisture) is popular because of its high yield.

In addition to the basic grains, the Middle East also produces a wide selection of fruits and nuts. Hazelnuts and figs are grown in Turkey; apples are found in the highlands of Lebanon; apricots, melons, and pistachios are grown in Iran; and, wherever hilly regions and moderate, dry weather occur together (as they do in the foothills of Asia Minor, Lebanon, and Israel), grapes are cultivated and harvested in large quantities. Oranges are the principal citrus fruit produced in the Middle East and represent a significant portion of Israel's export profits. They are also grown in parts of Iran, the Levant, and southern Turkey.

Even more important than the vine to the diet of many Middle Easterners are the date and olive crops. The olive represents a significant source of fat and is used in the preparation of a variety of tasty, nourishing dishes. Requiring considerable winter precipitation and long, dry summers, the olive tree is raised primarily in the valleys of southwest Turkey and, on a more limited basis, in Iran and along the coasts of Syria, Lebanon, and Israel. On the other hand, the date requires endless heat, meaning that crops thrive around the oases of the Arabian peninsula. However, the most abundant date harvests are obtained where either irrigation or rivers ensure a surplus of water. For this reason the district of Basrah, in southern Iraq, exports 80 percent of the world's supply of dates.

One of the most profitable commercial plants being grown in the Middle East today is Egypt's long-fibered cotton. Turkey and Iran, as well as other nations of the Fertile Crescent region, also raise cotton, but their annual yields are relatively modest in comparison to Egypt's bountiful harvests. Flax, hemp, and silk are produced in Syria, Iraq, Jordan, and Israel, but quantities are too small for market crops.

Some of the secondary crops produced in the Middle East are coffee, cultivated on the mountain slopes of Yemen; tea, raised along Turkey's Black Sea coast and the Caspian shore of Iran; and both sugar beets and sugarcane, harvested primarily in Turkey. Turkey also grows tobacco near its Aegean Sea coast, and small quantities of the plant are found in Iran, northern Iraq, and along the Levantine coast.

No survey of Middle Eastern agriculture would be complete without at least a brief look at those animals on which the pastoral and rural dwellers depend for food and income. Sheep and goats, numbering in the tens of millions, are found throughout the region, and it is believed by conservation specialists that their destructive grazing habits have contributed significantly to the disappearance of large areas of native vegetation. Nomadic tribes, who depend upon their livestock for survival, possess approximately 80 percent of these animals; the remaining 20 percent represent the herds and flocks of the settled farmers.

In comparison with cattle in other parts of the world, the cattle of the Middle East are generally not significant. They are small, and their milk yield is so low that most are used primarily as draft animals. It is not unusual to see donkeys and cows yoked together, pulling plows in the fields of the Middle East. However, in regions like the Nile Delta and the marshlands of southern Iraq the water buffalo is the principal beast of burden.

The horse is gradually becoming a rarity in the Middle East. The camel is still utilized by nomadic tribes in their long journeys across the deserts and arid steppe, but in rural areas the economical donkey has become the most common means of transportation. Animal husbandry does not include the raising of swine for domestic or commercial reasons, because the dominant Islamic creed prohibits the eating of swine. Small Christian communities raise swine locally. In Jordan, for example, the livestock commonly raised includes horses, asses, cattle, camels, sheep, goats, and poultry. Like farming, the raising of livestock primarily serves domestic needs although a marginal export market exists.

Resources

Oil is by far the most important mineral resource the Middle East possesses. No one knows exactly how great the oil reserves are, but it is apparent that they have not yet been fully explored. Middle Eastern oil is not equally distributed throughout the area. Some oil is found in Turkey, Egypt, Syria, and the State of Israel, but the truly large fields are located in Kuwait, Iraq, Iran, and along the Gulf in Saudi Arabia and the sheikdoms. Kuwait accounts for about 18 percent of the world's reserves, while Saudi Arabia accounts for 25 percent. The Arab world's oil reserves account for 56 percent of the world's total.[5] Following the organization of OPEC in 1973, Middle East oil became a vital concern especially for Western industrial nations. Oil-pricing policies and production requirements assumed crucial importance to the rest of the developing world.

A variety of mineral resources are found in the Middle East, but other than oil, only the red iron oxide and turquoise of Iran and the potash of Jordan are produced and exported in any quantity. Large deposits of coal and lignite exist in Turkey and Iran, but these beds have been exploited only in recent years. In addition to widespread but individually small pockets of gold, silver, copper, and iron ores, the Middle East also possesses considerable amounts of chromium and manganese and small amounts of antimony, molybdenum, mercury, and cobalt.

Other Middle Eastern resources include extensive basalt, granite, marble, porphyry, sandstone, and limestone quarries and the natural clays that have been used by many cultures to produce fine ceramics.

Industry

Before the oil boom, industry in the traditional Western sense was almost nonexistent in the Middle East. Outside the oil sector, the indifference of private investors and the shortage of trained administrators, skilled workers, and power have greatly limited the Middle East's ability to manufacture goods that can compete in price and quality on the world market. Only in Egypt, Israel, and Lebanon did textiles and other manufactured items represent a significant proportion of total exports. Nevertheless, there was a surge of industrialization brought about by such measures as state capitalism in Turkey and Iran, socialism in Egypt and Syria, tariff protection for private industry in Lebanon and Iraq, the investment of oil income in Iraq and Iran, and financial and technical assistance from abroad. In Egypt industrialization started in the 1930s, peaked in the fifties and sixties, and declined in the seventies and eighties. Now there is again emphasis on industrialization, primarily through the encouragement of the private sector, but the results have yet to be seen. In the 1970s, as a result of the acquisition of huge petrodollar revenues, the oil-exporting countries began to embrace ambitious modernization and industrialization programs in almost every major sector of their economies.

The growth of industry has resulted in the rise of a new working class. This group, though still small, has formed organized unions and influenced legislators to enact laws favorable to labor, thereby creating a working environment that may one day encourage further industrial expansion. A well-trained, satisfied body of workers is essential to industry, and benefits like workers' compensation and high wages are sure to attract and retain individuals. However, the number of people currently engaged in Middle Eastern industry is modest in comparison with the number working in agriculture. A survey in Egypt, a country with a relatively large proportion of industrial workers, indicates that less than 6 percent of the nation's work force are employed by industry. Even in those countries where oil production dominates the economy, usually no more than 1 percent of the labor force is actively involved with oil-connected enterprises. Nevertheless, the picture changed in the 1970s and 1980s.

The increase of oil production and export, however, overshadows industrialization. In 1963 Middle East crude oil production was recorded at 6,823.4 million barrels per day (mb/d). By 1973 this figure tripled to 21,152.6 mb/d. Four years later crude oil production reached its peak at 22,195.1 mb/d. However, the trend was not maintained; the 1983 crude oil production fell dramatically to 11,138.8 mb/d. Although production plummeted to a low of 9,778.5 mb/d in 1985, it jumped to 12,371.3 mb/d the following year.

The Middle East is still the world's major oil-producing region. Production trends indicate that the Middle East is capable of rapid industrialization because of huge revenues accrued from crude oil production. Moreover, there is reason to believe that this trend will continue for some time, even though minor fluctuations exist, because the Middle East is believed to have five-eighths of the proven oil reserves among OPEC nations: 1986 estimates show that OPEC members account for a total of 777,235.6 million barrels; the Middle East alone claims 535,937.7 million barrels of that figure.

Social Geography

Middle Eastern society is in the process of a socioeconomic and political revolution and is currently experiencing important and sweeping changes in its basic structure. Yet traditional social patterns, such as kinship-based groupings and the rule of Shari'ah (Islamic law), are generally more resistant in rural areas than in urban ones. Therefore, the process of change is uneven and must be considered separately for the urban dweller, the villager, and the nomad.

City Life

Although most of the population is rural, city life is a disproportionately strong influence in the Middle East. Urban developments are the centers of the economic, social, political, and religious activities of the area. In fact, the economic dominance of the cities has contributed significantly to the poverty of rural regions. Absentee landlords and merchants who control and manipulate the profits of rural produce have been able to accumulate most of the surplus agricultural wealth in the cities. In addition, the city is the locus of all political power.

One of the major problems of the Middle East, and of the Arab world in particular, has been the rapid growth of urban centers. Since the 1940s, the number of people moving from the rural areas of the Middle East to the cities has drastically increased. Among the reasons for this migration are the industrial employment, higher wages, free education, and improved medical facilities found in the cities. Increasingly the youth of the Middle East have been unwilling to remain in villages and have sought, instead, the opportunities and social stature of urban life. Of course, a high birth rate and a longer life expectancy have also contributed to urban growth along with migration trends. Urban populations show a wide range: from an estimated 700,000 people in Riyadh, at the low end, to Tehran, with more than 5 million and Cairo, with a 1986 census population of about 6 million in Cairo proper and 9 million in metropolitan Cairo.

Rural Life

Except in Israel, where it is estimated that 84 percent of the population lives in cities, the predominance of rural life is one of the primary features of Middle Eastern society. Approximately half the population lives in the countryside and is principally engaged in agriculture. Like the nomads, Middle Eastern peasants, or *fallahin*, generally live as their ancestors existed centuries before them. They live in villages near to or surrounded by their fields. The tools they use—the sickle, the threshing board, and the wooden plow—are the same tools that have been used to cultivate the land for more than 2,000 years. Until recently, the land peasants farm was the property of a relatively few powerful landlords, like tribal sheikhs and absentee owners. Before the 1950s approximately 70 percent of the fallahin were either tenants or sharecroppers. In conjunction with the land-reform programs, which have turned the fallahin into landowners, governments are encouraging the use of modern farming techniques and equipment and are attempting to replace the cash crop system with a food crop system. Moreover, industrializing trends are beginning to affect demographic shifts toward big cities.

Health and sanitation in the Middle East are no longer tragic problems. An increase in the number of health centers, clinics, and hospitals has played a major role in combating diseases once considered endemic. Infant mortality rates have decreased and life expectancy has increased in recent years. Despite much progress, considerable efforts are still required to extend health care to remote rural sectors.

Until recently, widespread illiteracy characterized Middle Eastern society, especially in rural areas. Government initiatives to establish compulsory education have improved the situation. The object is to provide a minimal level of education. Institutions offer incentives and easier access to advanced education, and generous foreign scholarship programs are offered by some Middle Eastern states. Educational institutions no longer confine themselves to Arab and Islamic studies. Subjects range from vocational studies, to the study of foreign languages, to math, science, and technology. The arts and sciences are becoming increasingly important in the educational system of the Middle East.

Nomadic Life

Like the urban dweller, the nomad too is in transition and is currently becoming a sedentary rather than a migratory member of Middle Eastern society. National governments have recently found it necessary to restrict the freedom of movement the tribes have enjoyed for centuries, and the threat posed by modern weapon systems has rendered the more warlike wanderers vulnerable even in their traditional strongholds, the desert and mountains. Moreover, as the area under cultivation has increased, the grazing lands upon which the tribes depend to support their livestock have rapidly dwindled. Consequently, many nomads have sought employment in the oil and mining industries, and others have joined military and public organizations. It appears that Middle Eastern nomadism will eventually disappear.

Nomadic existence centers around the raising of sheep and goats and the production of milk, butter, cheese, and wool. The various tribes depend heavily on their flocks and herds to sustain life, although the mobile and heavily armed tribesmen have traditionally supplemented their income with random but effective assaults on the outskirts of urban areas. For many tribes, raiding and pillage have long been an economic necessity—often the only alternative to starvation during years of drought when the grass has failed to replenish itself enough to feed their animals. Improved irrigation and a trend toward modernization are changing the nomadic lifestyle. Clearly the nomad's days are numbered.

The most important organization in the nomad's life is the tribe, which consists of a number of families who have been brought together through marriage and who follow a leader called a *sheikh* by the Arabs and a *khan* in Iran. The office of a sheikh or khan is decided partly by heredity and partly by merit, and it commands the loyalty of all members of the tribe. Although most tribes are found within the borders of the Middle Eastern states, they seldom recognize any government but their own, a practice that has often outraged central authorities. The tribe is usually large enough to survive in a hostile environment, but it is limited in size by the resources of the district it inhabits. Occasionally an exceptional leader has been able to combine the tribes into larger federations. These federations, however, have not lasted long, and they were generally marked by intertribal feuds and jealousies. On the whole, the nomad's way of life and social ideals, which include personal bravery and tribal stature, do not permit easy formation of extensive political unions.

There are two forms of nomadism in the Middle East. The "horizontal" nomads occupy the desert and follow the rain. During autumn and winter, seasonal precipitation extends the grazing area available for their sheep and goats, and the tribes are able to remain relatively stationary for long periods of time. However, during the summer months, they must either seek out distant water supplies for their flocks and herds or perish. The "vertical" nomads follow the vegetation that blossoms at increasingly higher altitudes during the summer in the mountainous regions of Iraq, Turkey, and Iran, and then they winter each year on the plains.

In order to remain highly mobile, nomads have only a few personal possessions. Their tents, customarily black, are woven of either goat or camel hair and are easily folded and moved; furniture is minimal and usually consists of a floor rug or mats and a few utensils necessary for daily life.

NOTES

1. G. Etzel Pearcy, "The Middle East—An Indefinable Region," *Department of State Bulletin* (March 23, 1959): 407–16; reprinted as Department of State Publication No. 6806, Near East and Middle Eastern Series 39.

2. Roderic H. Davison, "Where Is the Middle East," in *The Modern Middle East*, ed. Richard H. Nolte (New York, 1963), p. 29.

3. John S. Badeau, *The American Approach to the Arab World* (New York, 1968), p. 22.

4. For an analysis of Islamic Resurgence, see J.S. Ismael and T.Y. Ismael, "Social Change in Islamic Society: The Political Thought of Ayatollah Khomeini," *Social Problems* 27, 5 (June 1980).

5. See Ali Ahmad Attiga, *Interdependence on the Oil Bridge* (Petroleum Information Committee of the Arab Gulf States, 1988).

I

THE DYNAMICS
OF THE REGION

2

The Burden of History

Tareq Ismael and Jacqueline Ismael

Although historians disagree over the exact location of the birthplace of Western civilization, they do agree that it originated in
the Middle East, either in the Nile Valley or in Mesopotamia along
the Tigris-Euphrates River. From the earliest period, the area was
the crossroads of migrating peoples. Successive invasions into the
area made it a melting pot of races and cultures. The first of the
invaders, an Asiatic variant of the Mediterranean race called the
Sumerians, established a number of city-states between the Tigris
and the Euphrates rivers. The prosperity of these city-states attracted from the surrounding areas Semitic peoples who founded
the state of Akkad along the middle Euphrates about the beginning
of the third millennium B.C. For a thousand years Sumerian and
Akkadian states competed with each other. The threat of outside
invasion by the non-Semitic Elamites resulted in the unification
of all Mesopotamia by Hammurabi of Babylon about 1700 B.C.
During this same period, the Hamites established in the Nile Valley
a monarchical state which they were able to hold relatively undis-
turbed until about 500 B.C. when the Persians established their
empire. Semite tribes from Arabia, meanwhile, continued to fill
the area between Sumeria and the Nile, establishing states in the
area known as the Fertile Crescent.[1]

From 1700 to 100 B.C. the Indo-European invasions brought successive waves of conquerors, each of whom extended the empire
of his predecessors. Thus, the Persians, by 500 B.C., were able to
establish an empire bordered by the Indus River, the Black Sea,
and the western border of Egypt. The Persian Empire, a monar-

chical state, was effectively controlled by the appointment of satraps to the governorship of its territorial subdivisions and by the use of spies who watched the satraps and reported directly to the emperor. The Persians also built a highway, the Royal Road, from Sardis on the Aegean to their capital at Soussa. This road, excellently policed, both facilitated East-West trade and ensured communication within the empire.

One of the major problems facing the Persian Empire was the expansionist tendencies of the Greeks. The ultimate failure to control the Greeks was to have a dramatic impact upon the development of the Middle East. The conquests of Alexander the Great ushered in a new age not only for the Greeks but also for the groups who resided in the birthplace of civilization. It had been Alexander's wish to blend the cultures of Greece and Persia, and before his early death in 323 B.C. he was partially successful in Hellenizing the Middle East through his encouragement of intermarriage between his soldiers and the women of conquered peoples and his founding of a number of cities styled after those of Greece. After Alexander's death, the empire broke up into a series of kingdoms ruled by his generals. The Hellenizing effects of his conquest, however, were more permanent. For the next two centuries the Middle East continued to be an area wealthy in intellectual and artistic achievement but poor in political stability.

About the first century B.C. the Romans, then the most powerful people in the Mediterranean area, began to extend their influence into the Middle East through arbitration with the warring states there. Eventually the Romans established political control over the area except for the eastern part of Persia, where first the Parthian Empire and then the Sassanids predominated. The area remained under imperial regulation until the time of Constantine, when it fell under the authority of Constantinople.

Roman control of the Middle East, however, was never complete. The first centuries of occupation saw a number of large-scale uprisings, and the Parthians and Sassanids remained a constant threat to the security of first the Romans and later the Byzantines.

It might be expected that the spread of Christianity throughout the Roman Empire would have brought unity, but in fact it did not. From Constantinople to North Africa each area developed its own heresy, and the only link between them was that they were all split from Rome and the West.

Into this mass of political and religious strife came the Arab conquerors from the Arabian peninsula. The Arabs had formed economic ties between the city dwellers and their own nomadic bands. Thus, as the cities allied with the Arab tribes began to seek power on the basis of their position on the East-West trade routes, Western influence fell away.

Islam and the Islamic Empire

By the seventh century, Mecca, midway on the trade route between Yemen and Syria, was the principal center of the Arabian peninsula. It had become a wealthy and independent city which had achieved its position of eminence through trade and financial speculation in the Red Sea and eastern Mediterranean territories. The city maintained relations with the tribes in the surrounding area but carefully kept itself neutral in the conflicts between the Sassanid and Byzantine empires. The city government consisted of a council of clan leaders, but each clan was independent of the council and responsible for itself. Religion in Mecca was diverse, ranging from magic and pantheism to a clan-centered code of honor. The Arabs were steeped in idolatry, and Arabia was rife with tribal rivalry and warfare. Just as the land reached the height of rebelliousness, Mecca was at the eve of transformation.

In this environment, in the year 610 A.D., the Prophet Muhammad, a Meccan native, began preaching a religion of individual surrender to a monotheistic God. At first his movement drew a number of converts from the poor and the middle class; however, the wealthy feared that monotheism would lessen the number of pilgrimages to the Ka'abah, a pantheistic shrine, and would destroy the pilgrim trade. Most importantly the Meccan chiefs feared that this message of Muhammad would threaten the established order and challenge their authority. As a result, economic sanctions were taken against the new religionists, the Muslims, and they were persecuted so severely that their safety became endangered. The Muslims were sent to Ethiopia as refugees until the hostile climate changed. However, a worsening of the situation forced Muhammad in 622 to move with his followers to Medina, where, by acting as arbitrator for the city's clans and by consolidating his religion, he became the undisputed leader of the first Islamic city-state. This migration was called the *Hijra* and began the first year of the Islamic calendar. Eight years of warfare with Mecca followed, but finally that city was brought to terms and Muhammad returned as its master. It was during this hostile period that Islam spread throughout the Arabian peninsula and the social precepts of this new order were developed.

From the death of Muhammad in 632 until the establishment of the Umayyad dynasty at Damascus in 661, the Muslim leaders were chosen by the chief men of Mecca and Medina. Each of the four leaders chosen during this period—Abu Bakr, Umar, Uthman, and Ali—was named in his turn *khalifah* (caliph or successor) and functioned as both religious and political head of the Muslim world. During their years in power, these four men succeeded in completely entrenching Islam on the Arabian peninsula and wresting from the Byzantine and Sassanid empires the lands of Syria, Palestine, Egypt, Iraq, and Iran. Thus, the Islamic Empire expanded and rose to prominence both religiously and politically.

During the reign of the first four caliphs, a single family called the Umayyads had been gathering power through administrative ability. After the assassination of Ali in 661, this family established a dynasty that was to last for nearly a century. The Umayyads left four marks on the Islamic world: they moved the capital to Damascus; they added North Africa, Spain, and part of Asia to the empire; they reorganized the imperial administration; and they changed the elective caliphate to a hereditary system. The Umayyads at first partitioned the empire into five viceroyalties ruled by their appointees. Then, because of the lack of trained Arab personnel, they left the administration of each of these areas in the hands of those who had administered them before the conquest.

During the last half of the Umayyad reign, however, the Middle

East was torn by civil wars. Charges of corruption against the Damascene rulers aided the Abbasids, descendants of Muhammad, in their claim to the caliphate. In 750, Abu al-Abbas overthrew the Umayyads and founded the Abbasid dynasty. The Umayyads, however, retained control of Spain.

Following their rise to power, the Abbasids moved the capital to Baghdad and from there ruled, through their *wazirs* (viziers), their steadily dwindling dominions. In 788 an independent state was established in Morocco; in 800 the governor of Africa declared its independence; in the middle of the ninth century Egypt's own dynasties began. Finally, in the tenth century the Fatimids of Egypt succeeded in establishing a western Muslim world that stretched from Syria to the Strait of Gibraltar. And in the East all the Muslim provinces in and near India fell away from Baghdad. In the eleventh century the Seljuk Turks, fierce invaders from the East, seized the last of the Abbasid Empire.

Concurrent with the Abbasid political decline, however, was the development of a rich culture. Notable contributions were made to philosophy and poetry, and the distinct Abbasid architecture evolved—a style that features tall minarets and complex geometrical designs, which has had influence throughout the world. The works of Greek scholars were translated, studied, and supplemented, and work of original and lasting value was done in medicine, astronomy, and geography.

By the eleventh century both the Seljuk and Fatimid empires began to disintegrate into numerous petty states. Then, unable to present any organized resistance, these states watched helplessly as the European crusaders drove a wedge of control into Syria and Palestine during the twelfth century. The crusaders' fortunes in the Middle East were directly related to Muslim unity. Thus, when Salah-al-Din Alayyubi (Saladin) was able to regroup the torn Muslim world—starting with Egypt, then proceeding to Syria, northern Iraq, Hijaz, Nubia, and North Africa—he was able to extend his influence from the Nile to the Tigris. Upon his death, however, the crusaders gained back their lost territory and were able to hold it until the Mamluks gained firm control of Egypt. But even as the Mamluks were driving the Europeans from the

Middle East, they were required to meet a new threat. The Mongol hordes of Genghis Khan and his successors invaded from the East in a wave of destruction and conquest. They conquered as far as Damascus until in 1260 they were defeated and thrown out of Syria.

The Mamluk rulers of Egypt, the Turkish warrior slaves of Egypt's former rulers, established feudalism as the new social order. But the conquests of the Mongolian Turks, led by Timur Leng (Tamerlane), in the last part of the fourteenth century ended Mamluk control east of Egypt, resulted in a subdued and diminished Ottoman state, and left Iran dismembered and weak.

Ottoman Empire

When Constantine moved the Roman capital to Constantinople, he created a buffer state between Europe and the Middle East.[2] Originally the Byzantine Empire controlled the entire Middle East; but over its thousand-year lifespan the empire was reduced to a single city-state straddling the Bosphorus. Nonetheless, because of its strategic position, the impregnable city of Constantinople was able to maintain itself until the Turks captured the city in 1453.

From the time of the Seljuk invasions, the Turks had come to dominate the Middle East, largely at the expense of the Byzantines. By the last half of the twelfth century, the Sultanate of Rum (Rome) and the holdings of Salah-al-Din included the greater part of Islam. The Mongol invasions, however, destroyed both of these states. Then, about 1300, Osman, a Turkish chieftain, began to consolidate by conquest and alliance a number of small towns in Asia Minor. Although Osman died in 1326, the Ottoman Turks continued to expand their sphere of influence in the Middle East. In 1354 an earthquake destroyed the walls and fortifications of Gallipoli and thus enabled the Ottomans to cross the Dardanelles and gain a foothold in Europe. From there, aided by the chaos created by the Black Death, they were able to extend their dominion into the Balkans. At the same time, they pressed south and east, establishing their control over the greater part of Asia Minor. Ottoman expansion in the East, however, was met by Tamerlane. Tamerlane defeated Bayezid I in 1402 at the Battle of Ankara and then conquered to the west as far as the Mediterranean. Rather than holding Ottoman territory directly, in exchange for an oath of allegiance Tamerlane divided the Ottoman conquests of Europe and the easy holdings of Osman and Orhan I (Osman's son) in Asia among Bayezid's sons. Upon Tamerlane's death in 1405 the Ottoman *emirs* (leaders) asserted their independence of the Timurids, but the Ottoman state remained fragmented among Bayezid's four sons.

It was one of the sons of Bayezid, Mehmed I, who reunited the Ottoman state and set it again on the path of conquest. His grandson, Mehmed II, pushed into Hungary and southern Russia, completed the conquest of Turkey, and in 1453 captured Constantinople (renamed Istanbul), thus laying the foundation of the Ottoman Empire. Salim I added Syria, Palestine, Egypt, and Algeria. And finally, in the last part of the seventeenth century, Tunisia, the west coast of Arabia, and small holdings around the Black Sea and the Persian Gulf were brought into the empire, completing its period of expansion.

The Ottoman Empire was ruled from the sultan's court in Istanbul. The sultan was theoretically the absolute ruler of the state and head of the Muslim religion, but considerable power was exercised by the sultan's household. Also, the degree of local autonomy increased with the degree of remoteness from the administrative center at Istanbul. Because the Turks were a minority in their empire, administrators were drawn from any source, including nations outside the empire's borders. Officials, therefore, could be chosen on the basis of ability rather than on the basis of racial or religious considerations. Indeed, the corps of Janissaries, the famed bodyguard of the sultans, was composed entirely of Islamized Christians. Bribery was common in the appointment of officials, but a palace school was maintained for the education of those who would occupy the high positions of government, and thus it was ensured that the sultan and his immediate circle of deputies would be men capable of ruling.

The Ottoman Empire exercised considerable influence in European affairs, partly because of its encroachments on European territory and partly because of its control of the East-West trade routes.

Particularly strong were the Ottoman ties with the Italian city-states, which represented at that time the western terminus of the trade routes. But these ties were eventually weakened when at the end of the fifteenth century the Portuguese discovered a new East-West passage around southern Africa.

The sixteenth century also saw the development of Istanbul as a cultural center. The city was largely rebuilt, and it is still famous for its Ottoman mosques. A Turkish literature was developed during this period as both poets and historians were retained by the court. Also, Ottoman naval development in the Mediterranean led to advances in geography and cartography.

During the seventeenth century, however, the Ottoman decline was rapid. A combination of weak sultans, civil wars, and European expansion drove the Ottomans first from Europe and, in the following centuries, from North Africa. At the start of the First World War, the Ottoman Empire was reduced to Turkey, Mesopotamia, Palestine, and the fringes of Arabia. The Muslims expanded the Islamic Empire without consolidating power, and this is precisely what led to a fragile empire, its decay, and its eventual disintegration.

European Involvement[3]

In 1498 Vasco da Gama, a Portuguese navigator, reached India by sailing around Africa. In the years immediately following, other Portuguese retraced da Gama's route, establishing trading stations in the Persian Gulf and diverting much of the Eastern trade from the earlier route through the Middle East. For a time the Portuguese enjoyed a monopoly over the Cape route. The transport costs were as much as one-third less than those of the overland route via the Middle East. And to further inhibit overland transport, the Portuguese attempted to blockade shipping on the Red Sea and Persian Gulf. Thus, Lisbon quickly replaced Venice as the European clearinghouse for Indian goods. When military efforts by the Middle Eastern and European powers failed to destroy the

Portuguese trade, first Venice and then France and England signed trade agreements with the Turks to secure more favorable transport terms for their goods across Ottoman territory.

While France and England contended for the Middle East trade, England and Holland supplanted the Portuguese in the East Indies. But Holland, drained by its wars with the English and the French, was unable to compete with England; the Dutch withdrawal from the East left the British East India Company with a monopoly on the southern trade routes.

In the eighteenth century European expansion became more overt. As governmental authority broke down in the Far and Middle East, France and England sought to secure their trade through physical supervision of the sources and routes of that trade. England seized political power in large parts of the Far East and attempted to do the same in the Middle East. France countered in 1798 with Napoleon's expedition to Egypt. The defeat of the French fleet at Aboukir Bay, however, checked the French, and three years later they withdrew their army.

Napoleon's fall left England the dominant power in the Middle East, but the Egyptians had been impressed by the display of efficiency of the French expeditionary force to their country, and Muhammad Ali and his son, Ibrahim Pasha, laid designs to build the nucleus of a modern empire. Under the leadership of these two men, the Egyptians rapidly expanded into Sudan, Ethiopia, Palestine, Syria, and Arabia. British ties with the Ottomans, however, checked further expansion.

Having refused aid by Britain in modernizing their state, Muhammad Ali and Ibrahim Pasha turned to France. The French responded with trained administrators, military missions, aid in opening schools, and the training of young Egyptians in French colleges. Half of Egypt's trade, however, remained with England, and France's setback in the Franco-Prussian War left the English dominant once more throughout the Middle East.

Besides the modernization of Egypt, the French made yet another great contribution to Middle Eastern affairs. Building on a brief period of influence in the Ottoman Empire during the Crimean War, the French pressed for permission to build the Suez Canal. Granted permission by the Ottomans and supported by Russia and Austria, France was able to open the canal in 1869, thus linking the Middle East to the modern West. The Suez Canal was to open a new chapter of importance of the Middle East to the West and perhaps the world at large.

The incompetence and extravagance of Muhammad Ali's successors in Egypt resulted in the accumulation of an enormous national debt to the European powers. In 1879, therefore, France and England established dual political control of Egypt in an effort to secure their investments. When the Egyptians grew restive under this control, Britain in 1882 occupied the country and held all political power there until World War I.

Although British rule was helpful in reducing the Egyptian debt, the country itself was not improved much materially. Further, the use of English officials at all levels of control kept the Egyptians from developing the ability of self-rule.

In the nineteenth century the Ottoman Empire was the major area of European conflict. The Roman Catholics of France engaged with the Orthodox Christians of Russia in controversies over who should control the Christian holy places in the Middle East, and Russian expansionists desired to secure their entrance to the Mediterranean through the Bosphorus and to restore a Christian empire at Istanbul. Austria, fearing that Russia would outflank her from the south, wanted to check Russian expansion into Ottoman territory. England, too, was apprehensive about Russian expansion into the Mediterranean. In addition, both England and France were interested in Ottoman territory that lay astride the trade routes to their extensive commercial interests in the Orient. A series of small wars waged between these nations over Turkish territory kept any one of them from dominating the area.

In 1872 a serious threat to Anglo-French interests in Turkey appeared when the Ottomans brought in German investment and engineering to build the Balkan railway system. During the next thirty years, the Germans increased their influence in Turkey through extension of the railway and through trade agreements with the Ottomans.

The Twentieth-Century Middle East to World War I

European intervention in the Middle East during the nineteenth century fostered Arab nationalism. European armies, technicians, and administrators clearly demonstrated the abilities of, and the benefits accruing to, a modernized nation. Christian missionaries aided in establishing Arab schools, thus laying an educational foundation for modernization, and potential Muslim leaders were given the opportunity to observe and learn European methods in the academies of France and Germany. Moreover, Muhammad Ali's and Ibrahim Pasha's efforts toward Arab unification encouraged Muslims to consider the possibilities of establishing, and the advantages of operating, a modern Arab state.

The English occupation of Egypt spurred nationalism in that state. Given that British personnel were brought in to fill administrative positions, these posts were denied to educated Egyptians. Inspired by the gains of the Young Turks, Egyptian nationalists engaged in violent agitation for self-government.

Concerned for the security of the Suez Canal and their Egyptian investments, the British could not at that time accede to Egyptian demands for immediate self-government. In 1911, therefore, they reasserted their control of Egyptian affairs with the appointment of Lord Kitchener as administrator of Egypt. Kitchener initiated programs of legislative reforms designed to break down the power of Egyptian agriculturists. Although nationalist resistance was strong, an outbreak of violence was averted by the start of World War I.

The oppression and absolutism of the Ottoman sultan and the winds of change from Europe led to the growth of Turkish nationalism. In 1889 students at the Istanbul Military Medical College, led by Albanian student Ibrahim Temo, organized the Committee of Progress and Union (CPU), a secret society modeled after the Italian Carbonari societies. The movement quickly branched into the Military Academy, the Naval Academy, the Artillery and Engineering School, the Veterinary School, and the Civil College. With the blessing and support of the major ethnic and religious groups in the Ottoman Empire, the CPU led the revolution of 1908. The

Young Turk Revolution, which brought in its wake a declaration of the equality of all races in the Ottoman Empire, had stirred Arab nationalism, especially in Syria and Iraq. By 1909, however, conflict within the CPU divided its members along national lines and resulted in the growth of extremism on both sides. Centralization of government and Turkification of all elements within the empire became the covert objectives of the Young Turks. In the Arab world rapidly growing secret societies, which at first hoped to gain autonomy within the Ottoman Empire, now advocated complete independence. Moreover, German influence had grown with Turkish nationalism. Germany's *Drang nach Osten* (drive to the East) led to German aid in Turkish modernization, development of the Berlin-to-Baghdad railway, and the eventual emergence of Turkey as Germany's military partner.

The first months of World War I saw an uneasy truce in the Middle East, but in October 1914 the British began instigating Arab revolts in Arabia. In the celebrated correspondence between Sharif Hussain of Mecca and Sir Henry McMahon, British high commissioner for Egypt and the Sudan, McMahon promised the creation of an independent Arab state at the conclusion of the war. This state was to encompass the area demarcated on the north by a line drawn eastward from Alexandretta to the Iranian frontier and thence southward to the Persian Gulf and to include the entire Arabian peninsula with the exception of Aden. At the same time, however, the Allies were negotiating the division of both Turkish and Arab lands among themselves. The Constantinople Agreement of March 1915 gave Russia the right to annex certain areas in Asia Minor and Thrace while guaranteeing French and British interests in Turkey and Iran. The Treaty of London, signed in April of 1915, gave Italy territorial claims in North Africa and Asia Minor. Finally, in May 1916, the secret Sykes-Picot Agreement was concluded defining the exact territories to be taken over by Russia, France, and Britain and recognizing the spheres of influence of France and Britain in the Arab territories. In conflict with both the McMahon promises and the Sykes-Picot Agreement, the famous Balfour Declaration surfaced on November 2, 1917. This declaration, conceived without the consultation and consent of the Arabs, states that "His

Majesty's Government views with favor the Jewish people."⁴ And although "views with favour" was not a *promise* of a Jewish state, this paved the way for Zionists to claim Palestine. This declaration set the stage for a crisis in the Middle East that was to last to this day.

Precipitated by the Young Turks' declaration of martial law in Syria and by the execution and deportation of Arab nationalists, the Arab revolt of June 5, 1916, began. While hardly successful in mobilizing mass Arab support, this revolt was immensely helpful to the British in that it diverted Turkish reinforcements from facing the British advance through Palestine, ended German propaganda in Arabia, and forestalled the possibility of a German submarine base on the Red Sea.

Between Two World Wars

The Arab revolt of World War I had been purchased at the price of Allied promises of an independent Arab state. At the end of the war, however, each of the victorious Western European powers hoped to seize a chunk of Middle Eastern territory. After two years of nearly fruitless negotiations, the Treaty of Sèvres with the Ottomans was signed on August 10, 1920. Under this treaty Turkey renounced all claim to Arabia, Egypt, Mesopotamia, and Syria. Britain was given a protectorate over Egypt, a mandate over Palestine, and tutelage over nominally independent Mesopotamia. Syria was placed under a French mandate; and the rulers of Arabia were granted independence.

The end of the war saw the Allies in possession of Turkey. The occupation of that state was left in the hands of the Greeks until such time as the Allies might decide its future. But the Turks, led by Mustafa Kamal, took matters into their own hands. In 1920 the Turks raised the banner of revolt, and at the end of two years of warfare, they had forced the withdrawal of the occupying forces. The Turks established a new government, deposed the Ottoman sultan, and voided the legislation of his government. In 1922 they met the Allies at the Lausanne Conference to determine Turkey's future. The Lausanne Conference severed the last remnants of the Ottoman Empire from Turkey, but it left the Turkish Republic an independent state.

In 1923 Mustafa Kamal was elected president of the republic. A year later, he declared the official dissolution of the empire. Until his death in 1938, he directed the modernization of Turkey and encouraged the resolution of two problems concerning foreign interests: demarcation of the Iraqi-Turkish frontier in Mosul province, and foreign use of the Dardanelles and the Bosphorus. The first issue was resolved by awarding Mosul province to Iraq; in return, Turkey received £500,000 (British) from Iraq and a guarantee of 10 percent of all oil royalties paid to Iraq by the concessionaire for the next twenty-five years. An international agreement that allowed Turkey to fortify the Straits settled the second issue.

In the Fertile Crescent the French established a governorship in Lebanon. They agreed, in 1936, to make Lebanon an independent state, but later refused to sign the treaties accomplishing this. In Syria, also under French mandate, independence again was first promised and later denied, and dissension arose between the French and Syria over Syria's loss of Lebanon, Latakia, and the Jabel Druze.

The British occupation of Iraq had met with fierce resistance that led to British attempts to form a stable government in that country. In 1921 a kingdom was established, and the country achieved a state of semi-independence from England. Full independence, however, was not achieved until Iraq was admitted as a member to the League of Nations in 1932. Oil was the great issue in Iraqi politics, both international and domestic. The Iraqis turned this problem into a source of strength by basing their economy on oil concessions.

Palestine, occupied by the British, was torn by conflict between Arabs and Jews. Each group wanted an independent Palestine for itself. According to the 1931 census, Arabs constituted approximately 90 percent of the population; the remaining 10 percent was composed principally of Jews and a small minority of other non-Arabs. But Jewish immigration and effective Zionist representation greatly built up Jewish strength. With the immigration of skilled

Jews and with massive financial aid from the world's Jewry, Jewish settlements in Palestine flourished. British rule was a hopeless attempt to aid the Jews while protecting the rights of the Arabs.

Egypt continued after World War I as a British protectorate under martial law. Strong nationalist resistance, however, forced promises of eventual independence. The instability of Egyptian government, Britain's preoccupation with other matters, and British concern for the Suez made this a difficult step. But the Anglo-Egyptian Treaty of 1936 began the process of making Egypt an independent state.

Elsewhere, Great Britain maintained its influence on the southern coast of the Persian Gulf, and Ibn Saud consolidated the Arabian peninsula under his rule in 1927 and proclaimed himself king of Hijaz and Nejd.

Iran, an independent state at the start of World War I, successfully resisted British attempts to incorporate it into the British Empire and Russian attempts to secure Iranian territory after the war. Then in 1920 Reza Khan overthrew the Iranian government and attempted to establish a republic modeled after Mustafa Kamal's Turkey. Religious opposition, however, prevented this transformation, and in 1925 Reza Khan became shah.

Reza Khan's strength was sufficient to accomplish several reforms: the power of religion and of religious institutions was reduced; 15,000 miles of roads and the Trans-Iranian railway were built; efforts were made toward the improvement of irrigation and other agricultural methods; and a number of industries were initiated by the state. Also, the oil concessions to Britain were modified to bring greater Iranian control to and more profit from this important commodity.

In international affairs Iran sought close ties with Germany to protect itself from British and Russian encroachments. The advent of World War II, however, ended German influence and forced Iran to cooperate with Britain and Russia.

At its beginning, World War II was seen by most Middle Eastern peoples as a European affair that had little effect on them. Only Turkey saw itself in the path of aggression; but since German and Russian dominance were equally repugnant, Turkey maintained a careful neutrality. Iran attempted to tie itself to Germany, but England and Russia occupied the country, deposed Reza Shah, and forced Iranian cooperation. The collapse of France weakened French control in Lebanon and Syria, and attempts made after France's liberation to reassert that control were met by British intervention. Iraqi nationalists endeavored to capitalize on Britain's weakness in the early part of the war in order to stage a revolt, but they were unsuccessful. In Palestine, the Arabs were unconcerned with the war, but Nazi atrocities against the European Jews led to the creation of a Zionist Brigade and to frantic Jewish immigration to Palestine. This massive and illegal immigration in turn led to increased hostilities between Arabs and Jews, and Palestine erupted with terrorism. Egypt was used as a staging area for the British army, and Egyptian troops fought in the desert and in defense of Egypt.

At the end of World War II Britain remained the paramount power in the Middle East, maintaining effective control over Egypt, Palestine, Transjordan, Iraq, southern Arabia, and the Persian Gulf. But Britain emerged from the war a weakened state unable to withstand nationalist pressures fomenting in the states under its suzerainty. The episode of Britain's withdrawal from the Middle East and the forces acting within and upon each country in the area are taken up in Part 2.[5]

NOTES

1. For a survey of general Arab history see Bernard Lewis, *The Arabs in History* (London, 1950); Hamilton R. Gibb, *The Arab-Conquests in Central Asia* (London, 1923); Philip K. Hitti, *The History of the Arabs* (London, 1951); and Peter Mansfield, *The Arabs* (London, 1978).

2. For a survey of Ottoman history, see Sydney Fisher, *The Middle East: A History*, 3d ed. (New York, 1959), and L.S. Stavrianos, *The Balkans Since 1453* (New York, 1958).

3. For examinations of European involvement in the Middle East, see Carl L. Brown, *International Politics: Old Rules, Dangerous Game* (Princeton, 1984);

George Leneyoinski, *The Middle East in World Affairs*, 4th ed. (Ithaca, N.Y., 1980); J.A.R. Marriott, *The Eastern Question: An Historical Study in European Diplomacy* (Oxford, 1917).

4. Walter Laqueur and Barry Rubin, eds., *The Israel-Arab Reader: A Documentary History of the Middle East Conflict* (New York, 1984), p. 18.

5. See Tareq Y. Ismael, *The International Relations of the Contemporary Middle East: A Study in World Politics* (Syracuse, 1986) for a regional analysis.

3

The Political Heritage of Islam

Tareq Ismael and Jacqueline Ismael

Islam is not just a religious order. It is a complete way of life for the individual, the society, the state, and the nation. Islam does not recognize national, racial, or linguistic boundaries; it is a universal doctrine that does not permit a separation between the secular and the religious. The purpose of human creation is to "serve your Lord Who created you and those who were before you that you may become righteous" (Qur'an, 2:21). Thus, all human action and interaction within the Muslim community is by definition regulated by Islam.

There are two major sects of Islam: the dominant Sunni sect and the minority Shi'a sect. In addition to the theological differences between these sects, each represents a different school of political thought. There is agreement in both schools on the role and function of the state. In both, the establishment of a just society is possible only through the implementation of divine legislation, the *Shari'ah*. However, the schools disagree over the method of selecting the head of state. While both agree that a Muslim leader should be exemplary, Sunnism emphasizes the role of a consultative council, whereas Shi'ism emphasizes that the Muslim leader should come from the house of the Prophet and his descendants and must be chosen by God. The Sunnis refer to the Muslim head as *khalifah* (which literally means successor of the Prophet), while the Shi'a denote the head of the Muslim community as *imam* (which literally means spiritual leader).

The primary political unit in the Muslim world today is the nation-state, but the corresponding conceptual unit in Islamic law is the *Ummah*, the Islamic community. This community is the brotherhood of all Muslims and transcends national boundaries. In the past it has sometimes been a single political unit, though today it is primarily a religious and cultural one. It is held together by a common belief in *Tawhid*—the oneness and perfect unity of God—the *Sunnah*—the exemplary practice of the Prophet Muhammad—the Qur'an, the Shari'ah, and a variety of other common cultural patterns. Historically it was an underlying force in the formation and expansion of Islamic empires and in the more recent attempts to form a pan-Arab state.

The community concept, however, is incompatible with the reality of the nation-state. The Middle East rarely acts as a single political unit. Early Arab conquests led to the inclusion of diverse racial, linguistic, and cultural groups within the expanding territorial sphere of the Islamic brotherhood. The building of the Arab and Turkish empires led to the assimilation of some non-Muslims. European expansion in the nineteenth century also played a major role as it forced a potent injection of Western ideas and practices into the bloodstream of Islam. The result of these changes has been a diversification within the Islamic world, leading to the creation of several nation-states exhibiting marked differences. Today, forty-six Muslim countries constitute the Islamic Conference Organization, ICO, an attempt to assert the unity of the Ummah, to overcome national borders, and to promote the unity of Muslims throughout the world. Other world organizations like the Muslim World League also complement the objectives of the ICO by fostering greater cohesion and unity in overcoming the economic and social problems of the Muslim world.

Also shaping Islamic politics is the Muslim concept of equality. There is no priesthood in Islam serving as an intermediary between man and God, and because Islam covers all aspects of Muslim life, equality before God becomes, theoretically, equality before the law. Of course, racial, class, and gender distinctions exist in Middle Eastern states. Nonetheless, the theoretical equality of all Muslims leads to an awareness that all people have some sort of political rights. Non-Muslims, however, have traditionally been considered inferior to Muslims because they reject the rule of God that is applicable in Islam not only to the individual and to the church but to the state as well. The rise of the secular nation-state in the post–World War I era has resulted in reducing the role of religious belief in defining the rights and duties of the citizen. The rise of nationalism produced the nation-state as the central political unit, whereas in Islam the unit is the community of believers (Ummah).

The Prophet Muhammad and the Message of Islam

In the seventh century the Middle East was an area ravaged by constant warfare between the decaying Byzantine and Persian empires. The Arabian peninsula was a disunited area where individual cities flourished on the East-West trade routes. But in the vast areas between these cities there were only bands of desert nomads who survived by trading meat, milk, and livestock for the manufactured products of the cities. The Prophet Muhammad was born of a noble family belonging to the tribe of the Quraish in the year 569 A.D. He was married at the age of twenty-five. At forty he declared himself a messenger of God and proclaimed Islam as the religion and complete way of life ordained by Allah. Persecution drove him and his small community of Muslims to Yathrib, now modern Medina. Muhammad established the first Islamic city-state in Medina in 622 and became the undisputed head of state and leader of the Muslims. After consolidating power, Islam began to grow as alliances were made with the surrounding communities and tribes.

Muhammad then looked to Mecca. He initiated raids on Meccan caravans and, as a result, provoked a punitive expedition against himself and his followers. That expedition, called the battle of Badr, was the first all-out war between the Meccan chiefs and Muhammad. The chiefs failed. Muhammad and a small army of 317 ill-equipped men defeated the Meccan army of more than 1,000 better-trained and fully equipped combatants. Two major battles followed, bringing Mecca under Muhammad's power. Mecca was made the center of the new religion though not the seat of government, which remained in Medina. Shortly after his victorious return to Mecca, Muhammad died in 632. By the time of his death, all Arabia was brought under the dominion of the nascent Islamic Empire.

Muslim theologians generally make a distinction between three basic components of Islam: *Iman*, or belief, *Aamede*, or pillars; and *Amal a-Saleh*, or the doing of good deeds. The following are the essential religious beliefs of Islam: (1) Belief in the unity of Allah: "There is no God but Allah, and Muhammad is His Messenger." This creed of Islam is the central doctrine of the Qur'an. There is one God before whose judgment all persons are equal, and Muhammad is the Seal of the Prophets through whom God completed His favor and perfected religion, Islam, for the benefit of all humankind. (2) Belief in the angels of Allah. The angels are the messengers of Allah and, like people, they are his creatures and servants. Correspondingly, there are devils and *jinn*, who contrive to lead people astray. (3) Belief in the prophets of Allah. The Qur'an teaches that God sent messengers to all peoples throughout history to preach the unity of God and to warn humanity of the Day of Judgment. Muslims are enjoined to believe in all the prophets although only twenty-eight are mentioned in the Qur'an, including eighteen from the Old Testament and three from the New Testament. (4) Belief in the four Revealed Books: the Book of Moses, the Torah; the Zabur, the Book of David; the Injeel, the Book of Jesus; and the Qur'an, the Last Book, revealed to Muhammad. The Qur'an, the "Very Word of God," is the final arbiter and judge since scholars agree that this book retained its purity whereas the other scriptures were subject to human interference that renders them suspect. For Muslims, it is the Eternal Truth in its final perfect form. (5) Belief in the Day of Judgment. There will be a last judgment when each person's deeds will be weighed in the balance. Evildoers and disbelievers will be assigned to Hell, and righteous believers are assured eternal bliss in Paradise. There will be ranks in Paradise reflecting the level of piety and righteousness of each person. (6) Belief in the divine decrees of Allah. Everything that occurs is predestined by Allah, even human salvation, damnation, belief, and disbelief. Allah's will is everything, and the Muslim's only recourse is to throw himself upon Allah's divine mercy. Predestination in Islam, however, does not necessarily mean that one's fate is already determined in the absolute sense. In Islam, a person has the will and freedom to choose the right way if he so desires after he has transgressed. There is nothing in the concept that denies evildoers from entering Paradise if they repent and make amends. There is no guarantee of Paradise for the righteous if they become disbelievers later in life. In sum, the divine decrees of Allah encompass both good and evil, since without God's will nothing is possible.

There are five pillars in Islam that comprise the religious duties of the faithful Muslim. They include: (1) *Shahadah*—profession and practice of the creed, "There is no God but Allah, Muhammad is His Messenger"; (2) *Salat*—prayer five times daily, morning, noon, afternoon, sunset, and night; (3) *Siyam*—fasting during the month of Ramadan, the ninth month of the Islamic calendar, from dawn to sunset; (4) *Zakat*—almsgiving, explicitly enjoined by the Qur'an as the outward sign of piety and means of salvation; and (5) *Hajj*—pilgrimage to Mecca, required of every Muslim who can afford it, at least once in his or her lifetime.

The "doing of good deeds," as prescribed in the Qur'an, directs every aspect of human life whether social, political, economic, or religious from birth until death. It distinguishes what is right from what is wrong by specifically delineating conduct that is required, conduct that is permitted, and conduct that is forbidden. This advanced moral code has succeeded in bringing a sense of brotherhood to heterogeneous peoples.

Islam has undoubtedly been the greatest single factor in the development of the Middle East,[1] and because of Muhammad's unique position as the Seal of the Prophets, almost all that is Islam can be ultimately traced back to him. The analogies, the traditions, and the Sunnah all derive from the words and actions of Muhammad. The concepts of both centralized authority and rule by God are drawn from his practices in ruling Medina. Religious tolerance and the use of existing administrators in conquered territories, both of which were standard practices in the later empires, were techniques that Muhammad himself used in the exercise of power.

The Islamic State

The Islamic state[2] is a political institution initiated by the Prophet
Muhammad for the purpose of organizing the Ummah, preserving
the faith, and maintaining and enforcing justice through Islamic
Law according to the word of God. It can be examined in the
context of ten interlocking systems: the value system, the normative
system, the ideological system, the division of labor and specialization, the status-role system, the regulative system, the socialization
system, the power-authority system, the enforcement system, and
the maintenance system.

The Islamic value system is based on the Qur'an,[3] the revealed
word of God, and the Sunnah, the exemplary practice of the
Prophet. All pre-Islamic values contrary to Islam were seen as repugnant and were rejected. Islam enjoins freedom, equality, cour-
age, patience, loyalty, mercy, and justice. Over and above these,
Islam prescribes *Taqwa*—the fear of God, which will ensure all
other values and virtues. Duty to oneself, to one another, and to
God became an inseparable trilogy in the value system of Islam.
These virtues became the prototype of the Islamic value system
not only because the Islamic state was built upon the foundation
of pre-Islamic Arab society, but also because the Qur'an gave a
dominant position to the Arabic language. Arabic philology became the basis of the religious sciences. In the first four centuries
of Islam, Muslim literature was written almost entirely in Arabic.
Hence, the literary and social heritage of the ancient Arabs permeated Muslim literature. Their virtues were idealized and their prov-
erbs popularized.

The principal political institution of the Bedouin, the tribe,
did not become a permanent part of the Islamic system. The
ethnocentricity of the tribal structure is inconsistent with the
Muslim concept of the state as the community of all believers
wherein all loyalties, tribal or otherwise, are superseded by the
Muslim brotherhood. It was the absorption of large numbers
of non-Arab, multiracial elements without the tribal allegiances
of the Arabs that helped the state to develop politically beyond
its tribal structure.

Ideally all Muslims are equal; all their interpersonal relations are ordered by the Qur'an and formulated in the Islamic law. But the rapid spread of Islam in its first centuries precluded putting these ideals into practice. The attempt to organize the expanding empire and to assimilate the new elements within it led to compromises. New normative systems had to be incorporated into the state in order for the Muslims to deal not only with non-Islamic peoples but also with non-Arab Muslims within the state. In many cases this was accomplished by retaining the preexisting norms in a conquered area. The conquered peoples kept to their own behavior patterns and conformed to Islam only in its most obvious aspects. In other words, their social and cultural lives were not substantively transformed.

Considered from an ideological perspective, the foundations of the Islamic community are legal, not economic. Modern notions of ideology are basically secular and particular; the Islamic notion of community is holistic. Theoretically, Islam upholds the highest form of democracy through *Shura*, or mutual consultation, which keeps the state in constant contact with the people. There is no fixed tenure of the rule of the caliph. He can rule until his death or can be deposed if he is unfit to rule because of his personal or administrative conduct. Although the Qur'an contains no systematic presentation of political doctrine, there does emerge from the Sunnah of Muhammad, which synthesized Islamic beliefs and practice, a coherent and formal institutional structure.

To handle such day-to-day administrative functions of an expanding empire, specialists were needed. This resulted in a division of labor based upon administrative specialization. Although it was customary to retain the preexisting administrations in conquered territories, this practice made a central administration for the empire difficult. The Umayyad, Abbasid, and Ottoman empires, each in its turn, introduced administrative techniques to deal with the forces of fragmentation of a large, heterogeneous empire; but each ultimately succumbed to centrifugal forces. The Ottoman Turks, the last of the region's successful empire builders, created a bureaucracy and trained specialists to staff it for the purpose of administration. The Ottomans also maintained a palace school in order to ensure that the sultans and their advisers would be adequately trained for directing the administration of the empire.

Thus, administrative function in the empire became a basis for status distinction based upon achieved expertise rather than prescribed traits. Expertise provided the means for upward mobility. Men of many skills were needed for the maintenance of the empire, and such men were rewarded with honors and wealth. But the most distinct status-role differentiation occurred when the Seljuk Turks invaded the Middle East and established a feudal aristocracy under the Ottoman dynasty. In the sixteenth century, race became a determinant of status and role. As might be expected the Turks occupied the top level of society. Because Islam conceived of no intermediaries between man and God, the only religious specialization was in the field of legal interpretation and in the office of the khalifah.

Other bases for status distinction within the empire were religious affiliation and personal status. Monotheistic disbelievers in Islam are called "Ahl al-Thimmah," which literally means the guaranteed people because Islamic Shari'ah does not allow discrimination against them. Though not allowed to participate in some functions of the Islamic state, they enjoy guaranteed protection of their persons and wealth and all other rights. In return for this protection, they are required to pay a special tax to the state. They do not, however, pay the zakat.

Slaves were another distinct group. The slave's status was relative to the status of his or her master. Although Islam did not outlaw slavery, it demanded that the slave be treated the same as the master. Muhammad clearly and categorically ordered the people to treat their slaves as they would themselves. They were allowed to marry and have families so long as they remained loyal to their masters. Because slave and master were treated equally, the slaves of the Islamic state cannot be compared to those under non-Islamic governments. Reflecting this, under the Ottoman Empire, a class of slaves, the Mamluks, rose to rule Egypt and Iraq. This was not a unique or isolated circumstance, but only one example of many.

Islam's legal code, Shari'ah, governs the Islamic state. Shari'ah, or Islamic law, is derived from three sources. The first is the Qur'an, the revealed word of God. According to the Qur'an, Allah is the supreme law-giver. The Law, contained in the Qur'an, comprises the first and fundamental elements of Islamic laws. The second source of Islamic law is the Sunna, which is based on the Prophet's sayings, actions, and decisions. Whatever matters the Qur'an appears not to cover and whatever issues remain ambiguous in the Qur'an were addressed by Muhammad and became part of the Shari'ah. The third source of Islamic law is called *ijmá*, or consensus. Only the *fuqaha*—jurists, who are highly trained in Islamic jurisprudence—are allowed to make up the ijmá. Nothing in the consensus of the jurists of Islam can contravene the Qur'an or the Prophet in spirit or in substance. Thus, the Shari'ah is actually an all-encompassing code of ethics that regulates the Muslim's religious, political, social, domestic, and private life. It is a legal, moral, and divine document all at once since all laws from the Qur'an, the Prophet, and ijmá are based on the concept that Allah is the true lawgiver and His law is unmitigable. The Shari'ah and the constitution are not only synonymous but are in fact the same thing.

Two other methods of determining legislation were devised to help address the increasingly complex administrative problems of an expanding empire. First, *qiyas*, or analogies, were drawn from the Qur'an and from the traditions to meet the needs of new situations, and legal decisions based on the principles of the Qur'an and the Sunnah could be made if there was a consensus, or ijmá. Second, Muslims were allowed to engage in *ijtihad*, or reasoning. The principles of qiyas and ijtihad introduced into Islam the means of interpretation and provided the basis for philosophic debate, intellectual growth, and social adaptations.

The process of cultural transmission in Islam has generally proceeded on two levels. On one level there is written transmission of laws, literature, and science. These writings have been preserved, studied, and expanded by a literate minority clustered mainly around a few centers of learning. On the other level there is oral transmission which has been the major means of socialization. Most Muslims, whether they are born into Islam or are converts to it, learn their culture not only by the usual method of observing the practices of those around them, but also by listening to scholars who devote their lives to researching, studying, and memorizing their law and their history.

The mosque and the *ka'abah* are the main centers for socialization. Because congregational prayers are rated twenty-seven times better than praying alone, Muslims are encouraged to visit the mosque and pray in groups for the five daily prayers. Moreover, once a week Muslims are enjoined to perform the Friday prayer, which provides an even greater forum for community participation than the daily prayers. Problems and issues affecting the community are addressed in the sermons. The mosque sponsors two major Islamic festivals: *Eid ul Fitr*, which marks the end of fasting, and *Eid Adha*, which marks the completion of hajj. Obviously, these two annual events draw large gatherings.

The ka'abah is where Muslims from all over the world convene to perform the pilgrimage or the *umra*—lesser pilgrimage. Today pilgrims of diverse nationalities, races, and languages enter Mecca by the millions. Pilgrimage is observed once every year, and there are lesser pilgrimages as many times as possible. Thus, Islam provides an institutionalized socialization system. Its principal aim is the unification of the Ummah in all its varied dimensions.

The hierarchy of power and authority in Islam[+] are three-fold: God is the Absolute Power; His Messenger Muhammad is his delegated earthly authority; and the khalifah, successor of the Prophet, is the authority thereafter. At no time can the khalifah's rule contravene Muhammad's prerogatives; at no time can the absolute authority of Allah be negated. Thus, the khalifah governs the Islamic state as a successor to the Prophet, who governed for the cause of God. Although power and authority are reflected through the state, which is an instrument of God, it is in the person and office of the khalifah that power is concentrated. In Islam, power is not diffused; the khalifah commands obedience.

Muhammad, the Prophet of Islam, was also the head of the state. After his death several "successors of the Prophet" were elected by leading Muslims to serve as head of both the religion and the state. Thus was initiated the central Islamic institution of the khalifate, which endured until 1924. The last of the elected khalifahs was supplanted by the Umayyad family, which established a dynastic khalifate, only to lose it to the Abbasid family. The Abbasids ruled Islam until the establishment of the Ottoman Empire. Under these dynasties the khalifah was the religious and political head of Islam, employing viceroys to administer the territorial subdivisions of the state. But it was also during this period that imperial subdivisions broke away from the empire.

The Seljuk Turks reunited the empire under a new absolutist institution, the sultanate. The khalifate was retained, although it was shorn of its power, as a means of legitimizing the new institution. By the beginning of the fifteenth century, however, the two had become one. The sultanate, with its bureaucratic central administration, remained an absolutist government at the head of a feudal aristocracy until the beginning of the twentieth century.

The enforcing system in Islam depends on obedience to the ruler. It is not unlike the regulative system or the power-authority system. It is assumed that disobedience to the ruler results in anarchy. The ruler, however, is not above the law. For this reason the Islamic state has had religious courts to interpret the law during most of its history. The power of the courts has always been limited, and the enforcing power has generally been in the hands of the ruler and his subordinates.

A concept central to both the enforcing system and the power-authority system is the Islamic view of the human being as the best creation of God but also morally weak . Unless directed, people are incapable of leading an orderly life. Thus, there must be, within the state, some force capable of restraining people from following their own impulses. Moreover, the state is empowered to execute the commandments of Allah. The penal codes of Islam are drafted on the basis of the Shari'ah, and provision is made for both executing the law and for showing mercy or clemency. Every person has the right to justice; in fact, it is the object of the state in Islam to ensure it. And because order is a necessity, it is generally assumed that the authority imposed by a bad leader is preferable to the anarchy that would accompany his overthrow. Some Islamic scholars disagree with that point of view, but, on the whole Muslims have been oriented toward the acceptance of authority. However, there is a basis for resistance to the ruler in Islam. He should conform to the code of ethics laid down in the Qur'an. If he does not, the Ummah has the right to overthrow him, for the purpose of government is to ensure the temporal well-being of mankind according to the Shari'ah—God's Law—and not the law of any man.

An institutional maintenance system, which is made up largely of the other nine systems, can be divided into two categories: physical-economic maintenance and cultural maintenance. The Islamic state was born amid battles for a portion of the East-West trade routes; battles and trade routes provided its physical and economic maintenance. In its first centuries the state expanded rapidly by conquest until, under the Ottomans, it controlled almost all of the East-West trade. Since then the Middle East has attempted, with an increasing lack of success, to provide for its security through trade concessions. In recent years, the Middle Eastern states have been more successful in maintaining their political and economic security through oil concessions. Following the oil shocks in the 1970s, states in the region became more assertive in developing their capabilities. Education, health, housing, transportation, communication, and the attempt to modernize industry and agriculture are all issues that states must address. The disciplined forces of the police and the army are necessary as well to maintain the system as a whole.

Cultural maintenance is also nourished by the belief that Islam is the community of all Muslims, through the faith in one revelation of all law, and the belief in the legitimacy of all central authority. These beliefs curtail the development of heretical sects and limit the political power of those sects that emerge.

Islam Today

The extreme bureaucratization of the Ottoman Empire sapped the strength of medieval Islam, ended Islamic political expansion, and initiated a period of economic, political, and cultural stagnation in the Middle East. At the same time, Western Europe was experi-

encing technological growth, political expansion, and the advent
of liberalism, and when Ottoman power was withdrawn from vast
areas of the Middle East the European powers flowed into those
areas. The European penetration not only resulted in an influx
of Western ideas and attitudes but also contributed to the decline
in the vitality of Middle Eastern culture.

The political ebb of the Muslim world produced a strong reaction throughout the Middle East. Diverse reform movements were
started, ranging from those attempting to impose a strict adherence
to the letter of Qur'anic law to others seeking to change the basic
doctrines of Islam itself. A particularly powerful reform movement
occurred in Turkey during the nineteenth century. It did not, however, have the force necessary to overthrow the Ottoman established order. It was not until the beginning of the present century
that the Turkish nationalist movement overthrew the Ottomans
and made modernization feasible in Turkey. Since that time the
forces of nationalism and modernization have swept through the
rest of the Middle East, bringing benefits and problems similar
to those they brought to Turkey.

A major problem in the Middle East has been reconciling the
modernization process with the social values of Islam. A serious
conflict occurred with the adoption of Western penal codes and
family law. A greater conflict still is the imitation of libertine Western social practices. This conflict was addressed in Turkey by divest-
ing the Shari'ah, the religious courts, of their secular authority.
The result of this move was the first real separation of church and
state in Islam. It opened the door to secularization and led the
government to assume the prerogative of changing the social structure whenever its needs and desires run counter to the tenets of
Islam. Today the trend is reversing somewhat. Militant Turkish
Muslims are advocating a return to Islamic law. While not opposed
to modernization and material advancement, they are opposed to
the Western social ethics that they believe accompany the process
of modernization.

Since the Iranian Revolution in 1978–79, many Muslim political
movements have strongly pressed for state reform along the lines
of the Shari'ah. The more militant among them advocate a com-

plete transformation to a purely Islamic state. Some Islamic movements in Egypt, Syria, Lebanon, Sudan, and North Africa reflect
this radical fundamentalist tendency in Islam.[5]

NOTES

1. Tor Andrae, *Mohammed, The Man and His Faith* (New York, 1936) provides
an examination of the life of the Prophet of Islam. Also see Hamilton A.R.
Gibb, *Mohammedanism, A Historical Survey*, 2d ed. (New York, 1968).

2. See Tareq Y. Ismael and Jacqueline S. Ismael, *Government and Politics in Islam*
(New York, 1985) for an examination of the concept of the Islamic state.

3. Mohammed Marmaduke Pickthall, *The Meaning of the Glorius Koran*, 7th ed.
(New York, 1959) is considered one of the better translations of the Koran.

4. See Mehran Tamadonfar, *The Islamic Polity and Political Leadership: Fundamentalism, Sectarianism, and Pragmatism* (Boulder, 1989) for a theoretical
analysis of power and authority in Islam.

5. For studies of contemporary Islamic activism, see Edward Mortimer, *Faith
and Power: The Politics of Islam* (New York, 1982); Robin Wright, *Sacred Rage:
The Crusade of Modern Islam* (New York, 1985); R. Hrair Dekmejian, *Islam
in Revolution: Fundamentalism in the Arab World*, 2d ed. (Syracuse, 1989).

4

The Legacy of Nationalism

Tareq Ismael and Jacqueline Ismael

Nationalism as a political ideology is a fairly recent phenomenon in the Middle East and at the turn of this century was still only nascent. Since that time, however, the development of the concept has been rapid and has proven to be both a constructive and a destructive force in the Middle East. For example, reform and modernization have often been the first goals of the several indigenous Middle Eastern nationalist movements (Turkish, Arab, Iranian), and these efforts to reform and to modernize have contributed to the civil and social advancement of the area's inhabitants. However, ethnocentrism, irredentism, and national sovereignty have also been integral parts of the nationalist programs, and these aspects of nationalism have resulted in conflict and upheaval, as, for example, in the cases of Turkish versus Arab nationalism within the Ottoman Empire, Zionism versus Arab nationalism, and Turkish, Arab, and Iranian nationalism versus European imperialism.

The four major Middle Eastern nationalist movements are the Arab, Turkish, Iranian, and Zionist.

Arab Nationalism

Arab nationalism has been described as the "principal movement through which the Arab peoples are seeking to reconstruct the foundations of their life, after centuries of suspended animation."[1] It has rapidly spread throughout their world and has generated an invigorating force in a fundamentally stagnant political climate. The response of nationalism to the challenge of modernization has been a decisive factor in determining the fate of the Arab people in this century.

Modern Arab nationalism has deep roots. Its inspirations are the achievements and culture of early Islam, but it is somewhat fragmented. In contrast, Islam transcended national and other boundaries and makes a claim for the entire Muslim *Ummah*, or community. Whereas Arab nationalism is the sum total of all the Arab states, Islamic nationalism is concerned with the whole nation of Muslims. Before the advent of Islam the focus of Arab patriotism and loyalty had been either the family or the tribe. Arabs did not feel themselves part of any other larger unit, either socially or politically. Islam drastically changed their political and social focuses. As the armies of Islam began those seemingly inexorable marches that were to create the great Islamic empire—an empire that would eventually stretch from India to Spain—Arabs began to consider themselves more and more part of the larger Islamic community.

Of course, the Islamic community had an essentially supranational orientation, and the rich Islamic culture that developed during the Middle Ages was a synthesis of many cultures. But because the Muslim had to read the Qur'an and pray in the language of the Prophet Muhammad, Arabic became the common language of Muslim civilization. As a result, the culture of that civilization came to be regarded as Arabic. Thus, all of those who shared in common the Arabic language and the culture of the Muslim civilization came to regard themselves with pride as Arabs, a feeling not too remote from the modern sense of national consciousness.

However, by the thirteenth century the Islamic empire lay in ruins, and its fourteenth century successor to power, the Ottoman Empire, devised an administrative technique that tended to nullify nationalist sentiment and to emphasize sectarian differences. The Ottoman millet system organized the subjects of the Ottoman Empire on the basis of religious affiliation rather than by cultural or linguistic characteristics. Thus, people who under the Islamic empire would have proudly considered themselves Arabs identified themselves instead, under the Ottomans, as Christians, Jews, or Muslims.

It must not be assumed that all traces of Arab civilization disappeared during the four centuries of Ottoman rule. Indeed, since the Ottoman Turks had adopted Islam and had made *Shari'ah* law an important part of their government, Arab culture and language not only continued to exist but played an important role in Ottoman society. Thus, when Napoleon invaded Egypt in 1798, elements of the earlier Arab culture were still very much present in the Middle East.

Even though the inspiration of modern Arab nationalism was the culture of early Islam, the actual birth of that nationalism is usually traced to Napoleon's invasion of Egypt. The event itself did not result in a general Arab awakening, but it marked the beginning of a steady influx of the Western concepts, processes, and techniques that did finally spark the Arab renaissance and awakened many Arabs to the manifold disadvantages of Ottoman rule and the threat of Western imperialism. An increasing amount of Western intervention accompanied the influx of Western modes; and these European encroachments on what was essentially Arab territory, and the resulting exploitation of Arab resources, raised Arab ire against the Ottomans who seemed unable to protect them from European depredations.

The activities of two Albanians, Muhammad Ali and his son Ibrahim, helped to kindle an Arab renaissance. Muhammad Ali ascended to power in Egypt shortly after French withdrawal early in the nineteenth century and made Egypt virtually independent of Istanbul. Unquestionably one of the greatest rulers of his time, Ali introduced important reforms in education, agriculture, industry, commerce, sanitation, and social custom. The reforms in education were of particular significance to the revitalization of the Arabs. Primary and secondary schools, preparatory schools, a medical college, and a polytechnic school staffed predominantly by Egyptians were established. Many Egyptian youth were sent to Europe for a Western education, and schools were opened in Egypt for the training of civil servants.

Complementing his reforms in education, Muhammad Ali established a government printing press at Cairo in 1822 and thus made Cairo the intellectual center of the Arab world. By 1850 the press had printed over three hundred books in Arabic, Turkish, and Persian. It also printed newspapers in both Arabic and French that not only disseminated Western ideas but also gave the Arabs a vehicle through which they could regenerate their own literature.

At the same time that Muhammad Ali was introducing his reforms in Egypt, his son Ibrahim was encouraging modernization in Syria. Having succeeded to the governorship of Syria in 1833 as a result of his successful military campaign against Ottoman forces, Ibrahim embarked upon a program of reform similar to that of his father in Egypt. Sydney Nettleton Fisher writes of Ibrahim's eight-year rule in Syria that "taxes were regularized, justice was more sure for people of all religions, commerce was encouraged, privileges for foreigners were less abused, education was stimulated, law and order were prevalent."[2]

Ibrahim's administration came to an end in 1840 when the British forced Muhammad Ali to withdraw his son from Syria. Nevertheless, Syria remained the cradle of nascent Arab nationalism. As a result of Ibrahim's edicts, Syria was opened to American Protestants and French Catholics who were allowed to establish missionary schools. By 1860 the American missionaries had established thirty-three schools in Lebanon, Syria, and Palestine, and in 1866 the influential Syrian Protestant College in Beirut (now the American University) opened its doors. The French missionaries also founded many schools in the area, including the University of St. Joseph at Beirut in 1875. Because these schools taught in Arabic, they helped to revive the Arabic language as a medium of expression and communication for Arab writers and intellectuals and thus fostered the intellectual awakening that was to culminate in the Arab nationalist movement.

The tremendous demand for education that resulted from the establishment of schools in Egypt and Syria was not confined to those two countries but spread in unprecedented proportions throughout the Arab world. This demand was met partially by a great increase in the volume of printed material. Publishing houses and newspapers were established in many of the major cities, and the great volume of material printed became both a means for and a measure of the spread of nationalism throughout the Arab provinces of the Ottoman empire.

Educational societies to facilitate inquiry into Arab history, art, and literature were also organized during this period. The Society of Arts and Sciences was created in 1847 with the help of American missionaries, and the Jesuits organized the Oriental Society in 1850. Generally, however, Muslim Arabs refused to join these two groups because of their foreign Christian missionary affiliations. But in 1857 the Syrian Scientific Society was established on a nonsectarian basis, and under its auspices Christians and Muslims joined together to foster and develop their common Arabic heritage. From this society came Arab nationalism's first rallying cry, Ibrahim Yaziji's "Ode to Patriotism," a poem appealing to the Arabs to unite and to revolt against Turkish oppression.

The first organized response to Ibrahim Yaziji's appeal for unity and revolt came in the form of secret societies which sprang up in Beirut (the center of the movement), Damascus, Tripoli, and other cities. Their primary activity was the posting of placards which urged the Arabs to insurgence. Such urging proved to be premature, however, since there was not yet a sufficiently wide-spread sense of Arab national consciousness among the people to rally them to armed revolt and, as a result, the secret societies proved short-lived. Nevertheless, these secret societies did serve an important purpose, for their placards contained not only statements urging the Arabs to rebellion but also specific demands that served as a model for the Arab political programs that would be formulated later. Included in these demands were the independence of Syria in union with Lebanon, the recognition of Arabic as a national language, an end to censorship and the removal of other restrictions on the freedom of expression, and the use of only locally recruited units for local military service.[3]

Although the growing sense of Arab national consciousness received its chief impetus from the Arab resurgence in Syria, it was also stimulated by the pan-Islamic revival occurring in Egypt during the same period. Jamal al Din al-Afgani, the founder of the pan-Islamic movement, had advocated that one of the Islamic states be strengthened to the point that it could unify the Muslim world and thus free it from foreign domination. He did not care which Islamic state united the world of Islam, and it remained for Abdul Rahman al-Kawakebi to draw the distinction between Arab and non-Arab Muslims and to advocate that the Muslims would be united under a Quaraish-born Arab caliph established in Mecca. Kawakebi's proposals captured the imagination of the Arab world and contributed in no small way to the gradual change from Christian to Muslim leadership in the Arab national movement.

After the British occupation of Egypt in 1882, however, Egyptian leaders became preoccupied with the removal of the British; thus, it was in Beirut and Damascus that the search for Arab emancipation continued. At the time of the Young Turk's revolt in 1908, Arab leaders hoped that the Ottoman program of the Society of Union and Progress would bring about decentralization of the empire and give the Arabs an equal voice in the conduct of the empire. Thus, for a time, the Arabs sought emancipation through cooperation with the Young Turks. As a measure of their sincerity the Young Turks pressured Sultan Hamid into appointing Sharif Hussain as governor of the Hijaz, keeper of the holy places and prince of Mecca. When this appointment was made in 1908 the Ottoman Arab Fraternity was created as a society for the defense of the Ottoman Constitution and the promotion of Arab welfare. The society was barely created when in 1909 it and other non-Turkish political groups were forced to go underground by the Young Turks' program of centralization and Turkification.

Numerous Arab societies, some clandestine and some public, developed for the dissemination of Arab national ideas. Notable among them were the Literary Club of Istanbul, the Ottoman Decentralization party in Cairo, *al-Kahtaniya*, and *al-Jam'iyah al-Arabiyah al-Fatat*, of which the former two were public, and the latter two subterranean. The Literary Club, founded in 1909 and recognized by the Committee of Progress and Union because of its ostensible cultural rather than political objectives, played a significant role in that it "provided centres in which Arabs from all parts of the empire felt at home and talked freely in an atmosphere in which minds relaxed and the traffic of ideas could move."[4] Its membership reached thousands, and branches were established in Syria and Iraq.

The second public group, the Ottoman Decentralization party, was founded in Cairo in 1912 for the purpose of winning equality and autonomy for the Arab provinces within the framework of the Ottoman Empire. Branches were established throughout Syria, and close contact was maintained with other Arab nationalist associations. This organization provided the Arabs with the first extensive political machinery that could coordinate their activities and maintain concerted and continuous pressure to achieve a specific political program.

Al-Kahtaniya, a secret society organized in 1909, also had a well-defined program, advocating the creation of a Turko-Arab empire on the Austro-Hungarian model. But it was short-lived, and its chief contribution to the Arab nationalist movement lay in its attempt to enlist Arab officers serving in the Turkish army into the nationalist movement.

Of these major organizations, al-Fatat, a clandestine society organized by Muslim Arab students in Paris in 1911, was the only one to reject fully the idea of collaboration with the Turks and integration into a decentralized empire. It worked for creation of a sovereign Arab state and within a short time became an effective and widespread force. When in 1913 an interfaith Committee of Reform won public acclaim and enthusiasm for its open circulation of a plan for Arab autonomy, with the consequence that it was disbanded and many of its members arrested, al-Fatat took the initiative to convene the first Congress of Arabs at Paris. Representatives from most of the Arab nationalist organizations participated under the sponsorship of the Ottoman Decentralization party. The Paris Platform which they promulgated was a moderate program calling for reform within the empire to bring the Arabs and other non-Turkish nationalities a greater amount of local autonomy. As a sop to the Arabs, the Turks ostensibly accepted this program, but it remained unenforced.

Partly out of this hoax was born a secret society, *al-'Ahd*, organized by Aziz Ali al-Misri, an Egyptian major on the Ottoman general staff who had been a founder of al-Kahtaniya. Al-'Ahd advocated essentially the same program as al-Kahtaniya, and in 1914 the Turks arrested al-Misri on a trumped-up charge of treason in the Italian campaigns in Libya and sentenced him to death. Although he was subsequently pardoned after intervention by the

British, al-Misri's arrest and trial not only outraged the Arab leaders but aroused the masses. With this act of tyranny the Turks destroyed any hope for Arab-Turkish cooperation. The Arab national movement now fully crystallized in a drive for an independent Arab state.

Although the various nationalist groups now had unanimity of purpose, unanimity of action against the Ottoman government was more difficult to achieve. However, the advent of World War I helped to coalesce the many factions into a united front behind the leadership of Sharif Hussain, who favored cooperation with the British and the Allies in return for an independent Arab state. But even though the various factions were united under the leadership of Hussain, many of them still feared that cooperation with the Allies would result in European domination. They believed that a Turkish defeat would assuredly result in the dismemberment of Arab lands by the French and the British unless some guarantee for the creation of an independent Arab state was agreed upon by one or more of the Allied powers. Therefore, in 1915 the Arab revolutionists drafted the Damascus Protocol, which embodied their demands for an independent Arab state that would encompass all of the lands of western Asia that were culturally and linguistically Arabic. In return, the Arabs would revolt against the Ottoman Empire. This protocol was transmitted to Hussain and provided the basis for the controversial correspondence between Hussain and Sir Henry McMahon, the British high commissioner of Egypt. McMahon accepted the conditions of the Damascus Protocol on behalf of the British government, and on June 5, 1916, the Arab revolt was launched.

Thus, when the Paris Peace Conference convened in 1919, Prince Faisal attended as the representative of a people who had made a significant contribution to the Allied war effort. Armed with Allied promises of Arab independence—the Hussain-McMahon correspondence, Britain's Declaration to the Seven (a reaffirmation of Britain's pledge made to seven Arab leaders in Cairo in June 1918), President Wilson's Fourteen Points, and the Anglo-French Declaration of November 1918 (again reaffirming Allied promises) —Faisal prepared to demand the fulfillment of those promises. But

Britain had made other treaties and agreements conflicting with Arab aspirations, most notably the Balfour Declaration of 1917 and the Sykes-Picot Agreement of 1916, and did not intend to fulfill its pledge to the Arabs. In an attempt to forestall British and French designs to dismember the Middle East for their own advantages, President Wilson sent the King-Crane Commission to Syria and Iraq to determine the wishes of the people regarding their future rule. Two recommendations, both directly relevant to these agreements, were strongly urged in its report to the peace conference. The first stressed that the unity of Syria (which up to that time included Palestine and Lebanon) be maintained, because "the territory concerned is too limited, the population too small, and the economic, geographical, racial, and language unity too manifest, to make the setting up of independent states within its boundaries desirable, if such division can possibly be avoided. The country is very largely Arab in language, culture, traditions, and customs."[5] The second concerned the establishment of a Jewish national home. The commission reported that the "anti-Zionist feeling in Palestine and Syria is intense and *not likely to be flouted*."[6] It recommended that the Zionist program be greatly reduced because it could be carried out only by force of arms.

Meanwhile, in realization of French and British intentions to disregard Arab aspirations and with hopes set upon the King-Crane Commission, Arab nationalist leaders in Syria organized elections and convoked the first Arab parliament on July 2, 1919. It is known as the General Syrian Congress, and its resolutions may be briefly summarized:

(a) Recognition of the independence of Syria, including Palestine, as a sovereign state with the Amir Faisal as king; recognition of the independence of Iraq.

(b) Repudiation of the Sykes-Picot Agreement and the Balfour Declaration and of any plan for the partition of Syria or the creation of a Jewish Commonwealth in Palestine.

(c) Rejection of the political tutelage implied in the proposed mandatory systems; acceptance of foreign assistance for a limited period provided it did not conflict with national independence and unity, preference being given to American or—failing America—to British assistance.

(d) Rejection of French assistance in any form.[7]

In March 1920 the congress declared the independence of Syria and Iraq and demanded the evacuation of foreign troops. However, in April the Allied Supreme Council, meeting at San Remo, disregarded the congress's decisions, Allied promises, and the King-Crane report and divided the Arab provinces into several mandates: Syria and Lebanon under France, and Palestine, Transjordan, and Iraq under Britain. Also, the Balfour Declaration, so abhorrent to the Arabs, was reaffirmed.

The effect of the mandate system on the Arab nationalist movement was most dramatic.[8] Under the Turks the Arabs had at least enjoyed a uniform political status (except for parts of the coastal fringe of the peninsula). Now they were fragmented into a multiplicity of states, each one subjected to the political institutions of its particular mandatory power. Thus, Iraq and Transjordan, under Britain, were monarchial with parliamentary government, and Lebanon and Syria, under France, were republican. Palestine remained without any definite political character. The Arabian peninsula alone remained independent but was itself carved into five relatively weak states, which were later unified under Ibn Saud.

As a result of the mandate system, the nationalist movement fragmented and each group became preoccupied with the struggle for power and control within its own locality. Hence, a separate history began for each country. But all Arabs shared the bitter disillusionment with the results of a war that had played so piteously with their dreams of independence and had reduced them from the status of dissatisfied citizens under Ottoman hegemony to hapless subjects under colonial suzerainty.

Although this sense of disillusionment was a common bond that united all Arabs in sympathy, it was not sufficiently strong to regenerate the Arab nationalist movement, and it was not until the end of World War II that the nationalist movement again fused into a program of united action. The occasion for this united action was the Palestine-Arab revolt of 1936. In fact, the first violent expression of Arab feelings occurred on Easter Sunday in April 1920. Arabs revolted again in May 1921. After a relatively quiet period, Arabs broke out in revolt for the third time in August 1929. The major all-out rebellion against British occupation and Zionist-sponsored immigration was carried out between 1936 and 1939. Committees for the defense of Palestine were organized throughout the Arab world, and in 1938 the various groups merged to form the World Interparliamentary Congress of Arab and Muslim Countries for the Defense of Palestine.

During World War II, unrest continued throughout the Arab lands, resulting in the abortive coups of Rashid Ali al-Gailani in Iraq and General Aziz Ali al-Misri in Egypt. In recognition of this fomenting nationalist dissatisfaction, Anthony Eden, the British foreign minister, declared in May 1941 that Great Britain realized that "many Arab thinkers desire for the Arab peoples a greater degree of unity than they now enjoy. . . . His Majesty's Government for their part will give full support to any scheme that commands general approval."[9] In response to Eden's declaration, Nuri al-Sa'id, Iraqi prime minister, circulated his own plan for the creation of a Greater Syria, which was to include Syria, Lebanon, Palestine, and Transjordan, and for the formation of an Arab League to include any Arab states that might join. The concept of a Greater Syria was opposed, but the idea of an Arab League gathered support and by 1945 the Arab League pact was formalized with Iraq, Syria, Lebanon, Transjordan, Saudi Arabia, and Egypt as its members. Every Arab state subsequently joined as it achieved independence, and by 1972 the league had twenty-two members.

The purpose of the Arab League[10] was to promote cooperation among the member states in communications, health, economics, extradition, and cultural and social matters. It guaranteed each member's sovereignty and could force no member to take any action. Although the league initially aroused enthusiasm, its failure to organize the Arab states effectively to oppose the Zionists during the Palestine war discredited the organization among Arab nationalists.

The creation of more than one million Palestinian refugees as a result of the establishment of the State of Israel in May 1948 had greater ramifications than simply the condemnation of the Arab League. The Zionist victory led many youthful nationalists to condemn Arab society as a whole and to attempt, within a decade of the Palestine war, nationalist revolutions in Syria, Jordan, Iraq, Lebanon, and Egypt. Today all Arab states have achieved national independence except one. British intrigue and a military victory gave Palestine over to the Zionists. The UN Partition Plan in 1947, which further paved the way for the proclamation of the State of Israel in Palestine in May 1948, kept alive the struggle for Palestinian Arab nationalism. It is the principal Arab national struggle that exists today.

The nationalist movements that came to power in the 1950s and 1960s were dedicated to the concept of Arab unity as a means to regain control over the course and pattern of Arab development. The new nationalists were more militant and aggressive in their outlook than the old nationalists had been—pointing to the defeat of Palestine as an example of the ineffectiveness of the old men and their methods. The new nationalists were dedicated to restructuring the regional and domestic environments.

The most radical change occurred in Egypt after the Nasserist revolution of 1952. Nasser's influence extended far beyond Egypt and throughout the Arab world. His restructuring of Egyptian society, his opposition to imperialism, and the attractiveness of his vision of a resurgent Arab world appealed to the region's young —so much so that regimes throughout the Arab world defined and legitimized themselves largely by following his principles: republicanism, neutralism, socialism, and Arab unity.

Nasser's status (and consequently the stature of the new nationalism) grew by leaps and bounds with his stand against imperialism —the nationalization of the Suez Canal Company, the purchase of Czechoslovakian armaments after the West's refusal to sell arms to Egypt, and Egypt's stand in the Suez crisis. Ultimately, it was not anti-imperialism but the tenet of Arab unity that was to determine the success or failure of Arab nationalism. The most extensive attempt at Arab unity was undertaken in 1958 when the United

Arab Republic—the union between Egypt and Syria—was undertaken (see chapters 8 and 13).

It was during the short life of the UAR that many of the illusions of the nationalists were replaced by the brutal realities of politics. The republic proved to be unworkable for a number of reasons, most prominent of which were the incongruities between the political, economic, and social systems of the two states.

The failure of the UAR proved to be a huge blow to Arab nationalism though not a mortal one. Nasser remained firmly in control in Egypt, the Ba'ath controlled Iraq and Syria, and other nationalist parties remained influential throughout the 1960s and 1970s. The movement experienced a resurgence after the 1967 and 1973 Arab-Israeli wars but lost much of its lustre as a resurgent Palestinian nationalism began to take on a greater share of the Arab struggle against Israel.

Throughout the 1970s and 1980s the Arab states continually lost ground to Israel as Israel remained in military occupation of Arab lands seized in the 1967 war and regularly violated the sovereignty of other Arab states.[11] Perhaps more damaging, however, was the inability of ruling nationalist regimes to establish legitimacy and effectively rule their societies without resorting to violence and brutality, and their inability to achieve any sort of meaningful and lasting political or economic development. The result of these failures is that the movement has been seriously undermined and has lost many adherents. It is the contention of many that it is the failure of Arab nationalism and nationalist regimes that has led to the resurgence of Islamic fundamentalism. Iraq's invasion of Kuwait on 2 August 1990 may well have dealt a final blow to Arab nationalism, for it exposed the fact that the internal forces dividing the Arab world had prevailed over those uniting it.

Turkish Nationalism

In the eighteenth century Ottoman control in the Middle East began to fail. Since Turkish administration had been highly centralized in Istanbul with only a network of feudal overlords and governors to control the provinces of the empire, two problems arose.

First, the governors, who were semi-autonomous because the regions they controlled were generally far removed from the administrative center, made repeated attempts to increase their provinces' autonomy. Second, the provinces remained non-Turkish in population and culture and eventually developed local nationalisms of their own.

The central administration itself also began to fail. The sultans had long had the prerogative of appointing favorites to ministerial posts and of accepting gifts for favors. So long as the sultan was the only one operating in this manner, little harm resulted, but when the entire bureaucracy began following this practice, the government became paralyzed by nepotism and corruption.

European military penetration in the Middle East and later the presence of missionaries and commercial interests brought with them Western culture. Symbols of Western culture such as dress and manner were adopted by many of the educated in the urban centers, but of far more importance was the influx of Western thought which sparked a Turkish intellectual revolution. One of the fruits of this intellectual renaissance was a new literature that transformed the nationalist ideas of European liberals into political programs.

During this period of European expansion into the Middle East, Turkish leaders had ample opportunity to observe and compare the more efficient Western administrative machinery with their own. This comparison made it clear to some of those leaders that administrative reform was both possible and necessary.

Two schools of reform emerged within the empire, both influenced by the Europeans. One school, the idealists, felt that the adoption of Western governmental procedures (along with the philosophy underlying those procedures) would lead to the economic and industrial development necessary to bring Turkey to equality with the Western nations. The other school, the realists, felt that technological development was necessary first. Such development, they felt, would force governmental change. The Ottoman administration actually followed both programs, attempting from the top of the administrative pyramid to bring about the use of modern Western tools and techniques at the lower governmental levels.

The first task of the government in its effort to reform was to break the stranglehold of the conservative elements in the army. For this purpose a special artillery unit, loyal only to the sultan, was devised. This unit surrounded the barracks of the famed Janissary Corps, the stronghold of conservatism, and annihilated that force. Immediately after it destroyed the Janissaries, the unit traveled throughout the country and purged the rest of the army in a similar manner. Once the conservative elements were eliminated, a new army was created, one that supported the government in its reform attempts.

Backed by its modern army, the government was able to issue two decrees limiting its own powers: it gave non-Muslims equal protection under the law, and it reorganized corrupt governmental agencies. Although neither decree was ever fully implemented, and although the pressure for reform waxed and waned periodically, these measures increased governmental efficiency considerably. Hand in hand with these reforms, government support was provided for fledgling newspapers and publishing houses, and the number of schools was increased for the purpose of raising literacy.

Finally, in 1876, Midhat Pasha, then grand vizier and last of the great reformers, succeeded in introducing a constitution establishing a two-chamber parliament. However, the sultan, Abdul Hamid II, used the Russo-Turkish war of 1877–78 as a pretext to regain absolute control of the state through the emergency powers clause of the constitution. The parliament was rendered powerless and Midhat Pasha and the rest of the reformers were dismissed and then murdered.

Throughout the reform period,[12] concepts of nationalism were being developed. During the first half of the century, the terms for fatherland and nation began to acquire specific reference in terms of the Ottoman state and to take on patriotic overtones. Thus, in 1860, Sinasi, an Ottoman journalist, was able to write an article that discussed the interests of the fatherland and spoke of an Ottoman nation within that fatherland.

Namik Kamal, a gifted contemporary of Sinasi, also wrote of an Ottoman nation within the empire, but he wished that nation to be Islamic as well as Ottoman. Namik Kamal firmly believed that Muslim values and traditions would be reconciled with his own concepts of nationalism, parliamentary democracy, and individual freedom. He was, in fact, so anxious to preserve the best of Islamic tradition that he suggested the tie of Islamic brotherhood become the means of implementing modernization not just in Turkey but throughout Asia and Africa.

Abdul Hamid II's return to despotism, which ended the reform movement, was followed by the establishment in Seneva of secret societies which became centers of nationalism. Many of these societies espoused pan-Turanianism, a belief that the Ottoman Turks were part of a larger Turanian race that occupied large portions of Russia, central Asia, and China. The pan-Turanianists fostered racism by concentrating on the ancient history of Turkey and the supposedly original Turkish language. Pan-Turanianism, however, was countered by Ottomanism, a concept that stressed the equality of all subjects of the empire regardless of race, nationality, or religion. The secret societies were also divided between those who favored the continuation of centralism and those advocating a movement toward decentralization.

In 1907, at the Ottoman Liberal Congress in Paris, all of these groups were united under the newly reformed Committee of Progress and Union. The committee, consisting mostly of army officers, government officials, and professional men, was dominated by the ideas of Ottomanism and centralization. Its program was to oppose the government of Abdul Hamid in every possible way, and in the 1908 revolution the committee forced a return to parliamentary government and sponsored a resurgence of the programs of modernization and reform.

The next noticeable factor in the growth of Turkish nationalism was the outstanding success of the Turkish army during and immediately after World War I. The Turkish success in repelling the Allies at Gallipoli and in driving the Greek army of occupation from the country brought feelings of pride, already strong in the intellectual centers, to the peasant communities. The common people began to feel pride in regarding themselves as Turks.

But the complete formulation of Turkish nationalism as it was to be practiced under the government of Ataturk came from the pen of the sociologist Ziya Gokalp.[13] From the philosophy of the

French sociologist Emile Durkheim, Gokalp drew the idea of society as a reified concept. But he rejected a multinational society in favor of a Turkish one, for he held that a state which consisted of two or more cultures would necessarily disintegrate when the separate cultures were reasserted. For the same reason he made a distinction between Western culture and Western civilization, and he rejected the former while accepting the latter.

Gokalp's program, called Turkism, consisted basically of two elements. The first of these was a conscious return to a pure Turkish culture. The Turkish language was to be used, particularly in prayers, and a return was to be made to the presumably superior morality of the ancient Turks in the areas of national patriotism and family relations. The second element was Gokalp's plan for the modernization of Turkey. First he advocated that the power of the religious courts would have to be broken in order to deliver Turkey from theocracy and clericalism. Then he wrote that an "economic patriotism" must be fostered, emulating the prosperity of the ancient Turks but using the productive forces of industrialism and capitalism, with occupational unions and guilds operating as corporate persons. It was assumed that government aid would be necessary to the development of industry.

Thus, as the Ottoman Empire was about to die, many intellectual and political foundations for modern Turkish nationalism were in place, and on them Kamal Ataturk was soon to build a new Turkey. Nationalism in the republican era is addressed in chapter 5.

Iranian Nationalism

The territory of the modern state of Iran (known as Persia before 1935) has been strategically important for centuries. Iran sits squarely on the old East-West trade routes, and because of this a great deal of wealth has passed through the area. In modern times, Iran has been coveted by both Russia and England. Control of Persia would have provided Russia with Persian Gulf ports for trade and naval activity, and it would have provided England with a link between the Near East and Far East segments of the British

Empire. These two powers competed for control of Iran in the nineteenth and twentieth centuries, but fear of provoking a major war kept them from attempting physical occupation. Instead, each sought to manipulate political and economic interests in Iran and exploit its wealth through trade concessions. This foreign competition promoted greed, corruption, and conflict in Iran, eroding the legitimacy of the institutions of state and undermining the stability of the society.

During the nineteenth century, Persia was particularly vulnerable to foreign inroads. The rerouting of East-West trade through the Suez Canal deprived Persia of one of its major sources of revenue. Political corruption and foreign exploitation completed the job of reducing most of the country to poverty, and Persia fell into a state of anarchy. The shah's control was largely limited to his capital city, and the countryside was controlled by tribal leaders. In an effort to fill this power vacuum, the Russians organized the Persian Cossack Brigade. It served both to keep order in the capital and to protect Russian interests in Persia.

In 1890 a group of British merchants obtained a fifty-year concession for the production, sale, and export of tobacco; as tobacco was a major industry in Persia, the concession aroused deep outrage in the public and triggered riots all over the country. Religious leaders issued a *Fatwa* (juridical opinion) against the concession, and the shah was forced to cancel it. Britain demanded compensation of £500,000 (British) for the cancellation as stipulated by the agreement and arranged for Persia to borrow this sum from the British Imperial Bank at 6 percent interest. Customs receipts of the Persian Gulf ports were used as collateral to secure the loan, and for the next forty years Persia was burdened with this debt. Thus, through the British Imperial Bank, Britain established a foothold in Persia.

At this time, three groups began to emerge as political forces: the clerics, the merchants, and the intellectuals. In 1906 these groups accomplished a nearly bloodless revolution and forced the shah to institute a constitutional government under parliamentary control. With this success, however, the coalition fell apart, and the shah, with foreign backing, was able to crush the movement.

In 1907 under the Anglo-Russian Agreement Persia was divided into two spheres of influence. This agreement was bitterly resented by Persians, and the country was plunged into civil war as Britain and Russia backed reactionary elements which were united with the shah in an attempt to remove the constitutional limits on his power. The nationalist forces prevailed, however, and the shah was dethroned in 1909 and replaced by his son.

It was in this period that oil was discovered in southern Persia and the Anglo-Persian Oil Company (APOC) established. In traditional British imperial style, the British government set out to establish the company's virtual sovereignty in its areas of operation by supporting the autonomy of local leaders against the central authority of Tehran. APOC began construction of pipelines, refineries, and port facilities at Abadan, and by 1912 the first oil was exported. After converting their navy to oil, the British became strategically concerned with APOC, and in 1914, just before the outbreak of World War I, the British government acquired 51 percent interest in it. The British government now had formal vested interests in Persia, and British policy there was dictated by these interests.

At the outbreak of World War I, Persia declared her neutrality. The Russian occupation of Azerbaijan in the north and the British occupation of the south, however, made Persia virtually an ally. The Russian withdrawal from Azerbaijan in 1917 (as a result of the revolution) left a power vacuum the British aspired to fill by bringing Persia under full British control. To this end, Britain proposed in the 1919 Anglo-Persian Treaty to train the Persian army, build railroads, negotiate a loan, and reorganize government services. The treaty was opposed by nationalist groups and never ratified because of public opposition.

In February 1921, Sayyid Ziya al-Din Tabatab'i, a journalist, took over the government by coup and made himself prime minister. To appease the nationalists and dispel charges of being a British agent, the day after he seized power, Tabatab'i denounced the 1919 Anglo-Persian Treaty and signed a Treaty of Friendship with the new Soviet state. To accomplish the coup, Tabatab'i had found it necessary to ally himself with Reza Khan, an officer of the Persian

Cossack Brigade, and continued opposition from the court, the landowners, and the nationalists (who believed the coup had been engineered by the British) left Tabatab'i entirely dependent on Reza Khan's cossacks. This dependence enabled Reza Khan to strengthen his own position to the point that he was finally able to exile Tabatab'i and to declare himself prime minister.

Reza Khan used his position as prime minister to consolidate Persia's military and police forces, and then used those forces to secure Persia's frontiers and to quell its restive tribes. In 1924 he tried to establish a republic. This move was defeated by clerical opposition arising from fears of secularization. In 1925, in order to meet that opposition, Reza Khan became Reza Shah Pahlavi. As shah he had unlimited power. To appease popular nationalist sentiment, he attempted reforms modeled somewhat after those of Ataturk in Turkey. Rapid westernization was attempted through improvements in communications, education, industry, and transportation, but little attention was paid to the agricultural base of the economy. Unity and stability were achieved, but the British stranglehold on Iran's economy limited the extent of change. Reza Shah attempted to negotiate better terms for Iran in the oil concession, and some improvements were grudgingly accepted by Britain.

Just before World War II, Reza Shah began building ties with Nazi Germany: German technicians were brought in to organize administration, agriculture, and industry; German teachers were secured for Iranian schools; many Iranian students were sent to German schools; and, finally, commercial ties were developed between the two countries. By 1939 over 40 percent of Iran's trade was with Germany.

Reza Shah had hoped that by building strong ties with Germany he could offset British and Soviet influence in Iran. The result was quite the opposite. The USSR, fearing for its southern border, and England, fearing for its eastern empire, occupied Iran. They did agree to withdraw their troops within six months of the signing of an armistice. During the occupation, the Allies forced Reza Shah to abdicate in favor of his son, while they themselves took over the administration of the state.

The end of the war did not bring the withdrawal of all the occupation troops. American and British forces withdrew within the agreed time, but Soviet troops stayed to support a Soviet-engineered revolt in Azerbaijan. Ahmad Qavam, then premier in Iran, obtained the withdrawal of Soviet forces by agreeing to form a Soviet-Iranian oil company and to recognize an independent government in Azerbaijan. Then, through a series of maneuvers, Qavam succeeded in reoccupying Azerbaijan with Iranian troops and in having his agreement with the Soviets voided by the Iranian parliament. The Iranian government was once more in control of the country.

The next problem to be tackled by the government was that of capitalizing on its oil resources. While the Anglo-Iranian Oil Company, AIOC, secured a huge revenue from its Iranian operation, Iran received only about 1 percent of its profits. This inequity was a primary source of public ire against Britain. In 1949, a coalition of nationalist groups formed the National Front, headed by Muhammad Mossadegh, an Iranian intellectual and charismatic nationalist leader.[14] Under the banner of the National Front, Dr. Mossadegh won a parliamentary seat in the 1950 elections. A total of eight National Front members won parliamentary seats, forming in effect a small but vocal opposition in the *Majlis* (the Iranian parliament). In April 1950, the government brought in an agreement with AIOC that made no concessions to Iran and preserved AIOC's near-colonial authority there. Outraged at AIOC's intransigence over negotiating better terms, a parliamentary committee demanded nationalization of Iran's oil resources.

The issue threw the government into crisis. While the shah and his cabinet, on behalf of AIOC, attempted to have the agreement passed through the Majlis, the demand for nationalization gained increasing popularity with the public. In March and April 1951 there were mass demonstrations in Tehran demanding nationalization. To pacify public demand and forestall open rebellion against the government, Muhammad Mossadegh was elected prime minister in May by an overwhelming majority in Parliament, in effect forcing the shah to appoint him. His first move was enactment of the nationalization resolution, unanimously approved by Parliament.

In response to the Iranian nationalization,[15] Britain and the international oil cartel organized a boycott that made it impossible for Iran to market its oil. From 1951 to 1954, Iran was unable to market any oil, and the loss of revenue produced great economic hardship in Iran. In 1954, an American, CIA-engineered military coup overthrew the Mossadegh government and imprisoned Mossadegh and other nationalist leaders. Nationalization was rescinded. The nationalist movement was crushed, and the shah became a virtual dictator, with unlimited American support, increasingly relying on an elaborate secret police establishment to check political opposition. For the next three decades, any expression of Iranian nationalism was brutally suppressed, and nationalist sentiment was channeled to religious outlets. The explosion of the 1979 revolution in Iran was an outcome of this long-term suppression. This revolt is discussed in chapter 6.

Zionism

Modern Zionism is a sociopolitical and national movement. One of its main goals is the ingathering of the Jews as a nation in Palestine. Some of the more radical Zionist factions advocate an expansionist settler-colonizer objective in the Middle East and the expulsion of the indigenous Arab population. Zionism derives its inspiration from a particular interpretation of the Judaic religion, viewing the covenant established by God with Abraham, Isaac, and Jacob as assigning the land of Canaan to the Hebrews "for an everlasting possession." It also bases its claim on the fact that the Hebrews once inhabited Palestine. Certain symbolic elements in Judaism dealt with their ancient glories as a nation, religious festivals commemorate events in this history, and Jewish liturgy is permeated with prayers for a return. In the late nineteenth century, Zionism was transformed from a spiritual to a political movement and was translated into a cardinal principle of Jewish nationalism.

Zionism's political viability developed as a result of anti-Semitism in Europe, particularly among the East European and Russian Jews who suffered manifold disabilities and frequent persecutions. One of the manifestations of political Zionism at the time was Leo Pinsker's pamphlet *Auto-Emancipation*, published in 1882. Pinsker made the argument that legal emancipation was useless because it did not carry with it social emancipation, and that in order to achieve the latter, the Jews must establish their own nation. In the same year, Pinsker helped establish the organization of *Hovevei Zion* (Lovers of Zion), which founded the first Zionist colonies in Palestine supported by funds from abroad, followed by other settlements that were mostly inhabited by East European and Russian Jews. The movement, however, remained a religious-philanthropic undertaking until Theodor Herzl transformed Zionism into an organized political movement.

Herzl, a Hungarian Jew acting as a correspondent for a Viennese newspaper, was troubled by the anti-Semitism he witnessed while covering the Dreyfus trial in Paris. In 1895 he published *Der Judenstaat (The Jewish State)*, arguing that the Jewish problem could not be solved merely by immigration because Jewish minorities would eventually be persecuted wherever they existed. Herzl considered that a "Society of Jews" might acquire a national territory in either Argentina or Palestine and organize Jews in the diaspora for migration to their new home.

In 1897, Herzl organized the first World Zionist Congress in Basel, Switzerland, attended by over two hundred delegates. This congress established the World Zionist Organization, the "Society of Jews" prescribed by Herzl in *Der Judenstaat*, and formulated the "Basel Program," which stated that "the aim of Zionism is to create for the Jewish people a home in Palestine secured by public law."

Herzl, as leader of the World Zionist Organization, attempted through diplomatic channels to get one of the major powers to sponsor a Jewish home in Palestine. In Germany and Turkey he met with little success. The British, however, were more sympathetic. In 1903 they offered what is now Uganda as a site for a Jewish home. Zionist opposition to this offer was so strong that Herzl, who favored acceptance, supported Uganda only as a temporary home. Nevertheless, the Seventh Congress of the World Zionist Organization rejected the offer completely after sharp de-

bate. From that time on the Zionist organization became unaltera-
bly committed to establishing the national home for the Jews only
in Palestine.

During this period of diplomacy by the World Zionist Organization, other Zionist organizations were established to facilitate Jewish immigration to Palestine. The Jewish Colonial Trust was established in 1901, and the Jewish National Fund was set up about
the same time; both organizations purchased land in Palestine for
settlement by European Jews.[16]

The Zionist movement, however, was not without opposition
from within the Jewish community. The ultra-Orthodox Jews opposed the military and political ambitions of the Zionists on religious grounds. They believed that only a very small segment of
total world Jewry would return to Zion, and that the return could
occur only through divine intervention. Even stronger opposition
came from the Reform Jews, who viewed Judaism as a religion
and not as a race. Their views primarily represented the assimila-
tionist tendencies of the Jews in Western Europe, England, and
America who feared that Jewish nationalism would legally and
morally compromise their positions as citizens of their respective
states. Thus, a split developed among the Jewish people over the
problem of nationhood.

At the outbreak of World War I, the Ottoman government
clamped down on Palestine and declared the Zionist movement
a subversive element. During the war Jewish leaders gave financial
support to the Allied governments in an effort to gain Allied sympathy. Of greater importance toward that end, however, were the
contributions of Dr. Chaim Weizmann, a chemistry lecturer at
Manchester University and a Zionist leader. During the war, he
gained influence in England by developing a process for producing
acetone, an ingredient of the explosive cordite used in artillery
shells. Dr. Weizmann used his influence to gain the support of
British leaders for the Zionist cause, while U.S. Supreme Court
Justice Louis Brandeis and Rabbi Stephen Wise, American Jewish
leaders, convinced President Wilson that he should support the
now favorable British position on Zionism. As a result the British
issued the Balfour Declaration of 1917, which stated:

His Majesty's Government *views with favour* the establishment in Palestine of a national home for the Jewish people and will use their best endeavours to facilitate the achievement of this object, it being clearly understood that nothing shall be done which may prejudice the civil and religious rights of *existing non-Jewish communities in Palestine or* the rights and political status enjoyed by Jews in any other country. [emphasis added]

At the time of the declaration, Arabs constituted 92 percent of the total population of Palestine.

In 1917, Palestine was freed from Ottoman control, but the Allied powers had made several conflicting agreements and understandings over the disposition of the freed territories: the Sykes-Picot Agreement dividing the Middle East into spheres of influence for the Allied powers; the Balfour Declaration, discussed above; and the Hussain-McMahon correspondence promising the Arabs an independent state in the Arab lands of the Middle East. Out of these antithetic agreements and declarations arose the bitter struggle between Jewish and Arab nationalisms. The Arabs, no less than the Zionists, have a religious and historical attachment to Palestine. According to Muslim belief, Jerusalem is a sacred city. Perhaps even greater in importance to the Arab is the fact that Palestine had been continuously occupied by a primarily Arab population since 640 A.D. Furthermore, at the close of World War I, Palestine's population was comprised of 620,000 Arabs (of whom 550,000 were Muslims and 70,000 Christians) and 50,000 Jews (the majority of whom were culturally Arabs). The Arabs feared that unlimited Jewish immigration would displace the Arab population and eventually make the Arabs a minority in a wholly Jewish state. The Zionists, on the other hand, considered the Balfour Declaration the equivalent of a *promise* of a Jewish state in the whole of Palestine by Great Britain.[17]

The fate of Palestine thus remained undecided until 1922, when the League of Nations placed the territory under a British mandate, giving the British the "full powers of legislation and of administration, save as they were limited by the terms of this Mandate" and instructing them to work with "an appropriate Jewish agency" on matters affecting the establishment of a Jewish national home. The Zionist Organization was recognized as that agency, and the Jews set up a quasi-state within the mandated area. (The activities and organization of the Jewish quasi-state are discussed in greater detail in chapter 12.)

The advent of World War II sharply curtailed the Zionist activities aimed at the creation of a Jewish state in Palestine. Hitler's persecution of the European Jews caused both the Zionist Organization and the non-Zionist Jews of Palestine to expend most of their energy in support of the Allied war effort. Over 100,000 Palestinian Jews volunteered their services to the Allies, while those who stayed at home committed the agricultural and industrial resources they possessed to the war effort.

The Zionists also put considerable effort into supporting the illegal immigration of European Jewish refugees from Hitler's persecutions. This effort led to increased friction among the Jews, the Arabs, and the British. The indigenous Palestinian-Arabs, inflamed by swelling Jewish immigration and the fear that Palestine would become a Jewish state rather than an Arab state, demonstrated and rioted against the Jewish population and British occupation. To quell the unrest the British attempted to restrict Jewish immigration, and their naval patrols intercepted many refugee ships and sent the occupants to British colonies. In retaliation for these actions, the Stern gang, a small band of Jewish terrorists, maintained a private war against the British.

The revelation at the end of World War II of the attempted extermination of European Jewry caused world opinion to swing to the support of the Zionists. Inspired by the same horror, the Jews themselves concentrated all of their efforts on the immediate illegal immigration of European Jews to Palestine. British attempts to limit the immigration led to open clashes between them and the Jews and to the arrest of many Jews.

By this time Palestine was becoming an unbearable administrative and financial burden to the British. President Truman's commitment during the election campaign of 1948 of his support for the immediate immigration of 100,000 Jews into Palestine led

Great Britain to declare that Jewish disarmament must precede any large-scale immigration.[18] The Zionists' military organizations, the Haganah, the Irgun, and the Stern gang, answered the British demand with a military campaign.

Anxious to be rid of its burden, Britain placed the problem of Palestine before the United Nations. A UN investigating committee sent to Palestine to study the situation recognized that Arab-Jewish cooperation was unlikely. Consequently, in 1947, the UN, without the consultation and consent of the indigenous Palestinian-Arab population, voted to partition Palestine into an Arab state, a Jewish state, and an international zone in and around Jerusalem. The brewing civil war between Arabs and Jews broke out full-scale immediately following the partition proclamation. In the midst of this strife, on May 14, 1948, David Ben-Gurion, head of the Jewish Agency, announced the establishment of the State of Israel. Thus, the "Society of Jews" that Theodor Herzl, the founder of political Zionism, had envisaged in 1895 was achieved within fifty-three years but only at catastrophic expense to the Palestinian people.[19]

As detailed in chapters 11 and 12, the series of events that led to the foundation of the State of Israel in 1948 made refugees of one million Palestinians and led the Middle East into an era of tension, instability, and war. Thus far, five major wars have characterized the conflict: (1) the first all-out war of 1948–49, when Arab states declared war on the newly founded State of Israel; (2) the 1956 Suez crisis, when Britain, France, and Israel invaded Egypt; (3) the 1967 Six-Day War, when Israel launched a major offensive against Egypt, Syria, and Jordan, a major defeat for the Arabs since large sections of territory and more than one million Palestinian residents (most of them already refugees) came under the direct control of the Israeli military authorities, remained under military occupation for almost a quarter of a century, and remain so to date; (4) the October 1973 war when Egypt and Syria attempted to regain lost territories from Israel; and (5) the 1982 full-scale Israeli invasion of Lebanon (see chapter 9 for details).

The utopian idealism associated with Israel's creation has since given way to self-criticism, doubt, and increasing polarization. Zionism today is much different than the Zionism of Herzl and Pinsker, for Israel has seen the rise of extremist nationalists, unhappy with the status quo, who seek a radical solution to the Palestinian problem—if necessary through violence and terror—by removing the Palestinians from Israel's political landscape. For the proponents of extremism, such as Ariel Sharon, Rafael Eitan, and Meir Kahane, the roots of Israel's difficulties lie in its inability to deal effectively with the Palestinians within Israel and the occupied territories. To them, the Palestinians are an obstacle and a hindrance to the realization of the Zionist goals and need to be removed from Israel by forced mass deportations to other Arab states, or other means.

At the other end of the political spectrum is the Zionist left. Made up of educated, secular Jews, this group advocates the exchange of land in the occupied territories for peace. For the proponents of peace, Israel's difficulties lie in the intransigence of Israeli policy vis-à-vis the Palestine Liberation Organization, PLO. Concerned with the erosion of traditional Jewish values attendant upon the role of occupier, the liberal intelligentsia that makes up the principal constituency of the peace movement advocates some accommodation to Palestinian aspirations to end the violence endemic in military occupation.

NOTES

1. Hazim Zaki Nuseibeh, *The Ideas of Arab Nationalism* (Ithaca, N.Y., 1956), p. 207.

2. Sydney Nettleton Fisher, *The Middle East: A History* (New York, 1966), p. 282.

3. George Antonius, *The Arab Awakening: The Story of the Arab National Movement* (New York, 1939), p. 84.

4. Ibid., p. 109.

5. Ibid., Appendix H, p. 445.

6. Ibid., Appendix H, p. 449.

7. Ibid., pp. 293–94.

8. Philip S. Khoury, *Syria and the French Mandate: The Politics of Arab National-*

ism, 1920–1945 (London, 1987) provides a detailed case study of Arab nationalism and the French mandate; Bassam Tibi, *Arab Nationalism*, 2d ed. (London, 1990) examines the impact of Arab Nationalism on social and political change in the period following World War I.

9. George Kirk, *The Middle East in the War* (London, 1952), p. 334.

10. See Tawfiq Hasou, *The Struggle for the Arab World* (Boston, 1985) for a detailed study of the Arab League.

11. For examinations of the impact of these events on Arab Nationalist thought, see Tareq Y. Ismael, *The Arab Left* (Syracuse, 1976) and Issa J. Boullata, *Trends and Issues in Contemporary Arab Thought* (Albany, 1990).

12. Roderic H. Davison, *Reform in the Ottoman Empire: 1865–1876* (Princeton, 1963) provides an examination of the Ottoman reform movement.

13. See Ziya Gokalp, *Turkish Nationalism and Western Civilization*, trans. Niyazi Berkis (New York, 1959) for a presentation of Gokalp's political thought; see Uriel Heyd, *Foundations of Turkish Nationalism: The Life and Teachings of Ziya Gokalp* (London, 1950) for an examination of Gokalp's life and work in a historical context.

14. Farhad Diba, *Mohammed Mossadegh: A Political Biography* (London, 1986).

15. For detailed examination of Iranian nationalism, see Richard W. Cottam, *Nationalism in Iran* (Pittsburgh, 1964); and Ervand Abrahamian, *Iran: Between Two Revolutions* (Princeton, 1982).

16. Conor Cruise O'Brien, *The Siege: The Saga of Israel and Zionism* (New York, 1986) for a detailed history of Zionism.

17. Neil Caplan, *Futile Diplomacy: Early Arab-Zionist Negotiation Attempts, 1913–1931* (London, 1983) provides an examination of early Zionist diplomacy.

18. See Samuel Halperin, *The Political World of American Zionists* (Detroit, 1961) for an examination of the influence of Zionism on American foreign policy.

19. Walid Khalidi, ed., *From Haven to Conquest, Readings in Zionism and the Palestine Problem until 1948* (Beirut, 1971) provides a collection of readings on Zionism from different perspectives.

II

COMPARATIVE
GOVERNMENTS

The Northern Belt

5

The Republic of Turkey

Walter Weiker

Turkey is unique among Muslim Middle Eastern states in several ways. It has been a republic for more than sixty years, longer than any other in the area, and it has been a multiparty democracy for four decades. Although there have been three "interruptions" in which the armed forces assumed power for the purpose of "repairing" Turkish democracy, the most notable thing about all of these incidents is that the military kept its promise to return power to civilian hands. How these achievements came about and how they equipped Turkey to face the challenges of the future are the topics to be addressed.

History

The political system and the problems of contemporary Turkey are deeply rooted in Turkish history. The Ottoman Empire dominated the Middle East and brought the Turks power and prestige for more than five centuries before it succumbed to the onslaughts of nationalism and imperialism in the nineteenth and early twentieth centuries. During the same period, however, important foundations were laid for the modernization that was to be the basis of the Turkish republic.

Turkic tribes began to move from central Asia into the Black Sea region and Anatolia in the eleventh century, and by the thirteenth they dominated those areas. By the early fifteenth century they had moved well into the Balkans, and in 1453 they put a final end to the Byzantine Empire by capturing Constantinople. Ottoman expansion continued under such sultans as Suleiman the Magnificent (1520–66), bringing under its hegemony all the Arab areas including much of North Africa. Ottoman power twice reached the gates of Vienna, in 1529 and 1683, but both times failed to breach the walls of the city itself. Thereafter European military power began slowly to drive the Turks back, and in 1699 the Ottomans were forced to sign the Treaty of Carlowitz, the first time they were not the victorious party.

By the end of the eighteenth century the empire was increasingly under siege. Napoleon's invasion of Egypt in 1798 triggered the detachment of Egypt from Ottoman control, and during the nineteenth century one after another of the Balkan peoples broke away to form their own states. These would prove to be salutary developments, however, because they impelled the Ottomans to examine their situation and to seek ways to save the empire. The reforms they attempted to inaugurate have been termed "defensive modernization," and while they did not, of course, succeed in their ultimate purpose of saving the empire, they did lay the foundations for much of the reform that Kamal Ataturk was to introduce in the twentieth century.

The initial reforms concentrated on the military, one of the foundations of the Ottoman system. Instructors and technology were sought in the West, and a number of new professional schools were established in Istanbul, including one for military medicine. Ottoman officers were also sent to Europe for training and study. It became apparent, however, that much of the key to the empire's strengthening lay in social and political reforms, and a succession of reform attempts was launched by the sultans. The first notable event, under Mahmud II, was the abolition of the Janissary Corps in 1826 and its replacement by an army that was more modern, less politically conservative, and more loyal to the sultan.

Politically, the Ottomans sought to attract loyalty from the non-Muslim Greeks, Armenians, and Jews who lived in Ottoman territories and who possessed important economic and political skills. They would accomplish it through the *Hatt-i Sharif of Gulhane*, or Rescript of the Rose Chamber, promulgated in 1839 by Mah-

mud II, which proclaimed the equality of all Ottoman subjects before the law and promised that laws would be enforced
justly and honestly.

A variety of schemes for implementation followed during the
next half century, but few had real effects. Equality remained a
fiction because neither the Ottomans nor the non-Muslims really
wanted it. The former were unwilling to modify the basic position
that Islam is doctrinally superior. The latter were not interested
because they often occupied good positions by being exempt from
military conscription and by being able to invoke the protection
of European powers. Islam remained one of the pillars of the Ottoman state. In the Balkan areas and the regions near Russia the
minorities also continued in their efforts to gain their own political
independence. Reformers among the military, bureaucracy, and
intelligentsia were frequently beset as well by conservative Muslim
forces, including the *Ulema* and many local notables. The reaffirmation of Gulhane in the *Hatt-i Humayun* of 1856 did not achieve
much more.

The next reform attempt was potentially more significant because it was designed to give all subjects of the empire a role in
governing. In 1876, at the urging of Midhat Pasha, one of the most
successful Ottoman provincial governors and an astute statesman,
and a group of intellectuals, writers, and journalists who became
known as the Young Ottomans, an Ottoman constitution was developed. In the following year, 1877–78, the first Ottoman parliament was convened, but it accomplished little, in part because most
of the real power remained in the hands of the sultan and because
there was no bureaucracy in place to implement significant economic or social programs. Sultan Abdul Hamid II had "handed
down" the constitution reluctantly anyway, and he soon found opportunity to circumvent it and to prevent the parliament from
meeting again for thirty years. The sultan did, however, begin on
his own to improve education, to sponsor measures to improve
communications and transportation, and to establish some industry.

The reformers continued their efforts as best they could, but
in 1908 the Young Turks revolted. Led by officers, bureaucrats, and

intellectuals, they took power from the sultan, who was to be made into a constitutional monarch. The 1876 constitution was reinstated and the second Ottoman parliament convened. The organization that became the dominant political party was known as the Committee of Progress and Union (CPU). There was vigorous multiparty politics until 1913 when the CPU succeeded in overwhelming all its opponents. New efforts at social and economic development had some effect, but they were interrupted by, among other things, the Balkan wars, which detached the few remaining European provinces from the empire. In 1914, under the leadership of Enver Pasha, Turkey entered World War I on the side of Germany, and four years later defeat ended the Ottoman as well as the Austro-Hungarian empires.

The Turks were, of course, not finished. In the face of attempts by the victorious Allies to dismember Anatolia and Thrace (the Arab parts of the empire had been detached by both Allied and indigenous forces), Turkish nationalist leaders who had moved to Anatolia began to organize and to rebuild a Turkish army. They were motivated in part by the Allies' encouragement of Greek forces to attempt to annex a part of Anatolia. Under the leadership of Mustafa Kamal (later Ataturk), the most important Turkish military hero of World War I as well as an able politician who had gained experience during the Young Turk period, the nationalists brought the War of Independence to a successful conclusion in 1922. They organized a political structure that became a provisional government and that was able to oust the collaborationist sultan as well as to replace the punitive Treaty of Sèvres with the Lausanne Peace Treaty, reestablishing full Turkish sovereignty.

On October 29, 1923, Ataturk and his colleagues established the Republic of Turkey and began a process of social and economic change not seen in the Muslim Middle East before or since. The decade of the 1920s was momentous. Under the leadership of the Republican Peoples Party (RPP), Ataturk promulgated what have become known as the Great Reforms. His basic aim was to turn the face of Turkey from the east toward the west and the modern world. On March 3, 1924, the Grand National Assembly formally abolished both the sultanate and the caliphate (which the Ottoman dynasty had claimed since its early years). Soon thereafter came a change in the day of rest from Friday to Sunday, a decree to wear Western dress (in particular laws against wearing the fez, which among other things allowed men to follow the Islamic practice of praying with the head covered while at the same time touching the forehead to the ground), and new civil, criminal, and commercial codes drawn from European models. One of the most far-reaching steps to detach Turkey from its past was the 1928 substitution of the Latin alphabet for the Arabic script in which Ottoman Turkish had been written. Perhaps the most important reform of all, however, was secularization. Declaring that the ʿUlema was only a backward force, Ataturk divested religion of its power by taking control of all education, closing the Shariʿah courts, disbanding religious orders and brotherhoods, and making all religious functionaries state employees. He also discouraged religious observance, and his authority was such that many of his colleagues in reform supported him by changing their own behavior.

Politically the republic was centered on the Grand National Assembly, a unicameral legislature with unrestricted powers in accord with the principle of "Sovereignty Belongs Unconditionally to the People." Ataturk became president of the republic, and through the RPP, the sole political party after the opposition was ousted by some loyal Republican but more conservative colleagues in 1924, he was able to take total control. In 1930 Ataturk felt that the country was ready for the next step in its political development. In the face of a severe economic crisis, which came with the worldwide depression, he saw his opportunity and persuaded several of his colleagues to establish an officially sponsored opposition party. The Free Party was to challenge the government in the assembly, to bring the RPP to account, and to debate economic and political affairs. Under the leadership of former prime minister Fethi Okyar, Ataturk's friend, the opposition was vigorous, and soon expanded its activities as local elections approached. It quickly became apparent, however, that the Free Party was becoming a vehicle for all those who opposed the republic itself, including religious fundamentalists, and the venture into multiparty politics ended after only ninety-nine days.

It was followed by the years of "tutelage for democracy." One of the shortcomings of the 1920s reforms was that they had not reached below the political elites and into the general population. Among the new politics that Ataturk undertook was insertion of "independent deputies" (not members of the RPP) into the assembly to criticize the government vigorously in public and to teach the leaders and public alike the concept of "loyal opposition" (the RPP had not shown itself tolerant of this during the Free Party period). Another was to seek to bring wider elements of the general population into political life through a series of community centers known as *halkevleri* (people's houses), which were to be models for self-administration by the members, as well as institutions for general education and political indoctrination. He also attempted to reorganize the RPP to emphasize public service as one of the criteria for advancement.

There were also several important efforts directed toward refocusing social and political doctrines and orientations. (1) Language reform: Following the change in alphabet already mentioned, the Turkish Language Association now sought to "Turkify" the language by casting out many Ottoman terms that had been "borrowed" from Persian and Arabic and replacing them with the "pure Turkish" discovered by teachers and students sent to villages. As a result of the zeal to reform, for a while many Turks had to use glossaries to read their daily newspapers. The pace of change was considerably slowed, but even now "old" and "new" Turkish remains a political football between the left and the right. (2) History reform: Extensive research into Turkish history was conducted in an attempt to tell the story of the Turkish nation rather than that of the Ottoman dynasty. The new history, which was taught in schools, was instrumental in implanting a strong sense of nationalism. (3) The development of an ideology: Eventually known as Kamalism, it contained six points, or "arrows," four of which were closely defined and not subject to interpretation. The first point is republicanism, that "sovereignty belongs unconditionally to the nation" and would be exercised through the Grand National Assembly. The second point is nationalism, under which pan-Ottomanism, pan-Turkish, pan-Islam, and other "internationalist"

ideologies were banned, and under which policies to develop national pride were legitimated. The third point is secularism, the
disestablishment of all religions from temporal pursuits, such as
education and law, or from legal authority, and the placing of them
under government supervision. The fourth point is popularism,
which in addition to "popular sovereignty" stressed the mutual obligations of state and individuals to each other and envisioned formal equality through things like abolishing the titles of bey or
pasha.

The other two arrows were more open to discussion: etatism,
the idea that the state should play an active role in the economy,
and revolutionism, vaguely defined to mean the summation of the
spirit of all the Ataturk reforms.

Kamalism was to serve Turkish development in two ways. One
was to draw fairly definite limits on dissent and radicalism. The
other was to allow debate on many specifics, such as the proper
measures through which the state was to further the growth of
the economy.

In addition to these policies, the 1930s saw major efforts at economic and social development, including the rapid expansion of
education, transportation, and communication, and as much industrialization as was possible with still limited resources.

Ataturk died in 1938. He was succeeded by his long-time colleague and prime minister, Ismet Inonu. After stringencies during
World War II, pressure built for the relaxation of restrictions on
political opposition, and in 1946 four prominent RPP members
formed the Democrat Party (DP). They won a few seats in the
election that year but continued to build strength and in 1950 out-
polled the RPP, which, to the amazement of many inside and outside Turkey, quietly handed over the reins of power.

The Democrat decade saw change in some important Ataturk
policies as well as a period of rapid economic and social growth.
Among the important areas modified was secularism. Although
virtually all Turkish leaders of both parties accepted the principle,
many in the DP thought that Ataturk had gone to excess in its
implementation. They also found that in the general population
the attachment to Islam remained strong, and here was a sphere

in which a good deal of political capital was to be made. There followed, then, restoration of religious education in the schools. (Actually, in the face of rising opposition, the RPP had made the initial concessions, allowing religious instruction if parents requested it, so that the Democrats had only to say that it would be given to all students except when parents requested that their children be exempt.) Government funding for mosques was also increased, and the government no longer discouraged religious observance. There was not, however, any attempt to end secularization in general. The state still controlled education and law, and secularism in Turkey today remains deeply rooted.

Economic doctrine was a second area of major change. Under the statist policies of the RPP virtually all industrialization had been controlled by the state and its bureaucracy. Under the Democrats, primary emphasis was given to encouraging private entrepreneurs. At the same time a period of very rapid growth began, partly because of fortuitous conditions. A sizable surplus of funds was available because imports were scarce during World War II, the United States began large-scale aid under the Truman Doctrine, world grain prices skyrocketed because of the Korean War, and the DP under the leadership of Adnan Menderes was willing to engage in considerable deficit financing. One of the results of these policies was rapid inflation. With increasing urbanization came the integration of more and more of the population into the mainstream of national life. Another result was the great popularity of the DP, which won decisive electoral victories in 1954 and 1957.

Some of these things were fatal to the DP. In 1959 the economy became very unstable and was normalizing only after persistent intervention by the World Bank at the behest of Turkey's creditors. In the face of these frustrations, which showed signs of spilling over into the newly urbanized public, and of increasing opposition from the old RPP, the government became more oppressive, taking a series of strong measures against the RPP, the press, the universities, and others. On May 27, 1960, the armed forces ousted the Menderes regime.

The officers who formed the National Unity Committee (NUC) were intent on restoring democracy, however. Believing fully in the Ataturk doctrine of civilian rule, they set out to reform the constitution and electoral law. Despite the enthusiasm of some of the commanders and their supporters, they made minimal effort to change economic and social policies. As promised, after eighteen months they returned to the barracks, though the leader, General Cemal Gursel, was elected president.

The basis of the new constitution (for what came to be known as the Second Republic) was a set of strong checks and balances to prevent a recurrence of the authoritarian rule of the DP. It included the addition of a Senate, a Constitutional Court, and an electoral system based on proportional representation. As a result of the latter, three parties that competed for the old DP votes split their support, enabling the RPP to return to power at the head of a coalition. By 1965, however, the Justice Party (JP), one of the would-be successors to the DP, had won a clear victory, again bringing to power social and economic conservatives. Under Prime Minister Suleyman Demirel, the JP carried on many of the same social and economic policies of the DP, and it repeated its election triumph in 1969.

A new economic crisis loomed in 1970, coupled with greatly increased hostility between the JP and both the opposition RPP and the JP's own rivals on the conservative end of the political spectrum. This time when the armed forces stepped in to pressure the government to be more effective it was not in the form of direct intervention but through "coup by memorandum"—a warning to Demirel, who resigned. Many in Turkey were also troubled by the vigor of Turkey's first radical leftist party, the Turkish Labor Party (TLP), which had emerged under the auspices and in the atmosphere of the 1961 constitution. It had obtained only 3 percent of the vote in 1965 and 2.7 percent in 1969, but the fact that its closure by the Constitutional Court came shortly after the 1971 "memorandum" was only coincidental. Between 1971 and the 1973 election Turkey was governed by a series of "above-party" cabinets.

The 1973 election was significant because for the first time in the multiparty period the RPP increased its share of the vote over a previous election. There were several reasons why the voters finally became more receptive to a moderate left-wing party. One was that in the previous year the RPP had retired the last representative of the Ataturk team, Ismet Inonu, who despite his competent leadership had also been known as particularly militant in imposing some of the unpopular reforms. He was replaced by an attractive young campaigner, Bulent Ecevit. A second reason was social change itself and the waning of the older issues of secularism, together with the increase in the number of urban workers and the strength of trade unions that were not averse to economic and social policies like those of the DP and JP, which could be seen as serving mainly the interests of business groups and traditional landowners. A more ominous reason why the RPP became the biggest single party was the splintering of the moderate right into bitterly rival factions and the appearance of two parties on the radical right for the first time: the religion-based National Salvation Party and the neo-fascist National Action Party.

With these events a period of serious instability began. In early 1974, after long negotiations, the RPP formed a coalition with the NSP, solely on the basis of both coming to power, since the two parties shared almost no policy views. When Turkey invaded Cyprus that fall, Ecevit tried to capitalize on it by calling a new election, but the moderate conservative assembly majority prevented its dissolution and instead formed a patchwork coalition of their own, with Demirel again at its head. In the 1977 election the RPP again improved its position, but despite being the largest party, it was the only one on the left, and the JP was able to combine with the radical right to stay in power precariously. That meant, however, making increasing concessions to the National Salvation and National Action party demands, particularly on social, educational, and religious matters. Within the RPP, meanwhile, a strong faction that sought to pull Ecevit farther to the left gained considerable power, so that virtually the entire political spectrum was fragmented, with increased radicalism on both ends.

These events brought Turkey to its most severe government crisis and culminated in the third military intervention on September 12, 1980. The crisis had three components. One was the economy. As a result of spiraling world oil prices and global recession, and the Demirel government's careless spending, some aspects of the

Turkish economy had nearly collapsed. Turkey's foreign debt had risen so high that its credit deteriorated to the point where its checks would hardly be honored in any world markets. Shortages were everywhere, and the government's desperate tactic of printing money resulted only in worse inflation.

The second component of the crisis was government paralysis. With no majority party and with the utter inability of any of the parties to work together, no important economic and social problems were addressed, and at one point it was not even possible for the assembly to organize itself by choosing officers or to elect a president of the republic, even after fifteen ballots. The third aspect of the crisis was endemic urban guerrilla violence between rightist and leftist radicals. In 1979 more than 5,000 Turks lost their lives.

The 1980 military intervention, therefore, was welcomed by virtually the entire country, and under the leadership of General Kenan Evren and the National Security Council the officers set out once again to "repair" the fabric of democracy. The results, in direct response to what were seen as the roots of the political breakdown, have been far-reaching and have been what some people call "supervised democracy," which has governed Turkey since the armed forces once again returned power to the political parties on November 19, 1983.

The thrust of the restructuring has been to maintain democracy while curbing the chief abuses that led to the 1980 crisis. The main features of supervised democracy are restrictions on the political activities of private institutions, concentration of more power in the presidency than in the assembly (the Senate, created under the 1961 constitution, was abolished as were some other checks and balances), an electoral system that minimizes party fragmentation, and stringent curbs on radical political expression on both the right and the left. After completion of the new constitution a referendum on November 7, 1982, approved the new charter and simultaneously elected NSC chairman General Kenan Evren to a seven-year term as president. On November 6, 1983, the first election of the Third Republic took place. Because one of the reforms had been to abolish all of the old political parties and to ban their leaders from politics for periods of up to ten years, the election was contested by three new parties. Perhaps the most significant result of the election was that the Nationalist Democracy Party (the one which the armed forces signaled that they favored) finished third, a result widely interpreted as a show of independence by the Turkish people.

Today Turkey is a country of 301,000 square miles. Its population in 1985 was approximately 51 million, and the growth rate for the years 1980–85 was 2.8 percent. The country is now about 54 percent urban, and the population is 99 percent Muslim. The most significant minority is about 12 percent Kurds living in the eastern part of the country. There are also a few Alevis in several central Anatolian provinces.

Government Structure

Turkey is governed by a unicameral Grand National Assembly of 400 members elected for five-year terms. It has all of the powers normally given to a parliament. The head of state is the president, elected popularly for a seven-year term. The government is headed by a prime minister and a cabinet chosen from the Assembly. The judiciary, including a Constitutional Court, is independent. In regard to local government, Turkey is a unitary system divided into 71 provinces. Governors are appointed by the central government and are assisted by provincial councils that are elected but have few significant legislative powers. Mayors and councils of cities and towns and village headmen and councils are also popularly elected.

One of the areas of reform that received attention in the 1982 constitution was "discipline" of the governmental institutions. Under the Ataturk constitution of 1924 the Assembly had unrestricted powers, with no checks and balances (in the name of absolute popular sovereignty). That worked well when Ataturk himself governed, but it also gave opportunity for political repression by the Democrat Party during the 1950s. The 1961 constitution, therefore, included an extensive array of checks and balances (a Senate, a Constitutional Court, an electoral system, and autonomy for many institutions such as universities and government-run television and broadcasting). Its permissiveness was thought to have been one of the causes of fragmentation, radicalism, and government paralysis, and the 1982 Constitution took a middle ground.

One change is that the president has considerable power to act independently of the Assembly. He can call new elections in the event that the legislature is deadlocked on important matters. He can also name the prime minister and "accept his resignation" relatively independently of Assembly action. The president is also given strong veto power and extensive authority to declare one of several kinds of national emergency whereby he is able to rule by decree in certain areas.

A second area of reform changed the internal rules of the Assembly to speed deliberations. Among the changes, for example, are the establishment of a quorum of one-third (it had been half), provisions for the expulsion of members for nonattendance, and the establishment of time limits for important actions like the national budget. The Senate, established by the 1961 constitution, was also abolished. Other reforms in "rules" were directed at party instability, which had frequently plagued the Assembly. For example, there are restraints on party-switching. If a deputy now resigns from his party, a frequent occurrence during the factionalism of the 1960s and 1970s, he may not join another party during his term, may retain his seat only as an independent, may not take a cabinet post, and may not be a "central contingent" candidate of any party in the next election. (Up to 5 percent of a party's candidates may be selected by the central leadership and not subject to the processes of candidate selection by party members voting in each province.)

The Electoral System

The Assembly is elected on the basis of multimember constituencies, which are for the most part provinces except that some of the bigger provinces are subdivided. In order to prevent fragmentation from occurring, the proportional representation system (in which voting is by party lists) has been modified to include two thresholds: the district level, where a party must get a minimum of more than one d'Hondt system quotient, and the national level, where the party must get a minimum of 10 percent to be represented at all. (This appears to be among the highest thresholds in the world.) A party, in order to run in a national election, must be organized in at least half of the country's provinces. Parties organized on the basis of communism, socialism, or theological doctrines are not allowed.

Interest Groups

Interest groups are prominent on the Turkish political stage. One of the "abuses" that the military regime of 1980 sought to remedy was what some have called "overpoliticization" of Turkish society, and one of the probable causes of this was interest group activity. Thus, in the Third Republic all private associations are forbidden to engage in political activity, including maintaining relations with or contributing funds to political parties, joining political rallies or demonstrations, and taking positions on political issues—in other words, anything that is outside of the purposes for which the associations are organized, such as promoting professional standards or engaging in collective bargaining. Singled out for special mention were trade unions, professional associations, and the universities. Considerable radical tendencies had been evident in all of them before 1980.

The major interest groups continue to be active, however, if not directly in politics, then certainly in pursuing the interests of their members vis-à-vis the government or other spheres. The major interest groups are labor and business.

Although no accurate figures are available, it is generally estimated that over 50 percent of Turkish workers now belong to trade unions. Most belong to the Turkish Confederation of Trade Unions, *Turk-Iş* formed in 1952. It is generally moderate in its views, and at various times labor has supported both modern leftist and moderate rightist political parties. Turk-Iş has been active in collective bargaining and intermittently in other efforts to improve the conditions of workers, though it is also true that a considerable amount of the improvement in wages and working conditions in Turkey has come about because the major parties vigorously sought labor support.

Under the 1961 constitution, Turkish workers received, for the first time, the right to strike, though they had been promised that right under both the RPP and the Democrat governments. (The RPP had been strongly populist but also had a basic doctrinal hostility to any associations built on social class.) Strike activity erupted several times during the 1960s and 1970s either when there were economic stringencies or when there were specific antilabor policies on the part of Justice Party governments. Employers could circumvent strikes by recruiting workers from among the large numbers of unemployed or those who opposed some of the leftist tendencies of the unions. The latter were found in the many small enterprises that still characterize the Turkish economy. Under the 1982 constitution the right to strike is retained, but there are prohibitions against jurisdictional strikes, sympathy strikes, or strikes that can in any way be construed as political.

Before 1980 there were also the radical Revolutionary Trade Unions Confederation (DISK), which enrolled an estimated 20 to 25 percent of the workers and which was militant and visible, and the conservative National Trade Unions Confederation (MISK), which was much smaller. Both were banned in 1980.

Business is represented by several organizations. The oldest and largest is the Union of Chambers of Commerce and Industry. It was organized in the 1920s, and many categories of business are required to belong. Under various laws the Union has allocated import quotas among specific enterprises and certified the qualifications of applicants for a variety of government benefit programs. It also carries on many research and development activities, and while it has often sought to speak for the business sector as a whole, it has not had formal authority to do so or to engage in collective bargaining (which has been limited to the level of individual enterprises).

A newer organization is the Turkish Industrialists' and Businessmen's Association (TUSIAD). Formed in 1971, it represents the biggest and most modern enterprises, including the large holding companies. Among its activities are extensive research and professional consulting, and it issues frequent statements analyzing economic problems, particularly in regard to import and export policies.

A third major group is the Confederation of Artisans' Associations (*Esnaf ve Sanatkar Dernegi Konfederasyonu*). It represents an estimated 3 million artisans and is especially strong in many provincial cities and towns. It has often been active in combination with other conservative groups on behalf of "social tone" policies such as in education.

Other interest groups exist as well. Agriculture is represented by several organizations, including the Union of Chambers of Agriculture and the Turkish Cooperatives Association. Almost all professions have organizations (and in the recent past groups like teachers and police had two, one on each end of the ideological spectrum, so allegations of overpoliticization were not unfounded). There is also a small but active and growing women's movement.

Political Parties

Although all of the political parties that were in existence in 1980 were disbanded by the military regime, new ones organized for the 1983 election. It is useful, nevertheless, to describe them briefly because their histories help indicate some of the important directions that Turkish politics may follow.

The *moderate left* has been represented since the beginning of the republic by the Republican People's Party. Founded by Ataturk, it ruled as the single party until 1946, when it presided over the transition to multiparty politics. It was defeated in 1950 and since then has been in and out of power, as detailed earlier. During nearly sixty years of existence it had only three leaders, Ataturk, Ismet Inonu, and Bulent Ecevit. It always included a variety of political tendencies, but the only major defection came in 1967 when fifty-two senators and deputies who were critical of Ecevit's "left-of-center" platform split and formed the Reliance Party under the leadership of Turhan Feyzioglu. In the mid-1970s the party leadership also came under strong pressure from factions who wanted to move even farther left. The RPP's leadership has been drawn largely from bureaucrats, professionals, the educated urban classes, and, to some extent, from the military.

The reasons for both its defeat and its resurgence are instructive. The party's defeat in 1950, despite its having been the long-time representative of Kamalism, can be ascribed to several factors. One was that much of the drastic modernization was for some time disliked by many traditional groups in Turkey. Another was that during the single-party period the party and its agents were often autocratic in imposing the new ways. A third, already mentioned, was that the leaders of the Democrat Party in 1950 had come out of the RPP itself, so they were legitimized despite being dissenters. The RPP's comeback after 1973, in turn, was in response to several things, including policy failures of the Justice Party and social change that made conservative economic and social policies less appealing to the urban workers (and to some new leaders). Despite the fact that since 1973 the RPP was several times the biggest single party, the moderate left never received a majority of the votes, and the internal factionalism made it often ineffective in governing as well as in opposition.

The *moderate right* has been represented chiefly by the Democrat and Justice parties, which governed Turkey for most of the multiparty years. The fortunes of the strongly pro–private enterprise DP of 1946–60 under the leadership of Celal Bayar and Adnan Menderes were detailed earlier. The JP, founded in 1961 and led for most of its tenure by Suleyman Demirel, followed similar policies, and for most of the period it was the largest of the several parties that competed for right-wing votes. Because it was largely drawn from the business sector and from landowners and local notables in provincial towns and cities, its leadership contrasted to that of the RPP.

The dominance of the moderate conservatives was initially because of their opposition to the RPP on grounds of both the RPP's authoritarian behavior and its radical (for that day) programs. The moderate right's continued popularity was based on the rapid economic growth of the 1950s and 1960s and on the political skill of many of its leaders. Their decline was connected to their later inability to solve important economic and social problems, to severe factionalization, and to the general waning of the importance of a conservative "social tone" as social change and ambition became more widespread. (Defections from the DP and JP were frequent.) In 1955 a group of liberal intellectual critics formed the Freedom Party, which lasted for several years. In 1961 the JP split the vote with the rival New Turkey and Republican Peasants Nation parties, and during the 1970s it was severely damaged by defectors who organized a Democratic Party to challenge it. Most of the splits were factional, often based on the personal appeal of strong leaders. It was usually difficult to heal them in spite of relatively few important policy differences. In 1980 the personal enmity between Demirel and RPP leader Ecevit was said to be one of the reasons why the major parties were unable to cooperate in any way to solve some of the serious problems of the economy and of law and order.

The *radical left* has been represented only by the Turkish Labor Party. A Marxist group organized in 1961, it was strident but usually responsible in its criticism of the government. It won only 3 percent of the vote in 1965 and 2.7 percent in 1969, but its radicalism did not sit well with most Turks, and the party was disbanded by the Constitutional Court in 1971 on grounds of subversion. The other radical party, the Unity Party of the late 1960s, represented mostly central Anatolian Alevis.

The *radical right* was represented by the small Republican Peasants Nation Party and the Nation Party until 1969. In 1973, however, there appeared for the first time a party that ran primarily on a religious platform, the National Salvation Party (earlier the National Order Party), although it also took positions on economic issues and spoke strongly in favor of social and religious tradition. Headed by the colorful Necmettin Erbakan, the NSP received 11.8 percent of the vote in 1973, enough to hold a strong position in the Assembly and to make a coalition with the RPP for several months. While some observers were alarmed at the NSP's vote, others were heartened that it did poorly, and the views of the latter were supported when the NSP vote in 1977 dropped despite the severe social problems that might have motivated voters to support a religion-based party. The NSP was disbanded with the other parties, and under the new constitution it is unlikely that another party based on a religious platform will be allowed.

Some of the votes that the NSP lost went in 1977 to the neo-fascist National Action Party led by Alparslan Turkes, a veteran of the 1960 National Unity Committee. Its program emphasized anticommunism, nationalism, morality, and populism, and it provoked great anxiety when it appeared to be among the main organizers of the radical right-wing guerrillas who caused much of the urban violence in the late 1970s.

Three new parties competed in the 1983 election. On the moderate conservative side is the Motherland Party (*Anavatan Partisi*), which won 45 percent of the votes and 211 Assembly seats. Like its predecessors, its program centered on free enterprise and individual freedom, and its foreign policy would continue ties not only to the United States and Europe but to the Middle East and other Muslim countries as well. Its economic policy advocates increasing exports and encouraging private foreign investment. The MP outran its moderate conservative rival—the Nationalist Democracy Party—in part because it was led by Turgut Ozal, a well-known and colorful personality who had been deputy prime minister for economic affairs under the 1980–82 military regime and who received much credit for Turkey's economic recovery, which began in that period. The NDP, in contrast, was led by the relatively mild retired General Turgut Sunalp and had what many consider the additional handicap of being the clear choice of the members of the junta. In 1984 an additional party, the True Path Party, emerged on the moderate right.

The moderate left in the form of the Populist Party won 30 percent of the vote, a figure not far from what the moderate left had often gotten in earlier elections, and 117 seats. Led by Necdet Calp, a career civil servant, its program stressed social issues such as working conditions and tax reform, as well as problems of economic development and national security. In 1984 additional leftist parties began to appear: the Social Democracy Party (SODEP) led by Erdal Inonu, son of Ataturk's colleague and long-time RPP leader Ismet Inonu, and the Democratic Left Party (DSP) led by Rahsan Ecevit, wife of the former RPP leader. Merger talks among the three are reported periodically.

The Role of the Military

The political role of the Turkish armed forces is perhaps unique in the Middle East. Despite having intervened three times since 1960, they have always seen their role as one of "repairing" Turkish democracy. What is most striking is that their efforts have indeed been primarily of that nature. Although many of the officers had views on social and economic policies, they have seldom sought to impose them before returning power to the political parties.

One reason is that Ataturk strongly insisted that the military had no formal place in politics, and in fact in 1923 he forced those officers who were also members of the Assembly to choose one or the other position. A second reason is that the officers share the genuine commitment to democracy of most Turks. A third cause is experience. One of the lessons of the 1960–61 National Unity Committee was that the imposition of more liberal programs than the DP had followed would have met with a considerable dissatisfaction by both the general population and important political forces, without whose support the commanders could not have effectively governed an increasingly complex society. In 1971 and 1980 as well, the military understood that broad societal participation had become both desirable and necessary for national growth and development, and that if the commanders were to be seen as autocrats their ability to lead would be impaired.

On the other hand, the military can be expected to retain a strong watchdog role. The 1980 intervention and the structural changes made in its wake signaled clearly that the perceived defects of the institutions and of many civilian political leaders would not be allowed to recur. This is probably acceptable to most Turks as well, who welcomed the coup when it signaled the end of the urban guerrilla violence and the beginning of economic recovery and social stability. A strong role for the National Security Council in periods of national unrest (from a variety of causes, including economic emergencies) is built into the 1982 constitution. (It should be added that the armed forces act as an interest group on their own behalf. Not unexpectedly, they have made sure that military salaries and amenities are among the best in the country.)

The Role of Religion

Perhaps one of the most notable achievements of the Turkish republic is in defining the role of religion. As discussed earlier, secularization was one of the policies that Ataturk was most determined to implement, and he succeeded to a degree probably unequaled in the Middle East. Advocacy of any reversal in the severance of religion from formal legal or political roles has, of course, been illegal during the entire republic period. Most significant, however, is that despite the continuing deep religiosity of most of the Turkish population, the demands for the incorporation of religion-based values in society and social institutions have been moderate. A true modus vivendi has been reached, and people who are religious and people who are not have become generally tolerant of each other. Few in either group can be classified as "militant."

Turkey's political history is responsible. In Ottoman times the Turkish 'Ulema was usually a conservative force, and frustrated much reform. Ataturk reacted largely to this past record, and he always insisted that secularism was based not on the contention that Islam was undesirable but only that it needed to be modernized. When the multiparty period came (and Ataturk himself was no longer in power), the role of religion became a pressing issue because of its continuing popularity, but, as noted above, not even the conservative Democrats were willing to try to make changes that could be construed to reverse the basic secularist foundation of the state. Even the RPP saw the need to allow at least some resumption of religious education. Two other important forces were also at work, however. One was, again, rapid social change and the realization that things like secular education, economic growth, and personal freedom were of greater importance to many Turks than government enforcement of a conservative "social tone." The second was the pluralist nature of Turkish society, together with the fact that no group ultimately had power to impose radical social views on other segments of the nation. It is still debated in Turkey whether Ataturk went too far in his initial religious reforms, and there are still a few who resent those policies. But for the most part it is agreed that the combination of initial radical policies with later social change and political pluralism has resulted in a situation unique among Islamic countries.

(This is not to say, of course, that religion is not evident in Turkey or that there is no discussion about its role. Religious literature is for sale everywhere. There is religious education not only in the public schools but in state-run Islamic training schools up to high school and college and in private Koran courses. Mosque attendance on Fridays is high, and during Ramadan many keep the fast, including large numbers among the middle levels of the bureaucracy and private businesses. There are also periodic outbursts of protests by both small fundamentalist groups and militant secularists, but on the whole a general attitude of mutual tolerance pervades the scene.)

The Economy

Economic crises have been associated with the periods of instability, and one of the qualifications of the current prime minister, Turgut Ozal, that most attracted Turkish voters is his experience in the State Planning Office and in other posts related to the economy.

The Republic of Turkey began with an economy both poor and underdeveloped. After a period during the 1920s when Ataturk encouraged private enterprise, there came a decade of etatism in which the government took an active developmental role (almost to the exclusion of the private sector) that included two five-year development plans, and in which a good start was made toward industrialization. The DP in 1950 followed policies of strong stimulation of the private sector and presided over a period of rapid but unstable growth and considerable inflation through investment largely from internal sources and deficit financing. The most serious crisis came in the mid-1970s, partly as a result of skyrocketing world oil prices but also as a result of too rapid expansion financed partly by heavy foreign borrowing. The Democrat and Justice parties were also particularly cool to the idea of central planning, though a State Planning Office has existed since 1961.

The Turkish economy has, of course, grown substantially under the Republic, and in the early 1980s per capita income passed $1,000, putting Turkey into the ranks of the "middle developing" countries. Maturity has its costs, however. Many problems have to do with Turkey's relationship with the world economy. For many years the primary orientation was toward import substitution, and it is only since the late 1970s that Turkey has begun to become more export oriented. This is particularly important, given that in 1963 Turkey signed a protocol agreement with the European Community envisaging eventual full membership, a goal supported by all Turkish political parties. This will entail major improvements in the efficiency of Turkish industry and agriculture and in the quality of its products. Unemployment, estimated at around 20 percent in the early 1980s, is still partly mitigated by the presence of almost a million Turkish workers in Europe and the Middle East, but that situation is unstable. The rapid urbanization, which puts a strain on infrastructural and investment resources, is not likely to be eased soon and the economy will remain a major political problem.

Foreign Policy

There are several important foreign policy issues for Turkey. The most volatile is the problem of Cyprus and of relations with one of Turkey's traditional rivals, Greece. Cyprus, populated by about 80 percent Greeks and 20 percent Turks, was an Ottoman possession until ceded to Great Britain in 1878. When Britain left in 1960, the island became an independent republic but was plagued with constant communal strife. In 1964 a group of Greek ultranationalists attempted to take over the island's government, whereupon Turkey threatened to invade. A strong warning from U.S. President Lyndon Johnson stopped them. After more trouble Turkey did invade in 1974, an action that precipitated a U.S. arms embargo, which lasted until 1980. In the face of continued failure to agree on a single government structure, Turkish Cypriots proclaimed the Turkish Republic of Northern Cyprus in November 1983. In 1990 the stalemate continued with little promise of resolution.

There are also disputes with Greece. Hostility between Greece and Turkey goes back to at least the middle of the nineteenth century when Greece broke away from the Ottoman Empire. It was most aggravated immediately after the end of World War I when the Allies invited the Greeks to join them in the dismemberment of Turkey, and the victory over Greece was one of the events of the Turkish War of Independence that the Turks most welcomed. A major population exchange involving Greeks and Turks living on the Thracian border took place in the early 1920s, and a variety of issues have remained and resurfaced since that time. Among the most troublesome is jurisdiction over the continental shelf of the Aegean Sea, with its mineral and oil resources.

Another foreign policy issue is relations with Europe and the United States. Ataturk sought to turn Turkey's face toward the modern West and away from the traditional East, and those efforts have continued. Turkey is now a member of a number of European institutions. In 1952 Turkey also became a member of the North Atlantic Treaty Organization and was a partner in the Central Treaty Organization when it existed between 1955 and 1979. Turkey is currently moving toward membership in the European Community. Relations with the West have not always been smooth, however. Turkey has often felt that its importance as the southern flank of NATO has not been sufficiently appreciated by the other alliance members, particularly since the collapse of the pro-West government of Iran in 1979. Turkish workers have been welcomed in Europe but have also remained at the bottom of the social scale there, partly because of vast cultural differences.

Difficulties in relations with the West have led since the early 1970s to closer relations with other countries of the Middle East. This tendency became more pronounced as the Turks experienced an increasing need for Middle East oil, and as they sought support for other foreign policy issues like Cyprus. The Muslim countries, on the other hand, sought opportunities to capitalize on a shared religion and to get support for their own foreign affairs policies. Since the late 1970s Turkey has played a considerably more active role in the Middle East, with the exception of the Arab-Israeli dispute, on which Turkey has sought to stay uninvolved. (Turkey has maintained diplomatic relations with Israel, albeit marginally, since 1950.) Economic relations with the Middle East have grown rapidly with 35 percent of Turkish exports now going to that area and with the presence of over 200,000 Turkish workers and contractors there.

Conclusion

Perhaps the most important characteristic of the Turkish body politic in the mid-1980s is a strong commitment to democracy. It comes from several sources. One is that democracy is the norm among the countries with whom the Turks seek the closest association. Another is the strong democratic legacy of Ataturk. But equally important is that Turkey's rapid development into a complex, participatory nation. Because so many groups compete for power and resources and none has been able to gain dominance, all have come to accept the need for bargain and compromise. High among them is what many see as a continuing danger of anarchy and disorder, coming from radicalism on both the right and the left, and over-politicization. The changes in the policies structure made after the 1980 intervention were designed to remedy some of these threats to stability and orderly growth. It remains to be seen if Turkey has found political formulas under which both vigorous democracy and sufficient authority can exist simultaneously.

6

The Islamic Republic of Iran

Marvin Zonis
Cyrus Amir Mokri

Iran, formerly Persia, has played a continuously significant role in Middle Eastern and international politics for centuries. Because of its geographic position, it has been a focus of both imperialist and cold war rivalries. As one of the most powerful oil-producing nations, it has been a major factor in the policy-making councils of OPEC. Most recently, its Islamic revolution has had a formidable impact not only on the ideological currents in the Middle East and the Islamic world, but on international politics as well.

The Iranian revolution of 1978–79 must be counted as one of the most significant political events of the twentieth century and as one of the classic revolutions of world history. The revolution overthrew His Imperial Majesty Muhammad Reza Pahlavi, Shahanshah, Aryamehr—King of Kings and Light of the Aryans—as he came to call himself. The shah, as he was known in the West, was the world's most powerful reigning monarch. He was, as well, America's staunchest ally in the Persian Gulf and commanded an armed force which, along with Israel and Turkey, was the most powerful in the Middle East. Under his direction, the economy experienced explosive growth as the shah spearheaded OPEC's dramatic raising of the price of oil.

But during the revolution the shah acquiesced, with great reluctance, to the demands of virtually the entire Iranian people and left Iran on January 16, 1979. Even more dramatic events would follow in rapid succession. On February 1, Ayatollah Rouhollah Khomeini, the seventy-six-year-old Muslim cleric who had become the symbol of opposition to the Pahlavi dynasty, returned to Iran from nearly fifteen years in exile. In less than two weeks, the Pahlavi dynasty collapsed. The Imperial Guards—the elite military units charged with responsibility for defending the throne—retired to their barracks rather than confront the armed opposition to the rule of the shah.

The effects on international affairs of the newly formed Islamic Republic of Iran were not long in coming. On November 4, 1979, the American embassy in Tehran and many of its personnel were seized. In defiance of international law and diplomatic protocol, the Americans were accused, but never tried, of spying and other illegal activities and held captive for 444 days. In the next month, on December 27, 1979, the Soviet Union invaded Afghanistan. In the name of defending Islam, Iran began supporting the Shi'ite segments of the Afghan resistance movement. On September 22, 1980, after months of terrorist operations and cross-border shelling, Iraqi troops flooded across the frontier and invaded Iran, sparking a devastating war that ravaged each country until July 1988, when Iran accepted United Nations Resolution 598 calling for a cease-fire. During nearly eight years of war, senior officials of Iran's revolutionary regime, committed to the export of Iran's Islamic revolution and to the destruction of the international interests of both the United States and the Union of Soviet Socialist Republics, sponsored terrorism outside Iran and supported terrorist groups throughout the Muslim world. Ayatollah Khomeini, the "ruling jurist" of the regime, insisted that Iran seek to defeat and humiliate the United States, which he referred to as "the Great Satan," as well as the Soviet Union, the "Lesser Satan," in the process of liberating oppressed peoples throughout the world.

The Iranian revolution's consequences for the internal politics of Iran have been dramatic. Iran's current leadership has supervised the implementation of fundamental changes in its social, political, economic, and cultural institutions. In addition to eliminating the monarchy and changing virtually all other institutions, the regime has sought to infuse all aspects of Iranian life with what the clerics of the regime have defined as an Islamic spirit. Perhaps the most basic change they have sought to implement is the destruction of the Western culture the shah had done so much to disseminate during his rule.

The changes imposed on Iran by the Islamic regime, with the ruthlessness and brutality of a triumphant revolutionary movement committed to an all-encompassing ideology, are meant to conform to a particular conception of an "Islamic" state. Thus, for example, the new legal system has been based on tenets of Shi'a law as interpreted by Ayatollah Khomeini and his clerical allies. Perhaps most important of all, political power is allowed solely to those who demonstrate utter loyalty and strict adherence to the new Islamic ideology.

In assessing the domestic changes that have taken place in Iran since the revolution, one cannot ignore the monumental effect of the war with Iraq. The leaders of the Iranian regime committed virtually all of Iran's resources to the defeat of Iraqi president Saddam Hussain. Despite this commitment, there was no victory, either militarily or diplomatically. Since both sides pursued a military strategy of attrition, each attempting to wear the other down to defeat, economic installations were a favorite target of missile and bombing raids. As a result, tremendous damage was done to Iran's infrastructure, including the destruction of the oil refinery at Abadan, the largest of its kind in the world, and the virtual destruction of one of the world's largest petrochemical complexes.

More important was the human cost of the war. There were an immense number of casualties—dead and wounded, both on the battlefield and in the cities, shelled by long-range Iraqi artillery or bombed by Iraqi missiles. Furthermore, Iran has lost millions of its population through emigration, as members of its middle and upper classes sought to escape the brutality and hardships caused first by the revolution and then by the war.

Confronting the human and material toll of the conflicts is the most significant challenge for the post-Khomeini Iranian political leaders and the Iranian people. Relief for the Iranian people, furthermore, cannot be accomplished without the consolidation of power at the center of the regime.

Ayatollah Khomeini's death in June of 1989 produced anticipation of political turmoil. But the succession was carried off with great finesse. Hojjat ul Islam Ali Akbar Hashemi Rafsanjani was elected to the presidency by an overwhelming margin, while Hojjat ul Islam Ali Khameini, the former president, was promoted to *faqih*, or jurist, the position formerly held by Khomeini (and promoted to the superior clerical rank of Ayatollah in the process). The challenge for Rafsanjani is to consolidate power in the face of the efforts of the so-called Islamic radicals within the ruling clergy. They seek to impart Iran's revolutionary zeal to Muslims everywhere, particularly in Lebanon. The outcome of the internal Iranian struggle has yet to be decided.

Description

Iran is a large country of some 628,000 square miles, approximately the size of Texas, New Mexico, Arizona, and California combined or equivalent to the total areas of England, France, Germany, Italy, Belgium, Holland, and Denmark. Its lengthy boundaries with its neighbors give it a strategic position. To the east, Iran shares a common border of 500 miles with Pakistan and a border of similar length with Afghanistan. To the north, Iran and the Soviet Union meet for some 700 miles east of the Caspian Sea and nearly 500 miles west of the Caspian, with Iran's Caspian shore approximately 400 miles long. To the west, Turkey stretches for 240 miles and Iraq for another 750, before the border reaches the Shatt-al-Arab waterway and the Persian Gulf. Along the south, Iran has a coastline of more than 850 miles on the Gulf.

The people of Iran, 36 million as reported by the census in 1976 but estimated to have grown to nearly 50 million by 1988, reflect the diversity of their geography in their religions, languages, and ethnic backgrounds. Over 98 percent of the population is Muslim, an overwhelming majority of whom belong to the Shi'a branch of Islam. Sunni Islam, nevertheless, is practiced in Iran, especially by the Kurds in the northwestern province of Kurdistan. Before the revolution, other religious minorities practiced freely and sometimes, despite their limited numbers, played a major role in the economic and political life of the country. These minorities included Zoroastrians, Armenian and Assyrian Christians, Jews, and Bahais. After the revolution, however, life for the minorities became extraordinarily difficult, as restrictions were placed on their religious practice, the use of their indigenous languages, their right to operate their own schools, and their participation in political, economic, and social life.

In addition to religious differences, there are striking linguistic and ethnic differences among the Iranian population. The name Iran, which means "the land of the Aryans," belies the Turkic, Mongol, and Semitic peoples who have mixed with the original invaders of the Iranian plateau, who were apparently speakers of an early Indo-European language and, thus, called "Aryans." Examination of a map of Iran (which has recorded the population distribution by linguistic or ethnic groups) reveals the astounding heterogeneity of the people—to the northwest, Turkish-speaking Azerbaijanis; to the north, Gilani and Mazandarani; to the northeast, Turkomans and Kurds; to the southeast, Baluchis; to the south, Qashqais, Lurs, and Bakhtiaris; to the southwest, Arabs; to the west, Kurds. The interior of the country, the central plateau surrounded by the Zagros and Elburz mountain ranges, is the home of Farsi-speakers (Persians). Iran, then, is a combination of ethnically or linguistically distinct peoples whose minorities inhabit the border areas of the country. These non-Persians who live on the peripheries of the country are cut off from the Persians on the great central plateau by high mountain ranges. More of a threat to the Persian majority is the close proximity of the minorities to their kin across Iran's national borders, which present no natural obstacles to physical movement. The result has been mistrust in Tehran of the border peoples, fear of political relations with neighboring powers, and constant concern for the dismemberment of the country. Every Iranian regime has feared the centrifugal forces that threatened to tear apart the country and has acted in a ruthless centralizing fashion, exercising strong central control to maintain the unity of the diverse peoples of the land and prevent their succession, either to join with their fellow ethnic or linguistic kin across Iran's borders or to declare an independent state in a mountain redoubt on the periphery of the central plateau.

History

The most dominant foreign-policy objective of Iran for the past two centuries has been to avoid colonial control. Much of Iran's recent history can be understood in those terms. From the arrival of the European powers following the invasion of Egypt by Napoleon in 1789, Persia has been considered a prize. During the eighteenth and nineteenth centuries, France, Great Britain, and Russia competed for influence at the courts of the shahs. For the French, Persia represented a potential ally in its struggles with the British in India. When those struggles waned following the establishment of complete British hegemony, French interest diminished, leaving the field to the British and Russians.

From the late sixteenth to the early twentieth centuries, Britain's interests lay chiefly in protecting the northwestern approaches to India—the only possible invasion route unimpeded by formidable mountain ranges. With alterations of governments and circumstances, British policy fluctuated between an aggressive pursuit of active control over the Persian government and a passive policy seeking only to prevent Russia from doing the same. Russia seems to have pursued a variety of interests at different periods—from control of territory for strategic interests to capturing warm water ports on the Persian Gulf to simple economic imperialism.

The outstanding achievement of Persia during these centuries was to preserve its independence. It did so by refining the art of playing one foreign power off against the other, especially during the last half of the nineteenth century. Fearing for Persia's security, the shah would turn to the Russians for support. When Russian influence threatened to become too great, the shah would turn to the British. When the British demanded a concession in return, perhaps the right to build railroads in Persia, a concession that the shah was unwilling to give, he approached the Russians and urged them to demand a similar concession. Then he could return to the British and promise not to award the Russians rights for constructing railroads if the British did not press their demands. Thus, no concessions were granted and Persia retained its independence.

Two developments altered this balance. First, foreign powers learned to make complementary rather than conflicting demands. No longer could the shah refuse to grant demands for concessions on the grounds that the other foreign power would lose out. By the end of the nineteenth century, there were both British and Russian banks, British and Russian trading companies, British and Russian capitulations (the right of citizens of those countries to be tried by their own rather than Iranian courts), and British and Russian supervisors of Persian customs in order to assure that their revenues were used to repay loans from the two governments to the shahs—an endless array of institutional control over Iranian life by both of the Great Powers.

In addition, Britain and Russia were drawn together by the fear of a recently united and restless Germany. They determined to settle their extra-European differences and concentrate on the new challenge. After considerable negotiations, they signed a treaty in 1907 which resolved the outstanding differences between the two states in all the countries in which they had unsettled and conflicting interests. The treaty dealt with Persia as well. It divided Persia into "spheres of influence." The Russians were given a virtually free hand in northern Persia, including the capital, Tehran, and the central city of Isfahan. The British were allotted a small zone in the southeast of the country, flanking British India. In between was a large neutral zone that included the city of Shiraz.

Nationalists feared the treaty would lead to a break-up of the country. It might have happened had the Russian revolution not occurred and Lenin renounced all imperial claims made by the czars. At the same time, British ineptitude and the rise of strong central Persian leadership preserved Persian independence in a time when the rest of Asia was under colonial control.

Persia had become an astute player in the game of international politics. When an outside power threatened, an appeal was made for protection to a second power, hostile to the first. When the British and the Russians appeared to have coordinated their policy toward Persia, the shahs turned to Germany to counter their power. In the same way the United States became a second power in post–

World War II Iran. True to form, as the late shah, Muhammad Reza Pahlavi, perceived the Soviet threat diminishing and his own internal political position' strengthening, the value of the United States decreased. The shah turned to the USSR in order to counterbalance American influence and the overwhelming dependence of Iran on the United States. The shah's foreign policy, at least during the 1960s, manifested a return to a pattern of foreign policy familiar to Iran. Had the shah maintained that pattern in the 1970s, instead of fulsomely embracing the United States, he would have offended his people less.

Two additional themes run through modern Persian history. First, there is the significance of the Constitutional Movement of 1905–9, which resulted in the first regulation of the political affairs of any Middle Eastern state by a formal constitution. The movement was partly a reaction to the granting of concessions by the shah and the government to foreign companies seeking to exploit Persia in the latter part of the nineteenth century. Concession-hunters from Great Britain and Russia competed for the right to control Persia's foreign trade, to develop its natural resources, to build railways and bridges, and to monopolize any economic undertaking that promised sizeable economic benefit. While the shah had practiced the art of preserving the independence of Persia through the balancing of concessions, by the end of the century Persia had lost considerable autonomy to British and Russian subjects. A significant segment of the merchants and the secular and clerical intelligentsia feared for the diminishing integrity of Persia and the increasing disdain with which Persia was treated by other powers.

Perhaps even worse in the eyes of many of the activists in the struggle for a constitution to delineate and limit the otherwise completely unconstrained powers of the shahs was the total corruption of the monarch and his court. It had become clear to many Persians that the overwhelming reason for granting concessions to foreigners to develop Persia's economic potential was to finance the indulgences of the royal court. The shahs could not extract enough resources from the Persian people to finance the royal expenditures.

Instead, they sold Persia's sovereignty to foreigners in exchange for what amounted to paltry bribes. This resulted in the stupefying backwardness of Persia at the end of the nineteenth century.

Into this situation stepped a large number of foreigners bent on securing highly favorable concessions from the shah—concessions which were strongly opposed by some ministers, leading *Ulema* (religious scholars), clergymen, and merchants who formed the basis of the constitutional movement. In the summer of 1906, more than 15,000 Persians, including merchants and religious leaders, encamped on the grounds of the British legation in Tehran and took *bast*, or sanctuary, from their own government. The ultimate result of these pressures and others was the shah's granting permission for the writing of a constitution and supplemental laws that would define and limit his own powers and would create a *Majlis*, a parliament with lower and upper houses.

With the monarch's acceptance of the constitution, Persia seemed headed for a period of internal stability and independent foreign policy making. In fact, the next two decades marked an astounding increase in the very processes the constitution was designed to counter. Muzaffar al-Din Shah Qajar died shortly after the ratification of the constitution. His successor, Muhammad 'Ali Shah, dedicated himself to fighting the constitutional movement. Subsequent years were marked by occasional violent struggles between the nationalists pressing for full implementation of the constitution and the more conservative and reactionary elements who sought its abrogation. A nationalist triumph seemed assured by the forced abdication of the recalcitrant Muhammad Ali. But continuous intervention by the British and the Russians, the fact that the successor king was not of age and was supervised by a series of more or less reactionary regents, and internal dissension and rankling on the part of the nationalists kept the country divided and weak as World War I engulfed Persia.

Ahmad Shah, now of age and ruling without a regent, signed an agreement with Britain making Persia virtually a British protectorate, persuaded, to some extent, by the payment of monthly British subsidies to his London bank account. But the Majlis refused to ratify the 1919 treaty, arguing that it was the institution that represented the independent national status of Persia which the treaty would, in effect, end. The Majlis retained its adamantly nationalist line until 1921, when the British finally realized the impossibility of attaining agreement to the treaty they had first proposed in 1919. After formally withdrawing it from consideration, Great Britain announced its intention to withdraw its occupying troops as well. Shortly before the British withdrawal, a detachment of the Persian Cossack Brigade led by Reza Pahlavi, in conjunction with a fiery Persian journalist, Sayyid Ziya al-Din Tabatab'i, marched from Qazvin to Tehran, staged a coup d'état, and installed a new government with Sayyid Ziya as prime minister and Reza Pahlavi as minister of war. The role of the British in the coup d'état remains an unsolved puzzle of recent Persian history. Many argue that the British were responsible for the coup, believing that, if they could not directly control Persia, their interests would be better served by a strong centralized government in that country. After the coup the British withdrew their troops, leaving Persia, for the first time in decades, at its own mercies and confronted by the need to put its own house in order.

It soon became clear that Reza Pahlavi would be the center of power. He was personally aggressive and controlled the only organized military force in the country—the Cossack Brigade. Reza Pahlavi began consolidating his power. He sent Sayyid Ziya into exile and installed himself as prime minister. Then, in 1925 he did the same for Ahmad Shah, the last Qajar monarch, and crowned himself Reza Shah, the first ruler of the Pahlavi dynasty. From his coronation until his abdication in 1941, Reza Shah ruled with a firm hand and in an increasingly tyrannical, arbitrary, and venal fashion though Iran also experienced many substantial achievements during his rule, including a period of rapid development and modernization in the educational system.

Reza Shah began the state-directed development of Iran and established a strong central government with control over the farthest reaches of his domain, processes which continue unabated to the present. Yet Iran's new state power and armed forces were insufficient to defend the country against invasion in August 1941 by the USSR from the north and Britain from the south. After the German invasion of the USSR the two states had grown fearful of increasing German influence in Iran and the possibility of a German dash through the USSR, across the Caucasus, and into a sympathetic Iran, thus depriving the Allies of Middle Eastern oil resources. In addition, the Allies needed a transit route free from German submarines to supply war materials to the Soviet Union. Iran, with Reza Shah's newly built railroad, was the obvious choice. Without offering significant resistance, the Iranian army collapsed in the face of the coordinated invasion.

With the collapse of the Shah's army and the presence of British and Soviet forces in Tehran, the Allies were in a position to demand the abdication of Reza Shah. He was replaced by his son and crown prince, an inexperienced young man of twenty-one, Muhammad Reza Pahlavi. The chaotic years of World War II, characterized by weakness of the throne, foreign occupation, economic disintegration, and savage attacks on the twenty-year rule of Reza Shah, highlighted the insecurity under which Muhammad Reza assumed his kingship. Supported by the occupying powers and by many of the elite, including the military generals who had served his father, the shah continued to maintain a tenuous grip on the throne while trying to eliminate his many internal enemies.

Following World War II, Iran experienced a repetition of the patterns that characterized the end of the previous global conflict. The Soviet Union violated agreements it had signed with Britain and the United States by failing to withdraw its troops from Iran within six months of the ending of hostilities. With Soviet troops stationed throughout western and northwestern Iran, two "autonomous people's republics" were established in the Iranian provinces of Azerbaijan and Kurdistan. These appear to have been Soviet attempts to prepare Iran for dismemberment and eventual incorporation into the Soviet Union. The illegal Soviet occupation of Iran and the establishment of the people's republics were the first events of the cold war and also the first case brought before the Security Council of the newly established United Nations. Intense diplomatic pressures from the United States, Great Britain, and Iran in that forum as well as extremely shrewd diplomatic maneuvering and negotiations between Iran's prime minister at the time, Ahmad Qavam al-Saltaneh, and the Soviet Union resulted in the withdrawal of Soviet forces, the reoccupation of those provinces by Iranian troops, and the collapse of the republics.

Iran was once again free of foreign armies, and Muhammad Reza Shah Pahlavi turned to his two principal tasks—strengthening his political and economic bases of support. Yet for more than a decade internal political turmoil hindered his attainment of those goals. In 1949 an abortive assassination attempt on his life was followed by the outlawing and repression of the Iranian Communist party. Simultaneously, the National Front, a growing movement under the direction of Mohammad Mossadegh, became more insistent on the need to nationalize the Iranian oil industry and to wrest its control from the hands of the British government, which owned a majority of the shares in the Anglo-Iranian company. In addition, a third group, the *Fada'iyan-i Islam*, an Islamic political organization espousing violence and terror to achieve its ends, became increasingly active, supporting the anti-British fervor that increased following British moves designed to punish Iran after it nationalized the Anglo-Iranian Oil Company in 1951.

Mossadegh demanded ever greater authority from the shah in order to cope with the mounting economic crisis, while the shah was increasingly pressured by his supporters to curb the excesses of the prime minister. In 1952 the shah dismissed Mossadegh and appointed Qavam al-Saltaneh, hoping to resolve the diplomatic impasse with Great Britain and the domestic political and economic crises. Mossadegh's popularity, however, was at its peak and thousands of demonstrators rioted in Tehran to protest his dismissal. Mossadegh was reappointed, and a direct confrontation between the shah and his prime minister became inevitable.

In the following months, Mossadegh's position gradually weakened as many of his political allies defected. With the internal situation deteriorating and the *Tudeh*, the Iranian Communist party, becoming overtly more active, the British and the newly elected Eisenhower administration in the United States became concerned over what they perceived to be menacing threats to Western interests. The intelligence agencies of the two states designed a coup d'état, enlisted the support of the shah, and infiltrated operatives into Tehran to set the process in motion.

As part of the scheme, the shah formally dismissed Mossadegh, as was his constitutional prerogative, in August 1953. But Mossadegh refused to accept his dismissal, instead arresting the officer who had presented him with the shah's rescript. Panicked, the shah fled the country, stopping in Baghdad and then traveling on to Rome. But the coup went ahead, despite CIA reservations. General Fazlollah Zahedi, one-time ally of the prime minister but more recently in hiding because of a warrant for his arrest, had been selected by the British and Americans to succeed Mossadegh. With the fall of the premier, Zahedi was installed and the shah and his empress returned from abroad.

After the elimination of the most serious threat to his rule, the shah began consolidating his personal power. One of the most important steps he took was to purge the officer corps of the armed forces. Hundreds of officers were dismissed or arrested, accused of membership in or sympathy for the Communist party. Although the purge was used as the occasion to oust officers loyal to Mossadegh, the vast majority of the ousted military personnel belonged to the "Officers Club" of the Communist party. Then, the shah turned to neutralizing communists and Mossadegh supporters throughout Iran. He began to experiment with new forms of control.

From 1957 to 1960 a royally chartered and directed two-party system was created. One party was to serve as the government while the other was to perform the functions of the "loyal opposition." Both parties were directed by close personal friends of the shah. Not surprisingly, they failed to provide any meaningful channel for political expression and were quickly dismissed as the "Tweedle-dum" and "Tweedle-dee" parties.

The 1960 elections to the Majlis, however, revealed that the shah's control over the political system was still tenuous and his support unreliable. As the elections were held in stages across the country, political disquiet and complaints of electoral corruption were widely voiced. The shah responded by canceling the elections. The cancellation, however, only fostered demands for new elections free of police control.

The second round of elections began in January 1961, and they were as widely criticized for electoral corruption as the first ones. Nonetheless, they were completed and the shah convened the new parliament. It was immediately boycotted by important independent political leaders, students closed the University of Tehran with widespread demonstrations, and a revived National Front sponsored an ominously successful general strike. The shah responded to the mounting political chaos and the growing power of dissident politicians by taking a number of apparently liberalizing steps without, however, allowing any fundamental diminution in his own power. For example, he renewed the sale of crown lands to the peasants who were farming them. He dismissed a number of unpopular military officers, including the chief of the supreme commander's staff, the chief of army intelligence, and General Teimour Bakhtiar, director of the secret police, the State Security and Intelligence Organization, known by its Persian acronym, SAVAK.

The quiescence that followed was only temporary. Tehran teachers soon went on strike demanding higher salaries. They demonstrated in front of the Majlis to press their demand. Clashes broke out with security forces and one of the striking teachers was killed. The population was again galvanized and again the shah responded, this time by appointing as prime minister Dr. Ali Amini, popular with the demonstrators for favoring limitations on the power of the throne and widely reputed to be devoted to civil liberties and possessed of impeccable personal integrity. By the end of the year, however, Amini had failed to satisfy any section of the politically active population. He had been unable to induce the shah to call new parliamentary elections and was reduced to ruling by decree. He was able to do little to alter the political or economic priorities that the shah had established or to bring the National Front into political activities. With the shah's initial distrust of Amini, it was clear that his time was running out. Following a budgetary crisis, Amini resigned and the shah asked his closest boyhood friend, Asadullah Alam, to form a new government.

Alam was the only man in Iran the shah trusted. At that time, the only other person in Iran the shah trusted was his twin sister, Princess Ashraf, and even she had been rumored to be interested in arranging the succession to the throne of her own son. With Alam's appointment, the shah turned to securing his throne through a program of reform, known as the White Revolution, which included such measures as land reform, worker profit-sharing, and suffrage for women. The White Revolution was submitted to the people of Iran in a referendum, which was overwhelmingly approved.

Again, however, domestic harmony was disrupted with the outbreak in June 1963 of three days of nationwide urban rioting, touched off by the arrest of Ayatollah Rouhollah Khomeini. Khomeini had come to public attention in 1961 for his outspoken opposition to the government. Later, he criticized the shah's land-reform program and suffrage for women and accused the shah of being an agent for the international Zionist-Jewish conspiracy. Pictures of Khomeini covered the bazaars of Iran during the 1963 religious holidays of Muharram, a time of increased passions as the devout anguished over the martyrdom of Imam Hussain, grandson of the Prophet Muhammad. The shah's authorities waited until the early morning hours of June 4, after the end of the holy days, and arrested Khomeini. Rioting ensued and spread to other cities, but it was ruthlessly suppressed in a matter of days with considerable loss of life.

Iran's Economy under the Shah, 1960–1978

Throughout the 1970s and until the fall of the shah in 1979, Iran's economy was characterized by a level of growth virtually unprecedented among industrializing nations. Economic expansion was not, however, a new phenomenon in Iran. During the 1960s the country experienced steady, impressive economic growth, with the GNP rising at an annual rate of 8 percent. The boom of the 1970s, however, was of a different order altogether. It produced a 14.2

percent increase in GNP in 1972–73, a 30.3 percent increase in 1973–74, and an incredible 42 percent rise in 1974–75.

The single crucial factor driving Iran's rapid growth was a decade-long rise in world oil prices, a trend in part orchestrated by the shah. Iran's hard line on pricing was a major factor behind the Tehran-Tripoli agreements of 1971, when OPEC first took control of prices from the major oil companies. And it was the shah who in December 1973, at an OPEC meeting convened in Tehran, announced that Arab OPEC producers would end their embargo of oil shipments to the West, imposed to protest support for Israel in the October 1973 war with Egypt and Syria. But the cost of ending the embargo would be a nearly fourfold increase in the cost of petroleum. From 1971 through 1973, OPEC drove the price of a barrel of oil from $1.75 to $11.75, producing an historic transfer of wealth from oil consumers to OPEC states.

Not surprisingly, the effects generated on the Iranian economy and on Iranian society in general by these increasing revenues were pervasive and dramatic. They were also poorly managed. The stress they created increased popular discontent with the shah's regime and provided a vital impetus to opposition forces.

For the shah the new wealth provided the resources to transform Iran into an economic showcase of the industrialized world and the most powerful state in the region. Turning away from the emphasis on agricultural reform and rural development that had dominated economic policy since the White Revolution of 1962–63, the new oil-wealth-based goal of the shah was captured in the slogan "Sweden by the year 2000." Iran was to leave the Third World behind and become an industrially developed state providing a full range of welfare benefits to its citizens. The main impetus behind this transformation was the state itself, the leading actor in Iran's industrial development. Before the oil price increases of the 1970s, almost 40 percent of industrial investment originated in the public sector. By the mid-1970s, however, Iran's fifth development plan, covering the years 1972–75, called for the state to provide fully 60 percent of investment in industry. Aided by this large-scale commitment of state resources, Iran's industry grew during the 1970s at an average rate of 15 percent per year. Industry occupied an increasing segment of the labor force as well, with 2.5 million people employed in industry by 1977.

By almost any standard, the growth of the Iranian economy in the 1970s was remarkable, although achieved only at considerable costs. The overwhelming reliance on oil revenues and the rush to industrialize produced serious social and economic dislocations resulting from a lack of coordination, poor planning, corruption, and a general disregard for the social consequences of economic policy. Industrial-sector development was erratic, accompanied by problems with supply, distribution, and marketing. These difficulties, as well as the disruptive consequences of the rapid economic transformation itself, generated widespread popular discontent.

Perhaps most important in fostering public dismay was the increasingly widespread awareness of the unequal distribution of the benefits of the economic boom. A small circle of elites, with the shah and his family at the center, captured many of the gains. A group of urban entrepreneurs was created who became, by Iranian standards, fabulously wealthy and spent their money conspicuously. The opulence of the shah and his court and courtiers and that of the newly rich proved deeply offensive to the rest of the Iranian population. The ostentatious villas, luxury German automobiles, French and Italian fashions, gold wristwatches, and diamond necklaces were perceived to be the fruits of corruption and to signify the abandonment of Persian culture. The idea of the disastrous consequences for Iran of slavish imitation of the West was to become increasingly popular through the 1970s. This theme became central to the writings of Ali Shariati, whose essays and speeches fed the fervor that led to the revolution and found their place in the lectures of Ayatollah Khomeini as well.

The increase in oil revenues had led to more serious problems throughout the country, however. A fundamental problem stemmed from the belief that somehow oil revenues alone would solve all of Iran's economic and social problems. The opportunity provided by the large income from oil to develop other parts of the economy, therefore, was not used effectively. There was great waste through corruption and poor planning. As a result, the returns on capital invested fell far short of expectations. One consequence of the inefficiency of the economy was that income from oil, which was supposed to be used for capital investment, had to be spent to import consumer goods. Prominent among the consumer items purchased from abroad with oil money was food, which was in short supply because of a neglected agricultural sector, disastrous land reforms, and the drive to turn Iran into a major food exporter.

All the while, accelerating levels of economic growth, fueled by burgeoning oil revenues, put tremendous strain on Iran's economic and communications infrastructures. Power brownouts and blackouts, overwhelmed railroad and truck transport, paralyzing urban traffic jams, and choking urban pollution added to the discontent of the population. There were massive shortages of skilled labor and a ubiquitous problem of inefficient management. Many Iranian workers lacked education and/or skills. Although impressive strides had been made in expanding the education system as well as instituting on-the-job training programs, Iran's labor force was still inadequate to accomplish the plans of the shah. Foreign managers and workers were imported in its stead. The sight of so many foreigners getting the desirable jobs in the economic boom alienated many Iranians, who felt rejected by their own government.

The people of Tehran were treated to an additional dismaying sight. The shah, early in the development rush, took to traveling above Tehran by helicopter. He seemed to have further isolated himself from Iranian realities by never setting foot on the streets of Tehran. The shah's flight from Tehran's reality by helicopter was indicative of a major feature of the country in the 1970s. Throughout the decade it appeared that the shah had ever more difficulty distinguishing the grandiose from the merely grand. His ambitions to turn Iran into a major regional superpower had been fired by the oil boom. He was greatly encouraged in this by the West, in general, and the United States, in particular. As America retreated from its global commitments after its defeat in Vietnam, President Richard Nixon determined to maintain U.S. interests through regional allies. The shah was to be that ally in the Persian Gulf. During a 1972 visit, the president pledged that the United States would sell any nonnuclear weapons system the shah wished to buy, a privilege extended to no other state—neither America's NATO allies nor Israel. The shah did not hesitate to order the most sophisticated weapons, especially large numbers of the most electronically advanced American fighter aircraft—purchases made possible because of the sharp increase in oil revenues.

Major problems accompanied the military purchases, however. Military expansion diverted a broad range of human and material resources from the civilian sector. The Iranian military wasn't prepared to handle sophisticated military equipment in the numbers the shah had ordered. As a result, foreign, particularly American, military advisers were brought to Iran by the thousands to supervise the use and deployment of the new weapons systems. They appeared to many Iranians as a threat to the indigenous and particularly Islamic culture of Iran with their utter, even contemptuous disregard for the local values and customs.

Furthermore, weapons purchases fostered massive corruption. To facilitate their sales, American weapons manufacturers would frequently offer lucrative "commissions" to important Iranian officials. Those American manufacturers who did not offer appropriate financial inducements found Iranian officials asking for them, usually in the form of direct payments to foreign bank accounts. This further perverted the acquisitions process as weapons were bought with an eye more to the size of the "commissions" than to Iran's defense planning and strategic requirements.

By mid-1977 excessive and unregulated growth had produced serious inflation. The government introduced a series of policies meant to bring the economy under control. But the most obvious results of the policies were economic recession and increasing levels of working-class unemployment and disaffection. The convergence of these economic pressures with the escalating political crises of the period contributed significantly to the swift erosion of the regime's legitimacy and the equally swift coalescence of a revolutionary opposition bent on bringing down the shah. As the opposition gathered force, economic leverage was increasingly brought to bear in a widening circle of strikes, walkouts, and factory closures. When the shah left Iran in January 1979, the Iranian economy was virtually at a standstill.

The failures in the economic field, however, did not stop the shah from believing that his country was on the verge of economic and military greatness. This was shown most dramatically at the extravagant commemoration of 2,500 years of Iranian kingship held at Persepolis in 1971.

Five years after the Persepolis celebrations, the shah was to take another step that proved even more offensive to his people. He abolished the calendar—the same calendar in existence in much of the Islamic world, which counted the days from the flight of the Prophet Muhammad from Mecca to Medina. In its place, the shah declared the *Shahanshahi*, or imperial calendar, which was dated from the supposed accession to the throne of Cyrus the Great.

After the fall of Prime Minister Mossadegh, the shah's government had become increasingly repressive and intolerant of opposition. Political parties were all more or less controlled by the state. Perhaps more serious though was the influence of the shah's secret police, SAVAK. Its reputation for violating the human rights of its apparently larger and larger number of victims was virtually unique. As the 1970s wore on, the cruelty of SAVAK appeared to increase and the regime faced an unparalleled challenge from urban guerrilla groups, the most important of which were the *Fada'iyan-i Khalq*, an offshoot of Mossadegh's old National Front, and the *Mujahedin-i Khalq*, an Islamic group with socialist leanings.

The shah tried to respond to the mounting discord in Iranian society as many other rulers had before him by transforming domestic politics through the creation of a state-sponsored single-party political system. The shah announced the formation of the *Rastakhiz*, or Resurrection party. He declared that Iranians were free to join or reject membership in the party but that all loyal Iranians would join and those who chose not to were, by definition, disloyal and should leave the country. According to the shah, the mission of *Rastakhiz* was to create a unified, harmonious society under his benevolent rule, but the Iranian people were unimpressed. Rather than extracting the shah from his political difficulties, the new political system exacerbated them.

By late 1976 the shah had reached a crucial impasse. At home he was faced with mounting political problems. Internationally, he was fearful of the effects of the election of Jimmy Carter and his program of fostering human rights internationally and limiting the sale of weapons to the Third World. The shah responded with a bold decision—to liberalize. Over the course of 1977, he lifted the constraints on the expression of political opinion and especially the rights of his subjects to voice their criticisms of the government and its demands. He declared the imperial system and his person immune from this new openness. But as Iranians, especially the intelligentsia of Tehran—both secular and clerical—came to realize that the threat of the dire punishments previously visited upon those who criticized the government had been removed, their complaints began to escalate. The policy of openness and participation failed. In fact, it backfired. The opposition seized the opportunity to voice its demands, gained momentum, and became a revolution.

The Revolution

The explosion began in early January 1978. On January 9, in response to an article critical of Ayatollah Khomeini, clerical students and teachers began marching in Qum in support of Khomeini. The police opened fire on the demonstrators, and several died. The number of those first deaths in the revolution and all subsequent deaths was bitterly contested by the regime and the opposition. While the government claimed that eight had been killed in Qum, the opposition claimed that more than a hundred had been martyred.

In Shi'ite custom, the major memorial service for the deceased is held forty days after death. Forty days after the deaths in Qum, crowds marched in the streets of Tabriz. Those demonstrations grew into widespread rioting and lasted a weekend. There was not only great bloodshed but destruction of scores of public buildings and businesses associated with the regime or with the West.

The next major turning point in the revolution was the torching of a movie theater in Abadan in August 1978. The exit doors had apparently been chained and locked shut. Fire trucks arrived late, with malfunctioning equipment. As a result, the firemen watched as the movie house burned down with four hundred patrons unable to escape a fiery death. The cause of the fire has not been conclusively established to this day. But the local authorities clearly bungled their investigation, while the government responded ineffectively by arresting a few suspects. By then, the situation was out of control. The opposition charged that SAVAK had set fire to the cinema in order to discredit the opposition. A mark of how disastrously the political opinion had turned against the shah was that the charges were received with widespread sympathy.

After a short but tumultuous period the government imposed martial law. The military brutally suppressed all opposition to the move, most dramatically at a rally in Tehran's Zaleh Square, which resulted in a large number of deaths. "Black Friday," as the event came to be known, served to crystallize the hatred of many for the regime of the shah. It also symbolized a bloodthirsty regime disdainful of the sentiments of its people.

At approximately the same time, the Iranian government began pressuring the Iraqi government to expel Khomeini, who was living in forced exile in the Shi'ite shrine city of Najaf. The Iranian government hoped that distancing Khomeini even farther from Iran would calm the increasingly explosive political situation. President Saddam Hussein acquiesced to the Iranian demand and forced the Ayatollah out. He was refused entry by Kuwait and at the beginning of October 1978 was accorded temporary political refuge by France, from where he was able to monitor and influence events in Iran.

On October 31, 1978, the shah's regime received a decisive blow —the oil workers went on strike. Oil production fell from almost 6 million barrels per day to slightly more than 1 million barrels, just enough, the oil workers claimed, for internal consumption. Without foreign exchange to finance crucial imports and to co-opt much of the population, the government would soon be brought to its knees.

Meanwhile, the revolutionary forces were beginning to accept the Ayatollah Khomeini as the undisputed leader of the revolution. Khomeini, in turn, was adopting a hard line, accepting nothing short of the dismantling of the monarchy. He forbade any negotiations or compromise with the shah's government. Almost all opposition members heeded his call.

The major voice within the opposition to resist Khomeini's call was Shahpur Bakhtiar, who had been appointed prime minister by the shah in January 1979, in a desperate last-minute effort to preserve his throne by bringing elements of the opposition into the regime. But the tactic failed. Shortly thereafter, the shah left Iran for the final time, departing for a "vacation." On February 1, 1979, Ayatollah Khomeini returned in triumph from nearly fifteen years in exile, and within a matter of days, the fifty-four-year-old Pahlavi dynasty collapsed.

The seemingly unified opposition to the shah masked the reality of irreconcilable ideological differences between the revolutionary forces. The falling out and subsequent ruthless struggle for power began almost immediately after the overthrow of the monarchy.

Mahdi Bazargan was appointed by Khomeini to head the interim government after the fall of the shah. He was a Western-trained engineer, committed to Islam and to democracy, in a Western sense, and in favor of measured, not radical, change. He tried to restore the economy by encouraging people to relinquish their revolutionary euphoria and return to work while he normalized relations with foreign countries. Bazargan failed, however, because his moderation did not satisfy the mobilized masses of the Iranian population and certainly not the leaders of the more radical secular and religious groups. They called for an immediate, comprehensive, and dramatic change of the entire Pahlavi political, economic, and social system.

Bazargan tried valiantly to check these demands by isolating the extremists while accommodating them where necessary, but he could not survive. Despite his earlier assurances, Khomeini failed to offer Bazargan his wholehearted support and even occasionally criticized the prime minister. Furthermore, Bazargan could not deal with the radical Islamic groups because they had become institutionalized in "revolutionary committees." These committees appeared in city neighborhoods and virtually all workplaces only days after the overthrow of the monarchy. The revolutionary committees were blessed by Khomeini and became the principal means of governance throughout society. They determined policy and maintained order, but they were not susceptible to control from the center. They brought local order but national chaos, and their remnants are still to be found in the Islamic Republic, where there has yet to be a full coalescence of central rule around the established political system.

In addition to the local committees, national policy was being determined not by the prime minister and his cabinet, but by the Revolutionary Council, a group whose members were unknown to the public. As it turned out, Bazargan was a member, but he and his colleagues were outnumbered and constantly outmaneuvered by the clerical members of the council, who demanded radical change in Iranian society.

Only when Bazargan concurred with the wishes of the Revolutionary Council and the committees was the government able to accomplish its goals. The most significant early event in the history of revolutionary Iran occurred when there was near universal consensus to hold a referendum on the form of the new regime. Ayatollah Khomeini urged all Iranians to vote for an Islamic republic, "not one word more nor less." The Ayatollah feared that a vote to establish a simple "republic" would mean the formation of a secular republic from which the clergy would be excluded as governors. On the other hand, the establishment of an "Islamic democratic republic" might also lead to the exclusion of the clergy and the domination of the system by Marxists. By then Ayatollah Khomeini was being referred to as the imam, in effect a successor to the Prophet Muhammad. With the religious charisma implied by that title, Khomeini's counsel carried the day, and the Iranian people overwhelmingly approved the establishment of the Islamic Republic of Iran.

Next there was controversy about a new constitution for the Islamic Republic. After a draft constitution was prepared by the Bazargan government, Khomeini asked for a national plebiscite, similar to the one held on the Islamic Republic. Khomeini apparently had approved of the draft and believed the Iranian people would too. But in the case of the constitution, Khomeini's populist measure backfired. Most organized political groups demanded that there be discussion and debate over the drafted constitution by an assembly elected by the people. When Ayatollah Shariat'madari agreed, Khomeini relented, but not without taking steps to see that the constitution that emerged from the Constituent Assembly would meet with his approval. The elections were managed by the Islamic Republic party (IRP), composed of clerics and Khomeini devotees and directed by Ayatollah Muhammad Beheshti, one of Khomeini's most able lieutenants. IRP supporters won an overwhelming victory in the elections to the Constituent Assembly. While Ayatollah Montazeri, another Khomeini devotee, was elected chairman of the assembly, its day-to-day business fell into the hands of the vice-chairman, Ayatollah Beheshti. A far more ruthless and capable organizer, Beheshti produced a new constitution radically different from that produced by Bazargan and his supporters. The new constitution institutionalized clerical rule in an Islamic Republic and was to be guided by Khomeini's doctrine of *vilayat-e faqih*, the rule of the Islamic jurist, or Khomeini himself.

The final blow to Bazargan's prime ministership came a few days after he had met with Zbigniew Brzezinski, the national security adviser to President Carter, at a conference in Algiers. On November 4, 1979, the one-year anniversary of the first killings of students on the campus of Tehran University by the troops of the shah, students calling themselves "Students in the Line of the Imam" seized the U.S. embassy. Bazargan resigned two days later. Khomeini had rejected Bazargan's resignations on previous occasions. This time he accepted.

It was in this chaotic situation that elections were held for the presidency. In January 1980 Abul Hasan Bani Sadr, whom Ayatollah Khomeini referred to as "like a son," became president in a landslide, winning over 70 percent of the vote. But neither his convincing victory nor Khomeini's admiration meant that Bani Sadr would have any more authority than did Bazargan. In fact, the subversion of Bani Sadr by the clerics began almost immediately after his presidential victory. The Majlis, for example, passed legislation outlawing groups that had not voted in favor of the Islamic Republic or the constitution. This included almost all leftist groups who had supported Bazargan and then Bani Sadr, as an alternative preferable to the direct rule of the clergy. The Majlis legislation touched off rallies and street battles among groups seeking to preserve their political and—it was becoming increasingly clear—physical existence as well.

Bani Sadr's lack of control over the streets was exacerbated by the fact that Khomeini had been appointed chief justice of Iran's Supreme Court, and Ayatollah Abd al-Karim Musavi Ardabili, an ideological comrade of Beheshti's, had become the attorney general. With law enforcement in the hands of those very people who were working toward his ouster, there was little that Bani Sadr could do to preserve his rapidly waning power.

Not only could Bani Sadr not solve domestic problems, he was equally ineffective in foreign policy. For example, although he seems to have desired to bring about an end to the crisis fueled by the seemingly endless captivity of the fifty-two American diplomats, he failed. Bani Sadr had support from neither the groups outside the government who were holding the hostages or from the key influentials, such as Khomeini, who tacitly supported them. The American diplomats were eventually set free but only after the radical clerics had consolidated their power and the war with Iraq had begun. The hostages had served their domestic political purposes and were impeding Iran's efforts to repel the Iraqi invaders. Their release did not, however, ease the tensions between the president and his clerical opposition. Bani Sadr roundly criticized the negotiated agreement that set the hostages free. He argued that the Algiers Accord produced less for Iran than he would have been able to obtain had he been allowed to resolve the crisis earlier. His criticisms further infuriated his clerical enemies.

The climax to the conflicts between Bani Sadr and the Islamic Republic party came over issues concerning the war with Iraq. Khomeini had appointed Bani Sadr commander-in-chief of the armed forces. The clerics, however, soon concluded that Bani Sadr's association with the armed forces presented the danger of a coup d'état against the Islamic Republic. Then a struggle for control of the military began with a severity that made the previous internal conflicts of the Islamic Republic appear trivial.

The IRP convinced Khomeini that since the president needed the counsel of the whole nation on the war effort, a Supreme Defense Council should be appointed. Khomeini consented and appointed Ali Khameini's, a senior cleric of the Islamic Republic party to the council. Khameini's became the center of the anti–Bani Sadr conspiracy and was, eventually, to replace Bani Sadr as president of the Islamic Republic.

By June of 1981 the clerics had underway a carefully orchestrated process to dispose of the president. They had managed to persuade Khomeini to withdraw publicly his support of Bani Sadr. The parliament voted to impeach the president and Bani Sadr was replaced. The motion passed easily and Raja'i replaced Bani Sadr.

By December 1982 the opposition was largely defeated and Khomeini called for an end to the terror. By then, the Islamic Republic party had succeeded in monopolizing political power. Iran was launched on "Islamification," as Ayatollah Khomeini defined that goal. The regime did not hesitate to use brutality if it perceived that such actions were needed to accomplish what it had come to regard as a sacred goal. But while the clerics managed to achieve dominance over all domestic opposition political forces, they were bedeviled by two problems that impeded their efforts to achieve their version of an Islamic state—the war with Iraq and conflicts within the ruling clerical elite.

The War with Iraq

Iran and Iraq can boast of enmities of very long standing. Iran has been the world's center of the Shi'ite sect of Islam since the sixteenth century, yet the holiest shrines of Shi'ism are located in Iraq. In addition, the Kurds live across the border between Iran and Iraq, and each state has manipulated the political aspirations of the Kurds as an instrument of its own foreign policy. Another age-old dispute has been the border of the two states in the south. There the countries are separated by the Shatt-al-Arab waterway formed by the confluence of the Tigris and Euphrates rivers in Iraq. Iraq has sought to lay claim to the Shatt because it links Basrah, Iraq's second largest city, to the Persian Gulf. Similarly, Iran has sought to control the waterway, known in Persian as the *Arvand Rud*, because it is the only direct exit to the sea for the exports from the Abadan oil refinery, once the world's largest.

In the early 1970s, the two states came to military conflict as the shah armed the Kurds to further their separatist ambitions from Iraq. Iraq responded by controlling the Shi'ites more tightly and by expelling Iranians from their country. Eventually, cross-border shelling and air raids began. In June of 1975, President Houari Boumedienne of Algeria successfully intervened and mediated an agreement between the two countries. The agreement restored peace and open borders between the two countries and the shah ended his support for the Kurds. For the remainder of the rule of the shah, the relations between the two countries were positive.

With the institution of the Islamic Republic, however, old enmities returned, with several new twists. For one, Ayatollah Khomeini remembered personally the harshness with which President Hussain had treated the Shi'ites during the years of conflict between the two countries. He had, as well, the personal memory of Hussain's attempt to preserve the rule of the shah by expelling Khomeini from Najaf. In addition, the majority Shi'ite population of Iraq and its shrines convinced the Iranian clerics that Iraq was the country in the world most likely to experience the second Islamic Revolution and, thus, prove the authenticity of the Iranian experience as a global model and not a purely local phenomenon. As a response to these challenges and for a number of domestic reasons, President Hussain sent the Iraqi armies into Iran on September 22, 1980. Iraq proceeded to occupy more than 4,000 square miles of Iranian territory, including the important port city of Khurramshahr.

Khomeini publicly urged the Iraqi Shi'a community to join their Iranian brothers in revolutionary action. It was soon clear, however, that it was only a matter of time before the Iranians would succeed in expelling the invaders. First, there was no mass uprising of the Arabs of Khuzistan to welcome the invading Arab troops. Second, the war served to bind the Iranian population to the Islamic Republic. Rather than leading to the downfall of the regime, as the exiles and Saddam had hoped, the invasion aroused powerful sentiments of Iranian national patriotism and vested them in the revolutionary regime. Ayatollah Khomeini could then call upon both Islam and Iran as symbols to mobilize the population behind his regime. Third, Iraqi logistics and supply lines became hopelessly inefficient as the Iraqi armed forces moved deeper into Iran. The progress of the invasion was halted less by the resistance of the Iranian armed forces than by the inability of the Iraqis to sustain their armed forces in combat distant from their home base. Iran was given a crucial opportunity to prepare for and mount a counterattack.

Within a year Iranian troops had been able to launch a series of offensives and by June 1982 had succeeded in driving the Iraqis out of nearly all the occupied territory, including the destroyed city of Khurramshahr and the devastated Abadan refinery. Following that triumphant series of military operations, Ayatollah Khomeini and the Supreme Defense Council made a fateful decision. Rather than seeking an end to the war, they determined to carry it into Iraq, overthrow Saddam Hussain, and establish an Islamic Republic under the occupying troops of Islamic Iran. From 1982 to July of 1988, the war degenerated into a war of attrition, with neither side able to make decisive advances, despite numerous ground, sea, and air assaults. Though Iran possessed numerical superiority, this advantage was nullified by Iraq's technological superiority. By drastically increasing the cost of the war to the Iranian people and economy, Iraq pressured Iran to accept a cease-fire or end the war.

The Iranian will to continue collapsed in 1988 because of the tremendous human and economic costs of the war. To the amazement of virtually all Iranians as well as all observers of Iranian politics, the government of Iran announced that it was willing to accept United Nations Security Council Resolution 598 calling for a cease-fire in the war, and a cease-fire was officially signed between the two combatants in July 1988.

Like the end of the crisis with the American diplomats, the Iranians ended the war on less favorable terms than they could have received earlier. When Iranian armies appeared more formidable and threatened to overrun Iraq and perhaps invade Kuwait and Saudi Arabia, Iraq's chief financial backers, the Arab states of the Gulf, were willing to consider massive repatriation payments to Iraq. In order to buy an end to the war and Iranian beneficence, Arab chiefs of state had indicated a willingness to entertain multibillion dollar repatriations to Iran. But with Iran's acceptance of the cease-fire in 1988, after it had been defeated in the air, on the battlefield, at sea, and in its capital, the Iranians received nothing for accepting the cease-fire. There has yet to be an agreement for the exchange of tens of thousands of prisoners of war, let alone for a permanent peace. There is unlikely ever to be an agreement for reparations.

As a consequence, Iran has finished the war economically and emotionally spent. Its communications, educational, and economic infrastructures have been virtually ignored since the rule of the shah. Many of the major industrial projects initiated by the shah but unfinished at the time of his ouster were damaged by Iraqi raids, making their completion problematic. Even more of the operating industrial facilities have suffered damage. Meanwhile, having completely terminated all birth-control programs on the grounds that they were a Western plot to weaken the strength of Islam, the Islamic Republic has experienced booming population growth and even more rapid urbanization. In short, the Islamic Republic faces daunting challenges left by the war as well as by the death of the Ayatollah Khomeini.

Exporting the Revolution

Very soon after the fall of the shah, Iran's revolutionary leaders made it clear that they hoped the revolution would spread to the world, beginning with neighboring Islamic nations. They argued that their revolution went beyond the concerns of Iran, for it was a liberation movement that symbolized the struggles of all oppressed peoples and nations against their oppressors. Counted among the oppressors are all states considered to be enemies of Iran, especially the two superpowers (the "Satans"), European states (especially the UK and France), and regional client governments, such as Israel, Iraq, and Saudi Arabia.

Iranian leaders did not, however, limit themselves to talk. They soon began to channel efforts into spreading the revolution. In assessing the role of the Islamic Republic in exporting its revolution, it is important to distinguish between its general calls for revolution and its attempts to help Shi'a movements abroad.

In their general call for international revolution against the "oppressors" or their agents, the Iranian leaders have embraced such movements as the Western Sahara Polisario movement, the Palestine Liberation Organization (PLO), and opposition movements in other Islamic countries like Saudi Arabia. They have sponsored annual conferences in Tehran on the general theme of liberation struggle, inviting representatives of any "liberation" group they could find. Ultimately, the call for revolution on a grand scale failed in the Islamic countries. There are many reasons for this. Part of the failure may be ascribed to the essential Shi'a quality of the Iranian revolutionary message. While Ayatollah Khomeini always spoke on behalf of the entire Islamic world, even all the "oppressed," he drew his images and his examples from the history of Shi'ism. Despite his universal claims, therefore, the particulars of his message did not resonate strongly with non-Shi'a. But the generalities of liberation from oppression did clearly resonate and Iran's examples did fire the imagination of many Third World movements.

Yet, a decade after the success of the revolution in Iran, there have still been no successful emulators. Other factors besides the content of Iran's specific message are responsible. One has to do with the growing perception that Ayatollah Khomeini was bent on vengeance rather than liberation. His steadfast refusal to end the war with Iraq and the growing impoverishment of Iran also reduced the appeal of its revolution. A second factor is the great sophistication with which other rulers began to treat their internal opposition after the disastrous example of the shah. The lessons drawn from the fall of the shah have been many. But most other states seem to have come away with one overriding set of beliefs —crush the Islamic opposition elements unwilling to work within the existing system while encouraging the "legitimate" Islamic forces, i.e., those willing to accept the existing system.

The leaders of the Islamic Republic have been more active in supporting various Shi'a groups, financially and otherwise, most significantly in Lebanon, Iraq, and Afghanistan. To Lebanon, for example, they have sent a steady supply of money, weapons, and even troops from the Revolutionary Guardsmen to bolster and sustain the position of *Hizbullah*, the Party of God, the most ardent proponents of an Iranian-style revolution in Lebanon. Similarly, they supported the Shi'a opposition to Saddam Hussain, a group called *al-Da'wa*, the Call. The Iraqi leadership partially justifies its invasion of Iran on the grounds of Iranian support for al-Da'wa terrorism meant to overthrow the Iraqi regime. Finally, the Iranian government has aided the Islamic guerrillas of Afghanistan against their Soviet invaders, but Iranian assistance has been directed solely to the Shi'a resistance groups based in Iran and not the Sunni groups headquartered in Pakistan.

Despite their efforts to promote general or Islamic revolution abroad, Iranian leaders have failed. Even their efforts to export Shi'a revolution have been without success. With the exception of Iraq, where they form a majority, the Shi'a constitute a minority of the population. Even in Lebanon, where they are estimated to be the single largest group in the country, they still do not constitute more than one-third of the total population. The ability of the Shi'a minorities to enlist the support of the dominant groups in the population or to overwhelm their numerically and politically superior opponents has proven limited. Given the failure of Iran in its war with Iraq and the death of Ayatollah Khomeini, it is difficult to envisage the circumstances where other Shi'a revolutionary movements are likely to be successful.

The Political System of the Islamic Republic of Iran

Iran's political system, although boasting the trappings of a Western system—a parliament, prime minister, president, and cabinet —also possesses an institution particular to the Islamic Republic, *vilayat-e faqih*, the guardianship or rule of the jurist. All decisions made by the government are subject to that individual's approval. Following the death of Khomeini, Ayatollah Khameini became that jurist. The constitution specifies that upon his death, his successor will be chosen by an elected body. In the absence of a universally accepted successor, a council of from three to five *faqihs*, jurists, can be chosen. Khomeini is alleged to have originally specified Ayatollah Hussain Ali Montazeri as his choice for jurist but toward the end of his life, Khomeini and his son, Hojjat ul Islam Ahmad Khomeini, who ran his father's office, fell out with Montazeri. Montazeri resigned from all involvement in public life and withdrew to Qum. Thus, when the Ayatollah died, there was widespread anticipation of political turmoil because no one senior cleric was admired by enough of the ruling clerics of the Islamic Republic. Many assumed that the turmoil would result in violence and even civil war.

With the withdrawal of Montazeri, Rafsanjani was able to establish a firm lock on power. Appreciating the extent to which the Islamic constitution created a system of multiple and overlapping political responsibilities, Rafsanjani induced Ayatollah Khomeini to appoint a body to suggest modifications to the constitution as the Islamic Republic approached its tenth anniversary. The new drafting body proposed a substantial increase in the powers of the president, including the elimination of the office of prime minister. After the death of the Ayatollah, these changes were approved in a national referendum, which coincided with Rafsanjani's election to the presidency. Whether these changes are enough to facilitate his consolidating power remains to be seen.

Another major institution that has been the subject of serious attack has been the *Shura-yi Nighaban*, the Council of Guardians. Its task is to determine the compatibility with Islamic law of all legislation passed by the Majlis. The Council of Guardians has refused to legitimate a number of major bills pushed by the prime minister and president, including bills accelerating land reform and nationalizing foreign trade and industry. The basic controversy concerns the role of the private sector in Iran and, conversely, the relative power of the state over Iranian economic life, with the council protecting the interests of the society and private sector against the desires of the government to monopolize ever more power and control. The controversy between the government and the council has become so great that the government is nearly paralyzed. On numerous occasions, Ayatollah Khomeini was beseeched to exercise his prerogatives as faqih and issue a definitive judgment on these issues, but he steadfastly refused. Finally, he appointed a committee of representatives from conflicting factions, charging them with responsibility for resolving the impasse. Months after their appointment, however, there has been no change. The Islamic regime is as deeply mired in controversy and political paralysis as it has been for years.

Challenges of the Future

With the conclusion of the war with Iraq, the Islamic Republic of Iran faces two major challenges—reconstructing its devastated economy and managing the succession to Ayatollah Khomeini.

The economy is in ruins, the educational system a shambles, oil revenues inadequate, and technically trained personnel and managerial talent in short supply, partially as a result of the massive "brain drain" following the revolution. Most Iranians feel dismayed and cynical at the failure of the Islamic Republic to realize its revolutionary aspirations.

No rebuilding plan will begin, however, until the political situation is stable. President Hashemi Rafsanjani has not succeeded in controlling the members of the ruling clergy who seek to export the revolution through violence. Nor has he yet been successful in fashioning an overall plan for the reconstruction of Iran following the war with Iraq. Lacking the popular charisma of the Ayatollah, Rafsanjani is unlikely to be able to bully his adversaries into silence or grudging acceptance of his domination. There are even more profound conflicts outside the ruling clergy. Numerous political groups that have been excluded from participation in the Islamic Republic are eager for an opportunity to participate in the system.

The two strongest nonclerical movements seem to be that of Reza Shah Pahlavi II, the son of the late shah who has appointed himself successor to and ruler of the Pahlavi dynasty, and the *Mujahedin-i Khalq*, led by Mas'ud Rajavi. It is clear the ruling clerics fear these groups inasmuch as they have resumed a wave of executions since the acceptance of the cease-fire with Iraq. Both the United Nations and Amnesty International have officially censured the Islamic Republic for these new executions, which may number in the thousands. The regime was desperate to eliminate as many of its opponents within the country as possible before the death of the failing faqih.

Despite the profound opportunities for turmoil, the Islamic Republic has successfully celebrated its tenth anniversary as well as navigated the succession following the death of the Ayatollah. Now its greatest challenge is to begin to deliver the economic rewards its people appear to demand after ten years of revolutionary fervor and war. There is still no sign that the Islamic Republic can deliver such benefits. But after its astounding accomplishments—none more noteworthy than its having retained power—it would be folly to dismiss the chances for its success.

III

COMPARATIVE GOVERNMENTS

The Fertile Crescent

7

The Republic of Iraq

Tareq Ismael and Jacqueline Ismael

Iraq is a relatively new state situated on an ancient land. Roughly the size of California and with a population of close to seventeen million, Iraq is one of the largest Arab states. Its geographical position at the northern end of the Arab Gulf situates it on the borders of two non-Arab states—Turkey and Iran—both of whom dwarf Iraq in terms of size and population.

Iraq is composed of four major geographic regions: desert in the west, rolling uplands on the central plains of the upper Tigris and Euphrates rivers, highlands in the north and marshland in the south. The central plains are the most agriculturally productive region of the country because the deposits of silt left by the rivers have caused the soil to be rich in nutrients. Agriculture has declined in importance in the last few years as oil has become Iraq's economic lifeblood.

Arabic is the official language of Iraq, though Kurdish is spoken in the northern and northeastern regions. The interplay between the dominant Arab population and the Kurdish minority has greatly affected Iraqi history. Iraq is 73 percent Arab and 21 percent Kurdish. Arabs are evenly distributed throughout the country but the Kurds are concentrated in the mountainous northern regions. There is also an important religious diversity in the country that has had historical and political significance. Ninety-five percent of the total population is Muslim, about equally divided between the two major sects of Islam, Shi'a and Sunni.

While the modern history of the contemporary state of Iraq dates back to 1932, when it was admitted to the League of Nations as

an independent state, the history of the region is ancient. Mesopotamia, the historical name of the region, is considered one of the
original cradles of civilization; it was situated in a river valley where
centralized government first emerged and literate culture first
evolved.

Mesopotamian history was tumultuous from its ancient beginnings. Centered in the fertile valley of the Tigris and Euphrates
rivers and at the crossroads of three continents, both agriculture
and commerce prospered, fueling the constant interchange of peoples, products, and ideas. Numerous city-states flourished, variously cooperating, competing, and warring with each other for
protection, dominance, and hegemony. Empires emerged and
faded, marking the rise and decline of successive civilizations: Sumerian (ca. 2900–2350 B.C.), Akkadian (2350–2159 B.C.), Babylonian
(1894–1594 B.C.), Kassite (1680–1157 B.C.), Assyrian (ca. 953–605 B.C.),
Sassanid (226–637 A.D.), and Arab.

The Arabs arrived in Mesopotamia in 633 A.D., and the region
was one of the first conquests of the Arab Empire newly emerging
from the Arabian desert under the banner of Islam. Following the
death of the Prophet Muhammad, the center of the empire shifted
from Arabia to the Fertile Crescent. In 762 A.D. the reigning caliph,
Ja'far al-Mansur, founded Baghdad as the capital. For the next five
centuries, the Abbasid dynasty (750–1258) ruled the expanding empire.

While this historical record constitutes the prologue to the story
of modern Iraq, its influence on the contemporary government
and politics of the state is indirect. The direct historical antecedents
of Iraq as a modern state can be broadly demarcated by two interre-
lated historical processes: the steady decline of the Ottoman Empire and the steady expansion of the power of Great Britain in
the Middle East. Iraq had been a province in the Ottoman Empire
since the early sixteenth century, but in the early nineteenth century
Britain began chipping away at Ottoman hegemony in the Middle
East to protect, consolidate, and expand its own empire centered
in India.

British strategic and commercial interests in Iraq were a century
old by the time World War I began. As long as Turkey was friendly

to British interests and hostile to German and Russian interests, Britain was willing to tolerate Turkish rule in Mesopotamia. The pro-German leanings of the Young Turks and the German interest in constructing a Berlin/Baghdad railway evoked increasing alarm after 1908 in view of the potential threat to India. The British government, therefore, became increasingly concerned about establishing a direct sphere of influence over Iraq. A British expeditionary force was dispatched to Iraq in 1915, which, despite having little Arab support and suffering numerous military setbacks at the hands of the Turks, managed to subdue the entire country by 1918.

Iraq was initially the administrative preserve of the India office, which ruled with great arrogance, high-handedness, and insensitivity to local aspirations. A rigged plebiscite was held in December 1918 affirming the Iraqi people's desire for a British mandate. At San Remo, in September 1919, France agreed to forgo its claim to Mosul and to recognize the British right to rule in the former Turkish *vilayets* (provinces) of Baghdad, Basrah, and Mosul, in return for a British withdrawal from Syria. The two powers reaffirmed the British ascendancy in Iraq at San Remo in April 1920. The League of Nations never ratified the British mandate submitted in 1920, when Britain informed the League council of its intention to govern Iraq in accordance with bilateral agreements evolved during the preceding two years.

The Monarchical Period (1921–1958)

In reaction to the San Remo decisions, a popular nationalist revolt erupted and engulfed the entire country. Fighting was fierce, and casualties on both sides were high. By October 1920 efforts to quell the revolt had already cost the British Exchequer 30 to 40 million pounds. In October 1920 the new high commissioner, Sir Percy Cox, announced the British government's intention to facilitate the establishment of a national government in Mesopotamia. A truce was called, and representatives of nationalist forces and other prominent Iraqis were invited to cooperate in establishing an independent state.

A provisional council of state was formed to nominate a monarch. Faisal Ibn al-Hussain, the former king of Syria who was ousted by the French in 1920, was selected. The council of state also proclaimed in July 1922 that the Iraqi monarchy should be "constitutional, representative and democratic . . . limited by law." Faisal was proclaimed king of Iraq on August 23, 1921, after another rigged plebiscite in which he drew over 98 percent of the votes cast. An Anglo-Iraqi Treaty—the first of a series—in October 1922 set out the basic features of the Iraqi government and thinly disguised Britain's hegemony over Iraq behind the facade of a constitutional monarchy. A great deal of effort was expended in Baghdad and London on formulating an organic law that would preserve a balance of power between the monarch and the Iraqi Constituent Assembly. The first elections to the assembly were held between October 1922 and February 1924. The assembly convened in March 1924 to consider the draft of the Organic Law. The king approved the measure in March 1925.

Considerable power was vested in the king, who presided over parliament, issued writs for a general election, confirmed and enforced laws, supervised their execution, and could claim extraordinary powers under martial law. The king could pass measures intended to maintain public order with the approval of the council of ministers, and authorize public expenditures not outlined in the budget. The king selected and dismissed the prime minister and appointed cabinet ministers on his recommendation. He appointed members to the Senate and was also supreme head of state and commander in chief of the armed forces.

The cabinet was collectively responsible to the parliament; the prime minister was required to present his resignation to the king if parliament passed a vote of nonconfidence and individual cabinet ministers had to resign if the parliament expressed lack of confidence in them. Parliament was bicameral, consisting of the elected Chamber of Deputies and the numerically smaller appointed Senate. The Chamber of Deputies functioned on the model of the British House of Commons in all essential respects, whereas the Senate functioned as does the House of Lords.

Beneath the facade of autonomy, the British High Commission

in Baghdad retained a great deal of power, including the right to appoint advisers to the Iraqi government (although most of the lower-level civil servants consisted of native Iraqis, the upper echelons, particularly the top administrative posts, were occupied by Britons); to assist and train the Iraqi army; to protect foreigners domiciled in Iraq in accordance with the practices of English law; to advise Iraq on fiscal and monetary policy; and to manage Iraq's relations abroad.

A series of Anglo-Iraqi treaties ensued in January 1926, December 1927 (drafted but not ratified by the Chamber of Deputies), and June 1930, which gradually circumscribed British control over the country. By the terms of the 1930 treaty, British advisory privileges were terminated; British military bases and military transit privileges were maintained; Britain continued to train and equip Iraq's army; and Iraq was permitted to maintain diplomatic representation abroad and conduct its own foreign policy independent of Britain, with regular consultations with the Foreign Office. The treaty took effect on October 3, 1932, the date of Iraq's admission into the League of Nations, and is cited by many sources as the date of official Iraqi independence. Other sources cite the first Anglo-Iraqi Treaty of October 1921, which created the state organization.

Despite the internal conflicts, Faisal I ruled until his sudden death in 1933. He was succeeded by his son Ghazi. Amid nationalist turmoil, the young king died in a car accident in 1939, and his four-year-old son, Faisal II, was left to inherit the throne. An uncle, Abd al-Illah, was appointed regent. Nuri al-Sa'id served Abd al-Illah in successive cabinets, heading a quarter of them (fifteen out of sixty) until the 1958 revolution. Both men were staunchly pro-British and came to symbolize British imperialism in Iraq. Nuri al-Sa'id controlled Iraq with an iron fist and suppressed all political opposition.

In 1941 pro-British politicians in Iraq were temporarily replaced by anti-British, pro-Axis nationalists. However, Britain moved swiftly to reinstate its proxies back to power and to integrate Iraq into its war efforts. Between March 1946 and January 1948, negotiations led to a new Anglo-Iraqi treaty between Baghdad and Great

Britain. However, popular opposition prevented the signed treaty from being ratified.

With the rise of the Cold War in the aftermath of World War II, the United States sought to fill the power vacuum in the Middle East left by the decline of British power in the area. The construction of a mutual defense alliance, the Baghdad Pact, linked with NATO and SEATO, was the main thrust of U.S. strategy. The Baghdad Pact included Britain, Turkey, Iran, Pakistan, and Iraq. Strong popular opposition developed quickly in Iraq against Iraq's involvement in the alliance, which was viewed as a Western-sponsored strategy to stem the rising tide of Arab nationalism. In spite of this, Nuri al-Sa'id led Iraq into the pact in February 1955.

Throughout the monarchical period, social conditions in Iraq —indeed, in the entire Middle East—continued to deteriorate. Poverty was rampant in Iraq, particularly among the peasantry, even by Middle East standards. According to official Iraqi statistics, in 1957 the average life expectancy of Iraqis was pathetically low: between thirty-eight and forty years. As a consequence, 50 percent of the population was below twenty years old. By 1957 the cost of living in Iraq soared to a fivefold increase. On the eve of the 1958 revolution, a significant 80 percent of the population was still illiterate. There was one doctor for every six thousand Iraqis. Seventy-five percent of agricultural land was owned by less than 1 percent of the population, and 85 percent of peasants were landless.

Coupled with the constant political conflicts and the social and economic crises of Iraq was the attendant foreign domination of the country. Although Iraq gained independence before all of the other Arab states in the region, it appeared less autonomous. Consequently, the four main opposition parties, the National Democratic party (NDP), the Iraqi Communist party (ICP), the Istiqlal party, and the Ba'ath party (all illegal parties functioning underground) coalesced to form the National Unity Front (NUF) on March 9, 1957. The immediate aims were declared as (1) removal of Nuri al-Sa'id from power, (2) withdrawal of Iraq from the Baghdad Pact, (3) freedom for all political prisoners, (4) removal of all restrictions against political parties, and (5) support for the non-aligned movement. Within sixteen months, on July 14, 1958, a revolution toppled the monarchy, and Iraq was declared a republic.

The 1958 Revolution

The formation of the United Arab Republic (UAR) on February 1, 1958, represented a triumph for the forces of pan-Arab nationalism in the Arab world in general and posed a serious threat to the conservative monarchy in Iraq in particular. Iraq's unpopular and oppressive regime had failed to meet effectively the fundamental socioeconomic problems of the majority. In response to the political and ideological challenge posed by the formation of the UAR, the Iraqi government joined with the Jordanian monarchy on February 14, 1958, to form the Arab Hashemite Federation, a union in which the two Hashemite kingdoms pledged to support each other. When events in Jordan reached crisis proportions during the summer of 1958, it became necessary for Iraq to fulfill its pledge, and the government ordered army units to proceed into Jordan to support King Hussain. Instead, Colonel Abd al-Salam Aref (on behalf of the clandestine Free Officers' Movement in the army) ordered his unit not into Jordan but into Baghdad, and on the morning of July 14, Aref led a coup against the Iraqi government. The Baghdad populace, jubilant at the downfall of the monarchy, poured into the streets. Scores were killed in the mob violence, including King Faisal, Crown Prince Amir Abd al-Illah, and Nuri al-Sa'id. However, order was quickly restored, and by the evening of July 16 the country was under the firm control of the military. A republic was proclaimed, and a new government was formed under the leadership of Brigadier Abd al-Karim Kassim.

The first concern of Brigadier Kassim and his chief aide, Colonel Aref, was to consolidate their power by cementing the coalition of broad-based political support that the revolution initially enjoyed. A council of sovereignty representing the Sunnis, Shi'ites, and Kurds was established as a symbol of unity and the tripartite head of state. The first cabinet was chosen so that its members would bring a broad spectrum of political opinion into the new government. The National Unity Front played a major role. Brigadier Kassim became prime minister and commander-in-chief of the Iraqi armed forces, and Colonel Aref became deputy premier, minister of the interior, and deputy commander-in-chief. Preparations were made for a general amnesty for political crimes committed under the old regime. While a people's court under Colonel Fadil Abbas al-Mahdawi tried and sentenced leading members of the old regime, exiles returned from abroad. There was little resistance to the new regime, and it appeared that Kassim and Aref had successfully unified the nation behind their government. However, the increase in political activity and the emergence of forces previously suppressed led to conflicts before the dust had settled.

On July 26 a constitution was proclaimed for the state. Pronouncing Iraq to be an independent Arab republic, the constitution gave all executive power to the council of ministers, as well as, with the approval of the council of sovereignty, all legislative power. All laws were declared to continue in force until amended or canceled.

The Struggle for Power

Almost immediately there arose a three-way struggle for power among the pan-Arabists, the Iraqi nationalists, and the communists. This struggle first manifested itself in the problem of determining the nature of UAR-Iraqi relations. Aref supported a union with the UAR. Opposed to this pan-Arab view were the National Democrats, the communists, and their supporters. The communists, supported by the Kurds, opposed any merger with Egypt and by extension Syria primarily because of Gamal Abdal Nasser's opposition to communism. Iraqi nationalists, jealous of Iraq's sovereignty, also opposed any merger.

Kassim initially intended to seek closer relations with the UAR than had the monarchy, but he was also determined to maintain Iraq's independent status. His refusal to submerge the state into a larger political entity was to some extent a result of his desire to maintain power and become the symbol of Iraq's revolution. More fundamentally, however, Kassim was cognizant of the country's heterogeneous social characteristics, which are unique in comparison to other Arab states. Minority groups, Kurds, Turks, and other smaller groups were not sympathetic to an exclusively pan-Arabist program, for it posed an implicit threat to their cultural autonomy. Also, the Shi'ite majority did not like the prospect of being further immersed in the national political life of a federation with other Arab states, most of which are predominantly Sunni.

Therefore, in attempting to unify the country Kassim rejected the pan-Arab approach of Nasserism. A propaganda battle with the UAR resulted, as bitter as any between Nasser and the Hashemites had been, which caused a power struggle between Kassim and Aref. Kassim prevailed and on September 12, 1958, Aref was removed from his position as deputy commander-in-chief of the armed forces. On September 30 he was also removed from the cabinet along with two supporters and was appointed ambassador to Bonn. An uprising in his regiment was quelled on October 5, and on October 12 he left the country. He never took up his post in Germany, and upon his sudden return to Baghdad on November 4 he was arrested and accused of plotting against the security of the state. The pan-Arabists were now out of power and a good number of them were arrested. In February a sentence of death was pronounced upon Aref and Rashid Ali al-Gailani (a hero of the 1941 revolt), and in protest six ministers representing the right-wing nationalists left the cabinet. The Ba'ath and the Istiqlal parties were no longer represented in the government. These two groups, along with other disenchanted pan-Arab nationalists, subsequently formed a coalition, the National Front, as a means of gathering their forces against Kassim.

To counter the growing strength of the anti-Kassim nationalists and Nasserites, Kassim began to lean heavily upon the support of the left, including the well-organized Communist party. As a result of Kassim's complacency toward their activities, the communists were able to expand their influence considerably. They created front organizations, such as the Association for the Defense of the Rights of Iraqi Women, the Partisans of Peace, and the Democratic Youth Association. They organized labor syndicates, farmers' associations, and student unions. They infiltrated the paramilitary Popular Resistance Forces (formed in August 1958), and they were even able to gain control over the mass media through the appointments of pro-communists as press censor and as head of radio-television.

Even more significant and fateful was the appointment, late in 1958, of the well-known communist sympathizer, Colonel Taha Hajj Ahmad, as director of military planning in the ministry of defense. Colonel Ahmad was able to subordinate the entire ministry and, through the creation of his own intelligence channels, suppress opposition. Furthermore, communist-controlled committees for the defense of the republic were set up in almost every department of the government and functioned as spy networks to rout out political renitency. Through these machinations the communists were able to bring about the removal from government and the arbitrary arrest of many pan-Arab nationalists and Nasserites by early 1959. Needless to say, these purges had a debilitating effect upon government administration, removing some of the most able officials and leaving the survivors timid and cautious. More fundamentally, however, Kassim, in cooperation with the communists, isolated political opposition from legitimate channels of protest and helped consolidate nationalist unrest.

The conflict with the nationalists came to a head in early March 1959 when Colonel Abd al-Wahab al-Shawaf, a pro-Nasserite who opposed the growing influence of the communists, used his Mosul-based troops to stage a revolt against the government. However, the Iraqi air force raided Mosul, and the revolt, which was poorly organized, failed. Shawaf was killed during the raid.

As a result of Colonel Shawaf's abortive attempt at revolution, Kassim felt that communist distrust of the pan-Arab nationalists was justified; thus, the communists were allowed to intensify their purge. Scores of pan-Arabs, civilian as well as military, were implicated in the attempted coup and were either killed or arrested. The purge even reached into the highest echelons of government, for Muhammad Mahdi Kubbah, head of the Istiqlal and member of the council of sovereignty, was placed under house arrest. The communists had reached the peak of their power.

The threat of nationalist strength, especially Nasserite and Ba'athist, appeared to be effectively curbed. But in circumscribing nationalist power, Kassim had established a modus vivendi with the communists and had allowed them considerable freedom of maneuver. Now they began to demand a greater voice at the policy-making level of government. By the end of April 1959, a campaign by the communist press demanded full communist participation in the government. Minister of economy Ibrahim Kubbah, an independent Marxist, and minister of health Dr. Muhammad Abd al-Malik al-Shawaf urged the inclusion of communists in the cabinet. Although Kassim voiced his disapproval of these demands, he appointed the noted communist Dr. Naziha al-Dulaimi as minister of municipalities. The delicate balance of political forces that Kassim envisioned, and for which purpose he had suppressed the nationalists, appeared to be crumbling. But he was not a communist and had no intention of allowing their ascendance. His opportunity to diminish their power came on July 14, 1959, the first anniversary of the revolution, when rioting broke out in northern Iraq between Kurdish tribes and Turkoman townspeople. The communist-controlled Peoples' Resistance Forces aided the Kurdish demonstrators. Kassim, fearful of the power of the paramilitary People's Resistance Forces and outraged by the communist manipulation in this affair, disarmed and disbanded the organization. The Communist party, in an effort to extricate itself, indulged in extensive self-criticism in July 1960. Nevertheless, further actions were taken to curtail communist influence, including the removal of Ibrahim Kubbah, and later Nazih al-Dulaimi, from the cabinet. General Ahmad Salih al-Abdi, military governor-general of Iraq, became the nemesis of the communists through 1960 and 1961, during which time he further diminished their influence.

Kassim had at this point subdued both communists and pan-Arab nationalists, but he had also alienated both groups. His flirtation with the communists, moreover, incurred the distrust of most of the nationalist elements. Thus, within a year after he took power he had lost the trust of most of the civilian groups who had provided his revolution with support. Evidence of this fact was provided on October 7, 1959, when members of the Ba'ath party made an attempt on Kassim's life that placed him in the hospital until early December. Despite the alienation of many active politicians from his regime, he did establish an equilibrium of sorts, for in January 1960 political parties, which had been prohibited since 1954, were again permitted to organize under certain restrictions. No military officers or government officials were allowed to join, and the organizations were not allowed to use a military or paramilitary structure. Parties were allowed to operate under licenses granted by the minister of the interior. Of the first four parties to apply, three were granted licenses including the National Democratic party, the Democratic party of Kurdistan, and the Iraqi Communist party (actually a minority splinter group of the Communist party paid for and supported by Kassim in an attempt to undermine and deny recognition to the majority party). Subsequently, the Iraqi Islamic party and the Progressive National party, the latter an offshoot of the National Democratic party, were also granted licenses.

Two events occurred in 1961 that significantly weakened Premier Kassim's internal and international positions. First, the Kurdish leader Mulla Mustafa Barzani launched a rebellion against Kassim's regime and by September controlled some 250 miles of territory in northern Iraq. The government began an offensive against the Barzani group, but the Kurds maintained their position. The war became protracted, and the apparent inability of the government forces to bring it to a successful conclusion created dissatisfaction among many army officers. The Ba'athists, strengthened in Syria by the fall of the UAR, capitalized on this dissatisfaction and proselytized their more militant ideology to many in the army. As a result, Kassim's hold on the military, whose loyalty was essential to the maintenance of his regime, began to wane.

The second event occurred on June 25, 1961, when Kassim announced his intention of annexing newly independent Kuwait, which had been part of the vilayet of Basrah in Ottoman Iraq. Not only was this action vigorously denounced throughout the world, but it was particularly abhorred by all members of the Arab League.

The 1963 Coup d'État

Internally and diplomatically isolated, Kassim was in a most unstable position. But his opposition was also divided and fragmented, and he was able, albeit somewhat precariously, to maintain his hold until early 1963. The Ba'athists, meanwhile, used the interim period to organize a coalition of all nationalist and independent groups in an anticommunist and anti-Kassim front.

When they were ready to strike, they set up Colonel Abd al-Salam Aref (released from prison in November 1961) as the figurehead of their National Revolutionary Command Council (NRCC). On February 8, 1963 General Kassim was overthrown by a coalition of the army, the Ba'ath, and other pan-Arab groups. He was killed the following day. The Ba'athists named Aref president of the Republic, but real power lay with the premier, Ahmad Hasan al-Bakr (one of the more recent military proselytes to the Ba'ath party), his cabinet (primarily Ba'athists with a few nationalists), and the National Revolutionary Command Council (made up principally of Ba'athist Party leader). Trials and executions of communists, pro-Kassim elements, and others, along with a purge of the army and civil bureaucracies followed the coup.

The Aref government was nominally pro-Egyptian, and talks were begun following the Ba'athist coup in Syria (March 1963) in regard to a union between Iraq, Syria, and Egypt. Conflicts again arose, however, because of traditional rivalries and conflicts of interest. Although an agreement for eventual union was signed on April 17, Nasser and the Ba'athists were soon at odds. Subsequently, on May 13 non-Ba'athists were forced out of the cabinet, and the Iraqi government took on a strongly anti-Nasser disposition. President Nasser declared the U.A.R.'s withdrawal from the tripartite union pact in July 1963. On October 8 a Syro-Iraqi military union was announced which was to bring the two Ba'athist-controlled states into closer association.

Ba'athist Dominance

Now in control of a major part of the Fertile Crescent, the Ba'athists seemed to be prepotent. However, in Iraq there were two factors that augured ill for the party. First, there was widespread dissatisfaction in the military, which in Iraq is the essential element to the maintenance of power. The creation of a paramilitary national guard shortly after the coup was the primary cause of this dissatisfaction. The Ba'athists apparently used the organization as a measure to counter potential army dissidence and as a means of purging the population of political opposition. The organization became quite powerful, reportedly exceeding fifty thousand members, and many officers considered its existence and activities an affront to the military and were distrustful of this curtailment of their influence.

The second factor was an ideological split in the party ranks. By November 1963 two factions emerged in an intraparty power struggle—the so-called moderates and extremists. The extremists, under the leadership of deputy premier and minister of guidance Ali Salih al-Sa'adi, had control of the Revolutionary Command Council (RCC), the highest authority in the land, and the national guard. The extremists demanded the immediate and total application of socialism to Iraq, uncompromising continuance of the fruitless and costly campaign against the Kurds, relentless opposition to President Nasser, and suppression of all internal political opposition. On the other hand, the moderates led by Hazim Jawad, minister of presidential affairs, and Talib Hussain Shabib, minister of foreign affairs and supported by many among the military, were not so ideologically dogmatic and felt that accommodation and reconciliation should temper the government's policies.

On November 4, 1963, the moderates, in collaboration with President Aref, engineered a meeting of the regional command of the

Ba'ath party and elected a number of their group to important posts of party leadership. Simultaneously, al-Sa'adi and some of his supporters in the council were expelled from the country. Fighting then erupted in Baghdad within the national guard between members supporting the two factions. In an attempt to maintain party unity, Michel Aflaq and members of the National Command of the Ba'ath party (based in Syria) came to Baghdad and proceeded to renounce the election. They proclaimed the National Command the rulers of Iraq and expelled Jawad, Shabib, and others. They were unable, however, to resolve the differences paralyzing the party. On November 18 President Aref, supported by disaffected military elements, took advantage of the consequent weakness of the Ba'ath administration and ousted the party from the government. Aflaq and his associates returned to Damascus, but the struggle ended only when the Ba'athist National Guard surrendered to the army.

The Aref Regime

Aref's new cabinet retained some Ba'athists but was primarily composed of army officers and technocrats. Aref retained the presidency and appointed himself chief of staff, a month later assigning the post to his brother, General Abd al-Rahman Aref, and assigning the premiership to his close friend and confidant, Lieutenant General Taher Yahya, the former chief of staff.

At first President Aref was strongly pro-Nasser and went so far as to establish a Joint Presidency Council on May 26, 1964. On the sixth anniversary of the creation of the Republic of Iraq, July 14, 1964, the government took some momentous steps toward implementation of the union. The first was the establishment of the Arab Socialist Union of Iraq, hailed by President Aref as the "threshold of the building of the unity of the Arab nation under Arab Socialism." The Charter or Basic Law of the ASU of Iraq was identical in most respects to the charter of the Arab Socialist Union of the UAR. The four publicly active political groups in Iraq at the time—the Arab Nationalist movement, the Arab Socialist party, the Socialist Unionist movement, and the Democratic Social Unionists—were dissolved and absorbed by the Arab Socialist Union of Iraq.

Also on July 14, 1964, all banks and some thirty large business firms were nationalized by the government; 25.5 million Iraqi dinars were paid by the government in compensation (I.D. 1 = $2.80 U.S.). An economic establishment was formed to supervise the nationalized industries. All of these measures were designed to bring Iraq closer in aims and structure to the UAR in order to make the union foreseen by the agreement of May 26 viable. The first meeting of the UAR-Iraq Joint Presidency Council was held on July 15, 1964. True unity proved as elusive as ever, for although plans for union were announced on December 20, 1964, the pro-Nasser ministers resigned from the Iraqi cabinet in July 1965.

On April 13, 1966, President Abd al-Salam Aref was killed in a helicopter crash and was succeeded by his brother, Abd al-Rahman Mohammed Aref. The new president inherited the same basic socioeconomic and political problems that had thwarted all of Iraq's governments since World War II. In an attempt to solve at least one of them decisively Abd al-Rahman Aref undertook a massive spring offensive against the Kurds, involving some 65,000 troops and air bombardment of Kurdish strongholds. Aref's prime minister, the moderate Dr. Abd al-Rahman al-Bazzaz, the first civilian premier since the 1958 revolution, then offered the Kurds significant concessions. Outraged at this capitulation to the Kurds, the armed forces forced Dr. al-Bazzaz's resignation in favor of General Naji Talib. By May 1967 Aref had taken the office himself. Meanwhile, the Kurdish problem remained unsolved.

Iraq under the Ba'ath

As the Arab-Israeli June 1967 war approached, Iraq moved closer to the other Arab states. But the loss of the war heightened already intense frustrations, and in July 1968 President Abd al-Rahman Aref's regime also crumbled under a military coup. As a result of the coup, the Ba'ath party again returned to power under the leadership of Ahmad Hasan al-Bakr (the former premier, and later vice-president under the first Aref). Saddam Hussain, a powerful civilian Ba'ath party leader at the time, was generally considered the real power behind al-Bakr. Under President al-Bakr, he gradually consolidated his power by assuming the posts of vice-chairman of the Revolutionary Command Council, assistant secretary-general of the Regional Command of the Ba'ath party, and assistant secretary general of the National Command of the Ba'ath.

The Ba'ath regime that came to power in 1968 has proven to be the most resilient yet of the republican era, surviving all challenges to its authority through a combination of ruthless suppression of opposition and benevolent cooptation of dissatisfaction. In 1979 Ahmad Hasan al-Bakr stepped down as president of the republic, secretary-general of the Ba'ath party (regional command), chairman of the Revolutionary Command Council and commander in chief of the armed forces. He was succeeded by Saddam Hussain, who has since continued to centralize power in his hands, suppressing all opposition to his personal authority. In July 1990 he was proclaimed president for life by the National Assembly.

Between 1968 and 1980, the foreign and domestic policies of Iraq emerged fundamentally from the pan-Arab socialist ideology of the governing Ba'ath party. The central objectives of Ba'ath ideology —unity, freedom, and socialism—were pursued in both the internal and the external arenas. However, the war with Iran, which began in September 1980 and continued to July 1988, forced significant modification of Iraq's "ideological purity" in practice. In other words, as a result of the political, economic, and social exigencies produced by the war, the regime's policies veered from their ideological objectives. This was reflected in domestic policies of social development and foreign policies of regional and international relations.

In the sphere of domestic development, prewar economic policies reflected the Ba'athist goal of building an independent economy based on a strong socialist infrastructure. The Ba'ath government's drive for economic independence had several dimensions:

the establishment of sovereignty over oil resources and production; economic self-reliance in the internal market; and economic diversification.

Iraq's nationalization of the oil industry in 1972 was the realization of the first dimension. Economic self-reliance focused on Iraq's heavy dependence upon imported goods. Instead of importing goods and services required by the existing industries, the government gave priority in industrial development to the creation of industries that filled this function. Also, priority was given to industries that depended upon locally produced raw resources. In this way an industrial infrastructure independent of external suppliers was encouraged.

On the third dimension, economic diversification, the Ba'ath government undertook large-scale development projects geared to diversify its role in the international market. Iraq's rich sulphur resources were being developed with the creation of a sulphur extraction and refining industry. In addition, Iraq's abundant phosphate resources were being developed in the framework of a fully integrated industrial project. Hence, unlike many Third World countries, rich in raw resources, Iraq at the time (1968–80) was deliberately moving away from its role in the international economy as a raw resource exporter and developing a fully integrated and diversified industrial base with these resources.

The socialist transformation of the economy occurred in conjunction with the push for economic independence and self-reliance. While Ba'ath socialist ideology does not prohibit private enterprise, it places such activity in a role secondary and subsidiary to state enterprise. Financed by the wealth produced by the oil sector, the socialization of industry in Iraq progressed rapidly under the Ba'ath. While there was virtually no viable socialist sector when the Ba'ath came to power in 1968, by 1978 it was a dominant sector.

In the social sphere, Iraq's efforts to build an independent socialist economy with a self-sustaining rate of growth were complemented by social policies aimed at transforming the semitribal, semifeudal relations of production entrenched by centuries of exploitation, colonialism, and imperialism. Ideologically, the transformation of social relations from a tribal-feudal framework to a modern industrial socialist framework was the explicit objective of social development. Social policies in the areas of education, health care, labor relations, and family reflected these goals. From 1968 the quantity and quality of all social services to Iraqis improved substantially. For example, expenditures on medical services increased 40 percent from 1968 to 1974.

From 1968 to 1980, Iraq pursued socialist development under conditions of capital surplus rather than under the conditions of capital shortage which confound development strategies in Third World states. However, the prolongation of the Iraq-Iran war drastically changed this. By 1983 the material costs of the war were estimated to be about $1 billion per month. It transformed Iraq from a capital surplus nation into a debtor nation and a foreign-aid dependent. It was estimated by Western economists that Saudi Arabia and the Gulf emirates had given Iraq financial assistance of about $60 billion by the end of the war in 1988 (official Iraqi sources put the figure at less than half that). While the implementation of development projects continued throughout the war, the ideological fulcrum of development strategy—self-reliance and independence—had been checked. In fact, the effort to sustain development during the war increased economic and political dependence on external sources.

With the end of the war, Iraq had accumulated a foreign debt estimated at $55–$80 billion. In response to pressures from lenders, Iraq undertook economic liberalization—including privatization of some state industries, abolishment of socialist-inspired labor laws, and deregulation of private enterprise. In the political sphere, pressures toward liberalization were also evident. Elections were held in 1984 and 1988 and Hussain promised multiparty elections in the near future. He also pledged to introduce a new constitution that would be accepted or rejected by referendum.

The Constitutions of 1958, 1964, and 1970

Although several Iraqi constitutions have promised at least quasidemocratic institutions, powerful executives, as a close perusal of the constitutions of 1958, 1964, and 1970 will indicate, have been a fact of political life in Iraq and democracy a political doctrine subversive to the state. For example, the constitution of July 26, 1958, vested the prime minister with the central role in government. It established a figurehead presidential council (Article 20) that Kassim dominated. The council of ministers (cabinet) was entrusted with the legislative function, subject to the formal approval of the presidential council (Article 21). The individual ministers and the council of ministers were made collectively responsible for administrative and executive functions (Article 22). In this system, Kassim, as prime minister, defense minister, and commander in chief of the armed forces, controlled the means of government, and the primary function of the constitution was simply the legitimization of his rule. Power was not diffused.

According to the April 1964 constitution, the president was to be elected by a National Revolutionary Command Council (NRCC), which itself was made up of high-ranking army officers (Articles 55 and 42). This council—theoretically supreme in making policy—was to be consulted by the president and was to endorse his decision before he could declare martial law or a state of emergency, or declare war or peace (Articles 48 and 49). Further, the NRCC must approve presidential assumption of emergency powers (Article 51). The republican council, which acts for the president in case of his absence from the country or his inability to serve, is composed of three members of the NRCC (Article 53). Impeachment of the president is also the province of the NRCC, a two-thirds majority of that body being required for an indictment (Article 60). The president is also enjoined by the constitution to form a national defense council (Article 50).

Despite these constitutional restrictions on presidential power, Abd al-Salam Aref still succeeded in making the presidency the most powerful office in Iraq. The 1964 provisional constitution invested the president with the powers of commander in chief of the armed forces, appointer of the premier, deputy premier, ministers, and civil servants, and sole retainer of executive power. The cabinet was left with a primarily administrative function. Legislative power was vested in a National Assembly, which has never met, nor have elections ever been held for it. In fact, the vagueness of the constitutional provisions for such a body indicate that the idea was never a serious consideration.

When the Ba'ath returned to power in 1968, the 1964 constitution was superseded by a new constitution in September 1968. This was supplanted by the provisional constitution of July 16, 1970, which in part was a modification of the 1968 constitution. Almost two decades later, the provisional constitution of 1970 was still the basic law of the land.

The 1970 constitution provides for a government system with three branches: executive, legislative, and judicial. The executive branch is composed of the Revolutionary Command Council and the president, who chairs the RCC. The RCC is the supreme body in the state (Article 37), invested with the power to elect the chairman of the council, who becomes the president of the republic; select new members of the RCC from the Regional Command of the Ba'ath party (Article 38); promulgate laws and decrees (Article 42); and conclude peace (Article 43); approve the budget (Article 43); and exercise many related powers (Article 43). The president is the commander in chief of the armed forces and exercises power through a council of ministers that he appoints (Articles 57 and 58). The National Assembly (Articles 47–56) was not formed until 1980, when the first elections for it were held. Since then, elections have been held every four years. The judiciary (Articles 62–63) consists of civil, criminal, religious, and specific courts. All judges are appointed by the president.

Foreign Policy

Iraq's foreign policy has been polarized on two axes since early in the century. The first axis concerns Iraq's relations with other Arab states, chiefly Egypt and Syria. The second is the Great Power axis—first with Britain until the 1950s and then with the United States and the Soviet Union. The move from the thoroughly British-oriented policies of the monarchy to the nonaligned policies of the republican era has been a step away from cliency toward independence, as the Iraqis see it, but the inter-Arab and Great Power influences remain strong just the same.

The Monarchy

Before the revolution of July 14, 1958, the foreign policy of Iraq was tied closely to that of Britain. Nuri al-Sa'id, the guiding spirit of the government, was pro-British and anti-Communist. This orientation and Nuri's concern with the prevention of rapid social revolution in Iraq placed the state in opposition to Egyptian policies. The opposition of the monarchy to Nasser's revolutionary regime and its fear of liberal influences led to the formation of the Arab Hashemite Federation between Iraq and Jordan (both Hashemite kingdoms) in 1958, when the establishment of the UAR raised the threat of Egyptian hegemony.

The Kassim Regime

After the revolution the Kassim regime changed Iraq's foreign-policy orientations. Kassim was initially pro-Nasser, but conflicts in two areas of policy led to a renewal of the hostile stance previously taken. First, there was conflict within the revolutionary government as to the permissible extent of pro-Nasser policy. This conflict ultimately led to the dismissal of Aref and to increased suspicion of pro-Nasserites in Iraq. This pattern of a warming and then dramatic cooling of relations with Egypt repeated itself several times in the following ten years. Second, the growing friendship of Kassim for the USSR led Nasser, who was at odds with the Soviets at the time, to suspect Soviet aims in the Middle East.

Kassim's most notable impact in foreign affairs was the near isolation of Iraq from its neighbors and, indeed, from the entire international community. UAR-Iraqi relations were the first fatality. From the time of Abd al-Salam Aref's fall in September 1958, relations between the two states began to decline, and they were finally severed in March 1959. Iraq's relations with another neighbor, Iran, also deteriorated in 1959. In a treaty of July 5, 1937, Iraq had recognized Iranian sovereignty over certain roadsteads on the east side of the Shatt-al-Arab. In December of 1959 Iraq demanded the return of these roads. Iran refused to accept these demands, and relations between the two states became strained.

Jordan had broken relations with Iraq after the 1958 coup and had abandoned the Arab Federation in August of the same year. In October of 1960, however, relations improved. Jordan formally recognized the Kassim regime; and road, post, and telegraph contacts were resumed. In December the two states restored normal diplomatic relations.

But Iraq became further isolated among the Arab states in the summer of 1961. In late June Kuwait became independent, and a few days later Iraq laid claim to this small neighbor. The claim was based upon Kuwait's status as part of the Ottoman vilayet of Basrah in the nineteenth century. The Kuwaitis appealed for aid from the United Kingdom when Iraq made threatening military movements. The British landed troops in Kuwait, and the UN Security Council met to consider the situation. The Kuwaiti position was supported by the United States, Saudi Arabia, Iran, Jordan, and the UAR in addition to Britain. On July 12 the Arab League voted to support Kuwait with an Arab force, and on July 19 the British began to withdraw their troops. When Kuwait was admitted to the Arab League on July 20, Iraq boycotted further meetings. The Saudi Arabian, UAR, Sudanese, Jordanian, and Tunisian governments sent 3,300 troops to Kuwait two months later, successfully deterring the threat of any military action by Baghdad.

In retaliation for their support and recognition of Kuwait, Iraq severed relations with Jordan, Japan, Iran, Lebanon, the United States, and Tunisia in 1962. Finally, the Kurdish Rebellion, which began in 1960 (see the section on the Kurdish question), led to Iraqi charges of Turkish complicity with the Kurds in August 1962, and the withdrawal of the Turkish ambassador on August 23 completed Iraq's isolation in the Middle East.

East-West Relations. Within a few hours after the July 14, 1958, coup, Kassim announced that the new republic's foreign policy would be based on neutralism and nonalignment. Of course, the most immediate ramification of this policy concerned the Baghdad

Pact. Although Iraq did not formally withdraw from the pact until March 24, 1959, it did not actually participate in the affairs of the group after July 1958.

By August 1958 the Kassim regime had been recognized by most states, including the United States and Britain, and had in accordance with its neutralist policy established relations with the Soviet Union and the People's Republic of China, as well as with other communist states. For the first time, then, Iraq was provided with an alternative to dealing with the West, and the initial period after the revolution witnessed many commercial and cultural agreements with the socialist camp. A major technical and economic cooperation agreement was signed with the USSR in March 1959. This agreement provided for the Soviet Union to extend a loan and for engineering and technical staff to build factories in Iraq. Despite Britain's announcement in May of its intention to provide Iraq with arms and military planes, Iraq withdrew from the Sterling Area in June and refused further U.S. military aid. For the duration of the Kassim regime (July 1958–February 1963) Iraq continued to expand technical, political, economic, and cultural relations with the socialist bloc. At the same time, relations with the Western bloc continued to cool.

The Ba'ath Regime

After the coup d'état of February 8, 1963, the new Ba'athist government immediately initiated a foreign policy aimed at reestablishing Iraq in the mainstream of pan-Arab politics in accordance with Ba'athist ideology. A government spokesman announced that Iraq would seek friendlier relations with those Arab states antagonized by Kassim. Iraq returned to the Arab League fold and on February 16 attended a meeting of the League, the first time it had done so since July 20, 1961. A friendlier attitude was also adopted toward Kuwait, with the new government renouncing the Kassim claim on Kuwait.

Nasser's government was among the first to recognize the new regime, and on March 14 President Aref spoke in favor of a UAR-

Syria-Iraq union. A tripartite conference held in Cairo supported the idea. By April word of an agreement was released. The official announcement of a projected union came on April 17, and the Iraqi cabinet and National Revolutionary Command Council approved the agreement. However, the Iraqi cabinet reshuffle in May, a move that ousted non-Ba'athists from that body, once again foreshadowed serious strains in UAR-Iraqi relations. Although the ideal of unity continued to dominate political polemics, it appeared evident that the consolidation of Ba'athist rule was being placed above the formation of a union.

By late summer the two Ba'athist regimes of Syria and Iraq had moved closer together and away from the UAR. On September 2 a joint communiqué announced closer Iraqi-Syrian cooperation in several areas, especially defense, and in the following month a Supreme Defense Council was formed by the two states. Meanwhile, relations with the UAR grew very strained, and the Arab news media in Damascus, Baghdad, and Cairo began making charges and countercharges. It is also interesting to note that the Ba'athist regime's relations with the Soviet Union were also under considerable strain as a result of the Ba'athist purge of local communists.

When Aref took the helm of the government on November 15–18, 1963, he attempted to reverse the trend established by the Ba'ath and once more restored UAR-Iraqi relations. By May 26, 1964, a Joint Presidency Council with a secretariat in Cairo had been formed between Iraq and the UAR. On October 16, 1964, plans for a unified political command between the two countries were made known, and the following December the actual creation of such a command was announced. But the seemingly perpetual oscillation of UAR-Iraqi affairs proved to be too pertinacious for even so ardent a Nasserite as Aref. In July 1965 the inevitable pendulum began its swing back as the pro-Nasser ministers resigned from Aref's cabinet and relations between the two states began to deteriorate.

Some improvements in Iraq's foreign affairs were made in this period. The Kuwait question was resolved, and trade agreements with Kuwait were reached in February and again in the autumn of 1964. Relations with Iran, tense because of border conflicts and the Kurdish problem, improved with the decreased activity along the Iraqi-Iranian border after June 1966. Agreement was reached on a number of issues, and a cultural and trade agreement was projected.

Iraqi forces, although in scant numbers, participated in the Arab-Israeli war of June 1967. As a direct result of the war, Iraq broke diplomatic relations with the United States. Relations were not resumed again until November 1984.

The Ba'athist regime that took power in July 1968 had difficulties in inter-Arab politics, particularly with Syria and the UAR. The enmity among these governments was not overt, however, because of the desire to maintain at least a facade of unity in the face of the prevailing Arab-Israeli crisis. The new government had some success in creating better relations with Iraq's non-Arab neighbors, Iran and Turkey. Within the international sphere, the government took a strong anti-Western stand because of the Arab-Israeli crisis; Iraqi-Soviet relations were also somewhat strained as a result of the Ba'athist regime's conflicts with the Kurds and the Iraqi Communist party. Yet, this relationship was soon to improve.

In May 1969 the most significant aspect of Iraqi-Soviet relations began when General Hardan al-Tikriti, Iraq's defense minister, visited Moscow. Huge military aid and arms purchases were secured. In addition, economic and technical cooperation was established. Moreover, on July 4, 1969, Iraq and the Soviet Union concluded a technical agreement. On March 3 of the following year a permanent Soviet-Iraqi committee was formed to supervise economic cooperation between the two countries. Besides these agreements, more than a dozen arrangements dealing with a variety of technical, cultural, and other matters were reached.

Discernibly significant ties between Iraq and the Soviet Union continued until 1972. On April 9, Soviet Premier Elexi Kosygin visited Baghdad and signed a fifteen-year Treaty of Friendship and Cooperation with Iraq. The Soviet Union traditionally supported the Kurdish leadership, but the treaty ended this support. Iraq could now deal with this important domestic problem without the fear of Soviet support for Kurdish resistance.

Though Soviet-Iraqi relations were close, the Iraqis lacked ideological commitment to the Soviet cause. For Iraq, a close relationship with the Soviets was a pragmatic policy that did not stand in the way of Iraq's desire to forge economic and trade ties with the West. Iraq was especially interested in a good economic relationship with Western Europe, but the Arab-Israeli conflict interfered.

The first two agreements that the European Council (EC) signed with Israel in 1964 and 1970, respectively, heightened the concern of the Arab bloc with respect to the EC's position in the Arab-Israeli conflict. Arab states became even more critical of the EC when a third agreement between the EC and Israel was concluded in 1975. This agreement made Israel the first state to be accepted by the EC free-trade area. The pro-Israeli leanings that characterized the EC's policy on the conflict aroused Iraq's concern over the implications of dramatic increases in oil prices over a short period. Iraq believed that high oil prices would strengthen America's relationship with Western Europe and Japan rather than weaken them. Thus, they feared that the Arab states who boycotted the West would be alienated by U.S. pressure on its allies.

As a result, Iraq called for a strengthening of the Euro-Arab dialogue in order to seek a European policy distinct and separate from that of the United States. Iraq argued that fostering good relations with Western Europe coupled with a strengthening of the relationship with Third World countries would be in the best interest of the Arab world. Indeed, the rise in the amount of Arab petrodollars seemed to have propelled this expectation. Improved economic relations with the West were characteristic of the oil boom period.

Thus, in many ways, Iraq began to move closer to the West in the 1980s. This did not completely separate Iraq from the Soviet Union, because the Soviets remained Iraq's main international supporter, weapons supplier, and commercial creditor. However, events were soon to shift Iraq farther to the West.

The Iraq-Iran War

The beginning of the Iran-Iraq war in 1980 led to a noticeable moderation in Iraq's foreign policy on both the regional and international levels. Regionally, the war dramatically altered the structure of the balance of power. Before the war, Iraq's basic policy was disdainful of the area's conservative monarchies. However, because of the pressure the Iraqi regime found itself under once the war was underway, it sought the help of those very monarchies. Both Libya and Syria supported Iran in the war, and Iraq turned to the conservatives. For their part, the conservative regimes were more than willing to support the Iraqi effort given the effects that an Iranian victory would have had in the region. Saudi Arabia and Jordan fully supported Iraq logistically, financially, and militarily, and all of this support was vital to the success of the Iraqi war effort. Jordan and Egypt contributed "volunteer" forces to Iraq despite the fact that only a few years earlier Iraq was an avowed adversary of both. Even Kuwait, which had been threatened by Iraqi claims to its territories after independence, fully supported Iraq and was instrumental in gaining U.S. support for Iraq. In February 1989 Iraq joined with Jordan, North Yemen, and Egypt in creating the Arab Cooperation Council—a body designed to promote the unity of Arab economies—and thus linked itself more closely to two of the region's conservative regimes.

Caused by a number of factors—religion, nationalism, and geography—the war dragged on for eight years. While the casus belli of the conflict was control over the Shatt-al-Arab waterway—a strategically and economically important access route to the Gulf—its causes were historically rooted in age-old patterns of ethnic, religious, cultural, and territorial rivalry and ideologically rooted in the contemporary political dynamic between Iran's revolutionary Islamic regime and Iraq's secular pan-Arab nationalist regime. The issue of who fired the first shot is really a red herring because the outbreak of conflict was inevitable given the nature of power dynamics in the region. At the outset of the war, Iraq scored rapid military gains and occupied a large area of Iranian territory.

It was only a year later, in September 1981, that Iranian forces—vastly outnumbering the Iraqis—were able to counterattack in a force sufficient to undermine seriously the Iraqi position. By June 1982 the Iranians had forced Iraq to withdraw from Iranian territory, and by July 1982 Iranian forces were invading Iraq.

The Iranians mounted a number of offensives in southern Iraq aimed at cutting Basrah (Iraq's second largest city and only port) off from Baghdad. Iranian forces were never completely successful at achieving this objective, because the Iraqis relied on superior weaponry, innovative defensive tactics, and chemical weapons to repel Iranian attacks. Iraq also attempted to force Iran to accept a cease-fire or some kind of U.N.-sponsored settlement throughout the war's later stages by attacking Iran's economic infrastructure and Iranian morale. Shelling and air raids on major Iranian civilian targets came to be known as "the war of the cities."

Iraqi attempts at cutting Iran's economic lifeline centered around shifting the focus of the fighting away from land battles toward the tanker war—a tactic to prevent Iran from exporting its oil through the Gulf. It was this ploy that ultimately internationalized the war and brought the United States and the Soviet Union into the conflict, as the superpowers attempted to keep the Gulf open for shipping. By 1988 the economic and human costs of the war became too much to bear for both combatants. A UN-sponsored cease-fire was reached on July 19, 1988, and negotiations for a peace settlement began in Geneva on April 21, 1990.

Internationally, the Iran-Iraq war resulted in a major shift in Iraqi policy away from the Soviet Union and toward the West because of the need for financial assistance. By the end of the war, the regime was entirely concentrated in the hands of Saddam Hussein, and pragmatism had replaced ideology as the rationale of policy. After the war, Iraq's major trading partners, Japan, Italy, France, West Germany, and Turkey, secured a long-term loan of $20 billion U.S. for Iraq. In addition, the United Kingdom, Austria, and even the United States granted Iraq substantial agricultural credits.

The Kurdish Issue

The Kurds have long been important players in Iraqi domestic politics because of demands for national autonomy that have been consistently opposed by Baghdad. The Kurds have maintained a high degree of ethnic, linguistic, and cultural identity that has manifested itself in the desire to form a Kurdish national state of Kurdistan encompassing parts of Turkey, Syria, Iran, and northeastern Iraq.

The desire for autonomy has a long history, and it appeared that Kurdish demands would be met after the fall of the Ottoman Empire to the British in Iraq in 1918, but the British decided instead on direct administration of Kurdish regions through local officials. Officials in Baghdad had agreed to honor League of Nations recommendations that the Kurds be allowed cultural freedoms if they agreed to become part of Iraq. The government, however, vacillated on putting any guarantees to the Kurds in writing, and elements of a Kurdish national movement began to appear, led by Shaikh Mahmoud Barzani and, later, Mulla Mustafa Barzani. The movement, centered around the Kurdish Democratic party (KDP), dissatisfied with the government's pace of reform in Kurdish areas, demanded that more Kurds be brought into important educational and government positions.

Thus, when the government fell to Kassim in 1958, the Kurds, and Barzani in particular, saw the opportunity to speed the pace of change by cooperating with the new regime. Kassim went further than the preceding regime in granting and recognizing certain Kurdish rights. The Iraqi provisional constitution declared that Arabs and Kurds were partners in the Iraqi nation, and the permanent constitution guaranteed the national rights of Kurds within the framework of the entity of Iraq. Friction between Kassim and Barzani developed as a result of Barzani's demands for "local autonomy" within Iraq. Kassim responded with oppression, which met with armed Kurdish resistance in September 1961 and began more than a decade of confrontation between Kurdish nationalists under Barzani and successive Iraqi governments. Kassim responded by proscribing the KDP, which to that point had not taken part in the uprising. The conflict intensified with Turkish and Iranian support for the Kurdish efforts at ousting the regime that lasted until March 1963 and the coming to power of Aref.

The Kurds and the Ba'ath have had a long, stormy, and often violent history. Both have intensely distrusted each other's motives and intentions, though the Ba'ath distrusted the Kurds because of their particularist demands and their successionist desires, and the Kurds were fearful of the Ba'ath's pan-Arab ideology, especially the proposal to enter the tripartite union with the UAR and Syria. At the same time, though, the Ba'ath offered more to the Kurds than any previous regime had. When the Ba'ath returned to power in 1968, the resolution of the conflict by peaceful means was declared a major goal of the regime, but the suspicion of the party and the Kurds outweighed any constructive efforts on either side.

The Ba'ath sided with an anti-Barzani faction of the KDP, while Barzani received support from Iran, Israel, and the United States. Thus, the Kurdish problem also had important international implications for the Ba'ath. Through the late 1960s, the conflict became bloodier, more intense and entrenched. By 1970 the squabbling within the KDP and the war-weariness of the Kurds forced Barzani to accept Ba'ath peace proposals. An agreement was drawn up in March 1970 that gave the Kurds greater powers in Kurdish areas, and the government began a process of rebuilding areas destroyed in the conflict. It also called for a three-year transitional period.

Outside interference brought an end to what was a beneficial agreement. Iran, the United States, and Israel urged Barzani to demand more than the Ba'ath were prepared to give. A number of contentions developed, such as Baghdad's refusal to consider Barzani's candidate for vice-president and difficulties concerning the exact boundaries of a Kurdish territory. Outside interference ultimately heightened tensions caused by these difficulties, and, when the level of outside involvement became apparent to the Ba'ath, they moved swiftly to prevent the Kurds from achieving their goals.

By 1974 the Ba'ath believed the KDP was moving toward creating a state of its own within Iraq under Barzani's tutelage and proposed the establishment of the Autonomy Declaration of 1974, which gave Kurdistan limited political sovereignty and unilaterally implemented the March 1970 agreement. Barzani rejected the government's proposals, and full-scale conflict began in April 1974. With heavy American, Israeli, and Iranian moral, financial, and material assistance, the conflict proved to be a bloody and costly one, with both sides experiencing huge losses in the year it lasted.

After the Algiers Agreement of March 1975, the Ba'ath emerged victorious to the extent that it cut a major source of Kurdish support. In addition, the regime attempted to resettle entire Kurdish communities in order to create a cordon sanitaire between Kurdish areas and Iraq's borders with Iran and Turkey. While the exact number of Kurds that were resettled is unknown, it is clear that tens of thousands of people were removed from their villages, which were subsequently destroyed. This heightened Kurdish nationalist sentiments. However, with Barzani's flight from the country in 1975, his death in the United States in 1979, and the Iranian revolution, the Kurdish leadership found itself in disarray and was unable to mount effective opposition to Iraqi government measures at the time.

The Iran-Iraq war proved to be an opportunity for the Kurds again to press Baghdad on the issue of autonomy. Kurdish military action against the Iraqi government diverted troops from the main front against Iran. At the time, the KDP had disintegrated into a number of small factions. During the Iran-Iraq war, the Patriotic Union of Kurdistan (PUK), led by Jalal Talabani, was the main Kurdish opponent of the Iraqis. By 1983 both the PUK and the Ba'ath were weary of fighting each other, and they entered into a cease-fire agreement. Baghdad agreed to some PUK demands for halting the Arabization of Kurdish areas and agreed to discuss others. However, it seems that both Talabani and Hussain viewed the agreement as nothing more than short-term breathing space. Conflicts, though more minor than previous ones, again became common. To squash Kurdish resistance, the army used poisonous gas against Kurdish villages. Terrorized by this and other human rights violations, thousands of Kurds fled across the border to Turkey.

The Kurdish nationalist movement of the late 1980s found itself full of division and internal wrangling. The loss of the charismatic leadership of Barzani, the coopting of Kurdish elements by the Ba'ath, and widespread human rights violations succeeded in destroying the movement's unity and, to a certain extent, its strength. While it appeared that Saddam Hussain had gained the upper hand internally, the center of Kurdish resistance moved to Europe, where Kurdish human rights activists and the KDP are attempting to inform the international community about the plight of the Kurds. The Gulf crisis in fact sensitized international concern. In November 1990, a former Iraqi minister who quit the government in 1974, Sami Abdel Rahman, accused Saddam Hussain of responsibility for the murder of 50,000 Kurds in recent years and the expulsion of tens of thousands of Kurds from Iraq (*Khaleej Times* [Dubai], November 19, 1990).

The Invasion of Kuwait

On August 2, 1990, Iraq invaded Kuwait, and six days later Saddam Hussain announced its annexation to Iraq. (See concluding sections of chapters 13 and 17 for other dimensions of the Gulf crisis.) Before this dramatic event, Saddam Hussain had been threatening Kuwait, blaming it for driving world oil prices down by violating OPEC quotas and prices. Furthermore, border issues were increasingly contentious, and Iraq accused Kuwait of virtually stealing Iraqi oil from the Rumailah oil field. Over the summer, Saddam Hussain started a troop buildup along the border. Alarmed, the Arab League and Arab leaders—especially Husni Mubarak of Egypt, King Hussain of Jordan—attempted to mediate. Saddam Hussain assured them he had no intention of invading Kuwait. On July 31, a meeting between top-level Kuwaiti and Iraqi representatives, called by King Fahd of Saudi Arabia, was held in Jeddah. Kuwait was represented by the crown prince and prime minister, Shaikh Saad Abdullah al-Salim al-Sabah. Izat al-Duri, vice chairman of Iraq's Revolutionary Command Council and one of Saddam Hussain's closest confidants, represented Iraq and made it clear that Iraq's demands were not negotiable. Then, on August

2, Iraqi forces entered Kuwait, precipitating the first post–cold war international crisis.

The international response to the invasion was unanimous condemnation. Reaction, on the other hand, diverged into two streams, military and diplomatic. On the military front, President George Bush immediately committed America's military might to the defense of Saudi Arabia and initiated a massive buildup of American troops and armaments in the Arabian desert, code-named Operation Desert Shield. At the same time, he sought international participation in a military solution to the crisis. However, the international community was less than enthusiastic about a military solution. NATO members, except for Great Britain, gave only token commitments; the Soviet Union declined to participate unless the force was put under UN auspices; and Japan committed a small noncombatant contingent after considerable arm-twisting by the United States. By November 1990, four months after the invasion of Kuwait, the United States had a military force deployed in the Gulf that included troops from the following countries outside the Gulf (as reported in the *Khaleej Times* [Dubai], November 2, 1990):

United States	210,000
Europe	
Britain	15,000
France	10,640
Italy	1,000
Middle East	
Egypt	20,000
Syria	4,000
Morocco	1,200
Third World	
Pakistan	5,000
Bangladesh	2,500
Other	less than 500
(Senegal, Belgium, Netherlands, Greece)	

Iraq responded to the U.S. military threat on two fronts. First, it detained in Iraq between 5,000 and 10,000 foreign personnel of hostile countries, essentially holding them hostage against the threat of attack. Some were deployed around strategic sites as "human shields." Second, it revealed the destructive power in its military arsenal, which includes binary chemical weapons, antiballistic missiles, and supercannon, and encouraged rumors about nuclear and biological weapons capabilities. In other words, Iraq sought to make it clear that a military attack against it would result in a major conflagration. This twofold strategy did delay any precipitous military action but did not forestall the steady buildup of military forces and the consolidation of international support behind American military intervention.

One of Iraq's initial responses to the threat of military attack was the settling of accounts with Iran to reduce the risk of military engagement and the need for military deployment on its eastern flank. In a surprise move, on August 15, 1990, Iraq conceded all of Tehran's terms for a permanent peace. Iraq's crucial concession was the abandonment of its claim to sovereignty over the Shatt-al-Arab. The decision paved the way for a formal peace treaty. On October 14, Iraq and Iran resumed direct diplomatic relations. This rapprochement with Tehran raised fears in the West that Iran might side with Iraq in the event of war in the Gulf. While Iran condemned Iraq's invasion of Kuwait and has complied with UN sanctions, including the embargo, it has also called for the withdrawal of foreign forces from Saudi Arabia, the site of Islam's holiest shrines.

On the diplomatic front, the Soviet Union and most European Community members, spearheaded by France, worked to defuse a military confrontation and open channels for negotiation. To forestall a unilateral American military strike, the other four members of the UN Security Council agreed to support a set of resolutions condemning Iraq's invasion of Kuwait, demanding the unconditional withdrawal of Iraqi forces from Kuwait and the reinstatement of the deposed Kuwaiti government, and agreeing to an economic embargo of Iraq to enforce compliance. By November, the Security Council had passed ten resolutions against Iraq. The United States unilaterally undertook a military initiative to enforce the embargo. Meanwhile, top-level political and diplomatic missions—both official and unofficial—from the United Nations, the Soviet Union, France, Japan, Britain, China, Jordan and others shuttled between Baghdad, New York, and Washington in efforts to establish the basis for negotiations.

Iraq's response to diplomatic efforts have been essentially pragmatic and unpredictable. Its most significant diplomatic initiative has been the effort to link the settlement of the Gulf crisis with settlement of the Arab-Israeli conflict. Clearly an effort to find a formula for negotiations that would salvage Saddam Hussain's image in the Arab world and would vindicate withdrawal, the linkage was strongly rejected by the United States as an unreasonable and unthinkable consideration. However, Israel's massacre of Palestinians at Jerusalem's al-Aqsa complex, Islam's third holiest site, on October 8, 1990, may well have made the linkage thinkable in international circles (see concluding section of chapter 12).

Generally, Iraq's responses to diplomatic initiatives have involved efforts to weaken the international alliance poised against it. For example, most hostages have been released to encourage states with less belligerent inclinations; mediation efforts have been encouraged with conciliatory statements; the families of hostages were invited to spend the Christmas holidays in Iraq with their detained members, with guarantees of their safe passage from Iraq after the holidays. Iraq has also tried to encourage weakening of the international embargo by offering free oil to poorer states if they send tankers for the crude and to sell to others at half the market price. On November 18, Iraq issued a communiqué announcing plans to gradually release all hostages beginning December 25, the last departure to "take place March 25, 1991, if nothing comes to disturb the climate of peace" (quoted in *Khaleej Times* [Dubai], November 19, 1990). But most were released in mid-December.

Even as international diplomatic and military efforts continued, Iraq proceeded with the process of dismantling Kuwait and integrating it into Iraq. Stories of the pillage of Kuwait's wealth and suppression of internal resistance to the occupation were carried out of Kuwait by refugees fleeing the country and by returning hostages. By late October, satellite surveillance of Iraqi troop movements reported over 400,000 Iraqi troops dug into defensive positions in and around Kuwait. Meanwhile Saddam Hussain and George Bush carry on a game of brinksmanship. At this time of writing, the Middle East sits on the precipice of war, and it appears that each of the belligerents has backed his country into a corner. Whether the "balance of terror" that has resulted from all the saber rattling will forestall the ignition of a conflagration long enough for third party action to find some sane resolution can only be hoped for at this time.

REFERENCES

Hanna Batatu. *The Old Social Classes and the Revolutionary Movements in Iraq.* Princeton, 1979.
Uriel Dann. *Iraq under Kassim: A Political History, 1958–1963.* New York, 1969.
Rony Gabbay. *Communism and Agrarian Reform in Iraq.* London, 1979.
Edmund Ghareeb. *The Kurdish Question in Iraq.* Syracuse, 1981.
Philip W. Ireland. *Iraq: A Study in Political Development.* London, 1937.
Tareq Y. Ismael. *Iraq and Iran: Roots of Conflict.* Syracuse, 1982.
Maji'd Khadduri. *Independent Iraq: A Study in Iraqi Politics from 1932 to 1958.* 2d ed. London, 1960.
———. *Republican Iraq: A Study in Iraqi Politics since the Revolution of 1958.* London, 1969.
———. *Socialist Iraq: A Study in Iraqi Politics since 1968.* Washington, D.C., 1978.
Phebe Marr. *The Modern History of Iraq.* Boulder, 1985.

8

The Arab Republic of Syria

R. Hrair Dekmejian

The Syrian Arab Republic, ruled by the Ba'ath party since 1963, occupies an important geostrategic position in the Middle East. In the last two decades, Syria has emerged as a key player in regional politics by virtue of its strategic location, historical centrality in Arab affairs, and the activist leadership provided by President Hafiz al-Asad.

To a significant extent, the complex patterns of contemporary Syrian politics have been determined by the country's historical experience. Since early times, Syria has been the meeting place of opposing armies, conflicting cultures, and competing ideologies and religions. The resulting social and cultural transformation has produced modern Syria—a socially diverse country of about 10 million people spread over 71,227 square miles.

Prior to the twentieth century, the name Syria referred to the contemporary states of Syria, Lebanon, Israel, and Jordan—what is often called "Greater Syria." Located at the geographical confluence of three continents, Syria was ruled by successive empires —Assyrian, Chaldean, Persian, Greek, Roman, and Byzantine. The spread of Christianity made Antioch and Damascus major religious centers. The Arab conquest in 634 A.D. brought about the gradual Islamization of Syria, although large Christian and small Jewish communities maintained their existence as self-administered minorities under Islamic Shari'ah law.

The assassination of Ali, the fourth Caliph, in 676 A.D., and takeover of power by Mu'awiyah (the governor of Syria during the early Arab conquests) in Damascus marked the assumption of the Arab caliphate by the Umayyad dynasty. Under the Umayyads, Damascus became the capital of an Arab empire stretching from Spain to Central Asia. Syria's imperial period lasted only until 750 A.D. when the Abbasids overthrew the Umayyads and moved the caliphate to Baghdad. This brief imperial experience provided a powerful historical impulse for the Syrian nationalists of the twentieth century and has shaped the world view and policies of Syria's leaders in recent decades.

The establishment of Isma'ili Shi'ite power in Cairo under the Fatimid dynasty in 973 as a rival caliphate to the Sunni Abbasids of Baghdad made Syria the focus of intense ideological and military conflict. In the eleventh century came repeated invasions by Seljuk Turks and Mongols. Only the ascendancy of Salah al-Din al-Ayyubi produced a period of stability. His defeat of the Crusaders in 1187 at Hittin and unification of Syria and Egypt would serve as an important historical anchor and inspiration for the Arab nationalist movement of the twentieth century. Beginning with the thirteenth century, the Arab world was thrown into chaotic conditions under Mamluk, Mongols, and Turkic rulers. In 1517 the Ottoman Turks annexed Syria and controlled it until its liberation in 1918 by Arab and British forces under Marshal Allenby.

There was an expansion of Western influence in Syria under Ottoman rule brought on by traders, travelers, teachers, and missionaries. As a result, France and Britain were granted commercial, political, and legal privileges and extraterritorial rights. In 1861, the French sent troops to Lebanon ostensibly to protect the Maronite Christians, who were being massacred during a communal conflict. This act brought Lebanon under growing French influence, and gave it a sense of separateness from Syria.

The Struggle for Independence

In the last days of Ottoman rule, Syria had become the epicenter of Arab nationalism. Inspired by the West, the concept of nationalism first appeared in the writings of Christian-Arab intellectuals; it soon spread to the Muslim Arabs, led by the Young Turk party, who had become progressively alienated from the Ottoman regime because of its repressive policies toward Arab communities.

The ideology of Arab nationalism found many followers among

Syrian intellectuals who graduated from European and American-run colleges. In their quest for an Arab identity, these intellectuals focused on the study of Arab history, literature, and culture while rejecting Ottoman influences and institutions. These opponents of the regime formed a number of secret organizations to further their aims. The most important were *Al Jam'iyah al-Arabiyah al-Fatat* (the Young Arab Society) led by Prince Faisal, son of Sharif Hussain of Mecca, and *al-Ahd* (the Covenant), an association of Arab army officers dedicated to the cause of Arab nationalism.

Arab nationalists conceived of a Greater Syria—a nebulous formulation based on Syria's Umayyad past, roughly encompassing the territorial expanse of present-day Syria, Lebanon, Israel, and Jordan. During and after the halcyon days of the Arab revolt against the Ottoman Turks, this concept became fused with the even larger idea of a united Arab Kingdom encompassing Iraq and the Hijaz. Yet the victorious Allies were not prepared to honor their wartime promises of independence to the Arabs. President Wilson's attempts to modify the Anglo-French wartime agreements proved unsuccessful, as the two allies rejected the findings of the American King-Crane Commission regarding the Arab desire for independence.

Arab nationalist sentiment reached its apogee on March 8, 1920, when the General Syrian Congress proclaimed Syria (which at that time included Lebanon, Palestine, and Transjordan) an independent entity under the rule of Amir Faisal, the second son of Sharif Hussain of Mecca. A month later at the San Remo Conference, Britain agreed to the establishment of a French mandate over Syria as secretly prearranged by the Sykes-Picot agreement between France and Britain four years earlier. In July 1920, the French attacked Damascus and defeated the Arab forces at Maysalun. In exchange for acquiescing to the French takeover of Syria, Britain asserted control over the mandated territories of Iraq, Palestine, and Transjordan in March 1921. Britain made Faisal the king of Iraq and his brother Abdullah the king of Transjordan.

The postwar settlement left Syria in a state of geopolitical and ideological truncation, whereby the country's Sunni majority was cut off from its demographic extensions in Palestine, Lebanon, Iraq, Transjordan, and the Hijaz. Within Syria, the French encouraged fragmentation by dividing the country into provinces based on sectarian concentrations—Jabel Druze, Damascus, Aleppo, and Latakia (al-Alawin). Furthermore, the French created a Greater Lebanon that was ruled as a separate mandate, while the Alexandretta area was placed under a special regime as a prelude to its cession to Turkey in 1939. This French policy of "divide and rule" magnified Syria's communal differences and encouraged ethnoreligious separatist tendencies, thereby cultivating local and regional, rather than pan-Arab, sentiments.

From the onset the French faced unrelenting opposition from Syrian nationalists. Their sense of betrayal and disillusionment triggered insurrectionist movements in Jabel Druze, Damascus, Baalbak, the Hawran, and among the Alawis. Their opposition was based on many factors, including French suppression of political activity and civil rights, the division of Greater Syria into smaller units, and French reluctance to grant Syria its independence. In 1925 a nationalist rebellion spread throughout the urban centers and the Jabel Druze, only to be crushed in 1926. To appease the population, the French allowed the formation of an umbrella political organization—the National Bloc—composed of various nationalist groups. In the same year, elections were held to choose a legislative assembly and the National Bloc captured a large majority of the seats and adopted a constitution that provided for the reunification of greater Syria and the end of French control. In 1930, the French accepted the constitution except for the provisions calling for Syrian self-government.

During the early part of World War II, Syria was administered by the pro-German Vichy French regime, which was defeated in 1941 by British and Gaullist French forces. In 1943, Syria held its first nationwide elections, which brought the National Bloc to power under President Shukri al-Quwwatli. However, it was not until 1946 that Syria became fully independent after the departure of the French forces under strong British pressure.

The Quest for Arab Unity, 1921–1945

The territorial fragmentation of the Eastern Arab world (Mashriq) did not dampen the quest for a united Arab state centering on

Syria. During the interwar years three different schemes of Arab unity emerged—the Fertile Crescent plan and two different Greater Syria schemes. Each scheme is reflected in Syria's legacy of colonial fragmentation.

The Fertile Crescent plan originated in Iraq where King Faisal had become a symbol of Arab nationalist sentiment. After his death, Iraqi Prime Minister Nuri al-Sa'id became the main proponent of the plan aimed at unifying Syria, Lebanon, Palestine, Transjordan, and Iraq.

A rival unity project was the Greater Syria scheme advanced by King Abdullah of Transjordan in July 1940. Under this plan Abdullah would lead the unification of Syria, Lebanon, Palestine, and Transjordan. While both of these schemes had adherents in Syria, neither enjoyed widespread support since they tended to further the hegemonic interests of the Hashemite kings of Iraq and Transjordan.

The third plan was an alternative version of the Greater Syria scheme—one centered on an indigenous Syrian nationalism as distinct from Arab nationalism. Its foremost proponent was Antun Sa'adah, a Lebanese Christian from Brazil, who founded the Syrian Social Nationalist party (SSNP) in 1932, which advocated the establishment of a secular Syrian state encompassing Lebanon, Iraq, and the rest of the Arab East—the original territories of the Umayyad Caliphate. The party was suppressed during the late 1940s but reemerged soon after the outbreak of the Lebanese civil war as a faction of the pro-Syrian coalition opposing the Maronite-dominated government. Its ideal of Greater Syria continues to evoke support among those who are committed to building a strong Syrian state.

The Political Process, 1945–1970

Sociocultural Determinants

The political history of independent Syria has been shaped by several interacting determinants—geography, ideology, class conflict, ethno-sectarian differences, regionalism, military intervention, and the hegemonic pressures of the neighboring states and the great powers. The dynamic interaction of these factors produced a peculiar sociopolitical culture that tended toward instability.

Soon after independence, the polycentric tendencies encouraged by the French were magnified by internal and external social forces. First, there was the push and pull of powerful political and ideological forces radiating from the regional environment as Syria became the focus of an inter-Arab leadership struggle among Iraq, Transjordan, Egypt, and Saudi Arabia. The trend toward fragmentation was compounded by internal struggles for leadership among politicians as well as class conflicts within the urban centers and between urban-based large landowners, the peasantry, and the bourgeoisie. In the absence of sociocultural homogeneity, a unified political culture could not fully emerge.

After the French left, the National Bloc began to lose its cohesiveness. Its leadership, consisting of mostly Sunni and some Christian upper-class politicians, failed to develop strong roots among the diverse social strata of Syrian society. Two additional factors contributed to the demise of Syria's nascent democracy: intense pressure from neighboring Arab states to influence Syrian politics to further their irredentist objectives, and defeat of Syrian forces by the State of Israel in the 1947–48 war. The ill-trained Syrian army blamed its defeat on the civilian government, thereby triggering a series of coups d'état.

The first military regime that took power in March 1949 under General Husni al-Za'im was initially pledged to unify Syria with Iraq. This scheme was supported by the SSNP and the pro-Iraq People's party, but intense Saudi and Egyptian diplomatic pressures and financial aid induced Za'im to renege on his promise to seek the union.

In August 1949, General Za'im was overthrown and executed by Colonel Sami al-Hinnawi, who was pledged to unity with Iraq. In order to abort Hinnawi's unionist plans, the army effected a third coup d'état in December 1949, led by Colonel Adib al-Shishakli. These three coups were also influenced by extraregional forces. The Za'im regime was basically pro-French and pro-American in its orientation, while Hinnawi's pro-Iraqi stance enjoyed muted British support. Shishakli's policy toward the great powers tended to be neutralist and isolationist, while in the Arab sphere close ties were forged with Egypt and Saudi Arabia.

The two years after the December 1949 coup marked a return to a parliamentary government, which Shishakli manipulated through a civilian associate, Akram Hawrani. In 1950 a new constitution was adopted containing the systemic features of the 1930 constitution—a popularly elected unicameral chamber of deputies which would choose the president of the republic, who in turn would appoint the prime minister. Hawrani had succeeded in incorporating some radical welfare state and land reform provisions into the constitution to better the lives of ordinary people. When conservative politicians threatened to undermine Shishakli's power, he staged a second coup in November 1951, dissolving parliament and outlawing political parties, student organizations, and trade unions. To replace them, he established a single organization, the Arab Liberation Movement, and in June 1953 promulgated a new constitution and assumed personal power as president and prime minister. Shishakli's right-wing dictatorship created mass dissatisfaction and led to his overthrow in February 1954.

The Ba'ath and Pan-Arabism

Syria returned to civilian rule after Shishakli's overthrow. The free elections of 1954 brought to power some old guard politicians as well as many independents and Ba'athists. Despite its control of only 10 percent of parliamentary seats, the Ba'ath party presented a cohesive front because of its tight organization, populist ideology, and influence within the Syrian military.

The Ba'ath came into being through the fusion of several political groupings led by nationalist intellectuals and politicians such as Zaki Arsuzi (Alawi), Akram Hawrani (Sunni), Michel Aflaq (Orthodox Christian), and Salah Bitar (Sunni). Aflaq and Bitar had founded the Arab Resurrection party in 1941, which merged with Hawrani's Arab Socialist Party in 1953 to form the Arab Socialist Resurrection party—the Ba'ath. As the party's chief ideologue, Aflaq emphasized three dominant themes: pan-Arabism, socialism, and independence from colonialism. The party would strive to unite the Arab countries, which would pool their resources to achieve socioeconomic progress through a socialist economy.

As a secular, anti-establishment Arab nationalist movement, the Ba'ath appealed strongly to Syria's disadvantaged groups, many of whom populated the small towns and rural areas. These groups included Alawis, Druze, Isma'ili, and poorer Sunnis and Christians, for whom the party would provide opportunities for political and socioeconomic advancement. However, in its attempts to garner the support of these groups and to establish its political primacy, the Ba'ath encountered major rivals during the 1950s. They included Khalid Bakdash's Syrian Communist party and the growing force of a new pan-Arab movement led by Egypt's charismatic president, Gamal Abdal Nasser.

Aside from its organizational strengths, the Communist party enjoyed the support of key army officers, led by General Afif al-Bizri who became chief of staff in 1957. More consequential was Nasser, the dominant symbol of the unity movement throughout the Arab world, particularly among Syria's Sunni majority. From the Ba'ath's point of view, an alliance with Nasser could bring several political advantages. In view of his record of anti-communism in Egypt, Nasser could be expected to help the Ba'ath neutralize communist influence in the army. Also, a Nasserist connection could render the Ba'athi cause acceptable to Syria's Sunni population and nationalist elements both within and outside the army. Finally, in Nasser the Ba'ath would be allied with a legitimate charismatic advocate of the pan-Arabist creed. Despite Nasser's initial misgivings, the Ba'ath leadership persuaded the Egyptian president to agree to the establishment of a Syrian-Egyptian union—the United Arab Republic.

The United Arab Republic, 1958–1961

The formation of the United Arab Republic in February 1958 was an unprecedented event in modern Arab history. Under Nasser's leadership, the UAR generated intense emotions in virtually all sectors of Arab society. As the northern region of the new entity, Syria was strategically well located to influence the unionist movements operating in Iraq, Jordan, and Lebanon. Yet despite the great hopes that it generated, the Syrian-Egyptian union failed after three and a half years. Its longevity, compared with that of other Arab unity schemes, was a result of Nasser's grass-roots popularity and the strength of the Arab sentiment for unity. The factors responsible for its ultimate failure included the deterioration of Ba'athi-Egyptian relations, the incompatibility of Egypt's homogeneous Pharaonic political culture with Syria's multi-sectarian individualistic milieu, the heavy-handed modalities of Egyptian rule in Syria, the incongruity between Nasser's socialist-etatist policies and Syria's entrepreneurial economic culture, and Nasser's reluctance to use maximal coercion to preserve the union.

These factors transcend the Syrian-Egyptian unity experiment because they have been inherent in virtually every attempt at Arab unity. The first concerns an interelite conflict that has always been endemic in the Arab scene. The Ba'ath wished to rule Syria under the halo of Nasser's legitimacy but with a minimum of Egyptian interference. The Ba'ath soon found itself shunted by Egyptian administrators who preferred to rule through unpopular Syrian Nasserists. In practice, Egyptian rule was heavy-handed but not repressive. The Syrians resented the Egyptian determination to implement the July 1961 Socialist laws designed to nationalize the business sector. Ultimately, there was a clash of cultures between the dark-skinned bureaucrats from the Nile Valley and the free-wheeling Syrians. Syria proved to be far more difficult to govern than Egypt, which had a tradition of centralized authoritarian rule. Finally, the Nasserist vision of Arab unity seemed more attractive to the Syrians than its actual imple-mentation in the context of the UAR. Nor was Nasser satisfied with the union, despite the persistence of his personal popularity among the Syrian masses. A secessionist revolt led by conservative anti-unionist officers was not resisted by Nasser, who announced the dissolution of the union on September 28, 1961.

In retrospect, the demise of the UAR was the consequence of

objective social forces that militated against unity. The surprising fact was that the UAR lasted longer than any other Arab unity scheme. Indeed, it was difficult, if not impossible, to preserve the union, in view of its internal contradictions and the strong opposition from Arab ruling elites, the superpowers, and the West.

In the aftermath of the breakup sectarian interests reappeared with the reemergence of the Muslim Brotherhood, which had been proscribed under Nasser. On March 8, 1963, the Ba'ath returned to power through a coup in coalition with pro-Nasser unionist army officers. Yet the Ba'ath's subsequent overtures to Nasser to conclude a tripartite federal union of Egypt, Syria, and Iraq were rejected by the Egyptian president.

The Role of the Military

The protracted crisis surrounding Syria's political institutions since its independence made the military a crucial player in the struggle for power, despite its internal divisions. The Ba'ath was bent on strengthening its influence in the military by actively recruiting from the ranks of the junior officers. Indeed, the military, like the Ba'ath, had attracted members of Syria's underprivileged minorities since the days of the French mandate. The coups of 1949–54 were led by officers of Kurdish origin. During the mid-1960s officers from the Alawite, Druze, and Isma'ili communities had assumed leadership roles, along with Sunnis and Christians from lower-middle-class backgrounds. The military and the Ba'ath provided parallel opportunities for upward mobility and political participation for Syria's disadvantaged groups.

The Ba'ath's increasing reliance on the military to maintain power and the presence of many military officers in the party's ranks became a significant feature of the Syrian political system during the 1960s. The result was a symbiotic relationship between the party bureaucracy and the military establishment whereby the two institutions depended on each other for their common political survival. The events of the 1960s would show the military elite to be dominant over the civilians in the Ba'ath party and in the larger political arena.

In July 1963 the military purged pro-Nasser officers, and in April 1964 an anti-Ba'ath revolt was crushed in the predominantly Sunni city of Hama. In February 1966 the military's grip was strengthened when a faction led by General Salah Jadid overthrew the government of General Amin al-Hafiz and party leaders Michel Aflaq and Salah Bitar. After the Syrian defeat in the 1967 Israeli-Arab war, the Ba'ath political-military apparatus was split between factions headed by Generals Salah Jadid and Hafiz al-Asad. Jadid, as party chief, displayed a clearly ideological and activist orientation in domestic and foreign policy, while Asad, as defense minister, favored a more pragmatic approach. In November 1970 Asad moved to crush the Jadid faction, and in February 1971 he became Syria's first non-Sunni president.

Syria under Asad

In practice, the presidency under Hafiz al-Asad is the main repository of power in the political system. Asad has exercised close control over the army through his old military comrades, while trusted aids and relatives command special elite detachments that are used against the regime's internal enemies. His control has become close to total, and he has been highly successful not only in dominating the country's political scene but also in extending his influence throughout the region.

Soon after taking power, President Asad inaugurated a wide-ranging policy of "rectification" (tashih) in order to broaden his regime's legitimacy. His policies included a retreat from the radical socialism of earlier regimes by introducing economic liberalization to attract the support of the urban Sunni entrepreneurial classes; the ending of Syria's isolation by close cooperation with other Arab countries, particularly Egypt, Saudi Arabia, Jordan, Libya, and the Sudan; the appointment of Sunni officers and civilians to high-ranking positions to counter the minority image of the regime; and the restoration of a measure of constitutional life in which the Ba'ath and four smaller parties could play a role.

Asad's program of political and economic liberalization was well received. By expanding the Baʿath's societal base and establishing a popularly elected People's Assembly, Asad was able to stabilize Syrian political life to a significant degree. While maintaining his hold on the military and the party apparatus, he legitimized his power through a new constitution proposed in 1971 and approved in 1973 by a popular referendum. Meanwhile, Asad ended Syria's isolation from the Arab world by developing close relations with Egypt, Saudi Arabia, and Jordan as a prelude to the October 1973 Egyptian-Syrian attack on the State of Israel to regain Arab territories lost in the June 1967 war.

The 1973 constitution provided for a republican form of government in a "democratic, popular, socialist and sovereign state." It reaffirmed the Baʿathist ideological goal of Arab unity and referred to Syria as merely a part of one indivisible Arab nation.

The constitution stipulates that Syria's president must be a Muslim and that Islamic doctrine and jurisprudence (*fiqh*) are the main sources of legislation. At the same time, the Baʿath is defined as the "vanguard party in the society and the state." At the top of the constitutional division of power is the president, who is elected for a seven-year term by universal suffrage. The presidential nominee must fulfill four conditions: he must be at least forty years of age, be a Syrian Arab Muslim, be forwarded as a candidate by the Baʿath, and be nominated by the People's Council (parliament). Supreme power is vested in the president: he is commander in chief of the armed forces and has the power to appoint and dismiss the prime minister, other members of the cabinet, and even military officers. He has the right to dissolve the People's Council and can exercise legislative power when the council is not in session.

The constitution gave the People's Council substantial powers to make laws, debate policies, and dismiss ministers and cabinets by withholding votes of confidence. Also, the council acts upon the recommendation of the Baʿath party on the selection of the presidential candidate whose name would then be submitted to a popular referendum. In the periodic elections held since 1973, half a dozen parties have competed for council seats, with the Baʿath emerging as the dominant party. Similarly, the Baʿath has controlled at least half of the ministries in successive cabinets with the balance distributed among several Nasserist parties, communists, and independents united under the National Progressive Front.

The Ba'ath is not a mass-based political party but an ideological one. Membership has always been small and depends upon a vigorous selection process and ideological training. Theoretically, power lies with the party's National Command headed by Asad and composed of twenty-one members, half Syrian and half Arabs from other states. The National Command was envisioned as the government of a future unified Arab nation once unity was achieved. Because this possibility is remote and because Asad's desire is to strengthen his base of power, the National Command lacks any real influence.

Real power in the party is centered around the twenty-one-member Regional Command, also headed by Asad, which directs all party activity in Syria. Membership in the Regional Command is focused around Asad and the highest ranking members of his cabinet. Below the Regional Command is the Central Committee and nineteen branch commands that direct party activity at the local levels. The military wing of the party includes officers and enlisted men down to the level of battalion. This type of organization and party discipline has made the Ba'ath the primary tool of political socialization and stability in Syria since Asad's ascent to power.

Internal and External Challenges

The greatest internal challenge to President Asad has come from the Islamic fundamentalist movement led by the Syrian branch of the Muslim Brotherhood. Established in 1943, the Brotherhood was led by Dr. Mustafa al-Sibai, an associate of Hasan al-Banna, the founder of the Muslim Brotherhood of Egypt. Although the Brotherhood aimed at the establishment of an Islamic order in both Egypt and Syria, until the early 1970s the Syrian branch lacked the widespread support and militancy of the Brotherhood of Egypt, which had been suppressed by Nasser.

The first major confrontation between the Brotherhood and President Asad occurred in the spring of 1973 over the promulgation of a secular constitution. Pressured by riots, demonstrations, and strikes, Asad amended the constitution to stipulate that the president of the republic would have to be of the Islamic faith. However, the real target of the Brotherhood was the president himself who belonged to the Nusayri (Alawite) sect, which the Islamic fundamentalists regarded as heretical.

The Islamic opposition fizzled during the October 1973 war amid heightened popular feelings of Arab nationalism as Syrians united behind their president to fight the State of Israel. Despite the surprising vigor shown by the Syrian army, the Brotherhood criticized the regime for failure to recapture the Golan Heights and for joining U.S. Secretary of State Henry Kissinger's "peace process" that resulted in a disengagement agreement with the State of Israel on May 31, 1974. This agreement, followed by President Richard Nixon's visit to Damascus, produced an unprecedented Syrian-American rapprochement that lasted until the late 1970s.

The next challenge facing Syria was the outbreak of civil war in Lebanon in April 1975. President Asad intervened militarily in mid-1976 to check the PLO-led offensive against the Maronite militias—a move sanctioned by most Arab states and tacitly supported by the United States and even the State of Israel but not the Soviet Union. Initially, the outcome of Syria's intervention seemed conclusive. By deploying the Arab Deterrent Force, consisting principally of the Syrian army, Asad had succeeded in preventing the establishment of a radical pro-PLO regime in Lebanon. Indeed, such a regime could have been detrimental to Syrian interests by aligning itself with Iraq and Libya and increasing the likelihood of an Israeli attack on Lebanon. However, the Syrian position began to deteriorate as the Maronite militias, with the backing of the newly elected Israeli government of Prime Minister Menachem Begin, which took office in May 1977, turned against the Syrians.

Syria's difficulties in Lebanon and its economic problems at home provided the Islamic opposition an opportunity to destabilize the government. The Brotherhood accused Asad of acting as a surrogate for American, Israeli, and Maronite interests, but its overriding grievance was the prominent military and political position of President Asad's Alawi kinsmen and the concomitant erosion of Sunni power and status in the political system. Consequently, the militant wing of the Brotherhood, in alliance with smaller Islamic radical groups, declared *Jihad* (holy struggle) in 1976, employing hit-and-run tactics to provoke the regime into escalating its repressive policies. During 1979 Islamic terrorism intensified, and in March 1980 the Brotherhood and the smaller fundamentalist groups established the Syrian Islamic Front to unite their flagging efforts against the Ba'ath regime. August 1981 marked the onset of the third phase of armed struggle, culminating in the Islamic uprising in Hama during February 1982. After several weeks of fighting, the insurrection was crushed and parts of Hama destroyed. The revolt failed to trigger a general uprising; the massive losses suffered by the Islamic radicals neutralized a major threat to the regime.

The Syrian Economy

Syria's economy has undergone massive structural changes since independence. Syria lacked the resources and infrastructure necessary to capitalize fully on the stimulation of the economy brought about by the presence of Allied forces during World War II. At that time, its economy was dependent on supplying agricultural and locally manufactured goods to Allied forces. It was only when Syrian landowners began to channel agricultural profits into industrial enterprises that Syria began the long, and incomplete, road to development. Basic structural problems plague the economy and these difficulties have not yet been successfully addressed.

Syria has suffered from the rapid shifts in government policy that accompanied changes in regime through the 1960s and early 1970s. By the mid-1960s, nationalization of industry and foreign investments and land reforms marked the beginning of the socialization of the economy. As a result Syria suffered the loss of skilled workers and the flight of indigenous capital. Traditional business activities became marginalized as the state emerged in economic development policies that focused on industrialization and central planning.

Efforts to liberalize the economy were introduced and proved successful, although the greatest boon to the Syrian economy was the substantial increase in oil prices in the early 1970s. Syria's oil sector, small by Middle Eastern standards but significant nonetheless, grew at a rapid pace, as did the construction and manufacturing sectors. The government did not entirely abandon its economic role introduced in the 1960s, quite the contrary, the public sector remains the most important economic player. Liberalizing measures generally focused on promoting private sector investment and establishing of a number of free trade zones where imports and exports were tax free.

The greatest structural problems in the economy center on bureaucrat's attempts to deal with economic activity. Government personnel are clearly lacking in expertise and have not been able to address economic difficulties effectively. When the agricultural sector failed as a result of bad weather, as it did often in the early 1980s, the economy suffered severe setbacks as efforts at diversification had uneven results. The government faces a number of serious difficulties such as declining revenues resulting from slumping world oil prices, foreign exchange imbalances, weak export markets, large trade deficits, and the vagaries of Middle Eastern politics.

Syria's Foreign Relations

Syria's foreign policy has always been a key aspect of its political life given its historical legacy, commitment to Arab unity, limited capabilities, and hostile environment. Moreover, since Asad's rise to power, Syria's attempt to exert itself as a regional power on political, military, and ideological levels has stretched its capabilities to the limit in an effort to reach its objectives.

A central focus of Syrian foreign policy since independence has been its opposition to the existence of the State of Israel and, more recently, its efforts to reach a level of strategic parity with the Israelis. Syrian forces were part of the Arab army that attempted to prevent the partition of Palestine and attacked Israeli positions the day after Zionist leaders unilaterally declared an independent State of Israel. Syria was shocked by the Arab defeat and even more so by revelations of corruption and profiteering by its civilian political leaders. These events combined with the presence of 100,000 Palestinian refugees to make Syrian political life highly volatile, culminating in a period of political instability. Syria's foreign policy has thus had a profound effect on its domestic politics.

After 1948, the Syrian military began a rebuilding phase because of the instability caused by the Arab-Israeli conflict. Border clashes with the State of Israel were common. In the June 1967 Arab-Israeli war, the Syrian military was defeated and the State of Israel seized the Golan Heights—an untenable situation for Syria's leaders and an important factor leading to Asad's rise to power.

Between 1967 and 1973, Syria worked to challenge Israeli occupation of the West Bank, Gaza, and the Golan Heights. It supported the PLO militarily during Black September in Jordan and formed, through the auspices of the Ba'ath, a Syrian-sponsored, Syrian-manned guerrilla unit, *Al-Sa'iqa*. When Asad came to power he severely limited Palestinian activity in order to avert Israeli attacks on Syria. He also attempted to increase the professionalism and capabilities of the armed forces, largely with Soviet and Eastern bloc aid. The effort was successful to an extent; when it launched an offensive against the State of Israel with Egypt in 1973, the Syrian military was a formidable force. However, the offensive failed in terms of Syrian goals. For Asad, the offensive was designed to regain lost Arab territory and pride; for Egypt's President Sadat it was merely an effort to bring the State of Israel to the bargaining table, and he therefore directed Egyptian military activities to this more limited goal.

During the 1980s Syria's foreign relations have been marked by heightened turbulence in several multifaceted conflicts—the State of Israel's invasion of Lebanon, the Iraq-Iran war, and the Palestinian-Israeli confrontation. In facing these problems, President Asad had to play a complex role to sustain his regime and his country's national interests.

The State of Israel's first invasion of Lebanon in March 1978 and President Sadat's decision to seek a unilateral settlement with the State of Israel left Syria exposed. As a result, Syria, Libya, Algeria, South Yemen, Iraq, and the PLO formed the Arab Steadfastness Front, which met in Damascus in September 1978 to reject Sadat's peace initiatives. U.S.-Syrian relations had deteriorated when President Asad traveled to Moscow in October 1980 to sign a treaty of friendship to strengthen his military ties with the USSR, as a deterrent to the State of Israel.

Within the context of the Arab Steadfastness Front, the antagonistic Ba'athist regimes of Iraq and Syria sought to form a political and economic union in October 1978. The rapprochement came to an abrupt end in July 1979 as the two regimes resumed their confrontationist stance. When Iraq attacked Iran in September 1980, the Syrians broke with most other Arab states and supported Ayatollah Khomeini's Islamic government. Syria's ensuing isolation from the Arabs ended when the State of Israel launched a massive invasion of Lebanon in June 1982 as a direct challenge to Asad's regime.

The confrontation between Syrian and Israeli forces was limited to periodic clashes on the ground, although Syria was humiliated by the loss of much of its air force. Its losses prompted a major Soviet resupply of advanced weaponry, including a modernized air defense system, accompanied by a significant enlargement of the Soviet military presence in Syria. By mid-1983, the Syrian president was in a strong position to resist American and Israeli pressures to withdraw from Lebanon. Syria insisted on the abrogation of the U.S.-sponsored Lebanese-Israeli agreement, the total withdrawal of Israeli troops, and the establishment of a pro-Syrian regime in Beirut. Moreover, Asad and his Druze and Shi'ite Lebanese allies had successfully fought the Maronite militia and the fledgling American-trained Lebanese army. Meanwhile, the American peacekeeping force, backed by naval units, had committed itself to the survival of President Amin Gemayel's minority government. Indeed, there was little that American and Israeli military pressure could do to effect a Syrian withdrawal, short of a full-scale invasion of Lebanon. The sustained Druze attacks against the Lebanese

army at Suq al-Gharb, the killing of 241 U.S. Marines by a truck
bomb in October 1983, and Syrian anti-aircraft fire directed at U.S.
reconnaissance flights triggered ineffective American air and naval
bombing of Syrian and Druze positions. On another front, Syrian-
supported Palestinian forces had forced the evacuation of Yassir
Arafat and his PLO partisans from Tripoli.

The withdrawal of American, French, Italian, and British peacekeeping forces, the abrogation of the Lebanese-Israeli treaty, and
Israel's failure to impose its surrogates as rulers in Lebanon constituted major victories for the Syrians. By his defiance of the State
of Israel and the United States, President Asad had emerged as
the lonely defender of the Arab cause, a role that evoked considerable admiration and support from Arab nationalists. Despite these
successes Syria was unable to preside over the establishment of
a friendly regime in Beirut. Nor was it prepared to discipline the
Hizbullah and other pro-Iranian Shi'ite fundamentalist groups for
fear of jeopardizing the Syrian-Iranian alliance against Iraq.

Quest for Compromise, 1984–1990

The defeat of the Islamic fundamentalist challenge in 1982 and the
withdrawal of the State of Israel from most of Lebanon in 1983–
84 helped strengthen the Asad regime and brought a degree of
normalcy to the country. Yet the president's serious illness in November 1983 introduced an element of uncertainty concerning the
presidential succession. In view of Asad's central position since
1970, his illness created a power vacuum that triggered a struggle
among his top military aids. After regaining his health, the president took full control in mid-1984 and exiled the three top antago-
nists, including his brother Rif'at al-Asad who had been a symbol
of the regime's repressive policies. These purges were accompanied
by political and economic reforms to strengthen the regime's legitimacy. Despite growing economic difficulties at home, by the
mid-1980s the Syrian leadership had managed to strengthen itself
politically to confront the challenges of the late 1980s posed by
the transformation of the Soviet bloc, the ascendancy of Iraq over
Iran in the Gulf war, and the continuing quagmire in Lebanon.

While Syria supported the Intifadah, President Asad continued to oppose Arafat's leadership of the PLO, along with his peace overtures toward Israel. In Lebanon, the Syrians expanded and consolidated their military presence by weakening the pro-Iranian Hizbullah and containing PLO activities with the help of Amal and Walid Jumblatt's Druze militia. In Lebanon's crisis of presidential succession of September 1988, Syria supported Prime Minister Salim al-Hus's cabinet against General Michel Aoun's rival government. This stance led to protracted artillery duels between General Aoun's forces and the Syrian-led Lebanese militias. Despite economic difficulties at home and pressures from abroad, President Asad's government was determined to maintain its military presence until the conclusion of a new power-sharing agreement among Lebanon's warring sectarian groups, one that would accommodate Syrian interests.

The opportunity for such a compromise emerged at the Ta'if conference (November 1989) in Saudi Arabia, which provided for an intercommunal settlement in Lebanon to be followed by eventual Syrian withdrawal from the country. Under the Ta'if accords, Syria supported the election of René Mu'awwad as Lebanon's president. After Mu'awwad's assassination, Syria backed George Hrawi, who became president in late 1989 in the midst of intermittent clashes brought on by General Aoun's rejection of the Ta'if accords. The general's defiance of the Hrawi government, a government backed by Iraq, represented a new phase of Syrian-Iraqi rivalry in Lebanon.

Asad's quest for a foreign policy of accommodation in the late 1980s was dictated by major changes in Syria's international and internal environments. The transformation of the Soviet Union under Mikhail Gorbachev brought a sharp reduction in Soviet military and economic aid. Meanwhile, Syria's Iranian allies had been weakened by Iraq, which now sought to play a leading inter-Arab role. At home, the Asad government faced economic problems and a reduction of aid from the Arab Gulf states. These factors were instrumental in prompting Asad to undertake new policy initiatives: normalizing relations with the United States, strengthening inter-Arab ties, particularly with Egypt, permitting greater flexibility in seeking a Lebanese settlement, and even expressing a willingness to negotiate with Israel on outstanding issues such as the Golan Heights. Perhaps the greatest challenge facing the government at the threshold of the 1990s is how to relax political and economic controls at home so as to give free reign to the creative energies of the Syrian people in a secure environment. (See concluding section of chapter 17 for Syria's role in the Gulf crisis.)

REFERENCES

R. Hrair Dekmejian. *Islam in Revolution*. Syracuse, N.Y.: Syracuse University Press, 1985.

John F. Devlin. *The Ba'ath Party: A History from Its Origins to 1966*. Stanford, Calif.: Hoover Institution Press, 1976.

Stephen H. Longrigg. *Syria and Lebanon under French Mandate*. London: Oxford University Press, 1958.

Itamar Rabinovich. *Syria under the Ba'ath, 1963–1966: The Army-Party Symbiosis*. Jerusalem: Israel Universities Press, 1972.

Patrick Seale. *Asad*. Berkeley: University of California Press, 1988.

————. *The Struggle for Syria: A Study in Post-war Arab Politics, 1945–1958*. London: Oxford University Press, 1964.

Gordon H. Torrey. *Syrian Politics and the Military (1945–1958)*. Columbus: Ohio State University Press, 1964.

Nikolaos Van Dam. *The Struggle for Power in Syria: Sectarianism. Regionalism and Tribalism in Politics, 1961–1980*. 2d ed. London: Croom Helm, 1981.

9

The Republic of Lebanon

Nassif Hitti

The modern history of Lebanon as a political entity can be traced back to the end of the sixteenth century with the establishment of the Emirate of Mount Lebanon in 1590 under Fakhr al Din II of the Druze Ma'ns dynasty. In 1697, when the Ma'ns "became extinct in the male line,"[1] the Shihabs dynasty was founded by Bashir al-Shihabi, who was nominated by the Lebanese notables. Under the Shihabis (originally Sunnis, later many converted to Maronitism), the power of the Druze eroded as that of the Maronites ascended. The change over time in the sectarian balance of power contributed to the increasing tension between the two communities. In such an environment it did not take much meddling by the great powers to instigate a sectarian war between the Maronites and the Druzes in 1840–41, bringing about the end of the Shihabis' dynasty. The European powers in concert with the Ottoman Empire worked out a system for Mount Lebanon, that divided it into two new districts, one Maronite and the other Druze. The new administrative arrangements failed, however, and sectarian tension and violence, fueled by the same powers, continued until an agreement was reached in 1861 that featured a new organic statute for Mount Lebanon. Known as the Mutasarrifyah system, it granted the governorship to a Christian whom the Ottomans would name and divided Lebanon into a system of autonomous regions. The arrangement survived until 1915. Under the Mutasarrifyah system, Lebanon was divided from the coastal cities and the regions of Akkar and the Beka. These areas, although they had never formed an integral part of the empire, had until then remained for the most part under the control of the Ma'ns and the Shihabis.

In the early twentieth century, the Christians, in particular the Maronites, called for expanding Mount Lebanon to include the de facto controlled areas of the emirate. For the Lebanese nationalists, Fakhr al Din II is considered to be the first who unified the nation. Their concern over the growing Arab nationalist movement, along with economic insecurity and the geographic strangulation of Mount Lebanon, pushed the Maronites to demand the establishment of Greater Lebanon, despite the detrimental demographic changes that might result.

No sooner was Lebanon placed under the French mandate at the San Remo Conference in April 1920 than France proclaimed the establishment of Greater Lebanon. The new state included Mount Lebanon, the coastal cities, and four "Syrian" districts in the Beka region, not that different from the Lebanon of Ottoman times.[2] A constitution was proclaimed on May 23, 1926, and the first president was elected the same year, but leaders of the Sunni community were still calling for secession and union with Syria. On November 26, 1941, France declared the independence of Lebanon. The new Chamber of Deputies, elected in August 1943, amended the constitution, eliminating the articles referring to the mandate and the role of the high commissioner. France responded by imprisoning the leaders of the government, an act that prompted both Christians and Muslims to take to the streets in massive protests. Under pressure from this unrest and from France's allies (including Great Britain and the United States), the French liberated their prisoners on November 22, later proclaimed the official independence day of Lebanon.

The creation of Greater Lebanon did not alter the national loyalties of the vast majority of the Sunni community. There evolved two basic constituencies: a Maronite-dominated Lebanonist, or localist, constituency and a Sunni-dominated Arabist one. Amid the bipolarization, a political arrangement was needed to establish the parameters of the newly independent state. The formula that sidestepped serious debate on the issue of identity, concerning itself both with the Lebanization of the Sunnis and the Arabization of the Maronites, became known as al-Mithaq al-Watani, the National Pact.

The pact, never written down or clearly formulated, was a sort of modus vivendi whose various formulations and applications constituted the larger part of Lebanon's political life. An initial meeting was held between President Bishara al-Khoury and Premier Riyadh al-Solh in 1943 during which both agreed to build an independent and free Lebanon. The Christians promised to refrain from invoking the help of France, and the Muslims, in turn, promised not to call for union with Syria. A second meeting was held between the two leaders during which they elaborated the fundamental principles that constituted the pact: Lebanon is an independent republic; Lebanon is an integral part of the Arab world but has unique characteristics that encourage cultural ties with the West; the Lebanese vocation lies in cooperation with the Arab states, and Lebanon must maintain equilibrium in its relations among them without distinction or preference.[3]

These major points were enumerated many times in different speeches by President Khoury and Premier Solh. For Khoury, the pact was "nothing but a conciliation between two communities,"[4] a form of mutual deterrence in which both sides agreed to refrain from using their ultimate weapons: the Arab nationalism of the Sunnis, on the one hand, and the Lebanonism of the Maronites, on the other.

The Mithaq succeeded in perpetuating the delicate balance of power between the religious communities but failed to build a sound basis for national identity, as the events of 1958 and the ongoing war in Lebanon clearly demonstrate. Moreover, the Mithaq contributed to the immobilization that has characterized the Lebanese system since independence, an immobilization that both Christian and Muslim conservative forces praised for leading to stability, or rather, maintaining a status quo in which their political and socioeconomic privileges and interests were protected. The Mithaq was intended as a solution to what was assumed to be an inevitable conflict of identities between sectarian groups. Even today, a large constituency comprised of the traditional leadership of the Sunni and Maronite communities calls for the preservation of the spirit of the Mithaq. In the final analysis, however, there can be little doubt that while "the Mithaq was a bulwark against the disruptive potential of irrational confessionalism [it was] equally a roadblock that prevented the emergence of a rational and secular alternative to confessional politics."[5]

The Institutions of the State

The president of the republic is elected for a six-year term by the Chamber of Deputies, requiring a two-thirds majority in the first round or an absolute majority in the second round so long as a quorum exists. Though it is not indicated in the constitution, the ruling elites have agreed since independence that the three key offices of state should be distributed among the three main sects in the following way: the presidency goes to the Maronites, the premiership to the Sunnis, and the speaker of the chamber to the Shi'as. Among the prerogatives of the president is the right to dissolve the Chamber of Deputies and call for new elections. According to the constitution (Article 17) the president assumes the executive powers assisted by the ministers. Any decree must carry the signature of the concerned minister and the premier next to that of the president. Those who defend the presidency argue that the constitution (Article 60) correctly observes that the president cannot be held accountable in the exercise of his functions unless he violates the constitution or commits an act of high treason. Despite the legal constraints that parliamentary regimes impose on the presidency, that office developed into the strongest center of power in Lebanon. Thus the system could be labeled a presidential one. The president's mandate compared to that of the chamber, the fact that he has the upper hand in the political process of naming the premier and the ministers, and the enormous resources he commands through his office that allow him to distribute political rewards and benefits are factors that combine to tip the balance among the different institutions in favor of the presidency.

Before forming a new cabinet, the president consults with the different parliamentary leaders and groups, a process that involves considerable lobbying. The president then names the premier who traditionally contributes to the president's choice of ministers. The cabinet then goes to the Chamber of Deputies for a discussion of the Ministerial Communique—a set of proposed goals and policies—and finally a vote of confidence. If the vote is not positive, the president must renew consultations and present a new cabinet. The cabinet is structured to represent regional and sectarian interests rather than to meet the demands of interest groups.

The cabinet may convene ministerial councils that include all or some of its members to deliberate on certain issues, but, unless the president is present, the cabinet or Council of Ministers is not empowered as the executive body.

When there is disagreement between the president and the premier, the latter presents the resignation of his cabinet to the president. If the resignation is accepted, the premier continues to fulfill his responsibilities until a new cabinet is formed. A different kind of problem evolves when divergence on particular issues arises. Instead of presenting the cabinet's resignation the premier exercises his veto power by abstaining from signing decrees, thus paralyzing the executive body. The president may then invoke his constitutional right to form a new cabinet—a tactic which has proved certain to fail—or he may seek a political solution through accommodation and concessions. The bicameralism that emerges within the executive body in times of crisis is less a reflection of the institutional structure of the government than of the lack of national consensus that helps transform political issues into issues of national identity.

Legislative power is embodied in the Chamber of Deputies. The chamber, elected for a four-year term by universal suffrage, is a system of proportional representation based on sectarianism and regionalism and is invariably composed of a number that is a multiple of eleven in order to maintain the sectarian proportion of six Christian to five Muslim deputies. The chamber convenes twice a year in ordinary session. An extraordinary session may be convened by either a presidential decree or upon the request of the majority of members.

The notorious political ineffectiveness of the chamber and its marginal role in deciding crucial issues, especially in times of crisis, is largely the result of two elements: an electoral system fashioned to suit the interests of the locally based traditional leaders—thereby reinforcing and legitimizing sectarianism—and the traditional subservience of the deputies to the president and cabinet.[6] An astute observer of Lebanese politics has labeled this the "orphan complex" of the chamber: "the tendency of the deputies, in a non-party system which represents personal, regional and traditional interests, to assume the position of the President's clients, rather than to form and impose an independent policy consensus of their own in accordance with the substantial powers at least nominally granted them by the Constitution."[7] As a result, the power of government has become concentrated in the executive branch or, more specifically, in the hands of the president.

The political system in Lebanon can be considered a federation of religious communities. The state has abdicated its legal competence in certain areas to the communities; in other areas the religious and political leadership of the communities have usurped the role of the state. Fifteen different communities are officially recognized in Lebanon.[8] In a set of laws and decrees, the state has defined spheres of competence of these communities as well as their roles and functions. Thus, on April 2, 1951, a law was adopted by the Lebanese chamber "to delineate the competence of the Christian and the Israelite sectarian authorities," a law that strongly accentuated the sectarian regime by elevating these communities to the rank of political entities enjoying autonomy under their own by-laws.[9] The same kind of autonomy was granted to the Sunni community in the legislative decree of January 13, 1955, to the Druze community on July 13, 1962, and to the Shi'a community on December 19, 1967. The political establishment of the newly independent country institutionalized and consolidated sectarianism by making it the basis of the organization of the legal structure of the state. In turn the sectarian regime perpetuated its values and norms of political behavior through the same institutions and obstructed serious attempts at reform.

Contrary to the view that the separate Lebanese communities comprise different ethnic groups because "of the ascribed nature of sectarian identities in the Middle East and because the members of the religious groups consider themselves alike due to their common ancestry and are so regarded by others,"[10] the Lebanese share with each other such vital elements of identity as language and religion which cut across communal boundaries but differ with respect to ideology.[11] The socio-historical evolution of the different communities, particularly under the Ottoman empire, can be seen in the emergence of politico-ideological constituencies associated with certain sects or religions. The Lebanonist constituency became associated with the Maronites, and Pan-Arabism became associated with the Sunnis. Each constituency controlled its own agencies of socialization, such as schools and associations, and was able to promulgate its own conception of the history of Lebanon and its national destiny. Thus an already fragmented culture was reinforced by an environment in which national integration was an obsolete idea.

Some blame the failure of national integration on external factors and their "intervention in Lebanese sociopolitical affairs,"[12] but reasons for failure were essentially domestic, notably "the lack of consensus on fundamentals," the sectarianization of the state, and the legitimation of sectarianism.[13]

Political culture, wrote Sidney Verba, "consists of the system of empirical beliefs, expressive symbols and values which defines the situation in which political action takes place. It provides the subjective orientation to politics."[14] To speak of a Lebanese political culture in these terms is unrealistic. Witness, for example, the value system of the Lebanonist constituency, in which the Palestinian armed presence in Lebanon constitutes a flagrant violation of the ultimate value of sovereignty, while in the Arabist constituency, the Palestinians are welcomed as Arab brothers on Arab soil. Similarly, any policy at variance with an Arab power center committed to pan-Arabism is perceived by Arabists as a violation of the National Pact, while policies that lead to increased involvement in Arab politics in the name of the Arab cause is certain to be perceived by the Lebanonists as a violation of the National Pact. Perhaps the first to point out the inherent obstacles to national integration in the system itself was Georges Naccache, a journalist who criticized the pact as a negative consensus, writing in 1949 that "two negations do not make a nation."

The pact, the constitution, the different by-laws, the political customs and norms made Lebanon into a consociational democracy, "a government by an elite cartel designed to turn a democracy with a fragmented political culture into a stable democracy." Three conditions conducive to the establishment and maintenance of cooperation among the elite were present in Lebanon: the existence of an external threat, the presence of a multiple balance of power among the subcultures, and the low total load on the decision-making apparatus.[15]

It was the pride of the Lebanese political establishment that the system functioned smoothly and was able to absorb and contain crises, conditions that made Lebanon appear stable in relation to its Arab neighbors. Yet the elite were deaf to the warnings emanating from different sectors in Lebanon about the need to adapt to change at home and in the larger Arab environment. It was not willing to turn the state into an agent of national integration and sociopolitical reforms. The state in Lebanon was left to its traditional role of observer or, at best, of power broker between sects. Political sclerosis characterized the system.

The failure of the model[16] can be illustrated by measuring the performance of the system against the three factors mentioned earlier. First, the presence of an external threat became a source of conflict. There were different assessments of the character of the threat: was it the PLO's activities, Israel's expansionism, or Syria's Grand Design? Instead of cementing an agreement, the external threat destoyed what was left of a fragile consensus. Secondly, there occurred drastic change in the demographic balance of power among the sects. The sectarian distribution had favored the Maronites because of an apparently larger population based on a census taken in 1932, but the disproportionately high fertility rate among the Shi'as soon made the Shi'as the largest sect in Lebanon.[17] The Shi'as are now thought to number between 1.2 million and 1.5 million, while the Maronites are estimated at 900,000 and the Sunnis at 750,000.[18] This raised the divisive twin issues of increased participation by the Muslim sects and assurance of guarantees for the

Maronite leadership. Thirdly, and finally, the system was overloaded. The process of socioeconomic modernization generated first demands for reform, then alienation and discontent when the system proved unable or unwilling to reform.

The Socioeconomic Structure and Performance

The geopolitical location of Lebanon, its sociocultural characteristics, its liberal economic system (bordering on a savage laissez faire), the level of education and skills the population enjoys, and the prevailing conditions in the Middle East region shaped the Lebanese economy and greatly influenced the formation of its structures. The Lebanese economy is dominated by the service sector, which provides almost two thirds of the GDP; the remaining third is generated by the industrial and agricultural sectors.[19] The imbalance in the economy survived attempts at reform with only minor results in the industrial sector.[20] Lebanese industry expanded its production, but still failed to meet the needs of the import-reliant Lebanese market. The disparity between the degree of commodity concentration in Lebanese exports and imports supports the pair of generalizations that countries with laissez-faire economies "tend to specialize in what they export rather than in what they import"[21] and typically are more specialized with respect to the goods they produce than those they consume.[22] Next to the sophisticated service sector in Lebanon, including a surprisingly advanced banking system, the agricultural sector struggles to survive with primitive modes of production. Lebanon is a case par excellence of what economists call lopsided development.

The income distribution reflects the existing structural inequalities due to the sectoral imbalance. By the early seventies, 4 percent of the population earned 35 percent of the national income, the lower 50 percent received 20 percent of the income, and the income of the remaining 46 percent, that of the middle class, amounted to 20 percent of the total.[23]

The increasing disparity in the rate of growth between the different sectors of the economy and the system's unwillingness to counterbalance its effect considerably augmented the already large income gap among the socioeconomic classes and regions. Government favoritism toward the service sector was compounded by favoritism toward certain regions of Lebanon.

A potential economic crisis, which would almost certainly have led to the collapse of the Lebanese economy, was diffused by emigration. A vehicle of class mobility, emigration, through the remittances particularly of those in Africa and the Gulf region, greatly reduced both the problems associated with the balance of payment and the threat of an intolerable rate of unemployment. Serious problems developed, however, because of rural migration to the capital. The disintegration and the weakness of the agricultural sector and the security problem in Southern Lebanon due to the war of attrition between the PLO and the State of Israel prompted people to move to the cities, creating the infamous "misery belt" around Beirut.

In a society where class loyalty is still largely subordinated to parochial, communal, and national loyalties, the existing inequalities intensified the sectarian tension because the poor areas were predominantly Muslim, particularly Shi'a. A study of the Lebanese communities that found the non-Catholic and Catholic Christians ranked at the top of the socio-economic scale, followed by the Druze, the Sunnis, and finally the Shi'as, concluded that "some of the most pronounced differences between the religious communities are socioeconomic in nature."[24] Attempts at economic reforms were opposed by the Lebanonist constituency, which held the upper hand in the system, on the grounds that they endangered the Lebanese entity (al-Kyyan). Socioeconomic demands were manipulated and twisted into sectarian ones and so were never directly addressed, thus deepening the societal cleavages and sowing the seeds of the civil war that formally started February 26, 1975.

In a study on the performance of the Lebanese economy on the eve of the civil war, the author observes that the economy featured "an orderly and impressive financial growth" in purely quantitative terms. He remarks, however, the absence of important socioeconomic objectives that should have been sought, such as the creation of greater employment opportunities and the reduction of income inequality.[25]

Today, after thirteen years of war and especially after the Israeli invasion of Lebanon, the economy is in shambles, economic infrastructure destroyed, the agricultural sector devastated, a mass exodus undertaken, and the already small market fragmented. Lebanon's dependence on imports for even basic goods like food and fuel and the depression of the Lebanese pound produced a soaring inflation that made the currency virtually worthless; even small transactions today are in U.S. dollars. No serious economic medicine can be administered to Lebanon's ailing economy until a return to minimal political normalcy is achieved.

The Political Parties

Despite the presence of many parties in Lebanon, running the gamut from ultraconservative to extreme radical, there has never existed a multiparty system fashioned after any of the models of the various Western democracies. The political parties of Lebanon have not managed to act as agencies through which the demands of the populace are articulated and transmitted to the institutions of the state, a role which has been preserved for a traditional political elite that includes the secular leaders of different religious communities and the political bosses of regions where feudal relationships, though weakened, still function as tools of recruitment, still require allegiance to families with historical leadership status, or both. For this reason, parties have persistently been underrepresented in the chamber. The parties that succeeded in entering the legislative body were those that either represented specific ethnic interests, like the Armenian Tashnak party, or parties that are more or less leadership groups" like the National Liberal party and the Progressive Socialist party (PSP).[26] Whatever impressive organizational structure a party possesses, decision making remains the prerogative of the leader or founding father and the associates of his choice. The institutions of a party generally function as no more than rubber stamps for the leader's decisions; membership is maintained and expanded through a complex system of patron-client relationships.

Patron-client relationships characterize progressive parties as much as traditional ones. A figurehead gains support for his party less by espousing an ideology than by exploiting his position in the community. Paternalism is well entrenched in the political dynamics of Lebanon.

The war has had its effect on party politics in Lebanon in three different ways. First, it has led to the establishment of parties that are populist, anti-establishment, and progressive, rejecting the traditional rules of the game in Lebanon, like the Lebanese Forces and the *Hizbullah* (party of God). Second, the war has weakened other parties by shaking up their traditional power bases. Most of the prewar parties have suffered, the Phalangists and National Liberals party losing a large part of their constituencies to the Lebanese Forces and Amal to Hizbullah. Other parties, such as the *Najjade,* have virtually ceased to exist. Thirdly, parties were forced to accommodate their structures to the ideological and political environment of the war. Thus the three traditional parties that have lost their founding fathers, the *Kataeb* (Phalangist), the National Liberals party, and the Progressive Socialist party, are instituting structural changes to cope with new developments.

By differentiating among parties based on the socionational space addressed by each, the following three categories emerge.[27]

Trans-Lebanese Parties

Trans-Lebanese parties do not consider Lebanon to be a nation-state but part of a larger national entity. The relevant larger entity is Greater Syria for the Syrian National Social Party (SNSP) founded by Antun Sa'adah in the late thirties. A staunchly secular party that has members from different communities, the SNSP split during the war; both groups are still active politically and militarily. The Ba'ath party, founded in 1942, views Lebanon as an integral part of the Arab nation. In Lebanon there exists a Syrian Ba'ath and an Iraqi Ba'ath owing allegiance to Syria and Iraq, respectively.

The Hizbullah, founded in 1982, take *Dar al-islam* (the abode of Islam) as the proper place for Lebanon; this is a militant Shi'a party that calls for the establishment of an Islamic republic in Lebanon and closely identifies itself with Iran.

The Lebanese Parties

The Lebanese parties divide naturally into sectarian and secular groups. The *Kataeb* party founded by Pierre Gemayel in 1936 is a sectarian group dominated by Maronites that espouses an exclusive form of Lebanese nationalism. The Kataeb sees itself as guardian of the state and system and was, until the war, the largest and strongest sectarian organization in Lebanon. The National Liberal Party, founded by President Camille Chamoun in 1958, is ideologically close to the Kataeb but less structured and dominated by the charismatic Chamoun. And, unlike the Kataeb, the National Liberals count among their powerful members, traditional/conservative politicians who belong to the different Muslim sects, mainly Shi'as and Druze. The National Bloc party, led by Raymond Edde since 1949, was founded by Emile Edde, Raymond's father and president of Lebanon under the French mandate. The party is not well structured; it resembles a leadership group. It is worth noting that as a result of Edde's staunch anti-sectarianism, the self-exiled leader of the party has gained a constituency that cuts across sectarian lines and goes beyond his own party. All three of these parties consider Lebanon an integral part of the Arab world but hold different sorts of reservations about the level of commitment to Arab causes that Lebanon should maintain. They represent the Lebanonist constituency of the National Pact.

The Lebanese Forces, on the other hand, form a Christian party that opposes the views of the traditional Christian parties by rejecting the spirit of compromise embodied in the Pact; they consider the identity of Lebanon to be entirely distinct from Arab identity. Founded as a *force de frappe* of the Lebanonist constituency, the Lebanese Forces are the strongest political and military Lebanese organization. The originally Kataeb military organization established by Bashir Gemayel, went through an organizational metamorphosis and severed its ties with the party in 1985. It is now led by Samir Geagea flanked by a command council of young militants espousing a form of integral Lebanese nationalism. On the Muslim side, Amal (which stands for Lebanese Resistance Detachments), also called the Movement of the Deprived, was founded by a cleric named Musa al-Sadr in 1974. It is a strictly Shi'a organization that espouses Shi'a sectarian goals such as the need for a redistribution of the power among the sects to redress injustices from which the Shi'a community has suffered. Amal has become a major military force in Lebanon and is closely allied with Syria.

The Progressive Socialist party, founded by Kamal Jumblatt in 1949 and headed by his son Walid since 1976, is another major military force in Lebanon. The party, as its name indicates, began by advocating socioeconomic and political reforms. It profited from the traditional, sectarian, and secular leadership of the founder, who was able to appeal to both his Druze constituency, and the modernizing liberals and intellectuals. The party, which originally included both Christians and Muslims in its ranks and elite, has more recently been transformed into a sectarian party. What it gained in expansion of its power base among the Druze, for whom it now speaks, it lost in appeal to other communities, despite the fact that some of its top ranking officials remain Christian or Muslim. The party is an ally of Syria, but has been able, unlike Amal, to maintain a margin of maneuverability following policies that are not always in accord with Syria's.

Among secular groups, the Lebanese Communist party is the most important. Founded in 1922, the Communist party's influence was, for a long time, marginal in Lebanese politics. Its members are recruited from all socioeconomic groups and from different religious communities. Since 1969, it has gained an importance out of all proportion to its size by being vocal and active in the Lebanese National Movement, a loose coalition of progressive parties. The comparatively impressive organization and ideological sophistication of the Communist party pushed it into the forefront of the coalition.

The Organization of Communist Action founded in 1971 is the

second of the secular groups. Its origins can be traced to the political metamorphosis of the Arab Nationalist Movement. Redefining the "old" Arab nationalism by marrying it to Marxism-Leninism on the Chinese Marxist model, the organization was able in its first years to appeal to all those who were discontented with the Communist party. In the end, however, it failed to maintain its ideological distinctness from the party beyond rejecting the latter's alliance with Syria and maintaining an alliance with the PLO. Since the PLO's eviction from Lebanon, the organization has kept a low profile and witnessed the steady erosion of its power.

Sub-Lebanese or Ethnic Parties

The sub-Lebanese parties generally address the interests of particular ethnic groups. Among the Kurds there exist splinter groups (e.g., the Socialist Kurdistani Party) that have little impact in Lebanese politics and are generally exploited by Syria, Iraq, or Iran. The Armenian parties have been more successful; they are active and have a slight impact in Lebanese politics. The Tashnak party, for instance, a conservative Armenian group, was able to elect deputies to the chamber and have ministers in a number of cabinets in Lebanon. The Armenian socialist Hunchak party and the small Ramgavar party are also organized and active.

At least partly because of their socioeconomic status, the Armenians, unlike the Kurds, have been able to join the mainstream of Lebanon's political life.

Foreign Policy

One of the cornerstones of Lebanon's foreign policy has been a restrained engagement in Arab affairs and the retaining of a distinct national identity, a formula derived from the National Pact. It was Lebanon, a founding member of the League of Arab States, that succeeded (along with others) in obstructing attempts to inject elements of supranationality into the league's charter. The second cornerstone of Lebanon's foreign policy was its close association with the Western world. The open political system, the economic liberalism, and its historical and cultural tradition reinforced the Western orientation.

In terms of policy actions, Lebanon was supposed to abstain from getting involved in bloc politics in the Arab world. It was hoped that the Lebanese could strike a balance between the burdens of its Arab commitments and its specificity, a specificity that was defined negatively, in terms of the minimal possible commitment to a common Arab cause. It was Pierre Gemayel who adopted the slogan, "The strength of Lebanon lies in its weakness," which served as the basic tenet of Lebanon's policy toward the Arab-Israeli conflict (AIC).

Meanwhile the Lebanese foreign policy process has been overloaded by the geostrategic location of Lebanon, with the massive Palestinian presence in its south, which took on new importance in the AIC, and by the combination of a weak state and an open system whereby foreign policy and domestic politics are intertwined.

The Khoury Mandate (1943–1952)

During the mandate of the first president of independent Lebanon, Bishara al-Khoury, Lebanon did not face any divisive or controversial issues in its Arab milieu. It fulfilled its obligations when it joined the Arab states in the war for Palestine and followed those same states later by signing an armistice agreement with the newly established Jewish state. Al-Khoury's sensitivity to the Arab environment was behind his refusal to join the security plan sponsored by France and Britain aimed at entrenching the State of Israel's existence in the Middle East.

The Chamoun Mandate (1952–1958)

The Chamoun regime came to power in an era that featured increasing superpower involvement in the Middle East and the beginning of the Arab cold war, which pitted a nonaligned bloc headed by Nasser against a Western bloc centered around Iraq. Chamoun's unconditional identification with Western policies clashed with Nasser's Arab policy. Chamoun refused, for example, to sever diplomatic relations with France and Britain in the aftermath of the Suez crisis and later subscribed to Eisenhower's "containment doctrine." The tension with Nasser was reflected at home in the "Arabist" constituency where Chamoun's actions were perceived as a betrayal of the National Pact. Civil war broke out in Lebanon, the American military became involved, and the situation did not return to normal until the Chamoun regime ended.

The Shihab Mandate (1958–1964)

General Fouad Shihab, who came to power through an Egyptian-American understanding in 1958, instituted a reversal in Lebanese foreign policy. Assuming power in the year of the establishment of the Egyptian-Syrian union, Shihab grasped the lessons of Chamoun's unbalanced policy and the heavy domestic price it incurred. Seeking an entente with Nasser at the beginning of his regime, Shihab secured Egyptian approval of his foreign policy in exchange for a restrained realignment of the Lebanese position on Nasser's Arab policies. Shihab was able to maintain stability at home by agreeing not to oppose Nasser in the Arab world or support his foes.

The Helou Mandate (1964–1970)

The regime of Charles Helou maintained the spirit, orientation, and much of the leadership of Shihab's rule, but Helou was faced with challenges in the Arab world that he proved unable to accommodate without creating tension at home. The defeat of 1967 weakened Nasser, ushering in an era which saw the ascendency of the PLO and the beginning of a new era in the Israeli-Palestinian conflict for which Lebanon provided the main stage. In 1969, Helou temporarily averted a national crisis over the PLO's status in Lebanon by accommodating PLO demands in the Cairo Agreement.

The Frangieh Mandate (1970–1976)

Suleiman Frangieh came to power to reckon with an expanding PLO presence in Lebanon that commanded the support of an Arab world who found it convenient to fulfill its obligations to the Palestinian cause through Lebanon. An agreement with the PLO was reached in 1973, but the underlying conflict remained. In order to check the rapidly growing Palestinian influence in Lebanon, Frangieh turned to the Syrians, but he soon entangled himself in a bipolarization that pitted Syria against the PLO and its supporters, Iraq and Egypt.

The Sarkis Mandate (1976–1982)

President Elias Sarkis assumed office amidst a raging civil war. He maintained Frangieh's alliance with Syria despite tensions that arose as Syria tried to influence domestic policies. Sarkis avoided confrontation with Syria and attempted to temper Syria's influence by encouraging an Arab multilateral role in Lebanon. Syria, however, was already in a position to veto attempts by other Arab states to interfere in Lebanon. Lebanon was evidently becoming more an agent of other countries' foreign policies than an autonomous player in the international arena.

The Gemayel Mandate (1982–1988)

President Gemayel came to power after the assassination of his brother, President-elect Bashir. No sooner was the regime installed than Gemayel chose to align himself with the United States, believing that the Americans were the only ones capable of securing the withdrawal of all foreign troops from Lebanon. This policy, however, did little more than alienate Syria, and Gemayel was finally forced to abrogate the Lebanese-Israeli Accord. Gemayel spent the next years rallying between the Americans and the Syrians, failing to institutionalize a rapprochement with either and avoiding conflict with both. The Gemayel policy of waltzing between Syrians and Americans was a major factor in the destructive stalemate that Lebanon found itself in at the end of the Gemayel regime.

Current Affairs

If one divides and names the phases of Lebanon's "internal war" in terms of the forces that played the largest roles, we get the following divisions and labels.[28]

The Lebanese Phase

On February 26, 1975, a demonstration sponsored by leftist groups in the city of Sidon degenerated into a clash with the army when a leftist leader was shot to death. The leftist groups enlisted the support of the whole Arabist constituency on the issue. The government was paralyzed because of the differences that emerged over the role of the army in domestic matters. The crisis forced consideration of issues such as political reforms, abolishment of sectarianism, and the political privileges of the Maronite community.

The Palestinian Phase

The feelings of discontent and resentment among the Lebanonist constituency over the growing presence of the PLO and its "violation of the national sovereignty" provoked some of the existing parties to form militias of their own, creating a counter-force to the Palestinian armed presence. The government never attempted to obstruct the militarization process; indeed, some government leaders were known to support it. The rising political tension culminated in an incident in Beirut on April 13, 1975, between a Kataeb militia and the Palestinians. Fighting soon spread in Beirut; other groups took sides—the leftist groups and the Arabist constituency supported the PLO. Lebanese-Palestinian meetings mediated by Arab states failed to contain the fighting, and when the government decided to freeze the military activities of the PLO in southern

Lebanon, the PLO rejected the decision, the conflict escalated, and the fighting intensified.

The Syrian Phase

The signing of the second Egyptian-Israeli Disengagement Agreement in the summer of 1975 provoked a strong reaction from Syria, the PLO, and other Arab states who saw that the agreement tilted the regional balance of power in favor of the State of Israel. Syria settled on a policy which would bring together Syria, Jordan, Lebanon, and the PLO to compensate for the "loss" of Egypt. This allowed Syria to act as a mediator while its Lebanese surrogates fought together on the side of the PLO. The policy, however, required an extension of its influence over Lebanon, and Syria was growing nervous about a potential Arab role that could jeopardize its goals there. In January 1976, when the military balance began to favor the PLO-leftist alliance, the Israelis warned that a change in the status quo would lead to Israel's intervention. For Syria, a leftist takeover would both install a radical regime on its own borders and strengthen the PLO, making it less dependent on Syria. Such a scenario was as unacceptable to the Syrians as was the potential military confrontation with Israel. Hence the United States and Syria developed a common interest in containing the crisis. Syria chose to adopt a new moderate and balanced approach which earned it the support of the conservative Arab states and the approval of the United States, who, in turn, convinced the Christian militias to cooperate with Syria. The policy change also earned Syria the support of Lebanese President Frangieh. As tensions between Syria and the PLO-leftist alliance erupted in military clashes, Syria shifted its policy to support the Lebanonist constituency.

The Arab Phase

The PLO, at the beginning opposed to the Arabization of the conflict, was calling now for an Arab initiative to balance the Syrian offensive. At the request of Lebanon on June 1, 1976, the Syrian forces entered the country and the crisis became a Syrian-Palestinian confrontation. Algeria and Libya tried to mediate the conflict while Iraq and Egypt sided with the PLO. Attempts at mediation by Saudi Arabia, Kuwait, and the Arab League failed. Saudi Arabia was finally forced to use its influence with Syria to bring the latter to attend a mini-summit held in the Saudi capital in October. Egypt, Lebanon, the PLO, Kuwait, Syria, and Saudi Arabia were the participants. At the summit, an understanding was reached between Syria, and Egypt on the adoption of a strategy for a political settlement of the conflict. Syria succeeded in gaining Egypt's support for its presence in Lebanon under the nominal sponsorship of the Arab League. The PLO was left with no option but to accept the arrangement as a fait accompli. An Arab summit was later held in Cairo to extend a consensual Arab legitimacy to the arrangements worked out in Saudi Arabia.

The Israeli Phase

The situation in northern Lebanon returned to normal, but in the South a war of attrition developed between the PLO-leftist alliance and the "Christian" militias supported by the State of Israel. As the war intensified, the State of Israel warned that it would intervene directly to restore stability and drive away the Palestinians. The Egyptian decision in November 1977 to begin bilateral negotiations with the State of Israel drew the PLO and Syria together in a radical stand while the war in the South developed into heavy fighting, raids, and counterraids. On March 14, 1978, Israeli forces invaded Lebanon. According to the State of Israel, the aim of the invasion was the establishment of a ten-kilometer security belt along and inside its borders with Lebanon. The area was to be secured for the State of Israel's Lebanese allies. The Security Council of the United Nations adopted resolutions which led to the deployment of a peacekeeping force (UNIFIL) on March 24. Under mounting international pressure, the State of Israel began a phased withdrawal from southern Lebanon on April 11, linking its complete withdrawal to guarantees that the PLO would not return to the evacuated area and would end attacks against the State of Israel from southern Lebanon. The PLO agreed to cease its military activities in that area and the Israeli troops began their final withdrawal on June 13.

In April 1981, the Israelis warned the Syrians, engaged in fierce battles with the Lebanese Forces, not to escalate the fighting. The Israeli Air Force struck Syrian positions in the Beka valley and downed two Syrian helicopters as a warning to Syria not to increase its military presence in Lebanon or upset the existing configuration of power. The Likud government policy at the time consisted of support for the anti-Syrian Lebanese Forces in an effort to undermine Syria's influence in Lebanon and consequently mollify the PLO.

Despite attempts by both the United States and Saudi Arabia in the summer of 1981 to contain the war of attrition between the State of Israel and the PLO, the daily clashes and increasing tension were setting the stage for a new Arab-Israeli war. The State of Israel invaded Lebanon on June 5, 1982. A force of 20,000 men entered Lebanon from three directions, pushing through the western, central and eastern sectors. The UNIFIL units were bypassed without confrontation. Intensive fighting spread all over southern Lebanon while Syrians and Israelis faced each other in aerial combat. By June 12, the Israelis had occupied almost one third of Lebanon, and by the end of June West Beirut was under siege. Meanwhile, Americans were actively engaged with the concerned parties in working out the terms of a PLO evacuation from Beirut and the deployment of a multinational force (MNF). Despite successive calls by the UN Security Council, the Israelis stepped up military pressure on West Beirut that included psychological warfare. Finally the American plan was approved by all parties and the evacuation of the PLO from Beirut was initiated on August 21 under the supervision of a multinational force of American, French, and Italian troops. The force itself withdrew from Beirut on September 13. The very next day, President-elect Bashir Gemayel was killed at his party office in East Beirut, and Israeli forces moved into West Beirut under the pretext of maintaining order and peace.

The American Phase

The United States had been involved since the first days of the invasion, and the Americans were active on many fronts. First, they worked out a cease-fire between the Israelis and the Syrians. Second, through the Saudis and the Sunni leadership in Beirut, they settled with the PLO the modalities of the latter's withdrawal from Beirut. On the military front, the United States led the MNF in monitoring the safe withdrawal of the PLO. In effect, the 1982 invasion of Lebanon provided the United States with a golden opportunity to promote its grand design for the Middle East outlined in the Reagan Plan. The plan offered an American formula for the settlement of the Arab-Israeli conflict. It sought to weaken Syria, to eradicate the PLO's military power from Lebanon, to bring Lebanon into negotiations with the State of Israel, to stabilize Lebanon under American influence (thereby regaining the influence the United States had lost during the civil war), and, finally, to keep the Soviet Union out of the Middle East by weakening its allies and containing trouble spots that might provide opportunities for Soviet influence.

The U.S. goals were facilitated by Gemayel's pro-American orientation. On December 28, the Lebanese-Israeli negotiations began under the official auspices of the United States. The negotiations went through five stages: exploratory Lebanese-American talks on October 17; bilateral talks between the United States and Lebanon and between the United States and the State of Israel on the form and substance of the negotiations; formulation of the conference agenda that featured the points on negotiations; trilateral negotiations on different parts of the Lebanese-Israeli accord, which led to a stalemate in March 1983; and finally the shuttle diplomacy of the U.S. secretary of state beginning at the end of April and ending with the signing of the final text of the accord on May 17.[29]

When the Lebanese appeared reluctant to sign the accord, U.S. Secretary of State George Shultz stepped up American pressure, arguing that "we" cannot allow the Soviets and the Syrians to impose their veto.[30] Once the accord was signed, fighting erupted between the army and the opposition forces, and the United States was drawn into the conflict by summer. The American initiative had ended in shambles, alienating Syria and part of Lebanon, and forcing the Lebanese government into a high-risk, no-yield position. The United States was left alone when its Western allies sought disengagement from the Lebanese situation. Amid these developments, a conference on national dialogue among the warlords of Lebanon convened in Geneva (October 31–November 4), putatively to discuss possible reforms but primarily to ask President Gemayel to seek a way out of the stalemate with the Americans.[31] The Lebanese-American summit, held on December 1 in Washington, D.C., brought no results. In Lebanon in early 1984, the Syrian pressure was mounting, the fighting had intensified, and the army had begun to disintegrate along sectarian lines. Amal and the PSP extended their control over West Beirut and the Wazzan government resigned on February 5. The end of the American phase was sealed with the withdrawal of U.S. forces and the abrogation of the accord on March 5.

The Syrian Phase

Less than two years after its military debacle, Syria emerged as the main power broker in Lebanon. It orchestrated the fall of the Lebanese-Israeli accord and forced a reorientation of Lebanon's policy. Gemayel's visit to Damascus on February 29, 1984, ushered in a new era that forced the United States and its Western allies to recognize Syria's legitimate interests in Lebanon. The State of Israel also reversed the decision that linked its withdrawal to a simultaneous withdrawal of the Syrian and Palestinian forces. Meanwhile, in an attempt to bring the PLO in line with Syria's strategy in the AIC, Syria engaged in a war by proxy against the PLO through radical Palestinian factions and Syria's Lebanese allies. This was Syria's golden opportunity to try to bring Lebanon fully into its sphere of influence. It was important for Syria to mend the broken Lebanese regime and to promote a domestic settlement in Lebanon that would bring stability under its supervision.

Another conference on national dialogue was held in Lausanne on March 12–20. Syria's role this time was more that of mediator on domestic issues, as a consensus apparently existed concerning external issues. A government of national unity was formed on April 30, 1984, according to a Lausanne resolution but issues of contention between the different groups united in the government remained unsolved. Even problems between allies developed into military confrontation, such as the fighting between Amal and the PSP over the control of West Beirut. In order to contain the differences among its allies and create a counterweight to the Christian Conservative forces, Syria compelled the leaders of major opposition groups to join in an alliance that was officially formed on July 28, 1985, under the name of the National Union Front. The alliance, however, did not end the conflict between its two main pillars; Amal and the PSP engaged each other in fierce battle in November.

Syria again stepped up its pressure on the Lebanese parties and invited the leaders of the three main sectarian and military groups in Lebanon—the Lebanese Forces, Amal, and the PSP—to a conference to end the war. A peace project was adopted that called for reforms and closer institutionalized Lebanese-Syrian relations. The Tripartite Agreement, as it became known, provoked staunch opposition from the president, the Kataeb, and the majority of the Lebanese Forces, who considered it "a capitulation of Lebanon's sovereignty to Syria." In mid-January 1986, less than a month after its inception, the agreement became obsolete when a crucial figure in its formation, Elie Hobeika, was ousted from the leadership of the Lebanese Forces. The collapse of the agreement led to political paralysis and further disintegration of the government's institutions. The prime minister and the ministers of the opposition— Syrian allies—boycotted the president at the instigation of Syria; no Council of Ministers has been held since. Attempts at compromise failed to produce results; rigid bipolarization over the agreement was entrenched in a game of mutual veto.

The Relebanization Phase

Attempts at electing a pro-Syrian candidate to the presidency and another candidate supported by both Syria and the United States at the end of the Gemayel period were undermined by the Lebanese Forces and their allies, who used their influence in Parliament to prevent the formation of a quorum necessary to approve the holding of an election. Gemayel was thus compelled by General Michel Aoun, commander in chief of the Lebanese Army, and by the Lebanese Forces to name Aoun head of a military government. Executive power was entrusted to Aoun whose personal influence increased when a number of Muslim ministers he appointed to the cabinet refused to accept the appointment. Syria and Lebanese opposition groups rejected Aoun's government, preferring instead to recognize Selim Hoss as president. As a result, two parallel governments, each one claiming legitimacy, were formed. The country was being devastated as numerous third parties—the United States, Saudi Arabia, France, Algeria, the Arab League, and even the Vatican—attempted to break the stalemate.

On March 14, 1989, Aoun announced a war of liberation against the Syrian army in Lebanon, resulting in a new cycle of violence and bloodshed. Amidst these developments, an Arab League summit convened in Casablanca to form a tripartite committee composed of the heads of state of Algeria, Morocco, and Saudi Arabia to work out a settlement to the Lebanese crisis. The Arab option became an attractive alternative to many of the outside powers interested in the situation, and the committee was endorsed by the United States, the USSR, and the European Community. After intensive, and at times uneasy, consultations with numerous interested states and groups and with the different Lebanese factions, the committee was able to arrange a cease-fire and organized a meeting of Lebanese parliamentarians in Ta'if, Saudi Arabia.

The result of this meeting was the Ta'if Document, which centered around the concept of a National Reconciliation Charter based on a fairer power sharing agreement between the confessional groups. Aoun fiercely denounced the document but could not prevent parliament from formally approving it and electing René Mu'awwad as president on November 5, 1989. Mu'awwad was assassinated only seventeen days later and was replaced by Elias Harawi —a strong supporter of the Ta'if process and the resulting document.

While the international community rushed to recognize the Harawi government after the Mu'awwad tragedy, Aoun persisted in opposing not only the Ta'if document but the formal government apparatus as well. He refused to leave the presidential palace or to recognize the new president. A stalemate developed and when military action was initiated to remove him, Lebanon's internecine civil war took on a new dimension: Aoun's forces, backed by Iraq, battled government forces and progovernment militias, backed by Syria, in some of the bloodiest battles yet. On October 13, 1990, government forces and Syrian troops crushed General Aoun's resistance, and he took refuge in the French Embassy. President Harawi then moved quickly to reunify Beirut. Brandishing slogans of a militia-free Beirut, Harawi mustered popular support from a war-weary population for a voluntary disarmament of militias. By December, many militias had disarmed, and Beirut's barracades were dismantled.

NOTES

1. On the Ma'ns and Shihabis periods, see Philip Hitti, Lebanon in History, 3d ed. (New York: St. Martin's Press, 1967), pp. 371–97.

2. Kamal Salibi, The Modern History of Lebanon (New York: Frederick A. Praeger, 1965), p. xiii.

3. In Edmond Rabbat, La Formation historique du liban politique et constitutional (Beyrouth: Librairie Orientale, 1973), p. 522.

4. Ibid., p. 524.

5. Clovis Maksoud, "Lebanon and Arab Nationalism," in Politics in Lebanon, ed. Leonard Binder (New York: John Wiley and Sons, 1966), p. 241.

6. Ralph Crow, "Parliament in the Lebanese Political System," in Legislatures in Developmental Perspectives, eds. Allan Kornberg and Lloyd D. Musolf (Durham, N.C.: Duke University Press, 1970), pp. 274–75.

7. Malcolm Kerr, "Political Decision-Making in a Confessional Democracy," in Politics in Lebanon, p. 202.

8. Rabbat, pp. 75ff. These are Greek-Orthodox, Syrian-Orthodox, Armenian-Gregorian, Nestorian, Evangelical, Maronite, Greek-Catholic, Armenian Catholic, Syrian Catholic, Chaldean, Latin, Sunni, Shi'a, Druze, and Israelite.

9. Ibid., p. 102.

10. Paul D. Starr, "Ethnic Categories and Identification in Lebanon," *Urban Life* 7, no. 1 (April 1978): 114.

11. Georges Corm, *Geopolitique du conflit libanais* (Paris: Editions la Decouverte, 1986), pp. 161–62.

12. Edward Azar, "Lebanon and Its Political Culture: Conflict and Integration in Lebanon," in *The Emergence of a New Lebanon: Fantasy or Reality?* ed. Edward Azar et al. (New York: Praeger Publishers, 1984), p. 39.

13. Halim Barakat, "Social and Political Integration in Lebanon: A Case of Social Mosaic," *Middle East Journal* 27, no. 3 (Summer 1973): 301–18.

14. Sidney Verba, "Comparative Political Culture," in *Political Culture and Political Development*, ed. Lucien Pye and Sidney Verba (Princeton: Princeton University Press, 1965), p. 513.

15. Arendt Lijphart, "Consociational Democracy," *World Politics* 21, no. 2 (January 1969): 207–25.

16. See, for example, Richard Hrair Dekmejian, "Consociational Democracy in Crisis: The Case of Lebanon," *Comparative Politics* 10, no. 2 (January 1978): 251–65.

17. Joseph Chamie, "Religious Groups in Lebanon: A Descriptive Investigation," *International Journal of Middle East Studies* 11, no. 1 (1980): 179–80.

18. Gordon Barthos, "Lebanon Faces New Round of Savagery," *Toronto Star*, January 19, 1989, p. A.3.

19. Hamdy Ali and Nabil Abd al-Nour, "An Appraisal of the Six Year Plan of Lebanon 1972–1977," *Middle East Journal* 29, no. 2 (Spring 1975): 151.

20. Ibid., pp. 151–65.

21. Charles Kindleberger, *Foreign Trade and the National Economy* (New Haven: Yale University Press, 1962), p. 145.

22. Nadim Khalaf, *Economic Implications of the Size of Nations* (Leiden: E.J. Brill, 1971), p. 186.

23. Enver Koury, *The Crisis in the Lebanese System: Confessionalism and Chaos* (Washington, D.C.: American Enterprise Institute for Public Policy Research, 1976), p. 35.

24. Chamie, p. 181.

25. Samir Makdisi, "An Appraisal of Lebanon's Post-War Economic Development and a Look to the Future," *Middle East Journal* 31, no. 3 (Summer 1977): 267–80.

26. See Arnold Hottinger, "Zu'ama and Parties in the Lebanese Crisis of 1958," *Middle East Journal* 15, no.2 (Spring 1961): 127–40.

27. The chapter does not present an exhaustive list of the parties nor does it analyze their ideologies or policies. Both tasks are beyond the scope of the study. But it does shed light on the main parties with the view of drawing the map of party politics in Lebanon.

28. Internal is more exact than domestic in describing the war in Lebanon, for it is more encompassing in terms of players; see Antoine Messarra, *Prospects for Lebanon: The Challenge of Coexistence* (Oxford: Center for Lebanese Studies, 1988), p.24.

29. Ghassan Tuéni, *Une Guerre pour les autres* (Paris: Editions Jean Claude Lattes, 1985), p. 283.

30. Ibid., p. 328, citing Shultz on the "Soviet" veto; and Wadi A. Haddad, *Lebanon: The Politics of Revolving Doors* (N.Y.: Praeger Special Studies, 1985), p. 92. Haddad cited Shultz on the "Syrian" veto.

31. Haddad, p. 114.

ADDITIONAL BIBLIOGRAPHY

Cobban, Helena. *The Making of Modern Lebanon*. London: Hutchinson, 1985.

Evron, Yair. *War and Intervention in Lebanon: The Israeli-Syrian Deterrence Dialogue*. London: Croom Helm, 1986.

Gilmour, David. *The Fractured Country*. Oxford: M. Robertson, 1983.

Odeh, B.J. *Lebanon—Dynamics of Conflict: A Modern Political History*. London: Zed Books, 1985.

Picard, Elizabeth. *Liban: État de discorde*. Paris: Ed. Flammarion, 1988.

Randal, Jonathan. *Going All the Way: Christian Warlords, Israeli Adventures, and the War in Lebanon*. New York: Viking Press, 1983.

Salibi, Kamal. *A House of Many Mansions: The History of Lebanon Reconsidered*. London: I.B. Tauris and Co., 1988.

Schiff, Ze'ev, and Ehud Ya'ari. *Israel's Lebanon War*. New York: Simon and Schuster, 1984.

10

The Hashemite Kingdom of Jordan

Kamel S. Abu Jaber

Jordan is both a young and an ancient entity. Its history is inter-twined with the events of the Bible, the rise of the three great monotheistic religions, as well as ancient, medieval, and modern civilizations. Along its King's Highway running from Damascus in the north to the port of Aqaba on the Red Sea in the south, ancient civilizations flourished and great events occurred. The Arab Semitic people of Jordan can trace their history back to the second wave of Semitic immigration from central Arabia about 2900 B.C., followed a thousand years later by the Hebrews. Names that generate a variety of rich images, both biblical and modern, are associated with Jordan: Gilead, Rabbath Ammon, the giants or *Amalekak*, the Amorites, the Moabites, the Edomites, the Israelites and the Prophet Moses, the Assyrians, Chaldeans, Persians, Nabateans, the Greeks, the Romans, Christianity and Jesus Christ, Islam and the Prophet Muhammad.

The land of Jordan, as indeed the entire area of the Middle East, witnessed the rise of a new civilization that added the final touch to the character of the people and their land. Since the first battle between the rising Muslim civilization and the Roman legions led by the commanders of their emperor, Heraclius, at Mu'ta in South Jordan in 624 A.D., Islam has become not only Jordan's major religion but the fountain of its culture and customs. To the ancient struggle between Judaism and Christianity over the land and its soul another dimension was thus added. The Zionist infiltration and penetration of Palestine in the past century must be understood against this background. Many Arab intellectuals view this latest struggle over Palestine, in which Jordan is very intensely involved, as yet another modern crusade to capture the geographic, symbolic, and spiritual heart of the area.

The modern history of Jordan commences with the conclusion of World War I and the secret Anglo-French Sykes-Picot Agreement dividing Mesopotamia and Greater Syria into spheres of influence politely called mandates (not colonies) between England and France. The mandates were created by the dismantling of the last great Islamic empire, the Ottoman, which ruled the Middle East for four centuries, from 1516 to 1916. The Arabs fought on the side of the Allies in the hope that they would gain independence. Sharif Hussain of Mecca, great-grandfather to King Hussain of Jordan, leader of the great Arab revolt against the Ottomans, emphasized that Arab participation in the war effort was predicated on gaining independence upon the war's conclusion. The famous Hussain-McMahon correspondence clearly states Arab demands and expectations. The Sykes-Picot Agreement of 1916 and the 1917 Balfour Declaration, promising the British government's help to the Zionists in establishing a "national home" for the Jews in Palestine, set the stage for the subsequent turmoil and unrest that have beset the entire Middle East region since then. The King-Crane Commission had warned that the Zionist program in Palestine could not be carried out except by force.

In this atmosphere of imperial intrigue and division of spoils, along with a sense of betrayal on the part of the Arabs, the modern state of Jordan came into being. The British Colonial Office called for a conference of its principal Middle East experts to formulate a unified policy for the whole region. At the conference, held in Cairo on March 12–24, 1921, and attended by Winston Churchill, then colonial secretary, it was decided to offer the kingship of Iraq to King Faisal, while Prince (later king) Abdullah, Faisal's elder brother, was to be offered the emirate of Trans-Jordan. Churchill was to go to Jerusalem to discuss the subject with Prince Abdullah. The prince in the meantime had gone to Ma'an in south Jordan to lead a force of fewer than 2,000 men heading for Syria to try to restore his brother Faisal to the throne. Later Churchill persuaded the prince to rule over the area east of the Jordan with British assistance, and, on April 1, 1921, the new state of Jordan came into being. The British undertook to obtain from France a liberalization of its policy in Syria in order that an Arab government under Prince Abdullah might be established. The French were in no mood to change their policy, and Abdullah's dream of uniting Greater Syria was to remain unfulfilled throughout his life, a dream that was later to play a major role in inter-Arab politics of the region.

Abdullah came to a country that was a semiprimitive, largely desert domain with a small, illiterate, pastoral, and rural population. His immediate task was to assert central authority by abolishing the local governments established by the British, each with its own British adviser. Julius Abramson was appointed British resident and Jordan was granted £180,000 (British) as an annual subsidy. The 1923 London Agreement granted Jordan "independence," affirming its separate status and exemption from the provisions of the Palestine Mandate, though it was still under the administrative supervision of the British high commissioner. The British government issued a memorandum in September 1922, approved by the League of Nations, that specifically excluded Jewish settlement from the Trans-Jordan.

Political Development: Framework of Political Life

Two personalities have colored and dominated the history and politics of Jordan since its establishment in modern times: King Abdullah from 1921 to 1951 and King Hussain since 1953. Their style of leadership and ability to convert the once near-barren land into a modern state continue to leave an imprint on the land and its people. Abdullah's strong personality was instrumental in persuading the once independent tribal society to accept central authority. Still, five tribal rebellions took place in the 1920s, each of which was handled with force.

With a population of some 400,000 in 1921, Jordan's government was simple and direct. A civil service was slowly trained, and a small army headed by F. G. Peake, a British officer, was organized. In 1923 the police and army were combined into the Arab Legion with Peake Pasha as its commander. The government was centralized under a small executive council with British advisers that served as an administrative arm for the *emir*, the prince. A further step in granting a measure of self-government to Jordan was undertaken by the British in 1928. A Jordanian-British treaty was signed on February 20, 1928, relaxing, though not removing, British control over the government. A few weeks later, on April 16, 1928, a constitution called the Organic Law was promulgated providing for a two-step elected legislative council. The "powers of legislation and administration" were vested in the emir. "Above this native structure stood the mandatory government for Palestine and Trans-Jordan, represented in Amman by a permanent British Resident . . . [with] special prerogatives in regard to . . . legislation, foreign relations, fiscal matters and the protection of foreigners and minorities."[1] Only in 1934 through an amendment to the treaty did Jordan obtain the right to appoint consular representatives abroad.

Though vocal, local opposition to these arrangements was largely ineffective. The opposition organized the First National Conference, held in Amman on July 25, 1928. The *Istiqlal* (Independence) party composed of Jordanian and Syrian nationalists was quite vocal, while the other two parties, *al-Sha'b* (People) and *al-Nahdah* (Revival), were conservative and largely pro-government. Two additional parties were organized in the 1930s, *al-Tadamun* (Cooperation) and *al-Mutamar al-Watani* (National Conference), but they also lacked clear programs and were too organized around personalities.

Soon the country turned to the task of nation building, with the strong though moderate personality of the emir permeating its entire evolutionary development. Between 1928 and 1946, when the first Jordanian constitution was promulgated, five legislative councils were elected. Only the first was dissolved because of its opposition to the government. Writing of this period with some nostalgia, Sir John Bagot Glubb, better known as Glubb Pasha and the commander of Jordan's army from 1939 to 1956, says, "From 1932 to 1948 the whole of Jordan was one of the happiest little countries in the world . . . with the rest of the world in agony, with the neighboring Arab countries in constant upheaval, in Trans-Jordan for sixteen years nothing could go wrong."

Jordan's politics were indeed quiet, and the upheaval that was rocking neighboring Palestine because of increased Zionist militancy and the illegal immigration of Jews into that country did not exist there. Every Friday the emir opened his palace for the leaders and notables of the country to come and visit and consult with him on matters of the day. He established the paternal patriarchal system that is still in evidence in the style of leadership of his grandson, King Hussain.

It is interesting to note that between 1931 and 1946, all the members of the legislative councils were elected from only thirty-six prominent families in Jordan. During this period the politics of Jordan was dominated principally by local issues. The British resident, his advice, and the advice rendered through British advisers to the government constituted a very important center of power. The bureaucracy attracting the emerging educated class composed another center, while the army made up a third. The tribes and families constituted a fourth major center of power. Some of these tribe-family members were recruited to major positions in both the army and the bureaucracy, while their chiefs were coopted into senior ministerial posts and the legislative council. Above this whole structure stood, of course, the most important center of power, that of emir Abdullah, whose personality dominated the whole spectrum of politics. Gradually and surely, yet always willing to compromise, he succeeded in converting the tribal society into an emerging nation-state that, against all odds, was able to survive and prosper.

The Jordanian Parliament

Following World War II and in accordance with wartime promises by Britain, a new Anglo-Jordanian treaty was concluded on March 22, 1946. The treaty recognized Jordan's independence as a kingdom and ended the system of mandates. A new constitution was promulgated on February 1, 1947, and, accordingly, a new electoral law providing for a bicameral legislature was passed. Since then, the electoral law based on the principle of proportional representation has, with certain amendments, become the foundation of Jordan's political life. It provided for the election of Muslim, Christian, Bedouin, Circassian, and Chechen representatives. Though the 1947 constitution was an improvement over the 1928 Organic Law, it too fell short of national expectations. Among other things, it failed to make government responsible to the parliament, the *Majlis al-Ummah* (Council of the People). Only independents and the government-sponsored Revival candidates ran for the first parliament, dissolved on January 1, 1950, to arrange for new parliamentary elections following the union between Jordan, or the East Bank, and that part of Palestine not occupied by Israel in the 1948 war, afterward called the West Bank.

The Palestinians

With the creation of the State of Israel in 1948 and the subsequent advent of the first forced wave of Palestinian refugees into Jordan, the politics of the country entered a new phase. The newly arrived refugees, better educated and politically more aware than the Jordanians, though frustrated, bitter, and bewildered, injected an ideological element into the politics of the country. The earlier quiet, peaceful, happy atmosphere of which Glubb Pasha spoke was shattered and replaced by frenetic agitation and violence.

The addition of the West Bank and the influx of refugees into Jordan was more than a mere increase in the number of people in Jordan. The new arrivals infused intense stress into the political spectrum. Their goals of first liberating Palestine from Zionist domination and then achieving national self-determination were powerful rallying points. Thus, they responded with enthusiasm to the newly developing ideological atmosphere in the Arab world following the 1948 Arab-Israeli war and continuing through the 1950s. This was the period of the emergence of Nasserism, Ba'athism, the Muslim Brotherhood, *al-Tahrir*, the Liberation Movement, socialist ideologies, communism, and various strands of Arab nationalism. All these ideologies plus local ones had an impact on the now Jordanian-Palestinian nationalist elements in Jordan. No longer was the population of the kingdom as politically homogeneous as it once had been.

Locally, some personality-oriented political groups remained and contested seats in the parliamentary elections of the 1950s. *al-Hizb al-'Arabi al-Dusturi* (the Arab Constitutional party) and *Hizb al-Ummah* (the Nation party), both proregime groups, also ran candidates. In addition, an ideological party emerged—*al-Hizb al-Watani al-Ishtiraki* (the National Socialist party), led by Suleiman al-Nabulsi. This party attracted both the Jordanian and Palestinian intelligentsia. Thus, the elections to the second, third, fourth, and fifth parliaments of Jordan were infused with intense ideological debate, and for the first time genuine party lines emerged in the country. The opposition was legitimized by its popular following but also by the constitution of January 8, 1952, which made government responsible to parliament. Following the disturbances of 1956 through 1958, the government banned all political parties in Jordan with the exception of the Muslim Brotherhood, considered mainly a society rather than a political party. Following the ban the deputies ran as independents, more conservative and progovernment. Since then the regime has maintained its theoretical adherence to parliamentary government but with a definite shift of power from the legislative to the executive branch.

Two important events took place in the early 1950s in Jordan: the assassination of King Abdullah on July 20, 1951, and the accession to the throne of King Hussain on May 2, 1953. Though young, the new monarch proved to be a capable leader. Trained by his grandfather, he had acquired considerable political acumen, pragmatism, and vision. The five years after he assumed power was a period that witnessed an intense nationalist turmoil fueled partly by rising Arab nationalist sentiment and partly by repeated Israeli aggression along the armistice lines drawn after 1949. Also a point of contention was the American pressure to draw Jordan into the Baghdad Pact. In response, King Hussain dismissed General Glubb, Arabized the Jordanian army, and agreed to have Arab money replace the foreign subsidy to the Jordanian budget. In the mid-1950s and following the formation of the al-Nabulsi cabinet, there ensued a power struggle between progressives, inspired by Nasserite pan-Arabist ideas, and conservatives, headed by the monarchy and conservative elements. Following a series of confrontations between the king and the Nabulsi government, accompanied by street demonstrations, the king finally demanded and received the resignation of Prime Minister al-Nabulsi, an event that led to further disturbances. These events culminated in the rebellion of some army units at al-Zarqa camp, thirty kilometers north of Amman. The king thwarted it.

The Constitutional Crisis

The dismissal of the premier and the restoration of royal prerogative had a great impact on the political development of Jordan. Eliminating the ideological factor by banning the operation of political parties, these acts resulted in a return to the pre-1950 conservative hold on both cabinet and parliament. Since then, the king alone appoints the premier and decides the direction of major policies. Eliminating ideology from local debate and from the presentation of candidates for election has meant that only nonideological personalities or conservative individuals run for parliament.

The occupation of the West Bank by Israel in 1967 and the election of the ninth parliament in that year held back the formal political development of Jordan. A conservative parliament to begin with, it has become more so over the years. Given the occupation of the West Bank, no parliamentary election could be held. The ninth parliament's life was extended by constitutional amendment in the hope that a peaceful settlement of the Arab-Israeli conflict could be reached. When this still had not happened by the mid-seventies, the regime decided to convene an appointed National Consultative Assembly, which was, as its name indicates, purely consultative and mainly composed of conservative elements. Its two-year duration was set by law, and three such assemblies were convened. By 1984, seventeen years had passed since the 1967 occupation of the West Bank, and the deputies of the ninth parliament, long past their prime, were dying in rapid succession. In an attempt to maintain constitutional continuity a 1984 amendment to the constitution was passed allowing for the reconvening of this parliament. By-elections were to be held to replace the deceased deputies in the East Bank. A by-election for eight deputies was held in March 1984, and as each deputy from the East Bank dies, a by-election is held in his district to replace him. To replace deceased deputies from the West Bank, where elections cannot be held, members of parliament from both banks elect a candidate from a list of those interested.

This attempt at maintaining constitutional continuity has served the interests of preserving the conservative, nonideological status quo—a not unwelcome development as far as the regime is concerned. Defenders of these developments point out the fact that since the mid-1950s political stability has been achieved, and this in turn has permitted the evident genuine, socioeconomic development of the country. Whereas turmoil, unrest and instability have beset most neighboring Arab regimes, Jordan, it is pointed out, has been able to maintain its stability, develop in an evolutionary manner, and avoid the threat of violent coups witnessed elsewhere in the region.

Sociocultural Determinants of Politics

Studying the political development, indeed, the politics, of Jordan in terms of power—its distribution, location, and how it is practiced in the formal structure of decision making—does not tell the whole story. Judged along these lines alone, the state of Jordan may appear to be a repressive authoritarian regime. While it is true that political parties have been banned since 1958, they do in fact exist and operate, though discreetly and with the knowledge of the government and its security apparatus. A delicate balance, an invisible line delineating the limits, in addition to an awareness of the possibility of a quick clampdown, have created a self-imposed restraint on these parties, which in turn has permitted this legal-illegal coexistence. As long as this grey area is not violated, the parties are permitted to operate. Again, though legally banned, their leaders were called in by the crown prince, al-Hussaini, for an afternoon of consultation and exchange of views in the summer of 1987, and they do express their views in a variety of ways. The regime, however, remains the final arbiter—one that has succeeded, thus far, in avoiding the use of violence against its adversaries.

Though the powers of the Parliament were effectively reduced after 1958, it is not an entirely ineffective legislative body. It does force the government to explain its policies and defend its views and, on occasion, heated debates occur in which the government retreats or reconsiders its position.

In spite of the atmosphere of crisis pervading the entire area, and the fact that Jordan is surrounded by powerful neighbors on all sides, the regime continues to exercise power with self-imposed restraint. Public debate, though restricted, is not stifled and the newspapers, though operating under a stringent censorship law, are often an effective vehicle for debate. Rarely has the government made use of its authority because the newspapers exercise a form of responsible self-censorship.

The politics of Jordan can best be understood if this process of delicate interaction between the formal and informal is grasped. In the tradition of a paternal system, the regime is sensitive to the limits it must respect. When a formal decision is finally made, it has already taken into account what can be sociopolitically accomplished. It is thus that some opposition leaders, at various times formally tried and sentenced, were later pardoned, rehabilitated, and recruited into some of the highest positions of the state. No one drew the boundary and no formal agreement or proclamation was made but in the traditional Arab manner, everyone—government, opposition, and other political actors—knows the limits. This sense of self-imposed restraint exercised by the government, newspapers, and opposition has helped in the creation of a more liberal atmosphere than exists elsewhere in the region. Supporters of Jordan are aware that this liberal atmosphere is not based on established rights and can be ended by the regime at will; nevertheless, they stress that this system must not be judged against an absolute standard but one relative to the Middle East milieu in which the country exists.

One factor in the maintenance and the continuity of this system has been the quality of Jordan's leadership. The paternal approach of both King Abdullah and King Hussain, their personal disdain for the use of violence, and their attempt at keeping channels with the opposition open in the hope of rehabilitating and then co-opting some of its leaders have contributed to Jordan's political stability and legitimacy.

This semiliberal atmosphere in the political sphere has been reflected in the socioeconomic life of the country as well. In the early 1960s, a process of economic planning was introduced. The various plans since 1962 have emphasized the close cooperation, coordination, even partnership between the public and the private sectors. Private initiative is encouraged and the government invests in the economy only in cases where the private sector, for reasons of its own, will not invest. Such cases include primarily projects of principally social value, those that need very large investment that is beyond private sector means, or projects whose profit return is either low or has a long delay. Socially, the government plays a very active role but has relied on education rather than legislation to foster social change.

Old cohesive forces, the extended family, the tribe, the traditional demographic patterns have all weakened. Whereas almost four-fifths of Jordan's population lived in the desert or rural areas and small towns in 1948, now almost the same proportion live in urban areas. The shift to sedentary, urban lives has meant more than a change of domicile and the mode of making a living. It has reduced the role of the extended family and the tribe in determining modes of living and lifestyles. Nevertheless, old values from the Bedouin heritage or from the village have been carried to the urban areas: generosity, love and respect for the elders, valor, mutual help, and religiosity continue to be cherished and practiced. Islam continues to be the fountainhead of the customs, habits, and mores of the people. It is the standard against which individual and group behavior continues to be judged.

The fact that Islam incorporates in its precepts the concepts of progress and change, including social mobility, has been utilized as an impetus to accelerate the process of change peacefully. It is thus that the fatalism and the binding traditionalism that once characterized society have been modified in an evolutionary manner. Education, perhaps more than any other factor, has been a determining factor in the process of socioeconomic change. The educational revolution that began in Jordan in the 1950s has had a remarkable and enduring effect on Jordan's life. For example, traditional attitudes concerning women are rapidly changing. Women now have the right to vote and can be elected to Parliament. Since the mid-1970s women have been appointed to cabinet ministerial posts. Women now enjoy freedoms not known four decades ago and have opportunities in almost every walk of life in both the private and the public sectors. The veil that once confined them has been discarded.

Education, sedentarization-urbanization and modernization—though not westernization—have been the effective forces and determinants of change. The major external stimulus has been the continuous challenge posed by Israel, a challenge whose byproduct, the introduction of the Palestinians into Jordan, has been most important. The result of all these factors has been the shattering of the old socioeconomic order and the search for a replacement. Labor unions, professional associations, social and political clubs, women's associations, nongovernmental organizations have a permanent place in Jordan's life now, though no strong class consciousness seems to have developed yet. Socioeconomically, Jordan has, in the past four decades, leapt from a traditional, communal society to a consumer, service-oriented one. Changes in health, education, welfare, modern facilities, highways, and other infrastructure have been centrally planned, to a considerable extent.

The political game, formal or informal, is played within this fluid atmosphere that lacks rigid adherence either to an ideological precept, whether secular or religious, or to a set of rigid blueprints for political or socioeconomic change. Rather, policy reflects a pragmatic approach that eclectically manipulates the time and space dimension in the interest of stability.

Major Political Issues: Internal and External

The problems and major political issues facing Jordan internally and externally are often so interwoven that they are difficult to distinguish. Chief among the problems is the presence of the military-political power of the State of Israel in the area. After all, the State of Israel alone has been able to change the demographic and political composition of the area since the conclusion of the 1916 Sykes-Picot Agreement. No other external force has been as successful in reshaping the map of the area. Even the composition of Jordan waits on the resolution of the Arab-Israeli conflict. It is thus that the State of Israel continues to constitute both an internal and an external threat—internally, because of the Palestinian element in Jordan's population, and externally, because of the obvious threat the State of Israel continues to pose. That Minister Ariel Sharon and rightist expansionist groups within the State of Israel keep claiming that "Jordan is Palestine" only serves to further inflame passions.

Internally, the process of state consolidation and nation building commenced by King Abdullah is still an ongoing process, compounded in this case by Jordan's proximity to the Palestine problem and the passions and violence it generates. Law and order have been established, and, since the accession to the throne of King Hussain, the standard of living and the quality of life have been substantially improved. Statistics give an impressive picture of the scope of the socioeconomic development of the country.

One of the salient features of Jordan's economy is its continued heavy dependence on foreign aid. This factor, in addition to the inherent paucity of natural resources, has added to the challenges the country faces. Modernization has created its own sociopolitical tensions—a rising tide of expectations and rapid population growth. Jordan's population growth rate is one of the highest in the world.

Other internal political issues include questions relating to state legitimacy and the issue of popular participation. The powers accumulated in the executive since 1958 have, even in the absence of political parties and the weakened parliament, continued as issues debated within the country. While Jordan's modernization efforts have avoided the excessive model of the late Shah of Iran, which alienated his people from their culture and traditions, they have created their own tensions. A large middle class has arisen, composed of professionals, labor groups, an intelligentsia, and other groups. No institutional framework has developed to include them in the decision-making process. It is thus that any ideological debate that takes place often finds the extremes at opposite poles with the center silent or absent. This absence of responsible institutionalized debate has had an alienating effect on certain segments of this rising middle class and the intelligentsia. The demand for a true parliamentary system is also coupled with the issue of other civil and political liberties: free press, and the right to form political parties and other associations.

Among the most important internal political issues is what Arthur Day calls the Jordanian Palestinian Seam—a seam that often becomes a great divide between the two peoples.[2] Palestinians and Jordanians share language, religion, culture, and civilization. For most of the time they are one people and the seam remains merely that. It becomes a great rift at times when political issues, especially those dealing with the Arab-Israeli conflict, are raised. Living in the shadow of Israel's might, and its frequent use of that might, keeps the issue alive. Should the Arab-Israeli conflict be resolved in a way that satisfies the minimum national demand, this cohesion-cleavage process apparent in Jordan since 1948 would in time be resolved. In the meantime, this process remains a critical issue in the Jordanian political environment.

The general instability of the area, while an external issue, is also reflected internally. In this sense, Jordan is a creature and victim of its geographic location and demographic composition. The appeal of an extremism espoused externally is at times very strong. With Iranian fundamentalism on the one hand, and Israeli fundamentalism on the other, the balancing act within becomes more complicated. The leaders of both the State of Israel and Iran thunder like biblical prophets and, while headed in different directions, the fundamentalist content is the same. Fundamentalism, the argument goes, must be fought with fundamentalism. That is why the question of how Jordan's centrist position has been maintained takes on added importance. The issue of security, internal and external, is certainly a vital one, the more so considering Jordan's stability over the past four decades, a stability, indeed survival, that has often been in question. More relevant is the continued adherence of the regime to a generous measure of liberality. Adding to the uniqueness of the experiment is the regime's avoidance of the use of violence internally in spite of the many challenges and temptations. Although no one has been able to gauge its scope or depth, fundamental influence has been on the increase since 1967.

The major external political issues the country faces are just as complex and tension producing as those it faces internally. The Arab-Israeli conflict and the Lebanese crisis are most urgent and obvious issues. Jordan's very life is intertwined with the Arab-Israeli conflict on a daily basis. Since the Balfour Declaration of 1917 neither the region nor the country have known peace. In an attempt to find a permanent resolution to the conflict, Jordan insists that an international conference be convened made up of the five permanent members of the United Nations Security Council in addition to delegations from all the concerned parties in the region, principally the Palestinians. The settlement, Jordan insists, must be final, just, and honorable—one based on the principle of the exchange of land for peace embodied in UN Resolutions 242 of 1967 and 338 of 1973.

Jordan's view of the Lebanese crisis is one of brutal chaos caused by a combination of internal, regional and international factors that precipitated the total collapse of civil authority. That Israel has continued its occupation of large areas of the south of Lebanon is a major concern to Jordan. Jordan supported Syrian intervention in Lebanon at a particular stage to halt the civil war and to help initiate a Lebanese-Lebanese dialogue to end the crisis. Since then, however, Jordan has called for the withdrawal of all non-Lebanese forces from the country. Jordan's concerns are military, political, and human, ever cognizant of the threat of another conflict flaring up at so close a range.

Jordan has developed into a buffer zone surrounded by powerful states: Israel, militarily powerful; Syria and Iraq, militarily and ideologically powerful; and Saudi Arabia, financially powerful. The fact that Jordan was an active supporter of Iraq during the Iraq-Iran war put it on the front line of that conflict. Jordan's support was both political and military. Its port facilities, highways, and other such support facilities were placed at the disposal of Iraq.

Jordan, as part of the area, is affected by its general instability. One of the major concerns is how to maintain a moderate-centrist, basically pro-Western stand, in view of the realities of the situation. One such reality is the continued intransigence of the State of Israel supported unconditionally by the United States. The second reality is the seductive appeal of extremism in the area, both political and religious.

Foreign Policy: Regional and International

In writing about Jordan's foreign policy, Adam M. Garfinkle emphasizes three conditions that act as constraints: "The first concerns the crucial relationship between the ruling Hashemite hierarchy and Jordan's . . . 'Palestinian population'; the second concerns Jordan's economic well-being; the third concerns Jordan's internal and external security problem."[3] The three factors are of such importance that they determine the very survival of the regime, surely a first priority of Jordan's foreign policy. Survival is dependent, to a large degree, on finding an acceptable solution, a just and honorable settlement of the Arab-Israeli conflict.

Mr. Hassan Ibrahim, former Jordanian minister of foreign affairs, also adds another goal: that of striking a balance between Jordanian national and Arab national security. In this respect he emphasizes that in facing regional problems Jordan must continue to seek an Arab consensus. Jordan cannot ignore Arab opinion and has to operate within this framework, or at least in close proximity to it. The breakdown of Arab regional security since the mid-1970s has been a major concern of Jordan. Most of King Hussain's efforts in the last decade have been related to strengthening Arab regional security. Jordan's success in convening the November 1987 Amman Emergency Arab Summit must be seen in this context. Crown Prince al-Hassan's concern for regional security stems from his fear of Israeli intentions of balkanizing the area.

Since 1948 Jordan's foreign policy has concentrated on containment of this Israeli threat. This policy of containment took the shape of military confrontation in its first stage from 1948 to 1967. In its second stage, from 1967 to the present, it has taken the shape of working towards reaching a peaceful settlement to the conflict. Jordan believes that, should a settlement acceptable to both parties be reached, the hitherto deliberately undelineated boundaries of the State of Israel would be drawn. Thus far, the State of Israel has no defined boundaries. Jordan's search for peace is thus predicated upon the premise that the present military realities tilting so heavily in favor of the State of Israel should not be reflected in any final settlement if the settlement is to be more than another temporary truce.

In its attempts at reaching such a settlement, Jordan's efforts have been hampered, indeed thwarted, by the nearly total American support for the State of Israel. Since the early 1980s, King Hussain has repeatedly emphasized this aspect of American policy towards the region. This American posture has not only been a source of embarrassment for the moderate policies of Jordan internally but regionally as well. Jordan has been, some moderates point out, one of the staunchest pro-Western states since its inception in the region in 1921.

Factors of history, geography, and demography will, no doubt, continue to influence the way Jordan must conduct its foreign policy. Since 1967, Jordan has accepted every peace initiative to settle the Arab-Israeli conflict beginning with the Jarring Mission of 1967 and continuing through George Shultz's 1988 initiative. Since the early 1980s, the country has been working toward the goal of becoming a neutral state within the mercurial and shifting political configurations of the Arab states. Between the rival centers of power in Baghdad, Cairo, Damascus, and Riyadh, the task is not an easy one. In the meantime, Jordan continues to strengthen its relations with Islamic, nonaligned, regional and international organizations. Always, however, Jordan remains an active member and supporter of the League of Arab States and its various specialized organizations. While Jordan continues to be pro-Western, it has, over the past two decades, cultivated good relations with the countries of the Eastern bloc, particularly the Soviet Union and the People's Republic of China.

Epilogue

By 1988, it became evident that the Arab-Israeli peace process had come to a halt. For twenty-one years, Jordan, along with other Arab states, continued to pursue this peace policy through a series of concessions, ultimately appearing to be the party suing for peace, while the Israelis were pursuing their policy of escalating their demands, switching roles with the Arabs and making the conclusion of a meaningful peace agreement impossible.

It was perhaps with this in mind that King Hussain finally responded to the pressures of the PLO as well as those from other Arab states by declaring Jordan's legal and administrative disengagement from the West Bank on July 31, 1988. This action, in addition to the severe economic difficulties resulting in riots and demonstrations in various Jordanian towns and villages in April 1989, forms the panoramic background of the elections held on November 8, 1989. From 1967, when the State of Israel occupied the West Bank, until the disengagement decision, Jordan could not hold parliamentary elections since the area was under occupation. Now that the West Bank was disengaged, it was possible to resume the longstanding promise by the regime that Jordan would return to a parliamentary, participatory system of government.

In the background, and no doubt contributing to the disengagement decision, which in turn made parliamentary elections possi-

ble, was the Palestinian Uprising, Intifadah, against the Israeli occupation, clearly demonstrating the determination of the
Palestinian people to take the control of their destiny into their
own hands. Despairing of the willingness or ability of the Arab
regimes, singly or collectively (or, for that matter, of the entire
international community), to alleviate the heavy-handed Israeli occupation, internally they turned to the Intifadah in the West Bank
and the Gaza Strip and, internationally, to the PLO.

While economic difficulties, coinciding with the commencement
of the Intifadah and culminating in the April 1989 riots, form part
of the background of the 1989 elections, consideration must be
given to the internal pressure for democratization and openness
that was mounting as both political and economic difficulties escalated. Stopgap measures, the three successive appointed consultative councils, as well as the 1984 by-elections, while important,
could not stop the mounting demands for a larger and more meaningful role for the legislative branch of the government. The ever
increasing limitations on the freedom of speech and of the press
practiced by the Zaid Rifaʿi government after 1985 only added further fuel to the deepening crisis.

It is thus that the 1989 parliamentary elections have come to
constitute a significant happening, not only for Jordan, but, indeed, for the entire Arab state system. Free and unhindered, they
stand in stark contrast to the practices of most other Arab states.
Candidates from the extreme left, Communists, competed with
nationalists of various hues, Independents, Baʿathists, Muslim
Brothers, and various other Islamic fundamentalists. The resultant
Parliament, comprised of twenty-two Muslim Brothers, five
Communists/Leftists, and five members regarded as Arab nationalists, stands unique among Arab legislative bodies. Two more factors contribute to the uniqueness of this experiment. The first is
the fact that the elections were held at all, particularly in view of
the three converging crises facing Jordan at this time: the spiritual-
ideological crisis shared with other Arabs, indeed, with Islamic
states; the political crisis in the wake of the collapse of the peace
process and questions related to the role and place of the Palestin-

ian component in Jordan's life; and the more immediate and imminent economic crisis Jordan is presently undergoing.

The second factor adding to the singularity of this election process is that in spite of the success of Communist, pan-Arab, and pan-Islamic candidates, there emerged, albeit almost shyly, a purely Jordanian sense of belonging. It was as though, for the first time since the present boundaries of the states in the Middle East were set in the wake of World War I, and in response to imperialist desires, there is a tacit recognition and acceptance of these boundaries. This latest constitutional development is still in progress but it foretells a new and added support for the political legitimacy of the regime. Should the regime enter into a meaningful dialogue with these newly unleashed forces, who appear to be willing to abide by the rules of the parliamentary game, it will certainly add another dimension to the uniqueness of the Jordan experiment in the areas of socioeconomic and political development. (See the concluding section of chapter 17 for Jordan's role in the Gulf crisis.)

NOTES

1. For the text of the Organic Law, see Helen M. Davis, *Constitutions, Electoral Laws, Treaties of States in the Near and Middle East* (Durham, N.C.: Duke University Press, 1947).

2. See Arthur R. Day, *East Bank/West Bank* (New York: Council on Foreign Relations, 1986), p. 1.

3. Adam Garfinkle, "Jordanian Foreign Policy," *Current History* (January 1984): 21.

REFERENCES

Peter Gubser. *Jordan: Crossroads of Middle Eastern Events*. Boulder, 1983.
Hussain of Jordan. *My "War" with Israel*. New York, 1969.
Abdullah Ibn Hussain. *Memories of King Abdullah*. New York, 1950.
Valerie York. *Domestic Politics and Regional Security: Jordan, Syria, and Israel, the End of an Era*. Aldershot, 1988.

11

The State of Israel

Walter Weiker

Israel, although one of the world's newer states, lays claim to its statehood in part by virtue of an ancient identity. This combination goes far in accounting for its turbulent history, for the severity of some of its domestic and international problems, and for its strengths. Domestically, although Israel is a "modern" state, it must confront difficult problems of political structure and process, economic development and growth, and social issues of many kinds. Some are unique to Israel, but others are the same challenges faced by other countries in the Middle East. Internationally, the Arab-Israeli dispute is proving to be one of the most intractable issues in the postwar world. Despite these problems, Israel's record since its founding in 1948 is generally one of stability, growth, and expansion. The factors underlying this record and the resources on which Israel may be able to draw to solve its problems in the future are the subject of this chapter.

History

There has been a connection between the Jewish people and the land of Palestine since biblical times. Although Jewish sovereignty there ended nearly 2,000 years ago in the Greco-Roman period with the dispersal of the Jews to many parts of the world, there has existed the fervent hope and expectation that one day the Jews of the Diaspora (exile) would return to the Promised Land. Small Jewish communities were always to be found in Palestine amid its other inhabitants, especially in those cities with historic and biblical significance like Jerusalem, Safed, Hebron, and Tiberias. A concerted movement toward reestablishing Palestine as a Jewish entity did not begin until the late nineteenth century, however, when Russian and East European Jews began to organize a Zionist movement, partly spurred by the growing anti-Semitism that was often associated with the European nationalism of the period. The Zionists' first concrete and unified manifestation was a conference in Basle, Switzerland, in 1897 under the leadership of Theodor Herzl. It resulted in formation of the World Zionist Organization and the Basel Program, whose basic aim was "to create for the Jewish people a home in Palestine secured by public law."

Waves of Jewish immigration into Palestine began in the 1880s (with selective toleration by the Ottoman government), and by the turn of the century 25,000 Jews had arrived from eastern Europe. Between 1904 and 1913, approximately 40,000 more came (in what was known as the Second *Aliyah*, or ascent). A major turning point in the history of Palestine came in 1917 when the British government issued the Balfour Declaration, which "viewed with favour the establishment in Palestine of a national home for the Jewish people." The declaration took on particular importance when Palestine became a British mandate after World War I. It was a factor in stimulating the Third Aliyah (1919–23), which brought 35,000 immigrants, a small proportion of all the Jews living abroad but enough to make a major impact on Palestine. The Third Aliyah was important also because it included many members of several "young pioneer" movements who proceeded to intensify the establishment of *kibbutzim* and *moshavim* (collective agricultural settlements), which had been founded by the socialists of the Second Aliyah. The Fourth Aliyah, which brought another 67,000 immigrants, is usually dated 1924–28 and consisted in large part of Jews from Poland, who settled chiefly in urban areas and began considerable industrialization (although mostly in the form of workshops and small factories).

Simultaneously with immigration came the growth of institutions of Jewish self-government. British policy was to assign significant responsibilities for internal administration to each of the communities in Palestine (Jewish and Arab), and by the mid-1920s the *Yishuv*, as the Jewish community called itself, had all the trappings of a provisional government. Yishuv leaders established extensive contacts with Jewish groups abroad, saw to it that the World Zionist Organization and the Jewish Agency continued to function actively, and worked to liberalize British policy on immigration as the European Holocaust began to develop. With the failure to achieve a more liberal policy, they began to organize immigration directly.

Expanding immigration was not easy. The Arab people of Palestine had long opposed Zionist aims and immigration, seeing in it a threat to their own national aspirations. The Arab population began to oppose Jewish immigration, and considerable violence occurred between Arabs and Jews during the 1930s. Both Palestinian Arabs and Jews quickly developed their own armed forces, which would later go into action against the British as well. By the early 1930s, Britain had begun to realize the problems created by the Balfour Declaration, which also stipulated that nothing should be done that would "prejudice the civil and religious rights of the existing non-Jewish communities in Palestine," and the mandatory government sought to restrict immigration. Yishuv leaders succeeded only partially in persuading the British (and other governments) to enable more Jews to escape from Europe. During the Fifth Aliyah (1929–39), 250,000 Jews entered the country, almost all from central Europe and including a large number of professionals. A great many entered illegally. At the beginning of World War II, nearly half a million Jews constituted approximately 30 percent of the population of Palestine.

During World War II there was intense activity by Jewish communities of the world to enable more emigration from Europe, but it was largely unsuccessful and fewer than 100,000 Jews reached Palestine during the war years. Immediately after the end of the conflict and the world's awareness of the dimensions of the Holocaust (with the destruction of 6 million Jews by the Nazis, one-third of the world's Jewish population), pressures on Britain from the Jewish communities as well as from other governments increased even more. But Arab resistance also grew. By 1947 the British found that their mandate had become untenable, and they turned the entire matter over to the United Nations. After considerable debate and study that body adopted a plan to partition Palestine into Jewish and Arab states. The plan was accepted by the leaders of the Yishuv as the road to statehood but rejected by the Arabs, who saw it as a denial of their rights. It was, nevertheless, adopted, and after several months of serious disturbances in which the British tried only halfheartedly to make it possible for the partition to be orderly, the independent state of Israel was declared on May 14, 1948.

With independence came intervention by the armies of its neighbors, but despite the Arabs' superiority in manpower and resources they were not able to defeat the Jewish forces. A UN-sponsored armistice terminated the fighting in March 1949. The armistice lines somewhat enlarged the area that had been projected for the Jewish state in the partition plan. Because of Arab rejection of the plan to form the projected Palestinian Arab state, the bulk of what was to have been its territory came under the jurisdiction of the state of Jordan (except for the Gaza Strip, which came under Egyptian rule). During the fighting 2 to 4 million Arabs ordinarily resident within what was now Israel fled or were driven to these areas or into neighboring Arab states (there is still no agreement on the precise combination of reasons).

The institutions of the Yishuv were immediately transformed into a well-elaborated government. Also carried over were other institutions, the most important the Histadrut (General Confederation of Labor) and well-organized political parties. Several parties had their own paramilitary wings (the Hagannah, dominated by the Mapai, the *Palmach* of Agudat Ha'avodah, and the Irgun of the Herut Party, all of which were later incorporated into the Israeli Defense Forces), whose rivalry became intense and sharpened the existing gulf between the political right and left. The left, the democratic socialists of the second and third aliyot, dominated politically, and their power was confirmed in January 1949 when the election for the first Knesset (parliament) gave them just over half the votes. The secular nonsocialist parties led by Herut polled

Table II.I. *Immigration by Region of Origin*

Years	No. of immigrants	% from Europe-America	% from Asia-Africa
1919–48	452,158	89.6	10.4
1948–51	686,739	50.4	41.6
1952–54	54,065	24.0	76.0
1955–57	164,936	31.7	68.3
1958–60	75,487	63.7	36.3
1961–64	228,046	40.1	69.9
1965–68	81,337	46.1	53.9
1969–74	259,219	78.0	22.0
1975–79	124,847	81.8	18.2
1980–83	63,656	74.0	26.0

Source: Statistical Abstracts.

about 20 percent, religious parties 12 percent, and the remainder of the votes scattered among small parties, factions, and splinters. Chaim Weizmann, president of the World Zionist Organization, was elected the first president of the new state, and David Ben-Gurion, chairman of the Jewish Agency, leader of Mapai and perhaps the most charismatic of Israel's many colorful leaders, became prime minister.

Almost immediately after independence, immigration resumed at a rapid rate (table II.I). Within five years the population nearly doubled. The severe strains on the new state's resources were met to a great extent with a large amount of aid from Jewish communities abroad, particularly in the United States. Initial immigration was primarily from the European countries, where survivors of the Holocaust were waiting, but within a short time large numbers of so-called Oriental Jews from Asian and African (mainly Arab) countries were also arriving, motivated partly by long-standing emotional identifications with the Jewish people and the land of Palestine and partly by the increasingly difficult situations in their lands of residence caused by growing Arab resentment of the new Jewish state. International tensions were also increased by the Cold War. When East-West competition for influence in the region erupted in the Suez crisis of 1956, Israel joined Britain and France in invading Egypt. Although the action achieved many of its mili-

tary aims, its results were reversed diplomatically through the protests of both Russia and the United States.

Israel enjoyed relative domestic stability during these years. The
ability of political leaders to maintain continuity, coupled with an
extraordinary vigor for growth and cooperation generated by the
exhilaration and challenges of a new Jewish state, made this possible. Although Mapai never achieved an absolute majority in the
Knesset, Ben-Gurion and his colleagues maintained successful coalitions by making alliances with small religious parties, by sharing
power with others through such methods as assigning them functions like absorption of certain immigrant groups (which meant
that the coalition partners received not only subsidies but also opportunities to recruit the immigrants to become their voters), by
presiding over economic growth and skillfully allocating economic
resources, and by recognizing the need for national unity
generated by the international situation.

However, both internal and foreign problems soon began to
worsen. By the mid-1950s the proportion of immigrants from Asia
and Africa had increased to around two-thirds, presenting increased cultural divisions from the older residents (a subject discussed below), as well as new challenges for economic development. The hostility of the Arabs also continued to increase. In
1967 another turning point was reached with the Six-Day War, from
which Israel emerged militarily victorious over the armies of Syria,
Egypt, and Jordan. The most important result was that Israel
gained control over the Golan Heights, the Sinai Peninsula, the
Gaza Strip, the West Bank of the Jordan River, and all of Jerusalem
(which was reunified and made Israel's capital).

The war brought Israel benefits but also problems. Among the
positive results were a new wave of skilled immigrants from the
West, new resources of labor and oil in the occupied territories,
improved security, major increases in financial support from both
government and private sources abroad, and a surge in morale.
Other results of the war would prove more destabilizing. One was
the heightened development of the Palestinian problem. The nearly
1 million Arabs in the Gaza Strip and on the West Bank, who
came under Israeli control, presented major logistical and ideologi-

cal problems that later gave rise to the often violent debate about the territories' eventual permanent status, one that continues to this day both within Israel and around the world.

The situation came to a head once more in 1973 in the Yom Kippur War, which was for all practical purposes a military victory for neither side. For Israel, though, the repercussions were great. Failure to repeat the 1967 military performance brought about a sharp plunge in morale and a realization that failure to move toward permanent settlement of the Palestinian issue had been a costly error (assuming that a settlement had been possible, of course, which is debatable). Economically, it became necessary to devote an even greater amount of resources to defense than previously. Politically, allegations of failure to be prepared rocked the government and eroded public confidence in the ruling Mapai, exacerbating factional divisions that had appeared earlier as the institutions of the state matured. Simultaneously there was the worsening of social problems, including growing unrest among the Oriental Jews about their continuing lower-class status. Finally, there were serious economic difficulties, generated at least in part by the rise of OPEC and the accompanying world economic strains.

These problems, plus a number of political scandals and the rise to dominance within Mapai of relatively colorless successors to the charismatic state founders like Ben-Gurion and Golda Meir, led finally in 1977 to the electoral defeat of the Labor Alignment (as the socialist coalition was called) by the Likud, a coalition of conservative parties led by the Herut party and its veteran leader, Menachem Begin.

Probably the highlights of the first Begin government were the events that resulted in the Camp David Agreement of 1978. The Israelis were intent on dividing the Arab world and saw in Anwar Sadat the perfect opportunity to do so. Sadat, for his part, hoped to be seen as the man who brought peace to the Middle East. He took the initiative and visited Jerusalem on November 19, 1977. In the ensuing months negotiations took place between Israel and Egypt with the vigorous participation of the United States, culminating in the first peace agreement between Israel and any Arab country. The agreement suggested a way to evolve a formula for the future of the West Bank and Gaza, which will be discussed later in this chapter. Unfortunately, these negotiations have not gone forward as hoped, and Israel's security problems continue.

In the 1981 election the Likud increased its Knesset membership slightly, from 45 seats to 48. The Labor Alignment rebounded almost to equal the Likud, largely as a result of the demise of the Democratic Movement for Change, a group of liberal critics who had won 15 seats in 1977 but who were politically inept. The Likud again made a coalition with the religious and nationalist parties.

The period of the second Begin administration brought many problems into sharp focus. One was that the social cleavages between Ashkenazi (Western) and Sephardic (largely Oriental) Jews became directly involved in politics. The Likud sought consciously to exploit them in the 1981 campaign, the most strident election campaign in Israel's history. Another problem was the state of the economy. For reasons that included inherited conditions (debt service and the defense budget) but also because of internal political factors (the unwillingness or inability of the government to take needed reform and austerity measures), inflation rose to a level of over 400 percent by 1984, and Israel's foreign trade and balance-of-payment deficits skyrocketed. This was one of the major reasons for the Likud-Labor unity government of 1984.

The most dramatic single event of the second Begin government was the Israeli invasion of Lebanon in June 1982. Officially initiated in order to clear Palestinian forces from southern Lebanon, from which they had in the past launched attacks on northern Israel, the Israeli action quickly expanded to reach Beirut, and Israel's aims were widened to include the removal of the PLO from Lebanon entirely. "Operation Peace in the Galilee" proved more difficult than had been anticipated, however. The military arm of the PLO was indeed expelled from Lebanon, but its political presence was only weakened. Worse, Israeli casualties mounted as the initial attitudes of many residents of south Lebanon (many of whom were said to have considered themselves intimidated by the PLO) turned into hostility toward Israel's plans for creating a security zone by arranging for domination by the proxy South Lebanon army. The growing sense that continued direct Israeli military operations in Lebanon were futile resulted in the most intense internal debate over foreign policy that Israel had ever experienced, and in late 1985 Israel withdrew from all of Lebanon except for a small border security zone, relying for security instead on a general threat to return and on the presence of a small UN force.

The election of 1984 was held amid growing frustration over the situation in Lebanon as well as over the rapidly worsening economy and the lack of progress in solving the Palestinian problem. As a result, many voters turned away from the Likud, but instead of supporting Labor they increasingly voted for a series of small parties. Even after protracted negotiations, neither major party was able to put together a coalition. So, rather than once more having a weak government at the mercy of religious and radical parties, Labor and Likud agreed to form a government of national unity in which the cabinet posts would be divided equally and in which each party would occupy the office of prime minister for half the period before the next scheduled election in 1989. Despite serious differences between the coalition partners, this government, led first by Labor Party leader Shimon Peres, succeeded in arranging withdrawal from Lebanon and in enacting initial measures to solve the economic crisis. The results of the 1988 election were similar. Likud won 40 seats, Labor 39, the religious parties 19, and other minority parties 23. After long negotiations, another national unity government was formed by Labor and Likud. It lasted until early 1990, when a Likud-led government came to power again. Among other things, these results and the political confusion they created may have given new impetus to electoral reform.

Government Structure

The president is elected by the Knesset for a five-year term. While the office's formal powers are weak, it has important potential political influence. In the context of instability of the political party system, the president has recently had considerable leeway in choosing a prime minister–designate and influencing negotiations for coalitions. The president's unifying role has been further enhanced because all of the incumbents have also had impressive moral, personal, and sometimes scholarly stature: Chaim Weizmann, 1949–52; Yitzhak Ben-Zvi, 1952–63; Zalman Shazar, 1963–73; Ephraim Katzir, 1973–78; Yitzhak Navon, 1978–83; and Chaim Herzog, 1983–.

The unicameral Knesset is the center of governmental power. It is composed of 120 members elected for four-year terms, by proportional representation on the basis of a single nationwide constituency. Its functions and powers are those of legislatures in most modern states with parliamentary systems. A great deal of its work is done in a number of functional committees with a wide scope of authority.

The judiciary is divided between civil and religious courts. The latter exist for each denomination (Jewish, Christian, Muslim) and govern matters of personal status. Civil courts do not have the power to review laws of the Knesset (Israel has no formal constitution but instead is governed on the basis of a series of Basic Laws), but they are able to interpret statutes and to rule on the validity of administrative actions. In the latter function the courts have frequently taken an active and independent role.

The role of local government is relatively limited. Most tax powers are in the hands of the central government, which also supervises the activities of local authorities. Part of the centralization of power has been because of the electoral system whereby nominations for local offices could be controlled by the highly centralized national political parties. A 1975 reform provided for the direct election of mayors, the effects of which have included greater public accountability, frequently more vigorous local government, and the rise of an increasing number of Oriental Jewish leaders to political office. An interesting aspect of this change is that local office is becoming a pathway to national office, whereas in the past persons from national posts were frequently nominated for mayoralities— Jerusalem's mayor, Teddy Kollek, for example, who came to that post after many years as director of the prime minister's office.

The bureaucracy is ubiquitous, powerful, and almost legendary for its complexity of procedures. Israel is one of the world's most regulated societies. Initially highly partisan (in part because of the great importance of ideology in Israeli public affairs), it has become gradually more professional, though the levels of professionalism and competence vary a good deal among ministries and departments.

Although they are not government institutions, it is appropriate to mention here two other organizations of great importance whose functions can be described as quasi-governmental. One is the Histadrut, or General Confederation of Labor. A unique entity founded in 1920, it is a combination trade union, employer-entrepreneur, and social-educational-welfare institution. Its trade union department enrolls more than a million members, including homemakers. It negotiates as a single entity with the national government, and its agreements are usually then followed by most private employers as well. Its economic activities include numerous production companies, Bank HaPoalim (one of Israel's largest), marketing and insurance firms, and so forth. The Histadrut also administers the country's largest health and welfare funds. Since the time of the mandate much of its power has come from its close association with the Mapai, with which it has significant overlapping membership. In return, support by the Histadrut was an important factor in Mapai's ability to remain in power. Election to Histadrut office is through political party lists and proportional representation. All except the religious parties have usually participated. Despite the general electoral strength of the Likud, the Labor Alignment has been able to continue domination of the Histadrut so far.

The other extra-governmental but in fact quasi-governmental body is the Jewish Agency. Founded in the 1920s as the executive and representative body of the World Zionist Organization, it acquired all but official status during the mandate period and was the central agency through which immigration, land settlement, youth programs, and similar activities were carried out. It was also often the principal intermediary among the British government, many world Jewish groups, and the Jewish administrative bodies in Palestine. Since establishment of the state the Jewish Agency has continued to play a key role in many of these activities, including the channeling of much of the aid given to Israel by private Jewish communities abroad. The agency's headquarters in Jerusalem is the focus of many settlement activities. It has, however, come into increasing conflict with agencies of the Israeli state, particularly the ministry of absorption. Various Israeli groups have also felt that they were not adequately represented, and as a result a formula was developed in 1971 whereby there is now more "balanced" representation of Israelis and non-Israelis as well as various Jewish communities abroad.

Political Culture and Structure

Voter turnout has consistently been near 80 percent in each of Israel's twelve elections since 1949. Approximately the same level was recorded in all municipal elections. Political party membership, on the other hand, declined from 18 percent in 1969 to 8 percent in 1984.[1] All Israeli parties are of the "mass" type, and a recent study found that only about 6 percent hold party posts.[2] Asher Arian has remarked that the typical Israeli is one "who seems quite certain about the direction his country should take and who is quite articulate, perhaps even dogmatic, about his views . . . [but] on the other hand . . . [who] would be amenable to the emergence of a strong leadership 'in place of all the debates and laws.'"[3] Interest of at least this passing sort (and thus of potentially more active participation) is high, on the other hand, facilitated by high levels of literacy (approximately 90 percent in 1978), urbanization (90.6 percent of the Jewish population and 61 percent of non-Jews lived in urban localities in 1977), and media exposure (studies show that about 86 percent of the population read at least one daily newspaper, 77 percent read a newspaper every day, and 84 percent listen to the radio primarily for news and information).[4]

If general public participation beyond voting is relatively limited, institutions are far from quiescent. Interest group activity is both

Table 11.2. *Election Results, 1949–1988 (number of seats)*

Year	Socialist	Non-Socialist	Religious	Other
1949	65 (Mapai 46) (Mapam 19)	28 (Herut 14) (Liberals 7)	16 (single-list)	18 (Communist 4) (Arab 2) (other 12)
1951	60 (Mapai 45) (Mapam 15)	28 (Herut 8) (Liberals 20)	15 (NRP 10) (Aguda 5)	17 (Communist 5) (Arab 1) (other 11)
1955	59 (Mapai 40) (Mapam 9) (Ahd. Av. 10)	28 (Herut 15) (Liberals 13)	17 (NRP 11) (Aguda 6)	16 (Communist 6) (Arab 4) (other 6)
1959	63 (Mapai 47) (Mapam 9) (Ahd. Av. 10)	25 (Herut 17) (Liberals 8)	18 (NRP 12) (Aguda 6)	14 (Communist 3) (Arab 5) (other 6)
1961	59 (Mapai 42) (Mapam 9) (Ahd. Av. 8)	34 (Herut 17) (Liberals 17)	18 (NRP 12) (Aguda 6)	9 (Communist 5) (Arab 4)
1965	63 (Mapai 45) (Mapam 8) (Rafi 10)	26 (single list)	17 (NRP 11) (Aguda 6)	14 (Communist 4) (Arab 4) (other 6)
1969	56 (single list)	26 (single list)	18 (NRP 12) (Aguda 6)	20 (Communist 4) (Arab 4) (other 12)
1973	51 (single list)	39 (single list)	15 (NRP 10) (Aguda 5)	15 (Communist 5) (Arab 3) (other 7)
1977	32 (single list)	43 (single list)	17 (NRP 12) (Aguda 5)	28 (Communist 5) (Arab 1) (DMC 15) (other 7)

(continued)

Table 11.2—*continued*

Year	Socialist	Non-Socialist	Religious	Other
1981	47 (single list)	48 (single list)	10 (NRP 6) (Aguda 4)	15 (Communist 4) (Tehiya 3) (Tami 3) (other 5)
1984	44 (single list)	41 (single list)	12 (NRP 4) (Shas 4) (Aguda 2) (Morasha 2)	23 (Communist 4) (Arab 2) (Tehiya 5) (Shinui 3) (Civ. Rts. 3) (other 6)
1988	39 (single list)	40 (single list)	18 (Shas 6) (NRP 5) (Aguda 5) (other 2)	23 (Communist 5) (Arab 3) (CRM 5) (Tehiya 3) (Shinui 2) (other 5)

widespread and vociferous. Virtually every interest is organized. The groups, varying greatly in scope, type, and effectiveness, can be divided into several major categories (table 11.2).

Private interest groups are based on economic or social criteria, the aims of which are to protect the specific interests of their members. In the economic area, the most important players are the Histadrut and the Manufacturers' Association, the latter constantly visible both to the public and to the government, although its attempts at unified representation are often complicated by divergent interests within the private sector. There are also several active kibbutz federations. All professional groups are organized.

Public interest groups, such as the many concerned with the environment, public health, defense of citizens' rights, and so forth, are particularly numerous and active. Many get considerable funding from the government.

Ideological groups and extra-party movements, among which the most prominent are religious groups, represented by both associations and political parties; the Gush Emunim (Bloc of the Faithful), the organization of ideologically motivated settlers on the West Bank who are closely connected to religious groups and conservative political parties; and Peace Now, a mass movement urging a more conciliatory policy toward the Arabs in order to achieve a peace settlement.

The major targets of interest group activity are the bureaucracy and the political parties. Many interest groups have direct political party affiliations.

Political parties are central to Israeli politics. One writer has gone so far as to remark that "Israel's political system is, in many ways, of and by, if not for, political parties."[5] Another study found that party identification is the most important "determining factor" in voting decisions, though in recent years the rise and fall of numerous new small parties have complicated the matter.[6] This situation obtains because of (1) the great protection given to political parties by the Israeli electoral system, (2) Israeli political history (many of the parties were formed as far back as the mandate period and have carried over to the present, and frequently perform social, economic, and political services), and (3) the fact that many of the parties are strongly ideological and thus evoke much fervor. Because of these factors, the Israeli party system is characterized by fragmentation, both in the number of parties (some of which are really factions) and in the intensity of the divisions among them.

Both the centrality of parties and the great number of them are caused partly by the electoral system. Israel is unique because the country is a single constituency, with voting by party list. Although one study has shown that there is considerable negotiation within the parties in the process of composing tickets to take numerous political and local interests into account,[7] in the final analysis it is the national party organization that has the decisive hand. The electoral system also encourages fragmentation through an unusually low threshold wherein it is necessary for a party to get as little as 1 percent of the vote to qualify for a seat in the Knesset. There is some sentiment for electoral reform both to decentralize into more local constituencies and to raise the threshold, but it is not high on most political agendas.

The parties can generally be divided into several categories. The first is general, in which the most important division may be best described as socialist vs. nonsocialist, though there have also been important divisions on other matters, including foreign policy. This sector is generally organized into two major blocs (each of which contains a number of separate parties), the socialist Labor Alignment and the nonsocialist Likud. The second category is the religious parties. The third is radical parties, including Arab, communist, and several right-wing extremist ones. The following brief sketch of the most important parties will point up the unusually complex and cross-cutting nature of issues and interests, which has made Israeli domestic politics surely among the most volatile in the world. Perhaps paradoxically, at the same time Israel has had considerable government stability, having had only eight prime ministers in its 33-year history: David Ben-Gurion, 1948–53 and 1955–62; Moshe Sharett, 1954; Levi Eshkol, 1962–69; Golda Meir, 1969–74; Yitzhak Rabin, 1974–77; Menachem Begin, 1977–83; Yitzhak Shamir, 1983–84; Shimon Peres, 1984–86; and Yitzhak Shamir, 1986–.

Socialists

Socialist parties or blocs dominated by socialists were at the center of power from the mandate period until they were defeated by the Likud in 1977. Since 1968 they have been combined and known as the Labor Alignment.

The alignment's convoluted history illustrates well the volatile nature of the Israeli party system. Its major component is the Israeli Labor Party (ILP), which in turn is a combination of several other groups that have gone through various periods of unification and separation. The largest and oldest member of the ILP, in turn, is Mapai, formed in 1930 by a merger of two older groups, Achdut Ha'avodah (strongly based in one of the kibbutz movements) and Hapoel Hatzair. Virtually all the major founders of the state were Mapai members. Although organizationally united, the various components retained aspects of their individual identities, and during World War II Achdut Ha'avodah split away over issues of representation. For almost two decades after that, Mapai was able to maintain its organizational unity even though on many occasions it had to undertake extensive internal reorganization to overcome factional disputes. In 1965, however, as a result of the "Lavon Affair" (involving bitter recriminations over who was responsible for the failure of a security mission in 1954), several major Mapai leaders, including former prime minister Ben-Gurion, Moshe Dayan, and Shimon Peres, formed a new party, Rafi. By 1968 most Rafi members were sufficiently reconciled to join with Mapai (and Achdut Ha'avodah also returned to the fold) to form the ILP although remaining separate factions for a time. In 1969 the ILP, in turn, joined with Mapam (a Marxist-Zionist party founded in 1948 with strong roots in one of the kibbutz movements, which had steadfastly maintained its own identity despite considerable decline from its early position of second largest among the socialist parties) to form the Labor Alignment. The Alignment parties ran as a single list in the elections after 1969. After the 1984 election Mapam broke away in protest over Alignment cooperation with Likud to form the national unity government.

There are several reasons for the socialist parties' domination of Israeli politics for so long. First, they represented an ideology held by most of the Zionist settlers who immigrated to Palestine before World War II. Much of this ideology centered in the kibbutz movements that were one of Labor's most important bases of organized support. There have also been long-standing interlocking ties between Mapai and the Histadrut.

A second reason is that the Mapai, as the largest of several groups that have been in existence since the mandate period, stirred fond memories: it was the main voice against the British, and it counted among its members many of the charismatic, colorful leaders identified with the founding of the state.

A third reason is programmatic. Despite the numerous factional disputes in Mapai's history, one analyst has gone so far as to describe Mapai as programmatically "Israel's most pluralist party,"[8] an important reason for which is that Mapai's ideology is among the loosest of all Israeli parties. There is both considerable tolerance of program differences within the party itself and unwillingness to work together with parties whose emphasis might be different from Mapai's but with which a division of labor could be negotiated. For example, Mapai constantly acquiesces to having the religious parties as coalition partners, despite its own strongly secular orientation. This arrangement was possible because Mapai preferred religious parties to nonsocialist parties as coalition partners and because both Mapai and the religious parties agreed to refrain from trying to impose their wills on the areas of the other's central concerns, which were, respectively, economic and social organization and matters in religion-related spheres.

Despite all these assets, though, both long- and short-term factors overtook Labor in 1977: repercussions of the reversals in the 1973 war, over which the government of Golda Meir had had to give way the same year to a new one under Yitzhak Rabin; some personal scandals involving leading Mapai figures, including Rabin himself; the fact that the new leaders were far less colorful and charismatic than their state-founder predecessors; the worsening economy and the failure to make much progress on Arab-Israeli issues, which led to a widespread feeling that others at least ought to have a chance to solve these problems; the increasing political strength of Oriental Jews, who viewed Labor as largely representing Western and Ashkenazi Israelis; and reportedly, a general view (not dissimilar to what has apparently occurred in some other countries in analogous circumstances) that Labor had to be shown that its long tenure in office should not be taken for granted, that it had to be made clear that Labor did not "own" the state.

Nonsocialists

The role of the nonsocialists can also be described by examining reasons for both their rise and decline. The 1977 successors to the Labor governments were nonsocialist parties combined into a group called Likud. A 1973 evolution from an earlier (1965) bloc known as Gahal, its main components are the Herut (Freedom) party, the smaller Liberal party, and several splinter groups.

The Herut was founded in 1948 as the direct ideological descendant of the Revisionist movement, which had been organized in 1925 by the Russian Zionist Vladimir Jabotinsky. Many of Herut's members came from the Irgun Zvai Leumi, one of the several military groups that led the fighting against the British and the Arabs before the founding of the state. Menachem Begin, Herut's leader since its beginning, was one of the most colorful figures on the Israeli political stage until his retirement in 1983. Among Herut's chief programs are ardent nationalism and Zionism. Its anti-socialism is also important but has not drawn as much support. Herut's bases of support are diffuse. Its most solid single electoral foundation is among the Oriental Jews and similar groups, called by one analyst "lower-class nationalists."[9] They are variously adamantly anti-Arab, more religiously inclined than are Labor adherents, and cooler toward socialist ideology. Some are dissatisfied with their economic circumstances, and many have felt themselves excluded from political power by the East European and "veteran settler"–dominated Labor parties.

Herut's chief partner in Likud is the Liberal party. Before taking this name in 1961, it had a succession of name changes (Progressive, Independent, General Zionist) since its initial appearance in Switzerland in 1931. Based to a large extent in the business community, its chief program emphasis has been on nonsocialism and free trade. Despite this, the Liberals were in several coalitions with Mapai in the state's early years. In 1965 the Liberals joined Gahal, and in 1974 Likud.

Several factors contribute to the fragility of the Likud coalition. One is the specialization of the interests of the main partners (despite the fact that all share a general conservative outlook on both social and economic issues). Another is that the Likud is also the arena of competition between aspiring Oriental Jewish leaders like David Levy and the older leaders of European origin, who included Begin and his successor, Yitzhak Shamir. Likud has also been accused of being particularly zealous in exploiting the social divisions between Western and Oriental Jews. The latter have been the largest single base of Likud support even though Likud, as well as Labor, was run by Ashkenazim. The 1981 election campaign was one of particular bitterness. Likud's popularity among Sephardim has declined somewhat since then because of the Begin government's shortcomings and because of the increasing social mobility and heterogeneity of Israeli voters, which will be discussed. (Although ethnic factors have been important in Israeli politics, the party system was so strong that not until 1981 did a specifically ethnic party, Tami, emerge at the national level, receiving 2.6 percent of the vote.) Likud also contains an increasingly powerful far-right faction led by Ariel Sharon.

The Religious Parties

The second major category of parties has interests and appeal focused almost entirely on religious issues. For a brief period at the time of the founding of the state, four religious parties combined into the United Religious Front, but since 1950 this part of the Israeli political spectrum has been divided among several separate parties. Although as a group they have never received more than about 15 percent of the vote, their importance has been magnified because they have usually held a balance of power, and some or all have been members of every coalition government prior to the national unity government of 1984.

Up to 1981 the largest of these was the National Religious Party (NRP, or Mafdal), founded in 1956 out of two earlier groups, Mizrachi and Hapoel Hamizrachi. The latter had a Labor identification as well as a religious orientation. The NRP is Zionist and relatively moderate among the religious parties, and because of its stability produced some of Israel's best-known political figures (Joseph Burg and Moshe Shapiro, among others). In 1981, however, it was challenged and out-polled by several other parties, including the ethnic-based Tami, and the more conservative Shas, Aguda, and Morasha, all of which spoke for the increasingly numerous ultraorthodox voters. The religious issue in Israeli politics will be discussed further.

Radical Parties

The remainder of the Israeli political stage has at various times included one or more communist parties, several Arab parties, and numerous factions or splinters organized by the many strong personalities in Israeli public life. The factions come and go with great frequency. The most successful minor party was the Democratic Movement for Change, a reformist challenge to Labor, which won 15 seats in 1977 but whose members were politically inept and were reabsorbed into Labor by 1981.

In 1984 many Israelis were dismayed by the quasi-fascist Kach party of Rabbi Meir Kahane. Although it won only one seat in the Knesset, its noisy advocacy of expelling all Arab residents of Israel attracted a great deal of attention. When Israeli authorities dealt firmly with the party's militant public demonstrations in Arab villages, and when media support declined, Kahane's notoriety also decreased, though there are still concerns that renewed social and economic tensions can find their expression through Kach.

On the basis of these political characteristics, we are now in a position to examine major national issues and prospects for the solution of important public problems.

Issues in Israeli Politics

As remarked in the introduction, Israel as an old nation but a new state has compiled a remarkable record in many aspects of stability and development. We will examine here the major issues of Israeli politics and society both in terms of how effectively they have been handled to date and how they are challenges for the future. Some are issues that face every modernizing state, some are unique to Israel. To an important degree the major issues today have existed from the state's beginning: the economy, social and cultural integration, the role of religion, and the Palestinian question.

The Economy

At the beginning of the nineties, the Israeli economy is struggling to overcome serious difficulties. In 1985, before the Labor-Likud coalition enacted a package of stabilization measures, inflation was over 400 percent and Israel's balance of payments deficit was, in relative terms, almost the highest in the world. The deficit was managed only through large amounts of foreign aid and government borrowing. In 1986 a stringent program of wage and price controls had reduced inflation to around 30 percent, but even the coalition government proved unable to carry out other parts of the austerity program, particularly large cuts in the domestic programs budget.

There are numerous causes for the problems other than partisan political disputes, however. One is "natural": the lack of many natural resources. Others are due to particular circumstances, one the need to devote up to 30 percent of the government budget to defense and another to spend 12 percent on debt service. More controversial are those more directly attributable to policy choices made by Israeli governments, including what some people consider an excessively socialist welfare state and a standard of living that has been allowed to rise beyond what the country can afford.

On the whole, Israel's record in economic development is good. Among the most successful areas has been agriculture. Through the unique institution of the kibbutz and by making use of all available arable land and devising agricultural technology, Israel has become self-sufficient in many crops.[10]

Industry has also been successful. Because of limitations of raw materials, a relatively small domestic market, and limited investment capital, Israeli industry has grown along the lines of important consumer goods such as textile and food-processing, and high-technology goods which can take advantage of its highly skilled population and of innovative development into specialized export markets. Prominent among the latter are electric and electronic equipment and diamonds (which are 5–6 percent of Israel's industrial production). A high percentage of Israeli agricultural and industrial production must be exported.

Much of the root of the economic problems is political. In an effort to make more bearable the strictures imposed by the high defense expenditures, demand for raw material and consumer goods imports, and a higher standard of living than the country can perhaps afford, it was government policy for many years to "link" wages and salaries to inflation, to devalue Israeli currency constantly in the world capital market, and to make up the shortages of funds through massive foreign borrowing and printing of money. One of the aims of forming the national unity government of 1984 was to reduce the pressures on the individual political parties arising from their prospective popularity in future elections. But pending improvement in the basic defense problem and increasingly strong export competition from other countries, the difficult task of imposing austerity on the Israeli population remains.

Social and Cultural Integration

Although predominantly Jewish, Israel is among the world's most heterogeneous countries in many other social and cultural aspects. One of the foundations of Israel as a Jewish homeland and refuge from persecution has been the Law of the Return, whereby any Jew may enter the country and immediately become a citizen. The immigrants of the twentieth century have come from all parts of the world, bringing with them a range of diverse cultures from such sources as upper/middle-class Western Europe and the United States, postrevolutionary Russia, cosmopolitan Cairo, Algiers and Tunis, and some of the world's least developed countries, such as Yemen and Ethiopia. Each group has brought with it rich heritages of culture and tradition but also characteristics often unknown to their new fellow countrymen. They also required assistance in all aspects of resettlement and "absorption."

Many of their needs have been met in ways little short of extraordinary, considering the magnitude of the problems. Often with major assistance from both foreign governments and private Jewish communities abroad, housing, schools, and jobs have been created. Whereas in the 1950s large numbers of immigrants had to spend time in transit camps and other makeshift facilities, today there is a highly developed network of agencies and institutions which provide immigrants with needed service.

It is not only material problems that have produced challenges, however. Achievements have been impressive in social integration and the development of an Israeli identity, and most immigrants have evolved a solid feeling of "Israeliness." Much of this success has resulted from several factors: (1) the concept of the Jewish people and the belief that migration was a "return" to a land to which there was attachment going back to biblical times; (2) the sense of unity arising from having been pushed out of hostile homelands, a negative factor but one nevertheless important as a stimulus to a new unity; (3) the common experience of having been physically uprooted, of having to learn a new language and to establish new communities in every sense of the word, needs that gave strength to socializing institutions like schools; (4) the fact that the open nature of Israeli society has encouraged individual social mobility; and (5) intense personal socialization through the Israeli school system and the army. With few exceptions, all Israelis serve in the military, men for three years and women for two, and do several weeks of annual reserve duty to age fifty-five. Among the manifestations of social integration are numerous "mixed" neighborhoods in all Israeli cities and an increasing number of Israelis who marry persons from different cultural backgrounds.

But immigrants also put severe strains on social and cultural integration. Different communities brought with them greatly disparate levels of the traits needed to fit into the economic and social structure of a "modern" nation. Many Oriental Jews came with significantly lower levels of education, work experience, skilled occupations, and certain social orientations than was the case for those with European or North American origins. So, despite many opportunities for individual social mobility, many Oriental Jews have remained in the lower socioeconomic strata, and in the view of some analysts the rapid development of Israeli society and of the economy as a whole has led to the potential emergence of deep class divisions which all too often parallel differences in ethnic backgrounds. These divisions have been expressed periodically in protest incidents like the "Black Panther" outbursts by North African immigrants in the early 1970s and by political action such as strong Oriental Jewish support of the Likud and several recent small radical right-wing parties.

The divisive problems are difficult to resolve because while there are some short-run remedies, the solution may ultimately require large-scale redistribution of economic and social resources to speed up the "modernization." On a more positive note, many Israelis who at one time were oriented to integration in all forms have begun to show interest in preserving the cultures of the countries from which they came, and the "coat of many colors" is today as much an ideal as is the Jewish "melting pot."

Another difficult situation is presented by the Israeli Arabs.[11] Some 450,000 Arabs chose to remain in Israel after the founding of the state and to become Israeli citizens. Now numbering an estimated 550,000 Muslims, 100,000 Christians, and 75,000 Druze, they are concentrated in certain quarters of the major cities and in towns and villages in the north of Israel.

Israeli Arabs present the state with several problems. One is security. Despite the fact that they are full citizens and that many have good personal relations with their Jewish neighbors (and did so before the founding of the state), for security reasons Israeli Arabs had been under military jurisdiction for much of the period since 1948. They do not serve in the army and thus are ineligible for many benefits, such as those going to veterans. A gradual easing of restrictions culminated in a full ending of military jurisdiction in 1966 as it was decided that most Israeli Arabs are not disloyal. Concern rose again after the 1967 war, though, when Israeli Arabs began to come under pressure to support Palestinian demands for return of the territories captured by Israel, and there is currently a good deal of tension between Israeli Arabs and Israeli Jews.

A second problem is social integration. Israeli Arabs continue, for the most part, to live in their own villages and in their own districts in urban areas. They also have their own school system, newspapers, and other social and cultural institutions. Most also continue to occupy the lowest rungs of the social and economic ladder. They are enfranchised and have usually voted in large numbers (there are and have been several small Arab political parties) but are underrepresented in the Knesset as well as in high political offices.

There is some disagreement on the causes of Arab under-representation. Some contend that it is a result of deliberate, if unofficial, policies, others that the difficulty is rooted in modernization as well as in the insistence of Israeli Arabs that their own culture and heritage be vigorously maintained. There is no disagreement, however, that the problems are exacerbated by pervasive perceptions of unfavorable stereotypes among both Jews and Israeli Arabs. Recent surveys show that up to 70 percent of Jews believe that Jews should be given preference in university admissions, private and public sector jobs, and so on. Arabs are reported to consider all Israelis as hostile to them and their culture. These perceptions have been reinforced in recent years by growing sympathy among Israeli Arabs for the cause of Palestinian nationalism and the PLO, high birth rates among Israeli Arabs, Israel's severe economic problems, and the vocal, even if numerically small, support given to Rabbi Kahane.

A small Druze Muslim community is concentrated in about eighteen villages in the Galilee and near Haifa. The Druze are Arabic speaking but have a religion of their own which is kept secret, and they consider themselves a distinct community. Not directly a part of the large group of Israeli Arabs, they have a better record of integration with the larger Israeli society and economic and social mobility.

The Role of Religion

Israel is culturally a Jewish state. There is no doubt that this characteristic is a basic part of its identity, a powerful part of its unity and of its attractiveness to Israel's own Jewish citizens and to immigrants, and an argument for the continued support of Jews in other countries. As everywhere, however, the precise role of religion and religious institutions generates a great deal of debate.

While there is full religious freedom for non-Jews in Israel, the state's Jewish identity is expressed in a number of ways, both formally and informally. Most national holidays are based on religious observances like the Jewish New Year, the Day of Atonement, and Passover. In all but a few localities that exercise certain rights of local option, public transportation is suspended on the Jewish sabbath. All matters of personal status (marriage, divorce, inheritance, and so on) are administered by religious authorities (there are Muslim and Christian equivalents of the Jewish authorities). There are large state subsidies to religious institutions, including synagogues and *yeshivoth* (private religious schools), and a network of "religious-oriented" public schools is operated alongside "nonreligious" ones.

Controversy exists because of a combination of social and political factors. On one side, there is no doubt of the religious-nationalist connection: "94 percent of Israeli Jews affirm the attachment of Israel with Jewish peoplehood, culture, and history."[12] But it is also true, according to a survey in the early 1970s, that the great majority of Israelis identify themselves as either "nonobservant" (43 percent) or "traditional" (40 percent) and only 17 percent as "orthodox,"[13] while most matters related to religious administration are under the jurisdiction of the chief rabbinate, which is an orthodox monopoly. The nonobservant tolerate many restrictions at least partly because they have been able and willing to circumvent them (for instance, by using private transportation to travel to beaches on summer Sabbaths and holidays).

Another strain has resulted from the increasing proportion of ultraorthodox, who are immigrating in larger numbers than are less observant Jews and whose birth rate is considerably higher than the Israeli Jewish average. This factor and the apparently small likelihood that the Israeli electorate will produce a strong majority party have emboldened the religious parties in recent years to exploit their position in the balance of power in areas about which there are strong popular feelings. For example, while there may be little popular dissatisfaction with orthodox rabbinical rulings against autopsies and abortions, or against "conservative" or "reform" rabbis being allowed to perform marriages, there is increasing resentment toward large government subsidies to orthodox schools and institutions, toward wider exemption from military service for religious youths, toward orthodox demands to prohibit all sports events, radio, television, and so on, on the sabbath, and at the increasing boldness of the orthodox in pressing their demands through political demonstrations and violence. (There is also tension between the Israeli chief rabbinate and Jewish communities abroad, because outside Israel there are large numbers of "reform" and "conservative" congregations that resent restrictions by Israeli religious authorities in regard to recognizing the validity of "nonorthodox conversions" for purposes of the Law of the Return.)

The Palestinian Question

The history of the dispute over the territories of the West Bank, the Gaza Strip, the Golan Heights, and East Jerusalem was outlined earlier, and it is dealt with more extensively elsewhere in this book. Unfortunately for all concerned, it appears that solutions are getting more elusive rather than closer.

Viewing the range of possible formulas for a permanent disposition of the areas, at one end of the spectrum is an independent Palestinian state on the West Bank and Gaza, as demanded by the PLO. Resisting such a status is the one thing on which all Israeli political parties agree, on security grounds. The fact that some of these areas prior to 1967 were sometimes launching places for both Palestinian guerrilla attacks and for military operations by Arab countries, and the growing hostility to Israel among Arab residents of these territories, would make Arab autonomy acceptable to Israel only if the territory were demilitarized, a limitation unacceptable to the PLO.

The other end of the continuum is annexation of the West Bank and Gaza to Israel. Most proponents of this move base their claims on historical and religious grounds. They are a minority in Israel, and although they have become increasingly vocal and visible in recent years, most Israelis consider annexation undesirable because it would mean either adding enough Arab voters so as to endanger Jewish control of the Israeli state or it would make West Bank residents permanent second-class citizens, a tarnishing of Israel's identity as a democracy.

Between these poles a large variety of formulas all have proponents in Israel. On autonomy of the territories, there have been proposals such as the one made by Prime Minister Begin soon after the Camp David agreements that would have provided self-government in many social, economic, and local matters but not in foreign and military policy or on such things as water rights. Other formulas have proposed various degrees of association with either Israel or Jordan or both. The most widely publicized of these was President Ronald Reagan's 1982 proposal for association with Jordan, one turned down both by Israel and by most of the Arab states and the PLO.

Three sets of factors, for the most part the products of events that have taken place since 1967, seem to lie in the way of a settlement.

(1) In the "facts on the ground" view, Israel formally annexed East Jerusalem in 1980 and considers it no longer a subject of negotiation. In addition, large Jewish residential areas have been built in neighborhoods of the city that were formerly under Jordanian control. In 1981, Israel also annexed the Golan Heights, largely on security grounds, since that area had been the source of Syrian shelling of communities in northern Israel. On the West Bank, Israeli governments have authorized the building of over 125 settlements with more than 40,000 Jewish residents; it would be difficult for an Israeli government to remove them, were that to be a condition of an agreement. Also, in areas of the West Bank closer to Israel proper, numerous "bedroom suburbs" of large Israeli cities have grown up.

(2) The history of Israel-Arab relations in the West Bank and in Gaza have blocked agreements. Israeli policy has been to limit expressions of Palestinian nationalism and Arab hostility toward Israel by maintaining control over public meetings, Palestinian nationalist publications, and the activities of PLO officials. These efforts, plus the often provocative actions of militant Jewish settlers, have been contributed to the growth of Palestinian nationalism in the areas, to increasingly frequent clashes between West Bank and Gaza residents and Israeli troops, and to growing bitterness on both sides. Another Israeli policy has been to attempt to sidetrack PLO influence by seeking alternative leaders from among seemingly more moderate indigenous West Bank residents, but these efforts have failed. In 1987, what had been sporadic Arab demonstrations became large-scale and systematic disorders. The Intifadah (as it is known) has caused both sides to entrench their positions.

There are also economic complications. One is that Israelis have been allowed to purchase considerable amounts of land in the West Bank. Another is that a large number of Arabs from the territories are now employed in Israel, an arrangement important both to the workers' incomes and to the Israeli economy. Many doubt that an autonomous West Bank entity would be economically viable without massive foreign economic assistance.

(3) It has been impossible even to convene negotiations. At the base of this matter is interpretation of UN Resolutions 242 and 338. The former, adopted soon after the 1967 war, calls for "a just and lasting peace" based on both "termination of all claims and states of belligerence" and "the right of every state in the area to live in peace within secure boundaries," and on "withdrawal of Israeli armed forces from territories occupied as a result of the 1967 conflict." Resolution 338, adopted in 1973, calls for direct negotiations between the parties.

In addition to the practical problem of the return of territories because of "facts on the ground," Israel also maintains that it is impossible to guarantee "secure" boundaries except through continued control of at least certain parts of the territories, whereas the Arabs interpret "territories" to include "all."

In addition to such substantive points, there are formidable difficulties in agreeing on the format of negotiations. Israel has steadfastly insisted that she will not talk directly to the PLO until that organization recognizes Israel. In late 1988 the Palestinian National Council accepted UN Resolutions 242 and 338 as well as the 1947 UN partition resolution—enough for the United States to begin low-level contacts with the PLO but not for the Israelis, who countered with a proposal for elections in the West Bank and Gaza. The PLO in turn rejected this idea as Arab states and the Palestinian people view the PLO as the "sole legitimate representative" of Palestinians. As of mid-1990, the prospects of any of the parties moving from their positions are dim.

Other Israeli concerns with foreign affairs also focus intensively on matters of security. The initial reasons for the 1982 invasion of Lebanon were based on military threats, as have been Israeli efforts to keep sophisticated military equipment from the hands of the Arab states.

Israel has close relations with the United States and is the largest recipient of American economic and military aid. It also has close political and economic ties to Western Europe, and the EC is Israel's largest trading partner, though relations with individual countries have often been difficult. The Soviet Union, initially friendly to Israel, broke diplomatic relations during the 1967 war. Relations with Asian and African nations were also seriously damaged in 1967, and the Arab oil states succeeded in persuading most of them to sever relations and to send home the many Israeli technical assistance teams that had been at work. Ties to some African and Asian states have only gradually been restored. Israel also had close ties to the Shah of Iran before his fall.

Conclusions

In the 1990s there will again be major challenges: increasingly severe economic problems, which, in the views of many, require basic restructuring of the economy; frustration with fragmentation of the political party system and growing demands for electoral reform; continued lack of progress in arriving at a settlement of the Palestinian question; numerous implications of the end of the Cold War; and the successful absorption of what may eventually amount to 1 million Soviet Jewish immigrants.

Considering the many difficult problems that Israel faces, it is natural to wonder how this small state perseveres. The theme here has been that Israel could meet many of the challenges of building a new state because it has elements of cohesion arising from being an old nation and because it has many aspects of a developed state with which to confront problems of underdevelopment in some sectors of its society. Students of government and politics see Israel as particularly interesting because it faces both unique problems and some that are in essence only variations on challenges facing numerous other nations around the world.

Among Israel's strong elements is the uniquely powerful basis of its fundamental Jewish identity. Rooted in both religion and history, no other people have succeeded in maintaining their identity over as long a period of time and under as adverse conditions before finally achieving national sovereignty. Although there are many disagreements on what has constituted the foundations on which Jewish identity has rested, there is no doubt that it will continue to cement diverse elements within Israel and to bridge the gaps between the Jewish state and other Jewish communities in the world. Part of the cohesion comes, unfortunately, from negative elements, for example, the anti-Semitism that drove Jews together in their Diaspora communities and eventually in migration to Israel, and one of the reasons for outside support for Israel continues is that a refuge would be available in case of need. But religious and cultural identity have also been fused in more positive ways, as noted earlier.

Another sustaining factor has been the challenge of building a new society, much of which has been supported by the idealistic outlook of many of the builders. The numerous achievements in meeting the social, economic, and political challenges have also provided inspiration for even greater efforts. The more than half a century of work to put these ideals into concrete form has also brought to light many problems and areas in which the record is still inadequate. It is foolish, if not impossible, to make firm predictions about how well the remaining problems will be handled. What is sure, however, is that this dynamic society attempting to meet its challenges bears watching by policymakers in all countries, by students of politics, society and development, and by the world at large.

NOTES

1. Asher Arian, *The Choosing People*, p. 106.
2. Eva Etzioni-Halevy, *Political Culture in Israel*, (New York, Praeger, 1977), p. 76.

3. Arian, p. 215.

4. Etzioni-Halevy, p. 75.

5. Leonard Fein, *Politics in Israel* (Boston: Little, Brown, 1968), p. 67.

6. Arian, p. 114.

7. Steven A. Hoffman, "Candidate Selection in Israel's Parliament: The Realities of Change," *Middle East Journal* 34 (1980).

8. Fein, p. 78.

9. Arian, p. 211.

10. In addition to their economic importance, the *kibbutzim* have been perhaps even more interesting as social experiments. Intended to be the full embodiment of collectivist, egalitarian, intimate human associations, they were established in rural areas as fully self-sufficient institutions. Work was to be done by members of the community themselves, and decision-making was fully democratized with all members expected to participate. To enhance these factors and to avoid social stratification, all jobs were to be rotated among the members at given intervals. Another feature was cooperative raising of children. In order to become more viable many kibbutzim have recently added industries, and have moderated some of their collectivism in response to declining membership, but the kibbutzim remain the backbone of Israeli agriculture. A somewhat modified form of collective settlements are the *moshavim*, in which property is community-owned but in which families work individual plots and the social collective aspects are less intense.

11. This section does not refer to the Arabs living in the territories that came under Israeli control in 1967.

12. Charles Liebman and Eliezer Don-Yehiya, "The Dilemma of Reconciling Traditional Culture and Political Needs: Civil Religion in Israel," in *Politics and Society in Israel*, ed. Ernest Krausz (New Brunswick, N. J.: Rutgers University Press, 1984), p. 197.

13. Harold I. Greenberg, *Israeli Social Problems in Perspective* (Tel Aviv: Dekel Academic Press, 1979), p. 146.

12

Palestine and the Palestinian Question

Tareq Ismael and Jacqueline Ismael

No single issue in twentieth-century Middle East politics has been as robust and problematic as the question of national status in the land of historical Palestine. The reasons for this are rooted in geography, history, and the importance of Palestine in the religious consciousness of Muslims, Christians, and Jews. Besides being an important religious center for all three religions, the land stands at the crossroads of the Arab world, a bridge between the Mashriq (Arab East) and the Maghrib (Arab West). Jerusalem, besides its obvious place in Christian scripture, is the third holiest place of worship in Islam, so its role in political controversy has galvanized not only Arabs in the region (with whom the Palestinians share a historical and cultural bond) but Muslims the world over. (On the role of the land's religious significance for Jews in Zionist ideology, see chapters 4 and 11.)

In ancient times and throughout its long history, the land of Palestine was the site of different civilizations and the homeland of different peoples—Amorites, Canaanites, Arameans, Israelites, Philistines, Arabs. The earliest recorded civilization was that of the Canaanites. They were superseded by the biblical Hebrew tribes who invaded the region and, sometime around 1000 B.C., established a kingdom with Jerusalem as its capital. Jerusalem was destroyed by the armies of Babylon in 586 B.C. and rebuilt fifty years later. In the first century A.D. Jerusalem was again destroyed, this time by Roman occupiers, and the Israelites were exiled, dispersing throughout the world. With the Israelites gone, the area was gradually resettled by neighboring tribes.

By the end of the seventh century, Palestine was predominantly Arab and Islamic, with a small minority of Jews. Most Palestinians were Sunni Muslims; Christians, Druze, and Shi'ite Muslims constituted minorities. The region was overwhelmingly agricultural. In the early part of the twentieth century a small intellectual and professional class emerged. Life was centered around the principal cities of Jerusalem, Nablus, Nazareth, Acre, Jaffa, Ramallah, Hebron, and Haifa, where Palestinians concerned themselves with the same issues that faced other Arabs of the day.

Like most of the Arab world, Palestine became a province of the Ottoman Empire in 1516. This change in status had little direct impact on the life of the average Palestinian because throughout most of the Ottoman era, Palestine remained a relatively homogeneous, agricultural society. By the mid-1800s, the population of Palestine was estimated at over one-half million, of which 80 percent were Muslim, 10 percent Christian, and 5–7 percent Jewish.[1] However, by the turn of the century, tumultuous events were already brewing that would profoundly change the land of Palestine and the life of every Palestinian alive and yet to be born.

In the late nineteenth century two forces emerged, Arab nationalism and Zionism, that would determine the future of Palestine. The latter was a political movement that advocated the establishment of a Jewish national home in Palestine. The first large-scale Jewish immigration into Palestine began in 1881. The immigrants of the first Aliyah were mostly Russian Jews fleeing the pogroms that had followed the assassination of Czar Alexander II. While official Ottoman policy regarding immigration of this sort was restrictive, relations between Arabs and the incoming Jews were generally good and there was no measurable opposition to the immigration. Between 1897 and 1908 the Zionist movement established the infrastructure that would facilitate the Zionist colonization of Palestine. The Colonization Commission (1895), the Palestine Land Development Company (1895), and the Jewish Colonization Association (1891) were set up to acquire land and facilitate colonization. Financial institutions such as the Jewish Colonial Trust (1898), the Jewish National Fund (1901), and the Anglo-Palestine Company (1903) were then set up to aid these activities. Furthermore, the

Zionist movement set about gaining allies in their mission. In 1902, Theodor Herzl met with the Ottoman sultan, offering assistance with Turkey's public debts in exchange for settlement rights in Palestine. The Great Powers were also approached by the Zionists who argued that Jewish settlement in Palestine would serve to bolster European influence in the region.

Thus, between 1904 and 1907, the Jewish population in Palestine had swelled to 10–12 percent of the total,[2] and there arose increasing Palestinian opposition to Jewish immigration. Anti-Zionist protests in the Ottoman parliament and in the Palestinian press were accompanied by protests at the local level. A number of organizations were formed to oppose Zionist aims, *al-Hizb al-Watani al-'Uthmani* (the Ottoman National party, 1911) is one of the earliest examples. The halting of Zionist immigration appeared increasingly to require an end to Ottoman rule and the assertion of an Arab identity, and the issue came to be closely linked with the broader cause of Arab nationalism.

The outbreak of World War I served to shift the issue of Jewish immigration to Palestine further into the arena of Great Power diplomacy. The Turkish authorities expelled 28,000 to 32,000 Jewish immigrants (approximately 50 percent of Palestine's Jewish population) as enemy aliens.[3]

During World War I, Sharif Hussain of Mecca secretly negotiated with the British government through the British high commissioner in Cairo, Sir Henry McMahon, for a British promise of future Arab independence in exchange for Arab military action against the Turks. On October 24, 1914, McMahon promised independence for Arab territories including Palestine. On June 15, 1916, Sharif Hussain declared war on Turkey, an event\ subsequently termed "the Arab Revolt."

Meanwhile, in 1915–16, Sir Mark Sykes and George Picot, negotiating on behalf of the British and French governments, respectively, reached a modus vivendi on the future territorial disposition of Arab lands. The Sykes-Picot Agreement of 1916 called for the division of most Arab territory into either French or British control. Ultimately what proved to be the most important Allied position regarding the future of Palestine was taken in 1917 in the form of a letter from British Foreign Minister Arthur James Balfour to the English Jewish leader Lord Rothschild (for the content of the Balfour Declaration, see chapter 4).[4]

After driving the Turks out, British forces entered Jerusalem in December 1917 and were greeted as liberators. News of the Balfour Declaration and the heretofore secret Sykes-Picot Agreement soon altered the mood. When a British Zionist Commission arrived in Palestine in March 1918, it found evidence of widespread Arab nationalist and anti-Zionist sentiments. In January–February 1919 a Palestine Arab Conference met in Jerusalem to discuss the situation in Palestine. The conference ended with a call for Palestinian unity within an independent Arab Syria.

At the Versailles Peace Conference, both the Zionist movement and Sharif Hussain were represented by delegations. The Zionist delegation vigorously called for the establishment of a Jewish national home in Palestine, and in 1919 the United States set up the King-Crane Commission to investigate the situation. Although their report on Palestine revealed widespread support for Arab independence and expressed grave doubts about Zionist plans, the Versailles Conference adjourned without making a decision on the issue as the commission's report was not submitted to the conference.

In April 1920 six days of rioting in Jerusalem resulted in more than 250 injuries and nine deaths. In response, martial law was declared by the British authorities. At the San Remo Conference of the Allied Powers in that same month, Palestine was declared a British mandate. The preamble of the mandate echoed the pledge of the Balfour Declaration made in 1917, promising the Zionists a Jewish homeland in Palestine. The mandate also lent official recognition to "the Zionist organization" (Article IV) and charged Britain with facilitating Jewish immigration and encouraging "settlement by Jews on the land" (Article VII).

The Third Palestine-Arab Congress was held in December 1920. The conference's resolutions, although staunchly anti-Zionist, were largely uncritical of the British authorities. The Arab executive sent a number of representations to the British government in 1921–22 protesting Britain's pro-Zionist policies. British response, however, was to dismiss the legitimacy of such delegations and to declare that acceptance of the Balfour Declaration was a prerequisite to any negotiation. In 1922 Britain released a White Paper on Palestine in which it was stressed that British commitment to the Balfour Declaration, that crucial document with its promise of a Jewish homeland in Palestine, "was not susceptible to change."[5] As a result, an average of 6,000–8,000 Jewish immigrants entered Palestine each year for the first ten years of the mandate, despite insufficient agricultural land and high levels of urban Arab unemployment.[6]

Meanwhile, violent riots took place in Haifa (March 1921) and particularly in Jaffa (May 1921). Forty-eight Palestinian Arabs and forty-seven Jews died in Jaffa. The Fifth Palestine Arab Conference (August 1922) decided to pursue a strategy of constitutional opposition to British policy; it also called for a Palestinian boycott of the new constitution for Palestine and for a similar boycott of elections to the new legislative council. The latter boycott proved to be highly successful.

By 1922, the Jewish population in Palestine stood at approximately 84,000 (11 percent of the total population), and new immigrants continued to arrive by the thousands, peaking at 34,000 in 1925.[7] Zionist settlers in Palestine were pursuing a segregationist strategy. The Histadrut (Jewish Federation of Labor) was committed to a boycott of Arab produce and labor as an exclusionist policy to foster a self-contained process of Zionist development. Furthermore, the British mandatory administration determined the number of Jewish immigrants to be allowed entry into Palestine based on the number of jobs available for Jews. So, in fact, the rate of Jewish immigration was established by British administration on the basis of the absorptive capacity for labor of Zionist colonization.[8]

By the mid-1920s two major political factions had appeared in the Palestinian nationalist movement (which at this time represented a struggle for self-determination), corresponding to two of the area's most prominent families: the Hussainis and the Nashashibis. Hajj Amin al-Hussaini, Grand Mufti of Jerusalem and head of the Supreme Muslim Council, was rapidly gaining political prominence, complementing the Hussaini-dominated leadership of the Arab Executive Committee. In 1923 a National party was set up by the competing Nashashibi faction, together with a network of national Muslim societies and peasant parties.

A series of incidents that began in September 1928 were a flashpoint for major sectarian clashes between Muslims and Jews in August 1929. The violence lasted for nearly two weeks resulting in the deaths of 133 Jews and 116 Arabs. Palestinian notables were quick to distance themselves from the strife and to call for its end.

In reaction to the riots, the British government dispatched Sir John Hope-Simpson to investigate the problem. The Hope-Simpson Report on Immigration, Land Settlement, and Development was released in October 1930. On the issue of Arab unemployment, it concluded that "it is necessary that the existence of Arab unemployment should be taken into consideration when determining the number of Jews to be admitted." On the land issue it concluded that there was in Palestine "no margin of land available for agricultural settlement by new immigrants, with the exception of such undeveloped land as the various Jewish Agencies hold in reserve."⁹ The Passfield White Paper, the response of Britain's colonial secretary, Lord Passfield, to the Hope-Simpson Report, accepted most of its findings and recommendations. This acceptance elicited a storm of protest from British Zionist circles, and Prime Minister Ramsey MacDonald capitulated to Zionist pressures.¹⁰

Economic activity began to recover considerably in Palestine during 1931–32. This activity, coupled with increasing levels of anti-Semitism in Europe, led Jewish immigration to grow at even greater rates than during the Third (1919–23) and Fourth (1924–31) Aliyot. Accordingly, the Jewish population of Palestine—which comprised 174,000 persons, or 16–17 percent of the total in 1931 —began to increase at an annual rate of 2 percent compared to the non-Jewish population.¹¹

In October 1933, British troops opened fire on a Palestinian demonstration in Jaffa, igniting demonstrations throughout the country and precipitating a general strike. Meanwhile, the Arab nationalist movement galvanized around the Palestine issue, spawning new leadership and renewed political activity. In 1932 the Arab Independence (*Istiqlal*) party was formed in Palestine, signaling the demise of the moribund Arab Executive Committee. The latter, plagued by internal conflict, effectively collapsed in 1934. Other pan-Arab political bodies arose in the 1930s, particularly among the youth, the Arab Youth Congress the most influential example. The first half of the 1930s saw the creation of a number of clandestine armed groups that advocated guerilla warfare against the British and the Zionists.

In December 1935, British High Commissioner Waunchorpe released a revised proposal for a partly nominated, partly elected legislative council with an Arab majority. The Nashashibi's National Defense party accepted the proposals, as did the National Bloc and the Reform party. The Youth Congress and the Hussaini-led Palestine Arab party both rejected the proposals as insufficient although the latter's opposition was largely tactical.

The Zionist movement reacted to the legislative council proposals with hostility and actively lobbied against them. Pressure in London by the Zionists and their allies was successful, debates in the House of Lords (February 1936) and in the House of Commons (March 1936) proved unfriendly to the proposals, and the Colonial Office effectively withdrew them in July.

Riots on April 15, 1936, resulted in the death of three Jews and two Arabs. On April 20 a strike was organized in Jaffa, and a "National Committee" was formed in Nablus to organize a similar strike. Both received massive public support, so on April 25 the five Palestinian parties agreed to the formation of an Arab Higher Committee (AHC) to coordinate strikes and the numerous national committees. The AHC called for the general strike to continue until the British government agreed to end Jewish immigration, prohibit land transfers to Jews, and establish a national government responsible to a representative council. But in May the situation in Palestine grew more violent, exacerbated by a British decision to grant a new schedule of 4,000 immigration certificates to the Jewish Agency. In August a step was taken toward the improvement in the organization and training of Arab resistance after a Syrian revolutionary (and ex-Ottoman officer) Fawzi al-Din al-Kawukji entered Palestine with some 200 Syrian, Iraqi, and Trans-Jordanian volunteers and declared himself "Commander in Chief of the Revolt in Southern Syria (Palestine)." By September, Kawukji's leadership had been nominally accepted by six of the major guerrilla leaders.

The British responded to the initial strikes with the offer of a Royal Commission of Enquiry, but they steadfastly refused to make any concessions on immigration. Police activity and military reinforcements were also called in, and by summer British troop strength in Palestine had risen from 1,970 to approximately 20,000.[12] Mass arrests, demolition of houses, suppression of the Arabic press, and collective fines were all used in the attempt to end the disturbances.

By the fall of 1936, the guerrilla units were running short of supplies and support for the strike was slipping in many quarters. The mediation efforts of Arab leaders were now welcomed by the Arab Higher Committee, and on October 10, 1936, King Ibn Saud of Saudi Arabia, King Ghazi of Iraq, and Emir Abdullah of Transjordan issued identical appeals calling for an end to the strike and rebellion. The following day the Arab Higher Committee complied.

With the ending of the first phase of the revolt, the British government duly appointed a Palestine Royal (Peel) Commission on November 5. Colonial Secretary W. Ormsby-Gore refused, however, to suspend Jewish immigration during the course of the Peel Commission's investigation, and the Arab Higher Committee's subsequent presentation to the commission was relatively ineffectual. On July 7, 1937, the Palestine Royal Commission released its report recommending that Palestine be partitioned into an Arab state and a Jewish state. Certain areas of religious significance were to be retained under British administration.

Moderate Zionists were lukewarm to the proposals. More extreme Zionists protested vehemently against what they saw as the further division of Eretz Israel. The Arab Higher Committee (less the Nashashibi faction), and later the leaders of Saudi Arabia and Iraq, opposed partition, but Emir Abdullah supported it. The Nashashibi faction and the National Defense party—who had seceded from the Arab Higher Committee by July with the support of Abdullah—initially supported the partition plan. But the party and some Nashashibi-allied notables, whose regions would become part of the Jewish state, later reversed their position. Many Nashashibi supporters within the proposed Arab state maintained their backing of the plan. The split effectively destroyed the party. In early September a Pan-Arab Congress on Palestine was held in Bludan, Syria, at which delegates demanded an end to Jewish immigration and the mandate, and a British promise of Palestinian independence.

On October 1, 1937, the British district commissioner for the Galilee was assassinated. British authorities arrested hundreds of Palestinians and deported a number of AHC leaders to the Seychelles. Both the Arab Higher Committee and the various national committees were banned. Organized Arab resistance increased, support for which was coordinated from a headquarters in Damascus— al-Lujnah al-Markaziyya lil-Jihad (Central Committee of the Struggle).

The British government adopted a two-pronged strategy of military action and political conciliation. Palestine was placed under martial law. The British used a number of Zionist forces in the course of their activities, and British-Zionist military cooperation reached a new level. On the political front, in November 1938 the British government abandoned the partition plan and offered to hold a round table conference in London with Palestinian and Zionist delegations in attendance. An AHC delegation headed by Jamal al-Hussaini arrived in London in February 1939. The British, eager to pacify the Middle East in the event of a European war, made a number of concessions, including limitations on Jewish immigration and the establishment of Arab-dominated self-governing institutions. But no Arab consensus was reached. The conference ended in March without agreement.

In May 1939 the British decided to proceed without formal Palestinian approval and released the Palestine Statement of Policy (the MacDonald White Paper). They proposed a limit of 75,000 on Jewish immigration over the next five years, with Jewish immigration after that period contingent on Palestinian approval; the establishment of self-governing institutions; and the enactment of restrictions on the transfer of land. Both the Arab Higher Committee and the Zionists rejected the White Paper.

Indeed, by the time that World War II broke out, Arab resistance in Palestine was all but subdued. The British practice of exiling Palestinian leaders to the Seychelles left the movement virtually leaderless, and French authorities cracked down on Arab political activities in Damascus and along the border with Palestine.

Palestinian Nationalism, 1939–1967

The failure of the 1936–39 Palestine revolt severely weakened the organized Palestinian protest and struggle as material resources in the Palestinian community diminished considerably. At the same time, another area of Palestinian political activity was growing: the Palestinian trade union movement. Membership rose from 5,000 (1936), to 11,000–12,000 (1942), to 20,000 (1945).[13] The conservative Palestine Arab Workers Society (founded in 1925) and the more activist Federation of Arab Trade Unions and Labor Societies (1942) dominated the organization of Palestinian labor. Less successful was the Palestine Labor League (1927), controlled by the Zionist Histadrut.

Another focus of Palestinian political activity during this period was the Istiqlal, a number of whose leaders were readmitted to Palestine (after being exiled by the British) during 1939–41 on condition that they avoid political activity. The Istiqlalists purchased the Arab Agricultural Bank, renamed it the Arab National Bank, and used it (and its fourteen branches in Palestine) to continue nationalist activities. In 1943 the bank and its Istiqlalist owners organized the Arab National Fund, which sought to keep Palestinian land out of Zionist hands. The Istiqlal also obtained an interest in Palestine's second largest newspaper, *Falastin*.

In the second half of the war, two additional factors facilitated increased Palestinian political activity. The first was the lifting of the ban on political activity at the end of 1942. The gradual return of political leaders to Palestine led to the formal reemergence of a number of nationalist parties, including the National Bloc (February 1944) and the Youth Congress (April 1945). The Palestine Arab party was reconstituted in April 1944 under the formal leadership of Tawfiq Salih al-Hussaini.

The second factor that contributed to the reassertion of organized Palestinian nationalism was the creation of the Arab League. Musa al-Alami, a Palestinian observer sent to the Alexandria preparatory conference of the league in September–October 1944, succeeded in becoming a full-fledged delegate at the conference. At his urging the Arab League instituted a faltering boycott of Israeli goods, created a "Construction Scheme" to preserve Palestinian land and foster its development, and called for a Palestinian state to which the league's charter a priori granted membership.

Indeed, Britain's wavering support for the Zionist movement led the Zionists to set their sights upon a new—and ultimately more influential—benefactor, the United States.[14] Intensive pressure on the U.S. government was exerted by the Zionist movement. The American Zionist Organization made clear its aims in the so-called Biltmore Declaration of May 11, 1942, which explicitly called for unlimited Jewish immigration to Palestine; the formation of a Jewish army; and the establishment of a Jewish state in all of Palestine.

World War II benefited the Zionist movement in a number of ways. It served to bolster a Zionist military apparatus that had already grown rapidly during the Palestine revolt. During the war years 27,028 Jews in Palestine received military training in the British armed forces.[15] Thousands more were armed and trained by the British in Palestine as paramilitary police or auxiliaries. Still others received military training in various Allied armies.

The war further strengthened the powerful Zionist economic position in Palestine. By 1942 over 79 percent of industry in Palestine was Jewish-controlled. Palestine's Jewish population, which by this time accounted for approximately 30 percent of the total, received nearly 60 percent of Palestine's national income. In 1944 only 32 percent of Palestinian children aged five to fourteen attended school, compared with 97 percent of Jewish children. The Jewish infant mortality rate in 1942–44 was approximately one-third of the rate found among Palestinians.[16] A final factor that served to strengthen the Zionist movement during the war years was—with tragic irony—the Holocaust itself. The plight of European Jews proved highly influential in swaying public opinion in support of a Jewish state in Palestine.

Such factors, coupled with strong support by Winston Churchill, led Britain to alter its position regarding the future of Palestine once again. By 1944 the British cabinet had rejected postwar continuation of the policy set down in the 1939 White Paper and had returned to the concept of partition advocated by the earlier Peel Commission report. Opposition to partition from both Arab leaders and elements within the British government, together with the death of President Franklin Roosevelt and Churchill's electoral defeat, effectively killed the plan.

In 1945 the Zionist movement had made considerable political gains at the expense of the Palestinian nationalist movement. The Jewish community in Palestine was both well-armed and well-organized. The desperate predicament of hundreds of thousands of Jewish concentration camp survivors lent considerable political weight in Western countries to Zionist demands, though Western states failed to lower their own barriers to immigration for those Jews. Indeed, the United States actually raised its barriers and Canada, after being lobbied by Zionist leaders, only supported Zionist demands after it was made clear that the creation of a Jewish state would reduce the number of Jews wanting entry into Canada. In August 1945, President Harry Truman called upon the British government to grant 100,000 Palestine immigration certificates immediately to Jewish refugees in Europe. British reliance on U.S. economic aid accentuated the pressure.

On April 26, 1946, the Anglo-American Committee of Enquiry released a report calling for continued Jewish immigration if a settlement was reached, an end to the restrictions on land transfer which had been imposed by Britain in 1940, and the continuation of the mandate pending United Nations trusteeship, with the ultimate aim of a binational state. The committee rejected, however, both Jewish and Palestinian national aspirations on the grounds of their mutual incompatibility and Palestine's special religious significance. President Truman lent U.S. support only to the committee's recommendations regarding immigration. The concept of partition died once again, only to be resurrected by the Morrison-Grady Plan which focused on the concept of a federation.

In November 1945 the Arab League Council managed to impose upon the fractious Palestinian political leadership a new twelve-seat Arab Higher Committee dominated by the Palestine Arab Party. The re-formed Arab Higher Committee was then immediately recognized by the Arab League with the mandate government in Palestine following suit two months later.

In February 1946, Jamal al-Hussaini returned to Palestine and immediately set about reorganizing and enlarging the Arab Higher Committee, becoming its acting president. The Istiqlal and other nationalist groups protested this move and set up a rival body— the "Arab Higher Front"—in June of that year.

In May 1946, Hajj Amin made his way to Cairo. Both the Arab Higher Committee and the Arab Higher Front were dissolved upon league order, and a new five-member Arab Higher Executive was created under the mufti's chairmanship. Five additional members were added in January 1947. Since Hajj Amin was barred from entering Palestine, Jamal performed the role of acting chairman.

The focus of British policy in Palestine had shifted by this time to U.S.-British negotiations in London. The Morrison-Grady plan, which resulted from these bilateral discussions, called for a federalized Palestine under British trusteeship. The ultimate status of Palestine remained unclear within the plan, which provided for British control. Both Arabs and Zionists rejected the plan, though the latter accepted some form of partition in principle, with the promise of eventual Jewish statehood. The plan was never put forward.

Meanwhile, two Zionist terrorist groups, the *Irgun* and the Stern Gang/LEHI, stepped up their attacks against British and Arab targets; the former bombed Jerusalem's King David Hotel in July 1946 and killed ninety-one people. The Hagannah—under Jewish Agency direction and in formal alliance with the revisionist terrorist groups—also engaged in armed activity. In 1946 the strength of subversive Zionist military organizations in Palestine was estimated at approximately 67,000.[17] Violence by these groups in that same year accounted for over two hundred deaths.[18]

In contrast, the Palestinian population was largely inactive militarily during this period.[19] However, in October 1945 an independent military organization called *al-Najjadah* (the Helpers) was formed in Jaffa; by the end of the next year Palestinian armed strength probably stood in the hundreds, a mere fraction of Zionist mobilization.

In September 1946, Britain again attempted to place restrictions on the composition of the Zionist and Palestinian nationalist delegations, and both groups boycotted the London Conference in response. The Arab states—the only group (other than Britain) to attend—used the conference as an opportunity to propose the establishment of a Palestinian state within which a maximum Jewish population of 30 percent would be permitted. In the interim the Zionist movement had hardened its position still further, with the declared support from President Truman in October 1946.

Britain proposed a revised form of the Morrison-Grady plan, which envisioned regional self-government within an eventual unitary state. It was rejected by all parties. On February 14, 1947, the British government announced that it was referring the whole matter to the League of Nation's nascent successor, the United Nations.

The United Nations responded by creating a Special Committee on Palestine (UNSCOP) composed of eleven members which was to investigate and make recommendations regarding the question of Palestine. Arabs and Muslim supporters within the United Nations opposed the formation of UNSCOP arguing that an independent Palestinian state represented the only possible just solution to the issue. When UNSCOP subsequently visited Palestine in July 1947, the Arab Higher Committee (Executive) successfully called for a boycott of its proceedings by Palestinian groups and a general strike in protest.

In August 1947, UNSCOP made two sets of recommendations to the UN General Assembly. The first, the majority plan—endorsed by seven of eleven UNSCOP members—called for the partition of Palestine into a Jewish and Palestinian state together with an internationalized Jerusalem. Under the plan the Jewish community—which represented 31.7 percent of Palestine's population and which owned less than 6 percent of Palestine's land—would be assigned 56.4 percent of Palestine's territory.[20] Indeed, it was far from clear that Jews comprised a majority within the proposed Jewish state as a whole. UNSCOP also presented another proposal —the minority plan—endorsed by Iran, India, and Yugoslavia, which called for the establishment of a single federalized state within which Jewish and Palestinian units would coexist.

In September 1947 the General Assembly created an ad hoc committee to examine UNSCOP's recommendations, which in turn created subcommittees to consider separately the majority plan, other proposals, and conciliation. The Arab Higher Committee argued that Palestine should become an independent unitary state in accordance with the wishes of its Palestinian Arab majority. Any other "solution" would be unacceptable though the Arabs agreed to the minority plan at the eleventh hour while Zionists refused to compromise at all.

On November 25 the ad hoc committee approved by a vote of twenty-five to thirteen (with seventeen abstentions) a modified version of the UNSCOP majority plan. The United States placed tremendous pressure upon the UN's smaller members to support the proposals. The USSR—which had maintained an anti-Zionist position prior to the United Nations referral—also supported the partition proposal.

By a vote of thirty-three to thirteen (with ten abstentions) in the General Assembly on November 29, 1947, the partition plan was accepted. In an effort to appease public outrage throughout the Arab world at the ineptness of Arab governments in protecting the rights and welfare of an Arab population, the Arab League hastily organized a rag-tag army of volunteers. Untrained, uncoordinated, and poorly armed, this army paled in comparison to the well organized, sophisticated Zionist military machine. By May 1948, Hagannah's front-line strength exceeded 27,000, supplemented by 32,000 reservists, 5,000 members of the Irgun and LEHI, and thousands of other trained personnel.[21] Between January and May 1948 hundreds of tons of infantry weapons and ammunition, together with aircraft and armored vehicles acquired by Zionist groups, were smuggled into Palestine.

Fighting broke out between the Palestinian and Jewish communities immediately after the UN decision. Britain did little to halt the clashes. In January, the first 1,500 troops of the Arab Liberation Army began infiltrating Palestine from the surrounding Arab states. By February 1, violence in Palestine left over 2,500 dead and wounded.

On April 9, 132 members of the Irgun and LEHI, supported by a *Palmach* ("elite strike force") unit of the Hagannah, attacked the unarmed village of Deir Yassin and massacred 254 men, women, and children. Survivors were taken to Jerusalem, stripped and released on the streets. The massacre instilled terror within the Palestinian population and encouraged their flight.

The activities of the Irgun and LEHI complemented the Hagannah's official Plan Dalet, which was a thirteen-stage operation aimed at securing those areas assigned to the Jewish state by the partition resolution, as well as seizing additional territory. Radio broadcasts, loudspeakers, and word-of-mouth rumors were used to instill terror in the Palestinian civilian population. Villages and towns were attacked and their inhabitants driven out.

On May 14, 1948, the establishment of the State of Israel was formally announced. Contingents from Syria, Iraq, Trans-Jordan, Egypt, and Lebanon—totaling fewer than 15,000 troops—entered Palestine. The new state was given de facto recognition by the government of the United States and de jure recognition by the USSR on May 17. The nascent Israeli state not only resisted the much smaller and fragmented Arab forces but also expanded into areas assigned to the Arab state by the 1947 UN partition resolution.

The loss of Palestine in 1948 was to prove an event of major significance in the evolution of broader Arab nationalism. It raised questions about the ability of Arab governments to meet the most fundamental challenge: that of national survival. The reappraisal that followed hastened the end of the old order in Syria (1949),

Egypt (1952), and Iraq (1958). Under the impetus of the Palestine debacle, a strong current of Arab opinion concluded that the road to rectification lay through Arab unity. In the meantime, Jordan's ruler, Emir Abdullah, annexed those areas of Palestine under his control in December 1949 and renamed his country the Hashemite Kingdom of Jordan.

The only other area of Palestine that had not been incorporated into Israel, the Gaza Strip, came under Egyptian administration. In September 1948 the Egyptians permitted the holding of a Palestinian Congress in Gaza. Later, a "government" of Palestine was formed under Ahmad Hilmi Pasha; it was based in Cairo and played little role in Palestinian affairs.

Meanwhile, the State of Israel was rapidly moving to consolidate its position. A number of laws were passed enabling the Israeli government to seize control "legally" of the lands and property of those who had fled. Between 1948 and 1953, 370 Jewish settlements were constructed in the state of Israel, 350 on confiscated Palestinian land. Furthermore, Palestinians who had fled from their homes within what was now the State of Israel were refused permission to return. All Jewish immigrants, on the other hand, were promised Israeli citizenship under the 1950 "Law of Return." Some 740,000 Jews immigrated to the State of Israel during the first five years of its existence.[22]

In 1958 these developments helped lead to the formation of a union between Syria and Egypt, the United Arab Republic under the leadership of Egypt's charismatic president, Gamal Abdal Nasser. To the Arab world, unity now appeared as a concrete and achievable reality. To many Palestinians, it seemed as if such unity really did hold the potential for Palestinian liberation. Indeed, in 1955 the Egyptian army set up a number of *fedayeen* (guerrilla) units in Gaza composed of refugees and Palestinian members of the Egyptian armed forces. One year earlier, the Arab Nationalist Movement (ANM) was formed upon the foundations laid by earlier organizations.[23]

In the early 1960s the Arab Nationalist Movement grew closer, ideologically and organizationally, to Nasserism, but throughout the 1960s it continued to move to the left ideologically. By 1964 the ANM had adopted "scientific socialism" as a guiding principle. Although its major significance during this period was largely political, the ANM did not reject armed struggle as a weapon against the State of Israel. In 1964 it formed a "Palestine Region of the Arab Nationalist Movement" (also known as the "military grouping") to pursue such a strategy. By 1966 a portion of the paramilitary Palestine Region under Ahmad al-Yamani had formed the "Heroes of the Return," launching their first raid into the State of Israel in October of that year. At about the same time, the left wing of the ANM participated in the formation of a military organization, the Vengeance Youth, which carried out its first armed operation in May 1967.

The organizational nucleus of *al-Fatah* was established in Cairo in the mid-1950s by Abd al-Rahman Abd al-Ra'uf Arafat (Yassir Arafat), Saleh Khalef, and Khalil al-Wazir. The group subsequently expanded to Kuwait and other locations where the Palestinian diaspora could be found. Beginning in 1963 and for a few years thereafter, Fatah received logistical and other support from the Syrian military intelligence services and from the revolutionary government of Algeria.

On the night of December 31, 1964, al-Fatah's military wing, *al-Asifah* (the Storm), launched its first military operation against the State of Israel with an attack on an Israeli water-pumping station. Over the next twenty-nine months al-Asifah would claim responsibility for 175 military operations inside the State of Israel, making it the most militarily active of the Palestinian nationalist groups.[24]

During this period, a division grew between Arab governments, who sought to take the lead in seeking Palestinian rights, and the Palestinians themselves. The Palestinians were becoming more self-reliant and increasingly skeptical over the duplicity of conservative Arab regimes in dealing with the West, which after all strongly supported the State of Israel. The Arab solution to the Palestinian nationalist problem emerged in January 1964. The Arab League met in Cairo to discuss responses to Israel's plan to divert headwaters of the Jordan River and called for the formation of a "Palestinian entity" under the auspices of the Arab League. This "entity" subsequently took shape as the Palestine Liberation Organization.

Palestinian Nationalism, 1967–1987

Israel's defeat of the Arabs in June 1967 served to precipitate a visible split between Arab and Palestinian nationalism. The war's impact was major. In physical terms, the last vestiges of Palestine slipped from Arab control as 300,000 Palestinians fled their homes on the West Bank or in the Gaza Strip to join the Palestinian diaspora, dropping the proportion of Palestinian Arabs still resident in Palestine from 63 percent to about 50 percent.[25] In political terms, the inability of the Arab regimes to triumph on the battlefield raised critical questions about the ability of the pan-Arab orthodoxy to deliver Palestinian liberation.

What the Palestinian nationalists sought in the aftermath of the 1967 war was the revolutionary mobilization of the Palestinian people and the pursuance of a popular Palestinian armed struggle against the State of Israel. The emergent paradigm of revolutionary Palestinian nationalism maintained that the progressive Arab regimes (Egypt, Syria, Iraq), although "antagonistic to imperialism" and thus useful as allies, could make only limited contributions to Palestinian liberation because of their incomplete domestic social transformations. The reactionary Arab regimes (notably Jordan and Saudi Arabia) could make no such contribution and were bound to clash with the Palestinian revolution. More and more the PLO became prominent, and within the PLO, Fatah began to dominate the movement.[26]

As early as October 1968 the Fatah faction proposed a solution to the Palestinian problem. It called for the creation of a "democratic state in Palestine." Unlike the Jewish state, Israel, which limits citizenship and therefore meaningful democratic participation only to Jews, to the exclusion of others, Fatah insisted that all citizens in a democratic Palestine would comprise the state. In clear and categoric terms, Fatah called for nondiscrimination based on religious and ethnic lines. Citizenship was a sufficient criterion to ensure equally democratic rights for all Palestinians in the new state. Impressed by the vision and appeal of Fatah's proposal, the PLO adopted it as its official position in 1969, thereby asserting greater control over Palestinian affairs.

By October 1974, the first Rabat Arab Summit moved to recognize the PLO as the "sole legitimate representative of the Palestinian people." In the same year, at the invitation of the United Nations, Chairman Arafat addressed the General Assembly. The UN subsequently gave the PLO observer status inside the UN and all its accredited agencies.

PLO efforts to advance Palestinian nationalism were successful at the UN. In 1977, the UN declared an international day of solidarity with the Palestinian people. By 1980, the European Community resolved, in its Venice Declaration, that the PLO should be associated with negotiations leading to a resolution of the Arab-Israeli conflict. The community accorded greater legitimate rights to the Palestinian people and emphasized the crucial importance of the PLO.

By 1982, Palestinian nationalism entered a new phase of development, signaled by the full-scale Israeli invasion of Lebanon, aimed at crushing the PLO and Palestinian resistance to occupation of their land. The PLO's base was destroyed and the organization was removed from Lebanon and resettled in Tunisia. However, Palestinian nationalism was not weakened as Israel anticipated. The massacres at Sabra and Shatila refugee camps consolidated the support of the Palestinian people for the PLO and heightened international support for their cause. By this time, more than 128 countries recognized the PLO.

Following the Israeli invasion of Lebanon, the leadership of Yassir Arafat was seriously challenged both from within the PLO and from without. This struggle culminated in the dramatic siege at Tripoli when pro-Arafat PLO forces fought off, simultaneously, dissident PLO forces led by Abu Musa, the Syrian army which sought to end Arafat's influence in the organization, and the Israelis who sought to destroy it or at least drive it out of Lebanon. Arafat emerged from the battle still in control of the PLO, but the organization was weakened and in decline, its vitality dissipated by internal fragmentation and external challenge. The eventual demise of Yassir Arafat's leadership, the symbol of the PLO, and of the PLO itself, the symbol of Palestinian nationalism, appeared inevitable; and so it seemed that Palestinian nationalism had run its course. Then, in December 1987, the Intifadah erupted.

The Intifadah

The Intifadah (literally meaning the casting off of shackles) erupted on December 9, 1987, the day after an Israeli military jeep in Jubalya Refugee Camp in the Gaza Strip drove into a truckload of Palestinian laborers, killing four of them. The event precipitated spontaneous demonstrations in protest of Israeli military occupation and settlement policies, and these quickly spread throughout the occupied territories. Popular committees, organized to offer community services denied to the population by the Israeli military authorities in the occupied territories (health, sanitation, security), provided the organizational infrastructure and leadership for the Intifadah. The strategy pursued has been a campaign of civil disobedience (strikes and boycotts of Israeli goods) combined with acts of symbolic violence (rock throwing) aimed at the economic, political, and administrative disengagement of the occupied territories from Israel. Armed violence has been explicitly rejected by the Intifadah leadership.

The Israeli government responded to the Intifadah with force and intimidation in an effort to suppress public protest in the territories and restore military control. By January 1990 over a thousand Palestinians had been killed in the Intifadah, with an estimated 80,000 Palestinians wounded (many permanently injured) and over 50,000 held in administrative detention for periods of up to one year. The Israeli government has found the iron fist policy it adopted in response to the Intifadah unsuccessful and the Intifadah virtually irrepressible. Nevertheless, it has responded with even greater force, precipitating a split within the international community and within itself over the use of military force against an unarmed population and widespread reports of human rights abuses.

The Intifadah proved to be an entirely indigenous grass-roots movement that gained new sympathy in the international community for the plight of the Palestinians. The Intifadah leadership threw its support behind Yassir Arafat and the PLO as the symbols of Palestinian nationalism in the international community. This support renewed PLO legitimacy as the sole representative of the Palestinian people and reinvigorated Yassir Arafat's flagging leadership of the organization. Arafat responded to the mandate given him by the Intifadah by attempting to articulate the aspirations of the people of the occupied territories for a just peace with Israel that would end Israeli military occupation and allow the territories self-determination. As a result, at its November 1988 meeting in Algiers, the Palestine National Council (the governing body of the PLO) declared Palestine (comprising the occupied territories of the West Bank and Gaza) to be an independent state and implicitly recognized the existence of the State of Israel and UN Security Council Resolution 242 as the basis for peace negotiations. Yassir Arafat subsequently gave explicit recognition to the existence of the State of Israel, explicit renunciation of terrorism as a legitimate means in the Palestinian struggle, and formal acceptance of UN Resolution 242.

Israel, however, rejected PLO approaches and continued its iron fist policy in the occupied territories. Nonetheless, the strength of peace proponents in Israel greatly increased, and in early 1990, a split over the issue of peace brought down a fragile coalition government in Israel.

At the beginning of the Intifadah in December 1987, a Palestinian state appeared an impossible solution to the Arab-Israeli conflict. In 1990, it appears an inevitable solution. The debate has shifted from a matter of objectives to a matter of means.

The Palestinians and the Gulf Crisis

Iraq's invasion of Kuwait on August 2, 1990, elicited little sympathy among Palestinians in the Occupied Territories and the refugee camps of Lebanon and Jordan for the plight of Kuwaitis. In spite of the substantial moral and financial assistance Kuwait had given the PLO over the years, Palestinians regarded Kuwait as a reactionary state and exclusivist society more concerned with amassing oil wealth and protecting the status quo than with seeking justice for the Palestinian people or securing their human rights. On the other hand, the image of an Arab state taking on the United States, challenging Israel, and sponsoring the Palestinian cause elicited unqualified enthusiasm among Palestinians, especially in the Occupied Territories. Consistent with the sentiments of the people he represented, Yassar Arafat maintained a close personal relationship with Saddam Hussain throughout the crisis (though, in fact, the PLO joined other nations in denouncing Iraq's invasion of Kuwait). While his relationship with Saddam Hussain damaged the PLO's image internationally, it did refurbish Arafat's flagging image among Palestinians in the Occupied Territories. (On the Gulf crisis, see the concluding sections of chapters 7, 13, and 17.)

While Saddam Hussain's efforts to link Iraq's withdrawal from Kuwait to Israel's withdrawal from the Occupied Territories were initially dismissed in the international arena, Israel's October 8 massacre of Palestinians at Jerusalem's al-Aqsa Mosque complex highlighted the double standard being applied by the Security Council with regard to the Gulf crisis and the Arab-Israeli conflict and promoted a reconsideration in international circles. The European Community, for example, passed a resolution in the European Parliament condemning "the Israeli government for this latest massacre" and stating that both the Palestinian and Gulf conflicts should be dealt with according to international law and the resolutions of the UN Security Council (quoted in *Gulf News* [Dubai], October 12, 1990).

While the United States continued to oppose efforts to link an Iraqi withdrawal from Kuwait with the issue of Israeli occupation of the West Bank and Gaza, by mid-November it was widely recognized in international circles that agreement to discuss these issues in tandem was the only viable basis for negotiations that had been proposed. The U.S. concentration on a military strategy to resolve the conflict had overshadowed diplomatic efforts to find a peaceful solution. And although Iraq had softened its negotiating position in the face of the massive military buildup, its peaceful capitulation to U.N. resolutions outside of negotiations appeared remote. The only other option appeared to be war. Yet the United States remained resolute in its determination not to negotiate on the basis of any linkage between the conflicts. Nevertheless, from the time of the al-Aqsa massacre, the issue of the Occupied Territories was clearly an implicit part of the debate, whether by omission or inclusion. The statements by Israeli Housing Minister Ariel Sharon and Prime Minister Yitzhak Shamir on November 20 claiming the Occupied Territories are needed by Israel for settlement of the 2.5 million Jews expected from the Soviet Union highlighted this issue again.

NOTES

1. Janet Abu-Lughod, "The Demographic Transformation of Palestine," in *The Transformation of Palestine,* ed. Abu-Lughod (Evanston, Ill.: Northwestern University Press, 1971), p. 140. The Jewish population of Palestine included both indigenous Sephardic (Oriental) Jews, and Ashkenazi (European) Jews. The latter were largely made up of members of pious religious communities in Palestine supported by funds from the diaspora. Neville J. Mandel, *The Arabs and Zionism Before World War I,* (Berkeley: University of California Press, 1976), p. 29.

2. Elia T. Zureik, *Palestinians in Israel* (London: Routledge & Kegal Paul, 1979), p. 32.

3. Abu-Lughod, "Demographic Transformation," p. 141; Zureik, *Palestinians in Israel,* p. 33.

4. "The Balfour Declaration," in *The Arab-Israeli Conflict,* ed. John Norton Moore, vol. 3, *Documents,* (Princeton: Princeton University Press, 1974), p. 32.

5. "Churchill White Paper," ibid., 3:67.

6. The Hope-Simpson Report (1930) found that Arab unemployment "not only exists but is serious and widespread;" it also found that "[T]he Arab population has increased with great rapidity and the land available for its sustenance has meanwhile decreased by about a million metri dunums which have passed into the hands of the Jews," and that as a result there was "no margin of land available for agricultural settlement." See HMSO, "Palestine: Report

on Immigration, Land Settlement and Development" (Hope-Simpson Report) Cmd. 3686 (October 1930).

7. Abu-Lughod, "Demographic Transformation," pp. 142–43, 146–47.

8. For a detailed discussion, see Dan Tschirgi, *The Politics of Indecision: Origins and Implications of American Involvement with the Palestine Problem* (Praeger, 1983), pp. 1–17.

9. HMSO, "Palestine: Report on Immigration, Land Settlement and Development," pp. 139, 141.

10. Tschirgi, *The Politics of Indecision*, pp. 10–11.

11. Jewish immigration rapidly grew between 1931 and 1935:

1931	4,075
1932	12,553
1933	37,337
1934	45,267
1935	66,472

Abu-Lughod, "Demographic Transformation," pp. 150–53; Porath, *Palestinian Arab Nationalist Movement, 1929–1939*, 2:39.

12. In particular, the number of Jewish police (including supernumeraries) was increased by over 3,000. See Barbara Kalkas, "The Revolt of 1936: A Chronicle of Events," in Abu-Lughod, ed., *The Transformation of Palestine*, pp. 263–64.

13. Nicholas Bethell, *The Palestine Triangle* (London: Andre Deutsch, 1979), p. 83.

14. For a further discussion of this see Tschirgi, *The Politics of Indecision*, chap. 2.

15. See David Ben-Gurion, "Britain's Contribution to Arming the Hagannah," in *From Haven to Conquest*, ed. Walid Khalidi (Beirut: Mu'assasat al-Dirasat al-Filastiniyah, 1971), pp. 371–74.

16. Zureik, *Palestinians in Israel*, pp. 51, 56.

17. Hagannah: 40,000 static forces (settlers, townsfolk); 16,000 field army (Jewish Settlement Police); 2,000–6,000 full-time force (Palmach); Irgun Zvai Leumi 3,000–5,000; Stern Gang/LEHI, 200–300.

18. Bethell, *Palestine Triangle*, p. 297.

19. Ben-Gurion, *Israel: A Personal History*, p. 61.

20. "Report of Sub-Committee 2 to the Ad Hoc Committee on the Palestinian Question," UN Doc. A/AC 14/32 (November 11, 1947).

21. Much of their equipment was supplied by Czechoslovakia. See Arnold Krammer, "Arms for Independence: When the Soviet Bloc Supported Israeli," in Khalidi, ed. *From Haven to Conquest*, pp. 745–54, 861–63.

22. Hana Sinare, "How the Palestinians Became Refugees: Denial of Basic

Human Rights," *First United Nations Seminar on the Question of Palestine* (New York: UN, 1980), p. 59.

23. Walid Kazziha, *Revolutionary Transformation in the Arab World: Habash and His Comrades from Nationalism to Marxism* (London: Charles Knight and Co., 1975).

24. Fouad Jabber, "The Palestinian Resistance and Inter-Arab Politics," in *The Politics of Palestinian Nationalism*, ed. William B. Quandt, Fouad Jabber, and Ann Mosely Lesch (Berkeley: University of California Press, 1973), p. 172.

25. Edward W. Said et al., *A Profile of the Palestinian People*, pp. 16–17.

26. For a complete account of the clash of Palestinian nationalism with Arab conservative regimes, see Dan Tschirgi, *The American Search for Mideast Peace* (New York: Praeger, 1989).

IV

COMPARATIVE
GOVERNMENTS

The Nile Valley

13

The Arab Republic of Egypt

Tareq Ismael and Jacqueline Ismael

Egypt is an ancient nation with a rich culture and distinct identity that dates back thousands of years. Its contributions to science, culture, and civilization have had a profound and lasting effect on three continents—Europe, Africa, and Asia. For most of its history it has proven to be a significant actor in international and regional affairs.

Egypt is largely a product of the Nile River whose silt deposits enabled settlement along its shores dating back 8,000 years. From the banks of the Nile emerged an agriculturally based civilization that over time developed an organized system of government ruled by the pharaohs. It was under the pharaohs that the first Egyptian advances in architecture and science occurred and Egypt evolved into a highly sophisticated culture. Even under Roman rule the Egyptians flourished as a center of civilization and learning, and throughout the centuries that followed Egypt maintained its position at the forefront of world affairs. Only in the sixteenth century did Egypt begin to decline, when it became a province of the Ottoman Empire.

The Emergence of Modern Egypt

Napoleon invaded the Ottoman province of Egypt in 1798 with the hope of using that territory as a base from which to threaten the British Empire by attacking India. The plan was unsuccessful and Napoleon departed, leaving behind a French army of occupation. In 1801 this force was compelled to withdraw by the Turkish and collaborating British armies. When the British departed in 1803, Muhammad Ali, an Albanian junior officer, was left in control of several thousand Albanian and Bosnian troops. At that time, four forces were in competition for the control of Egypt: the Mamluks, the people of Cairo, the Albanian troops, and the Ottoman pasha. By 1805, playing one faction against another, Muhammad Ali had emerged as the strongest political leader, consolidating his power by crushing all opposition. He massacred Mamluk leaders in 1811 and in 1815 crushed a revolt among his own troops, thus completing the process of fortifying his personal power.

Ali's rule had profound effects on Egypt, especially in relation to the state's role in society. Under his control, the state treasury and administration were centralized, land was nationalized and redistributed, and facets of the state structure were modernized. After his death in 1849 his successors maintained these initiatives though the nation's resources were not able to meet the excessive demands imposed on the state by modernization. Ultimately, Egypt emerged from the modernization program seriously in debt—a situation which led to the British and French decision to support the deposition of Ali's grandson Ismail from power and expand their influence in Egypt.

Development of Egyptian Nationalism

During the 147 years that Muhammad Ali and his successors ruled Egypt, the idea of nationalism spread throughout the country. An expanding educational system was the main medium for the transmission of nationalist ideals. Nationalists questioned the traditional authority of Islamic leaders and suggested that the individual had a responsibility for the condition of the world in which he lived. The intellectual base necessary for a popular revolt had thus been laid.

The strongest movement against the British and French dual control of Egypt was led by Colonel Ahmad Urabi. Many of his followers were lower-ranking army officers, but Urabi was the son of a village peasant. Urabi's movement gained control of parliament as the national party and was powerful enough to force Ismail's successor, Tewfik, to guarantee a constitution. The party then called a national assembly and in 1881 drew up a moderate reform program. In 1882, however, Britain and France protested the formation of a constitutional government. They felt that Egypt's nascent nationalism would free her from European control and jeopardize their financial interests. Britain presented two ultimatums to the Egyptian government. Both were rejected. Thereupon, Britain invaded Egypt and Urabi's forces were overpowered.

Urabi's revolt was one of the most significant events in the development of Egyptian nationalism. It was a social revolution as well as a political movement because the peasantry and the new middle class were for the first time expressing themselves as a political force through their support of Urabi. They were signifying their dislike of both foreign intervention in Egyptian affairs and of the collaboration of their own leaders with foreign powers.

British Occupation

British rule in Egypt was strict. The Egyptians were allowed a legislative council, but real power was held by the British administration under the British consul general. The British began to organize Egypt's administration and reduce its debt, but these improvements were made at a cost. Social and political problems as well as education were almost entirely ignored. The British refusal to allow an increase in self-government led much of the nationalist movement to develop independently. This was especially true after Tewfik's successor, Abbas II, allied himself with the nationalist forces against the British. Eventually, however, he was persuaded to return to a traditional pro-British stance through the urging of Egypt's new British administrator, Sir Eldon Gorst.

Britain formally declared Egypt a protectorate in 1914. Over the next four years the country was used as a military base. Labor was conscripted, a large number of British forces (whose arrogance and ethnocentrism antagonized the native population) were brought into Egypt, and rampant inflation took place because of their ability to pay higher prices for commodities. Restrictions on the production of cotton were imposed, and confiscated crops were sold at huge profits. Thus, all levels of Egyptian society grew embittered toward the British. However, nationalist leaders were determined to hold their forces in check while the war lasted.

Two days after the armistice Saad Zaghlul (a prominent nationalist) and his followers formed the Egyptian delegation (*Wafd*) to present a demand for independence to the British commissioner, General Sir Reginald Wingate. Although Wingate urged his government to allow Zaghlul to proceed to London, permission to hear the Egyptian demands was refused. This gave rise to a popular revolution in 1919 throughout all of Egypt. The British were forced to allow the Egyptians to attend the Paris Peace Conference, where Zaghlul's delegation failed to secure Egypt's independence as the British protectorate was recognized by the attending nations.

Independent Egypt

Despite Zaghlul's failure in Paris, the British decided to take steps to ameliorate Anglo-Egyptian antagonisms. The English drew up a treaty of alliance with Egypt in 1920 to replace the protectorate. Both Zaghlul and the Egyptian people rejected the treaty, fearing a disguised continuation of British occupation. Realizing that Zaghlul would agitate against any treaty, the British deported him, and unilaterally terminated the protectorate in March 1922. Egypt became a monarchy under King Ahmad Fouad, but Britain continued to hold the reigns of power.

On April 19, 1923, the new king proclaimed Egypt a constitutional monarchy. Parliamentary elections were held the following January, and the Wafd party won a resounding victory. Saad Zaghloul became the first prime minister and immediately began to press Britain to renegotiate the 1920 treaty of alliance. In November 1924, the king dismissed Zaghloul's government. For the next decade, the palace and the British essentially controlled the official political agenda in parliament, while the Wafd led the nationalist struggle in opposition.

The Wafd returned to power in 1936 with a major electoral victory, forming an all-Wafd cabinet. The government immediately began to press Britain for a treaty to define the terms of reference of Anglo-Egyptian relations in order to establish Egypt's independence. On August 26, 1936, the Anglo-Egyptian treaty was signed in London and ratified by the Egyptian parliament the following December. Though the treaty did not free Egypt from British domination, it did limit British control and moved Egypt to the legal status of an independent state. As a result, on May 26, 1937, Egypt became a member of the League of Nations.

At the beginning of World War II, Egypt was once again turned into a British base. Although the upper echelon of Egyptian society prospered as a result of the war, the masses suffered severe privation analogous to their experiences in World War I. The British took drastic measures to keep Egypt neutral. Axis sympathizers were purged from the government, the palace was barricaded, and Fouad's successor, Farouk, was forced to hand over the reins of government to Mustafa al-Nahas, leader of the Wafd, to quell nationalist demands and secure public cooperation with the war effort.

By the end of the war, the Wafd was ousted from power. Thus began a long period of domestic instability and unrest that culminated in Egyptian demands for a revision of the Anglo-Egyptian Treaty of 1936.

These events and the creation of the State of Israel in 1948 substantially altered Egypt's perception of Britain. The treaty resulted in the presence of British troops in the Suez Canal Zone and in the Sudan. Determined to control itself, Egypt called for the complete withdrawal of all British forces. The Egyptians were especially concerned with the status of the Sudan because it controlled Egypt's access to the Nile.

In 1948, Egypt joined the Palestine war. The poor performance of its army against Zionist forces and corrupt government practices humiliated the Egyptian people, particularly junior army officers. Egypt considered Britain, above all, to be responsible for the establishment of the State of Israel. Against this tense background, the Wafd party regained power in 1950 and in 1951 abrogated the 1936 Anglo-Egyptian Treaty. It also declared Farouk king of Egypt and Sudan. Hostilities broke out between Egyptians and British, and in December, forty-three Egyptian policemen were killed during a British attack on the police barracks of Ismailia. Riots erupted in Cairo on January 26, 1952, "Black Saturday," in which most of the foreign quarter was burned. Farouk used the occasion to dismiss Nahas, thus throwing Egypt into its most serious political crisis in a generation.

Egypt in Revolution

On the night of July 22–23, 1952, a group of young army officers, calling themselves the Free Officers, led a successful coup against the government of Egypt. King Farouk abdicated on July 26 in favor of his son and went into exile. The Egyptian monarchy came to a formal end on June 18 of the following year when a republic was proclaimed.

The causes that led to the Free Officers' coup were numerous. Egypt's socioeconomic problems had become extreme by 1952 and the existing political structure had rendered them insolvable. Its economic problem was twofold: overpopulation and poverty. At the time of Muhammad Ali's suzerainty over Egypt, the country had a population of 3 million. By 1952 it had grown to about 20 million—an increase of 566 percent in little more than a hundred years. This tremendous increase had severe economic and social consequences. No attempts at modernization led to the expected trickle-down effects. Income inequalities increased, thereby exacerbating poverty, which led to high population growth. Egypt remained a desperately poor and underdeveloped nation whose masses were thoroughly and hopelessly impoverished. Poverty was further compounded by the concentration of landownership in a few hands. At the time of the revolution 71 percent of landowners had only 12 percent of the land and owned less than half a feddan each (a feddan is a little larger than an acre). At the other end of the spectrum, 191 owners possessed 9 percent of the land, owning between 1,000 and 2,000 feddans each. These landowners lived in the cities and were out of touch with conditions in the countryside where 80 percent of the population lived. This minority invariably controlled Egypt's political, social, and economic life.

The political scene was as stagnant as the economic scene. The monarchy had lost all remnants of popular support and the nationalist movement—symbolized by the Wafd—had lost its dynamism and credibility. The conservative old guard was not prepared to undertake the necessary economic or political reforms. All these factors, combined with dismay over British actions in Palestine and Britain's refusal to withdraw its forces from the Sudan or the Canal Zone, led to the revolution.

The Free Officers' Committee was primarily a group of young officers who had attended military college together and who had developed a broad secret organization in the army. The acknowledged head of the group was Gamal Abdal Nasser, the son of a post office clerk, and in order to obtain wider support they chose as their nominal leader the respected officer and distinguished soldier General Mohammed Naguib.

In the first months after the July coup d'état the Free Officers, under the leadership of their thirteen-man executive committee, the Revolutionary Command Council (RCC), attempted to reorganize the political system and restore order to Egyptian life. Politically, this meant weakening the system enough to make the economic and social goals of the revolution come about more quickly. Within months of the revolution, the parties of prerevolutionary Egypt were dissolved and a new constitution proclaimed. Obstacles to the revolution remained, of course, as the existence of the fundamentalist Muslim Brotherhood (the only remaining large political organization to survive the dissolution of the parties) prevented the RCC from consolidating the revolution.

All was not well with Naguib either, and he was replaced by Nasser in April 1954 after a short power struggle. Naguib was placed under house arrest in October after an attempt on Nasser's life, an attempt sponsored by the Muslim Brotherhood; Nasser used their involvement to disband the organization forcibly. Thus by late 1954, Nasser had reached the pinnacle of power, a position that was consolidated by revoking the Anglo-Egyptian condominium over the Sudan and evacuating British troops from the Canal Zone in 1956 after years of negotiations.

Negotiations with the World Bank and the United States began in 1955 over the financing of the Aswan High Dam project. This huge project was expected to increase Egypt's cultivable land by one-third and to supply sufficient hydropower to meet all of the country's projected needs. In July 1956, the United States withdrew its financial participation in the project in retaliation for Egypt's policies of positive neutrality and anti-imperialism (discussed subsequently under foreign policy). To keep the project from collapsing, on July 26, 1956, Nasser nationalized the Suez Canal to finance the dam.

Britain, France, and Israel invaded Egypt on October 29, 1956, under the pretext of securing the canal and protecting international shipping. World condemnation of the invasion, Soviet and Chinese threats to intervene, and a U.S. ultimatum to the tripartite alliance forced the withdrawal of the invading forces by March 1957.

The aborted invasion resulted in the unprecedented rise in the international stature of President Gamal Abdal Nasser and consolidated his role as the symbol and leader of Arab nationalism. Perhaps the most dramatic outcome was the formation of the United Arab Republic on February 1, 1958, based on a union between Egypt and Syria. Three weeks after its formation, on February 21, Nasser was elected the first president of the union—the pinnacle of Nasser's success and influence.

Nasserism

Practical considerations colored Nasser's initial approach to politics. The concerns of building a viable political order and maintaining the position of the Revolutionary Command Council were paramount. His main concern prior to the Suez crisis was the domestic security of his regime.[1] Even positive neutralism and the Suez situation were pragmatic responses to threatening circumstances.

After 1956, as events in Egypt began to impinge upon the politics of other states, there developed a more deliberate construction of ideological tenets and the application of these tenets to both domestic and foreign affairs. Thus the term Nasserism came into general use to explain the relationship between Nasser's ideas and

Egypt's internal and external politics. Nasser's thought was, to a large degree, typical of Middle Eastern political thought, and his role was simply that of the first effective articulator of policy with this general set of attitudes. The term Nasserism is misleading somewhat because the movement was neither originally nor exclusively Nasser's. Yet the force of Nasserism, its principles and the movement it designated, spread throughout the Arab world as a force to upset the status quo and threaten the balance of power.

The principles that Nasser forwarded were few and their applications varied as new situations arose, so that a firm appraisal of them is difficult. Three were notable. The first of these was anti-imperialism—the rejection of any form of foreign interference or influence in the Arab states. The second was pan-Arabism, a major influence on Nasser's ideas and policies. He believed that Egypt was an integral part of the Arab world, and the natural leader of the Arab states.[2] The third was social democracy. Nasser's regime was not notably democratic, and this goal may seem mere propaganda, but that was not the case. Nasser regarded democracy as the ultimate goal of his regime. However, political democracy depended on economic and social equality, and the achievement of such equality required stern measures that might preclude the immediate establishment of democratic institutions. Furthermore, Nasser contended that Egypt's experience with parliamentary institutions under the monarchy showed that the people of Egypt were not yet prepared for the proper use of democracy and had to be taught the necessary skills and enterprise. This step, he said, required firm leadership.

By 1964 the policies of Nasserism had profoundly affected Egyptian society. A provisional constitution enacted in early 1964 divided the powers of government between the president, the National Assembly, local judicial authorities, and the Arab Socialist Union (ASU). Nasser assumed the presidency in 1956, but his personality, energy, and leadership extended his authority far beyond any constitutional limits. He dominated the National Assembly, the cabinet, and the ASU; he appointed a number of vice presidents as well as the cabinet, members of which served as his administrative assistants. But he did not have complete control of the military

in the early years. Field Marshal and Vice President Abd al-Hakim
Amer held the real power in the army, especially between 1961 and
1967. Nasser regained control over the army after Israel's rapid immobilization of the Egyptian air force and the complete collapse
of Egypt's military defenses in the Six-Day War of 1967. Amer subsequently committed suicide. Following this, Nasser's control of
the army and security agencies was undoubted. His power was
based not on organization alone but on intense public loyalty. Institutional arrangements mattered little; in the United Arab Republic
the center of the government and political authority lay with Nasser
and his coterie of close associates. Thus, the UAR became a heavily
centralized state with all power focused on the leader.

Institutional arrangements were not unimportant. In October
1961, Nasser began to rebuild the political system of the United
Arab Republic. He believed that the National Union, as established
in Egypt in 1956 and taken up in Syria in 1958, failed because reactionary elements had infiltrated the organization and subverted it.
As part of a completely remodeled system of government, he
planned a new mass organization that would not be susceptible
to this sort of subversion. The ASU was to be created in place
of the old National Union. Its purity would be protected by a
requirement that half of the members of any representative body
of the ASU had to be workers and farmers.

On December 2, 1962, the statutes of the Arab Socialist Union
were approved by the National Congress of Popular Forces.[3] This
1,750-member body was established as the "supreme political authority" of the United Arab Republic. All public organizations and
the press were under its control. Its leadership selected the candidates for the National Assembly. It controlled the trade unions,
student federations, and other popular organizations. It represented an effort to bring revolutionary ideals to the younger generation and provide "a perpetual source of revolutionary van-
guards."[4] It provided an organization that was seen to embody
the principles of social democracy and to reach down to the grass
roots and serve as a mobilizing medium of the masses.

Aside from governmental structures and the ASU, the chief instruments of the revolution in Egypt were the communications

media and the control of access to them. The government maintained a monopoly of broadcasting services, and the press was controlled by the ASU. Political education was also provided by government-controlled publishing houses, television, and, of course, through the educational system where great strides were made in improving the quality and quantity of education available.

The efforts of the government of Egypt were directed at establishing a participant society whose members had the skills and values needed for modernization. Whether the methods used were appropriate to the task was a moot point.[5] In seeking to build his participant society, Nasser relied upon authoritarian methods. While this accorded well with Egypt's political traditions and was successful in the economic realm, the narrow range of meaningful political activities precluded the development of attitudes suitable for democratic politics. Nasser's reliance on authoritarian methods made impossible the use of any other means of governing.

Economic Policy

The first crisis of the revolution occurred little more than a month after the overthrow of the monarchy. The Free Officers had little in the way of ideological commitments, but they were committed to certain institutional reforms, especially in the system of land tenure. In early September 1952 a land reform program was proposed by the RCC to Ali Maher, who had been appointed prime minister. Maher and his civilian associates were not ready to attack the interests of the landowning classes; when he attempted to stall and dilute the reform he was removed.

Aside from land reform, the new regime followed traditional patterns in its economic policy. Although the RCC gave more emphasis to government investment in social overhead capital than the old regime had, no new principles of economic policy or social organization were established at this time. Government interference in the economy was limited to tax and tariff policy and the control of central banking through the National Bank of Egypt, a privately owned firm.

However, by 1957–58, government planning had become an economic reality in Egypt, a result of the nationalization of foreign assets in 1957 as a retaliatory measure of the Suez war. It seemed that economic development without government involvement was impossible. A National Planning Committee was formed to prepare a plan for reorganizing the economy. Though none of its recommendations were carried out, it laid the groundwork for the beginning of a series of five-year plans to begin in 1960.

The plans were the first sign of the government's increasing commitment to reorganizing the economy. The banking system was reorganized, and industrial development was encouraged through state provision of funds. High rates of economic growth were forecast, but distorted figures rendered growth estimates useless. The industrial sector did benefit from reorganization, and self-sufficiency in food produce was attained except for wheat.

By July 1961, three-quarters of capital investment was derived from government sources, and a series of nationalizations that took place the same year resulted in even more concentration of the economy in government hands. The tendency to socialism thus had been set in 1961, despite the fact that the attempt to spread nationalization to Syria led to its secession from the United Arab Republic. Whereas the government had done little to change the policies of the monarchy prior to the end of 1956, the reforms since were thorough enough to justify the comment that Egypt was on the road to a fully socialist and controlled economy.

Apart from socialism and planning, the other emphasis of the Egyptian economy under Nasser was on development. The two immediate problems in developing an economy are financing and planning. The first includes generating internal savings and dealing with problems of capital inflow, and the second subsumes such matters as sector emphasis and priorities. These problems were so complex that they proved difficult to overcome. Internal financing came mostly from government-provided investment capital derived from nationalized industries and tax revenues. The Suez Canal and import restrictions also raised capital but development funds came largely from foreign aid rather than internal financing. The United States and USSR were the largest contributors of both capital and technical expertise.

Foreign Policy

Within the context of policy determinants, several foreign policy principles evolved under Nasser's rule. The foreign policy of the United Arab Republic was founded upon eight basic principles: (1) adherence to the policy of peaceful co-existence, positive neutrality, and active participation in resolving international problems; (2) rejection of membership in cold war blocs or pacts, liquidation of all foreign military bases, and lessening of world tension; (3) assertion of the legitimate right of self-determination and liquidation of all forms of colonialism; (4) respect for the sovereignty of independent states and protection of the freedom and independence of their peoples; (5) exertion of all efforts for total disarmament, a total nuclear test ban, and solution of all disputes through peaceful means; (6) promotion of economic and cultural international cooperation; (7) respect for all international obligations within the framework of the UN Charter; and (8) respect for human rights and condemnation of the policy of racial discrimination.[6]

These principles may be categorized as positive neutralism (1 and 2), anti-imperialism (3, 4, and 8), and general expressions of goodwill derived from the UN Charter. The items in the last category had little real effect upon the foreign policy of Egypt except as a formal observance. The principles of positive neutralism and anti-imperialism, however, were major factors in determining the manner in which Egypt dealt with the rest of the international community. Positive neutralism evolved as a policy for nonaligned states at the Bandung Conference in April 1958. The concept was that to prevent the outbreak of a nuclear war, developing states should not be aligned to either of the superpower blocs but neither should they be passive watchers of international events. Instead, they should be actively involved in issues important to them and the world. Only in this way could they ensure their independence and have a real effect on global politics.

Anti-imperialism is closely related to the concept of nonalignment and was also a driving force in foreign policy because of Egypt's desire to be truly independent. The UAR belonged to no alliance and opposed (though unsuccessfully) the creation of Western-sponsored alliances throughout the Middle East.

These policy foundations manifested themselves in a number of ways. Nasser was highly active in both regional and global affairs by consistently supporting liberation movements in the Third World and by fighting all attempts by colonial powers to extend their influence, especially in 1956 when Britain, France, and the State of Israel launched a concerted military effort to weaken Egyptian control over the Suez Canal.

The regime's opposition to colonialism took the form of aid to independence movements in colonial possessions and diplomatic support for leaders of nationalist movements in Africa and the Middle East. Although the United Arab Republic at times became involved in the internal affairs of some Arab states (largely resulting from the vagaries of Nasser's pan-Arab aspirations), it had always been a concern of the regime to prevent interference by imperialist or reactionary powers in the affairs of other states.

Egypt's unique geographic location combined with the immense popularity of Nasserism raised Egypt to unprecedented heights of influence throughout the Third World, and especially in the Middle East. As a result of history, culture, language, and geography, the United Arab Republic placed the highest priority upon its relations with the Arab world and secondary importance on its African relations. The charter adopted in 1962 as an official expression of the United Arab Republic's national aspirations identified Arab unity, the pan-African movement, and Afro-Asian solidarity, in that order, as Egypt's main spheres of influence. The entire order was influenced by the UAR's East-West relations.

Relations with the Maghrib and Mashriq

Although Egypt lies in North Africa, its closest affinity has been with the Arabs of Asia. One reason is that historically, Egypt was linked to the east by trade and migration patterns. The deserts of western Egypt and Libya effectively separate Egypt from all of North Africa except Cyrenaica. Second, the Arab states of the east, like Egypt, border on or are in close proximity to the State of

Israel, so that the presence of that state constitutes a direct threat to them. The final factor was cultural: North Africans have had a much longer and more intimate association with Europe, particularly with France, and therefore have been more influenced by European culture than have eastern Arabs.

Two factors pervaded the United Arab Republic's relationship with the Mashriq: Nasser's concept of pan-Arabism and his view that Egypt should take the lead in that movement, and his position as a symbol of Arab nationalist ideals and pan-Arab aspirations. As such, he was able to evoke considerable popular support. The governments of Jordan, Syria, Iraq, and Lebanon all experienced mass demonstrations in support of the principles represented by Nasserism, and all of them were seriously threatened or, in the cases of Iraq, Yemen, and Syria, toppled by pro-Nasserite coups.

Two elements drove Egypt's pan-Arabist foreign policy: the desire for support from states of common interest, and the common cultural heritage and history of the states of the region, which lent strength to their perceptions of communality. The concepts of Arab socialism or social democracy were closely tied to pan-Arabism, as Nasser believed that unity was possible only when the gaps in development between Arabs were eliminated. To this end, from February 1958 until September 1961, Nasser's chief task was the creation of a union with Syria. It involved the integration of the political systems and, more fundamentally, the economic and social systems. The two states were highly dissimilar in tradition and culture, and to integrate their societies it was obviously necessary to integrate their institutions. Nasser attempted to export the principles and methods of the Egyptian revolution to Syria, but his attempt failed in September 1961 with a military coup against the Nasserites in Damascus followed by a proclamation of Syrian independence.

After the union with Syria dissolved, the United Arab Republic took a more cautious line with its Middle Eastern neighbors. Relations with Syria, Iraq, Jordan, and Saudi Arabia fluctuated between open hostility and cordiality. In the first period after the secession, the Syrian government, supported by Iraq, attacked Nasser continually. The Jordanian and Saudi governments also assailed the United Arab Republic. In August 1962 the republic temporarily withdrew from the Arab League under Syrian criticism. Egypt's prestige in the Arab world, despite continued popular support throughout the region, was at its lowest ebb.

In September 1962 a rebellion broke out in Yemen; Nasser immediately supported the rebels while the Saudi government supported the conservative forces. This return to the offensive on foreign policy initially restored much self-confidence to the Egyptian government and people. However, the war proved to be protracted, sanguinary, and costly.

By 1963 the pendulum had again swung in Nasser's favor. On February 8, 1963, the Iraqi regime was overthrown; its leader, General Kassim, was assassinated, and he was replaced by the pro-Egyptian Aref. On March 8 a coup in Damascus replaced the anti-Nasser government with men more favorable to Egypt. Unity negotiations soon began and a Tripartite Unity Agreement was signed. However, the Ba'ath party in both Iraq and Syria was not prepared to yield power rapidly, and the repression of Nasser's adherents in these countries led to Egypt's withdrawal from the agreement and renewed bitterness between Egypt and the Ba'athists. Following the Ba'athists' overthrow in Iraq, at an Arab summit meeting in January 1964, friendly relations were restored between Egypt and all the Arab states except Syria. The failure to settle the Yemen war led to renewed friction with Saudi Arabia, and relations with Jordan were tenuous.

Although tentative moves toward Arab unity continued, the prospects for unification were dim. Nasser firmly believed that the various states should have a unity of purpose and accomplish their internal revolutions successfully before real unity could be achieved. Even after the disastrous war of June 1967, Nasser was still the foremost leader in the Middle East.

Africa

The second area of concern in the United Arab Republic's hierarchy of interest was Africa. Several factors led to Egypt's involvement. The first was the historic and strategic interest of Egypt in the security of the water resources of the Nile. The second was the anti-imperialist policy of Egypt, which led to its involvement with African independence and nationalist movements. This support went beyond a principle of commitment; it was also motivated by strategic and geopolitical considerations.

Geopolitical concerns are seen most clearly in Egypt's relations with Sudan. Though Egypt rejected the idea of the "unity of the Nile Valley" following the 1952 revolution, the Sudan remained of paramount concern to Egyptian policy makers. While Cairo respected the Sudan's right to self-determination and had not violated its independence, it had guarded the Sudan's sovereignty from Western encroachments and attempted to maintain close relations. Moreover, the two countries reached agreements for the equitable division of the Nile waters and for cooperation on Nile projects. The Aswan High Dam project, for example, was made possible by a November 1959 agreement regarding division of the waters and the resettlement of Sudanese displaced by the project.

As well as supporting movements for Moroccan, Tunisian, and Algerian independence, Egypt provided a refuge and a base of operations for the leaders of many of the African independence movements. From 1954 to 1964 the efforts of the Egyptian government in this respect were of considerable aid to anticolonial movements. As the first phase of anticolonialism ended, this role diminished in importance, although the United Arab Republic continued to aid the South African nationalist movement as well as Holden Roberto's provisional government of Angola and was a major contributor to the Liberation Committee of Nine of the Organization of African Unity. These efforts established Egypt as a leader of the African nationalist struggle for independence.

Egyptian interest in Africa was pushed farther by Israeli efforts to penetrate the continent. The United Arab Republic had attempted at various conferences to counter Israeli penetration, primarily by portraying the State of Israel as an outpost of imperialism. By 1964, however, this policy appeared to be ineffective; the Black African states did not view the State of Israel as the threat it appeared to the Egyptians. Israeli economic penetration was viewed by such statesmen as Hastings Banda of Malawi as welcome aid and not a threat, unless it reached proportions which endangered the interests or autonomy of the state involved. However, the picture changed after the 1967 war, and by 1973 most African states had broken relations with the State of Israel.

The Third World

Egypt viewed the Third World as a countervailing force to the major power blocs. Although it constituted neither a bloc nor an alliance in the strict sense, it proved to be a cogent alignment of the smaller nations in their pursuit of an effective voice in the international community, particularly with regard to the cold war powers.

Egypt's assumption of a position of leadership among the neutralist nations meant that Nasser, like the other participants, had a platform from which to expound his ideas and a base of support at the international level. His concern with the neutralist nations was on both ideological and practical levels. He supported antiimperialist and independence movements, both because of a commitment to the principles involved and because it was in Egyptian interests.

Nasser stressed that the unity of all freedom fighters was an important factor for the success of any revolutionary movement.[7] Thus among the strong and fairly united group of neutralist states, Nasser found support for his policies and a means of advancing his country's international interests. At the same time, leadership in such a bloc gave the people of the United Arab Republic a sense of national pride.

East-West Relations

Nasser's relations with the West were influenced by his antiimperialist policies and the West's support of the State of Israel. His long-standing opposition to a Western-dominated Middle East defense alliance stemmed from this. That the dissolution of the Syrian union was caused by reactionary forces in Syria stemmed in part from his conviction that the West was primarily a force for reaction in the Middle East and used the State of Israel as a base to influence the region. Furthermore, the State of Israel was viewed as an outpost of Western imperialism. Inasmuch as the State of Israel was a Western creation and a thorn to Arab nationalism, continued Western support and maintenance of Israeli military superiority created a constant strain in Egyptian-Western relations and resulted in the entrance of the cold war into Middle East politics with the Czech arms deal of 1955. The deal was a result of Egypt's effort to offset Israeli military superiority in the region and the West's refusal to supply Egypt with arms. It represented the first Middle Eastern arms deal with the Socialist bloc and effectively ended the West's monopoly on the region's arms supply.

The relative decline in Egyptian-Western relations led Egypt and the Soviet Union to develop friendly ties. They supported each other diplomatically in many areas, particularly in Africa, but Soviet-Egyptian relations were merely on a formal state-to-state level. Nasser had little use for communists in Egypt or elsewhere in the Middle East and had consistently opposed them. By denying local communists any power, he thought himself to be well defended against any threat from the USSR.

Nasser maintained his position well in the narrow zone between East and West; he did not overcommit himself to one side or the other. After Suez he placed more reliance on the Soviet Union, but he also sought to exploit the Sino-Soviet split to maintain a balance. Although relations with the West were strained, there is little evidence that Nasser sought to cut himself completely off from the Western nations. The chief Egyptian concerns in foreign policy matters concerning the cold war were the maintenance of sovereignty, domestic development, and enhancement of Egyptian prestige. Egypt was willing to accept aid from either side. However, the tenets of positive neutralism proscribed permanent attachments to either one of the blocs. The freedom of maneuver gained by Egypt through these methods had allowed Nasser to pursue a number of prestige-building programs, such as the Aswan High Dam, which the Soviet Union financed after the U.S. withdrawal from the project in 1956. He was not totally dependent upon either side and thus could take risks not possible under conditions of dependency.

A key to Nasser's success at treading so precariously between East and West was in part a function of Egypt's geographic location, Nasser's ability to manipulate the Arab masses, and his leading role among the nonaligned nations. The interests of the West in the Middle East centered around the economic and strategic importance of this area; no guarantees were possible of its continued security without Egyptian cooperation. The interests of the Soviets were far more political than economic and related to Africa almost as much as to the Middle East; Nasser provided them with a link to both areas.

The primary key to Nasser's foreign policy in regard to East-West relations was flexibility. Although he had moved closer to the East over the years, and the June 1967 war with the State of Israel resulted in closer Soviet supervision of Egypt's military aid program, he still kept the lines to the West open.

The UAR and the State of Israel

Egypt's confrontation with the State of Israel was its central foreign relations problem. The Arab-Israeli conflict influenced almost every aspect of Egypt's external relations: It was the fulcrum of its Middle East policy, the arbiter of its East-West relations, and the propellent of its African policy. It had escalated to this magnitude over some two decades.

Nasser's initial opposition to the State of Israel—indeed, the opposition of Arab nationalists throughout the Middle East—stemmed from the irreconcilable aims of Arab nationalism and Zionism over the land of Palestine. The world's denial of the Palestinians' right to self-determination, even while recognizing the same rights of all other peoples under the UN Charter, violated a fundamental tenet of Arab nationalism—and of nationalism per se. The resulting degradation of the Palestinian population served as a constant reminder and ultimately a symbol of the struggle of Arab nationalism.

These were the considerations that motivated Egypt with regard to the State of Israel in the period immediately following Nasser's revolution. But they certainly were not central to Nasser's policies or problems at this time. Nasser's opposition to the State of Israel was primarily rhetorical. Egypt, or the entire Arab world for that matter, could pose no real threat to the State of Israel. The 1948 war had effectively demonstrated that the Arab East was no match for Israel. Small in terms of population, but thoroughly modern relative to organization and technology, Israel was able to defeat the Arab states and would likely outstrip them for a long time to come. Involved as Nasser was in an internal revolution to re-shape Egyptian society, he could little afford to take on Israel, although he did take on the responsibility of spokesman for Arab nationalism. After 1948 the State of Israel was a bête noire to the Arab states. Arab attacks against Israel were mainly rhetorical. Their only effective weapons were economic boycott, denial of passage through the Suez Canal, and diplomatic isolation from the Arab world.

The maintenance of the nation's security and territorial integrity were the sine qua non of the Egyptian government. The perception of Zionist policies as expansionist, the revelation of February 1955 that the State of Israel could indeed easily encroach upon Egyptian territory and the confirmation of October 1956 that it would do so, raised in Egypt the specter of gravely endangered national security. Israel was no longer merely the bête noire of Arab nationalism. It was no longer the source of the displacement and deprivation of the Palestinians. It now appeared as a formidable foe bent on territorial conquest. Thus it played a paramount role in Egypt's foreign policy. Indeed, Israel's June 1967 blitzkrieg against the Arab states deepened Egyptian fears and polarized both Arab and Israeli positions.

After Israel's occupation of the West Bank, the Golan Heights, the Sinai peninsula, and the Gaza Strip, Egyptian foreign policy distinguished between the Palestine problem proper and the Arab-Israeli dispute.[8] The official position was that the solution of the former could be reached only if the Palestinians themselves were a party to any settlement. As to the latter, the UAR accepted the

November 1967 UN resolution as a basis for the peaceful settlement of the conflict. A settlement would allow the UAR to concentrate once more on internal reforms and economic development, movements whose progress the war had severely arrested. Nasser asserted that if Israel evacuated its troops from the captive areas, the Arab states would favor a declaration of nonbelligerence; the recognition of the rights of each country to live in peace; the territorial integrity of all countries in the Middle East, including the State of Israel, in recognized and secure borders; freedom of navigation on international waterways; and a just solution to the Palestinian refugee problem. However, Nasser warned that if Israeli forces did not withdraw from Arab territory, there was the possibility of another full-scale war. He cautioned that Israeli withdrawal alone would not bring a settlement. Instead, if there was to be lasting peace, he insisted, Israel must permit the return of the more than one million Arabs who had been expelled from Palestine since 1948.

The Sadat Regime

Nasser died suddenly on September 28, 1970. He was succeeded by his vice president, Anwar Sadat. Sadat was one of the original Free Officers of Egypt's 1952 revolution, and, although he remained Nasser's protégé thereafter, Nasser never gave him a position among his coterie of advisors or in his government. Sadat's appointment to the vice presidency nine months prior to Nasser's death reflected more a ceremonial appointment to a powerless position than an appointment made after serious consideration of the problem of succession. In other words, Sadat's succession to power was one of those absurd accidents of history—an outcome of chance and happenstance rather than a dramatic historic movement.

Chance and his association with Nasser were Sadat's only claims to legitimacy. To consolidate his rule, Sadat immediately emphasized his loyalty to Nasser's principles in both domestic and foreign affairs and pledged to carry on Nasser's policies. The transition of power thus appeared smooth, but within six months Sadat purged the presidency of strong Nasserite elements so he could pursue unchallenged his own agenda for Egypt. Sadat struck the first challenge to the power base on May 15, 1971. He arrested and prosecuted ninety-one leading Nasserite figures on charges of treason. They included a vice president, a deputy prime minister, six cabinet members, four members of the Supreme Executive of the Arab Socialist Union and twenty-two members of its Central Committee, the chairman of the National Assembly, his deputy, and the head of the Public Security Agency.

The 1971 Permanent Constitution

Sadat described his action as a corrective step. Following the corrective step, Sadat's program began to crystallize, beginning with the promulgation of a new constitution in 1971. In essence, the constitution made no change in the political system set by Nasser. The Permanent Constitution defined Egypt as a "democratic, socialist state based on the alliance of the working forces of the people." However, one major change was the role of religion in the new order. Islamic jurisprudence was "the principal source of legislation." Sadat encouraged and supported the growth of the radical Islamic groups in the beginning of his rule. He also allied his regime with the old foes of Nasserism, essentially the Muslim Brotherhood and the old aristocracy represented by the New Wafd. This support of the religious groups had a political goal, that of combatting the Nasserist social base and, by the use of religion, the creation of a new social base to support the new regime under Sadat. By the end of his regime, Sadat clashed with his allies.

Economically, Egypt was defined as a socialist system. The constitution stipulated that a comprehensive development plan would organize the national economy in order to increase the rate of growth, raise the standard of living and reduce the income gap between rich and poor. The public sector was to remain the main agent entrusted with the implementation of this plan, and public ownership would be consolidated. Private ownership would be protected so long as it was free from exploitation and was not used against the people.

The constitution retained some key elements of the Nasserist state, including the establishment of the president as the most important political figure. In the constitution, legislative power is mentioned after presidential power, which indicates that it is subservient to the president's power. Legislative power was represented in the People's Assembly, which had 350 members at the time (and by 1990 had four hundred members) at least half of whom were required to be workers and farmers. The president had the right to appoint a maximum number of ten members to the assembly. Other members were elected by direct secret public balloting. The assembly's normal duration was five years, but the president could dissolve it after holding a referendum. The main tasks of the assembly were promulgation of laws (though the president also had the power to make laws), regulation of the state budget, and supervision of the performance of the cabinet. It had the right to address inquiries to the cabinet ministers or their deputies and to withdraw confidence from a minister or the whole cabinet.

The Search for Legitimacy

The strong performance of the Egyptian army in the October 1973 Arab-Israeli war gave Sadat sufficient legitimacy and popularity to pursue overtly the de-Nasserization of the Egyptian state. Thus, the October 1973 war marked a radical redirection of Egypt's policies—both foreign and domestic.

Egypt had suffered from a state of increasing economic deterioration that had lasted into the mid-1970s. As a result of the June 1967 defeat, Egypt had to bear the economic consequences of the closure of the Suez Canal, the loss of Sinai oil, a drastic drop in tourism revenues, and a great reduction in foreign aid. It also had to manage the expenses of rehabilitating the Canal Zone residents as well as finance the new military expenditures during the war of attrition. Although Egypt received considerable Arab aid after 1967, it could by no means make up for all those losses.[9]

In this context, in the October war, Sadat had in mind not only a military crossing but "an economic 'crossing' as well."[10] He called it *Infitah*—"the Opening." As Sadat said, "just as the crossing had brought victory on the battlefield, so this second crossing would bring victory on the home front in the shape of prosperity for all."[11] The objectives of the open-door policy were to direct the public sector, to implement the basic infrastructure projects that would serve the private sector, and to offer sufficient guarantees for the Egyptian private sector to encourage it to carry out productive investment and sufficient external resources to strengthen the national economy and enhance development.[12]

The open-door policy was initiated in 1974. It was followed by several other legislations which consolidated the new policy and transformed the internal structure of the Egyptian economy. In this transformation process, the public sector, despite its huge size, especially in industry, lost its hegemony and strength. It also experienced serious productive, organizational, financing, and distribution problems. Meanwhile, the private sector expanded, though its activities were mostly parasitic and far from productive. Finally, the encouragement of foreign trade led to an unbalanced trade relationship with the world, especially the West. It also resulted in a huge deficit in the trade balance brought about by the extravagant importation of consumer and intermediary goods and the reduction of exports.[13]

The new system had disastrous effects on the socioeconomic structure of society. While it led to the emergence of a new upper class, mainly merchants and middlemen, it also aggravated inflation to an unprecedented scale and threw a greater burden on the middle and lower classes.[14]

Western countries encouraged the Egyptian open-door policy by increasing their loans to Egypt. The United States became Egypt's prime lender and donor of financial assistance. That meant that the debt problem, besides having a dangerous effect on economic development, also gave way to serious political dangers. American loans were dictated by U.S. strategic and political interests. They could be used as a tool for political pressure to direct Egyptian policies to serve American interests. In fact, an AID Report to the U.S. Congress did assert that American financial support to Egypt starting in the mid-1970s served American interests in the region.[15]

The Multiparty System

In addition to the open-door policy, the Sadat regime sought to enhance its legitimacy and base of support by declaring that reform would be implemented by gradual evolution of a multiparty democratic system. In 1974, Sadat released a paper on the reform of the Arab Socialist Union that called for a total reassessment of the political system. The ASU, though not abolished, was to become the forum representing different social forces in the society, the final goal being the emergence of new political parties. In 1976, Sadat condoned the creation of three groups representing the right, the left, and the center. Thus, in the same year, the political arena witnessed the establishment of political parties for the first time since 1953: Egypt's Arab Socialist party (center), the Liberal Socialist party (right), and the Progressive Unionist party (left). From the beginning, most high officials joined Egypt's Arab Socialist party which came to be the regime party. The 1976 elections consolidated this trend, as Egypt's party won the majority of parliamentary seats.

In 1978, two new parties joined in the system: the National Democratic party, established by Sadat himself, and the New Wafd party. The first automatically became the majority party when most leaders and members of Egypt's Arab Socialist party joined it. Egypt's party was then voluntarily dissolved. Meanwhile, Sadat encouraged the establishment of the Socialist Labor party—a new leftist party to weaken the Unionist party.

Until his assassination in 1981, Sadat was the focus of the multiparty experience, starting with the formation of parties and including the establishment of his own party and harassment of opposition even inside the parliament. A few weeks before his assassination, the situation was critical: he was responsible for arresting opposition leaders, censoring the opposition press, and breaking into the headquarters of the opposition parties under the pretext that the opposition had instigated sectarian conflict.[16]

Sadat's handicapped democracy was also hampered by several laws that he enacted in order to impose restrictions on the activities of the opposition, such as the law of value protection, protection of home front, and social peace. Thus, in May 1978, the Wafd party dissolved itself while the Unionist party suspended its activities and newspaper. The regime also blatantly intervened in the elections of 1979. Finally, the new democratic experience received its hardest blow in September 1981, when more than 1,500 people from different opposition groups along the political spectrum were arrested by Sadat.

In May 1980, the Permanent Constitution was amended in the following ways to reflect Sadat's "liberalizing" measures in the economic and political spheres. (1) Rather than having Islamic jurisprudence as the principal source of legislation, it became the sole source. (2) The ASU was abolished and Egypt was declared to have a multiparty system. (3) References to "liquidating class differences" were deleted. Instead, there was the protection of legitimate earnings and a guarantee of equal distribution of public duties and responsibilities. (4) Instead of the president of the state being reelected for only one more term, he could be reelected for an indefinite number—a reflection of the decision of the People's Assembly to make Sadat president for life. (5) A seventh section, composed of two parts, was added to the Constitution. The first addressed the establishment and formation of the Shura Council, a new consultative body, the other addressed the press and established the composition and functions of the Supreme Press Council.[17]

Egypt's "Special" Relations with the United States

At the foreign policy level, since the June 1967 war, the "situation had been 'frozen' in favor of Israel, the Soviets would not attempt to change it while the U.S. 'held all the cards' in the dispute, and only American action could break the stalemate."[18] Thus, when

Sadat came to power, he attempted to restore the Rogers Plan. Later, he declared his readiness to conduct direct negotiations with the State of Israel provided it withdrew to the 1967 borders. He stated that he was also ready to expel Soviet advisors from Egypt if the United States would support his demands firmly.[19] Neither Sadat's peace proposals, his concessions to the State of Israel (in the form of promising recognition and direct negotiation), nor his expulsion of Soviet experts in 1972 induced the United States to play a more positive role in the Middle East to change the status quo. Hence, Egypt used the October War as a means of forcing the United States to act. The effort was largely a failure, and only Egyptian concessions resulted in any American movement. By January 1974, Sadat's attempts to improve Egyptian-American relations were formalized by the reestablishment of diplomatic relations with the United States and approbation of Secretary of State Henry Kissinger's peace efforts. President Richard Nixon "forecast an era of cooperation and prosperity" and promised Egypt more than $2 billion (U.S.) as investment capital.[20] Although that figure was exaggerated the American administration provided Egypt with an "overfinanced" aid program that made it second only to the State of Israel.

As Egyptian-American relations improved, relations with the Soviet Union steadily deteriorated. Sadat expelled Soviet experts in 1972. However, in that same year, as Egypt was preparing for the October War, he sought to guarantee the supply of Soviet arms. As a sign of good will, he agreed to make naval facilities in Alexandria and Marsa Matrouh accessible to Soviet ships in December 1972. Two months later the Soviets supplied the Egyptian army with surface-to-air and antitank missiles, which contributed to the Egyptian performance in the October War.

However, Sadat's economic and political opening to the West in 1974 aroused Soviet discontent. The Soviet press publicly criticized his open-door policy. Sadat, for his part, was busy strengthening ties with the United States and Saudi Arabia and made little effort to save Egyptian-Soviet relations from collapsing.[21] By September 1975, relations worsened as Egypt signed the Sinai II Disengagement Agreement with the State of Israel. The Soviets perceived this agreement as a deviation from the Geneva Conference course that the Arabs had agreed on and saw it as a step toward excluding them from a political settlement in the Middle East. In turn, they refused to respond positively to Egypt's economic and military demands until the political differences between the countries were settled.

The negative Soviet response to Egypt's demands was used by Sadat as a pretext to abrogate unilaterally the Friendship and Cooperation Treaty between Egypt and the USSR in March 1976. Sadat sought Western armaments and believed he could do without Soviet assistance. In August 1977, he took another unilateral step and decided to suspend all Egyptian cotton sales to the Soviet Union and the Eastern bloc, ending the bilateral trade protocols between Egypt and those countries. Relations reached a low point when Sadat began his peace process with the State of Israel. Finally, in September 1981, Sadat expelled the Soviet ambassador, diplomatic officers, and technicians, accusing them of taking part in a conspiracy to topple the regime.

After its pursuit of close relations with the United States and peace with the State of Israel, Egypt lost its leading role in the Arab world and in the nonaligned movement. Egypt's policy of allying itself with the West while almost completely severing relations with the Soviet Union and the Eastern bloc greatly reduced the country's credibility at both the international and regional levels. Thus, the Sadat regime succeeded only in limiting Egypt's maneuverability through lack of a balanced relationship with the superpowers.

Egypt's isolation, therefore, pushed the country further into the American fold. The United States was now Egypt's only source of political and economic support. The price of the support was Egypt's acceptance of American demands, including those of military bases in the country.

Sadat's Separate Peace with the State of Israel

These economic and political developments served to erode the legitimacy that Sadat had acquired after the 1973 war. The fatal blow, however, was his crippling of a united Arab front in the Arab-Israeli dispute by seeking a separate accord with the State of Israel, initiated by his trip to Jerusalem in November 1977. With the signing of the Camp David Accords in September 1978, the Sadat regime made enemies both with other Arab nations and among its own people, who saw the accord as surrender to Israeli occupation of Arab lands and aggression against the Palestinians.

Sadat's explanation was that peace would create both wealth and welfare for the Egyptian people who had sacrificed more than their share in the Arab-Israeli conflict. However, the subsequent policies of the regime served to refute such an argument. Economic problems lingered and became more pronounced. Moreover, Sadat's visit to Jerusalem destroyed the Arab regional system and isolated Egypt. After Egypt signed the Treaty of Peace with the State of Israel on March 26, 1979, other Arab states convened a summit conference in Baghdad and resolved to sever relations with Egypt and suspend its membership in the Arab League, the nonaligned movement, the Islamic Conference and the Organization of African Unity. The Arab League headquarters was transferred from Cairo, and loans and financial assistance to Egypt were terminated.

As Egypt was isolated from the Arab world, the State of Israel found itself with a freer hand in the area. It began planning for economic, cultural, and technological infiltration of Egypt. Peace with Egypt also presented Israel with the chance to expand its influence throughout the region with virtual impunity: the bombing of Iraq's nuclear reactor and the full-scale invasion of Lebanon in 1982 demonstrate this point.

Although there was some feeling of optimism among the Egyptian people at the beginning of the peace process, subsequent developments served to overshadow any kind of initial hope. The nationalist forces declared their opposition to the peace policy and rallied to the defense of the Arab identity of Egypt, believed to be subjected to severe attack by government agents and intellectual mercenaries.[22] These developments led to Sadat's regime losing its legitimacy with the Egyptian people and culminated in Sadat's assassination in October 1981 by the radical religious group Islamic Jihad. There was a noticeable absence of any display of sorrow among the Egyptian masses for his death.

Mubarak: Continuity and Change

As soon as Husni Mubarak came to power in 1981 following the assassination of Sadat, he made several statements that emphasized his concern with continuity and stability. One of his earliest steps was to deal with the acute economic problem facing the country as a result of the open-door policy. Accordingly, he called for a meeting of a broad section of Egyptian economists in order to examine and offer suggestions on solving Egypt's economic difficulties. Mubarak also stressed the fact that the open-door policy should concentrate on productive projects.

The economic situation worsened rather than improved, because of the lack of will on the part of the political leadership to implement those recommendations. As a result, housing, transportation, and inflation problems were exacerbated, and the foreign debt continued to rise. Under Mubarak, the Egyptian economy maintained its mixed character, and the basic tenets of the open-door policy were still operative.

On the political level, Mubarak attempted to expand the democratic process by immediately releasing political prisoners and rehabilitating opposition forces. He also declared a policy of open discussion with everyone and respect for the opposition, which during Sadat's time was severely attacked and slandered.[23] The political arena also witnessed the return of the Wafd party and the establishment of the Islamic-oriented Ummah party in 1983. Despite such efforts, however, several forces failed to be represented in the political system such as the Nasserites, the Leftists, and the religious groups, a fact which deprived the party system of its essence and continued to aid Mubarak's hold on power.

Parliamentary Elections

The 1984 parliamentary elections were controversial, and the results were challenged. Charges of violence and forgery were made by the opposition. Results showed that the National Democratic party won the majority of votes while the Wafd emerged as the only opposition party to garner enough votes to be admitted into the People's Assembly. In February 1987, Mubarak decided to dissolve the parliament and hold elections in April on the basis of the Supreme Constitutional Court's decision to declare illegal the state's electoral laws prohibiting independents running for election. The elections resulted in better representation of the opposition parties. Although the National Democratic party still retained a wide majority, the trilateral alliance among the Labor party, the Liberal party, and the Muslim Brotherhood enabled the alliance to win sixty seats (twenty-two for the Labor, thirty-four for the Brotherhood, and four for the Liberals) and thus become the prime opposition force in the parliament. The Wafd won twelve seats.

The 1987 election was also challenged by the opposition as being unconstitutional. In 1990, the Supreme Constitutional Court declared it invalid. That September Mubarak held a referendum on whether to dissolve parliament and hold new elections based on the court's decision or to let the existing parliament stand. Results unequivocally supported new elections. Mubarak dissolved parliament and scheduled new elections for November 29.

In the meantime, a new electoral law was promulgated to make the law consistent with the constitution. The new law, however, was immediately challenged by the opposition on the basis that it made judicial supervision of elections a practical impossibility. Opponents boycotted the new elections. Low voter turnout resulted. The ruling NDP won an overwhelming majority, which took 348 of the assembly's 444 seats.

Foreign Policy Orientations

In the Egyptian-Israeli sphere, Mubarak attempted to minimize interactions between the two governments, especially after the Israeli invasion of Lebanon and the State of Israel's reluctance to relinquish the Taba Strip to Egypt. These developments instigated the opposition forces to call for severing of relations with Israel and abrogation or at least suspension of the Camp David Accords. Mubarak's reaction was to emphasize the centrality of the Palestinian issue and Egypt's commitments to any treaties the country had signed.[24] In response to Israel's action in Lebanon, the president recalled the Egyptian ambassador to the State of Israel and called for an Arab summit to examine the new developments. Mubarak also declared that the Egyptian ambassador would not return to Israel until Taba was returned and Israel withdrew its forces from Lebanon. By early 1985, however, Egyptian-Israeli relations showed signs of improvement as official visits were exchanged and Israel participated in the Cairo Book Fair.

Since that time, relations have continued, though Egypt is careful not to appear to be too close to the Israelis. Thus, Mubarak has been careful to keep relations formal and sporadic. By the late 1980s, the focus of the relationship centered around the issue of elections in the occupied territories. Though the issue is at its root competitive (with both states trying to push their proposals on the other, on the Palestinians, and on the international community), there is a degree of cooperation as well. However, with the minimal contact between the governments and their formal nature, it is highly unlikely that this cooperation will deepen and give Egyptian-Israeli relations a dynamic of their own.

At the same time, Mubarak moved to enhance his relations with the Arab countries. In an interview he stated that "Egypt is an Arab country, we were neither Westerners or Easterners";[25] he further emphasized the fact that Egypt's return to the Arab fold was only natural.[26] In order to return to the fold, Mubarak ordered the cessation of any propaganda attacks against other Arab regimes even if they attacked the Egyptian regime. Officially, Mubarak believed that any restoration of relations with Arab states should be based on an Arab initiative since they were the ones who broke off the relations initially. Behind the scenes the story was different, as Egyptian diplomats and Mubarak himself worked feverishly to regain Egypt's credibility. As a result, Egyptian troops on the Libyan border were relocated, and Mubarak attempted to cultivate ties with Oman and Jordan, with which relations were eventually restored. Mubarak also stressed the historical links between Egypt and the Sudan, which transcended personal leadership.

In 1984, Egypt restored its membership in the Islamic Conference Organization after having been dismissed five years earlier. At the same time, bilateral relations between Egypt, Arab, and Muslim countries began to show considerable improvement. It was in late 1987 that the Arab League summit decided to give Arab countries the right to restore bilateral relations with Egypt, though it was a mere formality as bilateral relations had never completely ceased. Simultaneously, by 1990 Egypt restored formal diplomatic relations with all the Arab countries. In February 1989, the Arab Cooperation Council was established among Egypt, Iraq, Jordan, and North Yemen, reflecting that Egypt is no longer interested in allying itself with radical nationalist regimes and favors conservative, pro-Western regimes like its own. The restoration of its Arab League membership in 1989 also gave it an opportunity to influence other Arab states on a more formal level.

In order to exhibit some measure of independence, Mubarak moved to reactivate Egypt's role in the nonaligned movement by reestablishing contacts with all members and restoring Egypt's diplomatic relations with the Soviet Union in July 1983. By 1987, Egyptian-Soviet cooperation began to gain momentum in several fields. The Egyptian-Soviet Friendship Society was reestablished, and the Soviets agreed to upgrade a number of existing projects. In addition, a satisfactory settlement was reached with regard to Egypt's military debt to the USSR.[27] In addition, Soviet Foreign Minister Eduard Shevardnadze arrived in Cairo in February 1989 on a visit to the region to discuss Middle East issues and ensure a Soviet role in establishing a comprehensive peace settlement. During the visit, he urged a greater Egyptian role in bringing about peace in the Middle East.

Moreover, Mubarak participated in the conference of nonaligned countries which convened in New Delhi in late 1984. During the same period, Mubarak tried to illustrate the importance of national independence by calling on the United States to be more flexible regarding economic assistance to Egypt and by criticizing the American attitude and position on the Israeli invasion of Lebanon. Nevertheless, Mubarak did not embark on any fundamental change in policy that would reduce Egypt's dependency on the United States.

After nine years of rule, Mubarak achieved great success in his foreign policy. He reinstated Egypt as a member of the Arab

League and the Islamic Organization. Egypt became active in Third World forums, especially in the Organization of African Unity, which selected Mubarak as its head in 1989. At the same time, Mubarak was striving to maintain a delicate balance between Egypt's new commitments toward the peace process and the Americans, on one hand, and the regional commitments toward the Arabs and Egypt's national sovereignty, on the other.

Egypt and the Gulf Crisis

Egypt's efforts to strike a delicate balance between incompatible foreign policy commitments were thwarted by Iraq's invasion of Kuwait on August 2, 1990. When Iraq's confrontation with Kuwait over border and oil pricing issues first erupted in May 1990, Egypt attempted to diffuse the confrontation and mediate the dispute. President Mubarak and King Hussain of Jordan each visited Baghdad and Kuwait, and initiated the organization of a meeting between Iraq and Kuwait in Jeddah on July 31. On July 25, Mubarak announced that Saddam Hussain had assured him that Iraq had no intention of invading Kuwait. (On the Gulf crisis, see concluding sections of chapters 7 and 17.)

In the first week following Iraq's invasion of Kuwait, Egypt condemned the invasion and focused its efforts on containing the conflict within the framework of an Arab solution. To this end, Mubarak called for an Arab summit conference; one was held in Cairo on August 9 and attended by all the members of the Arab League except Tunisia. On August 10, the conference issued a final communiqué (1) condemning Iraq's invasion of Kuwait, (2) rejecting Iraq's annexation of Kuwait, (3) demanding the unconditional withdrawal of Iraqi forces from Kuwait and restoration of the legitimate government of Kuwait, and (4) committing the provision of Arab forces to the defense of Saudi Arabia and the Gulf states. The communiqué was not passed unanimously. Jordan, Algeria, and Yemen abstained, while the PLO, Sudan, and Mauritania expressed reservations. Only Iraq and Libya voted against it, and the other Arab states all voted in favor of it.

Following the conference, Mubarak abandoned efforts to contain the issue within an Arab framework and threw Egypt's lot in with American efforts to build a multinational force to legitimate its intervention and massive troop deployments in Saudi Arabia, code-named Operation Desert Shield. Egypt was the first Arab state to commit troops to the American operation, and its commitment was instrumental in reconciling international reaction. In fact, Egypt played a central role in the American strategy of legitimating military intervention under a multinational guise. While Mubarak initially only committed a token force of 2,000, by September 9 he had expanded this to two divisions, including mechanized and armored units. This made Egypt the largest contributor to the force after the United States and Saudi Arabia (see list of contributors in chapter 7). On October 29, Mubarak escalated Egypt's commitment even further, pledging unlimited military support, including war planes, to protect the Gulf Arabs from Iraq.

With a foreign debt of $45 billion, Egypt's economy was hit hard by the Gulf crisis. Its three major sources of foreign currency were all directly affected: Remittances of Egyptians working in the Gulf, estimated at $3.5 billion in 1989, represented Egypt's largest single source of foreign currency; tourism, the second largest source, was estimated to lose between $500 and $800 million in the 1990–91 tourist season alone as a result of the Gulf crisis; and Suez Canal tolls, down by 25 percent as a result of the economic embargo of Iraq which reduced oil tanker traffic through the Gulf (*Khaleej Times* [Dubai], September 1, 1990). It was estimated that Egypt would lose up to $4.5 billion in the financial year ending June 30, 1991 (*Gulf News* [Dubai], October 19, 1990). In exchange for Egyptian support of American policy in the Gulf, George Bush announced in September that the United States would cancel Egypt's $7.1 billion military debt. In addition, most of the countries of the Arab Gulf canceled Egypt's debts to them, estimated to be another $7 billion, and the Arab Gulf Cooperation Council developed an aid package for Egypt of between $1 and $2 billion annually (*Khaleej Times* [Dubai], October 26, 1990). Western Europe and Japan also developed substantial aid packages for the nations whose economies were directly affected by the economic embargo with Iraq. This combined aid not only ameloriated the economic impact of the Gulf crisis on Egypt but also helped Mubarak to reduce substantially the nation's foreign debt.

In exchange, Mubarak tied Egypt's policy in the Gulf crisis entirely to American strategy, abandoning any independent role or effort. In the Arab world, he served as the lynchpin of American policy, attempting to bring other Arab states into line with the multinational strategy, or at least quelling open opposition to it. While Syria and Morocco were the only other Arab states to send token troop deployments to the Gulf, after the August 9 conference serious efforts to contain foreign intervention and formulate an Arab plan for resolution of the conflict ceased. Only King Hussain of Jordan continued efforts in this direction.

To forestall any initiative in this direction through the Arab League, Egypt engineered a vote in an Arab League meeting called in Cairo in September to speed up the timetable for the transfer of the league's headquarters from Tunis to Cairo. The league moved to Tunis in 1979 after the Camp David Accords. The return of the headquarters to Cairo had been approved by all league members in March 1990 but was not scheduled to be completed officially until the following July. The decision to speed up the timetable to complete the transfer by November 1, 1990, was passed by a bare majority of eleven votes, which in effect represented the pro-American intervention coalition dominated by the six Gulf states and represented by Egypt. The move essentially paralyzed the possibility of any future mediating role in the conflict for the Arab League.

Egypt's role in mediating Arab opposition to the American agenda became apparent in its rejection of any linkage between Israel's occupation of the West Bank and Gaza and Iraq's occupation of Kuwait. Given the unwavering U.S. support of Israel, even the drawing of an analogy weakened the credibility of Bush's argument of defending fundamental principles of international law. Furthermore, beyond disaffiliating the Arab-Israeli conflict from the Gulf crisis, Egypt acted to deflect any criticism of U.S. policy vis-à-vis the Arab-Israeli conflict in the aftermath of Israel's October 9 massacre of Palestinians at Jerusalem's al-Aqsa mosque. In an emergency ministerial meeting on October 19 called by the Arab League to discuss the slayings, Egypt led opposition against a PLO-sponsored resolution accusing the United States of "bias towards Israel's policy of repression and terror" (quoted in *Khaleej Times* [Dubai], October 19, 1990). The resolution was rejected by a vote of eleven to ten, with the six Gulf states, Egypt, Syria, Lebanon, Djbouti, and Somalia voting against it.

Clearly reflecting his opposition to any effort to initiate an Arab peace process, on November 1 Mubarak rejected outright Soviet President Mikhail Gorbachev's call for an Arab summit to seek a peaceful resolution to the crisis. "If we are going to call an Arab summit," declared Mubarak, "while there is no clear vision, it will be a summit of insults. We reject summits of insults" (quoted in *Khaleej Times* [Dubai], November 1, 1990). And indicative of Mubarak's coordination with U.S. policy, on November 7 U.S. Secretary of State James Baker went to Cairo to discuss military plans with him. Shortly thereafter, the United States announced plans almost to double the number of its troops in the Gulf, to over 400,000.

In the atmosphere of heightened war tensions that the U.S. announcement produced, King Hassan of Morocco called for a "last chance" Arab summit. While Cairo did not forthrightly reject this proposal, and Husni Mubarak flew to Libya and Syria to confer with Colonel Qaddafi and President Asad, Egypt subsequently rejected the proposal, along with Syria and Saudi Arabia.

NOTES

1. Leonard Binder, "Egypt's Positive Neutrality," in *The Revolution in World Politics*, ed. Morton A. Kaplan (New York and London, 1962), p. 179.

2. *The Philosophy of the Revolution*, p. 85.

3. Text in the *Egyptian Political Science Review* 21 (December 7, 1962).

4. Arab Socialist Union, *Socialist Youth Organization* (Cairo, 1966), p. 53.

5. Leonard Binder, "Egypt: The Integrative Revolution," in *Political Culture and Political Development*, ed. Lucien W. Pye and Sidney Verba (Princeton: Princeton University Press, 1965).

6. United Arab Republic, *Statistical Handbook 1952–1965* (Cairo, April 1966), p. 265.

7. *al-Ahram* (Cairo), April 3, 1961, p.17.

8. *Christian Science Monitor*, February 14, 1970.

9. Galal Amin, *Qisat Duion Misr al-Kharijiyah Min 'Asr Muhammad Ali ila Al-Youm* [*The Story of Egypt's External Debts From Mohammed Ali Till Now*] (Cairo: Dar Ali Mukhtar, 1987) p. 67 (in Arabic).

10. David Hirst and Irene Beeson, *Sadat* (London: Faber and Faber, 1981), p. 202.

11. Ibid., p. 204.

12. *al-Taqrir al-Istratiji al-'Arabi*, 1985, referred to hereafter *The Arab Strategic Report 1985*, ed. al-Sayyed Yassin (Cairo: Al-Ahram Center for Political and Strategic Studies, 1986) p. 346.

13. Ibid.

14. Ibid., p. 317.

15. Ibid., p. 364.

16. The information on political parties is derived mainly from ibid., pp. 330–31.

17. Gisbert H. Flanz and Albert Blaustein, "Egypt," in *Constitutions of the Countries of the World*, ed. Albert P. Blaustein and Gisbert H. Flanz, (New York: Oceana Publications Inc., 1984), pp. 4–6.

18. John Waterbury, *The Egypt of Nasser and Sadat* (Princeton, NJ: Princeton University Press, 1983), p. 127.

19. Ibid., p. 400.

20. Ibid., p. 401.

21. Ibid.

22. Ibid., p. 395.

23. al-Sayed Yassin, ed., *The Arab Strategic Report 1987* (Cairo: Al-Ahram Center for Political and Strategic Studies, 1988) pp. 330, 338, 341.

24. Ibid., 398.

25. *al-Ahram*, 27.4.1982, p. 7.; 10.10.1982, p. 7; 13.9.1981, p. 3; 1.10.1981.

26. *al-Ahram*, 9.10.1981, p.6.; 10.10.1981, p.5; 2.11.1981, p.6; *al-Akhbar*, 10.2.1982, p. 1.

27. *The Arab Strategic Report: 1987*, p. 406.

14

The Republic of Sudan

Ann Mosely Lesch

Since attaining independence in 1956, the Sudan has experienced major shifts in its political system. Parliamentary institutions and democratic freedoms have been embraced by the Sudanese, but those processes have tended to degenerate into factionalism and indecision. The failure of parliamentary governments to resolve the underlying social and economic problems—derived from the heterogeneity of the population and the weakness of the economy—has resulted in their displacement by one-man dictatorships originating in the armed forces. When a ruler has proven incapable of solving the pressing problems, and popular alienation with his arbitrary rule has escalated, he in turn has been overthrown by a mass movement.

That cycle has been repeated and risks continue. The diverse and conflicting social forces remain a basic reason for the Sudan's endemic instability.

Social Characteristics

The Sudan is the largest country in Africa, covering a million square miles that range from desert and savannah in the north to impenetrable marshes and rain-fed hills in the south. Its 24 million residents differ profoundly in ethnicity, language and religion.[1] The more than fifty ethnic groups subdivide into approximately 470 tribes. In the north the principal groups are Arab, Beja, Nuba, Nubian, and Fur. Historically, many of the peoples were independent politically. The Sultanate of Fur in the far west, for example, controlled important trade routes leading into Africa and resisted, until 1874, the Turkish-Egyptian military forces that had entered central Sudan in 1821.

Nearly half the population identifies itself as Arab, which means that even if they originated from other tribes their primary language is now Arabic, they relate to Arab culture, and they are Muslim. The Arabs of the central Nile valley dominate political and economic life, holding the main government posts in Khartoum. They also play key roles in educational institutions, trade unions, and business establishments, as well as the armed forces' officer corps. As the largest and most centrally located ethnic group, Arabs wield a disproportionate influence over policy making and over the cultural identity of the country.

Some 6 percent of the population belong to the Beja, who are concentrated in the east. They live along the Red Sea and merge with tribes in Eritrea to the south. With their own dialect and particular customs, they have remained socially distinct. Nevertheless, the Beja share Islam with other northern Sudanese and participate in the *sufi tariqahs* (mystical orders) that are prevalent in the countryside. The Beja Congress has served as a political vehicle for the community, although it won only one seat in the 1986 parliament. Beja has also been elected through the Democratic Unionist party (DUP), which dominates eastern Sudan and is linked to the Mirghani family and the Khatmiyyah sufi tariqah.

The Nuba are another geographically localized group, concentrated in the western Nuba Mountains of Kordofan. They comprise nearly 6 percent of the population. The Nuba tend to be sedentary, living in villages in the hills apart from the Arab cattle-rearing nomads of the savannah. They have distinct languages but lack a single religious identity. Some adhere to traditional beliefs while others have become Muslim or Christian. Like the Beja, they sometimes form political blocs in order to advance their specific interests. Moreover, large numbers enlist in the armed forces, although few advance to officer rank. On occasion, their leaders have demanded political autonomy for the Nuba Mountains. In the elections of

1986, the Nuba-based Sudan National party gained representation in parliament under the leadership of the Christian preacher Philip Abbas Ghabboush. The party also attracted votes from the sizeable Nuba community living in the slums of Omdurman, twin city to Khartoum.

About 3 percent of the population is Nubian. They lived traditionally along the upper reaches of the Nile, bridging the Sudan and Egypt. The Nubians had independent Christian kingdoms prior to the Muslim conquest of Egypt. They have since converted to Islam but retain their own languages and culture. When the construction of the Aswan High Dam in the 1960s flooded their homeland, many Nubians were relocated to the central Nile region. They tend to be better integrated into the political and economic mainstream than the Beja and Nuba.

The Fur, inhabiting the far west, constitute only 2 percent of the population. They have a strong sense of identity, based on their geographical remoteness from the capital, their links with Chad and Libya, and their tradition of independence.

Thus, Arab identity predominates in the northern two-thirds of the Sudan. The Beja, Nuba, Nubians, and Fur live on geographical and political margins. Most of them share Islam with the Arabs, which contributes to a common outlook despite their ethnic distinctiveness. That area contrasts with the southern third of the territory, where relatively few Arabs live, where Islam is the minority religion, and where there is a wide variety of African tribal groups.

The Dinka is the largest tribe, comprising 40 percent of the southerners and about 10 percent of the Sudanese population as a whole. They are the most important political and economic force in Upper Nile and Bahr al-Ghazal, two of the three provinces that constitute the southern region. Other influential tribes in those areas are the Nuer (5 percent of the total population) and Shilluk (1 percent), who compete for influence with the Dinka. The southernmost province, Equatoria, contains a large number of tribes that differ in language, customs, and religions. They merge with tribes in the neighboring countries. In the south, political parties tend to be based on particular ethnic groups, a phenomenon that exacerbates the inherent fragmentation. Nonetheless, at key junctures southern political forces have found a common bond in relation to the north, and the north-south ethnic divide remains critically important.

Ethnic differences are based not only on racial characteristics but also on linguistic and religious differences. Arabic is the native tongue of only half the population, although it has become the lingua franca for government administration and commerce. Since barely 20 percent of adults are literate and only a quarter live in urban areas, the oral tribal languages remain important throughout the country.

Estimates of the religious composition of the population vary widely. However, it is generally assumed that about 70 percent are Muslim, concentrated in the north. Nearly a quarter follow traditional beliefs, especially in the south. No more than 7 percent are Christian, living primarily in the south but also in the Nuba Mountains and in northern cities. Some of the Christians are the descendants of merchants or officials who migrated in the nineteenth century from Egypt or Syria, but most are southerners who moved north in search of education and employment.

The Muslims are virtually all Sunni, but they belong to different sufi brotherhoods. Originally founded by local preachers, the brotherhoods have become complex organizations. They provide a focus of loyalty wider than the tribe and sometimes play an active role politically. The Khatmiyyah tariqah, for example, backed Turkish rule, welcomed the Anglo-Egyptian conquest, and provides the underpinning for the Democratic Unionist party.

The social and cultural diversity of the Sudan has been an important factor in the operation of its political life. The tension between the heterogeneity of the population and the dominance of the Muslim Arabs politically has caused frequent eruptions of civil strife. Moreover, the heterogeneity has contributed to the fragmentation of political forces. Given the ethnic and regional bases of most political parties, coalition governments have difficulty developing coherent policies to cope with the serious economic problems that the country has faced.

The Framework of Political Life

The Sudan became independent on January 1, 1956, after nearly fifty years of British rule.[2] Technically that rule took the form of a condominium with Egypt, which controlled most of the Sudan from 1821 to 1885. In fact, British administrators were in charge and policy was made in London. The Anglo-Egyptian troops had conquered the Mahdist state in 1898, an indigenous Islamic-oriented government that sought to ward off the encroachment of European and Ottoman imperialism.

During the colonial period, political life in the north revolved around the leading Muslim religious orders (*tariqah*) and the nascent urban educated population. The two key families were the Mirghani, head of the Khatmiyyah tariqah, centered in the grain-growing Kassala district, and the descendants of the Mahdi, organized in the Ansar movement under his posthumous son, Sayyid Abd al-Rahman.

At the end of World War II, the British recognized that they could no longer maintain their farflung empire intact and began to prepare the Sudan for independence. Elections for a national assembly were held in 1948 and 1953. An alliance of secular educated activists and Mirghani supporters defeated the Mahdist-based Ummah party in 1953, thus enabling the secularist Ismail al-Azhari to become the first prime minister.

Meanwhile, Britain had treated the south as though it was entirely distinct from the north. The Closed Districts Order of 1922 banned nonsouthern Sudanese from traveling to or living in the south unless they obtained a special permit. Britain removed northerners who had served in the southern administration, forbade Arab-style clothes in the south, and taught English instead of Arabic in the newly established schools. They also encouraged Catholic and Protestant missionaries to open schools and churches, whereas they banned Muslim schools, mosques, and preachers. These drastic measures were partly designed to stop Arab tribes from raiding the south for slaves, cattle, and grain, but they also severed natural trade ties and cultural interchange. The south was sealed off from the north and the inherent differences between the two peoples were exacerbated over twenty years.

The government altered the policy abruptly in 1946, when it acceded to northern pressure to keep the Sudan unified and to accelerate the transition to independence. Forced separation was suddenly changed to forced unity. All trade and travel restrictions were lifted, northern administrators and teachers were sent south, and Islamic preachers returned. At a conference of northern and southern politicians in Juba in 1947, southerners expressed their fear that the better-educated and more politically sophisticated northerners would dominate an independent Sudan. They requested either a delay in gaining independence or a federal system that would enable the south to rule itself.

Their fears seemed justified when no southerners participated in key decisions concerning independence and only six of the eight hundred senior administrative posts were allotted to southerners during the transitional period in the early 1950s. Moreover, a month before independence, the southern members of parliament refused to endorse the independence proclamation unless the south was granted federal status. They settled for a commitment from the government to examine the possibility of instituting a federal system; subsequently, nothing was done to implement the promise. Resentment was expressed by disturbances in the summer of 1955 among the Zande tribe and a mutiny of southern soldiers at Torit, who resisted orders to be transferred north.

Thus, important patterns of interaction among the political forces were established at the time of independence. The north-south divide was evident as was the competition between the Mahdist and Mirghani forces.

The First Parliamentary Period

The political system at the time of independence was based on the British parliamentary system, with a prime minister responsible to the dominant party in parliament. However, political life in the Sudan differed fundamentally from that in Great Britain. A foreign form of government, superimposed on a society, could not be expected to function smoothly.

Within two years, the system broke down and was replaced by direct military rule. The parliamentary government failed to establish legitimacy in the eyes of the public, failed to devise effective economic and social programs, and failed to cope with north-south tensions. In Great Britain, the parliamentary system's stability depended on a strong consensus among the public as to the rules of the political game and the existence of two dominant political parties; the Sudan lacked both of these characteristics. The ruling National Unionist party (NUP) soon fragmented over the issue of secular or religious rule. Within six months of independence, the government changed hands three times. Although a stable coalition was then formed by the two mass parties—Ummah of the Mahdists and People's Democratic party (PDP) of the Khatmiyyah—the alliance was weakened by personal rivalries. Nonetheless, the two parties did agree on one crucial point: the replacement of the provisional constitution, which was based on secular precepts, by one based on the *Shari'ah* (Islamic law). That agreement, in turn, alienated such secular parties as al-Azhari's NUP and the Communist party. In particular, the prospect of Islamic rule alienated the southerners. Their fears were compounded by the general agreement among northern politicians that the country should be unified and centralized administratively with minimal authority devolved on the regions. Although the southerners were joined by the Fur and Nuba in seeking federal status, their demands were brushed aside. When centralization was linked to Islamization, southern fears of northern dominance were compounded.

Thus, during the initial years of independence, the Sudan suffered from indecisive and fragmented governments. Civic tension was exacerbated by the growing trend toward Islamic rule. The public remained apathetic, distant from the maneuvers in Khartoum.

The Abboud Regime

The leaders of the coup d'état on November 17, 1958, were not sympathetic to the secularist or regional forces. They consisted of the high command of the armed forces acting in concert with the prime minister, Abdullah Khalil, and supported the Islamic orientation of the Ummah and PDP. They had grown impatient with the petty factionalism and inefficiency of the civilian politicians.[3]

Major General Ibrahim Abboud, commander in chief of the armed forces, led the coup and appointed himself prime minister. He established a Supreme Council of the Armed Forces, with a council of ministers subordinate to it. The majority of ministers were military officers who also served on the Supreme Council, thereby reinforcing military control. The junta immediately suspended the constitution, banned all political parties and trade unions, and closed the parliament. Nonetheless, several members of Ummah joined the junta's cabinet and key officers were active in the Khatmiyyah order.

However, the civilian politicians miscalculated their strength. Abboud swiftly consolidated power in his own hands. In fact, the general public welcomed the coup precisely because it shunted aside the discredited politicians.

Abboud's rule was challenged in March and May 1959 by senior officers who had been excluded from the Supreme Council, and in November young officers in the Infantry School mutinied. But the military remained largely united behind Abboud, as did the Khatmiyyah and Ansar movements.

Not until November 1960, two years after seizing power, did the parties begin to protest their exclusion from influence. Ummah and NUP submitted petitions requesting the return to civilian rule. The junta responded by holding elections for eighty-four local councils on a nonparty basis. But that gesture toward democracy was disparaged by all except the PDP.

Despite the ineffectiveness of the parties' criticism, the junta suddenly crumbled in October 1964. By then, the south suffered from full-scale guerrilla warfare that was abetted by Abboud's tough measures to transform society and impose a northern-dominated administration. Abboud believed that the way to unify the Sudan was to homogenize its people which, in his view, meant transforming the south into an Islamic society. He saw Christianity as alien, imported by foreign missionaries and lacking indigenous roots. He also expressed contempt for local languages and customs. Abboud made Arabic the principal language in southern schools, instead of English, and he sponsored the opening of Islamic schools and mosques.

Opposition from the north to the measures taken in the south appeared confined to left-wing groups, secular intellectuals, and minorities. They had few outlets for criticism and no influence over the regime. However, in September 1964, Abboud conceded publicly that military measures had failed to contain the civil war. He appointed a Commission of Enquiry to make recommendations for the restoration of harmony between the north and south. It provided the opportunity for civilians to demand fundamental reforms.

Students at the University of Khartoum insisted that the prerequisite to ending the fighting was for the military to relinquish power. They held large demonstrations despite the government's ban. The death of a student on October 22 fueled public fury and galvanized a broad range of civilians in the capital. The Professional Front, formed on October 25, included members of trade unions as well as intellectuals and left-wing politicians. The front called a general strike that paralyzed the capital. Junior officers sympathized with the civilians and delivered an ultimatum to Abboud. He was compelled to dissolve the Supreme Council and allow a transitional cabinet to be formed on October 30. Thus, authority was summarily handed over from a military junta to an all-civilian cabinet, half of whose members came from the Professional Front and half from the old political parties.

Even though the traditional parties had not played an important role in overthrowing Abboud, they quickly reasserted their influence. A mass demonstration by the Ansar in February 1965 forced the transitional government to resign in favor of a party-dominated cabinet. Ummah, NUP, and the relatively new Muslim Brotherhood controlled the government, and the Professional Front disintegrated.

The Second Parliamentary Period

Parliamentary elections were held in spring 1965—the first since 1958. The boycott of the PDP and the failure to hold any elections in the south skewed the results and enabled Ummah and NUP to form a coalition government with most of the seats in their hands.

The second experiment in parliamentary rule lasted four years, longer than the initial attempt but equally disastrous.[+] The politicians reverted to partisan wrangling, which was exacerbated by a split within the Ummah as the young al-Sadiq al-Mahdi challenged the leadership of his uncle al-Hadi al-Mahdi. Three different coalitions governed during that short time. Moreover, the parties renewed their debate on an Islamic constitution. PDP prepared a draft constitution in 1968, which it aimed to promulgate the next year. In so doing it poured fuel on the fire of the war in the south, deepening the demand for secession and undermining attempts to end the strife. The most promising effort had come with the Round-Table Conference of March 1965, but northern parties rejected even the minimum southern demand for a federal system.

By 1969 the legitimacy of the parliamentary system was even less than it had been in 1958. The south demanded secession; left-wing groups, professionals and trade unionists resented the power of the traditional, Islamic-oriented forces; and minority groups in the north, notably the Nuba, pressed for decentralization. Moreover, the junior officers who had catalyzed Abboud's resignation were disenchanted with the political trends that their action had indirectly enabled to emerge.

Calling themselves Free Officers and backing the Nasserite concepts of a secular, socialist, pan-Arab society, they engineered a coup d'e´tat on May 25, 1969. The coup was greeted by broad public support and, as in 1958, a sense of relief. The Revolutionary Command Council (RCC) was headed by Colonel Ja'far Muhammad Numairi, a longstanding critic of traditional political forces. The RCC dissolved the parliament, banned political parties, and annulled the constitution, as Abboud had done in 1958. But this time the RCC retired twenty-two senior army officers and arrested leading politicians. They set up a civilian cabinet responsible to the RCC, with a clearly left-wing cast. The prime minister was a respected former chief justice, Babiker Awadallah, and two leading southerners were included in the cabinet. On seizing power, the RCC claimed that their "May Revolution" was designed to return to the principles of the 1964 revolution, which the politicians had subverted. They stressed the importance of secular rule and recognition of the south's right to regional autonomy. Those views constituted a drastic shift from the attitudes of the parliamentary politicians.

Numairi's Rule

Numairi proved to be a master politician outmaneuvering all his rivals.[5] Over nearly sixteen years he deflected more than a dozen attempted coups, juggled parliamentary forces, and retained his grip on power. There were four main phases of his rule.

The first phase lasted from May 1969 to July 1971, during which time he used the support of the left to smash the traditional parties and began to reorient government policy toward the south. One of Numairi's first initiatives was to issue a declaration on June 9, 1969, asserting that he rejected the demand to homogenize the Sudanese population along Islamic lines. The declaration stated that the government "recognizes the historic and cultural differences between the north and south and firmly believes that the unity of our country must be built on these objective realities. The southern people have the right to develop their respective cultures and traditions within a united socialist Sudan."[6] Moreover, it stated that the south had the right to regional autonomy within the framework of a united country. Numairi rejected the rebels' demand for secession but encouraged them to accept federal status and offered to protect their particular culture and society.

During that first phase, Numairi relied on the socialist and communist officers of the RCC and their civilian allies. He sought to destroy the power bases of the political parties. When the Mahdist Ansar organized mass protests against the regime in 1970, the military bombed their headquarters on Aba Island. Thousands died, and the religious leader Imam al-Hadi al-Mahdi was killed as he fled to Ethiopia. The leader of the Ummah party, al-Sadiq al-Mahdi, went into exile. The unprecedented violence of the attack cowed the Khatmiyyah, while leaders of the Islamic Charter Front and NUP also retreated or went abroad.

Once Numairi crushed the religious forces he turned on his communist allies. In November 1970 he dismissed three procommunist officers from the RCC and arrested the party's leader. Communist-supported forces staged a countercoup on July 19, 1971, and detained Numairi for three days, but other troops rallied behind him and he regained power. He then proceeded to decimate the left, executing the three officers and the party leaders.

As the second phase began, Numairi had a narrow base of power. He had alienated both the religious right and the secular left, and in seeking to broaden his popular base and legitimize his leadership, he called a presidential referendum in 1971 in which, as the sole candidate, Numairi won 98.6 percent of the vote. He established a single mass party along the lines of the Egyptian political system in order to mobilize support. In elections for the People's Assembly in 1972, only members of the Sudanese Socialist Union (SSU) could participate. A constitution was promulgated in May 1973 which codified the new system. Numairi also cultivated support from technocrats and independent intellectuals with his plans for large-scale economic development and improvements in the social services.

In the meantime, Numairi made a bold political move by launching negotiations to end the war in the south. The government delegated a leading southern politician, Abel Alier, to contact the Anya Nya rebels led by Colonel Joseph Lagu. The ensuing peace conference, convened in Addis Ababa in February 1972, led to an historic accord. The entire southern third of the country was formed into one region with its own assembly and Higher Executive Council (HEC). The regional government was responsible for public order, internal security, and local administration over social, economic, and cultural matters. It had an independent budget with revenue drawn from local taxes and a special fund from the central government. English remained the principal language in the south, although Arabic was the official language of Sudan. The Anya Nya forces were absorbed into the regular army. That accord was embodied in the Regional Self Government Act, which was incorporated into the constitution in 1973.

The constitution affirmed that all citizens were equal and prohibited any discrimination on the basis of religion, race, language, or gender. Christianity and other "spiritual beliefs" should not be restricted or insulted. Thus, the constitutional structure erected by Numairi appeared to provide the basis for protecting the rights of non-Muslims and non-Arabs in the Sudan. It affirmed the idea that the country was heterogeneous in essence and that therefore an essentially secular political system was necessary.

Lagu became a major general in the Sudanese army and Alier, who was already a vice president, headed the transitional HEC in the south. In a bold stroke, Numairi resolved the principal schism in the Sudan and ended the seventeen-year-old civil war. He did so, in part, because he was able to silence the religious groups in the north. The move, in fact, provided Numairi with a new source of support from the southern public and troops.

Nevertheless, there were several attempted coups in the 1970s. Disaffected army officers tried to oust Numairi in January 1973 and in September 1975. A particularly serious uprising took place in July 1976, organized by a coalition of exiles, including Ummah, NUP, the Islamic Charter Front, and elements of the PDP. Arms and men were smuggled into Khartoum from Libya, but the coup was crushed and hundreds were executed. The fierce confrontation demonstrated that the opposition forces could not remove Numairi and that they lacked essential support within the armed forces. It also underlined the narrow base of Numairi's rule.

That awareness led Numairi to shift to the third phase. He met secretly with the prominent exile al-Sadiq al-Mahdi in July 1977 and reached an accord that would bring the northern political forces back into the public political arena. Their reconciliation agreement included the release of political prisoners, an amnesty for politicians living in exile, restructuring the SSU to allow the political forces to participate, and enhancing individual liberty and democracy. Under that amnesty, 3,000 people were released from prison and several politicians resumed their activities. Included among them, al-Mahdi and Hasan al-Turabi, head of the Islamic Charter Front, and Rev. Philip Abbas Ghabboush, leader of the Nuba Mountains group. The heads of the NUP and Ba'ath rejected the terms of reconciliation, suspicious that Numairi was not sincere in his offer of internal democracy.

The reconciliation was short-lived. The hope that the regime could be transformed into an institutionalized presidency turned into disillusionment as Numairi continued to manipulate the institutions for his own ends. The opposition parties showed their strength by winning half of the assembly seats in 1978 elections. Al-Mahdi subsequently resigned from the Political Bureau of the SSU and Ummah boycotted the elections in 1980. By 1981 the party was issuing manifestos calling for an end to one-man rule and the election of leaders accountable to the people.

Criticism also mounted in the streets and within the armed forces as Numairi's ambitious economic programs failed to benefit the country and prices soared. Moreover, lack of rain in the west brought the drought to disaster proportions by the mid-1980s. When the government instituted an austerity program in November 1981, which included reducing subsidies on wheat and sugar and raising gasoline prices, university student demonstrations spread to the marketplaces. The riots had to be quelled by the armed forces. When the military were called out again in January 1982 to subdue rioters, the leadership chafed at the use of force against civilians. The minister of defense led a delegation of officers to Numairi to protest against the harsh measures. In response, Numairi dismissed the minister (who was also first vice-president) and twenty-two senior officers, thereby shattering the military command. Omar al-Tayeb, head of internal security since 1977, became first vice-president, and Numairi assumed the defense portfolio himself.

During the third phase, southern support waned while Islamic fundamentalist support waxed. Southern politicians were alarmed at the reconciliation between Numairi and the northern religious-oriented groups. Since southern support was no longer vital for Numairi, they feared that they would lose the rights they had gained in 1972. Moreover, Numairi's manipulation of southern politicians through the regional assembly and HEC undermined the autonomy of the south.[7] Numairi dissolved the regional assembly in 1980, only halfway through its term, and replaced the HEC with a military regime in October 1981. The final step in undermining the regional institutions came on June 5, 1983, when Numairi abruptly issued a presidential decree that divided the south into three regions and dissolved the HEC. Any changes in the Addis Ababa Accord were supposed to be made only by a three-quarters vote in the national assembly and a two-thirds vote in a referendum in the south, but Numairi ignored those procedures. Since he was supported by politicians from Equatoria and by Vice President Lagu, he was able to implement the decree, but it signaled renunciation of the reconciliation of 1972 and accelerated the return to civil strife in the south.

Meanwhile, the Islamic Charter Front under Turabi maintained close cooperation with Numairi. It quietly gained control over key levers of power through its involvement in the SSU and People's Assembly and by giving party members important posts in government administration, schools, unions, and courts. Turabi served as attorney general and as a member of the parliamentary committee that was charged with adapting the legal system to Shari'ah. He sought to make himself indispensable to Numairi.

By the time the fourth and final phase began in 1983, Numairi had accumulated the senior positions in his own hands: president, defense minister, commander in chief, chairman of the SSU, and head of the official news agency. The SSU was a hollow shell, not an independent force. Turabi's Islamic Charter Front and Tayeb's security forces were the backbone of the regime, along with a group of southerners around Lagu.

Since 1979, Numairi had shown an interest in promoting Islamic social and political codes in the Sudan, a marked shift from his initial secular orientation. He even blamed the country's economic backwardness on the public's deviation from the true religious path.[8] In 1983, having been reelected president (unopposed) for the third time, he exercised his arbitrary power by first redividing the south and then decreeing Islamic law. On September 8 he promulgated a penal code based on the Shari'ah, as a first step to establishing an Islamic state. *Hudud* punishments, such as lashing, amputation, and stoning to death, were decreed for adultery, prostitution, theft, and possession of liquor, and special courts were established to hear the cases. Over the next year and a half, thousands were summarily flogged, and at least fifty persons had their right hand amputated.

Virtually all the political and religious organizations denounced the September decrees. The Catholic and Protestant churches argued that the decrees violated the constitution of 1973, which guaranteed equality and nondiscrimination among citizens, since the hudud were applied to Christians as well as Muslims and involved unequal status for non-Muslims in court. The decrees also undermined the Addis Ababa Accord and accelerated the southern resumption of full-scale guerrilla warfare against Khartoum.

The underground Communist and Ba'ath parties rejected the decrees as did the Islamic-oriented Ummah party. In fact, Numairi detained al-Sadiq al-Mahdi for fifteen months, during which time Ummah leaflets continued to assert that the decrees disfigured Islam and turned it into a punitive religion designed to protect an unjust regime. Many members of the SSU were disaffected, and there were rumblings of discontent within the armed forces. However, Turabi continued to back Numairi. Even though he had been taken by surprise by the timing and content of the decrees, he swiftly organized support for them and placed his cadres in key judicial posts in the Islamic courts.

On April 29, 1984, as opposition mounted, Numairi imposed a state of emergency. Security forces were allowed to search cars and houses without warrant and detain persons without charge. In June, Numairi submitted constitutional amendments to the assembly that would make him president for life and the infallible religious leader of the country. The Shari'ah would be the sole source of legislation, and non-Muslims would not have the same political and legal rights as Muslims.

The amendments caused a revolt among the normally docile members of the assembly, and Numairi was ordered to withdraw them. He also canceled the state of emergency in September 1984. But he retained the hudud punishments and special courts, which he began to use to silence political opponents. Communist, Ba'ath, and Nuba activists were arrested, and the leader of the pacifist

Republican Brothers was executed in January 1985. Numairi apparently did not dare act as harshly against the traditional religious parties; al-Mahdi was released in December 1984, and no leaders of the Khatmiyyah tariqah were detained, despite their assertion that the September decrees were a perversion of Islam.

Numairi may have also hoped to use those forces as a balance against Turabi's men, whose power he began to fear. As public opposition to the regime mounted, he tried to make Turabi the scapegoat. He blamed the Islamic Front not only for the harsh court sentences but also for the budget deficit and escalating famine. On March 10, 1985, Numairi arrested more than one hundred Islamic activists, including Turabi and most of the country's judges. This sudden move left Numairi without any popular base whatsoever. His only support came from a small group of corrupt advisors and from the security forces.

Numairi, the master manipulator, first used the left to destroy the religious right (1970), then turned against the left (1971) and created a new base by placating the south (1972). Once the south was securely behind him he reopened a dialogue with the religious right (1977) and then alienated the south (1983) while satisfying the demands of the Muslim fundamentalists. His political beliefs changed with each transformation in political alliances. A secular socialist in 1970, he saw himself as the religious imam by 1984.

At each stage, there were some politicians who were willing to play the game with Numairi. Therefore it was difficult for political forces to coalesce against the government. However, in the final years his ability to maneuver and play off political forces against each other was sharply diminished. When the showdown came in April 1985, there was no one left to back him.

The April Uprising

The uprising in 1985 bore similarities to the revolution of 1964 in that it began with student demonstrations and spread to the professional and trade unions.[9] The capital was closed down by a general strike, and the soldiers refused to confront the civilian demonstrators. In 1964 the junior officers acted against Abboud and the high command, whereas in 1985 the senior officers played a key role in removing Numairi and reining in the security forces. Numairi's departure for abroad facilitated the overthrow and reduced the likelihood of bloody confrontations in the streets.

On April 6, before Numairi was due to return, the high command announced that they had seized power in support of the civilian movement. They formed a Transitional Military Council (TMC) and a nonpartisan civilian Council of Ministers. Thus, unlike 1964, the military did not return to the barracks but rather instituted a one-year transitional government. This move was designed to restore order to the country and lay the groundwork for parliamentary elections in April 1986 that would transfer power to elected politicians.

The professional movements that had been crucial in the April uprising provided the leadership of the Council of Ministers. They had concurred on the need to overthrow Numairi but found it difficult to agree on other issues. In particular, they could not decide whether to rescind the September decrees. They suspended the application of the hudud punishments and closed the special courts, but a majority in the cabinet and TMC viewed their outright cancellation as blasphemous. They decided that action on such a delicate issue should be postponed until the assembly was elected.

Their hesitation deepened the alienation of southern political forces. Already, the Sudanese Peoples Liberation Movement (SPLM), which had led the growing revolt in the south since mid-1983, accused the transitional government of being little different from Numairi's regime. When the September decrees and division of the south were retained, their criticism appeared confirmed. Moreover, the TMC resisted negotiating with the SPLM to end the war, even though the generals were aware that it could not be won militarily.

Colonel John Garang, the leader of the SPLM, maintained that canceling the September decrees was an essential precondition for negotiations to end the fighting. The SPLM argued that merely modifying the Shari'ah would not satisfy non-Muslims, since the essence of discrimination would be retained. Garang stated in one interview: "Certainly the SPLM cannot be expected to enter a national dialogue to negotiate the best possible outcome of second class citizenship. Religious, racial, tribal or any other form of sectarian dictatorship in the Sudan is a recipe for disaster."[10] Only one meeting was held with the SPLM by the alliance of unions and political parties. They met in March 1986 in Ethiopia for intensive discussions that resulted in the Koka Dam Resolution, which asserted that the September decrees should be annulled and that a national constitutional conference should be convened to establish a new system of rule for the entire country. The SPLM sought a secular, federal system in which non-Arab Sudanese would have a proportionate share of power. That meeting came on the eve of the parliamentary elections and was never officially endorsed by the transitional government.

The Third Parliamentary Period

Meanwhile, the political parties had used the year's transition to reactivate their supporters and reorganize themselves. Dozens of parties sprang up with the attendant risk that fragmentation might be even worse than in the 1960s. Nevertheless, the power of the traditional parties reasserted itself.[11] Ummah, under al-Sadiq al-Mahdi, gained nearly 40 percent of the assembly seats, and the Mirghani-Khatmiyyah-linked Democratic Unionist party (DUP) attained 24 percent. Regional parties (Nuba, Beja and southern) and the Communist Party gathered only 15 percent of the seats as a whole, whereas Turabi's movement, renamed the National Islamic Front (NIF), captured 20 percent. Overall, Islamic-oriented politicians controlled 85 percent of the parliament, partly because escalating fighting prevented elections from being held in more than half of the constituencies in the south. It also reflected the continuing dominance of the Ansar and Khatmiyyah in the countryside and the consolidation of influence by the Islamic Front among educated middle-class residents in the towns.

Al-Mahdi was elected prime minister by the new assembly. After a month of discussions, he pulled together a coalition government with the DUP and four southern parties. The NIF formed a cohesive, articulate opposition bloc in parliament. Communist and Nuba MPs also criticized the government but from a weaker power base. The DUP was considerably more conservative than the Ummah in its political and economic views, calling for enactment of new Islamic laws and resisting the imposition of curbs on the big merchants and grain growers. The cabinet was paralyzed by conflicting trends.

During the next two years, the political balance shifted frequently as a result of the tug of war among contending forces. A weak caretaker government of Ummah and DUP, which was formed in August 1987, began moving toward stronger Islamic leanings in May 1988 when NIF joined the cabinet.[12] Turabi regained the post of minister of justice that he had held under Numairi. NIF's power appeared paramount in late December 1988, when DUP abruptly withdrew from the government. But that victory was short lived.

DUP had negotiated an accord with the Sudanese People's Liberation Army (SPLA) in November that provided for convening a constitutional conference, implementing a cease-fire, and postponing consideration of Shari'ah. The war-weary public welcomed the accord. In particular, the high command of the armed forces strongly affirmed their support. When al-Sadiq al-Mahdi failed to follow up on its terms, the officers issued an ultimatum on February 21, 1989. They compelled the prime minister to renounce the alignment with hardline NIF, form a broad-based government, postpone parliamentary debate on Islamic law until after the constitutional conference, and pursue vigorously the opening toward peace with the SPLA.[13] By summer 1989, intensive negotiations were under way with the SPLM and a limited cease-fire was in place, leaving the SPLA in de facto control of most of the south. Under the pressure of the military, the government in Khartoum was finally seeking reconciliation as a strategic aim, not merely a tactical maneuver.

The negotiations were stymied by a narrowly based military coup on June 30, 1989. The junta, led by junior officials in league with the National Isla?mic Front, instituted martial law, annulled the constitution, banned political parties, unions, and newspapers, and dissolved all nonreligious associations.[14] They reinstituted Shari'ah and hudud and explicitly opposed a peace accord with the SPLA based on a secular system. The military government arrested leading politicians and trade unionists, fired hundreds of military and police officers, and alienated all sectors of the society with their harsh and arbitrary measures. Since it lacks even external support, it appears doubtful that the government can remain in power for long. The third coup since independence has destroyed a third attempt at democratic rule, but it does not show any evidence of displaying the leadership and vision needed to lead the Sudan out of its morass.

Conclusion

The political institutions in the Sudan remain unstable, lacking clear legitimacy and not well utilized to resolve the underlying problems facing the country. The profound disagreement among the political forces concerning the basic identity of the country has been a crucial cause of that instability. So long as no accord is reached as to whether the constitutional framework should be Islamic or secular, governing institutions and political processes will remain fragile. Indeed, there may prove to be no consensus possible on that issue. At times, when secular constitutional rule has been in place, influential Muslim movements have sought to alter the system. When Islamic trends have been paramount, southerners have rebelled. The use of force has escalated tension and mutual animosity as well as drawn in outside powers and contributed to undermining the economy.

Various ways to resolve the inherent tension have been proposed. At one end of the spectrum lies the concept of Islamicizing the entire country, spreading Islamic beliefs among all the people so they will become a homogeneous cultural and political entity. Some have seen this as a gradual process, extending over generations, but others have urged government measures to accelerate and impose Islam. At the other end of the spectrum lies the concept of splitting the country into two independent states, a homogeneous Islamic and Arab north and an African south. That concept was favored by many southerners until 1972 and is currently espoused by some in the north who view the inherent tension as intractable. They believe that a definitive split would end the contradiction. Neither of these extreme resolutions is likely to be implemented, given that the former is more likely to lead to a violent reaction than to successful homogenization, and the latter would be opposed by all external powers as well as major internal political forces.

Various compromise formulae have also been proposed. One would establish Islamic rule in the north while allowing a different legal system to exist in the south. That has been proposed by the NIF and al-Mahdi but has been rejected by most southerners as perpetuating inequality and ignoring the problem of non-Muslim citizens in the north. Instead, some have proposed a broad decentralization of power throughout the country, which would accommodate regionally based ethnic groups in the north as well as the south, and a mechanism to ensure that all sectors of the population share power proportionately in the central government. That would require a reduction in the relative power of the Arab elite and is therefore resisted strongly by them. The compromise formulae are therefore difficult to establish and maintain, given the conflicting interests and orientations. Nonetheless, without some structural reform the different components of the society are caught in conflict. Strife undermines the Sudan's economic and territorial integrity, and destroys the stability of its political system.

NOTES

1. The analysis of the social forces is based on Ann M. Lesch, "Sudan," in *International Handbook of Race and Race Relations*, ed. Jay A. Sigler, (New York: Greenwood Press, 1987), pp. 263–67.

2. For historical background see Ann M. Lesch, "The Fall of Numairi," *UFSI Report* 9 (1985): 5, and P.M. Holt and M.W. Daly, *The History of the Sudan* (Boulder, Colo.: Westview Press, 1979).

3. Concerning the Abboud regime, see Ann M. Lesch, "Military Disengagement from Politics: The Sudan," in *Military Disengagement from Politics*, ed. Constantine P. Danopoulos (New York: Routledge, 1988), pp. 26–28.

4. On the second parliamentary period, see Peter K. Bechtold, *Politics in the Sudan* (New York: Praeger, 1976).

5. The discussion of Numairi's rule is based on Lesch, "The Fall of Numairi."

6. The declaration of June 9, 1969, is quoted in Ann M. Lesch, "Rebellion in the Southern Sudan," *UFSI Report* 9 (1985):5.

7. For details on the political manipulation in the south, see ibid., pp. 7–8.

8. On Numairi's turn to Islam, see Alexander S. Cudsi, "Islam and Politics in the Sudan," in *Islam in the Political Process*, ed. James P. Piscatori (Cambridge: Cambridge University Press, 1983).

9. For a description of the uprising and details on the transitional period, see Ann M. Lesch, "Transition in the Sudan; Aspirations and Constraints," *UFSI Report*, 20 (1985).

10. *Al-Sharq al-Awsa*, December 6, 1985, quoted in Ann M. Lesch, "Confrontation in the Southern Sudan," *Middle East Journal* 40 (1986): 412.

11. For the precise election results and formation of the government, see Ann M. Lesch, "Party Politics in the Sudan," *UFSI Report* 9 (1986).

12. The members of the cabinet are listed in *Middle East Economic Digest*, May 27, 1988, pp. 26–27.

13. *Sudan Times* (Khartoum), February 22, March 1, 5, 28, April 11, May 12, 28, 29, 1989.

14. Ann M. Lesch, "Khartoum Diary," *Middle East Report* 161 (November 1989): 36–39, and Anver Versi, "Another Shambles in Khartoum," *The Middle East* 181 (November 1989): 24–25.

ADDITIONAL BIBLIOGRAPHY

Abd al-Rahim, Muddathir. *Imperialism and Nationalism in the Sudan, 1899–1956*. Oxford: Clarendon Press, 1969.

Abu Hasabu, Afaf. *Factional Conflict in the Sudanese National Movement, 1918–1948*. Khartoum: Graduate College Monograph, University of Khartoum, 1985.

Beshir, Mohammed Omer. *Revolution and Nationalism in the Sudan*. London: Rex Collings, 1974.

Khalid, Mansour. *Nimeiri and the Revolution of Dis-May*. London: Routledge and Kegan Paul, 1985.

Malwal, Bona. *People and Power in Sudan—The Struggle for National Stability*. London: Ithaca Press, 1981.

———. *The Sudan: A Second Challenge to Nationhood*. New York: Thornton Books, 1985.

Voll, John Obert, and Sarah P. Voll. *The Sudan: Unity and Diversity in a Multicultural State.* Boulder, Colo.: Westview Press, 1985.

Warburg, Gabriel. *Islam, Nationalism, and Communism in a Traditional Society: The Case of Sudan.* London: Frank Cass, 1978.

V

COMPARATIVE
GOVERNMENTS

The Arabian Peninsula

15

The Kingdom of Saudi Arabia

Richard H. Pfaff

The Kingdom of Saudi Arabia is a twentieth-century political anomaly. Ruled by an extended family numbering in the thousands, it is governed much in the fashion of a family feudal estate.[1] The legitimacy of this state rests upon familial, tribal, and religious traditions that appear to be in antipodal relationship to those of a modern society. Academics used to quip that Saudi Arabia was "dashing up to the eighteenth century," implying that the values and institutions of the kingdom were too anachronistic to coexist with those prevalent in more modern societies. The Saudi regime is challenging this idea, contending that it is committed to establishing a society that will be both modern in its technological and industrial facets, and faithful to its basic social and political traditions.

Although the regime has introduced new administrative and economic institutions, it has done so only as needed and after due incorporation into the traditional framework. Saudi economic development plans, for example, always are prefaced with statements stressing that the purpose of such development is the strengthening of Islamic values and its associated traditions.

In the West a modern state is characterized by an ethos of science and technology, a territorial definition of community, and secular, political, and juridical modalities. Its political and social institutions are presumed to be purposeful and adaptive, with at least nominal attention given to humanistic and populist views. The Kingdom of Saudi Arabia contends that it already embraces such values or can introduce them without undermining the ideological foundation of the regime. The kingdom feels, therefore, that it can become a modern state without sacrificing customs and beliefs adopted at an earlier time and reflecting a different culture. It is too early to state whether Saudi Arabia will be successful in this regard, but if it can then this political system will be of interest far beyond its borders.

The entire Muslim world is currently caught in this challenge between modernization along Western lines and the basic values of Islam. Iran has suggested that the answer lies in revolutionary and fundamentalist Islam. In contrast, modern Turkey, Iraq, Syria, and Egypt are examples of Muslim societies willing to embrace Westernism in virtually all spheres of society. Saudi Arabia's approach is unique in that it espouses an Islamic answer that is non-radical, moderate in rhetoric, restrained in presentation, yet vehemently conservative in social and political ideology.

The key indicator of stability in any regime is its legitimate claim to the exercise of political power. In this regard legitimacy means a condition whereby the behavior of the ruling elite is perceived as appropriate by those subject to that elite. In the case of Saudi Arabia, the ruling family has forged strategic marital links with other elite groups and has adopted social behavioral patterns that have virtually eliminated major class distinctions.[2] Saudi dress, for example, makes the ruler virtually indistinguishable from the general Saudi public.

The Saudi Arabian allocation of privilege was largely ascriptive until recently. Prior to the discovery and development of petroleum in the country, the kingdom had largely a subsistence economy, supplemented by modest revenues from Muslims en route to Mecca to perform the pilgrimage and by episodic aid from Britain. It was even the recipient of U.S. aid during and shortly after World War II. So while distribution of economic wealth was ascriptive, there was not much revenue to divide. In fact, until 1954, the royal family did not draw a clear distinction between private funds and the public purse. Even today, all members of the royal family are salaried, and tribal, religious, and military leaders continue to receive royal largesse.[3]

The recent rise of what might be termed a technocratic class has produced persons seeking privilege based on their technological or managerial expertise. Together with more complex administrative and economic structures, this change has led to a relatively large salaried class. So far the affluence of the kingdom has enabled the regime to allocate ample economic privilege to both these new technocrats and those representing more traditional sectors of society. The regime has also been highly successful in recruiting technocrats into decision-making positions that have blunted much of the criticism of the government. Moreover, in recent years many princes have achieved a level of education that makes them "royal technocrats." They make an important bridge between the traditional rulers and the emerging technocratic community, particularly in the military and oil-related professions.

The kingdom's success in merging the imperatives of modernity with traditional values is also of global importance because over 25 percent of the free world's known oil resources are located within its borders. With an insignificant domestic demand, Saudi Arabia can export ten million or more barrels of oil each day to the industrialized West (including Japan). Since a petroleum industry needs comparatively few ancillary support industries and little infrastructure, the regime's oil affluence is less visible than might be expected. To a considerable degree, the limited penetration of Saudi Arabia's oil industry into the overall economy has enabled the regime to use the econological and sociological parameters of society to help sustain the kingdom's allegiance to its set of traditional values while it is modernizing.

The Setting

Saudi Arabia occupies the greater part of the Arabian Peninsula, encompassing an area of 1,226,480 square kilometers (865,000 square miles). Its southern border with the Sultanate of Oman, the United Arab Emirates, and Yemen is still undemarcated in many places. Within the Saudi kingdom live some 9 million people, about two-thirds of whom are Saudis.[4] By comparison, the state of Bangladesh, only one-third the size of Saudi Arabia, has a population ten times greater. The vast size of Saudi Arabia (as large as the United States east of the Mississippi) is deceiving. The Rub al-Khali, the great sand desert in the south of the country, is itself the size of Texas. Another desert, the Nafud, splits the kingdom, running from the northern stretches of the country down to the Rub al-Khali. It is the driest land on earth, relieved only occasionally by green oases, one of which, al-Hasa, is the world's largest.

Given the geographic character of the country, water is scarce. Only in Asir Province is there sufficient rainfall to sustain crops without irrigation. To ease the kingdom's water shortage, the government has expended considerable sums for the construction of desalination plants along both the Red Sea and the Persian Gulf.

The climate of Saudi Arabia is inhospitable. While the temperature varies according to the region, it is hot everywhere. In the central plains the temperature sometimes rises in excess of 120° F (49° C). Along the Persian Gulf the weather is somewhat milder but also more humid.

The lack of water, the difficult climate, and the barren landscape have left the kingdom relatively unpopulated, although not underpopulated for a desert economy. Although the exact population of the country is difficult to determine, the total number of Saudis is probably no more than 6 million. Of this total about 2 million are either nomads or villagers. Subtracting females and children from the remainder leaves a potentially productive adult male Saudi labor force of about 1.5 million. It is this limited labor supply that poses a major problem for the country as it strives to industrialize.

To overcome the kingdom's labor shortage, some 2 million expatriate workers from a number of other countries have been brought into the kingdom to do the work Saudis either will not or cannot do. Today they are literally running the country for the Saudis.

At the bottom of the economic scale of the expatriates are the Yemenis, perhaps as many as 1 million. They make up much of the blue collar labor force in Saudi Arabia. At the top of the economic scale are the Europeans and Americans who handle much of the upper level managerial and executive functions. In between are contract workers from South Korea, the Philippines, Bangladesh, Pakistan, and other Asian countries, as well as thousands from neighboring Arab states.

As the economy of the country weakened in the 1980s, many expatriate workers were sent home. This move was compatible with the government's policy of "Saudi-ization"—the replacing of expatriate workers with Saudi Arabians, particularly in the skilled and semiskilled occupations. Just how many expatriates can be replaced by Saudis will be the major question for the economy in the 1990s. Given the limited number of Saudis willing or able to work in needed occupations, it would appear that the kingdom will have a number of non-Saudis working in the economy for some time to come, particularly in the industrial and technical fields. In the interim the Saudis constitute almost a rentier class in their own country, with all the associated psychological and political implications of this situation.

Much of the population of Saudi Arabia is concentrated in three regions that together make up a sort of belt across the waist of the kingdom. On the Red Sea the important commercial city of Jiddah has a population (including expatriates) of almost 1 million. Inland in the same area are the Islamic holy cities of Mecca and Medina, as well as the resort town of Ta'if. In the center of the state is Riyadh, the capital of the country, also with a population approaching 1 million. Finally, along the Persian Gulf region is the Damman-Hofuf urban complex, including Dhahran and al-Khobar, totaling another million. Yenbo on the Red Sea and Jubail on the Persian Gulf are two cities the government is now developing into major industrial and petrochemical centers. In each of these cities, it is expected that more than half of the populations will be expatriates.

The Political Culture

While a sense of national identity is slowly taking form in Saudi Arabia, it does so within the context of older social networks involving tribal membership, sectarian affiliation, and, of greatest importance, the extended family itself. To a large extent the king-dom maintains its political stability and the regime maintains its legitimacy through a complex pattern of relationships that connects virtually everyone (excluding, of course, expatriates) into a rela-tively tight-knit sociopolitical community.

The central unit of this community is the extended family. Within the family each sex has its specific realm, with women playing a separate but not unimportant role in the social unit. The segrega-tion of the sexes receives considerable publicity in Western media, usually from a critical point of view. As society develops, the tradi-tional Saudi family framework may prove to be too anachronistic an institution. Viewed from the West the subordinate role of women appears to render them little better than chattel slaves. As Saudi women become more educated, they may demand wider rights of economic and political participation. At the moment, however, this male-dominated society shows no sign of allowing women any great expansion of opportunity other than in the field of education.

The restrictions on the freedom of women seem to be unneces-sarily onerous. Women may not appear in public unless properly attired, which for Saudi women (and foreign women, too) means heavily veiled and covered from ankle to wrist. Women may not drive motor vehicles (although Bedouin women do), may not travel without permission of a husband or male guardian, may be easily divorced by their spouses, and are generally kept isolated from the outside world. Unfortunately, the lives of most urban Saudi women are filled with banal conversation, child rearing, and household duties, with little real opportunity for career or personal develop-ment.

In earlier days much of this was defensible on the grounds that with less than 1 percent of the female population literate and the Saudi culture reflecting Islamic norms, women were left with no alternative life-styles. With the rapid education of women in Saudi Arabia today, however, the only defense of this traditional life-style for women appears to be that found in following Islamic custom as interpreted by the Wahhabi sect.

One reason for the Saudi reluctance to embrace Western-style equality for women is the culturally ingrained reverence on the part of the Saudi Arab for the past. If there is a single feature of the Saudi culture that has political significance, it is the penchant for tradition and the aversion to innovation. From setting fire to the first truck brought into the city of Ta'if in the early days of Ibn Saud's reign to the destruction of television transmitting towers during the days of King Faisal, the message has been the same. For the conservatively oriented Wahhabi, the introduction of new things into society could be the work of Satan. It always means another penetration into society by Westernism, the cumulative effect of which could be the erosion of the Islamic faith. It is in terms of this background that one can understand Saudi political culture.

That political culture is a mixture of three main ideas. First, there is *asabiyyah*, or tribal solidarity. Once identified as a positive attribute by the great Islamic historian Ibn Khaldun, asabiyyah, today, is viewed in Saudi Arabia as divisive and parochial tribalism. Ironically, it is a form of this corporate solidarity that is still to be found within the extended family, particularly the royal family. Such corporate solidarity is also the ideological cement holding Saudi nationalism together in the face of broader Arab nationalism.

The nexus between the corporate solidarity of the male-dominated extended family and outside society is manliness. One obvious way to give expression to such manliness is to have children, particularly sons. After the birth of a son, a Saudi father often takes the name "father of so and so." Thus, a father whose son is named Faisal becomes known as Abu Faisal, the father of Faisal.

The obvious challenge to the Saudi government is to be found in retaining these social values in a modern economic environment where occupational expertise, individual responsibility, and nuclear family loyalties replace Saudi traditional values. The ruling elite cannot adopt life-styles too much at variance with the traditional norm without weakening their own legitimacy—one reason why the behavior of the royal family at home and abroad is viewed with great sensitivity by the regime. The stories of Prince Fahd, later king, gambling and drinking in the south of France were not published inside the kingdom. Similarly, when the movie "Death of a Princess" (which dealt with the adulterous behavior of a Saudi princess) appeared in London, it almost led to the severence of relations between the kingdom and Great Britain. Since movies are banned in Saudi Arabia, it was never seen by the Saudi public, but there is still opposition to any such review of the private lives of the royal family.

Control over the distribution of information within the kingdom is an important tool in molding public perception of the regime. Public pronouncements invoking Islam, programming Saudi TV to give support to Islamic values, and careful monitoring of all news entering the kingdom are techniques used by the government to produce a favorable image of itself. It is for similar reasons that the educational system of the state is also kept under strict supervision by Riyadh.

Education

It is difficult for Westerners to grasp just how far the Saudis have progressed in the realm of education. As late as 1978, for example, less than 1 percent of women in Saudi Arabia were literate, and men had a rate only slightly higher. Even those who could be identified as literate faced a continual struggle to maintain that literacy. The kingdom was almost totally lacking in daily newspapers, periodicals, or books. Even today the library holdings for the entire country are less than what can be found in an average state university in the United States (figures for 1975 indicate a total of about 750,000 titles).[5]

Prior to the twentieth century there were no schools, public or private, in Saudi Arabia. In 1903 Haqq Muhammad Ali Zeynel founded a private school in Jiddah and another in Mecca. Later, in 1932, another private school, Dar al-Hadith, was founded in Mecca. But it was not until the discovery of oil and the receipt of massive oil revenues that Saudi Arabia could launch a major drive to bring free education to the general public. An official program calling for the educating of an entire society was started once oil money came into the government's coffers.

By the 1970s and 1980s new schools were being opened at the rate of one a day, and figures for student enrollment were equally impressive. By 1980 almost 1 million students were in primary school, a half million in secondary, and over 50,000 at a university or other advanced educational facility. While the quality of education is not always at a standard comparable to other Middle Eastern schools, it is a singular improvement over what existed before.

At the level of higher education, thousands of Saudis were sent to the United States, Europe, and other Arab states at government expense to attend college. Within the kingdom Riyadh University opened in 1957 and King Abdul Azziz University (Jiddah) in 1967. Saudi Arabia had seven universities by the 1980s.[6]

One adverse effect of education in the schools of Saudi Arabia today is the focus on mnemonic pedagogy. Critical analysis receives little emphasis. The school system tends to reinforce religious and traditional data with little attention given to a person's analytic abilities. With memorization the keynote of education, many students are able to recite the Qur'an word for word but have only limited powers of interpreting it. There is little room for experimentation or for any scholarly challenge of authority, whether in the scientific or in the political sphere. The iconoclastic posture, so familiar in the West, is absent for the most part in Saudi Arabia.

The Saudi educational system appears to be a structure established on premises that are incongruous with the industrial premises of modern society. It is impossible for the regime to do much else, of course, without endangering the entire edifice of its society. However, the current public policy of Saudi-ization may demand an educational system more reflective of modern pedagogy to put its graduates in tune with a modern industrial world.

The Arab of the desert has a rich, if sometimes violent, heritage. For the Saudi Arabians, whether nomads or city dwellers, that heritage is part of their own history. Much of the folklore, the customs, the habitus of the Bedouin,[7] dates back centuries before Islam, to what the Muslims call the *jahiliyya*, or period of ignorance.

With the rise of Islam all the dramatic events, theological dogma, legal tenets, and ethical dimensions of that great religion were absorbed into the habitus of the Saudi Arabia. The very presence of the Islamic holy cities of Mecca and Medina in the territory that would one day become Saudi Arabia has given added strength to the absorption of Islamic doctrine into the Saudi culture.

For much of the peninsula's history, life was, in Hobbesian terms, nasty, brutish, and short. Desperately poor, illiterate, and often ravished by disease, the Arab of the peninsula saw only in Islam the specter of an afterlife free of the vicissitudes of the human experience as he was forced to live it. He was—and is—ready to join with any force designed to sustain the purity of his faith. Therefore, when the Islamic reformer Shaikh Muhammad Ibn al-Wahhab sought refuge from his enemies with Sheikh Muhammad al Saud, the ruler of the principality of the Nejd, the spirit of Islam was easily united with the sword of the Sauds. For a time their alliance made "Wahhabism" the terror of the entire Arabian Peninsula.

The Wahhabi dogma is essentially that of two earlier Islamic reformers, Ibn Hanbal (d. 855) and Ibn Taymiyya (d. 1328). These men believed that Islam had strayed from its original purity. The teachings of the Qur'an and the way of Muhammad, as manifested in the *Hadith* (traditions of Muhammad), were being ignored: A return to the fundamentals of Islam was needed.

Toward the eighteenth century, Wahhabism burst out of central Arabia, threatening the very life of the Ottoman Empire. The Wahhabis preached a purified Islam that identified all but the true Wahhabi as *mushrikine*, or idolator. The Ottoman Empire, using the military arm of the Egyptians, ultimately crushed the Wahhabis and sent them fleeing back to the Nejd, where they were kept contained by tribes loyal to the Ottomans. Subsequent internecine conflict within the al-Saud family led to the loss of most of their domain, and in 1891 the Wahhabi family was driven from its new capital, Riyadh, and forced to take refuge in Kuwait. Then, in 1902, Shaikh Abdul Rahman's son, Abdul Azziz Ibn Saud (d. 1953), in a dashing sortie, recaptured his father's town with only a handful of followers. The dramatic story of his feat is part of the folklore of the kingdom today.[8]

In the early years of Ibn Saud's reign, the task of forging the tribal sheikhdoms of the Nejd into a single political community took all the Saudi ruler's energy. But the danger of frequent intertribal disputes, the tendency of tribes to war on each other for booty, and the inability of Ibn Saud to maintain an orderly domain without a stable military force led the new ruler to create a military institution that would at once give deeper religious fervor to his regime and at the same time provide him with a loyal military force. Thus, in 1910, Ibn Saud founded the Wahhabi *Ikhwan*, or brotherhood.

Ibn Saud's creation of the Ikhwan was an astute, insightful, and dramatic venture in a region accustomed to tribal divisiveness and conflict. But Ibn Saud's unique blend of charisma, piety, compassion, and daring enabled him to use the Ikhwan to his advantage. His state building was not the product of some architectonic design but rather the pragmatic use of available material, namely the Bedouin. By combining the tribesman's penchant for warfare with the religious fervor of Wahhabism, Ibn Saud's idea allowed the dynamism and the vitality of the Bedouin to become focused on loyalty to a system of beliefs inextricably interwoven with the legitimacy of the regime, itself.

The Ikhwan were settled into *hijrah*, or settlement colonies. The first such settlement was that of al-Artawiyyah, founded in 1913 by Bedouin from the Mutair, al-Harb, and al-Uraymat tribes. In subsequent years over 180 *hujar* (plural of *hijrah*) were founded, mostly in the Nejd. The Ikhwan colonies not only organized Bedouin into units that transcended particular tribes but also served as convenient locales for military training and organization. The colonies also functioned as a center for the propagation of the message of the Wahhabi doctrine of "unitarianism."

Each colony was brought under control of the ulema of Riyadh by the use of *mutawwa'ah* (religious instructors). This institution still exists with *mutawwa'ah* roaming the streets of Saudi cities today ensuring compliance by the populace with religious rites and duties.

The Ikhwan became the Saudi ruler's shock troops, supplemented by the usual tribal levies. The Ikhwans' reputation for fanaticism, coupled with their penchant for slaughtering their enemies in wholesale fashion, was sufficient in many cases to compel the surrender of a town without the Ikhwan firing a shot. As a result of the military prowess of the Ikhwan, Ibn Saud's domain increased rapidly. In 1913, al-Hasa Province (now the Eastern Province) was conquered. While not participating in the war, Ibn Saud was able during World War I to expand his domain to encompass the northern regions. Between 1924 and 1926, Ibn Saud captured the Hijaz and its holy cities of Mecca and Medina. Under the 1927 Treaty of Jiddah, Great Britain endorsed Ibn Saud's conquests, and the Saudi ruler was recognized as "King of the Hijaz and Nejd and its Dependencies." With the capture of Mecca and Medina the Saudi ruler also became the new protector of the holy places of Islam and host to the annual *hajj*, or pilgrimage of Muslims to Mecca.

The capture of the relatively more sophisticated Hijaz, negotiations with Great Britain (a mushrikine nation to the Wahhabis), and Ibn Saud's assumption of the title of "king" angered the Ikhwan who, if nothing else, stressed the absolute egalitarianism of Islam. In 1929 the Ikhwan revolted against Ibn Saud, and the Saudi ruler crushed the rebellion by defeating one of the Ikhwan's major leaders, al-Dawish, in the Battle of Sabila in March 1929.

The Wahhabi Ikhwan, now tamed and staunch supporters of the regime, were first reorganized as the regime's "White Army." Later they would become Saudi Arabia's national guard, serving, inter alia, as a counterfoil to the Saudi regular army.

In 1932, Ibn Saud officially united the several parts of his domain into the Kingdom of Saudi Arabia. Shortly thereafter, several American oil companies, led by Standard Oil of California, obtained concessions from the king to look for oil in Saudi Arabia, the discovery of which a few years later would make the Saudis rich. Until the oil began to flow, however, Ibn Saud's fortunes continued to be meager.[9]

The flow of funds into Ibn Saud's treasury was further restricted by World War II. Initially, the king was financially supported by American oil companies, but by 1945 the kingdom was led to seek aid directly from the American government. Saudi Arabia became qualified to receive aid after declaring war on Germany in March of that year. When oil revenues were resumed, Ibn Saud was able to establish and finance a small regular army and initiate an extensive infrastructural and bureaucratic program for his state.

The Structure of Government

The genesis of Saudi Arabia's political institutions is to be found in the tribal origins of the political system. The tribal leader, or sheikh, rules with the advice of other senior members of that tribe. His rule is not absolute: It is tempered by tribal custom and by the principles of Islam. He has no divine right to rule and retains his authority and legitimacy only so long as he can fulfill his functions to the satisfaction of the senior members. He wields what might be termed "contingent authority." Arab tribes also do not recognize primogeniture rights of succession; rather, the most qualified member of the ruling family is selected by the tribal leaders. The structure of government in contemporary Saudi Arabia is derivative of this tribal model.

The central political structure of the kingdom is the extended family clan of the great Anizah tribe, the Sauds. This royal family is the very raison d'e^tre of the state.

Following his visit to President John Kennedy in 1963, Faisal al Saud, then crown prince and prime minister (he would later become king), suggested that Saudi Arabia was a constitutional monarchy, with Islamic Law, or the Shari'ah, the kingdom's constitution. Members of the royal family are careful to give verbal acknowledgment of this arrangement whereby the ultimate sovereignty belongs to God and the political authority of the king is subordinate to the law of God. It is a personal feudal-styled political system, and one cannot understand the Saudi system unless this is kept in mind.

It is no surprise, therefore, to discover that there is a clustering of power at the top within the royal family. King Fahd serves as both king and prime minister. Prince Abdullah bin Abdul Azziz serves as crown prince, commander of the national guard, and first deputy prime minister. Prince Sultan is both minister of defense and second deputy prime minister. Royal family members, in fact, occupy most of the important cabinet positions with eleven of the top administrative posts held by princes, two by members of the bin Jiluwi family, and two by the al-Sheikhs. However, more and more technocrats are now filling important cabinet and subcabinet posts. Al-Khail, minister of communication, and Nisham Nazer, minister of petroleum, are two such examples. The several thousand royal princes exercise varying degrees of political influence. In real terms there are about forty-five princes who make up the central royal decision-making set.

The royal family also has blood ties with scores of other families. While custom dictates that the first bride of a prince be a cousin, there are no such restrictions on second, third, or fourth wives. Although the trend is toward monogamy, there is still a significant diffusion of royal blood throughout the kingdom. Given the importance of the extended family in the sociopolitical makeup of society, the broad base of the royal family provides another pillar of legitimacy for the ruling family, although not necessarily for any particular ruler.

The Council of Ministers

Originally the Saudi bureaucracy was made up primarily of the king's advisers, leaders of the major tribes, other male members of the royal family, and Wahhabi religious leaders. In 1931 Prince Faisal was made minister of foreign affairs, and a more institutionalized council of ministers was formed that same year. Over the ensuing years other ministries were formed until, by the end of the 1980s, there were thirty-five ministers in the Saudi cabinet. As of 1988, King Fahd was both king and prime minister, with Prince Abdullah crown prince and second prime minister. When King Khalid increased the size of his cabinet to twenty-six in 1979, a number of commoners joined the cabinet. In fact, only eight of the twenty-six ministries were held by princes. But the precariousness of tenure for commoners has been demonstrated several times in recent years. Kamal Adham was ousted as an adviser in 1975 after serving both Khalid and Faisal. In April 1984, Dr. Ghazi Gosaibi was abruptly ousted as minister of health, without explanation. A similar dismissal came to Shaikh Ahmad Zaki Yamani, the kingdom's long-time minister of petroleum.

Since political parties and organized interest groups are not permitted in Saudi Arabia, the Saudi bureaucracy is not subject to the same political pressures found in Western democracies. Saudi rulers have promised several times to establish a *shura*, or consultative assembly for Saudi Arabia. In 1983, King Khalid promised on Saudi television to form such a body but nothing transpired. Again in December 1984, the Saudi regime promised a shura would be formed. The Saudis even built a building in Riyadh for such an assembly, but it remains empty.

In the absence of such institutions as a shura, the process of politics is largely a function of gaining access to the decision makers. In this regard two traditions work to channel Saudi politics. The first is the *majlis*, or assembly. This institution is reflective of the Saudi concept of egalitarianism. Each day the king holds audience in a large reception room (majlis). In theory any male Saudi may approach the king seeking a redress of grievance. The process is quite ceremonial: petitioners approach the king, kiss his shoulder, and greet him, frequently by his first name. Meanwhile court members and other notables sit around the room in small groups sipping coffee. It was at such a reception that the young Prince Faisal bin Mus'aid assassinated his uncle, King Faisal, on March 24, 1975.

The majlis serves as an important source of feedback and allows the king to keep in touch with his subjects. It is doubtful, however, if it can convey to the king the depth of political dissensus that may surround a particular political issue. Saudis have a penchant for consensus, and long delays often accompany the decision-making process to such a degree that procrastination is substituted for action.

The Ulema

As noted, the Saudi executive branch cannot enact "laws" but only decrees under the doctrine of *urf* (positive law). As a result the

Saudi legal system is, in fact, a combination of shari'ah law, urf-generated decrees, and tribal custom. While Ibn Saud abolished tribal law, tribal customs still make up part of the combined Saudi legal corpus.

The Sunni *ulema*, or the kingdom's religious leaders, constitute an important structure of the Saudi government. For all matters covered by Islamic law, and this includes all matters of inheritance, divorce, marriage, child custody, and other matters of personal status, as well as criminal law, shari'ah courts hold jurisdiction. While the king serves as an ultimate court of appeal, he seldom overrides shari'ah judges.

By far the most recent additions to Saudi law have come by way of urf. Much of this additional law is based upon Western concepts of jurisprudence. While the concept enables the Saudi government to maintain the fiction that the shari'ah is the kingdom's only legal system, the introduction of Western legal norms cannot but undermine the hold of shari'ah law. The very fact that Western norms presume a different community operating in terms of different values makes coexistence of secular laws and shari'ah laws difficult. The shari'ah prohibition of interest, or the banning of transactions involving futures, has led Saudi businessmen to adopt a number of circuitous methods to realize in fact what is denied to them in terms of shari'ah law.

Since 1970 there has been a ministry of justice. In 1975 the Saudi court system was reorganized into a four-tier judicial hierarchy under this ministry. The lowest, or summary, courts were placed under a single *qadi* (judge) who handles most of the cases falling under shari'ah law. There are also two courts of appeal, a high court to hear special shari'ahs law cases, and a high judicial council. Paralleling the shari'ah court hierarchy is a set of secular courts culminating in a board of grievances. These courts handle cases arising under decree law.

Each ministry also exercises a degree of judicial authority. Thus, the Ministry of the Interior handles all cases involving motor vehicles. Arbitration boards exist to adjudicate commercial disputes, and the Ministry of Labor and Social Affairs handles labor disputes.

The parallel organization of the kingdom's decree law adjudication via the ministries and the shari'ah court system is but one step removed from their full integration into a single secularly administrated set of courts under the Ministry of Justice. The merging of shari'ah and decree law would surely follow such a step.

The Ulema have helped foster an obedient attitude on the part of the Saudi public toward the regime by lending religious support to the royal family. The Committees on the Encouragement of Virtue and the Prevention of Vice (the mutawwa) may be considered a nuisance by the more secularly minded, but they do reinforce the values underpinning Saudi political culture. The regime's awareness of the supportive role of the Ulema is signaled by the government's acceptance of their role in this monitoring of much of the daily life of the Saudi.

The Ulema's influence over Saudi television is an example of the regime bowing to religious influence, if not control, over the kingdom's mass media. Since the regime, itself, is bound up with Wahhabism, the Ulema are both a vehicle for providing the regime with continuous legitimacy and an institution standing somewhat apart from the regime itself.

The Ulema have participated throughout the life of the kingdom in important internal decisions. In 1964 they lent their influence to persuade King Saud to grant de facto political power to Prince Faisal in his role as prime minister and played an important role as part of a coalition with royal family members in deposing King Saud in favor of Prince Faisal. Again the Ulema provided a source of stability in 1975 after King Faisal was assassinated, facilitating a smooth transition to power of King Khalid.

While the Ulema are still powerful, their influence seems to be slowly waning. When the Grand Mufti of Saudi Arabia, Shaikh Muhammad bin Al-Shaikh, died in 1969, no one was appointed to replace him. Instead, a Ministry of Justice was created. No less ominous was the decision taken in early 1988 to date the Saudi budget in accordance with the calendar used in the West rather than the Saudi's Muslim calendar (*hegira*).

The "Opposition"

Identifying and assessing the political significance of opposition forces in an authoritarian regime such as Saudi Arabia is difficult. The government wields tight control over the flow of information, both within the kingdom and to the outside. Saudis do not enjoy civil rights in the way the West perceives them, and demonstrations of a political nature are proscribed. All these factors make it appear that all is calm within the kingdom.

One can, in theory, construct any number of potential opposition groups in the kingdom, ready to overthrow the ruling regime. But in fact there appears to be relatively little opposition to the government, with two notable exceptions. The first is from the military, the second from reactionaries on the religious right. However, so long as the Ulema support the regime, and so long as the mutawwas give the impression in public of reflecting a public policy that strongly supports Islam, it will be difficult to attack the regime strictly on the basis that it has strayed from Islam. The Shiʻite population in the Eastern Province is a problem, but it does not constitute a direct threat to the regime itself.

The seizure of the Grand Mosque in 1979 by a mixed Sunni-Shiʻite group led by Juhayman bin Saif al-Utaibi stirred up xenophobic passions. He preached that the Mahdi would come from the Qahtan family, and one Muhammad Qahtani was identified as the Mahdi by the al-Utaibi group. While the uprising was ultimately crushed, the attack on the very geographical epicenter of Islam challenged the regime's claim to be guardian of the Islamic Holy Places. In the following year there was an uprising among the Shiʻa. Bassam al-Saʻda, Ali Shawrokh, and Faisal al-Jamed, three Saudi Shiʻites who were killed for participating in this uprising, were subsequently identified as martyrs and their photographs distributed among U.S. colleges.

On July 31, 1987, demonstrations by Iranian Shiʻite pilgrims to Mecca led to violent clashes between Iranian fundamentalists and the Saudi security forces. Over 400 were killed, including 85 Saudi policemen. Such outbursts, whether from pilgrims to the holy places or by local dissidents, can be controlled by the regime without serious loss of legitimacy.

More serious and potentially more ominous for the regime is the whole question of how much modification to Saudi society can be tolerated without undermining the very edifice upon which the Saudi political establishment rests. From the first clashes in the 1920s to the clash between conservative Saudi princes and the government following the introduction of television during Faisal's reign, the sustaining of a delicate balance between progressives and the conservatives is a continuing challenge to the ruler. Usually, there is a de facto division of power between these two forces. Thus King Fahd, representing the progressive king of the ruling elite, is juxtaposed to the conservative Prince Abdullah, who serves as crown prince and heads the national guard. This conservative-progressive split of the royal family must not be exaggerated, however. Marriage between scions of one branch of the family and spouses drawn from the other wing are too common to permit clear ideological distinctions within the family. They do exist, but they only coalesce around specific issues. In the case of the military as an "opposition" group to the regime, the question, quoting Juvenal, is "who will guard the guards themselves?"

The Military Establishment

In the Middle East the most dangerous threat to the ruling regime has been, historically, the regime's own military. Since the end of World War II there have been more than a dozen coups within the Arab World, alone. If one adds failed attempts and conspiracies to promote a coup, the number increases to over twenty. Even within Saudi Arabia there have been several attempts on the part of the military to bring down the regime. But to Riyadh the rapid development of the military may be a Hobson's choice. Not to see the military expanded and modernized could lead to the regime's vulnerability to attack from outside, but expansion of the military admittedly could also breed a dangerous institution within the kingdom.

The 1929–30 suppression of the Ikhwan by Ibn Saud had established the Saudi ruler's hegemony over his kingdom, but his military establishment was primitive even by the standards of those days. During World War II the United States, anxious to secure an air base in the kingdom to meet its own strategic needs, agreed to provide the kingdom with economic aid. Then in 1951, upon renewal of the Dhahran air base agreement, the United States agreed to assist in the training of pilots for the incipient Saudi Air Force. The same year the United States began shipment of arms to the kingdom, sending in that year a total of $1 million worth of tanks and ancillary arms to Saudi Arabia. Since that date the United States has been the major supplier of military equipment to the Saudi regime.

The kingdom's small population, the vast territory to be defended, and the distance between urban centers dictated that the Saudis focus the modernization of their military on their air force. This strategic consideration meant that the Bedouin soldier would be of limited value in a military establishment where the armored vehicle and the jet airplane were rapidly replacing the rifle and the camel. This policy was given formal recognition when Prince Sultan, minister of defense, announced in 1964 that the kingdom would obtain the most modern missiles, up-to-date communication facilities, and jet fighters for the Saudi Air Force.

In the 1960s and 1970s the growth of the Saudi military structure was accompanied by several attempted coups. A September 1969 attempt led to the arrest of over two hundred officers and senior civil servants, thirty of whom were reportedly executed.[10]

In July 1977 still another coup was thwarted and 115 Saudi officers were executed for their participation in the attempts. What made this coup so significant was that it was not another attempt to topple the regime by supporters of radical Arab nationalism but rather the opposite. The rebels attacked what they claimed was the corruption of the royal family and, ominously, called for the creation of an "Islamic" republic, one "faithful to the Qur'an."[11]

The following year another coup was attempted. In this incident several Saudi princes, together with five of the army's leading officers, tried to seize power. While the rebellion was quickly crushed, the punishment meted out was more muted, probably because of the family links of the rebel princes. The rebels were exiled, and the officers allowed to "escape" to Libya.[12]

In 1979, after the fall of Iran's shah, unrest broke out within the Saudi armed forces, with the disturbance centered among the air force commanders at the Jubail Air Base in the Eastern Province. One of the conspirators in the rebellious group claimed they were inspired by Ayatollah Khomeini and that they hoped to replace the royal family with "one along the lines being followed in the Iranian republic."[13] Months later several junior army officers, allegedly belonging to a fundamentalist group known as the "Movement," were arrested for "anti-regime activities." On November 10, 1979, over 1,200 members of this group were arrested following demonstrations at the Grand Mosque, ten days prior to the seizure of the Grand Mosque as discussed above.

All these attempted coups and internal disturbances have done little to assuage fears on the part of the Saudi ruling elite regarding their military establishment. It was partly for this reason that the kingdom maintained 10,000 Pakistani troops in the kingdom for over a decade. Their departure in 1988 may have been dictated more because of the large number of Shi'ites in the Pakistani contingent (more than 10 percent) than because they were no longer needed.

It is also in response to the attempted coups against the Saudi government that it decided to retain the national guard or White Army, a group made up of those formerly with the Ikhwan, numbering about 40,000–50,000. The Saudi national guard is presumed to be more loyal than the regular army, or "Green Army." The national guard includes many tribesmen from the Nejd who are fanatic in their religious zeal and opposed to any "secular" regime. In addition to a sizable unit near Riyadh, the national guard also protects the oil fields in the Eastern Province.

The regular Saudi military numbers about 58,000, of whom some 14,000 are in the Saudi Royal Air Force. The air force, although relatively small compared to some of the kingdom's neighbors, is equipped with the latest aircraft, including AWACS, F-15 jet fighters, and air-to-air missiles.

The army consists of three armored brigades equipped with over

750 tanks. In addition there are mechanized, paratroop, and infantry brigades and a Royal Guard regiment. The army has 18 Hawk surface-to-air batteries in addition to regular anti-aircraft batteries. The navy is small, about 3,000 officers and men, and consists of one frigate and several coast patrol craft. This branch of the Saudi military is currently undergoing extensive development because of events in the Persian Gulf and the Iran-Iraq war. The Saudi navy is being trained primarily by the French. In the spring of 1989 the Saudis also began negotiations with the French to purchase up to eight submarines for the Saudi navy.[14]

The dramatic leap in oil revenues after 1973 provided the Saudis with abundant revenues to finance the kingdom's military buildup. The increased value of Saudi oil also provided a greater need to protect the country's underground riches. To meet its expanded targets, Riyadh turned again to the United States for assistance in training and arming the Saudi military. In April 1974 the Americans agreed to train the Saudi national guard and two months later established with the Saudis a "Joint Commission" to review the kingdom's defense needs continuously. The jump in the Saudi defense budget expenditures, the largest part of which went to the United States for the purchase of arms and for the service of the U.S. Corps of Engineers, indicates clearly that the government was going to build up its military even while closely watching political sentiments among the officer corps. Thus from the 1973/74 Saudi fiscal year to the 1980/81 fiscal year, budgetary outlays were as follows (in thousands of dollars):[15]

1973/74	988
1974/75	1,450
1975/76	6,510
1976/77	10,360
1977/78	11,569
1978/79	13,000
1979/80	14,268
1980/81	20,560

In 1984 Saudi oil revenue exceeded $84 billion and, taking into consideration the 1981 Saudi purchase of the costly AWACS aircraft, the government still spent more than $80,000 per capita on its military. The goal is to create a military capable of handling the most advanced weapons and technical equipment. Training requirements to handle this type of military hardware dictate a cadre of professionals not only highly sophisticated in the mechanics of military operation but also capable of making repairs in the field, adapting hardware to new environments, and integrating individual operations into a complex unit, sometimes under hostile combat conditions.

In addition the kingdom is constructing huge military "cities" such as King Khalid Military City at Hafi al-Batin and Asad Military City at al-Kharj. Major air bases were either built or upgraded at Tabuk, Khamis Mushat, Hafar al-Batini, and Dhahran.

Saudi requests for arms from the United States, particularly advanced jet fighters and modern missiles (Sidewinder and Maverick), is hotly opposed by pro-Zionist groups in the United States. Although these groups were unsuccessful in preventing Saudi Arabia from getting AWACS aircraft, their lobbying has been sufficiently powerful to lead the kingdom to seek arms elsewhere.

In April 1988, the Saudis were able to secure an undisclosed number of CSS-2 Silkworm missiles from China and in March of that year signed a multibillion-dollar deal with Great Britain for seventy Tornado fighter-bombers and their associated armament.

The growth of the Saudi military, particularly its air force, has been accompanied in recent years by a greater flexibility on the part of the Saudis toward their suppliers, making the dominant position held by the United States less secure. Events in the Persian Gulf during the 1987–88 period have underscored the importance of that region to the security of the kingdom, thus making the Saudi military more important than ever and, in turn, making it more politically significant.

Oil and Saudi Economic Development

With the discovery of vast quantities of oil in Saudi Arabia,[16] the kingdom had three choices regarding the use of its newfound wealth. It could slow the growth of its economy to a pace that would match its absorptive capacity; it could invest abroad in the fashion of modern Kuwait and plan on deriving much of the kingdom's income from foreign exchange earnings on its investments; or it could industrialize the Saudi economy. Saudi Arabia, for political as well as economic reasons, opted for the third choice: rapid industrialization.

For much of the period 1973–86, Saudi Arabia could not spend all its oil revenues, and huge sums were invested in Western banks. In doing so the Saudis left those funds unprotected against the very inflation that higher oil prices were generating. Moreover, in many cases development of the kingdom was accompanied by waste and corruption, overly expensive contracts concluded with Western contractors, and billions expended on frivolous or unnecessary "show-pieces." The Medina-Tobuk road was so poorly constructed in 1964 it had to be completely rebuilt in 1968.[17] In addition, millions were thrown away by members of the royal family and other rich Saudis in ostentatious displays of their wealth in the major cities of Western Europe and America. In time, this conspicuous consumption would be tempered by economic reality, but initially it generated some unseeming impressions of Saudi affluence. Early manifestations of conspicuous consumption, such as the Riyadh-Damman railway, fade into insignificance compared to such megaprojects as the King Khalid International Airport in Riyadh or the Hajj tent airport terminal in Jiddah.

The industrialization of the country was the product of several five-year economic development plans, the first covering the years 1959–64. In January 1961, a supreme planning board was established in the Ministry of Finance. Later the board became a separate ministry. Saudi Arabia is now in its fifth Five-Year Development Plan. Many of the projects launched in accordance with the several plans were turn-key projects involving high technology operation. To date, these projects are almost totally dependent upon expatriate labor, with the Saudi contingent occupying managerial positions marked more by title than by productivity. While this will surely change over time, the "psychology of the desk," whereby position supplants performance, is too prevalent among Saudis to suggest any basic change in their work ethic.

By the 1960s the infrastructural development of the country was under way, and the kingdom was dotted with schools, hospitals, roads, and lavish public buildings. When at the end of the 1980s the Saudis found themselves with insufficient funds to pay their expatriate staff and unable to secure local Saudi skilled labor, questions arose concerning the economic utility and viability of many of these elaborate projects. In fact, in the 1988/89 budget year, Saudi Arabia was forced to borrow from abroad to continue financing its economic development.

Unreasonable economic subsidies for agriculture and high military expenditures annually drain the kingdom of considerable funds. The government, for example, subsidizes the price of locally grown wheat to the extent that it is ten times more costly than the price of wheat on the world market. And extensive military expenditures add to the country's economic shortfall. The fact that the kingdom earned only $27 billion in the 1987/88 fiscal year compared to a high of $119 billion in 1981 indicates that the kingdom can no longer be economically profligate as it has in the past. The $50 billion in callable reserves held by the Saudis in 1988 are insufficient to sustain the kingdom forever. The Toyota has replaced the camel and the tower crane is as ubiquitous as the minaret, but a viable economy needs skilled labor which remains a virtual monopoly of the expatriates today.

Petroleum provided the kingdom the wherewithall to construct, ex nihilo, an industrial economy. However, things required to operate such an economy in 1990 are either absent or in critically short supply in Saudi Arabia. One problem is the kingdom's critical labor shortage and the need to include a role for women working alongside men. Another is the need to Saudi-ize the labor force, particularly for handling tasks requiring special skills. The government is aware of this problem and is striving to develop a skilled Saudi labor force, but the demand for such Saudi labor still greatly exceeds the supply. The entrepreneurial talent so important to an industrial economy is scarce; it is a product of a number of factors, but central to all of them is the architectonic confidence that the entrepreneur can change the world.

Finally, associated with the sentiment of entrepreneurship is that perspective of reality one identifies with modern science. Can Saudi Arabia build a modern economy without such a scientific mentality? It is doubtful. A policy of "spares instead of repairs" may be a short-term answer to the Saudi lack of labor expertise; it is not the building block of a viable economy.

The External Environment

In addition to internal forces challenging the legitimacy of the present regime, Saudi Arabia faces a number of threats from outside. The State of Israel surely counts as one such threat. When Israel attacked the Iraqi nuclear facilities at Osirak in 1981, it did so, in part, by violating Saudi air space. Had the kingdom's AWACS aircraft been under their control at the time (the Israeli aircraft were out of range of the American-controlled AWACS then operating within the kingdom), the Israelis may not have been able to route their aircraft over Saudi air space.

While the kingdom is staunchly anti-Israeli, the rhetoric from Riyadh is considerably greater than any action. The regime does support the PLO financially and politically, it does strive to bring the support of the Muslim world to the Palestinians, and it does assume a peacemaker role (e.g., the 1981 Fahd Plan to resolve the Arab-Israeli conflict) among Arab states. To date, however, the kingdom has not been a combatant in any Arab conflicts with the State of Israel.

A new development in 1988 may bring Saudi Arabia and the Jewish state into a more serious type of confrontation than clashes at the diplomatic or political level. It is the Saudi decision to acquire modern Chinese missiles with a capability of delivering nuclear warheads. While Saudi Arabia announced that its newly purchased missiles would not be nuclear armed and supported her announcement by signing the nonproliferation treaty,[18] the Israeli government has made it clear that it retains its option to make a preemptive strike against any Arab state that threatens the existence of the State of Israel. In developing greater defensive capability, the Saudi regime may also be inviting such a strike.

Iran is also a threat to Riyadh, both in terms of potential effects of the Iran-Iraq war and in terms of the spread of Islamic fundamentalism of the Shi'ite Iranian variety. This spread puts the regime in Tehran on a collision course with Saudi Arabia and its own version of Wahhabi Islam. Each country rejects the values of the West in favor of a set of values unique to their interpretation of Islam. But each state is ethnically distinct from and ideologically opposed to the other. The regime in Riyadh has been very cautious not to get directly involved in the Persian Gulf crisis of 1987–88, but it has sought to generate greater security for the kingdom in that region. This need was demonstrated following the clash on July 31, 1988, between Iranian pilgrims to Mecca and Saudi security forces just as earlier attacks on neutral shipping by Iran brought U.S. naval forces into the Gulf in 1987.

One way Saudi Arabia has sought to strengthen herself in the Gulf region has been through the creation in May 1981 of the Gulf Cooperation Council (GCC), the organization of the kingdom and the five Gulf sheikhdoms of Kuwait, Qatar, Bahrain, Oman, and the United Arab Emirates. While the GCC has marginal military capacity, its symbolic importance as a reflection of common Gulf policy among its members is important.[19]

American-Saudi relations make up the second way that Riyadh is striving to enhance its security in the Gulf, as well as to keep the State of Israel at bay. The American connection has been a close one. As early as 1942 the United States established a legation in Jiddah. Once World War II was over, the Saudis set up a legation in Washington, following the historic February 1945 meeting between Ibn Saud and Roosevelt in the Suez Canal aboard the U.S.S. *Quincy*.[20] Since then U.S.-Saudi relations have been measured along a spectrum involving the State of Israel and oil. When the State of Israel is not in conflict with its Arab neighbors and no embargo is placed against oil shipments from Saudi Arabia, relations between Washington and Riyadh are excellent. The relationship is a curious one, however. The Saudis are ready to buy arms for cash, but Congress is reluctant to sell the Saudis arms. The United States gives lavish political, economic, and military support to the State of Israel; Saudi Arabia considers the Jewish state among its most feared enemies. Saudi Arabia controls vast quantities of oil needed by the Western world, but until Iraq's invasion of Kuwait in August 1990, the United States was denied the bases, landing facilities, or rights to position military supplies in the kingdom. Saudi Arabia is seen to be an autocratic, tribal, and religious state in contrast to the liberal, democratic, secular character of America.

Conclusion

The challenge to Saudi Arabia is whether the regime can serve both God and Mammon at the same time. Despite some evidence of success, it appears that there is little incentive to sublimate Saudi religious sentiment to the whole industrial edifice of the kingdom.

Two small examples suggest the type of problems Saudi Arabia faces in this regard. In Riyadh the kingdom constructed huge, lavish, modern, air-conditioned government buildings, but the builders did not provide restrooms for women in these buildings. And in Jiddah a vast housing complex was built in 1985 for middle-income Saudis, but it remains largely unoccupied today because the builders did not install separate elevators for women.

Islamic fundamentalism is sweeping the entire Middle East, and the role of Saudi Arabia as the quintessential model of an Islamic society trying to achieve modernization without Westernization will be compared to similar efforts in Iran and elsewhere in the Muslim world. The Saudi kingdom has the wealth, it is not burdened by major ethnic, religious, or linguistic divisions, and it enjoys relative political stability. It might just be able to do it.

Iraq's invasion of Kuwait on August 2, 1990, presented Saudi Arabia with the most serious threat to the kingdom's security in its history. In response, Saudi Arabia sought American military protection and assistance in liberating Kuwait. (For a review of Saudi Arabia's role in the Gulf crisis, see the concluding section of chapter 17.)

NOTES

1. Saudi Arabia is the world's only political system named after the ruling family. The name reflects the role that community rather than territoriality plays in the mind set of the people of the Arabian Peninsula. This perception of the polity in communal terms is one reason why boundaries are not always precise and, where they do exist, are primarily the result of Anglo-Saudi agreements designed to prevent tribal raiding into territories once under British control or, more recently, to demarcate oil concession areas.

2. While behavioral excesses among Saudis abroad, including many of the royal family, have made world headlines, little of this news has been allowed to enter the kingdom. In recent years the public behavior of the Saudi elite, both within the kingdom and abroad, has been exemplary, given the wealth of most Saudis.

3. MERIP claims about $300 million a year is allocated to the members of the royal family, not including land grants and other transfers to family members. One favorite method of rewarding the deserving supporters of the regime is to give them receipts for crude oil which they can then sell to Western oil importers: *Middle East Research and Information Project* 91 (October 1980), p.10.

4. Population figures are more the product of the imagination than of the census taker in Saudi Arabia. There is an apocryphal story about an American census expert suggesting to Ibn Saud that he take a census. "Nonsense" replied the king, "a census is unnecessary. There are 7 million people in the kingdom." "Surely," the American responded, "there cannot be more than 3 million." "No," said Ibn Saud, "there are at least 6 million." With apologies, the American insisted that there could not be more than 4 million. Holding out his hand as if to seal a bazaar-style sale, the king said, "All right, five and a half!"

5. *Facts on File*, 1975.

6. An additional 15,000 Saudi students are studying abroad, some 12,000 of whom are in American colleges.

7. The term "habitus" is adapted from Pierre Bourdieu's *Reproduction: The Formation of Society* (London, 1978).

8. At age twenty-two Ibn Saud left Kuwait with forty followers. He left most of his supporters at date gardens at the edge of Riyadh, and with the remainder (fewer than thirty) attacked the governor as he left his fort at dawn. They were forced to wait for hours for the governor to leave the protection of the fort, and Ibn Saud's force spent the time praying, eating dates, and drinking coffee.

9. In 1937 Standard of California was joined by Texaco. In 1948 Standard of

New Jersey secured 30 percent and Socony-Vacuum 10 percent of ARAMCO, the extracting company in Saudi Arabia. In 1975 Mobil's share was increased to 15 percent. The *D.G. Schofield* took the first shipment of oil from Ras Tanura on May 1, 1939.

10. *New York Times*, September 8, 1969, reported that the rebels wanted to proclaim Saudi Arabia a "republic of the Arabian Peninsula."

11. Dilip Hiro, *Inside The Middle East* (New York, 1982), pp. 84–85. JQ 1758 A2 H54 1982.

12. Ibid.

13. See Helen Lackner, *A House Built on Sand* (London, 1978).

14. Earlier, in 1987, the Saudis also concluded a $2 billion deal with the French for arms, again, in part, because of Washington's reluctance to sell arms to an Arab state.

15. *World Military Expenditures and Arms Transfers, 1973–81*, ACDA, 1981, p. 66.

16. On January 9, 1989, Saudi Arabia announced that the size of its recoverable reserves were up to 51 percent from previous estimates and now totaled 252.38 billion barrels, more than one-fourth of the world's total.

17. Ramon Knauerhase, "Saudi Arabia's Economy at the Beginning of the 1970s," *Middle East Journal* 28 (Spring, 1974): 138.

18. In October 1988, Saudi Arabia formally acceded to the Nuclear Non-Proliferation Treaty.

19. See chapter 17 on the Arab Gulf states for a further discussion of the GCC.

20. The United States had granted recognition to Saudi Arabia in 1933 but did not establish a diplomatic post in that country until 1942. In October 1984 the U.S. embassy was moved from Jiddah to Riyadh.

16

The Republic of Yemen

On May 22, 1990, the Yemen Arab Republic and the People's Democratic Republic of Yemen declared the union of the two states to form the Republic of Yemen, ending more than 150 years of political division. According to the agreement, the merger between the two states will take place gradually over a thirty-month period. We will examine the political development of the Yemen Arab Republic and the People's Democratic Republic of Yemen separately, followed by an overview of the union and its planned political organization.

THE YEMEN ARAB REPUBLIC
Manfred W. Wenner

Until 1962, North Yemen was probably the least known and least "developed" state on earth. While this may seem unlikely in view of its strategic location on the Red Sea, it was a deliberate decision on the part of its Zaydi religiopolitical rulers to make it so. Determined to achieve autarky and create a purely Muslim state, the rulers of Yemen adopted and imposed measures and policies that were in keeping with centuries of Zaydi experience and tradition in the highland fastnesses of the country. These measures and policies were different from traditions and practices prevailing elsewhere—including other Arab areas of the Middle East. All other areas had experienced at least some measure of European administration, control, or influence during the preceding century—an experience Yemen had not had.

Any description and analysis of contemporary Yemen has to begin with an introduction to its past, and how its past has shaped and influenced contemporary conditions. The Yemenis have designed and introduced features and mechanisms that attempt to deal with what are perceived to be the inadequacies, the errors, and the undesirable features of the earlier system and of its leaders.

Two historical developments hold the key to an understanding of the political system that has developed in Yemen. The first is the rise of the Zaydi immamate, in the late ninth century. The mountains of Yemen became the home and refuge of the Zaydi sect of Muslims, and in their relative isolation the Zaydis and their leaders (imams) developed both the theoretical and the pragmatic nature of this key institution. Lasting about one thousand years (until the revolution of 1962), the immamate—for all of its variations in influence, power, and scope—dominated the Zaydis' perception of what a political system and its leaders could and should do.

The second development of importance was the two-fold occupation of Yemen by the Ottoman Turks, first from 1538 to 1630 and again from 1849–72 to 1918. Although this domination was by a Muslim power it introduced some administrative techniques, technology, and ideas that had been influenced by Europe and were therefore not in keeping with the traditions of the Zaydi-dominated highlands. One result was the development of an intense and highly motivated Zaydi-Yemeni "nationalism." It was manifested in the long campaign of two imams, Muhammad Ibn Yahya (b. 1839; imam 1891–1904), and his son Yahya Ibn Muhammad (b. 1869; imam 1904–48), both of the Hamid al-Din "house," to free Yemen from the foreign rule of the Sunni Ottomans.

The institutions that these two leaders revived or created during their tenure were in keeping with the perceived role of the imams in Zaydi Islam and their role in governance of highland Yemen. Moreover, especially in the case of Imam Yahya, who became the country's political as well as its religious leader when the Ottoman Empire was defeated and Yemen obtained its de facto independence in 1918, there was a specific plan, a specific set of political goals. These were an outgrowth of the experience with the Turks, with the presence of the British in the south, with his perceptions of the historic role of the immamate, as well as his perceptions of the responsibilities and functions of a proper Zaydi imam—in religious terms as well as in more "secular" terms—in order to establish his legitimacy.

It is precisely these institutions, the policy goals, and the means for accomplishing them, that the republicans later give as the justification for their revolution and the changes it sought.

The Geographical Background

The most important geographical features of Yemen are the long coastal strip (over 400 miles) known as the Tihama and the mountainous interior, which has a number of significant variations.

The Tihama, 12 to 30 miles wide, is a sandy, nearly waterless, extremely hot (and humid) area which makes up about 20 percent of the surface area of Yemen. Although its soil is fertile in some locations, the high temperatures and sparse water have combined to produce a landscape covered with only sparse vegetation. The population is a mix of Arabs and African peoples (Somalis and Danakils, for example), and the villages resemble those found on the western shore of the Red Sea, that is, they are largely made of biodegradable materials such as reeds. The larger cities— Hodeida, Zabid, and Bait al-Faqih—have predominantly traditional brick and cement buildings of the type found in all the major ports of the Red Sea region. In short, its population, its socioeconomic characteristics, and its life-style all differ markedly from what is found in the mountainous interior.

As one moves east, there is the first low range of hills, the foothills of the more massive mountains. Here the climate and the lifestyle begin to change: temperatures and humidity moderate, and a different set of crops from the tropical plants of the Tihama are raised. As one continues east, up any of the major river valleys, the hills gradually become massive mountains, intersected by deep gorges which eons of rain and erosion have produced and on whose floors, deep with silt and perennial streams, major crop-producing areas are found. Eventually, one reaches the great central plateau, with an average height of about 8,000 feet, surrounded by many mountains with peaks above 10,000 feet. If one proceeds farther east, the mountains begin to drop off again to the eastern desert regions, where the undemarcated border with Saudi Arabia lies.

A move from the Tihama to the mountainous highlands takes one through an equivalently diverse set of climatic zones, reflected most clearly in the crops produced: tropical fruits, tomatoes, and cotton in the Tihama, the melons, peaches, and other fruits and vegetables of the lower hills, the millet, corn, wheat and other grains of the intermediate plateaux, and the high temperate zone crops such as nuts, grapes, and pears. The ridges and mountains have produced perhaps the most diverse set of microclimates and attendant plant varieties imaginable in a space so small, roughly the equivalent of North Dakota or Greece. Furthermore, the difficult terrain and the inaccessibility of many hamlets, often deliberate, has produced distinct economic and social patterns, many of which manifest themselves in significant ways.

There is a pattern of decentralization unmatched in the contemporary world. It is, of course, a result of some obvious factors. (1) Transportation through and among the mountains of the interior is extremely difficult. It is hard to exaggerate the difficulty of constructing and maintaining adequate communications in such rugged terrain. (2) Developing and maintaining an adequate agricultural base is difficult. It has been accomplished through the construction of terraces on nearly all of the mountainsides. These terraces require constant upkeep to retain both their integrity and the soil's fertility. Maintenance can be neither ignored nor long postponed without drastic consequences for the agricultural base of the economy; the result has been a tradition of local self-reliance. (3) For much of Yemeni history, there has been a lack of effective, honest, and capable administration or government, especially for the population outside the major urban centers. The result has been the construction of easily defended houses and hamlets. In fact, most of the country's villages are closely clustered congeries of houses which are easily defended, and which occupy as little surface area as possible that might be used for producing crops.

These factors have contributed to the development of a complex of attitudes and values not particularly oriented or sympathetic to the outside world (which, in this context, may include villages only hours away).

Social and Demographic Characteristics

The Yemeni population may be divided in many ways—either in terms of analysis for contemporary social scientists or in terms that are meaningful for Yemenis and their society.

In historical terms, the oldest division, though probably the least significant at the moment, is between "northern" (Adnani) and "southern" (Qahtani) Arabs; the latter are the "pure" Arabs of the south of the peninsula, who lay claim to a more distinguished lineage. Though this distinction has been called relevant to feuds in other places in the Arab world (notably in Lebanon and Morocco), it is more important today in the two parts of Yemen than anywhere else. The distinction surfaced most clearly just before the revolution of 1962. Then, during the civil war (1962–70), it was used to rationalize specific alliances. The origins of the alliances, however, could be traced just as easily to more immediate differences between tribes, access to subsidies and weapons, the threat of retaliation by Egyptian forces, and similar reasons.

Of greater importance to today's events are the religious divisions among the Yemenis. The conquest of Yemen by Islam (begun by the conversion of some leading figures in the early seventh century) did not, of course, result in the immediate conversion of the entire population. However, since Islam itself suffered a major division within its own ranks shortly after the death of Muhammad, an important split survived in Yemen's Muslim community.

The Zaydis

As indicated, the most important event in Yemen after its conversion to Islam was the rise of the Zaydi immamate. The establishment of the religious (and later political) overlordship of the Zaydi sect has influenced the social structure, the attitudes, the entire life-style of highland Yemen. Because of the policies of various imams—past and early twentieth century—many aspects of the Zaydi vision and outlook were also imposed upon, or adopted by, those living in non-Zaydi regions.

The Zaydis are one of the three branches of the Shi'as; they derive their name from Zayd, one of the two grandsons of Hussain, who was one of Muhammad's grandchildren through his daughter's marriage to his cousin Ali. The Zaydis have never felt close to other Shi'as. Indeed, within Yemen and among many Sunnis, the Zaydis are known as the "fifth school" of Muslim jurisprudence because in practice and theology they are so close to the Sunnis.

The first of the Zaydi imams to establish himself in Yemen was al-Hadi ila al-Haqq Yahya. Because of the important role that Imam Yahya played in his lifetime—as spiritual leader, as mediator in ageless feuds, and so on—and because of his charisma, the Zaydis have, ever since, argued that the individual who fills the role of imam does so because of his personal merit, not merely as a descendent from Ali and Fatima (though that becomes the defining limit of the group from which the candidate must be drawn). A candidate for the immamate must fill a set of criteria and prerequisites before he may claim the title and, in any case, must be able to defend and keep the title from usurpers. The result is that the Zaydi community has always looked to charismatic, forceful, dynamic individuals as leaders.

One additional consequence of this history should be mentioned: the group from among which candidates for the immamate had to come were the *sadat* (plural of *sayyid*), that is, descendents of Muhammad. The sayyids, in other words, were an elite who enjoyed special privileges and status. Furthermore, as one of the two educated classes, they filled many administrative posts and were often the primary intermediary between the average citizen and any organized governmental activity. However, they were also considered, especially in the rural areas, individuals possessed of special spiritual and healing powers. Because of these special powers, they were often called upon as disinterested mediators in disputes and were under the general protection of the tribes in the district.

No census on the basis of religion has ever been undertaken in Yemen, so the relative numbers and percentages of the various sects are uncertain. It seems clear, however, that the Zaydis are the dominant sect in the central and northern highlands, as well as an important part of the population in the south-central highlands, and they have dominated the political apparatus of the state ever since the Ottomans specifically gave Imam Yahya administrative and judicial responsibilities in the early years of the twentieth century. Most observers suggest that they make up roughly half of the population, probably a bit less.

The Shafi'is

The Shafi'is of Yemen are Sunni Muslims, one of the four major schools of law. Although long more important in economic terms than the Zaydis (and probably still so), they have traditionally had considerably less political power, since they have no reason to accept the religious role of a Zaydi imam. In part because of these overlapping differences, there has often been friction between the sects.

The Shafi'is are found primarily in the Tihama, the foothills of the western mountains, as well as in the south and southwest. For many years, their links with the world outside Yemen were more extensive than those of the Zaydis. In part these links were a function of geography; that is, the Shafi'is had easy access to the Red Sea and the important port city of Aden in the south, which is an overwhelmingly Shafi'i area.

The Isma'ilis

The other Muslim sect with a presence in Yemen constitutes only a small part of the population today, though in the past it had considerably greater influence and numbers. The Isma'ilis, another branch of Shi'a Islam, are concentrated in the mountains west of Sana'a, around Manakha and the Jabal Haraz district. Since they are themselves a distinct minority within the larger community of Isma'ilis (for example, they do not recognize the position of the

Agha Khan), they do not play any important role in the contemporary social and political system. On the other hand, all of the republican governments have included at least one Isma'ili in the cabinet.
They number no more than 100,000.

The Jews

For centuries, Jews were the only non-Muslim community in
Yemen. Concentrated largely in Sana'a and in villages in the Zaydi
north, they were a highly visible and important part of the social
structure, performing many valuable functions because of their
skills. They were often subject to special laws concerning their
housing, clothing, and transportation and on occasion were subjected to more unpleasant policies.

In 1950–51, as a result of a combination of their own traditions
as well as the blandishments of Israelis seeking to accomplish the
ingathering of the exiles, the vast majority left for Israel. Today,
although there are still some Jewish villages in the north, their
numbers are probably no more than 7,500, and there are no Jews
at all in their former quarter in Sana'a.

Tribal-Urban Divisions

Overall, the most important distinction in a population could be
where one lives, since this is usually an indicator of important determinants of social organization and political power.

The most important form of social organization in Yemen is
the tribe. The Yemeni tribe is really a nation (in the original sense
of the word); it is a group of people with its own territory (and
the territorial limits of the vast majority of the Yemeni tribes have
not changed significantly in centuries), its own history, its own
markets, its own political allegiances and alliances, and its own
economic base. Nearly every tribe in Yemen long ago settled in
a specific area: hamlets, villages, and towns were founded, and
organized agricultural activity became the dominant way of life.

Over the centuries, the tribes have retained a tradition of self-
reliance, of independence from organized governmental authority,

and of disdain for the life of the urban dweller. It is primarily
the fact that the city dweller relies upon others—government officials and administrators—to fulfill such functions as personal safety
and the resolution of interpersonal disputes that the tribes see as
proof that city life is effete and demeaning. The fact that the tribes
engage in sedentary agricultural activity and participate in the economic system, which is, of course, oriented around urban centers,
is not perceived as contradictory; most market activity is done
through middlemen, allowing the tribes to perpetuate the myth
of their social, economic, and even political independence from
organized authority. However, even though reality may not match
belief, the tribes consider themselves the elite of Yemen—in part
also because of their ancestry.

Until the twentieth century, most of the tribal districts, because
of their rugged terrain and geographical isolation, had never come
under any centralized governmental administration or control.
Even under the most effective of the Ottoman Empire's administrators, only four of the major tribes in the highlands recognized the
Ottomans as their governors. After independence, one of the primary goals of Imam Yahya's government was to bring more of
these tribes under some form of control. And, although many were
prepared to acknowledge the theoretical suzerainty of the Zaydi
imam, very few were prepared to allow the imam's officials to play
roles and exercise functions that were perceived as traditionally
within the purview of either the tribes or their complex legal system.

Ironically, the civil war (1962–70) added to the power of the
tribes because both sides in the conflict depended on them for
manpower and saw them as allies in the contest for ultimate control
of the state. It was inevitable that, no matter who won, the tribes
supporting that side would demand recognition for their efforts
and would receive appropriate positions and perquisites in the new
order. The result has been that the major tribal confederation, the
Hashid, under its paramount shaikh, Abdullah al-Ahmar, is one
of the major supports of the republic (and the republic might not
even exist today had it not been for the support which it received
from the confederation). Though the central government has been

increasingly able to exert its authority in areas formerly completely under the control of the tribal shaikhs, it is still the case in the late 1980s that there are tribes, shaikhs, and areas that the government does not fully control and who choose where and when to support or resist governmental policies and personnel. Chief among these are some of the tribes of the Hashid Confederation, centered on al-Khamr in the mountains north of Sana'a on the road to Sa'adah.

In the past, friction and conflict between these independent tribes and the major urban centers was manifested in the delight and savagery with which the tribes would descend upon the cities during a civil dispute. Because the current government clearly recognizes their importance and indeed makes specific provision for their participation in policy making, their role and position remain as strong, if not stronger, than in the days of the imams.

Urban Divisions

Although it should be clear that the tribes are the political and in some respects the social elite of Yemen, they are not the only social category about which one needs to be informed to understand the domestic situation. There are, in fact, major social differences among the urban dwellers; though decreasing in importance as movement within the social system becomes easier due to the massive inflows of remittances, they nevertheless remain relevant.

Historically, though the names of the categories and their precise makeup differed from place to place (which led to some disagreements among early students of Yemeni society and should be seen as further evidence of the importance of regionalism in the Yemeni context), these are the "basic" classes.

(1) At the bottom, one finds both the descendents of slaves (*Abd*) and the *akhdam*, a caste-like group of presumed African origins, who perform the most menial and despised functions in the society, such as cleaning out the bathhouses, collecting garbage, and cleaning the streets.

(2) Somewhat higher are those who perform other tasks gener-

ally viewed by the Yemenis as low status: barbers, meat cutters, and so on.

(3) Somewhat higher still are those in the skilled trades: plasterers, masons, carpenters, glass cutters, metalsmiths, and so on. This category, which also represents some of the new skills like machinery operating, as well as some of the older skills previously in the hands of the Jews (silver and goldsmithing), has grown significantly in both numbers and as a percentage of the population as the economy has grown and changed from the 1970s to the present.

(4) Of marginally higher status are the owners of small-scale retail businesses and manufacturing enterprises.

(5) The "new middle class," to which all analysts of the Middle East have referred, contains technocrats, intellectuals (educators at all levels), journalists and other media professionals, army officers, and the educated bureaucrats and administrators in the rapidly growing public sector.

(6) The traditional upper classes are educated in the traditional fashion and institutions: the *qudat* (plural of *qadi*, the educated scholar and public official), the *hakim* (Islamic judge), and the *sayyids*.

(7) The *qubayl* (plural of *qabili*) are the tribesmen who are willing, on occasion and often only grudgingly, to acknowledge the special place and role of the sayyids.

The economic changes that have taken place in Yemen since 1970 have clearly affected certain aspects of this simplified outline of the traditional social structure. With the growth of remittances, many members of social groupings considered to be of low status have been able to buy land or other property and have thereby increased their prestige and their social status (especially if they leave their traditional place of residence). However, it should be noted that marriage patterns have continued along traditional lines and do not reflect the deemphasis upon traditional status groupings that has developed in the major urban centers. The beginning student of Yemen should beware of making simplistic equations concerning status and role, however; it would be far more accurate to say that status in Yemen today is a complex matter involving such elements as lineage, education, occupation, actual wealth, residence, land ownership, and current connections, and with whom one is considered eligible for marriage.

Positions within or in some way related to what the West perceives as "government" were restricted in practice to the sayyids and the qadis in the days of the immamate. In part, this restriction was a function of the special position of the sayyids within the system; in part it was due to the fact that the sayyids and the qadis were the only educated, literate class in the population. It was, inevitable, then, that whatever administrative, judicial, or regulatory functions were carried out, as well as such additional responsibilities as education and recordkeeping, would be in the hands of these two social groups. Today, the position of the sayyids has been substantially reduced; that of the qadis, however, has been barely affected by events since the revolution.

The Framework of Political Life

Prior to the revolution, all administrative and executive responsibilities were carried out by the imam. Under Imam Yahya, even such expenditures as the ink used in the few public schools required his personal approval. Under Imam Ahmad, things began to change slowly, but most governmental activities and actions were subject to arbitrary review and cancellation if the imam chose.

The first place where change was introduced was in the military. Even under Imam Yahya certain Yemenis were sent abroad to learn more modern military technology and techniques—to be used, of course, to enable Yahya to gain greater control of the state. Eventually, these military men were among the first to question the traditional system; nearly all were members of the groups that participated in the attempts to overthrow the imams, and many were among the leading figures of the republic in its early days.

The important thing to remember, however, is the fact that no real administrative cadres existed at the time of the revolution. In fact, one of the earliest tasks of the new government was to create the National Institute for Public Administration (NIPA) to train the personnel needed to carry out the multitude of tasks and responsibilities that it saw as one of the goals of the revolution. For years after the revolution, there was (and still is) a shortage of trained and experienced personnel to carry out the functions of a modernizing government—in the fields of health, education, transportation, and so on.

One long-term effect of the lack of personnel was that the economy was barely regulated, if at all. There is little doubt that the inclinations of the new leadership were also in this direction, which permitted the private sector to expand its activities at an incredible rate.

The Republic

On September 26, 1962, a collection of army officers and their civilian supporters shelled the "royal palace"; the revolutionaries then announced the creation of the Yemen Arab Republic and the end of the immamate as an institution. As it happened, the imam escaped and made his way into the northern mountains, where he was able to organize a counter-revolutionary effort.

His resistance produced a civil war that lasted for nearly eight years. The imam was able to retain the support of some of the major northern tribes. More importantly, he was able to gain the support of the government of Saudi Arabia, which saw the spread of republicanism and revolution on the Arabian Peninsula as an unmitigated evil. On the other side, the republic was immediately supported by Egypt. In short order, each side managed to gain additional support. Those supporting the imam, who were soon termed "Royalists," gained assistance from Jordan and Iran, both of which were also reluctant to see republican sentiment spread too widely and too quickly. Moreover, the British, who at the time were still in control in South Yemen, similarly supported the imam. Republican and more progressive governments and interests came to the support of the republic.

It was difficult if not impossible for the republic to begin the construction of a complete administrative infrastructure, a modern economy, as well as a new political system, while it was engaged in a fierce civil war. In the meantime the imam continued to lead a traditional government in the northern mountains. In the areas controlled by the republic, probably less than half the total land area of the modern state, the republicans and their Egyptian allies began to create and run governmental agencies and tried to supply the kinds of services associated with modern governments. These were, of course, rather rudimentary and limited in scope and effectiveness.

In 1970 the two major outside supporters, Saudi Arabia and Egypt, withdrew from the conflict and allowed the Yemenis to work out a mutually satisfactory compromise, and not until then did any real progress on a new political system begin. The efforts of the republicans up to that point cannot be called irrelevant; indeed, the basic outline of the new institutions and framework were in fact shaped during this period, and the people who were to become the major architects and governors of the postwar system first made their appearance during this period.

The Early Years

The major architect of the republican coup was an army officer, Abdullah al-Sallal. His subservience to Egyptian interests, the corruption that marred his administration, and his ineffective leadership had discredited him in Yemeni eyes by the mid-to-late 1960s. Leadership of the republic was transferred in 1967 to a Republican Council composed of three leading figures, Abd al-Rahman al-Iryani, Ahmad Muhammad Nu'man, and Shaikh Muhammad Ali Uthman. This change marks the political ascendency of moderates in the republican camp. Although the war was to continue for two more years, the outlines of the compromise and its outcome had become visible.

Perhaps the most interesting aspect of these developments is that while the nation was still engaged in a civil war, the leadership on both sides, who wished for a compromise and succeeded in imposing one on the military, were traditional civilian politicians. But the emergence of civilian leadership was not achieved without a price: in 1968 there was a major struggle for control over the direction and leadership of the republicans, in which moderates were pitted against a coalition of leftists. The moderates gained control, and the cost was domestic instability in the 1970s. The moderates were all Zaydis, perhaps inevitably because it was only they who were prepared and able to negotiate a real compromise with the totally Zaydi camp of royalists. Conversely, of course, nearly all of the supporters of the left were Shafi'is, which exacerbated the difference between the two sects. The conflict in the 1970s and 1980s broke out over the new incarnation of leftist opposition, the National Democratic Front, which was born in the mid-1970s and effectively eliminated from the domestic scene in 1982.

The Postwar Years

The compromise, as it has come to be known, specifically brought royalists into the government, and since there was widespread revulsion against Egyptian policies, it is not surprising that the immediate period after compromise saw a return to many of the traditional Yemeni religious, political, and governmental values and orientations—with one exception: the deliberate decision to avoid putting too much power in the hands of one individual, a clear reaction against the experience with the imams and Abdullah al-Sallal. In view of the traditional role of Islam in Yemen, it was not surprising that the constitution of 1970 specifically declared that the *Shari'ah* (Islamic law) had to be the source of all legislation and that members of the nation's public bodies had to be practicing Muslims. The special role of the *Ulema* (religious scholars) was acknowledged, and it was further stipulated that judges had to be selected from among the religious scholars.

In the first years of the government, many younger Yemenis who had been trained abroad and were committed to reform returned home and became active in the political system, thus creating in the Yemeni system a "new middle class." They sought to construct a liberal, socially conscious, and dynamic state, one that would take the lead in developing and providing the vast range of social services associated with modern, liberal, Western democracies. But these efforts soon ran into the opposition of the traditional elites and some of the powerful shaikhs of individual tribes who were similarly represented in the new institutions.

Most observers of the 1970–74 period would argue that the domestic instability of this period (represented by rapidly changing cabinets and prime ministers as well as numerous reorganizations), the tense relationships with Yemen's regional neighbors, and the financial problems made any lasting reform or political institution-building and development unlikely if not impossible. But there were a number of developments during this period that would have an impact on the way the government and its institutions evolved. Among these important initiatives were the founding of the central bank (1971), the creation of the Central Budget Bureau (1972) to begin to gain some control over the financial crisis, and, usually perceived as the most important, the creation of the Central Planning Organization (CPO). This last body was given responsibility for the formulation of national development policies and programs.

Eventually, however, it became increasingly clear that the al-Iryani government was incapable of dealing with the multitude of domestic and foreign problems in an effective manner. By 1974, the opposition, including the tribal alliances of the north, had lost their patience with the government and its policies, especially for failing to deal with what were perceived as major threats.

Thus it was that on June 13, 1974, a bloodless coup took place. Military officers took over the government in a move so smooth that many believed it had been planned and organized with the connivance of important figures in the government that was replaced. Usually known as the Corrective Movement, this coup marked the beginning of the institutions and processes that characterize the current state. Moreover, it marked the reentry of the military into politics.

Ibrahim al-Hamdi (1974–1977)

The army officers who organized the coup of June 1974 were led by Colonel Ibrahim al-Hamdi, a prominent figure who in the years since the revolution had performed both military and civilian functions. The officers termed themselves the Command Council, and among their first acts were suspending the 1970 constitution and the Consultative Council, dissolving the ineffective national political organization that had been attempted (the National Yemeni Union), and, of course, taking on all legislative and executive functions. They did, however, immediately appoint a new government and a new prime minister. All those appointed to ministries and cabinet-level positions had played important roles in prior governments, and the overwhelming majority were civilians.

Al-Hamdi's political skills were extraordinary. Within a few months he managed either to neutralize or to gain the support of practically every major domestic faction. He consolidated his position and fashioned a sufficiently strong and wide enough base that he could carry out the reforms and objectives he considered important: economic development, elimination of corruption, centralization of political control, and an end to the financial-economic irresponsibility and near chaos that prevailed in many of the ministries and their projects.

Perhaps his most important purpose was to centralize the political system. It must be remembered that the tribal shaikhs and regional notables had consistently benefited from the highly *de*-centralized system that early efforts at institutionalization had created—a system that accorded well with Yemen's political traditions. But al-Hamdi's first priority was to bring about a greater role for the central government in governance and policy making. To accomplish it, he had to curtail the power of many of the most important political elements in the country.

One could argue that Al-Hamdi's balancing act among the political, tribal, religious, and regional factions was bound to unravel eventually as such efforts nearly always do. In his case, he came to rely upon elements in the south and sources of support that were deemed "leftist," actively reformist, and supportive of significant change, and from that point his days were numbered. By 1977, his attempts were perceived—both by Saudi Arabia and nearly all of the northern tribes as well as some elements of the political center—as a dangerous game with South Yemen. On October 11, al-Hamdi and his brother (upon whom he had relied heavily for the loyalty of some special army units) were assassinated. We may never know who was directly responsible, but most analysts and the Yemenis themselves assume that it was an alliance of northern elements and their Saudi allies, that is, those who had the most to lose from al-Hamdi's continued rapprochement with South Yemen.

Ahmad al-Ghashmi (1977–1978)

The assassination of Colonel Ibrahim al-Hamdi brought to power another army officer, Colonel Ahmad al-Ghashmi. The most important fears of the Saudis and the northern tribes were allayed as soon as al-Hamdi's successor took office. The move toward improved relations with South Yemen was terminated; al-Hamdi's allies who were in influential positions were either removed or shifted to other responsibilities; and relations with Saudi Arabia improved perceptibly. Al-Ghashmi appeared to have little or no interest in devoting his energies to the development projects and plans that had occupied so much of al-Hamdi's time and energy. At the same time, however, he seemed to have some interest in developing institutions that would give his regime a measure of legitimacy. In February 1978, he appointed a ninety-nine-member Peoples Constituent Assembly (PCA), which consisted mainly of urban elements (not the tribal ones that had dominated the previous body), a move that indicated, if nothing else, the growing power and influence of urban elements. He abolished the Military Command Council, a decision that embroiled him and his successor in a major threat to the regime. One of the members of the MCC was Abdullah al-Alim, the highest ranking Shafi'i officer in the Yemeni army, who had close ties to al-Hamdi and strong support in the south. The abolishment of the MCC that ended his role in the government was seen as a deliberate diminution of the influence of the Shafi'is and the south, and Abd al-Alim rebelled. Al-Ghashmi sent his protégé, Ali Abdullah Salih, the military governor of Ta'izz Province, to deal with Abd al-Alim. The latter was unable to rally his supporters effectively. He committed a major blunder in dealing with some local elements seeking to mediate his dispute with the central government, thus discrediting himself and his principled position with respect to the government. Ali Abdullah Salih forced him to flee to South Yemen, thus eliminating the last major al-Hamdi supporter from any position of influence, civilian or military.

Overall, al-Ghashmi's tenure was not characterized by any major changes in al-Hamdi's general policies. He continued the preparations for the first five year plan and did not act to undermine or decrease the levels of support from foreign donors for development projects (an act that certainly would have produced disruptions in the slowly developing economy). His tenure in office was to be brief; on June 24, 1978, a briefcase bomb carried by an envoy from South Yemen killed him.

Reaction in Sana'a was swift, perhaps even practiced: a four-man Presidential Council was created consisting of al-Ghashmi's vice-president, Abd al-Karim al-Arashi; the prime minister, Abd al-Ghani; the chief of state, Ali al-Shayba; and Ali Abdullah Salih. After a brief period of intense political activity behind the facade of stability and peaceful transfer of authority, Colonel Salih appeared the victor and was elected as the new president of the republic and commander in chief by the PCA.

Ali Abdullah Salih (1978)

Although it was widely believed that Ali Abdullah was inexperienced, came from a tribe with too little influence in the system, and was too weak to withstand the blandishments and influence of the major domestic forces, he was able in 1990 to celebrate twelve years in office—longer than any other republican chief executive.

During that period, he has presided over the most far-reaching changes in the economy and social system in Yemen in more than a thousand years. Moreover, he has succeeded in treading a precarious middle path between various domestic and foreign forces with their own agendas for Yemen. All the while, he has managed to promote a measure of political development which, while slow in the eyes of many, has the overwhelming advantage of having given Yemen a measure of domestic stability—something it desperately needed after the turmoil of the end of al-Hamdi's tenure and the brief interregnum of al-Ghashmi.

Major Political Issues of the 1980s and 1990s

The definition of what is a major political issue in Yemen varies with the group affected and the region of the country—evidence that traditional divisions continue to be important. Nevertheless, it is possible to compile some broad categories of issues applicable to the entire country, though they should be seen as related and separated only for discussion purposes.

The Consequences of Oil

The role of oil revenues is always a subject of great interest to Yemenis. The dependence of the government upon the financial subsidies provided by the Saudis after the compromise—at first paid directly to the tribes, only later to the government as budgetary support funds—have made the Yemenis uncomfortable at best and resentful at worst. Although relations have nearly always been correct, frictions did develop as certain Yemeni leaders adopted policies that did not accord well with the Saudis' perceptions of their own interests—in Yemen, as well as in the southwestern corner of the peninsula in general. Therefore, the discovery of oil in the eastern desert in 1984 (and the first exports thereof in 1987) was of momentous importance to the Yemenis in both political and economic terms. There is the widespread hope and expectation that vastly increased government revenues will make it possible for the government to adopt a far more "independent" foreign policy and, furthermore, fund a more extensive and numerous set of development projects and programs.

The Economy

One of Yemen's most important problems in the early 1970s was the lack of any real source of foreign exchange earnings. Although Yemen is the ancestral home of such rare and desirable commodities as myrrh and coffee, international trade and production of these (and other) commodities has either disappeared, moved away, or been drastically cut back because of marketing and other economic

problems. Until the discovery of oil, Yemen's exports were minis-
cule, consisting almost entirely of small amounts of coffee, cotton,
and hides and skins—hardly enough to begin to cover the astro-
nomical demand for consumer goods, food, and other things that
the Yemenis now want (having been denied access to them until
recently). It is precisely the eruption of pent-up demand, which
had been stymied by the imams and then the civil war, that created
the buying explosion of the 1970s and the consequent unimaginably
huge deficit in the Yemeni balance of payments.

Luckily, Yemen simultaneously experienced its most profitable
export binge in centuries: its adult male population. During the
mid-1970s, hundreds of thousands of Yemeni males between the
ages of fifteen and forty-five left Yemen to find work in the oil
fields of the Gulf and construction projects in Saudi Arabia, not
to mention the agricultural fields of the San Joaquin valley and
the automobile plants of Detroit. Soon hundreds of millions, even
billions, of dollars flowed back to the families of the emigrants.
These remittance dollars funded the import binge; in fact, the rate
of remittances in the late 1970s was so high that Yemen ran a com-
fortable surplus in its balance of payments.

It was not to last. The drop in the price of oil that began in
the early 1980s had an inevitable impact on the number and scope
of the development programs among the Gulf states. Furthermore,
the Saudis, who had formerly preferred Yemenis as laborers, decided, after reflection (and after events such as the attack on the
Grand Mosque in Mecca, which had Yemenis as participants), that
it would be safer and probably even cheaper to hire foreign contract
labor (South Koreans, Thais, and Filipinos) who would fulfill their
contracts and go home without any participation in the social and
political life of the Saudi state. Soon, thousands of Yemeni laborers
began to return home, and the rate of remittances began to drop,
slowly at first, then more precipitously in the mid-1980s. This drop
led international lending agencies and donors to demand more
stringent domestic economic policies from the government and
a significant scaling back of the Third Development Plan.

For the moment, the situation appears to have stabilized. There
are still remittances flowing in; there is now some oil revenue flow-

ing in; and, there has been a decline in the rate of demand for consumer items. (This last change is partly because the first great rush of buying has abated somewhat and partly because of specific import policies that the government has been forced to impose.) However, as the statistics of income, government revenue, and expenditures indicate, complacency is not appropriate.

Foreign Policy Issues

Overwhelmingly, Yemen's foreign policy concerns revolve around its two neighbors, Saudi Arabia and South Yemen. As indicated, relations with Saudi Arabia have not always been friendly. The interests of the Saudis are relatively clear, if one bears in mind the orientation and politics of South Yemen: to minimize the influence of the South Yemenis, to keep (North) Yemen as a buffer between it and the People's Democratic Republic of Yemen (PDRY), and most important, to prevent North Yemen from falling into the orbit of the PDRY. These concerns mean that North Yemenis have to avoid becoming a puppet state for the Saudis or a proxy for their conflict with the South Yemenis. They have to adjust to the notion that they are, in effect, a buffer between the two.

Much to the dismay of the North Yemenis, their state has, in recent years, clearly moved to the periphery of the consciousness of the major powers, the United States and the USSR. It is the hope of the Yemenis that their high quality oil will help to obtain for them a status more in keeping with their own perception of their importance and role, both on the peninsula and in the wider Middle Eastern arena.

Political Stability

Although Ali Abdullah Salih has governed the domestic and foreign policies of Yemen for more than a decade, his government remains essentially a military one. It has not yet found or developed a basis of legitimacy that has the unwavering support of a majority of the population, though it appears to be trying hard. In view of the violent deaths of two predecessors and the many attempts to dislodge him, not to mention such organized efforts as the campaigns of the National Democratic Front, one must remain concerned, for the near future, about political stability and its effect upon development programs.

THE PEOPLE'S DEMOCRATIC REPUBLIC OF YEMEN

Tareq Y. Ismael and Jacqueline S. Ismael

South Yemen is a land of geographic, historical, economic, political, and social paradoxes. Geographically, it is isolated from the rest of the Arabian Peninsula by mountains and deserts, yet it is situated at the intersection of important Middle Eastern and African trade routes that date back to antiquity. Historically, the area has experienced a combination of isolation and interaction, of peripheralism and strategic centrality. On November 30, 1967, these geographic and historical paradoxes were inherited by the newly independent People's Republic of South Yemen (PROSY), renamed the People's Democratic Republic of Yemen in 1970. Politically, it is the only state in the Arab world to have officially embraced "scientific socialism"; socially, the traditional tribal-based structure underwent significant transformation in more than two decades of independence under a Marxist government.

The PDRY, encompassing 332,968 square kilometers, shared ill-defined and often disputed borders with three other Arabian peninsula states: the Yemen Arab Republic, commonly known as North Yemen or Yemen (Sana'a) to the northwest; Saudi Arabia to the north; and Oman to the east. It faces Somalia, Djibouti, and Ethiopia across the Gulf of Aden and the Red Sea. South Yemen has some of the most rugged and inhospitable terrain in the region, a fact that has had considerable influence on its social, economic, and political development—for example, it has only a small population of about 2.4 million.

Ethnically, its population is homogeneous, consisting primarily of Arabic speakers (90 percent) of the Mediterranean racial type.

A minority of non-Mediterranean Vedoids (Australoids), speaking a Semitic language related to but different from Arabic, are found in increasing numbers as one moves eastward in the hinterland, finally comprising a majority in the tribes of al-Mahrah. A similar ethnic group, intermixed with more recent African, Arab, and East Indian arrivals, can be found on the island of Socotra. Small African communities descended from former slaves or invaders are also found in the interior. Approximately 60 percent of the population is engaged in agriculture, and 10 percent are nomadic Bedouin.

Most of the indigenous population of South Yemen are Sunni Muslims, adhering to the Shafi'i school of jurisprudence. There are also, however, a large number of Zaydi Shi'ites in Aden, primarily immigrants from the north. Small Christian, Hindu, and Zoroastrian minorities are found in Aden and other coastal towns, reminders of a cosmopolitan colonial and mercantile past. South Yemen also has a small, two-thousand-year-old Jewish community, a remnant of the community that emigrated to the newly founded State of Israel in 1950, some 7,000 from Aden alone.

Independence in 1967 prompted the departure of British administrative and military staff and their dependents as well as much of the trading community, altogether about 80,000 people. Left behind were predominantly native Yemenis in the PDRY with a much-reduced Somali and East Indian minority in Aden.

Political Development

By the turn of the sixteenth century, Aden had become a major port of call not only for local trade but for ships en route to the Red Sea, East Africa, the Arabian Gulf, and India. The Ottoman Turks, warding off the Portuguese and other European intruders, captured Aden from its sultan in 1538. Napoleon's military campaign in Egypt (1798) rekindled European interest in Aden and its strategic position. By 1802, the British government had consolidated its influence on the mainland through a friendship treaty with the Sultan of Lahej, and in 1839, Aden was incorporated into the British Empire under the administration of the Indian government.

The Pre-Independence Years

The spread of steam navigation in the nineteenth century and the opening of the Suez Canal in 1869 made Aden an even more important port, and the British, spurred by visions of further conquest and riches, began to consolidate their position in the interior of South Yemen. Aden continued to increase in strategic and economic importance, which meant that a different political and administrative infrastructure was required to carry the weight of British interests in the Middle East and the Indian Ocean. Aden was therefore declared a crown colony in 1937, bringing the city under closer supervision, control, and administration of the Colonial Office in London. South Yemeni territories were divided into two large protectorates subdivided into sultanates, sheikhdoms, and tribal confederacies.

It was customary for the sheikhs of several tribal units to come together to select the sultan, usually from a ruling family (or families). The sultan's dependence on tribal support introduced a significant degree of accountability into the established political system. Under British colonialism, the sultan's position was virtually guaranteed by the overwhelming power of the British, in exchange for which the sultan and the existing elite pledged their support to British interests. A number of tribal revolts occurred between 1936 and 1959, but all were crushed by the British and their allies. Eventually, discontent with the status quo was channeled into an anticolonialist movement that ultimately drove the British from South Yemen and toppled the power of the traditional elite.

Popular resistance to the constitutional route to South Yemeni independence envisaged by the British government—leaving intact the power of the largely pro-British traditional elite—was stronger than in many other British colonies, largely for four reasons. First, the association between British colonialism and traditional Yemeni rule led to strong feelings of resentment toward London. Second, British involvement in the creation of the State of Israel in 1948 and in the Suez crisis of 1956 did much to discredit the colonial power. Third, the growing popularity of Arab nationalism—personified by Nasser—finally provided a unity previously lacking in the South Yemeni anticolonial struggle. And, fourth, the aims and struggle of the republicans in North Yemen against the reactionary regime of the past highlighted the alternatives available to the south.

In an attempt to appease growing pressures in the region, particularly those of Arab nationalism, the British initiated a series of discussions beginning in 1954 with sheikhs and sultans interested in the formation of a Federation of Arab Emirates of the South. This autonomous entity would have been tied to Britain by treaty, governed by a Yemeni Legislative Council (albeit in name only), and protected by the British army. A mass boycott of legislative council elections in 1959 and again in 1964 led to constitutional talks concerning the incorporation of Aden into an enlarged South Arabia Federation. Despite British efforts, nationalist demands for immediate independence grew louder and more organized—political efforts often led by the Aden Trade Union Congress (ATUC) and military efforts led by the nascent National Front for the Liberation of Occupied South Yemen (NF). Eventually the nationalists won international support for independence in the United Nations, in 1963 and again in 1965.

British efforts in the summer of 1965 failed to co-opt the accommodationist forces in the nationalist movement, and conditions continued to deteriorate until May 1967 when Aden's new high commissioner, Sir Humphrey Trevelyan, announced that Britain would grant South Yemen independence on January 9, 1968. With independence at hand, nationalist forces—the NF and the Front for the Liberation of Occupied South Yemen (FLOSY)— began to compete for postindependence supremacy. The ensuing civil war resulted in triumph for the NF, a Marxist-oriented socialist movement, which entered into final negotiations with the departing British. On November 30, 1967, the independent People's Republic of South Yemen was established.

The Post-Independence Years

The National Front and its successors—the Unified Political Organization of the National Front (UPONF, 1975–78) and the Yemeni

Socialist Party (YSP, 1978–) retained tight control over the apparatus of power in the country. Only two other organized political forces (both having ideologies consonant with those of the NF) were tolerated, the Popular Vanguard party (a Ba'athist party) and the Popular Democratic Union (a communist party). Both were subsequently co-opted within the ruling structure, joining the NF-dominated United Political Organization in October 1975 and remaining with the organization when it became the Yemeni Socialist Party (YSP) three years later.

It is important to understand the history of the National Front in order to understand its role and importance in the contemporary PDRY. Its predecessors include—from a complex array of parties and forces—the South Arabian League (SAL), the oldest major nationalist political group in South Yemen, which sought to unite the divided, British-dominated principalities of the south into an independent South Arabia; and the United National Front (UNF), originally in 1955 a coalition of SAL, trade union activists, and other nationalist groups, which called for independence from Britain, then, after the republican coup, unity with the North. The UNF found its support in Aden among the Yemeni petite bourgeoisie and the rapidly growing Adeni trade union movement (including ATUC, which established its own political wing, the People's Socialist Party [PSP] in 1962), and it stood in sharp contrast to the primarily hinterland and elite-based politics of its parent organization, the South Arabian League.

A third predecessor, which drew most of its support from urban workers, and especially rural and tribal populations, was established in June 1963 as the National Front for the Liberation of Occupied South Yemen. Following its initiation of armed struggle against the British on October 14, 1963, the NF gained so much strength in the countryside that it threatened not only British influence but also that of the traditional rural and tribal elites. Its anti-British stance won it additional support from Adeni workers.

Even before independence was achieved, as early as 1965, divisions in the NF party began to show. One group, heavily influenced by Nasserism and upholding social-democratic, Arab nationalist ideals, successfully dominated the party. A second consisted primarily of NF cadres fighting inside the country whose ideological out-look had been radicalized by the experience of armed struggle and whose position had grown increasingly distant from that of the formal leadership of the NF. These divisions were brought to a head in 1966, when Egyptian pressure led the first wing to an-nounce the merger of the NF with another Yemeni and Egyptian-influenced nationalist group, the Organization for the Liberation of the Occupied South (OLOS), forming the Front for the Libera-tion of Occupied South Yemen.

The second, more "radical" wing was against unity, opposing the program and composition of FLOSY, particularly its inclusion of sultans, princes, sheikhs, and members of the Adeni elite. Amidst strong party discord, the merger was signed by the NF leadership in 1966. But continued internal opposition to what was called for-eign interference in Yemeni affairs led to a reshuffling of NF leader-ship, resulting in the eventual domination of the "radical" forces later that same year. These forces succeeded in defeating FLOSY in a civil war that accompanied the withdrawal of the British so that, upon independence, the leftist version of the NF established itself as the sole governing power in South Yemen.

Despite its success in achieving South Yemeni independence, the NF continued to be plagued by internal dissension over the means of alleviating the economic and political problems facing the nas-cent country. The army in particular opposed not only the land reform policies of the leftists but, more important, their notion of militia formation, which would have challenged the army's privi-leged position. Less than two weeks after the Fourth Congress of the National Front in March 1968, where leftist leaders shored up their political strength, the army launched a coup, claiming it was saving the country from communism. Qahtan al-Sha'abi, ap-pointed president in 1967 for two years by the NF general com-mand, was reinstated as leader. But tribal dissension within army factions soon led to another coup, only two months later, which forced al-Sha'abi to resign. This period in South Yemeni history has become known as the Corrective Step of June 22, 1969.

Although the party and state apparatuses were now firmly in the control of the leftist wing of the National Front, the party had not yet developed the ideology, organization, and trained cadres necessary for the transformation of South Yemeni society. Nor had it yet solved the problems associated with tribalism, underdevelopment, hostile neighbors, and recurrent threats to internal security. In the decade following the Corrective Step, the NF underwent a structural transformation of its own, with the aim of rendering the organization ready and able to act as the socialist vanguard of the Yemeni masses.

In March 1972, at the party's Fifth Congress, several bylaws were adopted, including scientific socialism (which has, in practice, meant a sort of eclectic Marxism); the struggle against imperialism, Zionism, and reaction; democratic centralism, collective leadership, and the purging of counterrevolutionary and decadent forces; and a new centralist structure based on the communist model. In other words, the measures adopted at the Fifth Congress were meant to signify the NF's readiness to embark on the "national democratic stage of the revolution," within which the political preconditions for South Yemen's continued progress would be established, and the NF would become prepared for its final evolution into a bona fide vanguard party. The transition of the UPONF continued for three years until, in October 1978, the NF was superseded by the vanguard party, the Yemeni Socialist Party.

The political structure of the PDRY was set forth in the State Constitution of the Republic, which was drafted by leading party and government members with the assistance of both Egyptian and East German experts. Minor amendments were made in 1978 to allow the YSP to replace the NF, but the six original parts of the constitution remained largely intact.

Part I, "Foundations of the National Democratic Social System and the System of State," set the political foundations of the state, declaring the PDRY's commitment to Yemeni unity, to anti-imperialism and anticolonialism, and to the end of the "exploitation of man by man" and local reactionary feudalism.

Part II, "Citizens and Their Organizations," addresses the rights and duties both of the public and of mass organizations. All citizens were granted formal equality as well as a long list of rights ranging from the right to work to freedom of expression. Also included was the government's right to grant asylum to those struggling for national and social liberation abroad, protection that had been granted to members of Palestinian guerrilla groups.

Part III, "Organization of State Authority," outlined the structures and duties of the formal political organization of the state. The People's Supreme Council (PSC) was declared the formal state legislative body and source of sovereign authority, and was given a wide range of duties in foreign and domestic policy making. The Presidential Council was, until 1978, the senior executive of the PSC and the real focus of power in the PDRY; abolished in 1978, the council was replaced by the presidium of the People's Supreme Council, which never wielded the executive power held by its predecessor. Rather, state power shifted to the president and the PDRY council of ministers, which became the highest administrative and executive body of the state.

Part IV, "Democratic Law and Justice," Part V, "National Defence and Security," and Part VI, "Interim and Final Orders," complete the Constitution.

Upon independence, South Yemen was left virtually devoid of an organized civil service through which government policies could be enacted. The British and Indian colonial officials who had occupied the bulk of middle- and upper-ranking government administrative positions left the country at independence, and others followed after the Corrective Step. These changes, and the general lack of educated cadres in the country, left South Yemen with few civil servants who were not either corrupt, from elite backgrounds, or politically unreliable, having served with the prior colonial administration.

Thus, the Ministry of Labor (later of Labor and Civil Service) was given the task of overseeing the education and training of a new civil service. The service was thoroughly purged, and a new system of hiring by qualification and promotion by merit was adopted. These and other measures proved effective in building a relatively large and efficient government bureaucracy.

Like the civil service, the judicial system prior to independence was found ineffective. Court proceedings took place in English, legal personnel were largely drawn from the colonial elite, and, outside of Aden, tribal urf and Islamic Shariʻah legal systems predominated. The Ministry of Justice established People's Courts, land reform tribunals, and three levels of courts to correct these drawbacks—a Supreme Court, based in Aden; governate courts, in each of the country's governates; and local magistrates' courts, which dealt with family matters, civil disputes, and minor criminal, traffic, and by-law offenses. Parallel with this restructuring, the basis of a new legal system was established, drawing upon appropriate tribal, Islamic, and Crown Colony law as well as revolutionary legislation. For example, people awaiting trial may now be released into the custody of mass organizations, which also have the right to representation in the trial process itself.

Administratively, the country was divided into a number of governates (six by March 1980), which in turn were divided into directorates and subdivided into districts. Local governments were created to cut across tribal boundaries in order to weaken tribal identities. Two principles underlie local government: centralization (the governor holds central authority within each governate, retaining final authority over the smaller units) and popular democracy, in the form of elected People's Councils. In practice, however, "democratic centralization" has proved an uneasy combination, and centralization has usually been more effective than popular democracy.

Theoretically, the YSP was a vanguard of the people; it formulated revolutionary policy and then ensured that the state implemented it. This relationship was structured in a number of ways: it was enshrined in the constitution; there was an overlap of party/state membership; the state bureaucracy was monitored and controlled by the party bureaucracy; and mass organizations served to integrate party and state. Although South Yemeni party and state were theoretically two parts of a single system, tensions between party and state leadership constituted a source of political instability.

In addition to party-state tensions, problems of an internal nature had plagued the YSP, despite the rhetoric of party unity, since the Corrective Step of 1969. Notable among these were the execution of the former president, Salem Rubayi Ali, in June 1978; the sustained power struggle between three liberation-era figures—Ali Nasser Muhammad, Abd al-Fatah Ismail (exiled 1980–84), and Ali Antar—that followed Rubayi Ali's overthrow and continued until January 1986; and the January 1986 civil war, which saw Muhammad deposed, Ismail and Antar dead, and the emergence of new party and government leadership.

Political instability within the PDRY could be traced to five main causes. One comprised ideological differences: what the goals and tactics of the revolution should or should not be. Another involved tensions between the ideology of the party leadership and pragmatism of day-to-day executive officers. A third involved the persistence of tribal and other subnational loyalties, which were often manipulated to engender political support. Fourth, regional and international involvement in PDRY affairs—whether Soviet, Cuban, or Saudi—fomented disputes. Finally, personal conflicts in the PDRY led to dissension, sometimes violent, within the ranks of the party.

Foreign Policy

The foreign policy of the PDRY was largely shaped by two factors, its geographic location and its ideological orientation. Relations with neighboring states, by definition a function of geographic location, were alienated by the Marxist orientation of PDRY.

Relations with Oman were poor for most of the history of the PDRY because the PDRY supported the People's Front for the Liberation of Oman (PFLO), viewing its struggle as an Omani counterpart to its own struggle against the British and local feudalism. By 1976, however, the PFLO had been virtually crushed under the weight of Iranian, British, Jordanian, and Omani forces. Aden continued to support sporadic PFLO guerrilla actions until the two countries established diplomatic relations in 1983 and agreed to the exchange of ambassadors in 1985.

Saudi Arabia also posed serious foreign policy problems for the PDRY. It has always opposed revolutionary socialism on the Arabian Peninsula because of the dangers of such trends for its own conservative regime. After South Yemeni independence, Riyadh supported groups opposed to Aden and actively campaigned against Yemeni unity, still fearing the threats such unity might mean for the kingdom's security. Both direct and indirect confrontations continued until 1976 when the PDRY and Saudi Arabia finally agreed to establish diplomatic relations.

In the broader regional arena, the PDRY sought to build close political ties with "progressive" regimes and movements—Algeria, Libya, Syria, Iraq, Iran, the PLO, Arab communist parties, and Polisario—based on common opposition to imperialism, Zionism, and "comprador" classes. Aden's close ties with socialist Ethiopia have been based on the latter's ideological similarity to PDRY policies. The PDRY supported the Palestinian people's right to armed struggle, providing significant support at various levels to the PLO; it had particularly good relations with the left wing of the PLO, the Popular Front for the Liberation of Palestine (PFLP) and the Democratic Front for the Liberation of Palestine (DFLP), both of which were perceived to share common roots with the NF/YSP. Some tensions did exist between the PDRY and "progressive" Arab states—for example, the PDRY refused to support Libya's involvement in Chad or Syria's opposition to Yassir Arafat, but the most serious conflict existed between South Yemen and Iraq. The latter was implicated in the 1979 assassination of an Iraqi professor residing in Aden, leading to a PDRY storming of the Iraqi embassy; Iraq recalled its ambassador and the South Yemeni embassy in Baghdad was attacked; the PDRY arrested a number of people as Iraqi spies the following year; Iraq expelled Yemeni students in retaliation. The PDRY remained neutral during the Gulf war.

South Yemen maintained close ties with most Third World countries, closest with socialist states such as Cuba, Vietnam, and North Korea. Leading nonaligned and anti-imperialist states were also favorably regarded, the most important of which was India, for both political and historical reasons. The PDRY maintained ties with only five Western nations; its economic problems were probably responsible for those relations.

Diplomatic relations with the Soviets began almost immediately after independence but closer relations ensued after the Corrective

Step when ties with the entire socialist community grew. Such relations were important primarily at the political and economic levels although military relations also had an important place in PDRY-Soviet relations after a 1979 Treaty of Friendship and Cooperation was adopted by the two states.

Indeed, over and above the patronizing Soviet perception of the PDRY as a country in the infancy of scientific socialism, there existed several significant differences between the countries' foreign interests and policies: It was the Soviets who reequipped the North Yemeni armed forces in the aftermath of the 1979 war, enabling their subsequent assault against south-supported leftist forces; Aden has not allowed Sino-Soviet hostility to interfere with its relations with China, its most important socialist trading partner; and PDRY foreign policy differed significantly from the USSR's on the Palestine question and Polisario's struggle against Morocco in the Western Sahara.

After the 1986 upheaval that brought moderates to power, the PDRY began to moderate its foreign policy vis-à-vis its conservative Arab neighbors. In particular, South Yemen revived dormant aspirations for unity with North Yemen and sought closer relations in lieu of it. The push for unity had begun in earnest.

THE ROAD TO UNITY
Tareq Y. Ismael

Although Yemeni unity was formally supported by both the YAR and the PDRY, and despite North Yemen's support for South Yemen's liberation struggle, the gap between the two countries widened following South Yemen's independence. Reasons for this include the North's harboring of the remnants of FLOSY and other defeated groups as well as dissident splinters of the NF. This fact, combined with ongoing disputes concerning their shared border and control of Kamaran Island, led to a Saudi-fomented war in 1972.

A cease-fire was soon agreed on, but rapprochement between the two Yemens was stalled by the profound differences in ideological orientation. The 1977 assassination of the North's pro-unity president, Colonel Ibrahim al-Hamdi, only worsened the situation; the 1979 assassination of the North's pro-Saudi president, Ahmad Hussain al-Ghashmi, prompted a full-scale war. In February 1979, National Democratic Front guerrillas, in opposition to the YAR and supported by South Yemen's regime, advanced into North Yemen. Fighting lasted only a short time, and a new unity agreement, reached through negotiations, was announced in March 1979.

In 1981, a draft constitution for unity was declared, though ideological differences proved insurmountable. The 1986 fratricidal civil war in South Yemen virtually wiped out all of the ideological hardliners in the south; thereafter, South Yemen adopted a more pragmatic position on unity. In May 1988 an agreement for the joint exploration of oil resources in the Ma'rib (North) and Shabwa (South) border zone defused potential conflict over the border oil deposits. On November 30, 1989, North Yemen's president, Colonel Ali Abdullah Salih, visited Aden and negotiated an agreement to merger the two states within six months of the approval of the 1981 draft constitution by both parliaments. On May 22, 1990, unification took place.

Sana'a is the capital of the new republic. The constitution of the Republic of Yemen has 136 articles. It establishes a Presidential Council as the head of state (Article 82) and parliament as the highest legislative body (Article 40). The presidential council is composed of five members elected by parliament through secret ballot for five-year terms (Articles 82, 83). The council elects its president from its membership (Article 84). Parliament is elected for four-year terms (Article 43). All citizens eighteen years and older have a right to vote (Article 42). An independent judiciary is established (Article 120) under a judicial council (Article 123). A supreme court is the highest court of the land (Article 124). The council of ministers is the highest executive and administrative organ of the state (Article 102). It is composed of the prime minister

and his deputies and ministers who are appointed by the prime
minister in consultation with the presidential council and must be
approved by parliament (Articles 103–5). The council of ministers
is collectively responsible to parliament, and the prime minister
must resign if the majority of the cabinet resigns (Article 105).

The constitution guarantees fundamental human rights declared
in the UN Charter (Article 5). Political freedom and equality are
guaranteed (Articles 26 and 27). Torture is singled out as a crime
and is forbidden (Article 33).

The first cabinet of the new republic, headed by Haydar Abu
Bakr al-Attas (the last president of the PDRY), has thirty-nine
members, twenty-two from the north and seventeen from the
south. The Presidential Council, headed by Ali Abdullah Salih (formerly the president of the YAR), has two members from the north
and two from the south. The new cabinet is responsible to a
320-seat House of Deputies, created by merging the former legislative bodies of the two states, and adding representatives of other
recognized political interests (e.g., the NDF and former leaders
of the south).

Many details of the association remain to be worked out during
the 30-month transition period, but most observers are cautiously
optimistic in view of the tremendous enthusiasm and optimism that
the merger created. On the other hand, it should be noted that
there are interests in both states that remain unpersuaded of the
wisdom of unity and oppose the changes that unification can be
expected to bring to both regions.

Iraq's invasion of Kuwait on August 2, 1990, presented Yemen
with its first foreign affairs challenge as a unified republic. Serving
on the Security Council when the Gulf crisis erupted, and scheduled to assume the rotating presidency of the council in December,
Yemen's stance on the crisis assumed an international significance
not generally accorded to a small state. While Yemen upheld all
Security Council resolutions against Iraq, it opposed U.S. military
intervention in the region, and called for an Arab solution. Saudi
Arabia expelled two million Yemeni workers in retaliation. (For
details of the Gulf crisis, see concluding sections of chapters 7,
13, and 17.)

REFERENCES

Al-Moukif Al-Arabi, vol. 10, no. 424 (May 28–June 3, 1990).

Al-Watan (Sana'a), vol. 13, nos. 1, 2 (February 1990), pp. 16–18, 63–65.

Robert D. Burrowes. *The Yemen Arab Republic: The Politics of Development, 1962–1986.* Boulder, Colo.: Westview Press, 1987.

Tareq Y. Ismael and Jacqueline S. Ismael. *The People's Democratic Republic of Yemen: Politics, Economics and Society.* Boulder, Colo.: Lynne Rienner Publishers, 1986.

Tom Little. *South Arabia: Arena of Conflict.* New York: Praeger, 1968.

John E. Peterson. *Yemen: The Search for a Modern State.* Baltimore: Johns Hopkins University Press, 1982.

Robert W. Stookey. *Yemen: The Politics of the Yemen Arab Republic.* Boulder, Colo., 1978.

———. *South Yemen: A Marxist Republic in Arabia.* Boulder, Colo., 1982.

Manfred Wenner. *Modern Yemen,* 1918–1966. Baltimore: Johns Hopkins University Press, 1967.

———. *The Yemen Arab Republic.* Boulder, Colo., 1991.

17

The Arab Gulf States

Tareq Ismael and Jacqueline Ismael

The states of Kuwait, Bahrain, Qatar, the United Arab Emirates, and Oman—commonly known as the Gulf states—are addressed together because they are tiny states that are sufficiently similar in their patterns of government and politics to justify collective treatment. Furthermore, these patterns are shaped by the same forces of history, geography, and economics. We will look at these common forces first and then consider the individual states.

History

The Gulf states were relatively obscure in modern times until the discovery of their oil resources. They lay along the world's most ancient sea routes and were centers of intense commerce and trade for centuries. Pearling, fishing, boat building, and commerce were the main industries of the Gulf region until the discovery of oil. In the desert climate, agriculture, if it existed at all, was limited. Settled populations lived along the coasts and near the oases, and the interior of the Gulf region was desert, inhabited by nomads.

Although obscure to the Western world until the discovery of oil, the Gulf region has played a significant role in the West's domination of the Orient since the initiation of the age of imperialism. The hegemony of the British East India Company over India by the end of the seventeenth century initiated Britain's increasing efforts to dominate the Gulf to protect and expand its imperial interests. In 1798 Muscat was forced to sign a treaty with Britain, a treaty that in effect gave Britain control over the entrance to the Gulf. Between 1810 and 1820 a series of treaties were signed with local Gulf rulers under the pretext of safeguarding sea routes and combatting piracy and the slave trade. In reality they were destroying all indigenous resistance to British hegemony.

Between 1861 and 1899 Britain achieved colonial control over the entire Gulf through a series of treaties with local leaders (1861 and 1892 with Bahrain, 1891 with Muscat, and 1899 with Kuwait). Thus, by the late nineteenth century, the British had essentially turned the Gulf into a British lake.

By the beginning of the twentieth century the Gulf region was politically and economically part of the British Empire. Rather than administering the region directly as a colonial possession, Britain institutionalized its control of the Gulf by exploiting the historical tribal relations that had existed in the region for centuries. Within the framework of these tribal relations, government and politics were largely undifferentiated from the institution of kinship. As in tribal societies generally, government was essentially democratic and participatory. A ruling family (shaikhdom) held symbolic authority but not real power. There was no fixed line of succession within a ruling family. Community consensus essentially determined succession. The British subverted this natural tribal institution to function as a surrogate for British colonial administration.

Britain accomplished this subversion by aiding and abetting the transformation of the Gulf's ruling families into royal families. This was achieved by concentrating economic and political power in the hands of one ruler—one favorable to Britain, who readily exchanged authority based on community consensus for power based on British support. Succession was then limited to direct lines of descent from this ruler. The British guaranteed royal families' rule against internal and external challenges in return for their support and loyalty. This structure remained in effect even after the British formally withdrew from the entire Gulf (by 1971).

The impact of British imperialism on the patterns of government and politics in the region was twofold: all of the states of the region have royal families as the central and most powerful institution in their political structures, and the region is politically fragmented into independent states. Before the British replaced the institution of ruling families with that of royal families, political organization was based on tribal alliances, and divisions between polities were consequently loose, informal, and fluid—much like the Arabian Peninsula before Saudi unification.

Physical and Social Geography

The impact of geography on patterns of government and politics can be summarized in terms of geopolitical factors. The region borders powerful neighbors—Iraq, Iran, Saudi Arabia. It lies astride strategic transportation/communication links between east and west, north and south—overland, waterway, and air. Because of its geopolitical significance, which greatly exceeds its geographic and demographic size, the region played the role of political pawn in regional and international power games. In this century, it was coveted by neighbors (each at different times), sequestered by empires (first the Ottoman, then the British), and courted by social movements seeking to unify and restructure the Arab world (both nationalist and religious).

The geopolitical fate of the region was sealed by the British in the nineteenth century. At the same time that Britain secured the consolidation of internal power in the hands of rulers committed to British hegemony in the region, it also took over direct control of all foreign relations for the Gulf states. By protecting the authority of the ruling families against the claims of covetous neighbors and dissident social movements, Britain directly tied the geopolitical future of the Arab Gulf states to Western strategic interests generally and British interests specifically. With the decline of the British Empire and the rise of the American-dominated Western ideological bloc, the Arab Gulf region has remained firmly in the Western geopolitical orbit.

Today the common geopolitical interests of the Arab Gulf states are reflected in the Gulf Cooperation Council (GCC). The GCC was formed in May 1981 under the sponsorship of Saudi Arabia in reaction to the Iraq-Iran war, on the one hand, and Iran's aggressive sponsorship of the Islamic fundamentalist revolution, on the other. It represents a collective security organization under the tutelage of Saudi Arabia of the region's most conservative governments. The GCC constitutes, in effect, the active foreign policy of the Arab Gulf states and as such reflects their geopolitical position in the Saudi sphere of influence.

The GCC was formed to coordinate the policies of members in order to keep Gulf shipping lanes safe and secure and to provide collective security against Iran's efforts to ignite an Islamic revolution in the region. While Saudi Arabia cut all relations with Iran (Kuwait followed after Iran attacked it in 1987), the southern Gulf states, especially the United Arab Emirates (UAE) since October 1982, kept the lines of communications to Iran open and actively sought good relations with Iran's revolutionary leadership. At the war's end, all states immediately reestablished relations—a sign that they had shifted the focus away from stopping Iranian interference in their affairs to stopping expected Iraqi interference in the future.

Iraq is the only Arab state adjacent to the Gulf that is not a GCC member; it has never been asked or wanted by member states. GCC support for Iraq during the Gulf war was based on the strategic and political interests of the Saudis and the Gulf states.

The GCC has emerged as a tension-management forum for disputes between Gulf states. Major problems center around boundary disputes. Saudi Arabia is the focus of many of these disputes, having only recently settled claims with Qatar and the UAE. The UAE-Saudi Arabia territorial dispute has not been settled yet despite the 1974 treaty. This is clearly reflected in the UAE not having a map. The Oman-Saudi Arabia territorial dispute was not settled until March 1990. There is still a neutral zone between Kuwait and Saudi Arabia, as ownership of the territories has not been settled. More serious is the dispute between Qatar and Bahrain over ownership of a number of islands in the Gulf. There is a long history of conflict between the states that flared up most recently in 1986 when Qatari forces landed on the island of Fasht al-Dibal to stop Bahraini construction of a coast guard station. The incident culminated with Qatar's seizing nineteen workers on the island. Bahrain responded by massing its forces. The tense situation lasted nearly two months until, at the GCC's urging, both states agreed to stop hostile actions and rhetoric.

While the GCC has managed to coordinate the foreign policies of the Gulf states to a certain degree, differences on foreign policy issues are quite frequent, concerning, for instance, the U.S. presence in the region, the Soviet Union, and Iran. There is a UAE-Oman axis regarding Saudi Arabia, and Bahrain, Qatar, and Kuwait play on this. Regarding economic policy, the GCC has dismally failed to coordinate the Gulf states' economies. Because of their singular dependence on oil for generating government revenue, the states have concentrated their productive capacities almost solely on exporting oil. The result has been a concentration on export opportunities with Europe, Asia, and North America rather than other Gulf states. Even where there has been a high degree of coordination—in OPEC (all Gulf states but Oman are OPEC members)—this coordination has crumbled in the face of declining oil prices and severe economic recession, for example, the UAE refused to accept the quota allocated by OPEC.

Economy

The economy is entirely dependent on the region's role as a major oil exporter. Individual states have accumulated vast wealth as a result of oil sales, and each state has invested the wealth in exotic technologies and external investments according to its individual development plans. All of them are, however, totally dependent upon oil revenues. A legacy of British imperialism is that control over oil resources is invested entirely in the ruler's hands. Until recently there was little distinction made between state budgets and the private purse of the rulers. Under British influence, communal ownership was transformed into private ownership, but with the discovery and exploitation of oil, the position of the royal families throughout the Gulf became entrenched independent of direct British protection.

The economies of the Gulf states are all narrowly specialized around the production of oil and the management of the resulting financial capital which is far greater than their absorptive capacities can accommodate. The net result is high consumption in both public and private spheres and service-oriented economies based on consumption rather than production. The indigenous population of the Gulf states constitutes a pampered leisure class, with labor predominantly performed by migrant workers. The economies of the Arab Gulf states are integrated into the global economy as high-powered consumer economies—high-powered not because of the size of the market but because of the size of the bankroll. They are economically independent of each other, which increases their absorptive capacity for infrastructure technologies, and they are economically dependent upon the global economy for production, which increases their absorptive capacities for the renewal of infrastructure technologies.

Socially, economically, and politically, oil has been the dominant factor in the Gulf's development. Oil and oil revenues have fundamentally changed the Gulf. Prior to the discovery of oil, the Gulf was a culturally homogeneous region dominated by Sunni Muslims who migrated to the area from central Arabia. The tribes who settled in the Gulf consisted of uneducated and illiterate desert dwellers who were bound together by social connections.

The discovery of oil changed all this. The tiny uneducated populations of the Gulf states were unable to meet the needs of the oil industry, resulting in a tremendous influx of expatriate workers from Lebanon, Egypt, Palestine, India, Pakistan and East Asia. These expatriates have come to dominate the labor forces in all Gulf states. Since independence, the majority of Gulf workers in all sectors of the economy have generally been expatriates. The only significant sector of indigenous laborers is government, the second most important economic sector in the region, and this has become possible only recently as education levels of Gulf citizens have risen dramatically.

The influx of the expatriates during the boom years did much to enhance what little economic diversification there was by tremendously increasing the demands for consumer goods and housing—demands that would not have existed through natural population growth alone. The housing market experienced rapid growth. At the same time, expatriates put pressure on economic and social infrastructures: schools and hospitals had to be built quickly to handle the growing population, to keep them productive, and to ensure their children would be productive. All this growth was handled relatively easily during the 1970s when oil revenues made Gulf citizens among the richest in the world. With the decline in oil prices during the 1980s, the rapid growth in the expatriate population came to a halt. The housing market stalled, and the demand for domestically produced consumer goods fell dramatically. Tens of thousands of expatriates remain and constitute the majority of the population in several countries. In the UAE nationals constitute not more than 20 percent of the population; in Kuwait the nationals make up less than 28 percent of the population; in Saudi Arabia 50 percent; and in Oman 80 percent.

Kuwait

Kuwait entered the international arena as an independent state in June 1961 upon termination of its 1899 agreement with Britain. It did not take long for its independence to be challenged. The Kassim regime in Iraq renewed historical Iraqi claims to Kuwait. To retain sovereignty, the Kuwaitis received support from the British and, later, the Arab League. In 1968, when the Ba'ath regime in Iraq came to power, the threat from Iraq was based on ideological challenges more than on historical territorial claims. As a conservative monarchy with a strong pro-Western orientation, Kuwait represented an antithesis to the Ba'ath ideology. Ideological hostility was diluted somewhat by Kuwait's adoption of an Arab nationalist stance in regional issues such as the Arab-Israeli conflict. Kuwait was one of the first Arab states to sever relations with West Germany after Bonn initiated relations with the State of Israel; it sent troops to Egypt during the 1967 Arab-Israeli war, and it has always been a strong supporter of the Palestinian cause. Aside from these issues, however, Kuwait has more or less adopted a pragmatic approach to its foreign policy, as seen in its move to keep its British accounts after the 1967 and 1973 Arab-Israeli wars rather than moving them elsewhere.

Despite its small population base, Kuwait has been an important player in the Arab world. This is largely because of the Kuwait Fund—a foreign aid fund made possible by the wealth from oil revenues. The fund is distributed throughout the Third World by an arm of the Kuwaiti foreign ministry. In the Arab world, the fund has aided states right across the ideological spectrum and has been used by Kuwait as a means of coopting critics and opponents as well as rewarding friends and allies.

The Kuwait Fund was made possible by the discovery and export of oil. Oil revenues have been so high that the country has ranked among the world's top five in GNP per capita. Such wealth—the overwhelming majority of which is funneled to the government—in a country of some 1.8 million people means that the government is able to meet the majority of the economic and social needs of its citizens. The building of an economic and social infrastructure, including roads, schools, and hospitals, was completed quickly after oil revenues began to pour in, and Kuwaitis benefitted tremendously from the wealth generated by their country's primary resource.

Kuwait has recently suffered along with other Gulf states because of the decline in oil prices that accompanied the Gulf War during the 1980s (although not as much as other GCC members because of its investments). While the war never really threatened Kuwaiti territory (save for Iraqi mining of Kuwaiti waters in 1987), it did affect its ability to secure access routes into and out of the Gulf for its exports. Coupled with the drop in oil prices as a result of a decline in consumption, Kuwait entered a deep recession in 1982 that lasted until the end of the decade. The virtual collapse of the economy was symbolized by the collapse of the Suk al-Manakh—Kuwait's stock market—because of a lack of confidence in the economy. As a result, Kuwait sought to increase oil revenues and in 1987 began to ignore OPEC production quotas.

During the Iraq-Iran war, Iran made threats against Kuwaiti shipping and attacked a number of Kuwaiti tankers. As a result,

Kuwait approached the Soviet Union and the United States to assist in keeping open the export routes through the Gulf. The Soviets responded by lending the Kuwaitis a small number of vessels and agreeing to provide naval protection to Kuwaiti ships. The United States replied in kind and even reflagged a number of Kuwaiti tankers. Kuwait thus brought the big powers into the Gulf and hastened the end of the Iraq-Iran conflict by encouraging American support of Iraq.

As do other Gulf states, Kuwait's economy depends on oil, though diversification has been a primary developmental goal. The Kuwaitis succeeded in establishing a relatively successful financial sector when oil revenues were high, but many of the loans made by Kuwaiti banks have proved to be nonperforming. Other sectors such as heavy industry and services have also suffered and proved to be largely inefficient—all contributing to the economic collapse in the 1980s. In fact, between 1984 and 1986, the value of Kuwait's GDP fell 27 percent (*Middle East Report* 1 [1987]: 90).

Political Situation

Kuwait has a longer and deeper history of political involvement than any other Gulf state save Bahrain and has the honor of being home to the longest running national assembly in the Gulf. Early Kuwait was ruled by an oligarchy of noble families—all of which were Sunni Arabs—who selected a political leader from among themselves. One of the leaders was Sabah al-Jabir, whose family, the Al Sabah, has ruled Kuwait since.

The process demanded that the man chosen as leader was to rule in accordance with the wishes of the leaders of the other families. There was a high degree of consultation until the turn of the twentieth century when Shaikh Mubarak Al Sabah, who (with the help of the British) came to power in 1896, and his son Salim abandoned these informal lines of communications and sought to expand the family's authority throughout Kuwait. These attempts were met with considerable opposition. There were calls for a more formalized consultative body both from other leading families and from the merchant class. Shaikh Salim proved to be highly unpopular because of disputes with Ibn Saud (later king of Saudi Arabia) that had greatly affected Kuwait's relationship with Arabia. The decline in trade with Arabia and the resulting economic effects mobilized the merchant class to pressure the Al Sabah family to establish some kind of formal consultative body after Salim's death in 1921. The family agreed and the initial council was formed with twelve representatives of the merchant class, but it proved to be ineffectual and inefficient.

By 1928 the council no longer existed but demands for more democratic institutions did. Kuwait was exposed to the nationalist ideals that were so common in the Arab world at the time, and by 1938 demands for a new consultative council were renewed. Shaikh Ahmad (who replaced Salim) was unpopular in Kuwait, and his family's rule was challenged by elements in Iraq. In addition, a Saudi blockade of Kuwait initiated in 1923, the absence of any kind of development plan, and charges of financial incompetence led to a great deal of popular dissatisfaction with Shaikh Ahmad's rule.

Though political parties were banned, Kuwaiti exiles in Iraq formed the al-Sha'biba and the National Bloc, and other groups of all ideological persuasions began to spring up within the country. A number of Kuwaitis were arrested, and the level of discontent and dissatisfaction grew to include important notables and the British. The pressure was such that Shaikh Ahmad was forced to agree to form the Majlis al-Ummah al-Tashri'i. Members of the council came from a list of eligible voters from 150 Kuwaiti families who elected the fourteen-member council. The council was active during its six-month existence: it drafted an interim constitution, fought to reform the economy, and attempted to check the power of Shaikh Ahmad. It had attempted too much too soon, however, and was opposed by the conservative elements of society, who were still quite powerful. The council was replaced by a new twenty-member council (chosen from an electorate of four hundred) that was no longer an executive council, as the old one had been, but rather an advisory one. In the interim between councils, Shaikh

Ahmad rewrote the constitution and gave himself veto rights. This change was met with heavy opposition from the new council, which refused to meet until its original status was renewed. Shaikh Ahmad rejected the council's demand, and it was dissolved four months later.

The democratic movement remained in hiding until the 1950s, when, after a number of elections to ineffectual councils, political opposition proliferated. Egyptian expatriates began a Kuwaiti branch of the Muslim Brotherhood in 1951, which later gave rise to the Social Reform Society. Movements such as the Teachers Club, the pan-Arabist Cultural Club, and the Graduate Club emerged in the 1950s. Ba'athist ideology was brought in by Syrian and Palestinian workers, and Iraqi and Iranian communists were instrumental in starting the Kuwait Democratic Youth. But it was only after independence in June 1961 that an assembly was set up.

A Constitution

The decision to create an elected Constituent Assembly was largely the product of Emir Abdullah al-Salim, who replaced Shaikh Ahmad in 1950. The new assembly had twenty elected members and eleven cabinet ministers. Its principal role was to draft the country's permanent constitution. The constitution, adopted in 1963, declared Kuwait a hereditary monarchy under the Al Sabah family, whose ruler was to be a direct descendant of Emir Mubarak the Great. It placed restrictions on the ruler's power and guaranteed personal liberties, the right to social and economic welfare, and freedom of the press, residence, and communications. Through a separation of powers, executive power rested in the hands of the emir and the National Assembly. The National Assembly was to consist of fifty secretly selected members and all nonelected cabinet officers, who served a four-year term. A minister could be questioned by the assembly, and ministers were subject to votes of nonconfidence, though only the emir was allowed to call for the resignation of the entire cabinet or the prime minister.

National Assembly

Theoretically, the constitution is a contract between the ruler and the people, represented by the National Assembly. The emir must swear an oath to respect the constitution. The National Assembly has been suspended on three occasions after severely criticizing government policies and the integrity of its ministers. The criticism was such that the emir considered the existence of the assembly to be contrary to the interests of both his government and the country, and it was thus suspended, for the first time, in 1975.

The assembly remained suspended until 1981—four years after the emir's death and his replacement by Shaikh Jabir al-Ahmad. Shaikh Jabir was more open to the concept of the National Assembly, which, throughout its suspension, remained a popularly supported institution. The new National Assembly was accompanied by changes in the electoral laws that created more electoral districts. This change served the shaikh's personal interests by bringing more representation from Kuwait's conservative bedouin elements at the expense of Shi'a representation. Charges of gerrymandering were common, and the electoral results, giving bedouins twenty-seven seats while the Shi'as and nationalists were virtually shut out of the assembly, seemed to bear these charges out.

The same types of results were obtained in the 1985 election where the progovernment National Center Group (composed of bedouins and conservatives) maintained control of the assembly by winning nineteen seats. Combined with the seventeen cabinet members who sat in the assembly, progovernment forces controlled thirty-six of the sixty-five seats. Other groupings in the assembly included three members of the Democratic Bloc (a leftist group with origins in the Arab Nationalist Movement), two Arab Nationalists (liberals with Ba'ath leanings), three Kuwaiti Nationalists, three members of the Social Reform Society (Sunni Muslims affiliated with the Muslim Brotherhood), two members of the Heritage Revival Society (Sunni Muslims aligned with the al-Salafiya movement), and only one member of the Social Cultural Society (Shi'a Muslims).

Both the fifth and sixth assemblies were forced to deal with the difficult economic situation in which Kuwait found itself in the 1980s. The sixth assembly proved itself to be more vigorous in its examination of the system and succeeded in forcing the resignation of Justice Minister Shaikh Salman al-Duayi Al Sabah and almost forcing that of the oil minister, Shaikh Ali al-Khalifa Al Sabah, for financial mismanagement and impropriety. The assembly was so successful in its attacks on the government that it was suspended on July 1, 1986. Public demand for the restoration of democracy forced the ruler to announce the formation of a National Assembly with consultative powers as an interim step to the resumption of parliamentary democracy. On June 10, 1990, elections for the assembly took place. The assembly consisted of seventy-five members of whom fifty were elected by secret ballot and twenty-five were appointed. Twenty-seven members of the 1985 parliament boycotted the election, and a number of political groups did so as well.

Kuwait and the Iraq-Iran War

The Gulf war and Iran's initial successes in driving toward Basrah and occupying the Fao peninsula scared the Kuwaitis. Fearful of an Iranian victory, Kuwait had reversed its suspicions of the Ba'ath regime in Iraq by fully supporting and financing Iraq's war effort. Iran, in turn, began to sponsor attacks against Kuwaiti oil installations and other targets. A pro-Iranian group bombed the U.S. and French embassies in Kuwait, began to mine Kuwait waters, and fired a number of missiles into Kuwaiti territory. In 1985 the attacks became bolder when an attempt was made on the emir's life and attacks against oil installations and other pieces of the economic infrastructure began. Members of the group captured proved to be from Iraq and Lebanon though they were supported and sponsored by Iran. The Kuwaiti regime used this information to accuse Iran of terrorism.

In 1986 and 1987, Iran stepped up its attacks against Kuwaiti shipping. At the same time, the oil installation at the key Mina al-Ahmadi refinery and a number of cafés in Kuwait City were bombed. As a result attacks on Shi'as occurred in the Kuwaiti press, tens of thousands of Shi'as from other Islamic states were deported, and Shi'as were removed from sensitive positions in the oil industry, military, and police.

Kuwait under Occupation

On August 2, 1990, Iraq invaded Kuwait and six days later announced its annexation to Iraq. Saddam Hussain subsequently proclaimed Kuwait to be Iraq's nineteenth province and, in a systematic effort to obliterate Kuwait's national identity, initiated the dismantling of Kuwaiti political and economic institutions. Tens of thousands of Kuwait's 1.6 million expatriot workers fled the country in the wake of the invasion. Apparently encouraged by the occupying forces, the outflow of population continued unabated in the following weeks. By October 1, half of Kuwait's population—600,000 Kuwaitis and twice as many foreign workers—had fled the country (*Gulf News* [Dubai], October 1, 1990).

Following the invasion, Kuwaiti Emir Shaikh Jaber Al Ahmed Al Sabah and his government established a government-in-exile in Jeddah, Saudi Arabia. From there, they attempted to coordinate resistance to Iraq's occupation with regional and international efforts to liberate Kuwait and to take control of its substantial financial resources in foreign assets.

Kuwait's foreign assets, in effect, constituted an offshore economy. Since the sixties, Kuwait has been systematically ploughing its vast oil wealth into foreign assets. After the invasion, an asset freeze was clamped on Kuwaiti holdings by world governments to protect them from Iraqi seizure. Within three weeks of the invasion, the government-in-exile was in full control of its assets (*Khaleej Times* [Dubai], October 22, 1990).

In an effort to mobilize support of Kuwaiti nationals behind their exiled rulers, the Emir of Kuwait called a meeting of prominent exiled nationals. Held in Jeddah on October 13–14, the meeting was attended by about 700 Kuwaitis. Crown Prince Shaikh Saad Al Abdullah Al Sabah promised the delegation restoration of Kuwait's 1962 constitution after Kuwait's liberation, and urged politicians to silence differences in the interest of unity (*Gulf News* [Dubai], October 14, 1990). Eleven national reconstruction committees were established to initiate planning for the rebuilding of Kuwait's devastated infrastructure in the wake of liberation.

Bahrain

Bahrain is unlike any other Gulf state: It is a group of small islands twenty miles offshore of Saudi Arabia and Qatar. Its geographic position has greatly affected its political and economic development, as has the composition of its society. Iran has historically laid claim to Bahraini islands for both strategic and nationalistic reasons. In addition, the emergent Arab nationalist movement of the 1950s and 1960s was a greater threat to the Bahraini monarchy than it was to the monarchies of the lower Gulf states. Thus, Bahraini development took place in an atmosphere of hostility from outside powers and challenge from ideologies that disputed the position of the ruling family.

Internally, too, Bahrain has faced challenges. Bahraini society consists of four principal groups. Members of the traditional aristocracy, centered around the ruling Al Khalifa family, are Arab Sunni Muslims. The *hawala* are also Sunni but came to Bahrain from Persia over the last several centuries. These Sunnis constitute the upper classes of Bahraini society and include members of the ruling family, the aristocracy, and the commercial classes. The lower classes consist of Shi'a Muslims. Constituting a majority of the population (estimates range between 55 and 70 percent), these Shi'as are divided into Baharna and Ajam Shi'as: the Ajam migrated to Bahrain in significant numbers only in the last century, while the Baharnas, who are more numerous, are descendants of the original inhabitants of Bahrain. The majority of Shi'as live in Bahrain's rural areas and are poor. Though constitutionally equal to their Sunni countrymen, Bahraini Shi'as have long complained about the political, economic, and social stratification between the sects that has seen them dominated by the Sunni minority.

In many ways, Bahrain has had longer to develop than other

Gulf states because it was the first Arab state to export oil. Oil was first discovered in Bahrain in 1932 and exportation began only two years later. The significant socioeconomic force of oil revenues has been in effect longer in Bahrain than in any other Gulf state, though the depletion of its oil reserves means that Bahrain will be the first one to face an oil-less future. An economic downturn will be eased, though, because of recent discoveries of large gas deposits.

Bahrain remains dependent on its oil production as its major source of foreign currency, though the oil sector provides only around 20 percent of GDP. Bahrain has managed to diversify its economy to a greater extent than other Gulf states, especially in the finance sector, which in 1986 accounted for 24.5 percent of GDP. However, oil products accounted for 70 percent of government revenues, showing that the diversification that has taken place has not been sufficient to reduce Bahrain's dependence on oil for its economic welfare. Future economic prospects depend on many factors, but Bahrain has a better chance of diversifying its economy and surviving the end of the oil era because of its educated population and the quality of its economic and financial infrastructures.

The overseers of Bahraini economic development have been the Al Khalifa family who have dominated Bahraini politics. The family migrated to Bahrain from central Arabia in the 1780s and seized control of Bahrain after the collapse of Persian influence there. They imposed Sunni control over the remaining Shi'a population and were able to extend their influence throughout the islands. By the time the British turned the Gulf into a British lake, their supremacy was unchallenged.

Bahrain National Congress

Unlike other Gulf shaikdoms (where the populace has been historically apolitical), Bahrain has had a long history of political activity and was the first Gulf state to experiment with a national assembly in 1923. Though the supremacy of the Al Khalifa was unchallenged, the populace did take an active part in antigovernment protests. They were of two kinds: anti-British demonstrations by members of the merchant community who were dissatisfied with reforms undertaken at Britain's request, and demonstrations by Shi'as unhappy with the treatment they received at the hands of the Sunni majority. The protests gave rise to a Bahraini nationalist movement that formed the Bahrain National Congress in 1923 to demand a reduction in British influence in internal affairs and the establishment of a consultative council which would make the emir more accessible to public input. The Shi'a protest movement included demands for proportional representation on municipal and educational councils, but the British refused to act on the demands of all parties and made it clear that they firmly supported the status quo.

British intransigence did nothing to quell demands for reform. Combined with the fermenting political demands of Shi'as and the merchant classes for greater political participation, the 1950s and 1960s saw great numbers of Bahraini students returning home from abroad where they had invariably been exposed to socialist and pan-Arabist ideologies. The British were particularly despised because of events in Palestine and their unwillingness to bring about reform, and British interests were the subjects of strikes by Bahraini workers. The pressure exerted by the strikes and the growing politicization of society forced the government to act, and it established a number of committees to study the demands of the opposition. The result was the formation of three councils (health, education, and municipal) that were to be half elected and half appointed. To the government's embarrassment, members of the Higher Executive Committee (HEC)—formed by Abd al-Rahman al-Bakr, a student activist—swept the voting for the Health and Education Council, forcing the government to suspend voting for municipal councils.

The councils proved to be unworkable because of conflicts with the government. Al-Bakr was forced to leave the country, and the HEC changed its name after police crackdowns caused by an HEC-led general strike in protest of the political stalemate. The HEC was replaced by the Committee for National Unity with Ab al-Aziz al-Shamlan as secretary general at the end of the general strike. The stalemate between the government and the reform movement remained, and throughout 1955 and 1956 the reform movement tried to force change through a series of general strikes. These culminated in the return of al-Bakr to Bahrain. He, al-Shamlan, and others were subsequently arrested and their movement declared illegal.

Bahrain and the Arab Nationalist Movement

Political opposition was driven underground by the regime's repression. The repression had the effect of solidifying Al Khalifa control, though there is evidence that numerous Ba'ath, Marxist, and Arab Nationalist Movement cells were able to operate in Britain at that time. These cells grew to form the National Liberation Front of Bahrain and the Bahraini branch of the Popular Front for the Liberation of Oman and the Arabian Gulf. These cells were, nevertheless, small and unable to bring about an end to either British rule or the rule of the Al Khalifa.

Independence

The end of British rule in 1971 and formal independence of Bahrain brought reform of government structures. Bahrain's reaction upon independence was to join the proposed federation between the nine emirates but it subsequently decided to go it alone. Despite the creation of an Administrative Council during the turmoil of the 1950s, the executive power of the Al Khalifa remained supreme. A number of ministries were added, and the Administrative Council was renamed the Council of State. The council became the cabinet; members were appointed by the shaikh and represented the interests most supportive of him. Outlying areas—mainly Shi'a in composition—were administered by local officials chosen by the shaikh. Also accompanying independence was the formation of a Constituent Assembly that had as its primary duty, among others, the ratification of a newly drawn constitution. The assembly consisted of twenty-two elected members, who were appointed by the shaikh, and the twelve members of the cabinet. Ten were reformers or nationalists, and fourteen were Shi'as. The twenty members appointed by the shaikh ensured government control over the assembly and the passing of the Al Khalifa-authored constitution. In the constitution, which was modeled after Kuwait's, Bahrain was described as a hereditary monarchy whose ruler was to be declared on the basis of primogeniture. While there is a separation of executive, judicial, and legislative powers, the emir and the National Assembly are to share legislative functions. The emir can veto any bill passed by the assembly and has the right to appoint members of the cabinet. He can ratify laws; vetoed laws are sent to the National Assembly. The thirty-member assembly has the right to question any minister, and ministers are responsible to the assembly. Individual assembly members may initiate legislation, and the assembly as a whole must ratify the yearly budgets. Any principle of the constitution may also be challenged by the assembly—except the concept of hereditary rule—if the amendment is supported by a two-thirds majority.

The initial National Assembly included a bloc of popular candidates (including Ba'ath, Marxist, socialist, and Arab nationalist elements) whose goal was to broaden the institutions which, they hoped, would eventually lead to Bahraini democracy and involve Bahrain more deeply in Arab affairs. Opposing it was a bloc of conservative and religious leaders and independent members who supported the policies of the shaikh. The National Assembly was suspended in 1975 because of continuing labor unrest and government fear that the situation might lapse into turmoil similar to that of the 1950s. The government had to introduce a security law to deal with the unrest in the National Assembly, choosing to bypass the assembly and unilaterally impose the law. In 1975, the assembly was dissolved and the constitutional principle requiring new elections suspended.

The National Assembly remains suspended and has not reconvened. The emir has never shown a great affinity toward government accountability and seems quite willing to keep governing the country without any popular input into government policy. The Iraq-Iran war suspended most talk of reconvening the assembly, as Iranian influence among Gulf Shi'as (especially Kuwait) showed the emir that it was a risky proposition. The government responded to critics of their actions by replying that the average Bahraini is more interested in housing and jobs than in the National Assembly and that the government has been efficient in meeting those needs.

Qatar

Like the other Gulf states, Qatar's political development since independence has focused on the actions of its ruling family, and its economic development has resulted from oil wealth. Its development, however, has followed a slightly different path than that of its neighbors Kuwait and Bahrain because of differences in social and cultural homogeneity. These differences have resulted in Qatar's political development being marked by stability and a general lack of political activity among Qataris.

Qatari society is marked by tremendous homogeneity—the indigenous population is entirely Sunni—and it is bound together by centuries-old social networks that combine with the powerful influence of Wahhabism to make it politically and socially stable. Unlike other Gulf states, Qatari society has not emerged from a commercial tradition centered around coastal centers; rather, it has grown out of a Bedouin tradition with its center of influence in the interior. The tribes migrated to Qatar from what is today Saudi Arabia. Among them was the Maadhid, to which the current ruling family—the al-Thanis—belonged. First emerging as a powerful force during the introduction of Wahhabism to Qatar, the al-Thanis succeeded in rising to prominence by tying themselves to the interests of foreign and regional powers who were shaping the region's development. By the late 1800s, when Kassim al-Thani managed to defeat a superior Ottoman force sent to overthrow him, the position of the family was unchallenged.

At various times in its history, Qatar has been tied by the al-Thanis to the interests of the Saudis, the Ottoman Empire, and, finally, the British. These linkages resulted from two factors. The first is that Qatar is small, devoid of natural defenses and the basic capabilities necessary for self-defense. Historical enmity between Qatar and its neighbor Bahrain caused Qatar to turn to outside powers for protection against al-Khalifa claims. Ultimately, the interplay between the foreign and regional powers prompted the al-Thanis to agree to formalize their relationship with the British in 1916, when Qatar became a British protectorate.

The second reason the al-Thanis aligned themselves with foreign powers was to increase their influence in Qatar. Indeed, by the time that the treaty with Britain was signed, the position of the family was largely unchallenged. They had managed to play off foreign powers against one another to gain the best possible deal for Qatar and, in the process, began to construct the infrastructure through which they would rule the country into the 1990s.

When the British government announced its intentions to quit the Gulf by 1972, Qatar's first reaction was to join with other Gulf emirates in the formation of the Union of Arab Emirates. But it did not join, opting instead for sovereignty. This necessitated the formation of some kind of governmental structure, but the structure chosen was in reality no different than the one that had existed under the British.

Constitution

A provisional constitution was drawn up in 1970 and was subsequently amended in 1972 after the succession of Shaikh Khalifa to power. Though it was to be purely a transitional document, the original constitution still remains in force. In it, Qatar is described as a democratic Islamic Arab state that derives its laws from the shari'ah. Executive and legislative power lie in the hands of the emir. The constitution, however, provides for the creation of a Council of Ministers and an Advisory Council, which are designed to discuss issues and make recommendations to the emir on legislative matters. Constitutionally, the Advisory Council should consist of twenty appointed members in addition to the cabinet, but membership was expanded to thirty in 1975. There has never been an election for the council; there has only been one council since the constitution came into effect, and it is regularly extended by emiri decree. The council elects its own president, vice president, and standing committee.

Shaikh Khalifa has been careful to use the composition of the council as a means of extending his personal and familial influence. Members of the merchant community and important tribes hold seventeen of the thirty seats and thereby constitute a majority. The most important constituencies in the state are well represented in the council, and it appears from all accounts that its members are well respected and would likely be elected were an election ever held. The council's reputation speaks well for Khalifa's political acumen and shows the disinterest in reform in Qatar.

Economy

Economically and socially Qatar appears to be sound, but under the surface there exist many currents that could undermine the stability of the regime. Oil is, of course, the dominant force in the economy and the reason for the state's wealth, though Qatar is desperately trying to diversify its economy. Some 90 percent of economic activity in Qatar is generated by the government, and 95 percent of this comes from oil production. Though desalination and power projects and some heavy industry projects are under way, oil remains the lifeblood of the economy. The decline in oil prices during the 1980s hit the country hard, though not as hard as some other Gulf states. The recession convinced the Qataris that their future economic prosperity lies outside of oil, and they began the first stage of construction of the giant North Field gas project in 1987. The project, which is to culminate with the construction of liquid natural gas export facilities, is reported to be the largest concentration of oil-related natural gas in the world, and it is clear that, with the decline in price and importance of oil on the international markets, gas will have to become the new way to fill Qatari coffers.

Gas, however, will not solve the problem of dependency that haunts the economy. Despite all the wealth that oil exports have brought to Qatar and all the related health, social, and educational benefits, Qatar is resource-poor and depends on outside factors for its economic survival. Qatar depends on export markets for oil and will have to depend on similar markets for its gas exports, and it depends on foreign nationals for its labor force. There is no sign that any of these forms of dependence will end in the near future.

Oman

The Sultanate of Oman stretches over some of the most strategic territory in the Middle East. Lying at the entrance to the Gulf and the Gulf of Oman, the strategically vital Strait of Hormuz lies just off the tip of Oman's Ras Musandam. The hostile climate and geography of the region have determined much of Oman's history, and its development has been constrained by sea and desert.

Throughout much of their history Omanis have been led by an elected Imam. Most Omanis belong to the Ibadhi sect of Islam whose leader (the Imam) heads the state. The present dynasty (the Al Bu Saids) dates back to 1744, when the family managed to expel the Persians from what is now Oman. Trying to extend the influence of the family to the interior and southern reaches of Oman proved to be difficult—a fact that has colored much of Oman's political history. The family has managed to retain control despite opposition from within and from early Wahhabi interference from what is now Saudi Arabia, and despite the separation of the functions of the Immamate and the Sultanate (the separation of religious and civil authority), which occurred in 1783. The Sultanate, the seat of real political power in Oman, has remained in Al Bu Said hands while the Immamate is in the hands of the Hinawi tribe.

This arrangement, brought about largely through British influence in the 1800s, has had real and dramatic effects on Omani politics. The Sultanate had to fight very hard to extend its influence inland and into the southern reaches of the state while trying to prove itself the real leadership of Oman at the expense of the Immamate. The Hinawi have, until recently, resisted Al Bu Said attempts at controlling Oman—even going so far as to apply for Arab League recognition for the interior of Oman in 1954. Though the movement was defeated and the Sultanate managed to increase its influence among outlying tribes, the opposition to the Sultanate from the Immamate was not over.

As with other Gulf states, the discovery of oil marked a critical period in Omani history. The rapid influx of oil revenues after oil was discovered in 1962 led to societal demands for modernization. By 1968, oil revenues were such that Sultan Said Ibn Teimour began to put together a development and planning program. He was, however, a conservative man and was determined that whatever progress was made was to be undertaken slowly. At the time, Oman was one of the most underdeveloped areas in the Gulf: It lacked hospitals (it had one hospital plus a number of dispensaries), schools (it had three schools with one hundred students), and doctors, and its infant mortality rate was among the highest in the world.

Not only was the Sultan conservative, he was authoritarian as well. His inability to meet the needs of Omanis resulted in the formation of the Dhufar Liberation movement, whose goal was to free southern Oman from the rest of the Sultanate. Though the rebellion in Dhufar lasted well into the 1970s, the political situation changed with the overthrow of the Sultan in July 1970 by his son Qabus Ibn Said, who had been under house arrest since returning from school in England. Qabus pledged to modernize government structures and the economy, and to liberalize society.

While liberalization and modernization proceeded in fits and starts through the 1970s, Qabus managed to increase his personal influence within the ruling family and within Oman itself. By the end of the Dhufar rebellion in 1975, he had managed to extend the power of the Sultanate throughout the entire state—an accomplishment his father was never able to achieve. Sultan Qabus was autocratic, he ruled without any sort of consultative body, but he was more open than his father had been. He ruled on the basis of personal and tribal relationships that had developed before he came to power and that he had also fostered after coming to power. His rule during the 1970s succeeded in introducing basic economic and social infrastructures to Oman.

That situation changed in 1981 when the Sultanate of Oman's State Consultative Council (SCC) was established after Sultan Qabus formed a small ministerial committee to report on the feasibility of introducing a formalized consultative body. Initially, the SCC had forty-three appointed members though that number was expanded to fifty-five in 1983. Original members were selected by the initial SCC committee and names forwarded to the Sultan, who has accepted every nomination forwarded to him. The SCC president, a figurehead, is the only SCC member directly chosen by the Sultan and has always been a member of the cabinet.

Of the fifty-five members, nineteen are members of the government, and the Chamber of Commerce elects nineteen, eleven of whom are chosen by the committee. The remainder represent each of Oman's seven geographic regions; their numbers vary according to the population of the region.

The SCC has developed into a government watchdog, and its members are encouraged to criticize government policy at every opportunity. Ministers, chosen by the sultan and tending to represent all regions of Oman, are held responsible to the SCC and are expected to appear before it when called. The government cannot be subject to a vote of nonconfidence, and no one can question the ultimate rule of the Sultan.

Ultimately the SCC served as a means for Sultan Qabus to unite the state and bring in views from outlying regions. The Dhufar rebellion had a great effect on the sultan in his attempt to unite the southern and northern regions of the country. His main tactic has been to channel large amounts of money into the southern region, and to balance the development projects in the north with those in the south. While it may be politically wise, this scheme has little economic merit, and many of Oman's current economic difficulties can be traced to the waste of funds on inefficient projects that exist in the south.

On November 18, 1990, Sultan Qabus announced the formation of a Majilis Al Shura (consultative council) as a step to increase public participation in government. The council, scheduled to be functioning within a year, is to be entirely composed of representatives from Oman's forty-two wilayets (districts) and will have no government-appointed members (*Khaleej Times* [Dubai], November 19, 1990). The means of selecting representatives, as well as the powers and responsibilities of the council, were not announced.

Overall, Oman has emerged intact from the economic difficulties that face all Gulf states. It has avoided the lavish projects that have so infatuated its neighbors and has instead developed its infrastructure at a slow but steady pace. It has not been bound to OPEC export quotas because it refused to join the organization, leaving it free to set its own standards on the amount of oil it exports. Exports and revenues declined as the price of oil plummeted during the Iraq-Iran war. The government has been able to insulate the economy from the devastation that falling prices have wrought on other Gulf economies. In Oman 95 percent of GNP is derived from oil revenues.

Other important sectors whose growth has been stressed since the third Five-Year Plan are natural gas, the development of copper smelters in the north, coastal fisheries, and the agriculture. Before the discovery of oil, agriculture was the lifeline of the economy, and Oman's climate lends itself well to increasing production. However, increases in production rest on Oman's ability to bring irrigation systems to the interior of the country.

United Arab Emirates

The UAE was formed as a federation of the Omani-coast emirates in late 1971. These emirates and others had previously attempted to unify under British auspices but failed because of several obstacles. However, when the British government announced in 1968 its intention of quitting the Gulf by 1972, the rulers of Abu Dhabi and Dubai announced their intention to unite. Soon other Lower Gulf leaders expressed their desire to join the union, and by December 1971 Abu Dhabi, Dubai, Sharjah, Ajman, Umm al-Qaiwain, and Fujairah had joined to form the United Arab Emirates. Ras al-Khaymah joined the federation on February 10, 1972.

The union is in many ways a strange one. Despite the ethnic

and social ties that bind the people of the UAE together, the emirates differ vastly in size, wealth, and economic capabilities. Historically, Abu Dhabi (the most populated and richest of the emirates) and Dubai (geographically the largest) have dominated the union. Abu Dhabi's Shaikh Zayid Ibn Sultan al Nahyan has served as the UAE's only president and is considered one of the most powerful leaders in the Gulf region. Dubai's ruler, Shaikh Rashid Ibn Sa'id al Maktum, was the UAE's vice president and prime minister until he died in October 1990 and was succeeded by his son, Shaikh Maktum bin Rashid al Maktum. The smaller emirates are plagued by their small size and population and insufficient economic bases, which limit their ability to influence the direction of the UAE's policy.

Theoretically, there is a separation of powers in the UAE. The executive consists of the Supreme Council, the presidency, and the Council of Ministers. The Federal Supreme Council, composed of the emirs of each emirate, is the highest executive body in the federation and is chaired by the president. Each emir has one vote on issues before the council; a simple majority suffices on ordinary matters, but five of the seven members must approve substantial matters, and two of those votes must come from Abu Dhabi and Dubai. Therefore, though the power of Abu Dhabi and Dubai has been constitutionally balanced to some extent, they remain in a position to dominate the union.

They dominate also because of the tremendous power vested in the president. He signs laws, convenes sessions of the Supreme Council, appoints the prime minister, deputy prime minister, and cabinet, can end the term of any and all ministers, and can veto all motions brought before him. Shaikh Zayid's reelection at the end of each five-year term and the powers vested in the presidency reflect both his role and Abu Dhabi's position as the most powerful of the seven member states. This power concentration has not gone unopposed: one of the reasons Ras al-Khaymah did not join initially was because of the veto power that would be possessed by Zayid and Rashid. Shaikh Saqr, emir of Ras al-Khaymah, has been outspoken on this and other issues concerning the dominance of the two largest emirates, but, on the whole, the emirs of the smaller members seem to have accepted their dominance.

There have been, however, differences among the emirs. The UAE is a federal state, and the constitution gives the federal government exclusive jurisdiction over defense, finance, foreign affairs, the use of the armed forces (both externally and internally), and other important areas. (Defense was not unified until 1978, and despite the unification, Dubai's forces are not part of the federal defenses.) All powers not included in the constitution are controlled by the emirates which have, through this arrangement, retained many of the political and economic institutions that existed prior to union. Though the powers of the federal government are explicitly stated, this did not prevent it from trying to expand its areas of influence. It has also not stopped the emirates from squabbling among themselves.

The leaders of the smaller emirates must carefully balance their federal commitments with their local ones. The emirs are hereditary rulers who must rely on tribal support to stay in power. They must satisfy local needs in order to secure a local base of support, a difficult feat in a federal setting where federal policies often infringe on local interests. Such was the case in Sharjah in 1972 when many in Sharjah believed that Shaikh Khalid had grown too dependent on Abu Dhabi and wanted him to follow a more independent course.

The federal government has recently proved its willingness to interfere in the internal affairs of the emirates when Shaikh Abdul Aziz al-Kassim moved to depose his younger brother, Shaikh Sultan, as ruler of Sharjah because of financial profligacy and Sharjah's $1 billion debt. The Supreme Council of the UAE rejected the move and refused to recognize Abdul Aziz's rule of Sharjah. The crisis ended when the council would not recognize Abdul-Aziz and Shaikh Sultan agreed to reorganize Sharjah's administrative structure.

The federal national council is a consultative body of forty members. Members are proportionately distributed among the emirates with Abu Dhabi and Dubai having eight, Sharjah and Ras al-Khaymah with six each, and the remaining emirates having four each. A ruler is allowed to choose the members from his emirate. The majority are representatives of the commercial classes, and many from Dubai, Sharjah, and Ras al-Khaymah come from prominent merchant families. Members from the other emirates tend to represent the dominant tribes of the emirate.

As with other Gulf states, the future of the UAE is largely dependent on the success of its economy, though there are additional factors. If it is to succeed politically, it must learn to live with the differences among the emirates. In its first decade and a half, it has managed to do so because of the power possessed by Abu Dhabi and Dubai, and it appears that this trend will continue if the economies of Dubai and Abu Dhabi remain dominant. In the short term there is little doubt that the economies of Abu Dhabi and Dubai will continue to outperform those of the other emirates, though the decline in world oil prices, the failure of import substitution programs, and the failure of diversification could work to undermine their dominance.

The UAE is also similar to other Gulf states in that its economy is entirely dependent on oil revenues. While some of the emirates are less dependent on oil (Sharjah, Ras al-Khaymah, and Fujairah rely more on agriculture), all suffer similar difficulties—high debt, decreasing government revenues, and poorly performing oilfields. Attempts at diversification have failed, generally, and projects that are up and running tend to be inefficient and a greater burden than benefit.

The Gulf Crisis

The Gulf crisis precipitated by Iraq's invasion of Kuwait on August 2, 1990, transformed the Gulf region into a vast military encampment. (See concluding sections of chapters 7 and 13 for other dimensions of the Gulf crisis.) Within one week of Iraq's invasion, on August 7, the United States initiated Operation Desert Shield and began deploying troops and armaments to the Arabian peninsula. By the end of September, there were 130,000 American troops in the Gulf and about 50,000 troops from other countries supporting the American initiative. At the same time, U.S. armaments deployed to the region included 840 tanks, 650 planes, 300 armed helicopters, 44 fighting ships and four aircraft carriers, in addition to a number of Stealth bombers, a nuclear submarine, and SCUD and SAM missiles (*Gulf News* [Dubai], September 22, 1990).

The American arms buildup, which continued unabated throughout October and November, was matched by Iraq's redeployment of troops in and around Kuwait. By the one-hundreth day of the crisis, there were over 800,000 troops, and a vast array of high-tech weaponry facing each other in the Gulf. With a commitment of another 200,000 U.S. troops, the buildup continued. By late November, 3,360 tanks, 401 armed helicopters, 1,244 planes, 124 fighting ships, five aircraft carriers and 490 SCUD and SAM missiles were deployed against Iraq in the Gulf (*Khaleej Times* [Dubai], November 24, 1990).

The development of the Gulf crisis dramatically changed the Middle East political scene, essentially polarizing the Arab world into two camps: one supporting American military intervention to restore the pre-invasion status quo in the Gulf, another opposing such intervention. All of the Arab states accepted UN Security Council Resolutions 660 (August 2) and 661 (August 6) condemning Iraq's invasion of Kuwait, demanding the unconditional withdrawal of Iraqi forces, and supporting actions of the Arab League and Gulf Cooperation Council to secure an Iraqi withdrawal. Polarization, in other words, was over American intervention, not over condemnation of Iraq. Opposition to the Iraqi invasion was unanimous. An extraordinary session of the Arab League Council on August 2, 1990, unanimously condemned Iraq's invasion of Kuwait and rejected the use of force to solve inter-Arab conflicts. It also rejected foreign intervention in Arab affairs, and it was this issue that caused a split at the Arab summit conference in Cairo on August 9–10 (see chapter 13).

Headed by Saudi Arabia, the six members of the Gulf Cooperation Council (GCC) constituted the core of the pro-intervention camp. Saudi Arabia had called for American intervention in the first place. While all six members of the GCC accepted American troop and arms deployments on their territory and were in fact committed to covering most of the cost of the military deployment, Saudi Arabia took the lion's share by far. Egypt and Syria were the major non-GCC members in this camp. Both strongly endorsed

American military intervention and contributed troops to the multinational arm of the American military buildup.

Unlike support for American military intervention, opposition to it among the Arab states has been unorganized and uncoordinated because the degree and nature of opposition in this group varies. Ideologically opposed to U.S. intervention, the PLO and Libya are perhaps the most consistent critics of it, considering it a far worse calamity than Iraq's occupation of Kuwait; strategically opposed to U.S. intervention, Jordan and Yemen consider it dangerous and in the best interests of the Arab world to seek an Arab solution to the crisis. The rest of the Arab countries, except Tunisia, have taken positions more or less supportive of one camp or the other but have not positioned themselves prominently in either camp. Tunisia has abstained from taking any position, essentially avoiding direct involvement.

By mid-November, war in the Gulf appeared imminent. Diplomatic efforts—championed by King Hussain of Jordan in the Arab world and by Soviet President Mikhail Gorbachev in the international arena—had failed to avert the steady drive toward war. In early November even President George Bush confirmed for the first time that the U.S. buildup was to ensure not only an adequate defensive posture but also "an adequate offensive military option" (quoted in *Khaleej Times* [Dubai], November 10, 1990). In this atmosphere of impending conflagration, King Hassan of Morocco called on November 12 for a "last chance" Arab summit on the Gulf crisis. At first, reaction to the proposal from both Baghdad and the Gulf states was essentially negative. Then China's Foreign Minister Qian Qichen, in Baghdad on a Gulf peace mission to four Arab states, warned Baghdad that China would not veto a Security Council resolution sanctioning the use of force to implement earlier resolutions. Saddam Hussain then indicated he was prepared to "offer sacrifices for the sake of peace" and would participate in a summit (quoted in *Khaleej Times* [Dubai], November 14, 1990).

The next few days witnessed a flurry of diplomatic activity in the Arab world. Egypt's President Husni Mubarak flew to Libya and Syria. Soviet President Mikhail Gorbachev sent two personal envoys to Arab capitals. But by November 16, plans for a "last chance" summit floundered as both Saddam Hussain and Saudi Arabia put forward conflicting pre-conditions for a summit. Egypt, Syria, and Saudi Arabia then rejected outright the call for a summit. And even while the Soviet Union and Javier Pérez de Cuéllar, secretary general of the UN, attempted to revive the summit, U.S. Secretary of State James Baker sought support from Security Council members for a resolution approving the use of force to expel Iraq from Kuwait, a resolution the U.S. wanted to introduce in the Security Council before the end of November, while the U.S. ambassador still held the rotating post of council president and chaired its meetings.

AUTHOR'S NOTE

The library research for this chapter was done by the author's assistant, Michael Sondermann.

REFERENCES

Hassan Hamdan al-Alkim, *The Foreign Policy of the United Arab Emirates*. London, 1989.

Calvin H. Allen, Jr. *The Modernization of the Sultanate*. Boulder, 1987.

Hasan A. al-Ibrahim. *Kuwayt: A Political Study*. Kuwait, 1975.

Jacqueline S. Ismael. *Kuwait: Social Change in Historical Perspective*. Syracuse, 1982.

Ali Mohammed Khalifa. *The United Arab Emirates: Unity in Fragmentation*. Boulder, 1979.

Fouad I. Khoury. *Tribe and State in Bahrain*. Chicago, 1981.

Ragaei El-Mallakh. *Qatar: Energy and Development*. London, 1985.

Amile Nakhleh. *Bahrain: Political Development in a Modernizing Society*. Lexington, Mass., 1976.

———. *The Gulf Cooperation Council: Problems and Prospects*. New York, 1986.

Ian Richard Netton, ed. *Arabia and the Gulf: From Traditional Societies to Modern States*. New York, 1986.

Malcolm C. Peck. *The United Arab Emirates: A Venture in Unity*. Boulder, 1986.

A. O. Taryam. *The Establishment of the United Arab Emirates, 1950–85*. London, 1987.

John Townsend. *Oman: The Making of a Modern State*. New York, 1977.

VI

COMPARATIVE
GOVERNMENTS

North Africa

18

The Socialist People's Libyan Arab Great Jamahiriyah (SPLAJ)

Tareq Ismael and Jacqueline Ismael

Libya is a North African country and, with an area of 1.76 million square kilometers, the fourth largest state on the African continent. It is seven times the size of the United Kingdom or Germany or France and two and one-half times the size of the state of Texas. It boasts 1,900 kilometers of coastline with the Mediterranean Sea to the north. To the east, it is bordered by Egypt and Sudan, to the south by Niger and Chad, and to the west by Algeria and Tunisia. The country has five geographic regions: the coastal plains, the northern mountains, the transitional zone, the hinterland, and the oases.

The hinterland is largely desert and inland mountains. Deserts occupy a large portion of Libya, an estimated 750,000 square kilometers. Less than 2 percent of Libya's total land area is arable; it is concentrated along a narrow coastal strip. Approximately 4 percent of the country is considered semi-arid and is used chiefly as grazing grounds. The climate is temperate, with cooler temperatures in the northern mountain ranges and warmer temperatures southward. The hinterland is characterized by sand dunes and barren, rolling hills or tableland. The Libyan deserts form part of the vast Sahara Desert, which dominates most of North Africa.

Oases, the most important features of the deserts, are found in depressions where underground water is close to the land surface. They have severely restricted vegetation, mostly groves of palm trees. The Libyan oases are conspicuously separated into a northern and a southern series.

According to a 1988 estimate, Libya has a total population of 4 million people. Libyans, who are of Berber and Arab descent, constitute 97 percent of the nation's populace. Correspondingly, all Libyans adhere to Islam and follow the Sunni school of thought. Approximately 90 percent of the population is settled in 10 percent of the area, the coastal plains region. The three major cities boast 57 percent of the population: 31.4 percent in Tripoli, 14.5 percent in Benghazi, and 11 percent in Zawia.

Libya has been the object of successive invasions. The earliest were the Phoenicians, Greeks, and Romans, and the most significant was the Arab conquest in the seventh century which made a lasting impact in Libya's social topography. It became an Arab Muslim country and was part of the Ottoman Empire until 1911, when the Italians invaded and stayed.

The Allied victory in World War II brought an end to the Italian occupation in 1943, but Libya was no less free. At the end of that year, Britain assumed suzerainty over Libya and controlled, in particular, the eastern and western parts. France took control of the south. British rule was characterized by discriminatory practices which set indigenous Arabs at a serious disadvantage in favor of the small Italian and Jewish communities.

In 1951, a monarchy was installed and King Idris I proclaimed himself ruler of all Libya. Under his administration, Libya was granted independence on December 24, 1952, the first nation to achieve independence under the auspices of the United Nations and an achievement in which the British were credited with a major role. Libya was besieged by corruption, oppression, and mismanagement under Idris, and the social, economic, and political conditions largely attributed to the monarchy brought about his overthrow on September 1, 1969. The military junta that replaced him was known as the Unitary Free Officers, led by First Lieutenant Muammar Qaddafi. The revolution abolished the monarchy, proclaimed the Libyan Arab Republic, and established the Revolutionary Command Council (modeled after the Egyptian RCC) as the governing body of the newly proclaimed republic.

The revolution ushered in a new chapter in Libyan political, economic, and social life, both domestically and internationally.

The new regime's proclaimed goal was to move on a path toward social justice and democracy under the slogans of the new Libya: freedom, socialism, Arab unity, and anti-imperialism.

One of the principal aims of the 1969 revolution was to put an end to all foreign military installations in Libya. The following year the British withdrew from their installations in Tobruk and the Americans from the then largest air base outside of the United States, Wheelus Air Force Base. Foreign military presence had long vexed the Libyan people, and King Idris I suffered the brunt of the enraged Arab population in the country. Now, with the cessation of foreign military presence, Libya was proclaimed to be a truly independent Arab-Muslim nation by its new revolutionary leaders.

Political Development

Political development is a central theme of Qaddafi's ideology as elaborated in his *Green Book, the Third Universal Theory*. It is important to examine both the theory and practice of politics in Libya to understand the direction of the country's development. Politics in theory is often utopian, always rational, and likely sensible. The practice of politics, however, is often brutal, almost always disappointing, and likely nonrational (if not irrational). Assessing the difference between the theory and practice of Libyan politics reveals the constraints and obstacles of reality and the limitations of politics.

In Theory

The new regime abolished most of the governmental structures of the monarchy and constructed its own. The RCC retained some elements of the 1951 constitution, which Idris oversaw, but replaced most elements with the December 1969 Constitutional Proclamation. The proclamation, intended to serve as an interim constitution until a permanent one could be drawn up, vested supreme authority in the RCC and changed the state's name to the Libyan

Arab Republic. The RCC was formally defined as a collegial body to debate issues and policies until reaching some kind of consensus. It was given the power to appoint a Council of Ministers to carry out its policies. The council could draft legislation but could not promulgate it, a function reserved for the RCC.

This structure remained until 1977 when governmental institutions were reformed. The reform was accompanied by Qaddafi's return to a high level of involvement in the state's administrative affairs. By 1972 Qaddafi had withdrawn from his role as prime minister and left his more mundane RCC commitments to Abd al-Salaam Jaloud in order to concentrate on revolutionary activities. By 1977, this activity resulted in a redefining of Libyan society as a *Jamahiriyah* (loosely, a state of the masses). Accompanying this redefinition was an overhaul of governmental institutions. The RCC was replaced by a General People's Congress, led by a five-member General Secretariat, and the Council of Ministers was replaced by a General People's Committee. The theory behind the restructuring was to extend the regime's revolutionary base by increasing direct popular participation. Previously, the regime had attempted to do this by creating its own version of the Arab Socialist Union (modeled after Nasser's ASU in Egypt) which was to be the medium through which popular opinion would reach the RCC. The ASU was not defined as a political party but, rather, as a mass organization which would lead the nation. In actual fact, the ASU's purpose was to spread the ideals of the revolution. Its goals proved to be unreachable, given the apolitical nature of Libyans and the inefficiency of the ASU. To correct these flaws, a cultural revolution was declared in April 1973, followed by the creation of people's committees to be the instruments of the revolution.

However, with the 1977 reform, it was felt that neither the ASU nor the people's committees were effective enough in revolutionizing the citizenry. Accompanying the reforms was the creation of revolutionary committees composed of carefully selected members (usually committed youths) who were to guide the committees, educate Libyans, and raise public awareness of the state's ideology.

The political ideology of the new Libya was advanced in Qaddafi's *Green Book*. He concentrates on three main issues: the solution to the problems of democracy by institutionalization of the authority of the people; the solution of economic problems by the introduction of socialism; and the social basis of the third universal theory, which was aimed at restructuring the social relations of society along specific lines.

The first concern of the book is to examine critically the conception of popular democracy and the idea of the modern parliament. Qaddafi argues that the representative nature of the modern parliament is "undemocratic as democracy means the authority of the people and not an authority acting in their behalf." In fact, he argues that representation by a highly selective and privileged elite is a falsification of democracy; indeed, he believes that "representation is an ironic denial of participation" and therefore defeats the objectives of democracy. He contends that the party system divides and alienates members of society into antagonistic and hostile classes with competing interests. It does not seek to unify the people, and, moreover, the most socioeconomically powerful elite who comprise the small minority of society prevails. Thus, the majority of the people are excluded. As a result, a party is an instrument to rule the people by a privileged few. It is precisely this use that makes it undemocratic because the party is only part of the people whereas the people are indivisible. As a result, according to the theory, rule by a particular group, class, tribe, or indeed party is tantamount to dictatorship, not democracy. Consequently, the theory suggests that the masses should "struggle to put an end to all forms of dictatorial rule."

The solution advanced by *The Green Book* is the establishment of the General People's Congress instead of a parliament, which would ensure that democracy remains the "supervision of the people by the people." Popular congresses, therefore, are viewed as the only viable means to achieve real democracy.

Parliamentary democracies and all that accompany them are considered undemocratic. For instance, plebiscites are seen as another deviant form of democracy, and media and press behavior often represent the interests of the ruling elites. Qaddafi argues that the media should be democratic, free, and accessible to the whole society equally since they are a means of expression of the society as a whole and not the privilege of the powerful and influential. Thus, the basic assumption of the idea of revolutionary Libya was to abolish the prevailing systems that made a mockery of democracy. True democracy was to be sought through and by means of popular congresses.

With respect to the second concern of *The Green Book*, the solution to the economic problems in society, socialism was advanced because of the "decadence" of capitalism. Capitalism exploits voraciously and leads to a concentration of wealth in the hands of the ruling elite.

According to the socialist doctrine advanced by Qaddafi, production has three basic factors: machines, workers, and raw materials. These factors are exploited in capitalism, and the worker is dehumanized, which is not only counterproductive but immoral. The factors of production need to be used justly to provide the basic needs of man—food, housing, clothing, and transportation. Thus, the social factors of production suggest that economic activity should be geared to satisfy the needs of people. Since capitalism does not work toward this end, socialism is prescribed as the solution to the economic problems of society. It is argued that because of the decadence of capitalism or any other system of exploitation, "natural law has led to natural socialism" as the only means of resolving economic problems.

As for the third concern, the social basis of the third universal theory, religion, family, and tribe comprise the foundations of society. Ideally, since tribes and religions can divide society, the nation should be a single family or tribe practicing a single religion because the relationship that "binds the family, is that which binds the tribe, the nation and the world." In other words, a common set of unifying factors could ensure a strongly close-knit and unified nation. It is for this reason that a common religion is perceived as essential to the survival of the nation state and indeed the nation of mankind.

Especially important to the concept of the social basis of the third universal theory is the notion of a unified and harmonious nation. Thus, the social relationship based on this theory will, taken to its logical conclusion, lead to the objectives of the third theory. This theory calls for a reorganization and restructuring of the social structures and relations of society. For instance, equality of the sexes and races should not be based on their ability to provide equally for themselves. Women are not considered to be inferior. They are equally part of the nation, and minorities must be accorded the same rights as others. In fact, their "rights must be guaranteed," and encroachment of these rights is considered an act of injustice necessitating prompt redress. Among other ideas, education must be "free and non-coercive." Thus in keeping with the objectives of the third theory, society should have only those values that contribute to a just, unified, and harmonious nation. Those that threaten and indeed subvert these objectives should be abolished by one means or another. The Libya that followed the revolution was envisioned as one that strives toward this end— first for the nation and then for the rest of mankind. A falsified democracy, a voracious exploitative economic system, and an un-natural social order must give way to socialism, the People's Congress, and an undefined religion, respectively. This approach is thought to be the solution to the problems of all societies.

Under Qaddafi, Libya unremittingly pursued a program aimed at establishing "true democracy" in lieu of the modern notion of representative democracy. Direct participation by the people was greatly encouraged. In addition to these objectives, Libya embarked on a revolutionary economic policy aimed at bringing about development, progress, and equality. Although this path was termed "socialism," it was not Marxist or Leninist. Since Libya is a Muslim state, it is presumed that social policies characteristic of "socialism" were in fact based on Islamic ideals. Qaddafi believes that the idea of a just, unified, and harmonious nation had its beginnings long before Marxism or Leninism was conceived and that the social order and structure characteristic of the third universal theory can be traced back to the advent of Islam by the Prophet Muhammad. Revolutionary Libya could not escape its Arab and Islamic heritage. Thus, its concept of a just society clearly reflects this reality. Above all, however, Islam would seem to have played the most significant role in shaping the idea and indeed directing the future of a progressive Libya.

The claim that revolutionary Libya is largely a reaction to the defunct Libyan monarchy is not categorically an exclusive justification of Libya as it has emerged under Qaddafi. Failure of the old regime was also seen as a direct result of its deviation from Arab tradition and the abandonment of Islam as a complete and perfect way of life. Libya not only had to respond to the failings of an inept and corrupted monarchy; it had to rethink its strategy on development as it affects every aspect of Libyan life—economic, social, and religious, both the secular and the clerical. Ruthless exploitation, repression, poverty, and foreign domination and interference were perceived as only the symptoms of problems in Libya. The solution required revolution leading to a path outlined in *The Green Book*.

In Practice

Twenty years after the revolution, Libya remains firmly under Qaddafi's direct personal control, and he has succeeded in constructing an impressive political and security infrastructure around him to guarantee his hold on power. He remains the single most important player in Libyan politics and, despite reports to the contrary over the years, does not appear to plan any change soon. His control over the tools of the state is too strong for there to be any change of regime in the foreseeable future.

We cannot say, though, that his rule has been unopposed. In recent years, the level of popular discontent in Libya appears to have risen dramatically, and it has been centered around two factors. Firstly, there is the inability of Qaddafi and his Green Revolution to increase dramatically the standard of living of the ordinary Libyan to the levels promised by the regime. Economically, Libya has stagnated. Recent declines in oil prices, foreign economic boycotts, and the general failure of diversification schemes have severely strained the regime's ability to increase the standard of living of the general population. The regime cannot meet the high expectations of the populace.

Some of Libya's economic difficulties have resulted from a tremendously high level of state involvement in all spheres of everyday life, the second reason that discontent exists. Economically, private enterprise was all but eliminated as economic functions were centralized in the hands of the state. More seriously, state institutions evolved that were designed to secure Qaddafi's power. They included traditional schemes of internal security such as the police and armed forces but extended into the ideological sphere with the creation of revolutionary committees and revolutionary courts whose main purpose was to uphold the ideological purity of the state. Combined with recent economic declines, the increase in internal state security apparati led to an increase in popular discontent against state centralization.

As a response to this discontent and the political and economic stagnation within Libya, Qaddafi moved to liberalize the state in 1988–89 to try to bring disaffected Libyans back into the fold. This liberalization began with Qaddafi's declaration to the General People's Congress that he was prepared to release all political prisoners and to move to increase the human rights of all Libyans. In a second address to the congress in March 1988, Qaddafi called for an end to capital punishment (except for certain crimes such as treason) and the abolition of the courts operated by the revolutionary committees. One month later, the congress approved a charter of human rights that guaranteed freedom of expression for Libyans. The court system was revised by replacing the revolutionary courts with a People's Court and a People's Prosecution Bureau.

Attacks were also stepped up against the revolutionary committees, which had been accused of lawlessness in their upholding of the ideological purity of the state. A secretariat for Jamahiri Mobilisation and Revolutionary Guidance was created to bring the committees under more control and to check their activities. In addition, Qaddafi also announced that "all the institutions which are traditionally considered as state organs are to be abolished"— including the police, the army, and the internal security apparatus.

Though the roles of some state institutions have been reformed and others have been abolished, Qaddafi is clearly not able to go as far as his statement would indicate. The reforms that have been undertaken were designed not so much to redefine the state's role in Libyan life as to give the people just enough to curb their discontent with the state. It is doubtful whether these reforms will go far enough to accomplish that, and, in the final analysis, the result of the reforms will most likely be a strengthening of Qaddafi's hold on power, not a weakening of it.

Economic and Social Development

In April 1973 a comprehensive five-point reform program was formulated. It espoused a dramatic restructuring of Libya's economy and society: the suspension of existing laws and the promulgation of new legislation; the implementation of Islamic thought; the distribution of arms among loyal citizens in order to protect the revolution, followed by the purging of political adversaries including communists and capitalists alike; an appeal to employees and officials to work to improve bureaucratic efficiency and end corruption; and the establishment of "popular committees" throughout the country to advance the agenda of the revolution.

Significant economic developments followed from this program in the principal sectors of the country through the next decade and a half. Oil exploration, industrialization and economic diversification, health and housing programs, education, agricultural expansion, transportation and communication facilities, and utilities such as electrical power generation characterized ambitious programs for the advancement, growth, and expansion of Libya. More recently, an immense project to create a "manmade river" between the Sahara and the coastal areas was undertaken. Estimated to cost some $25 billion, the project would create a network of pipelines designed to transport water from the vast underground reservoirs of the Sahara northward to Libya's population centers. The project, entering its second phase in 1990, is seen as a way to make Libya self-sufficient in food, and thus it meets an important requirement of the theory behind the revolution—independence through self-sufficiency.

Oil and Industry

Oil was first discovered in Libya by the Italians in the 1930s, but the burdens of World War II prevented further exploration and exploitation, and it was only in 1953 that oil companies were granted exploration rights. Recognizing oil as a vital economic resource, the Libyan Petroleum Commission issued legislation in 1955 for a profit-sharing venture in which the government and the companies would each keep 50 percent of the profits.

By 1964, an estimated twenty-five oil companies owned eighty-two land concessions and five marine concessions, and oil production was on the rise. The intensification of exploration in 1969 accounted for 2,396 wells that produced 2.5 million barrels a day (mb/d). Natural gas was discovered in large quantities, and its production capacity was measured at 12.5 million cubic feet per day. Exploration for other minerals in the country resulted in the discovery of potentially lucrative mines—iron ore, potash, gypsum, chalk, aluminum, limestone, sulphur, and coal.

In order to assume greater control of the principal sources of the national economy, the government nationalized 51 percent of the assets of all foreign oil companies in 1970, a move which resulted in annual revenues of $1.6 billion (U.S.). Two months later, Libyan oil was posted at $15.766 per barrel. The move by Tripoli to exercise control of its economy manifested itself further in 1974, when, on February 1, three U.S. oil companies—Texaco, California-Asiatic Oil Company, and Libyan-American Oil Company—were nationalized. In addition, Libya, in an attempt to preserve its oil wealth, reduced its production from 821 mb/d to 542 mb/d in 1975. Further legislation not only facilitated the nationalization process of foreign-owned oil companies in Libya but limited foreign participation rates to 19 percent and 15 percent for sea and land concessions, respectively.

The government's intensified involvement in the oil sector was further characterized by its ambitious refinery projects. Two principal objectives were outlined for these projects: to meet the needs of domestic consumption and to export surplus production. In addition, a fourfold program for the industrialization of oil was begun. It included the construction of ammonia, nitrogen fertilizer, methanol, and ethylene plants to meet both domestic and export needs. Following from the government's program of the industrialization of oil, the manufacture of synthetics and plastics was also seen as an important diversification strategy and a move away from "intermediary industries" to more advanced operations.

The priorities of the September Revolution necessitated, from the five-year plan, an allocation of L.D. (Libyan dollars) 387.5 million. This figure is, phenomenally, seventeen times the amount set aside for industry before the revolution. This budget was boosted by the transformation plan (1976–81) to L.D. 1.09 billion, and L.D. 143.5 million was targeted for 1976 alone. Indeed, the industrial sector was the largest investment of the SPLAJ; over five years L.D. 1.51 billion was expended. The new industrial strategy of Libya was governed by four basic goals: the creation of an independent national economy by removal of foreign control of industries; the diversification of its economy away from reliance on oil; the increase of its manufacturing capabilities by import substitution; and the creation of a capable indigenous public sector, which would increase Libya's indigenous industrial development projects.

In keeping with the objectives of the industrial strategy of revolutionary Libya, six basic sectors were endorsed for immediate attention. (1) Priority was given to the expansion of food commodities and the attainment of sufficiency in agricultural products, such as livestock and fish. (2) Building materials for housing and all projects were given greater consideration. (3) The establishment of metal industries was noted as an important component of growth and expansion, with particular emphasis on the production of heavy steel and iron products. (4) As an overall strategy for the oil and gas industries, the operation of chemical industries and their integration with the oil and gas industries formed an essential industrial strategy. (5) The expansion of the metallic, engineering, and electrical industries was seen as crucial in the production of intermediary components for domestic needs. (6) The SPLAJ endorsed the expansion of a geological engineering program aimed at exploration, discovery, and subsequent exploitation of other natural mineral resources, which could be seen as a move to shift emphasis from oil to other lucrative commercial minerals.

Thus the overall industrial strategy of the new Libya was comprehensive in nature and emphasized the construction of major projects. Examples of the basic industries are food, tobacco, textile, timber and wood, paper and printing, chemicals, oil, cement and building materials, metal, and handicrafts, all large-scale projects. Small to moderate industries pursued by the public sector are numerous.

The success of the larger projects has been uneven. By the late 1980s, industry, including the oil sector, accounted for 60 percent of the state's gross domestic product and almost 100 percent of exports. The entire economy, despite diversification attempts, remains heavily dependent on the oil sector for revenue and raw inputs. With the decline in price and demand for oil in the 1980s, Libya's single-commodity economy suffered greatly. Though the regime reduced spending on some sectors to counterbalance the effects of lower oil revenues, huge sums were spent on others (the "man-made river," for example). The result has been a significant balance-of-payments problem that has only recently eased with the stabilization of world oil prices.

Agriculture

Prior to the discovery of oil, 87 percent of the Libyan labor force was engaged in agriculture. Libya grows such staples as cereals, wheat, barley, olive, citrus fruits, figs, peaches, dates, pomegranates, prunes, apricots, apples, plums, bananas, groundnuts, tobacco, and almost all the varieties of vegetables. Pastoral activities remain the primary occupation of nomads and seminomads.

The oil boom brought great changes in Libyan agriculture, which now accounts for 2 percent of the gross national product of the country and absorbs 17 percent of the labor force. The regime claims that agriculture is the cornerstone of economic and social development, and the priority it has been given bears this out. In 1968 only L.D. 17 million were allotted for this sector, but after the revolution it received the second largest allocation from the five-year plan of the SPLAJ. L.D. 939.1 million were earmarked for Libya's agricultural sector. Moreover, the L.D. 1 billion Sirte fertilizer complex, postponed in 1985, is now proceeding. However, the agricultural sector remains a small, inefficient, and largely unproductive sector, accounting for 3 percent of the GDP. Libya can meet its food needs only by importing food.

Housing and Accommodation

The most significant early development in Libya's housing sector occurred in the three-year plan of 1973–75. The government allotted L.D. 722 million for the commencement of 80,000 housing units and L.D. 300 million as loans to citizens for the construction of 50,000 housing starts. In the more ambitious five-year plan of 1976–80, 150,000 housing units at an estimated cost of L.D. 150 billion were earmarked, L.D. 794 million was allocated for 1976 alone. Emphasizing the joint effort of the government and its people, 80,550 units were constructed by the public sector and the remaining 43.6 percent by the private sector.

Five basic projects characterized Libya's housing plan. (1) Public housing became a priority. As the most important aspect of the plan, 45 percent of all housing starts was undertaken by the public sector. The number of units projected was 36,500 in addition to 7,337 units scheduled for completion in the first year of the five-year plan. (2) Prefabricated housing became an important dimension of Libya's overall housing policies. The plan was to establish two large prefabricated housing factories in Tripoli and Benghazi, with an annual combined production estimated at 3,000 units, plus three other prefabricated housing facilities with annual output capacity of 4,000 housing units. (3) The Sheba housing project would produce 10,000 housing starts in the towns and villages of Sheba. (4) The rural shelter project, launched to meet the housing needs of the peasants and farmers in the reclaimed areas, would produce 8,250 housing starts. (5) The accommodation plan for workers and employees, a massive housing scheme, had 765,000 units scheduled for completion by the end of the third five-year plan of 1985–90. The proposal included several programs for the construction of public utilities, new integrated villages, and administrative blocks, and the principal beneficiaries are workers in the oil and electrical industry, though other industrial sectors also hope to benefit. However, because of the exodus of large numbers of foreign workers in the mid-1980s as a result of the decline of the oil sector and a resulting cutback in government spending, the housing industry has suffered an overall decline.

Transportation and Communication

Libya embarked on a program aimed at improving and expanding its transportation sectors. Since the revolution, the SPLAJ recorded substantial growth in transportation, with measured increases in aircraft and marked improvements in air service, and further expansion of the air fleet and airport facilities is envisaged.

Land transportation received special attention, especially public facilities. By the end of the three-year plan, 1,200 motor buses were owned and operated by the General Organization of Public Transport, and 1,000 additional buses were targeted. Transportation by rail was also designated a major priority. A railway network planned for both intercity and interstate runs was operating by the early eighties. The capital, Tripoli, is linked by rail and road to all the major cities and towns such as Sebha, Misurata, Tobruk, and Salum to meet internal transportation needs and is also linked via rail and road to Tunisia.

Water transportation is an important aspect of Libya's national economy, especially with respect to oil. Initially, L.D. 373.5 million was allotted for water transportation, L.D. 70.9 million for the first year. The major seaports of Tripoli, Benghazi, Qasr Ahmad in Misurata, Dernal Zuwara, and Brega were singled out for the plan, the principal aim of which was to improve facilities for ocean-going vessels. Import-export capacity of the ports was estimated at 30 million tons after completion. The total capacity of Libya's state-owned fleet is 35,400 tons. The aim of this aspect of the commercial fleet is to expand and strengthen trade opportunities between the SPLAJ and the rest of the world.

Electrical Energy

To meet the expanding needs of industrialization, growth and expansion of Libyan electrical capacity was needed. Accordingly, modern electrical power generating stations were constructed, and total electrical power capacity rose from 82 megawatts in 1968 to 272 megawatts in 1970. The dramatic growth and expansion of electrical power generation brought the nation's total electrical energy output to 1,000 megawatts by the end of the three-year plan. To achieve this standard, L.D. 217.8 million were expended but this achievement still did not meet the goals of the nation. The transformation plan earmarked L.D. 543.6 million for further expansion and upgrading of electrical energy in the Jamahiriyah. In the first year alone, L.D. 116.6 million were allocated.

Libya has always had a large energy surplus, given its small needs and large hydrocarbon resources that drive its electrical generating stations. Large sums have been spent on making electrical energy more cost-efficient and productive because of fears, especially during the days of low oil prices, that rising industrial power requirements might cut into oil exports. Agreements were signed with the Soviet Union to build an 800-megawatt nuclear power plant at Sirte. Libya, it seems, is able to mine enough uranium to fuel the plant, and it is focusing domestic energy around this plant.

Health and Welfare

The SPLAJ embarked on an extensive and ambitious health and welfare program. Based on the transformation plan, five major areas of need were identified. (1) In addition to upgrading and improving the nation's health service, seventeen more modern hospitals were to be built. (2) After achieving a standard of five hospital beds per 1,000 persons from the previous plan, this plan targeted an increase of hospital beds to 21,024 at a set rate of seven beds for 1,000 persons. (3) The plan expected to reduce the physician-patient ratios from 1 per 1,124 to no more than 1 per 1,000 patients. (4) According to population density, thirty health centers were scheduled for construction in association with one hundred dispensaries for remote areas. Emergency or otherwise urgent cases would be taken care of by means of air transportation. Thus, the government emphasized the need for improved, modern, adequate, and easily accessible medical care.

The government's principal objectives with respect to health and welfare were to provide adequate, accessible services in both preventative and corrective medicine. Moreover, it pledged to eradicate epidemic and disease. Thus, three priorities were targeted: the institution of free health care for all citizens; the realization of an adequate number of hospital beds; and a more ambitious program to manufacture medicine and pharmaceutical products locally in order to make them more easily accessible.

Social services in Libya are comprehensive and apply to both foreign workers and Libyans. Libyans receive free medical care and education, subsidized food, relatively inexpensive housing, and highly attractive workers' benefits, including injury and sickness compensation and pensions. Jobs are protected, and the unemployed and underemployed receive extensive benefits. These programs exist throughout the country and are, of course, a product of Libya's vast economic growth as a result of high oil revenues in the 1970s. Though revenues have declined, social services have largely withstood cutbacks.

Education and Literacy

The SPLAJ inherited major problems in education and literacy. After the revolution, the government considered these problems to be crucial to the growth, development, and expansion of the country. The government's motto became "Education for all." Education was seen as the principal vehicle for progress, stability, and social change. In affirming the importance of education, the government announced two basic programs designed to eradicate illiteracy: free and compulsory education through the preparatory levels, and the reduction of adult illiteracy. Expenditure for educational programs were estimated at L.D. 420 million. In the first year of the plan, L.D. 112 million were allocated to encourage rapid progress in this area.

From 1972 to 1973 enrollment in primary education increased by a dramatic 69.3 percent. By 1981, enrollment continued to increase modestly by 8.1 percent, and the actual pupil population numbered 577,654. Two universities were built, and registration revealed a student population of 3,460 before 1980. By 1981, this figure was increased by a modest 7.36 percent. Thus, although the greatest emphasis on education was placed at the preparatory, primary, and secondary levels, postsecondary education made significant achievements under the extensive educational plan of the SPLAJ.

Foreign Policy

Since the September revolution, Libya has attempted to pursue a foreign policy based on two fundamental principles: anti-imperialism and Arab unity. They became the imperatives of Libya's foreign policy. Practical considerations play a role in Libyan foreign policy as well, given the country's status as a small state with few capabilities outside of oil. The interrelationships between the realities that Libya faces and the principles that guide its foreign policy have meant that Libya is considered a kind of pariah state, given some of its seemingly erratic and impractical foreign policy moves and its hostile attitude toward the international system. In practical terms Libya has often operated outside of the norms of the international system since the revolution.

Anti-Imperialism

The imperative of anti-imperialism is partially a reaction to Libya's brutal experience as an Italian colony from 1911 to 1943, as a theater of World War II, and then as a country under military occupation by the British and French until 1951. Anti-imperialism as a principle of foreign policy represented not only a reaction by the revolutionary regime to the past but also a practical strategy to address the realities of big power geopolitics. Because of its location on the African coast of the Mediterranean astride Europe and the Middle East, foreign penetration and interference kept independent Libya weak, dependent, and underdeveloped, ruled by a corrupt and despotic regime that kept the population in poverty and ignorance, under the suzerainty of foreign powers. Military bases in Libya were the symbol of imperialism for Qaddafi's revolution and became the target of the nationalist, anti-imperialist struggle.

A treaty between the Libyan monarchy and the United Kingdom in 1953 preserved a British military presence on Libyan soil in return for financial aid, but relations faltered over Britain's conflict with Egypt over British occupation of the Suez Canal. Then a new agreement was concluded in April 1958. In 1954, Libya had also signed economic and military agreements with the United States, by which the United States secured a military base in Libya— Wheelus Air Force Base—which became the largest and most important American air base outside the United States. In return, the United States paid Libya $4 million a year during the period 1954–60, and $1 million annually thereafter. While the Libyan monarchy demanded greater compensation from the United States, the Libyan population became more hostile to the presence of the military base, especially in light of American support of the State of Israel and increasing hostility to Egypt's President Nasser, the unrivaled symbol of Arab nationalist aspirations. Soon after the revolution, Qaddafi terminated Libya's agreements with the British and Americans, which served to put an end to any foreign military presence in Libya.

Foreign oil companies were the other major symbol of Western imperialism. Occidental Petroleum, the most influential major oil company operating in Libya, had a virtual monopoly over exploration and production. Libyan oil reserves are large and the quality high. The oil is close to the surface and therefore cheap to extract. Companies like Occidental, Shell and ESSO extracted huge profits from Libyan oil, while Libya realized only modest royalty returns.

Qaddafi saw the foreign oil presence in Libya as a remnant of colonialism that stood in the way of the realization of his goal of achieving Libya's complete independence and self-sufficiency. So he undertook a struggle to curb the powers and influence of the foreign-owned oil companies.

For Libya, oil is more than simply a revenue generator; it is a vital foreign policy tool. A small state with limited capabilities has to use available resources to the fullest in order to achieve its foreign policy goals, especially Libya: It is an outsider in international affairs because of its erratic and hostile foreign policy toward the superpowers.

Libya has been a hawk on oil prices regardless of fluctuations in price and demand, and by the end of 1976 the price of its oil was the highest of all producing states. Its membership in OPEC and OAPEC has given it a forum to push for high oil prices, though demand, price, and revenues have fallen dramatically since the 1980s.

Arab Unity

Arab unity as a foreign policy imperative is closely related to anti-imperialism. Qaddafi has identified Arab unity as the best defense against imperialism. From that perspective, Arab unity is not only a romantic ideal but no doubt a seemingly sound strategy for a weak state in a coveted location. Alone, Libya is virtually defenseless against the machinations of big powers; allied with other Arab states, Libya would be in a stronger position to resist imperialist encroachments on its sovereignty. Theoretically, a united Arab world would be a formidable power.

To Qaddafi, the fate of the Palestinians reflects the naked objectives of imperialism, and the State of Israel represents the primary base of imperialism in the Arab world. Libya's traumatic history of Italian colonialism is deeply embedded in the consciousness of its people. It has increased their sense of affinity with the Palestinians and Libya's hostility toward the State of Israel (and its chief ally, the United States).

In practical terms, the principle of Arab unity has manifested itself in a number of ways, including repeated efforts at union with other Arab states, complete support of the PLO and Yassir Arafat, and efforts to enhance the military capability of Libya and other Arab states. In the mid-1970s, Qaddafi, with the approval of Egypt's President Nasser (before his death in September 1970), moved to mobilize Arab military capabilities to confront the State of Israel and liberate the occupied Arab territories. He called this the "pan-

Arabization" of the battle, and his efforts included a tour of Arab states to mobilize their military under one command.

The effort was fraught with disappointment for the young and idealistic Qaddafi, and he had to channel his efforts elsewhere because of the failure. First, he sought to increase Libyan capabilities by maximizing the state's only real foreign policy tool: oil. By maximizing oil profits Libya could accelerate its material support for the Palestinian liberation movement with arms purchases from the West. He could also increase Libya's status in the Arab world and in the struggle by greatly enhancing the state's military capabilities.

His second effort was directed toward achieving a more formal union of Arab states by pushing for a union of Libya, Egypt, and the Sudan. Though the Sudan bowed out, Libya and Egypt agreed to create a unified state with a unified political command in August 1972. The union was to be formalized in September 1973, but, again, reality forced its way into Qaddafi's idealism. This time personal suspicion between the leaders (Qaddafi and Sadat) doomed the union. Qaddafi's suspicion resulted from Sadat's handling of the 1973 Arab-Israeli war and the subsequent Egyptian-Israeli peace process.

Following the Camp David Accords between Egypt and Israel, Libya broke with Egypt completely: it eliminated diplomatic relations, called for Egypt's expulsion from the Arab League, and pushed for an extension of the Arab boycott against the State of Israel to include Egypt as well. As a result of Egypt's expulsion from the Arab League, Qaddafi began to increase Libyan connections with Syria and the PLO on a regional level and the Soviet Union on an international level. Given Qaddafi's intransigence on issues of Arab unity and anti-imperialism, Libya has been largely an outsider in Arab political discourse: it is seen as a destabilizing force by the region's more conservative regimes. This view has placed Libya on the fringes of the system, a position that does not suit Qaddafi well. Despite many failed attempts at union with other Maghrib states—for example, in 1974 alone Libya attempted separate unions with Tunisia, Algeria, Morocco, and Mauritania— Qaddafi's belligerent actions toward Chad have made many doubt his real intentions. Libya has staked claim to parts of Chad since 1974 for ideological reasons and economic gain from Chad's uranium. In 1989, Qaddafi began a concerted effort to reestablish Libya's relations with Egypt, to broaden its relationships with Arab regimes of all kinds, and to end the conflict with Chad. Again, he included moves toward unity—this time with the Union of al-Maghrib al-'Arabi between Libya, Tunisia, Algeria, Morocco, and Mauritania. Arab unity remains a primary foreign policy goal of the Qaddafi regime.

In both theoretical and practical terms Libya's strong anti-imperialist orientation has meant a policy of self-sufficiency and independence based on opposition to both superpowers and their ideologies. This policy has affected Libya's relations with both the United States and the USSR. The SPLAJ was initially hostile toward the Soviets, considered an imperial power that sought to dominate smaller states. The tone of the relationship changed only when Qaddafi sought closer ties with them to counter growing American influence in the region. The change toward the Soviets was not ideologically motivated but rather was purely pragmatic in nature as improvements focused solely on increased arms purchases from Moscow. This relationship grew in importance as Western nations became increasingly reluctant to supply Libya militarily.

Libya's relations with the United States have been much more volatile. The United States is seen as the chief imperialist threat to the Arab world and U.S. support of the State of Israel is the manifestation of it. The new revolutionary regime was not initially hostile to the United States, but American actions in the region and reaction to Libyan policy soon changed its orientation. American support for the State of Israel intensified Libya's hostility, especially after the United States refused to sell arms to Libya and halted the delivery of a number of aircraft. As the Carter administration became more hostile toward Libya in 1977 (largely because the United States sided with Egypt in its dispute with Qaddafi), the Libyans attempted to increase their connections with influential Americans to clarify their position and improve relations. It became impossible to do so after the U.S. embassy in Tripoli was sacked and burned in 1979 by rioters demonstrating against the siege at the Grand Mosque in Mecca.

Qaddafi initially welcomed Ronald Reagan's election in 1980 and anticipated an improvement in U.S.-Libyan relations, but the Reagan era was marked by unparalleled levels of rhetoric and military action against Libya. Reagan viewed Qaddafi as a Soviet pawn (a view carefully engineered by Sadat) whose pan-Arab policies were designed to increase Soviet influence in the region and destabilize regimes friendly to the United States. Libya responded with hostile anti-American rhetoric and accused the Americans of becoming more imperial in their actions. The situation worsened during Reagan's second term when Libya was accused of armed aggression against the United States after a 1986 terrorist attack at the Rome airport—an attack never reliably proven to have been planned, authorized, or carried out by Libya. The United States cut all economic ties to Libya, froze Libyan accounts in the United States, and attempted to force Americans working in Libya to leave. To Qaddafi, such actions were tantamount to a declaration of war, and he feared an impending U.S. invasion of Libya. He publicly announced that Libya would seek to increase ties with the USSR in response to the perceived threat of U.S. military action against Libya.

The war of words escalated into a military confrontation when U.S. naval forces began a series of maneuvers near the Libyan Gulf of Sidra, a move designed to provoke Qaddafi into military action. A confrontation did ensue, culminating in U.S. attacks on Libyan patrol boats and shore batteries in March 1986. A more serious one followed in April after the bombing of a Berlin nightclub for which the Libyans were again blamed. The United States responded by bombing Libyan targets, including Qaddafi's personal compound. Considerable international condemnation of the American action reduced active U.S. military provocation. With the initiation of the Bush administration, overt and open hostility between the United States and Libya subsided.

Revolutionary Activities Abroad

The view of many in the international community, one promoted by the United States in the Reagan era, is that Libya is a sponsor of international terrorist activities. This belief has gone a long way in isolating Libya in the international community. It is true that Libya under Qaddafi has been a strong supporter of revolutionary activity throughout the Arab world and elsewhere, largely because of Qaddafi's anti-imperialist and Arab nationalist views as expressed in *The Green Book* (though it also has pragmatic political purposes as well). Ideologically, the regime has been supportive of all efforts to bring about Arab unity, all efforts to oppose the State of Israel, all efforts to further the interests of Muslims, and all efforts to oppose imperialism. In practical terms this support has gone to a number of far-flung revolutionary movements in the region and abroad.

In the region, Qaddafi has been an active supporter of movements that oppose the "reactionary" leadership of Arab states in addition to the aforementioned support for the Palestinian liberation movement. Since the revolution Libya has supported movements in the Western Sahara (the Polisario) and has been accused of supporting covert movements in Egypt, the Sudan, and Tunisia. This support has taken the form of financing, training, arming, and supporting rhetorically the goals and leadership of these movements.

While the focus of the regime has been on revolutionary activities in the Middle East, Libya's activity has not been limited to the region. Libya under Qaddafi has long supported what it considers to be persecuted Muslims and those suffering under imperialism. It supported Pakistan militarily in its war with India in 1971, and, in the same year, it warned both the Guinean and Filipino governments that it would take action to protect persecuted Muslims in those states.

Libya has also been linked with a number of terrorist groups in the developed world, including the Bader-Meinhof gang in West Germany, the Red Brigade in Italy, the Red Army faction in Japan, the Irish Republican Army, and the Black Muslim movement in the United States. This support was said to include the financing, organization, and arming of these movements. Though Qaddafi has denied having any connection with them and has attempted to live down his reputation as a supporter of terrorist groups and activities, Libya was constantly linked to terrorist actions throughout the 1980s. It is still perceived by many international players as a sponsor of terrorist movements, and its relations with many states have been linked to its disavowal of these movements. The most obvious example of the connection between its activities and its isolation came in April 1984 when Britain cut off diplomatic relations with Libya following a series of attacks carried out in Britain against Libyan exiles opposed to Qaddafi. A British policewoman was killed after shots were fired into a crowd of demonstrators outside of the Libyan People's Bureau in London. The shots had come from the bureau.

This linkage plays a large part in Libya's international isolation, as does its intransigence on the Palestinian question and its rhetorical vilifications of those with whom the regime does not agree. By 1989, ending this isolation by seeking to establish closer ties with Western Europe and to improve relations with the United States became a primary foreign policy goal of Qaddafi. Regionally, there have been Libyan initiatives to end the conflict with Chad over the Auzo strip (which has caused years of hostility) and the dramatic improvement in relations with Egypt after the May 1989 Arab League Summit.

These recent efforts indicate a desire to break away from the perception of Libya as a state hostile to regional and global players. Whether they will result in a change of perception of the Libyan regime remains to be seen. Libya remains in essence a small and relatively powerless state. It has acquired its reputation because of its aggressive ideological position in foreign policy and lack of pragmatic realism. Every indication is that Qaddafi is attempting to portray Libya as a more reasonable player in international affairs.

Iraq's invasion of Kuwait on August 2, 1990, provided the opportunity for Libya to demonstrate its role as a responsible player in regional as well as in international affairs. While Libya asserted strong opposition to U.S. military intervention in the Gulf and supported the linkage of Israeli occupation of the West Bank and Gaza with Iraq's occupation of Kuwait, it did uphold Security Council resolutions against Iraq. (See concluding sections of chapters 7, 13 and 17 for a review of the Gulf crisis.)

REFERENCES

Jonathan Bearman. *Qaddafi's Libya*. London, 1986.

David Bundy and Andrew Lycett. *Qaddafi and the Libyan Revolution*. Boston, 1987.

John C. Cooley. *Libyan Sandstorm: The Complete Accounts of Qaddafi's Revolution*. New York, 1982.

John David. *Libyan Politics: Tribe and Revolution*. London, 1987.

Mahmoud G. El Warfally. *Imagery and Ideology in U.S. Policy Toward Libya, 1969–1982*. Pittsburgh, 1988.

Ruth First. *Libya: The Elusine Revolution*. Baltimore, 1974.

19

The Maghrib

Bahgat Korany

The term *Maghrib*, the Arabic word for where the sun sets in the west, designates the three countries of North Africa—Morocco, Algeria, and Tunisia. Sometimes Libya is attached to this group, sometimes not, a hesitation that shows the ambiguity of the concept. Reflecting how artificial state frontiers are as authentic lines of social demarcation, Habib Bourguiba (president of Tunisia until November 1987) suggested that staple food demarcates Maghrib from Mashriq. If people eat mainly rice, they are of the Mashriq; if they eat couscous—the staple soumoul starch—they belong to the Maghrib. This distinction provides no greater clarity than language or culture, for there are areas, like Darna, Eastern Libya, where people eat both.

The grouping of Morocco, Algeria, and Tunisia here is based on two criteria, the prevalence of a Berber subculture within these societies and the continuing presence of French culture due to French colonization.

The word *Berber* comes originally from the Greek *barbarizein*, to speak like a foreigner, with roughly the same meaning in the Arabic language. Berbers identify themselves as belonging to tribal confederations that speak different dialects, the prevalence of which increases from east to west. Almost no longer existent in Libya and Tunisia, Berber dialects are spoken by 20 percent of Algerians and 30 percent of Moroccans. On the second criterion, French colonization has been not only long but also so intense in its objectives and effects that Algeria was officially considered by Paris as forming a part of France, a Departement d'outre-mer (DOM).

Here we will examine both the general aspects common to the three countries and some peculiarities of each political system. In section 1, we emphasize common background variables related to geography, social organization, Islam's impact, and the role of external powers—all determinants of the evolution of politics and society of the three countries. In section 2, we concentrate on the political aspects of each political system. The emphasis is on the role of institutions and the relationship between the two pillars of governing, executive and legislative. The objective is to reveal the problematic relationship between state and civil society. In section 3, we come back to the general level to probe further two aspects of this problematic relationship: some examples of political elite concentration, and the dynamics of change in the political system as evidenced by Tunisia and especially Algeria's political restructuring from a one-party to a multiparty system for the 1990s.

Some Common Factors Influencing State-Society Relations

To understand the functioning of the three North African political systems analyzed here, we must consider four elements: geographical location, basic social organization, Islam, and the interaction between precolonial history and the subsequent European—especially French—penetration.

Geographically, the three countries vary in size, but their common peculiarity and importance stem from their locations between the traditional center of Arab events—the Mashriq—and Europe. Between Morocco's Tangier and Spain's Algeciras, there is only an hour and a half ferry ride. In fact, Morocco's capital, Rabat, is nearer Spain than any Arab capital. This proximity to Europe has affected some major historical patterns of this subregion. For instance, an Islamic empire—Andalusia—was established in the Middle Ages in the south of Spain. After its decline and the Christianization of this part of Spain, many Muslims returned to the Maghrib to become members of its ethnic groups and culture.

As mentioned, the original inhabitants of the Maghrib were Berbers. The land that they inhabited has not changed much over the ages. It has three fairly distinct regions. The coastal strip of more than 3,000 kilometers across the southern shores of the Mediterranean contrasts with its southern Saharan part which links the Maghrib with sub-Saharan Africa. Between these two lies a transitional zone that varies in size from one place to the other. "The vegetation of the Maghrib diminishes progressively from north to south as the rainfall diminishes. The Mediterranean zone represents about one-fifth of the total area of Morocco, Algeria, and Tunisia. This includes the Rif mountainous region of northern Morocco, the Atlantic-facing slopes of the Middle Atlas, the tall Atlas in Algeria, and the High Tall Dorsale (Fr. 'backbone') in Tunisia."[1]

These geographical characteristics had important social consequences. For instance, because of the uncertainty of rainfall, social and economic patterns were dominated not by settled agricultural communities but by the pastoralists—*les nomades*—who constituted almost a half of the population of Tunisia, the country that had the most established tradition of urbanization among the three. Consequently, "tribal structure was the most effective way of ensuring the cohesion of a pastoral group whose movement through space made it impossible to define itself with a reference to a precise territory permanently occupied."[2] The result is that tribalism continued to affect political culture and organization until modern times, accentuating the segmentation of society.

This segmentation is mitigated by the role of Islam. Islam came from the East, but in the process of spreading it became multiethnic and Arabized. Though this Arabization would also apply to the original inhabitants of the Maghrib, the Berbers, those in some mountainous areas and isolated spots continue to keep their original language and culture and thus keep alive the characteristics of a segmented society. In Algeria, for instance, estimates of Berber-speaking population range between 17 percent and 30 percent. It is important to reiterate that contrary to Lebanon, for instance, where parts of the population were Arabized but still kept their original Christian faith, the Berbers were Islamized but tended to keep their original (oral) language.

The fourth background element came also from outside, this time from the north. The French got the upper hand in their competition with the Spaniards and Italians and became the dominant colonial power in this region. They invaded and occupied Algeria in 1830 and extended their colonization to Morocco and Tunisia; by the end of the nineteenth century, settler-colonialism was firmly in place. Though initially centered around urban areas, the French army conducted several "pacification campaigns" in the interior and through land appropriation tried to restructure parts of the indigenous society. In addition to some obvious economic effects (e.g., the imposition of vineyards for wine production on an Islamic country), the basic effect of settler-colonialism was on language and culture. This externally generated change became most explicit in Algeria, which was simply incorporated into France. This Francization would deeply color the debate on Algeria's national identity and even, after independence, make of the question of Arabization a hot and often divisive political issue.

The Specificities of the Three Political Systems

Until 1988 the important distinction in North Africa was not between the two republican regimes of Algeria and Tunisia and the monarchy of Morocco. The distinction could be related rather to the specific bases of political legitimacy, that is to say "the extent to which leadership and regimes are perceived by elites and masses as congruent and compatible with the society's fundamental myths —those value-impregnated beliefs that hold society together."[3] Consequently, the demarcation line (until the political and constitutional changes in Algeria in 1989) was between Algeria's revolutionary-based legitimacy and the continuity-based legitimacy of Tunisia and Morocco. For instance, while Morocco's 1979 constitution has as its basic principle that the kingdom is "an Islamic State" and "a constitutional, democratic and social monarchy," Algeria's is based on the war of independence (1954–62). In its preamble it is recalled that "Algeria owes its independence to a war of liberation which will go down in history as one of the epic struggles in the resurrection of the peoples of the Third World. . . .[I]nstitutions which have been established since June

1965 are intended to transform the progressive ideas of the revolution into real achievements, affecting daily life, and to develop the content of the revolution by thought and action towards a definitive commitment to socialism." The three countries are, however, united by one basic characteristic of their political systems: the primacy of the executive branch of government.

Algeria

Until 1976 the Revolutionary Council in Algeria embodied the country's political legitimacy. At first with twenty-six members, it was later reduced to seventeen after the death or exclusion of some members. At the time of President Houari Boumedienne's death in December 1978, it had twelve members.

Colonel Boumedienne came to power in 1965 through a military takeover, or "Correction Revolution," that ousted Ahmad Ben-Bella, Algeria's first president, installed in 1962 when Algeria achieved independence. Whereas Ben-Bella counted on the FLN (Front de Libération Nationale, Algeria's only political party) and especially its political bureau, Boumedienne installed a Revolutionary Council. For its first three years, it resembled in its functioning the old political bureau. But after the 1968 purges of the old *maquisard*, homogeneity among its members increased and overlapping with the government was reinforced.[4] Indeed, it used to hold joint sessions with the government during times of important decisions.

As in Ben-Bella's presidency, concentration of power was characteristic of the post-1965 Algerian political system. Boumedienne was the head of the Revolutionary Council, head of government, minister of defense and—at least semi-officially—head of the party. During this period, the only institution that could resemble a legislative body was the "conference of Presidents of Popular Assemblies" (PPA), a result of the 1967 elections. It used to meet annually to discuss the government's balance sheet and provide a link between the top echelons of the executive and the masses, between the political center and the periphery. But the government would not allow this institution to function as a parliament. Instead, these annual meetings were used to inform the government of practical problems at the base and of how the government was perceived by the local elites and to inform the latter of the government's policies and their raison d'être. The same pattern of communication was used for the conference of the "nation's cadres," also meeting annually.

Even the 1976 constitution (with its various amendments) continued to affirm the primacy of the executive, especially the powers of the president. In addition to being secretary-general of the FLN, he is in charge of domestic and foreign policy. Though his decisions have to be ratified by a two-thirds majority of the assembly, it is not a problem since the assembly emanates from the party, itself dominated by the secretary-general, i.e., the president.

Even at the judiciary level, the powers of the president operate despite the constitution's insistence on the independence of the judges. For judges have to help in the "defense and protection of the socialist revolution," and, implicitly at least, the president has to make sure that it is done. Moreover, the president chairs the Magistrature's Council, which decides judges' appointments, transfers, and the path of their careers.

It is, of course, at the level of the executive itself that the president's powers are formidable and explicitly so. He presides over the cabinet, ratifies treaties, has the power of rule-making and even rule-application, is in charge of appointments to the highest military and civilian leadership positions, has the power of "pardon" and of canceling any legal consequences. According to a 1979 constitutional amendment, he can appoint one or more vice-presidents and a prime minister. But these people are more assistants to the president than independent political personalities (for the man in the street, the prime minister was called the "last" minister). However, on paper at least, the president has to contend with two main institutions: the People's Assembly and the FLN.

It was only in 1977—twelve years after Boumedienne's takeover —that general elections took place to fill the 261 seats of the National People's Assembly (NPA). According to the constitution, a member of the assembly is elected for a five-year mandate that is renewable. But contrary to the president he does not have the right to accumulate any other posts—even a ministerial one—so that he can devote himself to his post and achieve a high level of professionalism.

The assembly has two functions, legislation and control. At the legislative level, it is usually limited to enunciating "general rules" and "basic principles," and does not really affect the president's overpowering authority. He keeps the power to legislate by decree, especially during the long intersession periods. He has the power to propose bills on his own, whereas the assembly members have to regroup to propose one, and he still can veto a law even after its acceptance by the assembly.

The NPA's powers of control over the president are limited since he cannot be voted out. The members can decline to accept one of his proposed bills, but this is an unrealistic move because the NPA is controlled by the party and the president is its secretary-general. If the assembly vetoes one of the president's bills, he can dissolve it or punish politically any of the recalcitrant members.

The NPA's control function is thus mainly toward the cabinet: asking questions of different ministers, reviewing the budget, and offering constructive criticism. But it may also offer an inquiry commission to censure or denounce any governmental behavior touching the public interest. Moreover, the NPA has the power of control over "socialist enterprises of any nature."

At the basis of the NPA is the FLN, the only political party permitted by the constitution until institutional changes were made following the 1989 riots. The FLN's basic logic of organization is "democratic centralism." It is composed at the national level of the General Congress, the Central Committee, the Political Bureau, and the secretary-general. The congress is usually convened every five years, or when two-thirds of the members or the secretary-general asks for an extraordinary meeting. In case of emergency due to a vacancy in the presidency, the congress is convened ex officio. Among the many tasks of the congress, the most important are the discussion of the institutional aspects of the state, the election of the members of the Central Committee, and approval of the choice of the FLN's secretary-general from among the Central Committee members.

In the period separating the meeting of the different sessions of congress, the Central Committee (with its 120–160 regular members and 30–40 acting members) is the highest political body. It orients the country's general policy and makes sure that congressional decisions and recommendations are applied. It discusses the national plan and guarantees its application and discusses the reports of the Political Bureau.

A 1980 modification reduced the membership of the Political Bureau from 17 to 22 to 7 to 11 to strengthen its cohesion. It meets once a month instead of twice, as before, and is considered an executive organ of the Central Committee, to which it is accountable.

The Political Bureau is headed by the FLN secretary-general who chooses its members from among Central Committee members. Individually, bureau members are accountable to the secretary-general, whose authority is extensive. He convenes the congress, the Central Committee, and the Political Bureau and presides over the last two. He also proposes to the Central Committee the creation of permanent structures covering its different functions and is in charge of putting them in place. He is the one who in 1980 appointed Cherif Messadia as the permanent Central Committee secretary and dismissed him after the 1988 riots. It was also he who reduced the number of permanent commissions from twelve to five and defined their responsibilities.

Even though the FLN possessed institutionalized structures at lower levels in the country (from the cell to the *Kasma*, or municipality, to the *Muhafatha*, or governorate), the centralization of its functions was still the rule.

One of the major flaws of high concentration of different facets of power in the hands of one person (who is, in this case, both the president and the secretary-general of the only party permitted) is that if this person is not of high caliber, the whole system could suffer the consequences of his personal weaknesses. Moreover, with such concentration, power is bound to slip into the hands of the president's entourage and to increase the influence of different clans and their infighting. At this level, the February 1989 constitution effected some changes and could justifiably be labeled the "beginning of the second Algerian Republic."

Morocco

At the other end of the revolutionary/continuity scale is Morocco's political system, based on the king, commander of the faithful and descendent of the Prophet Muhammed. But Morocco—unlike the Arab kingdom of Saudi Arabia—is a constitutional monarchy that functions according to the tenets of the 1972 constitution, itself emanating from the Royal Charter of Public Liberties, the constitutions of 1962 and 1970, and the 1961 Fundamental Law.

All these documents define Morocco as a sovereign Maghrib state, an integral part of the grand Maghrib, with the monarchy —constitutional and democratic—as the source of all powers. The person of the king is almost sacred; he is described as guardian of the constitution, symbol of national unity, and protector of the rights and liberties of the citizens.

The king appoints and dismisses the prime minister and his cabinet, presides over the government, dissolves the Chamber of Representatives by a *dahir*, or decree, and can go directly to the people— against the wishes of the members of parliament if need be—by organizing referenda on questions he feels are important. He alone has the power to declare a state of emergency in a situation considered serious for the country or endangering the functioning of its institutions. He is also, of course, in charge of appointments to high military and political positions.

Succession as monarch is hereditary; usually the direct male descendent follows his deceased father, as Hassan II did after the death of Muhammad V in 1961. However, the king has the right during his life to designate a successor other than his eldest son.

Since the king is himself in charge of the government, his prime minister merely signs alongside the monarch and only for some laws and decrees. The result is that the different ministers act in fact as advisers to the king and may be changed quite frequently. Indeed, the average period of tenure among Moroccan ministers is around two years.

The 306-member Chamber of Representatives, or *Majlis al-Nawab*, is elected for four years. But only two-thirds of the members are elected by direct universal vote, the other third by an electoral college composed of advisers in the local government and of employers' and workers' associations.

The Majlis convenes for two sessions a year, each just exceeding two months, one beginning in October and the other in April. Laws can be proposed for discussion and approval by the king, the prime minister, or any deputy. If a government loses a confidence vote in the Majlis, it has to resign. In addition, the chamber participates in the formulation of global policy including the review of the budget, whereas policies of less importance are decided by royal or governmental decree.

But both the government—and also the king—have to contend with a major characteristic of the Moroccan political system: the existence of political parties. They are almost a dozen, reflecting a wide gamut of philosophies and practices ranging from Islamic fundamentalism to communism. For instance, each party participated in the election of September 14, 1984, with an average of six or seven candidates competing for the 204 seats of the Majlis to be decided by direct popular vote. Though in this case, as previously, the election results were contested, 67 percent of registered voters are said to have exercised their right to choose their representatives.

Many of these parties are either offshoots of or an amalgamation of previously existing parties. The most firmly established is the *Istiqlal* (Independence party). Despite its recent conflicts with the royal palace, it has been usually monarchical and reformist, and other political parties have often defined themselves in relation to the Istiqlal. The Constitutional Union (established in 1983), the Popular Movement (predominantly Berber), and the National Assembly of Independents are all promonarchy parties.

Among the strong opposition parties is the National Union of Popular Forces, established in 1959 by dissidents from the Istiqlal.

It is a coalition of leftist nationalists and heads of trade unions, usually concentrated in the big cities. But like the Istiqlal before it, it fragmented, and its dissidents formed in 1972 the Socialist Union of Popular Forces with a radical program asking for the nationalization of all means of production. The Party of Progress and Socialism is Morocco's Communist party.

The presence of these parties and their political maneuverability notwithstanding, the political process is dominated by the king and the palace, with their physical resources and the powers conferred on the king by the constitution. He commands wide support, especially in the countryside. For many in the "deep country," the commander of the faithful is still accepted as the focus of national identity and institutional continuity.

The king's political style has been consistent. To maintain his monopoly of political power, he has played different political forces against each other and made marginal any political party that does not accept explicitly the monarchical regime and the absolute preeminence of the king's political authority.

The disadvantage of this highly hierarchical and centralized system of political power is that the majority—whether among the urban proletariat or even the army—feel excluded from power, and their alienation pushes them to take to the streets (as in the 1984 bread riots) or to resort to "irregular political transfer" and attempt a military takeover (as nearly happened in both 1971 and 1972). Ironically, however, the political parties have adhered to the king, mainly in preference to the most probable alternative, an army takeover. A political context favorable to the king was provided by the 1975 Green March to integrate the Western Sahara with Morocco. The monarchy found its political legitimacy and influence quickly and highly reinforced. Consequently, the king decided to hold elections in 1977 (the first since 1963) and to launch a constitutional democracy in Morocco.

But in such a clearly hierarchical structure, democratization has its limits. Thus in September 1981, in the Organization of African Unity (OAU) Nairobi meeting, the king had to accept under international pressure the principle of a referendum in the Western Sahara. The Socialist Union of Popular Forces reacted and published a communiqué denouncing the king's readiness to abandon the "Sahara province." The party's secretary-general was immediately arrested and condemned to one year in prison. Though he profited from a royal pardon in February 1982, the message was clear: the limits allowed to political opposition are both narrow and immediate in application.

Similarly, when international pressure continued to mount and isolated Morocco, because of this Western Sahara conflict, the margin of maneuver for political parties widened again. Thus in 1983 the king invited six political parties to form a national government but still one that would accord with the wishes and rules specified by the palace. On October 30, 1986, when the daily *al-Bayan*—of the Party of Progress and Socialism—criticized the declaration of Redha Guedira, the king's adviser, that no political party should dissociate itself from the royal consensus, a decree stopped the appearance of the newspaper until further notice. In addition, both extremes of the political spectrum—Communists and militant Islamic fundamentalists—have seen in practice the limits of the democratization process. They have often been arrested, tried, and condemned.

Tunisia

In its main characteristics, Tunisia's political structure and organization are not very different from those of Algeria and Morocco concerning the primacy of the executive branch of government and the monopoly of effective political power by the president's royal palace. A slight difference is that former President Habib Bourguiba valued a pattern of political culture based on European liberal ideas to compete with Tunisia's Arab-Islamic heritage.

In the aftermath of Tunisia's independence (1956), the 1959 constitution confirmed the character of the regime as president-centered based on the Neo-Destour party (the sole inheritor to the old Destour since 1934). According to this constitution, the president of the republic is elected by direct universal vote for a five-year mandate, renewable for three consecutive terms. He enjoys exceptional powers and virtually monopolizes political authority. He is thus the protector of the constitution. He appoints the prime minister and the members of the cabinet who are all accountable to him. He defines general policy and is in charge of its execution. He even has a veto power over the laws voted by parliament since he can ask for a second reading (which necessitates approval by a two-thirds majority). He has the right to issue decrees, especially when parliament is not in session (which is in fact the major part of the year). He appoints high-level military and civilian personnel, declares war and makes peace, and ratifies treaties. Indeed, the National Assembly in 1974 received a draft law declaring Bourguiba president for life, which it duly approved in March 1975. In this situation, the existence of the cabinet does not radically change the president's monopoly of power. As in both Algeria and Morocco, the ministers become presidential advisers or assistants.

As for the National Assembly, or *Majlis El-Umma*, its 136 members are elected by universal vote for five years, thus making their mandate coincide with the president's. It holds two sessions per year, each not exceeding three months maximum, but it can be convened in an extraordinary session by the president or by the majority of its members. The president can dissolve the assembly in response to a vote withdrawing confidence from the government and then organizes new elections. But if the new assembly maintains the nonconfidence vote, the government has to resign. Otherwise, the powers of the assembly are indeed quite nominal.

The Neo-Destour party is the only one permitted in the country, and it overlaps with the government. Indeed, Bourguiba himself had been—until his removal in November 1987—president of the republic and head of Neo-Destour for more than thirty years, and political personnel go from government to party and vice versa. The party is essentially a mobilizational agency and functions more often than not as a governmental bureaucracy. Until the 1987 constitutional coup, the party's congresses convened at irregular intervals (1959, 1964, 1971, 1974), depending on the political context and Bourguiba's wish.

Other components of Tunisia's political structure exist but do not modify the main features of presidential monopoly. They obey the same hierarchical rules of functioning and owe allegiance to the president. For instance, the Council of the Republic (established in 1966 and comprising the president, cabinet members, and the Neo-Destour Political Bureau, and sometimes enlarged to include regional governors and heads of national enterprises) does not in the least compete with the president's prerogatives. Even at the level of the judiciary, the president appoints judges, but on the suggestion of the Judiciary Council.

The influence of Bourguiba—the *"combattant suprême"*—has been even more prevalent than his formal powers in the Constitution permit, and that is through his imprint on modern Tunisia's political culture. In fact, ever since his studies in France and his conciliatory approach toward decolonization, Bourguiba has adopted and propagated his theory of *étapisme*, gradualism or step-by-step struggle, and insisted on the importance of European liberal ideas in Tunisia's political fabric. According to this view, Tunisia's political philosophy is said to have been influenced since ancient times by both Rome and Carthage, which made of it a crossroads between Europe and the Arab world, based on Mediterranean heritage. Consequently, Bourguiba and members of his political elite collided with Islamic tendencies by emphasizing secular trends in modern Tunisia, to the extent that Bourguiba decreed the abolition of polygamy and asked his countrymen not to fast during the Moslem month of Ramadan.

The Tense Dialectics between Continuity and Change, State and Civil Society

Two important meeting points between the state as a set of institutions and a political apparatus and civil society with its various associations and pluralistic tendencies are (1) the characteristics of the governing elites (e.g., how representative they are) and (2) the evolution of the problem of political legitimacy.

The Case of Cabinet Elite

We have seen that despite the apparent differences between forms of political systems (republican versus monarchical), the dynamics of all three North African political systems are dominated by the executive branch. It is important, then, to have a closer look at some characteristics of this executive elite, as typified by cabinet members. After all, politics can "best be understood through a study of those who exercise power—those who make the decisions and rules that run society."[5]

In the equivalent of a master's thesis in the Faculty of Law at the University of Tunis, Munir El-Sharafy analyzed the 137 ministers participating in Tunisia's six cabinets since the country's independence and until the constitutional coup of November 1987 by General Zin al-Abidine Ben-Ali, then prime minister.

What strikes the analyst is the high level of skewedness in distribution, especially the concentration by region. Out of the country's twenty-one regions, four urban regions (Tunis, Monastere, Soussa, and Sfax) are represented by 86 ministers, i.e., 62.7 percent of the total number of ministers of 137. The three regions of Tetouan, Zaghwan, and Sidi Bou-Zin (which represent 7.26 percent of the population) did not have any ministerial representation whatsoever. They stand in contrast to Monastere, the town of Bourguiba's origin, which represents 4 percent of the population but had an average of 15.3 percent of ministers over the whole period—its ratio of cabinet representation compared to its population is almost 600 percent. Moreover, in Morocco there has been a similar dominance of Fassi (of Fes) elites, and in present-day Algeria there is over-representation of elites originating in Annaba, Bendjedid's town.

Another important characteristic of those elites operating the political system is that the great majority of them come from governmental service. Thus among the 137 Tunisian ministers, 116 (or 84.67 percent) are technobureaucrats (from the fields of teaching, justice, diplomacy, and the military). Consequently, there is the prevalence of a bureaucratic (as distinct from a political) belief system,[6] a strict adherence to rules, rather than innovation, for instance, and subordination to the boss rather than a tendency toward debating him. Thus what Zartman's data revealed in the early 1980s seems to be still valid: "The most important prediction of elite membership after higher education and male sex is shared experience with incumbent members of the core elite, although its form may be very diverse. Shared experiences may take the form of common education (Morocco, Algeria, Tunisia . . .); common regional origin (Morocco . . . but especially Algeria); common nationalist experience (Algeria); common occupational experience (Morocco, Algeria, Tunisia . . .); or family connections by blood or friendship."[7] It is too early to decide whether this pattern of elite concentration will change in the near future. For, despite appearances, change is prevalent in these political systems: both from the top (among state incumbents, e.g., Ben-Ali's assuming power) and from the bottom (the revolt of civil society, e.g., Algeria's mass riots of 1985, 1988, and 1989).

The Changing Basis of Political Legitimacy

While the legitimacy basis in Morocco is the king and his descendance from the Prophet Muhammad, the basis of legitimacy of the governing elites in the other two republican regimes lies in the winning of independence. But this source has its limits since it is much more time-bound. The clearest case is Tunisia's 1987 "constitutional" coup that removed Bourguiba after more than fifty years in politics, including more than thirty years as Tunisia's president.

Not only was the man at the top getting old and senile, but the regime itself was increasingly stagnant and in great need of change. When Muhammad Mzali was prime minister (April 1980–July 1986), he apparently thought of invoking Article 57 of the Tunisian constitution (which allows the prime minister to replace the president in case of death, illness, or absolute disability) to carry out the needed changes. But while legal justification was there, Mzali lacked the military power. Zin al-Abidine Ben-Ali came to possess both.

As a man of the Ministry of Defence (he became its undersecretary in October 1984) and of the police (appointed minister of the interior in April 1986), he could marshal the necessary means of physical power. Thus when the president appointed him prime minister on October 2, 1987, Bourguiba unknowingly put together in the hands of one man legal justification and physical power to change the regime both at and from the top. Moreover, since the immediate reason for change was the president's militancy against the Islamic groups and his pressuring of the prime minister to carry out strong action, Ben-Ali's coup could rally around its influential Islamic support—at least for some time.

Eight months after his constitutional coup, Ben-Ali was chosen president of the Neo-Destour Party, and in April 1989 he was elected president of the republic. Needless to say it was too early to affirm whether this change would bring about the necessary rejuvenation of the system after thirty years of independence, especially given the new problems increasingly affecting the basis of political legitimacy.

A similar situation prevails in Algeria. But the change this time came from the bottom after the intensification of popular protest and riots, first in 1985. The riots that followed three years later ("Black October," 1988) left 176 dead by official count. These widespread disturbances took many observers by surprise, for in the ocean of political instability characterizing the Third World, Algeria was perceived as an island of stability, an exception. In a world of legitimacy deficit, the Algerian government had it in abundance.

Algeria's Legitimacy Surplus. In the 1960s and 1970s, Algeria's strong legitimacy rested on a triple-sided base.

Historical legitimacy is represented by the FLN and NLA (National Liberation Army), which were credited with wresting independence from France after 132 years of colonization. It was a savage war (1954–62) that finally forced even the stubborn and proud De Gaulle to give up the popular conception of Algeria as an overseas French department. For such a decision, he faced a rebellion within his own army, but the price the Algerians paid was much higher: more than 1 million "martyrs." Thus at a time when other African parts of the French Empire were granted independence, Algeria's was fought for and won. It looked more real, and the government naturally profited from this hard-won legitimacy.

International leadership legitimacy: Since Algeria was capable of having its way and regaining its lost (Arab-Muslim) identity, it became a model, an exemplar—*montreur de conduite*. It was in Algiers that the Group of 77—the Third World trade union in north/

south relations—first met in October 1977 and established their charter, which still governs the Third World negotiating position with the developed north. The UN special session in the spring of 1984, which issued the NIEO (New International Economic Order) document, was summoned by Boumedienne—then chairman of the nonaligned countries. In fact, the NIEO document itself incorporates most of Boumedienne's opening speech. Algeria was thus encouraged to take the initiative in what seemed delicate issues. It was in Algiers in 1975 that the shah of Iran and Iraq's President Saddam Hussain met and successfully averted a potential war. It was also in Algiers in 1980 that the Americans and Iran's ayatollahs negotiated—with Algerian mediation—the freeing of U.S. hostages in Tehran after more than 400 days in captivity.

Developmentalist legitimacy: Algeria's role model development strategy was based on industrializing or heavy industry, especially on possessing independent financial capital—petrodollars. With the sudden rise in the price of a barrel of petrol from about $2 in 1972 to $40 in 1979, the Algerian government possessed the funds to industrialize and to urbanize. It was the omnipresent patron-state. But the 1980s would tell a different story.

Legitimacy Eroding. The end of the 1970s witnessed a change in political authority with the death of President Boumedienne. Even before overthrowing Algeria's first president, Ahmad Ben-Bella, in June 1965, Boumedienne—as the NLA chief—was a strong man in both preindependent and newly independent Algeria. The current president, Chadli Bendjedid, has maintained the same pattern of governability since he came to power in 1979 but without the political assets of his predecessor. In fact, Bendjedid was a compromise candidate in the presidential contest. It was then that the different factions in the Algerian political system were allowed to surface, and then clustered around two candidates: the foreign minister, Ahmad Boutaflika, advocating the injection of a limited market economy and a certain opening toward the private sector and thus representing the political center, and Mohammed Yahloui, the party man, representing ideological orthodoxy and the maintenance intact of the original socialist option and thus identified with the left. There was no right.

Among the more then 2,000 FLN delegates voting, neither of these two groups could guarantee the victory of its candidate. The army's 640 delegates were thus in a powerful position. They advanced their own candidate, Colonel Bendjedid, the most senior man in the highest rank.

Rather than innovating, Bendjedid continued the previous pattern of governing the country: extreme centralism around the presidency and authoritarianism from above. There were institutions without institutionalization, and political competition was limited to rivalry among political clans. Political structures continued to ossify until they had to be bypassed. Stagnation at the top of the political pyramid led to explosion at the bottom, hence the bloody October riots. It was an abrupt awakening of civil society, abrupt because early warnings were not heeded.

Legitimacy Deficit.   Indeed, for eight years there had been warning lights in abundance. In 1980, after intensive Berber demonstrations, the police shut down the Tizi-Ouzou University and detained 400 people. Other universities went on strike. In 1981, trouble continued in both southern and eastern regions of the country, with one dead, several dozens hurt, and more than 50 people detained for investigation. In 1985 various parts of the country had trouble at different times: April 22–28, Casbah (traditional district) inhabitants of Algiers demonstrated against insecurity, insalubrity, and lack of water; June 5–7, incidents ended in two dead and 56 hurt in Ghardaia (600 kilometers from Algiers) after a controversial distribution of land; October 31–November 1, new student protest in Kabylie. And in 1986 came the raging disturbances in Setif and Constantine. The years following also were troubled. The 1988 October events were, then, neither exceptional nor the most dangerous.

But in "Black October," everybody was surprised by the cruelty of the arm of repression—the army—that unleashed massive force to quell the protest. Hospital personnel were overwhelmed by the numbers of injured, especially youngsters. This heavy repression by a model "people's regime" was embarrassing and shocking, even for established French intellectuals who had spent their youth opposing their government's policy of a French Algeria.

But the army's bloody answer cannot alone explain Black October, for it begs the question as to why the regime overreacted. Clan infighting apart, the regime was nervous because it felt vulnerable. We thus come full circle to the basic Third World problem of governability.

The bases of the mentioned types of legitimacy were disappearing. Two-thirds of Algeria's population were born after 1962, as the legitimacy based on the "glorious" War of Independence is—for them—literally history or even prehistory. This is what many youths of Algerian origin shouted in the streets of Paris in their demonstrations against Black October. The north-south negotiations—Algeria's leadership arena—are in limbo. Algeria is abandoning its "Prussian" foreign policy and embarking on a rapprochement and a Maghrib union with Morocco, ignoring the Western Sahara Polisario's pleading, if necessary. Worse still, the omnipresent state is—following the decline of petrol prices from $40 to $15 a barrel—cruelly reminded of its internal economic fragility.

Thus while the Algerian state is finding it increasingly difficult to satisfy basic needs at the 1970s rate, its people's demands continue to grow. The satisfaction-demand gap widens, and the situation becomes critical. We could compare the government to an air traffic control tower, increasingly overloaded with demands to land and take off. The tower could make planes queue up but not indefinitely, or there could be accidents and crashes. Thus, outside help must be sought. Algeria borrowed on the international money markets, and has a present debt of $20.7 billion, with a cost for the last two years of $5.2 billion—with worse still to come.

Austerity measures have gone too far, shortages have been chronic, and some factories have been functioning at 30 percent of capacity for lack of spare parts. Whereas Algeria's population is growing by 3 percent a year, the economic growth rate is only 1 percent. Algeria is growing backward. The explosion of Black October was to be expected. It is not the scale of the protest but rather the difficulty of finding an immediate solution that fueled the crisis.

The Beginning of the Second Republic

President Bendjedid was conscious of the approaching crisis, and did introduce "economic reforms" to liberalize the economy. Not only did such measures anger the hardliners, especially within the ranks of the NLF, but they also created, in the short run, glaring income gaps that added to the other problems of suffocating statism, *nomenklatura*, bureaucratization, and nepotism. It is in this context that the increasing popularity of Islamic fundamentalism —which takes as a slogan the eradication of these ills—can be explained. Thus before they could be fully carried out, the government's economic reform policies were criticized from both the left and the right.

But Black October could become Algeria's spring. The riots would give the president the justification to get rid of opponents and follow his perestroika forcefully and effectively. Indeed, in October he got rid of Messadia—the permanent secretary of the FLN central committee—and some other apparatchiki, as well as General Lakhal Ayat of military security. The prime minister is now accountable to the National Assembly and not to the president as before. Authority of the people's representatives is thus on the ascendency. The draft of the new constitution voted on February 23 brings other new measures to rejuvenate the political system.

In comparison with the 1976 constitution, the constitution of 1989 is far more explicit about the bases and characteristics of Algeria's perestroika. The first article, which in the old constitution stipulated that the Algerian state was socialist, omits the word completely. Nowhere does it appear in the new text, nor do the words "FLN" or "the (1976) National Charter," the basic ideological-organizational infrastructure of independent Algeria.

A second major difference concerns fundamental freedoms and rights. In the new text, they are those of the "man and citizen." The old one had emphasized the collective aspect: fundamental freedoms and rights of the people as distinct from—and even op-

posed to—individualism, deemed petit bourgeois and even Western. It is in this sense that the constitution of 1989 marks a great
step by "recognizing that right to create associations of a political
character" (Article 40). This is the germ of multipartism that is
emerging in Algeria.

The third important difference concerns the role of the army.
In the old constitution, it was the focus of all of chapter 4 whereas
in the new it is only part of chapter 3 entitled "of the State." Previously, the army's task was to participate in "the country's development and the constitution of socialism." In the new text (Article
24), its role is technical: "to safeguard national independence, defend national sovereignty, the country's unity and territorial integrity." The depoliticization and professionalization of the army are
accelerated by confining it to the barracks.

There are other differences concerning the role of Islam in the
state, but the three mentioned indicate that a new era has started
in Algeria. Of the three basic poles of Algeria's political power
—the army, the party, and the presidency—only the last is left
intact and stronger after the 1989 February referendum.

However, if the old regime is discredited, the second republic—
replacing industrializing industry with democratizing industry—is
in its infancy. The debate over governability is not ending, but
starting, and many imponderables could still make it stumble on
the way.

Conclusion

Such legitimacy-building problems in the face of constant change
are not peculiar to Algeria or to the Maghrib countries but characterize all of the Third World. Because of the myriad of factors—
both indigenous and exogenous, geographical and cultural, structural and contextual—the relationship between state and civil society is continuously in flux. The search will continue to find the
happy solution to the problem of governability, a solution to satisfy
both economic and identity needs and achieve an acceptable combination of modernity and authenticity.

In this chapter, while being necessarily synthetic and selective, we have tried to attract attention to the characteristics of institutional organizations as well as to the dynamics of political practice, historical factors, and contemporary problems. While the three political systems could be differentiated by basic indicators concerning population or education data, republican or monarchical regime, number of political parties, or characteristics of institutional structure, they were found to share some common and basic political patterns: All accord primacy to the executive branch of government, especially centered on the head of state, all reveal a skewed pattern of elite distribution (political elites are not representative of the various regions or the different strata of society), and all are going through the throes of political change while searching continuously for the right mix of political legitimacy and governability.

Consequently, while academic research on these problems of governability continues, the problem of Maghrib political system-building and legitimation will persist and be debated—both inside and outside—through the 1990s and probably beyond.

NOTES

Research for this chapter was supported in part by a grant from the Social Sciences and Humanities Research Council.

1. Jamil Abun-Nasr, *A History of the Maghrib in the Islamic Period* (Cambridge: Cambridge University Press, 1987), p. 8.

2. Yves Lacoste, "General Characteristic and Fundamental Structures of Medieval North African Society," *Economy and Society* 3 (1974): 7.

3. Michael Hudson, *Arab Politics* (New Haven: Yale University Press, 1977), p. 2.

4. See William Quandt, *Revolution and Political Leadership: Algeria 1954–1968* (Cambridge, Mass.: M.I.T. Press, 1969).

5. William Zartman et al., *Political Elites in Arab North Africa* (New York: Longman, 1982), p. 1.

6. See Richard Little, "Belief Systems in the Social Sciences," in *Belief Systems and International Relations*, ed. R. Little and Steve Smith (Oxford: Blackwell, 1988).

7. Zartman et al., p. 8.

Table 19.1. Basic Data

Country	Area (km²)	Population, 1988 (millions)	Year of independence	Year of admission to UN
Algeria	2,381,741	23.80	1962	1962
Morocco	710,850ᵃ	23.92	1956	1956
Tunisia	163,610	7.80	1956	1956

Sources: The World Bank, *World Bank Atlas; Political Handbook of the World* (CSA Pub., 1985); *Middle East and North Africa* (London: Europa Publications); Le Monde, *Dossiers et Documents* (No. Sp.: "Bilan Economique et Social 1989"), January 1990.
ᵃ This Moroccan area includes the disputed territory of the Western Saraha, which covers 252,120 km².

Table 19.2. Ethnic and Religious Composition

Country	Ethnic subdivision			Religious subdivision		
	Ethnic groups	Total (000)	%	Religious groups	Total (000)	%
Algeria	Arabs	15,928	78.5	Sunni Muslims	20,168	99.4
	Berbers	3,936	19.5	Christians	81	0.4
	Europeans	81	0.4	Unknown	41	0.2
	Unknown	345	1.7			
Morocco	Arabs	12,307	59.6	Sunni Muslims	20,541	99.5
	Berbers	8,157	39.5	Roman Catholics	109	0.5
	Europeans and others	186	0.9			
Tunisia	Arabs/Berbers	6,250	96.0	Sunni Muslims	6,230	95.7
	Europeans	52	0.8	Roman Catholics	39	0.6
	Others	208	3.2	Other Christians	13	0.2

Source: Ammaire de L'Afrique du Nord (Paris and Aix-en-Provence: CNRS, various years).

Table 19.3. Gross National Product (GNP) per Capita ($ U.S.)

Country	1967	1970	1975	1980	1984	1985	1987	1988
Algeria	250	300	870	1,900	2,410	2,530	2,780	2,450
Morocco	190	230	470	800	670	610	620	750
Tunisia	210	250	730	1,300	1,270	1,220	1,210	1,230

Source: World Bank Report, 1989.

Table 19.4. Defense Expenditure as a % of GNP

Country	1965	1970	1975	1980	1983	1984	1985	1986	1987	1988
Algeria	3.50	3.50	2.20	2.10	1.80	1.80	1.70	1.70	1.70	1.50
Morocco	2.40	2.90	2.80	6.70	9.80	4.70	5.40	5.10	5.00	5.00
Tunisia	1.40	1.10	1.31	3.90	5.30	4.70	5.20	5.90	5.50	5.30

Sources: SIPRI, *Yearbook 1990: World Armament and Disarmament;* IISS, *The Military Balance;* IMF, *Government Finance Statistics;* World Bank, *Rapport sur le Developpement dans le Monde.*

Table 19.5. External Debt

Country	Total external debt (TED) ($ U.S. millions)					Total external debt as a % of GNP				
	1970	1975	1980	1985	1988	1970	1975	1980	1985	1988
Algeria	1,470	9,589	18,662	15,526	22,191	30.3	65.6	47.2	29.0	45.7
Morocco	958	2,409	9,265	14,998	21,454	24.3	25.6	50.7	124.6	117.7
Tunisia	863	1,757	3,689	5,250	7,060	61.6	40.6	42.2	64.4	73.9

Sources: The World Bank, *World Debt Tables, External Debt of Developing Countries* (1st supplement) (Washington, July 1989); Banque Mondiale, *Rapport sur le Developpement dans le Monde.*

Table 19.6. Debt Service

Country	Debt service as % of GNP					Debt service as a % of exports				
	1970	1975	1980	1985	1988	1970	1975	1980	1985	1988
Algeria	0.9	3.1	9.8	8.3	12.6	3.9	9.4	26.6	33.3	71.3
Morocco	1.5	1.5	6.5	8.6	13.4	8.6	7.2	36.5	32.3	45.6
Tunisia	4.6	2.3	4.9	8.3	13.8	19.5	7.6	12.9	24.9	34.1

Sources: The World Bank, *World Debt Tables, External Debt of Developing Countries* (1st supplement) (Washington, July 1989); Banque Mondiale, *Rapport sur le Developpement dans le Monde.*

Contributors

Kamel S. Abu Jaber is professor of political science, University of Jordan. He is the author of *The Arab Ba'ath Socialist Party* (1966); *The United States of America and Israel* (1971) in Arabic; *The Israeli Political System* (1973) in Arabic; *The Jordanians and the People of Jordan* (1980); *Economic Potentialities of Jordan* (1984); *Political Parties and Elections in Israel* (1985) in Arabic; and *The Badia of Jordan* (1987) and a contributor to *The Arab-Israeli Confrontation, 1967* (1969); *Government and Politics of the Contemporary Middle East* (1970); *The Future of Pastoral Peoples* (1981); *The Contemporary Mediterranean World* (1983); *Political and Economic Trends in the Middle East* (1985); and *Regional Security in the Third World* (1986). He is also editor of *Roots of Arab Socialism* (1964), in Arabic; *Levels and Trends of Fertility and Mortality in Selected Arab Countries of West Asia* (1980); and *Major Issues in the Development of Jordan* (1983). His articles have appeared in *The Middle East Journal, The Muslim World,* the *Arab Journal, Mideast, The Encyclopedia Britannica, Orient, The Third World Chronicle, Problems of International Cooperation, The Arab Perspective* and *The American Arab Journal.* He is currently editor of the *Journal of the Arab Political Science Association, al-Reem, (Journal of the Royal Society for the Conservation of Nature in Jordan).*

R. Hrair Dekmejian is professor of political science, University of Southern California. A graduate of Columbia University, he has served as consultant to the Agency for International Development, the Department of State, and the United States Information Agency. He is the author of many books and articles, including

Patterns of Political Leadership, Egypt under Nasser, and *Islam in Revolution: Fundamentalism in the Arab World.*

Nassif Hitti holds a Ph.D. in international relations and Middle East affairs and has taught at the American University of Beirut and the University of Southern California. He is the author of two books published in Arabic: *The Theory in International Relations* (1985) and *The Arab World and the Five Great Powers: A Futuristic Study* (1987). He is also the author of many articles on Arab and international affairs.

Jacqueline S. Ismael is a professor of social welfare at the University of Calgary. Her research interests include the Canadian welfare state and social development/social change in the Arab world. Her publications include numerous articles and book chapters and the following books: *Kuwait: Social Change in Historical Perspective* (1982); *Canadian Social Welfare Policy: Federal and Provincial Dimensions* (1985); *The People's Democratic Republic of Yemen: Politics, Economics and Society* (with Tareq Y. Ismael) (1986); *Perspectives on Social Services and Social Issues* (ed.) (1986); *The Canadian Welfare State: Evolution and Transition* (ed.) (1987); *Privatization and Provincial Social Services in Canada: Policy, Administration and Service Delivery* (1988).

Tareq Y. Ismael is professor of political science at the University of Calgary. He is the author of *Governments and Politics of the Contemporary Middle East* (1970); *The U.A.R. in Africa: Egypt's Policy under Nasser* (1971); *The Middle East in World Politics* (1973); *Canada and the Middle East* (1973); *The Arab Left* (1976); *Iraq and Iran: Roots of Conflict* (1982); *Government and Politics in Islam* (with J.S. Ismael) (1985); *PDR Yemen: The Politics of Socialist Transformation* (1986); *International Relations of the Contemporary Middle East* (1986); *The Communist Movement in Egypt* (1990). He is also coeditor of *Canada and the Third World* (1976) and editor of *Canadian-Arab Relations* (1984), *Canada and the Arab World* (1985), and *Middle Eastern Studies: International Perspectives on the State of the Art*

(1990). His articles have appeared in *The Middle East Journal, Current History, Journal of Modern African Studies, The Middle East Forum, Arab Studies, Europa Archiv*, the *Arab Historian, Palestine Affairs*, the *Canadian Journal of African Studies, Social Problems*, and the *International Journal*.

Bahgat Korany is professor in the Department of Political Science and director of the University Program of Arab Studies at the Université de Montréal. He has been visiting professor in many universities (Algiers, Dakar, McGill, Aix-Marseille) and a visiting scholar at Harvard and is on the editorial board of many specialized periodicals in the fields of international relations and development studies. A founding member of the Organization South-South Corporation (Beijing, 1983), he has published four books and thirty-five articles in such periodicals as *Revue francaise de science politique, Etudes internationales, International Journal*, and *Journal of the Social Sciences, World Politics*, some of which have been translated into Arabic, Italian, Spanish, and Chinese. His first book, *Social Change, Charisma and International Behavior*, was awarded the 1976 Hauchman Prize.

Ann M. Lesch, a graduate of Swarthmore College (1966) and Columbia University (Ph.D., 1973), teaches political science at Villanova University. She worked for the American Friends Service Committee, the Ford Foundation, and Universities Field Staff International in the Middle East. She is a member of the Board of Directors of the Middle East Studies Association and of *Middle East Report*. She is the author of *Arab Politics in Palestine, 1917–1939: The Frustration of a Nationalist Movement*, and she has written numerous articles on the Palestine problem, Egyptian politics, and the Sudan, including an analysis of Sudanese foreign policy in *Foreign Affairs* (Spring 1987) and an investigation of the civil war in the South in *Middle East Journal* (Summer 1986). She most recently visited the Sudan in July 1989.

Tim Niblock is senior lecturer in Middle East politics at the University of Exeter and joint director of the Research Unit for the International Study of Economic Liberalisation and Its Social and Political Effects. A former associate professor of political science at the University of Khartoum (1969–77), he was secretary of the British Society for Middle Eastern Studies between 1986 and 1990. He is the author of *Class and Power in Sudan: The Dynamics of Sudanese Politics, 1898–1985* (1987) and editor of, and contributor to, *Social and Economic Development in the Arab Gulf* (1980), *State, Society and Economy in Saudi Arabia* (1981), *Iraq: The Contemporary State* (1982), and, jointly with R. Lawless, *Prospects for the World Oil Industry* (1985).

Richard H. Pfaff graduated from the University of California at Berkeley after leaving the U.S. Army and then did graduate work at the University of Beirut in Lebanon. After getting his Ph.D. at the University of California, he joined the faculty of the University of Colorado at Boulder. He has lived one year in Iran, one year in Turkey, and one year in Lebanon and has also made a number of visits to Morocco, Libya, Egypt, Israel, Jordan, and Saudi Arabia. In 1970–73, Dr. Pfaff served as a consultant to the U.S. Department of Defense, International Security Affairs Division. He has also done contract research for the U.S. Arms Control and Disarmament Agency. He has published a book on Jerusalem, a book-length study on Cento, and a number of articles on politics in the Middle East. He is currently working on the role of science in the modernization of the Arab world.

Walter F. Weiker is professor of political science at Rutgers University. He is the author of *The Turkish Revolution 1960–61: Aspects of Military Politics* (1963); *Decentralizing Government in Modernizing Nations: Growth Center Potential of Turkish Provincial Capitals* (1972); *Political Tutelage and Democracy in Turkey: The Free Party and its Aftermath* (1973); *The Modernization of Turkey* (1981); and *The Un-Seen: The Jews from Turkey in Israel* (1988). He is coauthor and coeditor of *Continuing Issues in International Politics* (1973).

Manfred Wenner is currently professor of political science at

Northern Illinois University. He was educated in Switzerland, Austria, West Germany, and the United States and has degrees from Oberlin College and Johns Hopkins University (Ph.D.). After a period as a foreign policy analyst with the Congressional Research Service, he taught at the Universities of Wisconsin, California (at Berkeley), and Washington and at Salzburg College. He has published a number of articles on Yemen as well as *Modern Yemen, 1918–1966*, and the forthcoming *Yemen Arab Republic*. He was a founding member of the American Institute for Yemeni Studies, of which he has been vice president and president. His primary research interest remains the Middle East, but he has recently published and taught in Western European affairs and environmental politics.

Marvin Zonis teaches in the Committee on Human Development at the University of Chicago and has been a student of Iranian politics for nearly thirty years. He is the author of *The Political Elite of Iran*. **Cyrus Amir Mokri** is a graduate student in the Department of History at the same institution.

Index

Note: Arabic names are indexed in the form in which they are most familiar in the West. Generally, names from earlier periods are indexed under the given or first name, while more current persons are found under the last name. Last names beginning with "al" are alphabetized according to the element following this particle. (For example, al-Hussain, King Abdullah is found under Hussain, with the particle "al" retained in front of it.)